KARL MARX AND THE BIRTH
OF MODERN SOCIETY

Karl Marx and the Birth of Modern Society

The Life of Marx and the Development of His Work

VOLUME I: 1818–1841

by MICHAEL HEINRICH

translated from the German by Alexander Locascio

MONTHLY REVIEW PRESS

New York

Originally published as *Karl Marx und die Geburt der modernen Gesellschaft*
by Schmetterling Verlag GmbH, Stuttgart, Germany © 2018 by Schmetterling Verlag GmbH.
English translation by Alexander Locascio published by Monthly Review Press 2019
© by Monthly Review Press

Library of Congress Cataloging-in-Publication Data
Names: Heinrich, Michael, 1957– author.
Title: Karl Marx and the birth of modern society : the life of Marx and the
    development of his work / by Michael Heinrich ; translated from the German
    by Alexander Locasio.
Other titles: Karl Marx und die Geburt der modernen Gesellschaft. English
Description: New York : Monthly Review Press, [2019]—| Includes
    bibliographical references and index.
Identifiers: LCCN 2019017089 (print) | LCCN 2019018221 (ebook) | ISBN
    9781583677360 (trade) | ISBN 9781583677377 (institutional) | ISBN
    9781583677353 (hardcover)
Subjects: LCSH: Marx, Karl, 1818–1883. | Communists—Germany—Biography. |
    Communism—History. | Marxian economics—History.
Classification: LCC HX39.5 (ebook) | LCC HX39.5 .H4413 2019 (print) | DDC
    335.4092 [B] —dc23
LC record available at https://lccn.loc.gov/2019017089

ISBN cloth 978-1-58367-735-3

Monthly Review Press
134 West 29th Street, Suite 706
New York, New York 10001

www.monthlyreview.org

Typeset in Minion Pro

5 4 3 2 1

CONTENTS

For Karin (1955–2013), with whom so much began

PREFACE

For instance, *Meyer's Konversationslexikon* wrote a long time ago asking me for a biography. Not only did I not send one; I did not even reply to the letter.

—KARL MARX, LETTER TO LUDWIG KUGELMANN, OCTOBER 26, 1868 (MECW 43: 144)

Karl Marx probably would not have wanted a biography, and certainly not one planned for multiple volumes. He emphasized to Wilhelm Blos in Hamburg that "neither of us cares a straw for popularity. Let me cite one proof of this: such was my aversion to the personality cult that at the time of the International [meaning the International Workingmens' Association, 1864–1876] when plagued by numerous moves—originating from various countries—to accord me public honor, I never allowed one of these to enter the domain of publicity, nor did I ever reply to them, save with an occasional snub" (letter from November 10, 1877, MECW 45: 288).

This work is not concerned with a cult of personality. Marx is neither placed on a pedestal, nor is he condemned. Nor is history, not even the history of the creation of important theories, reduced to the influence of "great men." It is concerned with the historical process in which Karl Marx developed as a person, as a theorist, as a political activist, and as a revolutionary. This was a process in which Marx intervened not only through the publication of his analyses and commentaries, but also through the founding of newspapers and his efforts to reshape organizations such as the Communist League or the International Workingmens' Association.

Already in the last decade of his life, a broad and increasingly international reception of his work began that has continued up to today. In the twentieth century, multiple revolutions and state formations aimed at overcoming bourgeois-capitalist relations referred to Marx's theories. A huge number of political parties and groups that exhibited large differences and in part vehemently fought one another referred to themselves in the twentieth century as "Marxist." This enormous political influence was accompanied by a transformation of Marx the person by adherents as well as opponents into a positive or a negative icon. At the same time, Marx's extensive work was usually only taken up very selectively.

That which Marx published himself was only the tip of a gigantic iceberg that only saw the light of day gradually in the twentieth century. Every generation was familiar with a different set of "complete works" from which one could cherry-pick. Only now, at the beginning of the twenty-first century are we close to having an overview of Marx's complete works with the aid of the new, but not yet completely published, Marx-Engels-Gesamtausgabe (MEGA).

Whereas Marx emphasized again and again how time-bound all intellectual production is, his own work was frequently extricated from the conditions of its creation and regarded as a system of timeless statements. Marx's enormous learning processes, which repeatedly led to theoretical new beginnings and revisions, and above all left behind unfinished work, were often not really noticed. Marx had to always already be "Marx." In contrast, in the last few decades a necessary "historicization" was often spoken of: the necessity of placing Marx's life and work in historical context. This was in part an act of defense—the historicized Marx was to be an object of history with nothing more to say to us today. In part, this was also an obligatory exercise in order to continue on as before. But an adequate historicizing requires not only a change of one's line of vision, to the extent that one devotes more attention to the historical background; it's also a real research task in which this or that certainty is left by the wayside.

When reading many Marx biographies, one can get the impression that the statements about Marx were decided beforehand, and the biographical material merely serves to buttress already existing results. In contrast, I admit that the work on this biography over many years led to changes in my picture of the person, as well as his work and its development. And this research process is far from finished.

This first volume of this book deals with Marx's youth in Trier and his studies in Bonn and Berlin, with his doctoral dissertation as his first independent work. In some Marx biographies this is the material for one or two brief introductory chapters; things first appear to get interesting after that. I hope to disprove this judgment. The importance of Marx's school days, his attempts at poetry, his engagement with religion and the philosophy of religion, as well as his dissertation, seem to me to deserve a more exact consideration than hitherto usual, and the political processes and debates in Prussia in the 1830s have to be taken into consideration all the more. I do not at all wish to assert that this early phase is something like the key to Marx's life and work; there were enough shifts that weren't predictable. Nonetheless, the experiences and learning processes of Marx's student days constitute the background against which his journalistic and political influence plays out in the following years.

It's not just the subject of a biography that's historical; the person writing the biography is, with his questions and preconditions, also a product of his time and social conditions. One cannot escape such influence, but one can attempt to deal with it consciously. In the past eight years, I not only was able to participate in conferences in various countries, in Brazil, China, and India in particular, I also had the possibility of conducting seminars and workshops on Marx and to discuss with people active in various political and social contexts. The experience that I was able to gather, the various perspectives on Marx and his work that I got to know, have helped me to better understand the historical situation of my own judgments and to question my own apparent matters of course.

Language also belongs to those cultural influences that one first must be made conscious of as an influence. It has often been criticized that in German as well as other languages the male form is at the same time regarded as the universal one, encompassing both genders. Despite various attempts to overcome this, no alternative has been successfully established. I will attempt to explicitly state repeatedly that social struggles were led not only by men but also by women.

I would not have been able to write this book without help from others. For reading parts of the manuscript, for numerous suggestions, encouragement, and critique, I thank in particular Valeria Bruschi, Ana Daase, Andrei Draghici, Raimund Feld, Christian Frings, Pia Garske, Jorge Grespan, Rolf Hecker, Jan Hoff, Ludolf Kuchenbuch, Martin Kronauer, Sofia Lalopoulou, Christoph Lieber, Kolja Lindner, Urs Lindner, Jannis Milios, Hanna Müller, Antonella Muzzupappa, Arno Netzbandt, Sabine Nuss, Oliver Schlaudt, Dorothea Schmidt, Rudi Schmidt, Hartwig Schuck, Kim Robin Stoller, Ingo Stützle, Ann Wiesenthal, Patrick Ziltener. I thank Michael D. Yates and Martin Paddio at Monthly Review Press for their cooperation, patience, and understanding. Finally, I wish to thank Alexander Locascio for an excellent translation. I thank the Stadtmuseum Simeonstift Trier for the kind permission to use the portrait of Marx drawn by Heinrich Rosbach, as well as Johann Anton Rambouxs's painting of Johan Hugo Wyttenbach.

ON CITATION

Texts by Marx and Engels are cited according to the new Marx-Engels-Gesamtausgabe (MEGA) appearing since 1975 (Walter de Gruyter Verlag, Berlin) and the Marx-Engels Collected Works (Lawrence and Wishart, London). For the MEGA, the Roman number refers to the section, the Arabic number to the volume, and then the page. So MEGA III/1: 15 means the third section, first volume, page 15. In the case of the MECW, the volume number is followed by the page. So MECW 1: 46 would be Volume 1, page 46. If not otherwise indicated, emphases in quotations of Marx are by Marx.

WHY MARX?

A JOURNEY BY SEA AND A BOOK

The trip lasted more than two days. On April 10, a Wednesday, the *John Bull* had left London at 8 a.m.; on Friday, the steamship arrived in Hamburg at noon. The passage was stormy, and most of the passengers had taken to their bunks with seasickness. Only a small group had braved the storm in the common room, where they listened to a German passenger tell adventurous stories. He had spent the last fifteen years traveling through eastern Peru and had gone into territories that had barely been explored. With a cozy frisson, the audience listened to the anecdotes about his encounters with the indigenous inhabitants and their—for Europeans—so foreign customs.

One of the passengers entertained by these stories later wrote, "So cannibalic jolly, as 'twere five hundred hogs!" Whoever is wondering about this strange formulation should know that it comes from Goethe's *Faust*, one of this passenger's favorite books. The man in question was of neat appearance, about 5 foot 6 inches tall, and slightly stocky. His still very full but already grayed hair covered his head in even waves combed backwards, which emphasized his already broad brow. The only things as black as his hair used to be were his bushy eyebrows, from under which a pair of attentive dark brown eyes twinkled. His face was covered by a thick full beard, in which black and gray were mixed. The man was in his late forties, but the amount of gray in his hair and beard made him look about ten years older. He was an imposing presence. When he spoke, one could still hear the jovial inflection of the Mosel region, which indicated where he had spent his youth. This passenger was carrying the second part of a substantial book manuscript, which he wanted to hand over personally to his Hamburg-based publisher.

He could have, as he had done a few months before for the first part, sent this manuscript with the postal ship, but the matter was too important to him. The work on this book, which had taken many years, had almost ruined him in terms of his health and financially. And even worse, his wife and children had also suffered heavily under the constant strain and destitution, and were still suffering. In a letter, he had written that he had "sacrificed" his "health, happiness, and family" to this work. He was thus relieved that he could now finally hand over the finished manuscript to his publisher. After a few delays in the preparation and correcting of the galley proofs, the work was published in September of 1867, its title: *Das Kapital: Kritik der politischen Ökonomie* (*Capital: A Critique of Political Economy*).[1]

Twenty-three years earlier, in 1844, Karl Marx had begun preparatory work for a fundamental critique of economics. In 1845, he even had a contract with a publisher to write a two-volume work of *Kritik der Politik und Nationalökonomie* (*Critique of Politics and Economics*). At the time, Marx was an up-and-coming young author, who in 1842–43 as editor-in-chief of the liberal *Rheinische Zeitung* had had run-ins with the Prussian authorities, until the newspaper was finally banned. The young Marx was regarded as witty and educated in equal measure. While his "pointed pen" was regarded critically by Prussian censors, some publishers had an open-minded attitude toward him. Instead of actually writing this two-volume work, however, Marx (along with his friend Friedrich Engels) began a completely different work, which then remained in a drawer and published about ninety years later under the title *The German Ideology*. Marx did publish some texts in which economic questions played an important role, for example, in 1848, the *Communist Manifesto*, which became famous later. But the large work on the critique of economics was constantly postponed.

During the turbulent times of the 1848 Revolution, in which Marx played an important role as the author and editor-in-chief of the *Neue Rheinische Zeitung*, he didn't have time for long theoretical treatises. After the defeat of the Revolution, Marx needed to leave Germany with his family as quickly

---

1. For the details of Marx's trip, see the letter to Engels from April 13, 1867 (MECW 42: 356); on Marx's stay in Hamburg, Sommer (2008) and Böning (2017). "As '*twere five hundred hogs, we feel So cannibalic jolly!*" is sung in Auerbach's cellar in Goethe's *Faust*, Part 1. The letter mentioned was written by Marx to Sigfrid Meyer on April 30, 1867 (MECW 42: 366). Details on Marx's appearance are found in Kliem (1970: 15ff.). Franziska Kugelmann (1983: 253) mentions the "homey Rhineland dialect" (*gemütlichen, rheinländischen Dialekt*), though being from Hannover, she was hardly aware of the difference between a Rhineland dialect and that which was spoken in Trier and the Mosel area.

as possible. As was the case for many other political refugees in this period, London was for him the last, rather miserable, resort. The Marx family was only able to survive there thanks to the generous support of their friend Friedrich Engels.

In London, Marx also followed his plan of composing a comprehensive analysis of the capitalist economy. In a certain sense, it was in London, then the center of capitalism, that Marx recognized the amount of material that would be necessary for this analysis, and thus it would be years before he could even think of a finished publication. Not without difficulty, Marx found a publisher, but then delivered only a brief overture to the planned large work: two chapters dealing with the commodity and money, published in 1859 under the title *Zur Kritik der politischen Ökonomie. Erstes Heft* (*A Contribution to the Critique of Political Economy*). When Marx was on his way to Hamburg, to a different publisher, this work had already been published eight years before.

From the viewpoint of its impact, the short book published in 1859 proved to be a considerable misfire. Even close political friends of Marx were disappointed, since they could not recognize any utility for their political struggles in the rather abstract and not always simple treatise on the commodity and money. Marx, who initially intended to publish a direct continuation of this overture, gave up this plan after a few years. Starting in 1863, he planned an independent work, *Das Kapital*, which was to consist of four books. He brought the second part of the manuscript for the first of these four books, titled *Der Produktionsprozess des Kapitals* (*The Production Process of Capital*), to his new publisher in Hamburg in April 1867.

Marx reckoned with a great success, since he had learned from the failure of 1859. He tried to keep the theoretical part more popular and understandable. The new work no longer dealt only with the commodity and money, but also with the capitalist process of production as a whole, containing concrete depictions of factory labor, the misery of working-class families, and the struggle to shorten the working day. Nobody could now lob the accusation at Marx that the whole thing was too dry and only appropriate for specialists.

Political changes had taken place as well. In September of 1864, the International Workingmen's Association (IWA) had been founded in London. Marx became a member of the general council of the IWA and soon became its leading thinker. In the following years, the IWA continued to gain support. Workers' associations and trade unions developed. All of this raised the hope that the conditions for the book's reception were now far more auspicious than for the earlier text. In his eulogy for Marx, Engels correctly emphasized: "For Marx was before all else a revolutionist. His real mission in life was to contribute, in one way or another, to the overthrow of capitalist society."[2] However, Marx carried out this mission not as fighter on the barricades or as a rousing orator, but rather by pursuing the path of a scientific analysis of capitalist relations. This was his sharpest weapon. A week after he left London to bring the manuscript to Hamburg, Marx wrote in a letter to Johann Philipp Becker concerning his book that it was "without question the most terrible MISSILE that has yet been hurled at the heads of the bourgeoisie (landowners included)."[3]

However, this first volume of *Capital* also did not have the success for which Marx had hoped. It would take four years for the first print run of 1,000 copies to sell out. Despite considerable effort, Marx was not able to complete the subsequent volumes of *Capital*. After Marx's death, Engels published the second and third volumes, in 1885 and 1894 respectively, from Marx's unpublished manuscripts, and the unfinished character of these volumes is readily apparent. With that, the three (theoretical) volumes of *Capital* were available (the fourth was to deal with the history of economic theory), but it would be decades before further important texts from Marx's unpublished papers would be published. Nonetheless, with his views and analyses, Marx had a comprehensive and lasting influence, both intellectually as well as politically, not comparable to that of any other author of the last two or three hundred years. For about a hundred years, many critics have triumphantly proclaimed again and again that "Marx is dead." But these repeated proclamations are the surest indicator of the opposite. If Marx were really intellectually and politically dead, one would not have to repeatedly invoke his demise.

"MARX" AS CIPHER

Why was Marx's theory able to gain such influence, why is it able to cause a stir again and again? One obvious argument against the possible relevance of Marx's theory is the time span between now and its emergence. Two of the most recent biographies emphasize precisely this point. Jonathan Sperber (2013) sees Marx as so rooted in the nineteenth century that his theories have no meaning for the present. Stedman Jones (2017) doesn't go as far as Sperber in his rejection of Marx's theories, but he is primarily concerned in showing the limits of Marx's thought, which supposedly remained trapped in the topics and questions of its time. But before concluding that Marx's theories are necessarily obsolete, one should first consider the relation

---

2. MECW 24, 468.
3. MECW 42, 358.

between the economic and political upheavals of the nineteenth century and our present.

Nowadays, in Europe or the United States, every ten or twenty years a new "age" is proclaimed. In the late 1990s, it was the "internet age," even though some had been speaking of the "computer age" since the 1960s. The "service economy" has also been rediscovered a few times. During the German economic miracle, or *Wirtschaftswunder*, of the 1960s the "consumer society" was trendy; in the 1980s it was the "post-materialist era." Labeling new technological or economic changes with a new "age" name connects with people's everyday experiences and brings media attention. However, a few years later, it becomes clear that the new era hasn't really come that far. In light of crisis, unemployment, and precarious employment, the all-too-pretty constructions of a post-materialist and post-capitalist era have lost much of their earlier plausibility.

It's all too easily forgotten how many fundamental social and economic structures, despite all changes, have remained the same, or have developed further within a predefined and discernible framework. Many of the technical, economic, social, and political foundations of modern European societies and of modern capitalism were created during the phase of upheaval that occurred between 1780 and 1860. Knowing how close the last phase of this time of upheaval is to those of us in Western Europe and North America, and how far we are from the period before 1780, can be made clear with a little thought experiment.

Let's imagine that an educated person from France or England in the year 1710 woke up 150 years later in France or England in the year 1860. This person would not only marvel at the many changes, but it would be difficult to explain to him or her what, for example, a telegraph or a steam engine is. After many millennia in which the horse (on land) and the sailing ship (by sea) were the fastest means of movement, now previously unimaginable quantities of people and goods were transported by locomotives and steamships in a much shorter time. Whereas this person from the year 1710 would only be familiar with small cottage industries, which were not much more than a continuation of handicraft workshops, now there would be enormous factories with gigantic machines and smoking chimneys at which to marvel. Whereas earlier, wage workers had only existed in the form of simple day laborers, and the vast majority of the population lived in the countryside, now an immense process of revolutionary change would be underway. The countryside would be emptying out while the cities would be constantly growing. The number of wage laborers (including masses of women) employed in industry would be increasing with tremendous speed. However, this new working class would not just be increasing numerically, it would be organizing itself in clubs and political organizations, demanding political participation. The "divine right of kings" was still being asserted, but it was radically doubted by broad swathes of the population; even religion itself had been losing considerable ground. Instead, the demands for popular sovereignty and universal suffrage were becoming widespread. The visitor from the year 1710 would have been familiar with newspapers, but primarily as an irregular medium published in small print runs, providing curious news for a small educated stratum of the population. In 1860, regularly published daily newspapers with large circulations were firmly established; they were the first instance of "mass media." Papers not only provided news but acted as a forum for publicly held important political debates. People's outward appearance also had changed radically. With a powdered wig, breeches, and silk knee stockings, a wealthy member of the bourgeoisie or aristocracy would not be particularly noteworthy in the year 1710 in England or France, in strong contrast to the year 1860. Such clothing would still be known, for example in the English court, but only for official occasions, and as a quotation from a past era.

It would be an entirely different case, on the other hand, if we would take a similarly educated person from the Western Europe of 1860 and transport him or her 150 years later to the year 2010. This person would also find himself or herself in an initially foreign and surprising world, but would have far fewer problems understanding contemporary conditions. If this person were a man, his clothing wouldn't deviate too much from ours. A man dressed like Karl Marx would hardly arouse attention walking through the streets of Paris or London today. Even the internet could be made understandable to this person rather quickly, as a more developed telegraph system, in which everyone has a telegraph connection at home and in which not only Morse code, but also pictures (photography was known in 1860) and sound could be transmitted. Steam locomotives had developed into electric locomotives and were even faster. And just as the steamship revolutionized travel by sea, "airships" have made possible the conquest of the air. Capitalist industrial enterprises have in part gotten even bigger and have more efficient machines. Popular sovereignty and universal suffrage (including for women) are no longer regarded as radical political concepts but are recognized in principle in many parts of the world, and more or less implemented (albeit not with the politically revolutionary consequences hoped for earlier). Mass media exist not only in print form, but also as electromagnetic "broadcasts" in the form of radio and television.

Whereas for the person transported from 1710 to 1860 the changes would constitute a deep break with pretty much everything he or she previously regarded as obvious and immutable, most of the changes could still be inte-grated into his or her range of experience. To a considerable extent, they are improvements and developments in that which is already familiar. If one considers the qualitative difference of the before and after—to just take one sphere—steam locomotives, steamships, and the telegraph are fundamental historical changes with regard to human mobility and communication over large distances. They mark a greater change than the airplane and internet do compared to the steamship and telegraph.

It's not an exaggeration to see in the economic and political upheavals that took place between 1780 and 1860, initially in Western Europe and North America, an epochal rupture in the history of humanity. The econ-omy was increasingly dominated by a *modern* capitalism, which not only dominated trade, as in earlier centuries, but also production, accompa-nied by recurring economic crises. Concomitantly, in Western Europe and North America an increasingly secular society emerged in the nineteenth century, one based upon the formal equality and individual freedom of citizens (later also of women and people of color) with considerable mate-rial inequality. This epochal rupture is still determinant for contemporary social and economic conditions, even if, considered at a global level, there's considerable differentiation in terms of varieties of capitalism as well as political systems.

Marx was a child of this epochal rupture, and his reflections on it were among the most outstanding ever made. With the expression "modern soci-ety," which I use in the title of this book, Marx aimed precisely at the differ-ence between pre-capitalist, pre-bourgeois societies, and capitalist, bourgeois societies. In the preface to *Capital*, he writes: "It is the ultimate aim of this work to reveal the economic law of motion of modern society" (Marx 1976: 92). Marx's analyses of modern society, to which not only *Capital* is devoted, and which are not at all limited to that "economic law of motion," are, how-ever, not available in a finished state; they exhibit important development, accompanied by considerable breaks and conceptual shifts. Thus, this book will discuss among other things the extent to which Marx, in his conception of modern society, rested upon a Eurocentric point of view, and the extent to which he succeeded in freeing himself from that point of view.

The assertion of capitalist relations in production (and not just their limited existence in trade, where they had existed for centuries) was the fundamental motor of previously unknown social and economic changes in Europe as well as worldwide: capitalism as a *mode of production*, once it emerged, had the tendency to expand and undermine pre-capitalist relations. However, the result of this process of expansion was and is not uniform. In the process of its historical consolidation, the capitalist mode of production was based not only on free wage labor, but also upon slavery and other forms of unfree labor, which have not completely disappeared today but are reproduced again and again (see Gerstenberger 2017). The political forms that accompanied capitalism were also extraordinarily diverse, and did not always develop in the direction of a parliamentary system, the separation of powers, and human rights, as, for example, the fascist regimes in Europe in the first half of the twentieth century made clear. Considered in a global context, "modern capitalism" shows itself to be anything but homogeneous.

In *Capital*, Marx examines the basic structures of modern capitalism, and not only in the limited economic sense that characterizes the doctrine of the field of economics today, but rather as a social relation, as the foundation of the dynamic of class relations and (social and political) class struggles. These basic structures of capitalism, which Marx had analyzed more comprehensively than anyone else, are of fundamental importance for most societies today. Yet his analysis is not at all limited to the conditions of British capitalism. These serve, as he emphasized in the preface to the first volume of *Capital*, only as an "illustration" of his "theoretical development" (Marx 1976: 90). At the end of the manuscript for the third volume, he states that the content of this theoretical development is "the internal organization of the capitalist mode of production, its ideal average, as it were" (Marx 1981: 970). So Marx is not concerned with a particular historical manifestation of capitalism, but rather with structures that are important for every manifestation of capitalism. To that extent, Marx's analysis, regardless of how one judges each of his individual results, is still relevant today, since it is ultimately about contemporary society.

But it's not just the thematic relevance of Marx's analysis that engages us with Marx's theory. Theories of society are never just pure analysis. They also are driven by the question of what human emancipation means, and in what sense we can speak of freedom, equality, solidarity, and justice, and under what social relations they are even possible.

For the bourgeoisie and its leading spokespersons in social theory, the possibility of freedom and emancipation had been given with the transcendence of feudal relations of dependence and privilege, with the implementation of the free market and free elections. With the chance to earn a fortune on the market and the possibility to vote out a disliked government, the emancipation of the individual as well as the political freedom of society as a whole had been realized for the bourgeoisie. The tremendous force of this liberal promise of happiness and freedom was last demonstrated in the 1980s and 1990s with the triumphal march of neoliberalism.

In opposition to this liberal promise of happiness, Marx maintains that the liberation from relations of personal domination and servitude of pre-capitalist epochs is not identical with the freedom from domination and servitude as such. In place of personal relations of domination, there emerge under capitalist conditions the impersonal, objective relations of domination, that "silent compulsion of economic relations" that Marx refers to in *Capital* (Marx 1976: 899). And the bourgeois state takes the place of feudal force. In that it guarantees, by its own "legitimate" force, private property regardless of the social status of the person, thus respecting the freedom and equality of citizens, it allows this "silent compulsion" to develop in the most effective manner.

With his own political activity as an editor of progressive newspapers, as a member of the Communist League and in the general council of the IWMA, but above all with his foundational critique of capitalism, Marx had a direct influence upon political developments. During his lifetime, and even more so in the twentieth century, large parts of the labor movement as well as numerous oppositional groups and parties oriented themselves in terms of Marx's conceptions, or, at least, what were regarded as his conceptions. "Marx" became a cipher that has become an integral part of political and intellectual development. Almost all fundamental political and economic projects that emerged and became influential in the twentieth century, whether progressive or conservative, had to deal in one form or another with Marx. "Marx" is the point of friction that has become unavoidable since the end of the nineteenth century.

At the same time, this point of friction was repeatedly concealed by its own effects and their metamorphoses. Not infrequently, Marx's critique was equated with "Marxism," with the manner in which this critique was taken up and became operative in the labor movement and the various left parties. This identification was powerfully advanced by the Communist parties that emerged after the Russian Revolution of 1917. The Soviet Union depicted itself as the result of Marxist-Leninist doctrine, whereby Lenin was regarded as Marx's fitting successor. Under Stalin, "Marxism-Leninism" became the legitimizing ideology of a brutal rule by the party over society and a no less brutal rule of the party leadership over the party. During the Cold War, both the Communist state parties and their bourgeois critics were united on at least one point: that the politics of Marxism-Leninism were the authentic expression of Marx's teachings. Marx was even held accountable for the worst crimes of Stalinism. Both in the East and the West, only small left groups, usually neither unified nor influential, emphasized the difference between Marx's critique and the various forms of official party Marxism and of authoritarian state socialism.

That Engels was the "inventor" of Marxism, as the subtitle of the German edition of Tristram Hunt's biography of Engels claims,[4] is a crude simplification. In contrast to the practice, especially within Marxism-Leninism, of regarding the works of Marx and Engels as identical, in which it's irrelevant who said what, since it's always supposed to hold for both, it's appropriate not to blur the differences between the two. But both Engels and Marx should not be reduced to what later generations have made of their writings.

With the collapse of the "really existing socialism" practiced in the Soviet Union and its satellite states, it appeared for a brief historical moment that Marx's critique of capitalism and "Marxism" in all of its varieties had also been finished off. Capitalism seemed to have survived its alternative. From now on, one could only work at improving really existing capitalism; every attempt to abolish it was doomed to failure, undertaken by those perpetually stuck in the past. At least, that was the widespread belief at the beginning of the 1990s. Since then, the destructive potential of globally victorious capitalism through its wars and crises has become increasingly clear and the insight that Marx's analyses are indeed not identical with what authoritarian political parties had declared them to be is starting to gain ground.

WHAT IS IT ALL ABOUT?

There is no lack of Marx biographies. Since the first comprehensive works by Spargo (1912) and Mehring (1918), more than thirty large biographies of Marx have been published. If yet another, comprehensive biography of Marx is to be presented, it requires some justification. That the older biographies are full of lesser and greater inaccuracies is hardly surprising. Some of the defects could have been detected by the authors themselves had they been a bit more careful in their research, but to some extent these defects only became obvious through later findings. The mere correction of existing mistakes would, however, be a weak justification for a new biography. The partisan nature of many Marx biographies—many followers glorified Marx the person and not a few critics attempted to supplement the critique of his works with evidence of bad personal qualities—is still not a strong argument for a new biography. To justify my undertaking, and to characterize what is conceptually new about it, I can offer three points.

The first point has to do with a phenomenon that I refer to as *biographical*

---

4. *Friedrich Engels: Der Mann, der den Marxismus erfand* (Friedrich Engels: The Man Who Invented Marxism). The original bears a considerably more precise title: *The Frock-Coated Communist: The Revolutionary Life of Friedrich Engels* (London: Allen Lane, 2009).

overestimation. Biographies tell the story of a person's life. Usually, they stake the claim of making the person familiar to the reader, of drawing a portrait with all human strengths and weaknesses. Franz Mehring, the great historian of early German social democracy, wrote in the introduction to his Marx biography: "The task which I set myself when I undertook this work was to present him in all his powerful and rugged greatness" (Mehring, xvi). Mehring was further assured by Marx's daughter Laura, since she, as Mehring mentioned in the introduction, "felt that I had obtained the deepest insight into his character and would be able to portray it most clearly" (Mehring, xv).

Other biographers might not state things so clearly, but often have the same pretension of being able to enter into the "character" of the person whose life they are depicting. Some support this claim with the assertion that they personally knew the subject quite well, while others argue that they were able to study intimate documents such as diaries or private letters. Thus, in the 1930s, the complete letters of Marx and Engels, which had just been published for the first time, served as justification for the work of many Marx biographers because now, finally, one had access to the private Marx. But this judgment is only valid in a limited way. Not all letters had been preserved, and indeed a number of letters of a purely personal nature were sorted out by Marx's daughter Eleanor after his death and probably destroyed.[5]

Many readers take the comprehensive claims of biographers at face value and believe after having read a biography that they know not only the profiled author, artist, or politician, but also the person. Although John Spargo and Franz Mehring, for example, had not known Marx personally, a biography can only fulfill the claim of revealing the "essence" or "character" of a subject in a fragmentary way. Every person has a sphere of thoughts, feelings, and desires of which he or she is more or less aware but does not share with anyone or with very few trusted people. As we all know from experience, our fears and hopes, vanities or longings for revenge, play an important role in what we do, without us necessarily revealing that to others. Through the careful evaluation of letters, diaries, and statements by friends and relatives, a biography can illuminate certain backgrounds or make it clear that a work or public intervention perhaps came to be in a way different than was previously commonly assumed. But we can never be sure whether we have found out all the motives and intentions of the depicted person. I am not referring here to a sphere of the "unconscious," but rather to that which is conscious

---

5. See Eleanor's letter of March 26, 1883, to her sister Laura (Meier 1983: 191).

to the person in question, what the person perhaps discussed within a close circle, but concerning which there is no longer any testimony.

The claim to present the essence of another human being is a massive over-estimation of the possibilities of a biography. However, it's an overestimation that comes naturally to mind. Dealing comprehensively with a person's life, reading their most intimate letters, penetrating their public and private con-flicts—this all creates the impression in the biographer of having achieved a deep familiarity with the profiled person. One believes that one knows the person depicted exactly, what they felt, why they reacted one way and not another. That's why many biographers tend to regard the suppositions that appear to them to be plausible as facts and to present them as such. That is fatal for the reader. If an author makes clear that he or she is expressing a supposition, then the critical reader is challenged to evaluate the plausibility of this supposition according to the state of his or her own knowledge. If, on the other hand, an author presents a matter as a fact proven by sources, then the reader tends to accept the matter, assuming that the author has carefully evaluated the sources. If the author does not distinguish between somewhat secure knowledge, more or less plausible suppositions, and mere speculation, and even augments them with vulgar psychology, then the border between biography and *biographical fiction* has been crossed.

This is then the first starting point of the present biography: *avoiding any biographical fiction*. That does not mean I will dispense entirely with suppo-sitions. I will distinguish exactly, however, between that which we can more or less assume to be true on the basis of the existing sources (the credibility of which will have to be discussed individually), that which we can only sup-pose (whereby the plausibility of each supposition must be discussed), and what we simply don't know.

The demand to distinguish between relatively secure knowledge on the basis of sources and mere supposition might sound obvious to some readers, whereas others who are familiar with more recent epistemological debates might object that the strict demarcation between secure historical facts and mere suppositions is not at all as simple as it sounds. But my point is not to give a green light to naive positivism, which believes that science can be reduced to the affirmation of facts. Rather, my concern is the manner of deal-ing with sources and reflecting upon the status of statements that are made on the basis of these sources. If one writes, for example, of the intentions con-nected with a specific act, then it makes a huge difference whether the ascer-tainment of this intention is based upon a self-description by the person in question, or whether it is merely a conclusion arrived at from certain clues. Such a difference should not be blurred in the presentation.

In many Marx biographies, the way in which sources are dealt with is questionable. Some authors, like Friedenthal (1981), for example, do not cite detailed sources at all for some statements, thus preventing them from being checked. Others provide sources, but do not work critically with those sources, satisfied that they are able to provide any kind of source at all for a specific statement. But when the source turns out to consist simply in a reference to an assertion in another biography, which in turn does not name a source, then the citation isn't worth much. In some Marx biographies, such as Wheen's (1999), there are a number of products of fantasy (I will refer to some briefly in the appropriate passages) that are simply given without a source. In contrast, Sperber (2013) has provided the Marx biography with the greatest number of sources thus far. On almost every page, there are multiple notes with bibliographic references, so that one has the impression that even the most minor statements are proven by sources. Unfortunately, this is not always the case. If one checks the references, then not unfrequently it turns out that the sources do not provide proof of the assertion in the respective passage. I will also deal with some of Sperber's fictions.

In this biography, I have attempted to provide the most reliable source possible for every important biographical assertion and, if necessary, discuss how reliable the source is. Furthermore, I've made the effort to distinguish exactly between that which the source proves and that which can perhaps be supposed on the basis of the source. Whereas many biographies are similar to an *Entwicklungsroman*, written from the perspective of an omniscient narrator, the present biography is at times more like a crime novel: what does a certain text say, how reliable is the statement of a third party, what can actually be concluded on the basis of a certain clue? These investigations do not always lead to a clear result.

The *second starting point* with which this biography can be justified concerns the relationship between life and work. There is still not a Marx biography that takes both life and work into account in equal measure. Most biographies make do with a short excursion into the work. Many biographers only have a superficial knowledge of Marx's theory, which doesn't stop some of them from making far-reaching judgments. One exception is McLellan's (1973) biography, which attempts a systematic consideration of Marx's work based on the author's expertise. A further exception is the three-volume double biography of Marx and Engels that was published by Auguste Cornu between 1954 and 1968, but which only goes up to the year 1846. For this period, Cornu's work has not yet been surpassed in terms of both comprehensiveness and detailed knowledge, even if in a number of individual points it contains factual errors and at times questionable judgments.

However, Cornu and McLellan's works were published before the (second) *Marx-Engels Gesamtausgabe* (MEGA) in 1975.[6] Currently, the most thorough examination of Marx's work using the second MEGA can be found in the biography by Sven-Eric Liedman, published in Swedish in 2015 and in English translation in 2018. However, the actual biographical aspect is treated in a somewhat cursory manner.

The importance of the second MEGA for the discussion of Marx's work can hardly be overstated.[7] If one considers Marx's works as a whole, then the texts that he did not publish himself in his own lifetime constitute, both quantitatively and qualitatively, a considerable portion. Their posthumous publication occurred with, in part, very long interruptions, so that since the end of the nineteenth century, every generation not only posed different questions to Marx as the problems changed with the times, but was also familiar with a different "complete works" of Marx. The individual editions were of widely varying quality in terms of faithfulness to the texts. The texts not published by Marx were worked out to different degrees. The early editors, starting with Friedrich Engels, who published the second and third volumes of *Capital*, attempted to make the posthumous texts more readable and, above all, more systematic, so that the edited text would more closely resemble the form for which Marx had been striving. But the editorial interventions, rearrangements, and reformulations were accompanied by shifts in substance; above all, the ambivalences and ruptures that one finds in the original manuscripts were overlaid. The reader received a more or less strongly edited text without clarifying the extent of the editing.[8] For that reason, with the (not yet finished) second MEGA, the works of Marx and Engels are for the first time actually available. They are *complete*, since all manuscripts and excerpts are published, and they are *original*, since the manuscripts are available in their original state, without editorial interference.[9] With the MEGA, for the first time we can deal with the works of Marx and Engels on the basis of a secure textual foundation; for each text, the apparatus volume outlines the

---

6. The first MEGA was begun by David Riazanov (1870–1938) on behalf of the Moscow Marx-Engels Institute, and the first volume was published in 1927 in Frankfurt am Main, Germany. The project was forcibly broken off in the 1930s, falling victim to Stalinism and German Fascism. Riazanov was shot by Stalin's henchmen in 1938. For more, see *Beiträge zur Marx Engels Forschung Sonderband 1*, 1997, and Hecker, 2000 and 2001.

7. When, in the following, reference is made to the "MEGA," the second MEGA is always meant.

8. Such editorial practices were not limited to Marx's texts, but were customary until the beginning of the twentieth century.

9. The MEGA follows historical-critical editorial principles; that is, all texts are published

condition of the text's emergence and transmission and thus the MEGA provides a wealth of biographically relevant information.[10]

But why should someone primarily interested in Marx's work read an extensive biography of Marx at all? Isn't it enough to deal with the arguments that Marx made? Despite all "Marxist" attempts at constructing a system, it cannot be overlooked that Marx's work remained a torso: most of the fundamental works are unfinished, and in part they consist of unpublished manuscripts. In this situation, it is common to refer to Marx's extensive letters, which partially provide substantive additions and explanations. But letters are completely different than published texts or unpublished manuscripts. In letters, one engages with friends, one attempts to explain something to acquaintances, or to convince publishers of a certain project. We must rely therefore on the biographical context to have an adequate understanding of letters and that which is stated in them or what, in fact, cannot be stated in them. But that isn't the only reason to occupy oneself with the biography, even if we are primarily interested in Marx's theories.

Marx's work is not just a torso; it is a succession of torsos. It consists of a continuous sequence of attempts that were broken off, of new beginnings that were not continued, or continued in another form. These different approaches contain not only thematic shifts and substantive tangents, but also, again and again, new theoretical conceptions and breaks with previous conceptions. Marx did not except his own work from critique. If we survey the development of his work as a whole, then both important continuities

---

completely, true to the originals, and with all variations (in the case of published texts, differences between individual editions; in the case of manuscripts, with deletions, replacements, and rearrangements). Text alterations by the editors are kept to a minimum and exactly documented. In addition to each actual volume containing the text, there is an apparatus volume, which in addition to text variations, subject explanations, and indices also contains an exact description of textual evidence as well as information concerning the publication and history of each text. The MEGA is structured into four sections: I. Works (except for *Capital*), II. *Capital* and preparatory works, III. Letters, containing not only letters by, but also to Marx and Engels, and IV. Excerpts, from books that frequently contain notes and commentaries by Marx and Engels. Within each section, the texts are presented in more or less chronological order. Section II, which contains Marx's texts concerning the critique of economics starting in 1857, is now completely available. Dlubek (1994), Hubmann, Münkler, Neuhaus (2001), Sperl (2004), and Neuhaus, Hubmann (2011) deal more extensively with the history and editorial principles of the MEGA.

10. For the time period up to 1843 that is dealt with in this first volume of biography, all relevant MEGA volumes in all sections are available. After that, there are a few gaps, but since the publication of the MEGA volumes does not follow their chronological order, there is no longer a phase of Marx's life for which there are no MEGA volumes.

as well as multiple strong ruptures can be recognized. In the last seventy years, many discussions revolved around whether Marx's intellectual development must be regarded as a continuous enterprise, in which no fundamental changes occurred after the *Economic-Philosophical Manuscripts* of 1844 (some claim after the *Critique of Hegel's Philosophy of Right* from 1843 or even after the Dissertation of 1841), or whether there was a rupture in the development, which is usually dated from the *Theses on Feuerbach* or *The German Ideology* from 1845.

It appears to me that both the continuity hypothesis as well as the notion of a break, with the widespread contrast between a "young" (philosophical, humanist) Marx and a "mature" (economist, scientific) Marx miss the complexity of Marx's work and his development. Marx always followed multiple thematic trajectories. Even if he became strongly occupied by political economy after 1843/44, this development did not necessarily progress toward *Capital* as the "major work." Alongside the critique of political economy, Marx was concerned, after 1843, with a critique of politics and the state. His investigations range constantly across multiple fields. And alongside the main lines, there is an abundance of intermittently appearing and disappearing offshoots. Among other things, Marx dealt extensively with mathematics and the natural sciences, with anthropology and linguistics, and again and again with historical questions. The breadth of this thematic diversity is made clear by the consideration of the countless newspaper articles that Marx wrote and, above all, his excerpt notebooks, which will be published in their entirety for the first time in section 4 of the MEGA.

Beyond that, Marx was not only a scholar who conducted research, but also a political journalist who composed an enormous number of articles for newspapers and journals. And he was a revolutionary political actor who entered into alliances, who participated in the construction of different organizations, and who was caught up in political conflicts that led to deep differences with former allies and to persecution by the state. However, scientific work, journalistic interventions, and political engagement were never neatly separated. The scholarly insights achieved by Marx influenced the direction of his journalistic and political activities. What is more, these activities often required interrupting the scientific work, leading to new themes and problems, and thus gained an influence upon the direction of his scientific research. To that extent, if one ignores Marx's life, one can only speak of his scientific-analytical work and its development in a limited sense. If we wish to know why Marx followed certain themes in his work and abandoned others, why there exists this multitude of terminations, new beginnings, and thematic shifts, then we have to deal with the political developments in which Marx was involved, the conflicts and debates to which he referred, and not least the at times turbulent circumstances of his life.

With that, we have arrived at the *third* starting point for the present biography: the manner in which the development of Marx's life and works can be situated in their historical context. Just about every biography deals with historical circumstances. Not infrequently, a biography promises in its subtitle to depict the person "and his times." There is no Marx biography that doesn't address the history of the nineteenth century, though frequently this remains limited to political history and doesn't constitute much more than the general background for telling the story of Marx's life. Precisely because the big milestones in the development of Marx's life and work are known, a more or less strong necessity of this development is assumed. But if one wishes to approach the breaks and contingencies, then their conditions need to be made clear. That is not just the case for the conditions of the story of Marx's life in the narrow sense, but also for the general conditions within which Marx's intellectual-scientific development occurs. Thus, not a few critics of Marx tend to disdain the originality of Marx's achievements and turn him into a second-class student of Ricardo, Hegel, or Feuerbach, without examining in detail the relation of Marx to these authors. In an exact inversion, many Marxists tend to inflate Marx. Ricardo, Hegel, and many others are named as sources, but their contributions are assumed to pale next to Marx's. Not infrequently, Marx's (later) judgments—not only about Smith, Ricardo, Hegel, and Feuerbach, but also earlier companions such as Bruno Bauer and Ferdinand Lassalle or later opponents such as Michael Bakunin—are uncritically adopted and made the measure of the presentation. But Marx's attitude toward the people named changed, sometimes multiple times. A simple judgment is not enough. And not least, Marx's judgments must also be subjected to critical scrutiny.

Marx's life and work can only be presented adequately if the contemporary conflicts in which Marx was involved do not shrink into mere background, and if both Marx's friends and enemies don't just become extras. That a biography of Marx must also deal in depth with the life and work of Friedrich Engels—who not only provided Marx with enormous material support, but was his most important discussion partner and comrade-in-arms for almost forty years—is a matter of course, as is the fact that his wife, Jenny von Westphalen, also played an important role. However, in a few phases of his life, other people as well were of great importance for Marx, and they also deserve detailed consideration.

To situate Marx comprehensively in the conflicts of his time, to make clear his original contributions as well as his intellectual dependencies and limits, is a task that has not been adequately performed in previous biographies.[11] For that reason, I will deal extensively not only with the politics, but also the science of the nineteenth century, with Marx's sources and his contemporaries, including a few that did not have any close relationship to him. This reaches a fundamental problem of biographical writing. Is it in fact possible to pick out a single person, a single life from history? For historicism, the dominant form of historiography, primarily in Germany, in the nineteenth and early twentieth century, this was self-evident, since one assumed that history was made by "great men" with which the biographer "empathized" in order to "understand" their actions. Biography thus became a central component of historical research and explanation. If, however, we take into consideration the importance of structural conditions within which social life occurs, then the matter is no longer so simple. In the debates that were conducted in the twentieth century concerning the possibility of biographical writing, a considerable skepticism developed, which in the case of the famous French sociologist Pierre Bourdieu led to a fundamental antipathy, since according to Bourdieu every biography rested upon the illusion of a demarcated life (Bourdieu 1998).

What is correct about this critique is that one cannot separate human beings from the conditions under which they act. Nonetheless, neither their actions nor thoughts are completely determined by the respective conditions; some things are made possible while others are made impossible, some things are suggested by circumstances while others can only be achieved by overcoming great hindrances. The preconditions of our thoughts and actions are not static; they are changed by human activity, which leads to the emergence of new possibilities for action, while the existing possibilities are altered. A person is not simply a fixed unity that, on the one hand, receives influences (in youth and during "maturation") and from which, on the other hand, effects emanate (in "mature" adulthood). But a three-part presentation based upon such a simplifying scheme often forms the foundation of many biographies: after the shaping of the person in youth and early adulthood, the focus is placed upon the direct effects upon the mature adult, and finally upon the last stage of life and the person's legacy (the indirect effects) of the person in question.[12] But the person (as well as the work) is not a fixed unity,

---

11. Here as well the work of Cornu (1952–68) stands out in comparison with all other biographies. But the depiction only goes up to 1846 and is based upon a level of knowledge more than fifty years old.

12. The three parts of Sperber's 2013 Marx biography also follow this schema: I. Shaping, II. Struggle, III. Legacy. In doing so, Sperber doesn't even try to offer a justification for the

but the result of a permanent process of social constitution occurring at different levels. To that extent, a biography is not just concerned with "understanding" a person, but also with the historical conditions, the course, and the consequences of this constant, unconcluded constitution process, and the work that always emerges anew and differently from it.

In the present biography, I have avoided the division into such crude life phases. In the division into chapters, I orient myself, on the one hand, upon the respective external conditions under which Marx lived, in which cities, with what activities, and, on the other hand, upon the development of his thoughts and work. Temporal overlapping between the chapters as well as looks ahead and looks back cannot be avoided. The fact that this biography encompasses multiple volumes is due to the scope of the material. But the division into individual volumes in no way involves presenting discrete phases of Marx's life or work, which is why I have numbered the chapters continuously through all three volumes.

---

arbitrarily drawn demarcations between these three phases (1847 and 1870). Especially in the case of Marx, it becomes clear how inadequate such a division is: well into old-age, Marx was not only eager to learn (older than fifty, he learned Russian in order to read economic literature from Russia), but also prepared to overturn his own conceptions. And his "struggle" does not begin in 1847, but at the latest after his studies, when he became editor-in-chief of the *Rheinische Zeitung* in 1842 and immediately ran into conflict with censors, until the newspaper was finally banned in 1843. And not only was *Capital* received as his "legacy," but the unpublished writings of his youth such as the *Economic and Philosophical Manuscripts* of 1844 were as well.

1

FORGOTTEN YOUTH
1818–1835

The young man made an impression, a tremendous impression: "Be prepared to meet the greatest, perhaps the only real philosopher living now. When he will appear in public (both in his writings as well as at the university), he will draw the eyes of all Germany upon him. . . . [He] is still a very young man, hardly 24 years old; but he will give the final blow to all medieval religion and politics; he combines the deepest philosophical seriousness with a cutting wit. Can you imagine Rousseau, Voltaire, Holbach, Lessing, Heine, and Hegel combined—not thrown together—in one person? If you can—you have Dr. Marx." (Hess 2004: xii)

Moses Hess (1812–1875), who wrote these lines in 1841 to his friend Berthold Auerbach, was six years older than Marx, and the author of two books in which he had attempted to give the most recent philosophy a political twist. The young Marx, in contrast, had at this point not published anything other than two poems. Nonetheless, his friends regarded him as a future star in the philosophical firmament.

The young man did not just make an impression upon his friends. Just twenty-four years old and without practical experience in any profession, in October of 1842 he was made part of the editorial staff of the *Rheinische Zeitung* in Cologne. This was not a small local rag, but rather the mouthpiece of the liberal Rhineland bourgeoisie. Well appointed with capital as a joint-stock company, the *Rheinische Zeitung* was on its way to becoming one of the most important German newspapers.

How could it be that the young Marx was able to make such an impression upon his environment so early in his life? Marx was born in 1818 in Trier, at the time a tiny little city in the far-western part of the Kingdom of Prussia. He spent his childhood and youth in Trier with numerous siblings, attended gymnasium,[13] received his first sparks of intellectual stimulation, and very early on made the acquaintance of his later wife, Jenny von Westphalen. Family, school, friends, the environment in which one grows up, experiences and conflicts during one's youth and childhood—all of this has a considerable influence upon a person's development. Early hopes and successes can have long-term effects just as much as early fears and failures. But we know nothing about the hopes and fears of Marx the youth. His childhood and youth, the phase of life before his Abitur exam in 1835, is "lost." Marx did not keep a diary or compose memoirs of his youth, and there are no eyewitness reports of his youth, no letters from third parties in which he's mentioned. Not even isolated observations by relatives, acquaintances, or teachers have survived. Even later, when Marx was a well-known personage, none of his fellow pupils published any kind of recollections concerning him. Only his youngest daughter Eleanor shared two small anecdotes after his death, both unspecific in terms of time period. Otherwise, only a few pieces of information can be gleaned from official documents.

WHAT WE KNOW FOR SURE

Karl Marx came into this world in Trier on May 5, 1818, a Tuesday, around two o'clock in the morning, as the child of Heinrich Marx and his wife, Henriette, *née* Presburg. That's what is recorded in the birth register of the city of Trier, which gives the child's first name as "Carl." (Monz 1973: 214).[14] Marx usually wrote "Karl"; the double name "Karl Heinrich" that shows up in many biographies was used only during his time as a student.[15]

---

13. *Gymnasium* denotes a secondary school at which pupils train for the *Abitur*, a qualification that allows recipients to attend university. —Trans.

14. On the following information, see, above all, Monz (1973: 214ff.) as well as the extensive collection of sources in Schöncke (1993).

15. He goes by the name "Carl Heinrich Marx" in 1835 on the registration form of the University of Bonn as well as on his leaving certificate from Bonn (facsimiles in Bodsch 2012: 15 and 160). At the University of Berlin, he enrolled as "Karl Heinrich" (facsimile in Museum für Deutsche Geschichte 1986: 26); this form is also found on the title page of his dissertation from 1841 (facsimiles in MEGA I/1: 9); in all other official documents, as well as his Abitur diploma from 1835 (facsimile in MEGA I/1: 471) and his marriage contract from 1843 (Kliem 1970: 141), one only finds "Karl" or "Carl." Marx also only used the initials "KH" for the collections of poems for his father and for Jenny (see chapter 2). The fact that the name "Karl Heinrich Marx" is still circulated is the result of decades of cribbing from two early, but

Karl was not his parents' first child; in 1815, their son Mauritz David and in 1816 daughter Sophie had been born. However, Mauritz David died in 1819. In the years following, further siblings were born: Hermann (1819), Henriette (1820), Louise (1821), Emilie (1822), Caroline (1824), and Eduard (1826), so that Karl grew up with seven siblings total. However, not all of them would go on to live long lives: Eduard, the youngest brother, was eleven when he died in 1837. Three other siblings were hardly older than 20 at the time of their death: Hermann died in the year 1842, Henriette in 1845, and Caroline in 1847. In all cases, the cause of death was given as "consumption" (tuberculosis), a widespread illness in the nineteenth century. The three remaining sisters lived considerably longer; they also survived their brother Karl. Sophie died in 1886, Emilie in 1888, and Louise in 1893.

Parents Heinrich (1777–1838) and Henriette (1788–1863) had married in 1814. Both came from Jewish families that converted to Protestant Christianity. Karl Marx was baptized on August 26, 1824, along with his then six siblings. At this point, his father had already been baptized; the exact date, however, is not known. His mother was baptized a year later, on November 20, 1825. On the occasion of the baptism of her children, according to the entry in the church register, she wanted to wait with her own baptism out of consideration for her still-living parents, but she wanted her children to be baptized (Monz 1973: 242).

Marx's father was a well-regarded lawyer in Trier, and his income allowed his family a certain affluence. Both the house on Brückengasse (today Brückenstraße), which the family rented and in which Karl was born,[16] as well as the somewhat smaller, but centrally located house on Simeonstraße that the family purchased in the autumn of 1819 and in which young Karl grew up, were among the better bourgeois homes of the city (Herres 1993: 20).

As the school tuition payments verify, the twelve-year-old Karl was accepted in the winter semester of 1830–31 to the Quarta, that is, the third grade, of the Trier gymnasium (Monz 1973a: 11). He took the abitur exam in 1835, at the age of seventeen; his Abitur tasks are, except for a poem that's probably even older, his earliest texts. We don't know whether Karl attended an elementary school. Elementary schools at this time were not particularly

---

incorrect, sources: Friedrich Engels had used this name in a biographical sketch written in 1892 for the *Handwörterbuch der Staatswissenschaften* (Political Science Handbook) (I/32: 182; 22: 337) as did Franz Mehring, who published the first comprehensive biography of Marx in 1918.

16. Marx's house of birth, a typical bourgeois Trier house in the baroque style, still stands as the "Karl Marx Haus," a museum.

good, and since Karl began with the third grade of gymnasium, he presumably received private instruction before his admission. The bookseller Eduard Montigny mentions in a letter to Marx from the year 1848 that he had once given him writing lessons (MEGA III/2:471).

Personal information about Marx's youth is only available from two anecdotes handed down by his daughter Eleanor. Twelve years after Marx's death, she wrote: "My aunts [Marx's sisters] say that as a little boy he was a terrible tyrant to his sisters, whom he would 'drive' down the Markusberg at Trier full speed and, worse, would insist on their eating the 'cakes' he made with dirty dough and dirtier hands. But they withstood the 'driving' and ate the 'cakes' without murmur, for the sake of the stories Karl would tell them as a reward for their virtue" (E. Marx, 1895: 245).

In a biographical sketch prepared shortly after Marx's death, Eleanor writes that he was "At once much loved and feared by his school fellows—loved because he was always doing mischief, and feared because of his readiness in writing satirical verse and lampooning his enemies" (E. Marx 1883: https://www.marxists.org/archive/eleanor-marx/1883/06/karl-marx.htm).

Eleanor reports that among Marx's earliest playmates was his future wife, Jenny von Westphalen, and her younger brother Edgar. The latter attended the same school as Marx and also received confirmation along with him on March 23, 1834 (Monz 1973: 254, 338). How the children's friendship came about and when it began, however, remains unknown. We know that Marx's older sister Sophie was friends with Jenny, but whether it was the two girls or the two boys Karl and Edgar who first made friends, or whether the children's friendship was first initiated through the friendly relationship between their fathers, is not known.

Edgar was the only classmate that Marx remained friends with for long after his school days. We don't know whether he maintained friendly relations with other classmates during his school days. But it would be somewhat hasty to conclude from this lack of knowledge that he had no friends, a point to which I'll return at the end of the chapter.

Eleanor also discloses that the young Karl was intellectually stimulated primarily by his father and his future father-in-law, Ludwig von Westphalen. It was from the latter that he "imbibed his first love for the "Romantic" School, and while his father read him Voltaire and Racine, Westphalen read him Homer and Shakespeare." The fact that Marx dedicated his doctoral dissertation rather emotionally to Ludwig von Westphalen in 1841 demonstrates how important the latter was to him.

That's everything we know for sure about Karl Marx from the time before his Abitur exam. However, we can factor in his environment, living conditions in Trier, his family relations, and school. Particularly with regard to his father and father-in-law, a few things have been discovered in the last few decades. Neither personal characteristics nor later developments can be deduced from his environment, but it constitutes an initial background against which the young Marx processed his early experiences.

TRIER BETWEEN IDYLL AND PAUPERISM

Marx was born into a provincial city. In 1819, Trier had hardly more than 11,000 inhabitants; furthermore, about 3,500 soldiers were stationed in Trier (Monz 1973: 57). This was not an especially large population, even if one takes into consideration that back then most people lived in the countryside and cities had far fewer inhabitants than today. Despite its small number of inhabitants, Trier, which was surrounded by a town wall until well into the nineteenth century, had a considerable spread. Construction was extensive, with many open spaces, which were used inside the city as farmland and gardens or as pastures. In 1840, the undeveloped spaces in Trier still outnumbered the developed ones, and alongside houses made of stone were one-story houses made of wood, in one neighborhood there were even "barracks the likes of which nearly no other tiny country town has" (Kentenich 1915: 746).

The Trier in which Marx grew up was characteristically rural; it had only two main streets, the rest of the town consisting of side alleys and little streets (ibid.: 747). How the conditions of buildings and hygiene must have been is made clear by the prohibitions of a police order from 1818 (reprinted in full in ibid.: 713ff.). The order said that from now on house construction would be allowed only along an established alignment; houses in danger of collapse (of which there were apparently not a few) had to be torn down; flues and stovepipes could no longer lead directly to the street but had to be extended to the roof; diverting sewage from kitchens, stables, and commercial enterprises onto the street was prohibited; also prohibited was pouring wastewater and emptying chamber pots onto the open street; and it was no longer permissible to slaughter pigs and calves on the street.

Within Trier, there were important remnants of Roman buildings; outside of the city there was an impressive landscape. Both were important for Marx's youth. Comprehensive lessons in Latin found vivid illustration in the Roman buildings and collections of classical antiquities, and the landscape was inviting for strolls and hikes. As can be gleaned from the dedication of his dissertation (MECW 1: 27), the young Karl had undertaken extensive hikes with his future father-in-law, Ludwig von Westphalen. The city's appearance at the time is depicted by Ernst von Schiller (1796–1841), the second-oldest son of the poet Friedrich von Schiller and a judge at the district court of Trier between 1828 and 1835. In a letter from June 1, 1828, to his sister Emilie, he wrote:

> Rather long, interrupted by many gardens, the city stretches along the right bank of the Mosel River, over which there runs a stone bridge of eight arches. At the northern end, the city is closed by the Porta Nigra, a gigantic building . . . within the city, on the eastern side, there stands on a gigantic square the palace of the 30th infantry regiment. In the south-eastern corner of the city there still lie the very large ruins of the Roman baths and the amphitheater. . . . In the south and the north of the city are the splendid buildings of formerly wealthy abbeys under imperial immediacy [a status granted by the Holy Roman Empire to give institutions autonomy from local rulers]. . . . On the left bank of the Mosel, right behind the bridge arise jagged rocks, red in color; between them are large almond and chestnut trees. Upon these rocks, one sees a hermitage and at its highest point, a lonely cross, from which one glances into the steep depths. Behind these rocks, high mountains project, with a beautiful high forest of chestnut, oak, and beech trees . . . between the rocks, there's a forest stream that flows into the Mosel which, from a distance of 15 minutes from its outlet, plunges from a height of 70 feet into a ravine where the sun never shines. Here it is splendid; constantly cooled, and with no sound other than the fall of the forest stream. On the mountains and rocks, one looks down upon the city as if upon a map. It is a quite beautiful valley. All of these natural beauties are so near that one can reach them and return within a few hours. (Schmidt 1905: 335)

Trier's History and Cultural Life

Trier, founded by the Romans around 16 BC, is one of the oldest German cities. In the first few centuries after Christ, Trier developed into one of the largest Roman cities north of the Alps, and in the fourth century was one of the residences of the Western Roman Emperor, with around 80,000 inhabitants. In the immediate vicinity of the most famous Roman building in Trier, the Porta Nigra, in Simeonsstraße, was the house in which Karl Marx grew up.

In the Medieval and Early Modern periods, the population of Trier declined drastically due to wars, plagues, and famine. In 1695, it contained fewer than 3,000 people (Kentenich 1915: 534). Since the Middle Ages, Trier and its surrounding territories had constituted an *electorate* (German: *Kurfürstentum*).

The archbishop of Trier was one of three spiritual electors who, along with the four secular electors, chose the German kings. Not only many churches and monasteries, but also the palace mentioned by Schiller, originate from the period of the electorate. Starting in the twelfth century in Trier, a prestigious relic was preserved, the "Holy Tunic," supposedly the tunic worn by Jesus. When this tunic is exhibited publicly, which is rarely, it attracts massive numbers of believers. Karl Marx's wife, Jenny, saw such an exhibition in 1844 during her visit to Trier, which she reported on.

The strong position of the Catholic Church in Trier was not shaken by the Reformation; at the beginning of the nineteenth century, Protestants in Trier were an infinitesimally small minority. The architectural consequences of Catholicism were characterized by Johann Wolfgang von Goethe, who got to know Trier in 1792, as follows: "The city itself is striking; it lays claim to possessing more ecclesiastical buildings than any other town of the same size; this it would be difficult to deny, for inside the walls it is crowded, nay, overwhelmed, with churches, chapels, monasteries, convents, colleges, and other buildings for knightly orders and fraternities to meet; outside it is beset by abbeys, institutions, and Carthusian monasteries."

Goethe had participated in the first military campaign against revolutionary France. The armies of the old monarchist Europe, the Europe that looked down on the new France with contempt, had to retreat before the cannonades of the Battle of Valmy, which would become famous. During the retreat, Goethe spent some time in Trier, where he made the acquaintance of a young teacher from whom he learned about the city during their walks together and with whom he enjoyed "many pleasant talks on scientific and literary subjects" (Goethe 1884: 176). This young teacher, Johann Hugo Wyttenbach (1767–1848), was for a good forty years or so after Goethe's stay the director of the gymnasium of Trier, where he taught the young Karl. We will return to him.

When Karl Marx was born, twenty-six years after Goethe's visit, the cityscape had changed considerably. In 1794, Trier was occupied by French troops. Revolutionary France had not only beaten back the monarchist powers but had made considerable territorial conquests. French rule brought a decisive revolutionary break to Trier, which fundamentally changed life in many areas. In 1798, French law, which was very progressive at the time, was introduced, followed in 1804 by the Napoleonic Code Civil. With that, aristocratic privileges were abolished, and all citizens were equal before the law. The hereditary subservience of the peasantry and guilds was abolished and the freedom to exercise a trade of one's choosing was introduced. Court trials were made public, and for punitive matters, juries were summoned; that is, there was a reliance upon the participation of citizens, which was reflected in verdicts. The power of the Church was restricted, and the obligation to wed before a civil registry office introduced.

From 1802 on, most of the monasteries and abbeys in Trier were abolished, and numerous buildings torn down. Most Church property was transferred to the state and subsequently auctioned off. Since individual Church properties were sold as undivided units, considerable means were required to buy them, which only the urban bourgeoisie possessed. After purchase, the properties were divided and further sold at a large profit. The consequence was an enormous growth in wealth of the already well-heeled ruling class (Clemens 2004).

Above all, after 1800 the French occupation was advantageous for industry and trade: Trier obtained access to French markets; sales to the French came from wallpaper manufacturers, a porcelain manufacturer, and multiple cloth factories produced for the French army (see Müller 1988). Furthermore, due to the continental blockade Napoleon enforced against England, these industries were protected against superior English competition. After Napoleon's failed Russian campaign, French rule ended. In 1815, at the Congress of Vienna, Catholic Trier, along with the Rhineland, was awarded to Protestant Prussia.

During the Prussian era, a number of prosperous and even a few very rich families lived in Trier. The description provided by Ernst von Schiller in a letter to his wife dated April 12, 1828, seems typical:

> The women preen themselves quite a bit, sometimes according to a taste rather strange to me. . . . They work in small circles and promenade parties, i.e., they knit. Fridays, from 5 to 6 o'clock, they go to Wyttenbach's history lectures. . . . Wednesdays during the summer, one spends the time from 5 to 8 o'clock in Gilbert's garden, where one drinks coffee and wine, listens to music, smokes, and knits. . . . Now and then on other days of the week, families, or sometimes the women alone, go to Wettendorf's cottage and enjoy coffee or chocolate. Every fourteen days, there's an evening entertainment with women hosted by the casino, where one mainly dances. Usually, however, one visits a family, at least once a week, that is to say one visits good friends. . . . There we drink tea and beer, play whist, smoke, and knit, and at half past 8 we eat salad, roast, tongue, cheese and the like and drink wine with it. After the meal, a pipe is smoked and then around 10 or half past 10, one goes home. (Schmidt 1905: 329)

Groß estimates the "top of Trier society" during this period as ten to twelve people: the generals of the garrison; the presidents of the district government and the courts; a few rich merchants, bankers, and landowners; and last but not least the Catholic bishop, Josef von Hommer (1760–1836). They often met over long Sunday dinners with exquisite ingredients, the reputation of which reached as far as Berlin (Groß 1998: 77).

Despite its small population, Trier had a diverse cultural life (for an overview, see Zenz 1979: 159–79). The "Society for Useful Research," founded in 1801, played an important role. In 1817, the Society was divided into natural history/physical sciences and historical-antiquarian sections, the latter dedicated, among other things, to the research and preservation of antiquities in Trier (Gross 1956: 93ff.) Wyttenbach, mentioned by Goethe, was a co-founder and for many years secretary of the Society; his archaeological studies made him well known far beyond Trier (ibid.: 102). He also founded the Trier city library, for which he rescued thousands of volumes from the secularized monasteries and abbeys of the immediate and distant environs, so that the library contained numerous manuscripts and old editions. The gymnasium he directed also housed a collection of coins, natural objects, and antiques. In his public lectures, mentioned by Schiller, he addressed the educated bourgeoisie or those parts of the bourgeoisie with an interest in education. The desire for education had increased enormously since the late eighteenth century; in a number of cities, there were more or less regular, public lectures by well-known scholars. The most famous were the "Cosmos" lectures that Alexander von Humboldt held in 1827–28 at the Berlin Choral Society, which were attended by over eight hundred people on multiple occasions (Humboldt 2004: 12). It has been established that the Trier gymnasium held evening lecture series on various topics starting in 1802 (Gross 1962: 34).

The poet Eduard Duller (1809–1853) from Vienna and his friend, the Silesian lieutenant Friedrich von Sallet (1812–1842), who also wrote poems, created a lively literary life in Trier from 1832 on (Gross 1956: 136). There was also a theater, in which during the 1820s and 1830s, alongside the classics by Schiller and Lessing, historical-romantic pieces as well as multiple operas were performed. Weber's romantic-horrifying *Der Freischütz* (The Marksman) was performed to great success on multiple occasions, including the year 1834 (ibid.: 129). It is quite possible that the young Karl, who composed his first poems during his school years, also attended one of the performances.

The center of social life in Trier was the Literary Casino Society (*Literarische Casinogesellschaft*) founded in 1818 (this is the "casino" mentioned by Schiller). Its statutes determined its purpose to be "maintaining a reading society connected to an association location for the convivial enjoyment of educated people" (quoted in Kentenich 1915: 731). In the Casino building, completed in 1825, there was a reading room that also contained several foreign newspapers. Balls and concerts, and on special occasions banquets, were regularly held (see Schmidt 1955: 11ff.). The sophisticated bourgeois stratum and the officers of the garrison belonged to the Casino. Karl's father, Heinrich Marx, was one of the founding members.[17] Similar societies, often with the same name, also arose at the end of the eighteenth and beginning of the nineteenth century in other German cities; they were important focal points for the emerging bourgeois culture. Critique of existing political conditions was also articulated here. In 1834, the Trier Casino was the scene of two political affairs, which we will address.

Social Relations

Trier was not the Biedermeier idyll that one might imagine from the depiction of its beautiful landscape or cultural life. The succession of French rule by Prussian rule had considerable economic and social consequences. Trier was cut off from the important French markets and, as a town at the extreme western periphery of the Prussian kingdom, ended up in an unfavorable peripheral position with poor transportation links to the rest of the empire. The Prussian government regarded the newly acquired Trier area primarily from a military-strategic viewpoint, as a deployment zone for troops in the case of a conflict with France (Monz 1973: 52). State means to support the local economy were not provided, especially as the government increasingly followed the precepts of economic liberalism: the free market alone would take care of economic development.

Many public authorities that had their headquarters in Trier under the electorate or the period of French occupation were moved to Cologne or Koblenz. The university closed under French occupation was not reopened; instead, a university for the Rhineland was founded in Bonn in 1818. Compared to the period of French occupation, the tax burden also increased considerably. Prussia had to finance the costs of war, and disproportionately burdened the Rhine province. The land tax was raised a great deal compared to the period under French occupation, whereas noble landowners in East Prussia were largely exempt from it. The newly introduced taxes on milling and butchering led to an increase in the price of foodstuffs, primarily affecting the poorer sections of the population (Heimers 1988: 401). All this did not exactly contribute to making the primarily Catholic population of

17. See the list of names from the protocol of the general assembly called for January 28, 1818, printed in Schmidt (1955: 88).

Trier, which had accommodated itself well to French rule, into adherents of Protestant Prussia. Conversely, the Prussian government had a great distrust of the city, which it suspected of strong sympathies for France (see Monz 1973: 110ff.)

At the beginning of the period of Prussian rule, the Rhineland experienced strong economic decline, as did the Saar-Mosel area. Trier and the Trier countryside were hit particularly hard. The cloth trade, which had earlier produced for the French army and employed over 1,000 workers, a porcelain manufactory that had employed over 100 workers, and a woolen blanket manufactory now no longer had sufficient sales volume and had to cease production. Only small businesses remained (Heimers 1988: 402).

The sales difficulties were not just a consequence of the loss of French markets. After the repeal of the continental blockade, which had prevented the sale of English goods on the continent, local producers were exposed to superior competition. Thus, the iron industries in the Eifel and Hunsrück regions, the two largest industrial areas in the vicinity of Trier, registered steep declines. In the Mosel valley, the poverty of which had already been reported upon in the eighteenth century (Monz 1973: 45), there were also great problems. The Mosel winemakers had initially profited from Prussian rule. The Prussian customs law of 1818 practically granted them a monopoly, so that their cultivation area was markedly expanded. However, the greater quantity of wine was accompanied by a decline in quality. When Prussia concluded customs agreements with Hesse and Württemberg in 1828 and 1829, southern German wines largely displaced Mosel wines from the Prussian market. Poverty increased considerably among Mosel winemakers and, in the 1830s, their situation worsened considerably because of the founding of a German customs union. In the early 1840s, Marx made the poverty of Mosel winemakers widely known through his reporting for the *Rheinische Zeitung*.

So, since the end of the 1820s at the latest, the entire Trier region found itself in drastic economic decline. The situation of small-scale business in Trier was also impaired, since the surrounding region was its primary market. The well-off strata in Trier were confronted by numerous impoverished artisans and a broad mass of poor and partially unemployed workers, who lived in overpopulated residential areas. Their desperation was reflected in an increase of begging, a rising number of civil cases, the auctioning of household possessions, liens, and increasing prostitution (Monz 1973: 83ff.). In Trier, the new social phenomenon that spread throughout all of Western Europe in the first half of the nineteenth century was becoming clearly visible: *pauperism*. Poor people had of course existed in the past. But as a consequence of early industrialization, large sectors of the population were impoverished, including workers and artisans who had previously been able to feed themselves through their work. It wasn't clear how these people would ever again be able to escape poverty. In Trier, about a fourth of the population was completely dependent upon public relief and private charity. The country almshouse was already threatened by overcrowding in 1826. Four years later, a grain repository was founded that was financed through the issuing of shares. Sales from a public repository were intended to influence bread prices and provide for the poor. In 1831, a soup kitchen was established. Heinrich Marx was apparently also moved by the social misery; he bought two shares in the grain repository. Only sixteen wealthy citizens bought more; usually, only one share was bought (ibid.: 96ff.).

The mayor of Trier for many years, Wilhelm Haw (1793–1862), constantly emphasized the poverty of large parts of the population in his administrative reports to the government, and he demanded supportive measures from government agencies. But the Prussian government, under the influence of economic liberalism, did not approve such measures, or at least not to a sufficient extent. As can be gleaned from Haw's reports, the "middle classes" were also threatened by poverty. He wrote that they concealed their poverty on the surface, but the number of foreclosures and liens revealed the true situation (ibid.: 73; Schiel 1956: 10).

In a detailed examination of tax registers, Herres arrives at the result that for the years 1831–32 that in good times 20 percent, and in bad times 30 percent of Trier households were directly dependent upon public support. Around 40 to 50 percent of households did not live below the poverty level, but their situation was precarious. Accidents or illness could suddenly plunge them into poverty (Herres 1990: 185). The poor lower strata, or strata threatened by poverty, therefore encompassed about 80 percent of households.

To the middle and upper strata—and only they were recorded in the tax registry—belonged the remaining 20 percent of households with an income of over 200 taler a year. Among them, there were considerable differences in income and wealth. Around 10 percent of all households (therefore half of all households subject to taxation) had an annual income of between 200 and 400 taler. Around 8.8 percent had an income between 400 and 2,500 taler. The truly rich households with an annual income above 2,500 taler comprised around 1.2 percent of all households, around 6 percent of households taxed (ibid.: 167). According to the tax registries evaluated by Herres, the two richest citizens of Trier had an annual income of about 30,000 taler. Mayor Wilhelm Haw, who showed considerable engagement on behalf of the issue of poor relief, had a total income (from his office, but primarily from property) of about 10,000 taler; the Catholic bishop Josef von Hommer

ANNUAL INCOME OF TRIER HOUSEHOLDS 1831–1832 (ACCORDING TO HERRES 1990)	
1.2%	over 2,500 taler
8.8%	400–2,500 taler
10%	200–400 taler
80%	less than 200 taler (poor or threatened by poverty)

8,000 taler. Ludwig von Westphalen and Heinrich Marx had annual incomes of 1,800 and 1,500 taler, respectively. Hugo Wyttenbach, the director of the gymnasium, had an income of about 1,000 taler (ibid.: 189ff.). On the basis of this data, one can make an overview (above) of income distribution.

Under the impression of conditions in Trier, one of the first pieces of socialist writing in Germany was written in 1825: "What Could Help?" (*Was könnte helfen?*) by Ludwig Gall (1791–1863). Gall, employed since 1816 as a secretary of the district government in Trier, was influenced by the ideas of the early socialists Robert Owen (1771–1858), Charles Fourier (1772–1837). and Henri de Saint-Simon (1760–1825). In the preface to his text, Gall vividly describes the miserable living conditions of workers. He saw the cause of social problems in all-powerful money: workers were completely dependent upon those who disposed of money. However, Gall did not aim at a complete revolutionizing of social relations or the abolition of money. Rather, with the aid of the state, he wanted to improve the position of the poor vis-à-vis the rich. The state should employ the poor and beggars with useful labor, thus making it possible for them to feed themselves. The poor also were to be strengthened by cooperative institutions supported by the state. In a publication founded in 1828, of which only the first number was issued, Gall propagated his ideas, but they did not find any great reception in Trier. We don't know whether the young Karl Marx was familiar with Gall's writings (on Gall, see Dowe 1970: 43; Monz 1973: 105ff.; Monz 1979).

The issue of poverty remained topical in Trier throughout the entirety of the 1820s and 1830s. It also played an important role in the detailed depictions of Trier life initially published anonymously in 1840 as letters to the publication *Trierer Philantrop* and soon after as a book. The author was Johann Heinrich Schlink (1793–1863), district court councilor in Trier and friend of Heinrich Marx. Schlink wrote that, regardless of the equality before the law introduced by the French, there were "three main classes" in society, namely:

1. the people (day laborers), 2. the middle class, 3. the upper bourgeoisie with public officials (*Beamte*) and the officer corps . . . among the

lowest class I count all people who feed themselves from the daily earn-ings on the work of their own hands and who possess no property (day laborers). It is very numerous, and the current slump in many trades brings them in a great dilemma, so that widespread poverty is becom-ing noticeable.... In order to help themselves during this hardship, they bring their household articles to the pawnshop, often in the illusory hope of recovering them ... moreover, the tendency to consume alco-holic beverages increases; the family falls increasingly further behind and soon can longer survive without the aid of the poverty commission or of the hospital.[18] (Quoted in Kentenich 1915: 759.)[19]

Schlink did not just describe conditions; he also sensed an ominous future: "Meanwhile, pauperism is increasing everywhere to such a degree that it occasionally rises up as a threat, so that one will ultimately have to set a limit to the further expansion of the proletariat" (ibid.: 761). Behind the compas-sion for the misery of the poor there is a noticeable fear that one day the masses could forcefully struggle against their fate; this fear was widespread within the bourgeoisie at the time. In Marx's case as well, one comes across traces of this fear during his activity as editor of the *Rheinische Zeitung*.

KARL MARX'S PARENTS

Karl Marx came from a Jewish family that on his father's side had brought forth numerous rabbis. However, his parents converted to (Protestant) Christianity. The question of what role Jewish tradition and Christian bap-tism played for Karl Marx suggests itself. In part of the biographical literature, this question is not addressed at all. In another part, it is regarded as the key to Marx's psyche and sometimes to his work, whereby Judaism and baptism are usually regarded in a completely ahistorical way. But Jewish heritage and conversion to Christianity meant something different at the beginning of the nineteenth century than it did fifty or a hundred years later. Before we can deal with Karl Marx's family in greater detail, it is necessary to address the political and social upheaval experienced by Jewish communities in Western Europe at the beginning of the nineteenth century.

---

18. Until well into the nineteenth century, hospitals were often not only responsible for the ill, but also for infirm elderly people and the poor, who could at least obtain a warm meal.

19. Kentenich writes of an anonymous author. On Schlink's authorship, see Schiel (1954: 15).

The Position of Jews in the Eighteenth and at the Beginning of the Nineteenth Century

In the estate-based society of the eighteenth century, unequal access to power, influence, wealth, and income were not determined solely by inherited wealth, but also by estate codes and legal regulations. Not just one's concrete conditions of life, but also what one was allowed or forbidden to do, largely depended upon whether one was born into the estate of the nobility, bourgeoisie, or peasantry. In everyday life, there were numerous privileges and prohibitions, which even regulated questions of clothing: for example, only dignitaries of the city, such as doctors, aldermen, council members, and mayors, were allowed to wear velvet and silk; all other citizens, regardless of their wealth, had to content themselves with cloth.

In this estates-based society, most Jews lived under extremely precarious conditions. Due to regulations of the guilds, which did not admit Jews, they were denied the possibility of practicing a number of trades. Since Jews were prohibited from owning land, agriculture was also out of the question as a way of making a living. So only commercial and financial transactions remained as an option. The legal status of Jews was also insecure. Jews were regarded as foreigners who were only tolerated to the extent that one could hope to gain economic advantages from doing so. Their right to take up residency in a place had to be bought again and again through payment of dues, protection money, and special taxes.

Within the Jewish population, there were considerable social differences. There was a world of difference between the small upper stratum of prosperous "court Jews," who conducted long-term services on behalf of a princely court, a slim middle stratum, usually of merchants and bankers, so-called *Schutzjuden*, who had "letters of protection" from the respective lord of the domain that guaranteed them certain rights, and the large Jewish underclass that, largely without legal protection, were mainly employed as servants and service staff or lived at the margins of subsistence from hawking and petty commerce (Reinke 2007: 9ff.).

A vivid impression of the treatment of Jews in the eighteenth century is conveyed by an order issued by Friedrich II in 1744 concerning Jews in the Silesian capital of Breslau. Consider that this Prussian king, who had invited Voltaire to his court, was actually one of the more progressive rulers of his day. He had heard, it says, that "an effusive swarm of all manner of Jewish people had crept in and spread out, and that there have arisen from the practices of the same, both as secret trade and transformation . . . not only considerable disadvantages for our royal coffers, but also manifold detriments

to the loyal estate of merchants found in our capital of Breslau." He therefore
resolved "to deal with this miserable state of affairs by means of the present
law, to expel the entire dissolute Jewish people from the city, except for those
well-regarded Jews who conduct trade honestly that are indispensable and
necessary to the mint of Breslau . . . and who also might be useful to maintaining the important trade with Polish Jews; their trade and change shall be
limited in such a way . . . that essential disadvantages cannot arise therefrom
for our merchants" (quoted in Reinke 2007: 11).

The contempt with which Jews were met is made very clear here. The
"Jewish people" as a whole are classified as "dissolute," and are to be "expelled,"
regardless of how long they have lived in the city. But even those that are
admitted to conduct trade "honestly" are only allowed to do so to the extent
that they are useful to the state and no disadvantage arises for "our merchants," that is, established German merchants.[20]

The majority of the Christian population regarded Jews with a deep distrust rooted in the centuries of anti-Jewish tradition during the Middle Ages.
The everyday life of the great majority of the Jewish population was not only
characterized by their insecure legal status, but also by greater and lesser
humiliations and affronts at the hands of their Christian neighbors. It was
regarded as a truism that with few exceptions, Jews were "morally depraved"
or were morally far inferior to their non-Jewish neighbors. This truism was
still shared by those Enlightenment thinkers of the late eighteenth century
who, like Christian Wilhelm von Dohm (1751–1820), were engaged on
behalf of improving conditions for Jews. What was new about this conception was that it regarded Jews—given improvements to their poor legal and
social situation—as being at all capable of such "civic improvement" (see
Reinecke 2007: 13ff.).

A fundamental change was introduced with the French Revolution. In
France, it initially brought full legal equality for Jews. In 1791, the National
Assembly abolished all special laws regarding Jews and granted all (male)
Jews the rights and obligations of (male) French citizens. In the course of
French conquests, legal equality for Jews was extended to other territories
in Western Europe, for example, the formerly German territories on the
left bank of the Rhine, to which Trier belonged. However, this equality was

---

20. The decree quoted was in no way an exception. Hostility to Jews was a constant of
Friedrich's II's entire reign (Breuer 1996: 143ff.). Things looked no better under the rule of
Maria Theresia, the Catholic counterpart to the protestant Friedrich: in 1745, at her initiative,
all Jews were expelled from Prague, with the argument that they had allegedly supported the
Prussian enemy during the war (ibid.: 149).

largely retracted by 1808 by Napoleon. As a reaction to the accusation that Jews engaged in land speculation and dubious financial transactions, debts owed to Jews were reduced or even entirely abolished. Furthermore, Jews were now required to obtain "patents" to practice many professions, and these were only granted to those possessing a good reputation. In Jewish and Christian liberal circles, this was referred to as the "décret infâme," since individual accusations were not investigated; rather, Jews were again accused as a collective of being dishonest and usurious (Jersch-Wenzel 1996: 28).

In other states as well at the beginning of the nineteenth century, there was increasing discussion about equality for Jews, in which economic considerations played an important role. In Prussia, after the devastating defeat against Napoleon in 1806, a process of modernization of the economy, administration, and legislation was set into motion, which led in 1807 to the abolition of serfdom and in 1810 to the freedom to practice a trade of one's choice. After Wilhelm von Humboldt had demanded in a report from 1809 immediate, and not just gradual, legal equality for Jews (Humboldt 1809a), an edict was issued in 1812 that granted partial equality to Jews: Jews living in Prussia were declared to be Prussian citizens, supposed to receive the same rights as the Christian majority. Jews were permitted to practice any profession, as well as to purchase land, as well as to teach, if they had the necessary qualifications. Whether Jews were to be allowed access to all parts of the civil service was left open by the edict, deferring the issue to a regulation to be issued in the future (Jersch-Wenzel 1996: 32ff.).

In general, the early nineteenth century in Western Europe showed signs of a societal opening: Jews could practice many more professions than earlier and were subject to considerably less legal discrimination. They no longer had to stand at the margins of society leading a merely tolerated and endangered existence; now they had the prospect of really belonging to society.

Within the Jewish community, there were considerable changes during the turn of the century. In the second half of the eighteenth century, a Jewish current of the Enlightenment had emerged, the "Haskala," the most important representative of which was Moses Mendelssohn (1729–1786) (Graetz 1996). The Jewish upper class, comprising well-off merchants, bankers, and factory owners, increasingly converged upon the values, culture, and patterns of behavior of the Christian bourgeoisie, which was forming at the same time. This development reached a high point around the turn of the century in the Berliner salons: primarily women from rich families invited well-known personalities from the fields of literature, science, and philosophy to their homes, where a comparatively unconventional conviviality was possible beyond the limits of estates or religions, and one could debate without coercion over literature and philosophy. Not a few of these salons were started by young Jewish women. The most famous were Henriette Herz (1764–1847) and Rahel Varnhagen (1771–1833).

Jews were still excluded from the emerging clubs and societies, reading societies, and Masonic lodges through which German (educated) bourgeois society developed. But at the beginning of the nineteenth century, the possibility existed to a far greater extent than previously for Jews to begin an academic education and acquire social recognition through their professions and educations. Among the first generation of Jews who made use of these new possibilities for educated middle-class social ascent was the father of Karl Marx, who during Napoleonic rule studied law and became a lawyer.

With the defeat of Napoleon and the Restoration that followed, the extensive legal equality for Jews in the German territories formerly occupied by France was partially revoked. The validity of Napoleon's discriminatory edict from 1808 was confirmed under Prussian rule, and the Prussian edict of 1812, which had granted Jews partial equality, was now applied more restrictively. Jews were excluded from the civil service, whereby "civil service" was understood rather broadly. Jews were not only prohibited from becoming teachers, judges, and officers; they also were not allowed to be lawyers or pharmacists (Monz 1973b: 176). The Prussian interior minister, Friedrich von Schuckmann (1755–1834), even fundamentally called into question the edict of 1812: "There are certainly individual Jews that are lawful and respectable, and I know some myself; but the character of this people as a whole still constantly consists of perfidious vanity, filthy avarice, and cunning swindling, and it is impossible for any other people that respects itself with national spirit to regard this people as equal" (quoted by Monz 1973: 32).

As can already be gleaned from this statement, not only did the legal situation of Jews worsen after 1815; in Germany, fundamental opponents of the emancipation of Jews increasingly expressed themselves. Particularly influential was an essay published in 1815 by the Berlin historian Friedrich Rühs (1781–1820), which was reprinted in 1816 in a second, expanded edition. Rühs conceived of the German nation as a community based upon ancestry, customs, language, and ultimately (Christian) religion. Since Jews allegedly stood outside of this community due to their religion, they could not be granted equal participation in social and political life (Rühs 1816). In an extensive review, the Heidelberg professor of philosophy Jakob Friedrich Fries (1773–1843) agreed with this argumentation and even intensified it. Both Rühs and Fries had as their goal the conversion of Jews to Christianity and thus their complete assimilation into the German people. Whereas Rühs wanted to allow Jews unwilling to convert to stay in the country without civil rights, Fries favored deporting them, and also advocated that converted Jews should be subject to restrictions for a few years (prohibiting them from engaging in financial transactions, for example) before they could be recognized as full-fledged citizens (Fries 1816). In the case of Rühs and Fries, we are no longer dealing with the religiously motivated hostility to Jews of the Middle Ages and Early Modern period (anti-Judaism), but rather with a post-religious, secularized hostility to Jews (anti-Semitism). In the case of Rühs and Fries, this anti-Semitism is motivated in an ethnic and national way, but not yet in terms of biological racism (see Hubmann 1997: 176ff.). In the case of anti-Judaism, a person's Jewishness ends with their conversion to Christianity. Ethnic and national anti-Semitism regards converted Jews with considerable distrust; one is not sure whether converted Jews have really made a turn toward the cultural and religious community of a nation, but the possibility is fundamentally recognized. For racist anti-Semitism, conversion and cultural assimilation is irrelevant, since it assumes that supposed racial characteristics cannot be shed.[21]

In the course of the deterioration of the economic situation, in the summer of 1819 there were violent pogroms against Jews in many parts of Germany, commonly described as the "Hep Hep Riots": looting and attacks on Jews were frequently accompanied by the cry *"Hep-Hep Jud' verreck!"* (roughly: "Hep-Hep, die Jew!") (Jersch-Wenzel 1996: 43ff.).

The fact that Prussia was largely spared from these riots does not mean, however, that there was no anti-Semitic sentiment there. Not only established circles, but also oppositional tendencies, such as the student fraternities that formed after the anti-Napoleonic wars, were in no way free of anti-Semitism. The ethnic and national anti-Semitism propagated by Rühs and Fries increasingly won adherents, but also encountered decisive critics.[22] The question of "Jewish Emancipation" remained controversial for decades. It also constitutes the background of an article Marx wrote in 1843, "On The Jewish Question," a text that in the twentieth century was sometimes described as anti-Semitic. We will return to this.

---

21. Up to today, the usage of the concepts of anti-Judaism and anti-Semitism has remained inconsistent. Frequently, every form of hostility to Jews is described as anti-Semitic, but that flattens out important historical differences. For a differentiated discussion of the concepts of anti-Semitism and anti-Judaism. see Heil (1997).
22. Critics of these anti-Semitic notions included not only Jewish writers such as Saul Ascher in his *Germanomanie* (1815), but also Protestant theologians such as Johann Ludwig Ewald (1816, 1817, 1821) or Heinrich Eberhard Gottlob Paulus (1817). Also notable is the satirical critique by the Count of Bentzel-Sternau (1818).

The Family and Education of Heinrich Marx

Heinrich (originally Herschel) Marx, born on April 15, 1777, in Saarlouis,[23] was the second child of Mordechai (also named Marx Levi, ca. 1746–1804) and his wife, Chaje Lwów (also Eva Levoff, ca. 1757–1823). The couple had a total of eight children. Mordechai was initially the rabbi of Saarlouis, then from 1788 until his death the rabbi of Trier, where he succeeded his late father-in-law, Moses Lwów. The latter had been a rabbi in Trier since 1764. In the meantime, we now know that among the ancestors of Moses Lwów were not only further rabbis of Trier, but also well-known Jewish scribes.[24] Apparently, the family of Heinrich Marx was aware of this rabbinical tradition. In the biographical appendix of Georg Adler's examination of Marx's critique of political economy, published in 1887, he reports: "Karl Marx's cousin, Dr. phil. Marx in Breslau, to whom I owe the information about Marx's family, provided me with a very comprehensive collection, partially comprising legal decisions on the basis of the Talmud, and partially comprising theological treatises composed by the mentioned rabbis" (Adler 1887: 226n1).[25]

Rabbis were not just ministers and teachers; they also functioned as legal scholars within the Jewish community, which could autonomously regulate its internal affairs up through the late eighteenth century. With regard to the outside world, they were representatives of their communities. The high prestige of rabbis frequently did not entail a correspondingly high, or even sufficient, level of income; not infrequently, they had to practice another profession in order to earn money. Karl Marx's grandfather, Mordechai, also exercised his office under impoverished conditions (vgl. Rauch 1975: 23) and

---

23. For a long time, there was uncertainty about the year of birth and day of birth of Heinrich Marx. In the census of 1802, his age was given as seventeen years, which would make the year of birth 1785. On the death certificate of 1838, his age was given as fifty-six, which would make the year of birth 1782. Mehring also gives this year, and many Marx biographers have taken it over from him. MEGA I/1 also states it in the register of persons. For the wedding in 1814, however, Heinrich's brother Samuel confirmed that Heinrich was born in April 1777 in Saarlouis (Monz 1973: 217n33). Finally, Monz was able to find Heinrich's leaving certificate from the law school in Koblenz, in which the date of April 15, 1777, is given (Monz 1979a: 133).

24. Wachstein (1923) and Horowitz (1928) have compiled the fundamental information about the Lwów family. Brilling (1958) was able to find out a few things about Mordechai's ancestors. This information was slightly supplemented and corrected in terms of smaller details by Monz (1973: 215ff.) and Wilcke (1983: 775ff.).

25. This cousin was *Moses Marx,* born in 1815, a son of Heinrich's older brother Samuel (on Moses Marx, see Schöncke 1993: 58ff.). Horowitz (1928) addresses some of these treatises.

was active as a merchant (Monz 1973: 242). After his death, the position of rabbi initially remained unoccupied, until finally his oldest son, Samuel, (1775–1827), became the rabbi of Trier.[26] Samuel declared in 1808 that he and his siblings wished to take the surname Marx. Up until the beginning of the nineteenth century, it was frequently the case that Jews did not have definite surnames.[27] In France, taking on a fixed surname became a requirement in 1808; in Prussia, the edict of 1812 made doing so the precondition for legal equality. Samuel's family was not the only one in Trier bearing the name Marx. In Catholic areas in particular, the name Marx, from "Markus," was widespread.

Mordechai's widow, Chaje, got married again in 1809, to Moses Saul Löwenstamm (1748–1815), the chief rabbi of the Jewish community in Amsterdam. She lived with her second husband in Amsterdam, but still maintained contact with her children in Trier where in 1823, only a few days after Karl's fifth birthday, she passed away.

As rabbi of Trier, Mordechai lived with his family in the synagogue building along Weberbach Street. The building was dilapidated and too small (Monz 1979a: 126). Heinrich Marx grew up there under modest and confined conditions, from which he apparently wished to free himself. As his sparse allusions in his letters to his son Karl testify, this was not an easy path. He wrote to Karl, who was studying in Bonn, in November 1835: "I should like to see in you what perhaps I could have become, if I had come into the world with equally favourable prospects" (MECW 1: 646). The less favorable prospects were not just his impoverished family situation, but also discrimination as a Jew (see the letter to the Immediate Justice Commission quoted below). In another letter to Karl from August 1837 he wrote: "I received nothing from my parents apart from my existence—although not to be unjust, love from my mother" (MECW 1: 674). Apparently, with the exception of motherly love, Heinrich lacked emotional support for his path in life. His relationship to his father was probably not close, otherwise he would have spoken of the love of his parents and not only of that from his mother.

Nothing is known about the religious and political attitudes of Heinrich

---

26. Samuel was married to Michle Brisack, who was born in 1784 in Luneville and survived her husband by more than thirty years; she died in 1860 in Trier. The couple had a total of seven children (Monz 1973: 219).

27. In Europe over the course of the Middle Ages, initially among the nobility, and then among wealthy urban citizens, sobriquets became surnames, which was an advantage in tracing inheritance claims. In some rural areas, family names first became established in the seventeenth and eighteenth centuries. Jewish communities got by without fixed surnames.

Marx's father. We know a bit more about Heinrich's brother Samuel, who followed his father as the rabbi of Trier. In 1807, Samuel participated in the "Grand Sanhédrin" in Paris, an assembly of Jewish notables, called by Napoleon, concerned with questions of religious rights as well as the future development of the Jewish communities and the expansion of professional possibilities for Jews. Samuel was apparently so impressed that in the same year, during a celebration of Napoleon's birthday in the main synagogue of Trier, he called upon the Jewish youth to learn skilled trades, agriculture, and the sciences (Rauch 1975: 21).

Samuel's younger brother Heinrich apparently wanted to follow this call. Nothing is known about his youth and early adult life. What is certain is that Heinrich was secretary of the Jewish consistory in Trier between 1809 and 1810 (Kasper-Holtkotte 1996: 313n322; Monz 1979a: 126). In 1811–12 he worked as a translator at the legal court of Osnabrück. There, he attempted in vain to receive permission to take the required exam for aspiring notaries (Monz 1981). In 1813, he studied at the law school of Koblenz, which was established in 1806 under French rule, and obtained the "certificat de capacité" on November 8, 1813 (Monz 1979a: 133). This was the lowest qualification offered, requiring merely one year (divided into three trimesters) of study of criminal and procedural law (Mallmann 1987: 122). However, Heinrich did not enroll during the first, but rather the second trimester, which indicates that he already had prior juridical knowledge (Monz 1981: 60). This is also indicated by another document. In January of 1811, the Jewish consistorium of Trier complained to the French administration about the setbacks encountered by Jews. One of the examples given was that of Heinrich Marx: although he had successfully graduated from the *Zentralschule* (for law) in Koblenz, he could not find employment (Kasper-Holtkotte 1996: 383n34). So Heinrich Marx must have enjoyed legal training prior to 1811.[28]

---

28. Sperber (2013) portrays Heinrich Marx as a liar: "His aspirations to study law—marked by almost certainly false claims to have studied at the School of Law in Koblenz before he was enrolled there, and to have studied law in Berlin before the University of Berlin was actually founded—were greater than his ability to do so" (Sperber 2013: 24). Sperber, in a note to this statement (2013, 443n16), names Kasper-Holtkotte (1996: 383) and Schöncke (1993: 123) as sources. The former cited the administrative appeal by the Trier consistorium. Why the statement contained within it, that Heinrich Marx successfully graduated the Zentralschule in Koblenz, is supposed to be false, is never explained by Sperber. The notion that the consistorium, in an administrative appeal, would make false statements about the brother of the rabbi, is not very plausible. Rather, one can assume the opposite: that the case of Heinrich Marx was mentioned because it was certain that the facts provided were correct. Sperber's second assertion, that Heinrich Marx claimed to have studied law in Berlin, is not quite

Heinrich Marx's activity as an *avoué* in Trier from January 1814 is attested (Monz 1979a: 134f.). Avoués were tasked with preparing courtroom trials and writing legal documents. Advocates (*Advokaten*), who had finished a longer course of study, then pleaded before a court. Above all in Germany, where such a division of the legal profession was unknown before the French occupation, avoués were regarded as half-educated and did not enjoy much respect.[29] As Heinrich Marx's memorandums show, his knowledge went far beyond that of an avoué, so that it's plausible he studied more than just the two trimesters in Koblenz. His knowledge was obviously recognized: since 1816, Heinrich Marx was an advocate; in 1820, he was appointed as an attorney (*Advokat-Anwalt*; this profession was able to perform all the activities of a lawyer) (Monz 1973: 256).

There is no surviving picture of Heinrich Marx. But he looked similar to his son Karl (without a beard, however, since beards were not fashionable in the early nineteenth century). Karl Marx's youngest daughter Eleanor reports on a photograph of her grandfather that her father always carried, but which he did not wish to show to strangers, since it did not bear enough similarity to the original. Eleanor remarked upon the photograph: "The face appeared quite handsome to me, the eyes and forehead were the same as those of the son, but the section around the mouth and chin was more delicate; the whole face was of an expressly Jewish, but beautifully Jewish, type" (E. Marx 1897–98: 240).[30]

---

correct. In the passage cited by Sperber, Schöncke presents the submittal made by Heinrich Marx to the Prefect Keverberg from January 15, 1813, with regard to issuing a citizen's card. In this submittal, Heinrich Marx mentions that after reaching the age of majority, he had resided in Berlin due to "studies" (*etudes*), without further specifying these studies. By age of majority, Heinrich probably did not mean the age of twenty-one, but rather reaching the age of thirty in the year 1807—from this point, according to French law, one could marry without parental permission (see Monz 1981: 63). Even if one assumes that by "studies," Heinrich meant legal studies, Sperber's attempt to accuse Heinrich Marx of being a liar is based upon inadequate knowledge of the historical facts. Public lectures that made it possible to "study" existed in Berlin before 1800. After the University of Halle was closed by the French in 1806, a few professors moved to Berlin and began to give public lectures in many subjects, even before the founding of the university. Theodor Schmalz (1760–1830), the later founding rector, held lectures in law starting in 1807. The topics mentioned by Köpke (1860: 141; reprinted in Tenorth 2012: 39) prove that they weren't popular lectures but specialist lectures in law. So legal studies in Berlin were possible years before the founding of the university.

29. On legal education in Koblenz, as well as on Avoués, see Mallmann (1987: 61, 114, 122).

30. This photograph, according to Eleanor, had been made from an old daguerreotype. Since Heinrich Marx had already died in 1838, it could not have been a daguerreotype of Heinrich himself, but must have been taken from a painting. In a letter from December 1863, Marx

Henriette Presburg, the Mother

On November 22, 1814, Heinrich Marx, already thirty-seven years old, married Henriette Presburg, who was eleven years younger and from Nimwegen in the Netherlands. Henriette was born there on September 20, 1788, as the daughter of Isaak Presburg (1747–1832) and his wife Nanette Cohen (ca. 1764–1833). She also had three younger siblings, David (1791–after 1829), Markus (also known as Martin, 1794–1867), and Teitie (1797–1854), who was later named Sophia and married Lion Philips (1794–1866) (Monz 1973: 221; Gielkens 1999: 37). Karl Marx is supposed to have maintained a relationship to the Philips family in later years. The grandchild of Sophia and Lion founded the Philips Corporation, which still exists, in 1891.

How Heinrich and Henriette met is not clear. It's quite possible that Heinrich's mother played a role, since she lived in Amsterdam with her second husband. The marriage seems to have been harmonious for the most part; any sort of tensions or conflicts are not known. In the only surviving letter from Heinrich to his wife, from August 12, 1837, he addresses her as "My dear good Hansje" and concludes rather sentimentally with "Farewell, my dear, second, better self" (MEGA III/1: 313). And Heinrich wrote to Karl on September 16, 1837, that he counted himself among the rich, since he "enjoy[ed] the love of an incomparable wife" (MECW 1: 682).

Not much is known about Henriette. The first information we have originates with Karl Marx's daughter Eleanor, who wrote to Wilhelm Liebknecht: "Mohr's mother, née Presburg, was a Dutch Jewess. In the beginning of the 16th century, the Pressburgs, taking their name from the town of Pressburg, migrated to Holland, where the sons of the family were Rabbis for centuries. Mohr's mother spoke Dutch; up to her death she spoke German faultily and with difficulty" (Liebknecht 1896/1908: 165). Eleanor's statement that Marx's mother came from an old family of rabbis is repeated in many biographies. However, it cannot be stated with absolute certainty whether the ancestors of Henriette Presburg were in fact rabbis, since the verified family tree does not reach very far back (see Monz 1973: 223, 228).[31] It is possible that Eleanor was mixing up Karl Marx's mother with the mother of his father Heinrich: concerning the latter, one can say

---

reports to his wife, Jenny, that his mother had bequeathed "father's portrait" to his sister Sophie (MECW 40: 499).

31. With reference to similarities of name and the precondition that the ancestors of Isaak Presburg were rabbis, Monz surmises a certain lineage that would yield a distant relationship between Karl Marx and Heinrich Heine (Monz 1973c: 224–29). However, this conjecture is marked by considerable uncertainty.

with certainty that she came from a family "in which the sons were rabbis for centuries."[32] Henriette's father, Isaak Presburg, in any case was not a rabbi, but rather a "reader" (*Vorleser*) and "cantor" (*Gazzan*) of the Jewish community in Nimwegen. He was a textile merchant, money changer, and seller of lottery tickets, and apparently became rather wealthy from these activities. In 1814, he was able to free both of his sons from military service by paying for replacements, and in the same year, his daughter Henriette received a considerable dowry worth 20,000 guldens for her marriage to Heinrich Marx (Gielkens 1999: 32). Heinrich and Henriette were probably only able to establish their household on the basis of this dowry, since Heinrich was just beginning his activities as a lawyer, and probably did not have any meaningful savings.

The fact that Henriette's knowledge of German remained deficient for her whole life is made clear by her surviving letters.[33] These letters are concerned with everyday matters and do not allow one to make any conclusions about whether she had any intellectual interests. John Spargo, who even before Franz Mehring had written the first larger biography of Marx, had already concluded that "she was a simple, good-natured soul of the domestic type with no particular intellectual gifts" (Spargo 1912: 26). Subsequently, this judgment was simply adopted by most biographers of Marx (see for example Cornu 1954: 53; McLellan 1973: 4; Padover 1978: 13), or even intensified: Wheen (1999: 12), without providing new evidence, even makes her "an uneducated—indeed only semi-literate—woman." Mary Gabriel (2011: 16) also writes of "Henriette Presburg, who was neither educated nor cultured." The newest variant of devaluing Henriette comes from Sperber, who claims that Heinrich Marx wanted a career and participation in public life, but that his "Dutch wife" and her "very household-oriented version of female Jewish piety" did not fit (Sperber 2013: 31). However, Sperber does not provide evidence for this specific piety, nor for the assertion that Henriette did not fit into the bourgeois world of Trier. There is no indication that she did not, for example, participate in the balls organized by the casino society and the city. On the contrary, a letter reveals that dancing was not so unusual in the Marx family. To her somewhat ailing son Karl, she wrote in February–March 1836: "Dear Carl, do not dance until you are quite well again" (MECW 1: 652).

32. Family tree with details on who worked as a rabbi can be found in Monz (1973: 222).
33. The letters to Karl are available in MEGA III/1; letters to her Dutch relatives are printed in Gielkens (1999).

The image of Henriette as an uneducated housewife should be met with considerable doubt.[34] The remarks in the letters from Heinrich Marx make it clear that Henriette was a concerned housewife and mother completely devoted to her growing family. The young Karl must have seen things similarly, and described them as such in a lost letter from the year 1837, which his father answered: "You yourself have described so beautifully the life of your excellent mother, so deeply felt that her whole life is a continual sacrifice of love and loyalty, and truly you have not exaggerated" (MECW 1: 675). In the first letter by Karl still available to us today, from November 10, 1837, she is described as an "angel of a mother" and a "grand and wonderful woman" (MECW 1: 20). Karl's sister Emilie also wrote in 1865 concerning her mother: "She cared, trembled, and suffered so much for her children" (quoted in Schöncke 1993: 341). But it would be hasty to accuse Henriette without further ado of being uneducated and not particularly intelligent. There are a few indications to the contrary. For example, in a letter written in November of 1835 to Karl, who had just started his studies in Bonn, she displays a certain ironic wit. After admonishing him in a loose, chatty tone to maintain cleanliness and order, she continues: "Please let me know everything about your household. Your amiable Muse will surely not feel insulted by your mother's prose, tell her that the higher and better is achieved through the lower" (MECW 1: 649). And a remark on Napoleon III in a letter to Sophie and Lion Philips from February 2, 1853 (Gielkens 1999: 145) makes clear that she followed political developments attentively. Karl's sister Sophie is the source of the characterization of their mother as "small and delicate, very intelligent" (quoted in Schöncke 1993: 556).[35] The statement made by Marx's daughter Laura in 1907 to John Spargo that Marx's mother, when asked about her belief in God, answered that "she believed in him not for God's sake, but for her own" (MEJ 8, 1985: 300) is not exactly an indication of the lack of wit of which most Marx biographers accuse her.

A notable statement was also made by the adult Karl Marx, who soon after the death of his father already fought with his mother over the inheritance. Ever since this conflict, he had a distanced relationship toward his mother and spoke negatively of her. After a visit to Trier in the year 1861, however, he reported to Ferdinand Lassalle that his mother had also intrigued him

---

34. Heinrich Gemkow (2008: 506n33) and Stedman Jones (2016: 45) are among the few biographers who criticize this onesidedness of this predominant image of Marx's mother in the biographies.

35. In 1883, Sophie was admitted to a psychiatric clinic. The statement is found in the admission questionnaire of the clinic.

"by her exceedingly subtle esprit and unshakable equanimity" (MECW 41: 283). There is no indication that this statement was meant ironically. Marx's mother appears to have in fact possessed a "subtle esprit."

However, his mother's "esprit" was primarily channeled toward her own advancement and that of her children. Thus, shortly before his fiftieth birthday, Marx wrote to Engels: "Half a century on my shoulders, and still a pauper. How right my mother was: 'If only Karell had made capital instead of etc.!.'" (MECW 43: 25) A remark made by Marx's son-in-law, Paul Lafargue, also points in this direction: "His family had dreamt of him being a man of letters or a professor and thought he was debasing himself by engaging in socialist agitation and political economy, which was then disdained in Germany" (Lafargue 1890: 91). That the family was ashamed of his socialist agitation can only be a reference to Marx's mother and possibly his siblings, since Marx's father had already died before he became politically engaged.

As emerges from a letter from June 4,1860, sent by Jenny Marx to Ferdinand and Louise von Westphalen (Hecker/Limmroth 2014: 267), Marx's mother appears to have been prepared, in spite of all familial and political differences, to financially support him in disputes, such as in 1859–60 in his libel suit against Karl Vogt (ibid.: 16). Also, during the already mentioned visit to Trier in 1861, his mother destroyed Marx's IOUs, and as the latter emphasized in a letter to Engels from May 7, this did not occur because he had asked her to: "I myself said nothing to her about money matters and it was she who took the initiative in this connection" (MECW 41: 279).

Even if the available information is not sufficient for a detailed depiction of the personality of Karl Marx's mother, it is clear that the dominant image in the literature of a vapid and uneducated housewife cannot be correct.

Heinrich Marx's Memoranda

Heinrich Marx's talent for legal argument as well as his political attitudes emerge from two remaining memoranda that he composed in 1815 and 1816–17. After the Congress of Vienna, the Rhineland had become part of Prussia, but it was not clear if Napoleon's edict from 1808, which entailed considerable discrimination against Jews in various areas, would continue to be valid. On June 13, 1815, Heinrich Marx presented a memorandum to the Prussian governor-general, von Sack, in favor of declaring the decree invalid.[36]

---

36. "Some remarks on Napoleon's Decree of March 17, 1808, on the occasion of the fortunate unification of our country with the Royal Prussian Monarch" (*"Einige Bemerkungen über das napoleonische Dekret vom 17. März 1808 bei Gelegenheit der glücklichen Vereinigung unseres*

In an introductory remark, Heinrich Marx emphasizes he does not desire to provide a treatise in favor of his coreligionists, since he does not regard it as necessary, since: "tolerance is the order of the day. To whom would it occur in the 19th century to say one should be intolerant toward Jews? And why? Perhaps because they are circumcised and eat unleavened bread during Easter? Such a person would appear ludicrous, and a weak mind would rather appear malicious than ludicrous" (Schöncke 1993: 141). If one considers how widespread anti-Jewish sentiment was, one cannot resist the impression that there is a certain amount of irony deployed here. However, the arguments made probably arise from a completely non-ironic intention. In the face of enlightened thought preaching tolerance, prejudices against Jews indeed appear ludicrous. Since the time of Friedrich II, the Prussian state had made precisely this claim of being "enlightened," and Heinrich Marx is referring to the consequences of this claim. However, he does not only refer implicitly to the claim to Enlightenment by the Prussian monarchy. In his cover letter to the appeal, he refers to the Prussian king as "the most enlightened statesman" (ibid.: 146). The consequence suggested by Heinrich Marx is therefore that this monarch would appear ludicrous were he to yield to prejudice against Jews.

Concerning those who propagate prejudices against Jews, he states clearly: "Human well-being and public spirit float on the tongue of every scoundrel, even if these scoundrels have accumulated treasures at the cost of helpless widows and orphans and abandoned good, hardworking families to misery. These wolves in sheep's clothing are for the most part the ones who strike out mercilessly against their confrères in Israel. If one were to believe them, the basis for their hatred is the lower level of humanity of this race and their sole heart's desire its regeneration. But they are actually so prejudiced against the descendants of Jacob because they occasionally encounter Jewish good-for-nothings on their path, and have to share with them" (ibid.: 142). Heinrich Marx admits that accusations leveled at individual Jews might be justified. He adds, however, that this is also the case with individual Christians, which brings him to the further observation: "The gentle spirit of Christianity could often be obscured by fanaticism; the pure morality of the Gospels sullied by ignorant priests" (ibid.). A similar argumentative strategy is already found in his cover letter, where he initially concedes: "I am far from claiming that no measures are necessary in order to make my co-religionists worthy of the

---

Landes mit der königlich-preußischen Monarchie"), first published by Kober (1932). There, one also finds an extensive presentation of the provisions of Napoleon's decree. The appeal was republished in Schöncke (1993: 141ff.).

fortune of being citizens." He then adds almost angrily: "But not by stifling every seed of good with degrading treatment does one arrive at a laudable goal. On the contrary, the good must be encouraged, and evil destroyed at the root. But only a fatherly government can and will do so" (ibid.: 147).

Heinrich Marx analyzes Napoleon's edict in detail and shows that it contradicts a number of elementary legal principles. Above all, he decisively opposes the notion of misbehavior on the part of individuals leading to the punishment of an entire group. A "wise lawmaker" would find means of determining the guilty party. "And if he is unable to, then he would prefer to throw a veil over petty vices than issue a condemnation of thousands of his subjects . . . but a punishment that affects an entire sect can have as its motive only the most abhorrent intolerance." And he adds that if there is usury, then the absolute severity of the law should be applied, which would presuppose that there are laws against usury, "which, incidentally, would be a very salutary restraint for some uncircumcised individuals as well" (ibid.: 145).

This memorandum shows Heinrich Marx as somebody who is not only well versed in the law, but who also knew how to argue in a clever and quite self-confident manner. An answer has not been preserved. Since the decree was retained, Heinrich Marx probably did not make any friends in the government with his words, since he had made it very clear what he thought of any monarch who would confirm the decree he criticized.

Heinrich Marx presented a further piece of writing at the turn of the year 1816–17 to the immediate justice commission (*Immediat-Justiz-Commission*) for the Rhine provinces. This commission was supposed to examine how the "Rhenish law" valid in the Rhine provinces (that is, what was left of French law) could be aligned with Prussian law. For this purpose, it called for proposals. Heinrich Marx sent the commission a position statement on the commercial courts (printed in Schöncke 1993: 154ff.).

The commercial courts inherited from French rule were only occupied by merchants; they were supposed to issue judgments exclusively with regard to the commercial disputes of merchants and bankers. Heinrich Marx spoke out against the commercial courts, since he regarded it as an ill that there were special courts at all. According to him, the commercial courts were privileged courts, only there for a specific "class" (ibid.: 154). Furthermore, it was problematic that the courts were led by juridical laymen, who also pursued their own economic interests. Thus "that advocate" who "had the misfortune of reprimanding one of these Croesuses" would have his words fall upon "deaf ears" (ibid.: 160).

The commission was impressed by the arguments and recommended that the author publish his text in the renowned publication *Niederrheinischen*

Archiv für Gesetzgebung, Rechtswissenschaft und Rechtspflege (Lower-Rhenish Archive for Legislation, the Study of Law, and the Administration of Justice), which only occurred in a few cases (Mallmann 1987: 176). Heinrich Marx agreed to the publication but asked that his name and home city not be disclosed, since he feared that this piece of writing would not be advantageous to him in Trier. In light of the content of the text, which aimed to take away some of the privileges of the merchants, as well as its not exactly friendly characterization of those "Croesuses," this fear was not entirely unfounded. In his letter, all his bitterness concerning the experience of constant affronts as a Jew is expressed: "But unfortunately, my conditions are such that as the father of a family I have to be somewhat cautious. The sect to which nature chained me does not, as is known, enjoy any particular esteem, and the local province is not the most tolerant. And if I had to endure much—some of it bitter—and use up almost the entirety of my small fortune until one could resolve to believe that a Jew might have some talent and be legitimate, then it can certainly not be held against me that I have become somewhat shy" (letter from January 17, 1817, printed in Schöncke 1993: 151). His wish was granted, and the article was published anonymously in 1817.

Heinrich Marx sent a further memorandum, dealing with usury, to the minister of justice, Friedrich Leopold von Kircheisen (1749–1825), on June 30, 1821. In the cover letter he writes: "The ardent wish to contribute to the elimination of such a low as well as harmful vice, namely that of usury" had occasioned the "short treatise" (Schöncke 1993: 171). So far, this piece of writing has not been found; what remains is merely the brief answer by Kircheisen from July 27, 1821, in which its receipt is confirmed and the minister notes that he had "recognized with pleasure the good will" to proceed against "the sins of your race" (ibid.: 172). Since one can assume that Heinrich Marx was not concerned in particular with "Jewish usury" but rather with usury in general, the answer by the minister of justice, reducing usury to a "sin" of the Jews, is an example of the nastiness with which Jews were constantly confronted.

Baptism

The legal changes experienced by the Rhineland as a new province of Prussia had a direct effect upon the Marx family. Since Jews were no longer admitted to the civil service and the profession of lawyer was considered part of the civil service, Heinrich Marx's future was uncertain.

The president of the Higher Regional Court, Christoph Wilhelm Heinrich Sethe, who gave a report on April 23, 1816, on the number of Jews in the

Rhineland judicial system, recommended that the government issue a special permit for the activity of the three Jewish lawyers, one of whom was Heinrich Marx. He pointed out that the president of the administrative court of Trier had issued "a very laudatory testimonial" with regard to Heinrich Marx and characterized him as follows: "Lots of knowledge; very diligent; good speech; and quite legitimate." Sethe himself mentions an article that Heinrich Marx submitted to the governorate in Aachen, and which reveals his "brain and knowledge" (Schöncke 1993:148).[37] However, the Prussian minister of justice, Kircheisen, refused to issue a special permit. The interior minister, Schuckmann, expressed himself in exactly the same way (Monz 1973: 247). For Heinrich Marx, this meant either giving up his profession or, like many other Jews during this time, get baptized.[38]

The exact date of Heinrich Marx's baptism is unknown. It would be informative, however, since we could read from it how Heinrich dealt with the pressure placed upon him. In his biographical sketch of Karl Marx from 1892, Friedrich Engels stated that Heinrich Marx and his family converted to Christianity in 1824 (MECW 27: 332), which Mehring and other biographers accepted. In 1824, however, only the children were baptized. It was entered into the baptismal record that the father had already been baptized by the chaplain Mühlenhoff. From 1817 to 1820, Mühlenhoff was a military chaplain in Trier, so the baptism must have occurred in this period. Stein (1932) suspects that the baptism had already occurred in 1816–17: after the report by Higher Regional Court President Sethe from April 23, 1816, and before the founding of the Lutheran-Evangelical congregation in Trier in the middle of 1817, since after its founding there would have been no need to be baptized by a military chaplain. This period of time for the baptism (that is, before Karl Marx's birth) is accepted in all newer biographies. However, Monz (1973: 243) had already pointed out that it was a united military and civilian congregation, so that a baptism by the chaplain would have also been possible after 1817. Since the church records of the military congregation are first available from the year 1820, and no baptism of Heinrich Marx is registered, Monz concludes that the baptism occurred between April 23, 1816, and December 31, 1819 (ibid.: 245).

The most probable solution to the puzzle is provided by an interesting incident from the history of Trier's Jews (see Laufner 1975). On June 21,1817,

---

37. This article has not yet been found. It cannot be the memorandum to Governor General von Sack from the year 1815, since Sack had his headquarters in Düsseldorf. So Heinrich Marx wrote at least four treatises.
38. Legal equality for Jews first came with the imperial constitution (*Reichsverfassung*) of 1871.

Heinrich Marx was appointed, along with Samuel Cahn, to the Commission on the Settlement of Jewish Debts (*Judenschulden-Tilgungskommission*). These "Jewish debts" were special taxes imposed on Jews, originating from the time period before the French occupation and were collectively paid by Jewish communities. The Commission was to account for all Jewish citizens and distribute these tax debts along with the accumulated interest among them, not a particularly thankful task, and one that promptly brought complaints. In one of the complaints, the question was raised as to why the name of Heinrich Marx did not show up in the distribution list drawn up by Samuel Cahn. In his answer from April 3, 1819, Cahn justified this by pointing out that because Heinrich Marx had performed so much gratis labor for the Commission, his exclusion from the list was merely a small compensation. There is no mention of any conversion to Christianity, so one can assume that Heinrich Marx was not yet baptized at this time. If one follows this assumption, Heinrich Marx was baptized between April 3 and December 31, 1819, relatively late: three years after the rejection of a special permit for Jewish lawyers.

A baptism in the year 1819 could explain another, somewhat unusual event, as Schöncke (1993: 562) elaborates. On August 12, 1819, Hermann was born as the fourth child of Heinrich and Henriette, not in Trier like the other children, but rather in Nimwegen. One can assume that pregnant Henriette would not have undertaken the trip from Trier to Nimwegen without a sound reason. The reason might have been to personally inform—not just through a letter—her parents that her husband had just been baptized, or was just about to be.

That Heinrich Marx's baptism was compelled by his professional situation is beyond doubt, as Karl Marx's youngest daughter Eleanor confirmed to Wilhelm Liebknecht (Liebknecht 1896/1908: 165). If Heinrich Marx had refused baptism, his endeavor over many years to obtain a legal education and a career as a lawyer would have been for nothing. Without this profession, he also would not have been able to feed a family. To that extent, he really had no alternative than to be baptized. But the question remains as to how difficult it was for him to make this step, and whether the baptism constituted a break with his family and the foundation of a conflict with his son Karl, as some authors claim.

Apparently, Heinrich Marx attempted to delay the baptism. Perhaps he believed he could still avoid it. And when he finally allowed himself to be baptized, he was initially the only one in his family. All of this speaks against the notion that he regarded the baptism as a voluntary act or even as a step toward emancipation, as Mehring speculated (Mehring 1962: 3). On the other hand,

Heinrich Marx did not appear to have an especially intense attachment to the Jewish religion. When, after his death, a notary conducted an inventory of his personal library, only one Hebrew book is listed, which is not further specified (Schöncke 1993: 294). As emerges from a letter from November of 1835 to his son Karl, who was studying in Bonn at the time, Heinrich Marx believed in God, but adhered to an enlightened Deism. He recommended to Karl a "pure faith in God," which "Newton, Locke, and Leibniz" had believed in (MECW 1: 647). This fits well with Eleanor's observation that Marx's father was a man "strongly imbued with French eighteenth-century ideas of religion, science, and art" (E. Marx 1883). He probably did not adhere to any particular religious practices, so baptism probably did not plunge him into a conflict of religious conscience. But he likely regarded it as bitter and degrading that he was forced into being baptized in order to practice his profession. Eduard Gans (1797–1839), one of the most important Hegelians, who despite excellent scholarly qualifications was only made a professor after being baptized (and who would later become one of Marx's academic instructors in Berlin), expressed what many educated Jews no doubt felt when confronted with baptism as an indispensable precondition for working in the civil service: "If the state is so narrow-minded that it won't permit me to be of service to it in a manner befitting my talents unless I make a profession of faith that I don't believe in, and that the minister also knows very well that I don't believe in, then it shall have its will" (quoted in Reissner 1965: 36).

It is quite possible that Heinrich Marx regarded his baptism with similar feelings. The postponement of his baptism could have been an attempt to evade this hypocrisy demanded by the state. It is also possible that he wanted to spare his still-living mother and his brother—active in Trier as a rabbi— any sorrow. About his mother, Heinrich Marx wrote, "how I have fought and suffered, in order not to distress them [Heinrich Marx's parents] as long as possible" (MECW 1: 674), which might be a reference to the baptism. Henriette had also indicated during the baptism of her children that she wanted to wait on her own baptism out of consideration for her still-living parents. However, she then allowed herself to be baptized a year later, even though her parents were still alive.

It is not clear why Heinrich and Henriette's children were baptized in the year 1824.[39] On the one hand, the fact that Heinrich's mother had died in 1823 might have played a role. On the other hand, Karl, the oldest living son, was now of school age. Jewish children who went to Christian schools

---

39. We don't know whether the baptism was accompanied, as is claimed in some biographies, by a great celebration. There is no indication of this.

were so aggressively teased by other children that even the district government issued an order prohibiting this (see Monz 1973b: 181). The decision to baptize the children at this point in time might have sprung from the desire to spare them this teasing at school. However, it's not clear whether the children visited an elementary school (*Elementarschule*) at all, or received private instruction.

In Catholic Trier, the Marx family did not convert to Catholicism, but rather to Protestantism. For Heinrich Marx, tending toward rationalism and the Enlightenment, Catholicism, with its saints and belief in miracles and relics, probably was out of the question compared to Protestantism with its more rationalist orientation.[40]

Blumenberg (2000: 11) and above all Künzli (1966:42) claim that after the baptism, Heinrich Marx made a break with his family. However, there are no indications of this. Künzli simply asserts that when somebody comes from an old rabbinical family and converts to Christianity, then this must lead to a familial break. The only hint regarding familial relationships is from August 1837. From the spa in Bad Ems, Heinrich Marx wrote to his wife: "Give warm greetings and kisses to the dear sister-in-law [the wife of his late brother Samuel] and her children" (MEGA III/1: 313). Künzli cannot dispute that familial relations at this time were untroubled, so he suspects that Heinrich Marx was seeking closer contact again due to "the apostate's feelings of guilt." (Künzli 1966: 43). However, this talk of a rapprochement assumes that a break occurred in the first place. But Künzli is unable to provide any evidence for this break or for the alleged feelings of guilt. Heinrich Marx had a close relationship not only with his brother's family, but also with other members of the Jewish community. The distinguished Jewish doctor Lion Bernkastel was the family doctor to the Marx family (see letter from May-June 1836 MEGA III/1: 297). Furthermore, Heinrich Marx and Bernkastel shared ownership of a vineyard in Mertesdorf (Monz 1973: 252).

Professional Success and Social Recognition

Heinrich Marx was a reputable lawyer in Trier. He must have had good relationships with his professional colleagues. The godfathers and godmothers of most of his children were lawyers and their wives. Karl's godparents were the attorneys Johan Friedrich Bochkoltz and Johann Paulin Schaak (Monz 1973: 257). In a letter to his son Ferdinand from January 1838, Ludwig von

---

40. However, in the form of Pietism, there was also a countermovement to rationalism within Protestantism. The young Engels was raised in a Pietist household (see volume 2).

Westphalen reported that Heinrich Marx was ill, but that he was so popular that his colleagues would take over his cases for him (Gemkow 2008: 520). Karl Marx later mentioned that his father was "for many years *bâtonnier* of the *barreau* there"; that is to say, the president of the bar in Trier (MECW 41: 96).

Heinrich Marx probably had especially close relationships with the attorneys Ernest Dominik Laeis (1788–1872) and Johann Heinrich Schlink (1793–1863), already mentioned in this section on Trier. In 1824, Laeis and his wife were among the godparents to the children; in 1834, Laeis and Schlink had Heinrich Marx's death certified at the registry office, and in 1842 both were among the witnesses when Marx's sister Sophie married the lawyer Wilhelm Robert Schmalhausen (Monz 1973: 257, 231n19). After Heinrich Marx's death, Schlink became the legal guardian of the children who were not yet of age, Karl among them. Back then, one became a legal adult at the age of twenty-one.[41]

When in 1825 Mayor Wilhelm Haw, in his capacity as chair of the Commission on the Settlement of Jewish Debt, was sued by some Jewish citizens because of their payment obligations, Heinrich Marx was Haw's lawyer (Laufner 1975: 13), which also indicates his high reputation. Finally, in the year 1831, Heinrich Marx was granted the title "judicial council" (*Justizrat*) by the provincial government (Schöncke 1993: 215). Only fifteen jurists from the courts of Trier, Cologne, Aachen, and Koblenz obtained this title (Mallmann 1987: 174).

Heinrich Marx's own ethos, inspired by Kant and Fichte, is expressed especially clearly in one of his letters to his son Karl, who was studying in Berlin: "The first of all human virtues is the strength and will to sacrifice oneself, to set aside one's ego, if duty, if love calls for it, and indeed not those glamorous, romantic or hero-like sacrifices, the act of a moment of fanciful reverie or heroic feeling. Even the greatest egoist is capable of that, for it is precisely the ego which then has pride of place. No, it is those daily and hourly recurring sacrifices which arise from the pure heart of a good person, of a loving father, of a tender-hearted mother, of a loving spouse, of a thankful child, that give life its sole charm and make it beautiful despite all unpleasantness" (letter of August 12–13, 1837, MECW 1: 675).

Professional success was also reflected in a certain level of affluence. In 1819, Heinrich Marx was able to buy a house on Simeonstraße. According to the tax information evaluated by Herres, Heinrich Marx was assessed in 1832 as having an income of 1,500 talers annually (Herres 1990: 197), thus

---

41. Schlink's guardian status emerges from the documents concerning Heinrich Marx's estate, printed in Schöncke (1993: 287); there is further proof in Gemkow (1978).

belonging to the upper 30 percent of the Trier middle and upper class that had a yearly income of more than 200 talers (ibid.: 167). Since this middle and upper class only comprised around 20 percent of the population (ibid.: 185), the Marx family, in terms of income, belonged to the upper 6 percent of the total population. With this income, the family was also able to accumulate a certain level of wealth, owning multiple plots of land used for agriculture, among which were vineyards. For wealthy citizens of Trier, ownership of vineyards was a popular retirement provision (Monz 1973: 274). The Marx family also employed servants. In the year 1818, there was at least one maid (Schöncke 1993: 161); for the years 1830 and 1833, "two maids" are documented (ibid.: 295).

However, Heinrich Marx was not at all satisfied with what he had achieved in life. He wrote to his son Karl: "In my position I have also achieved something, enough to have you, but not enough by far to satisfy me" (letter of August 12–13, 1837, MECW 1: 677).

FROM THE PROMISE OF A CONSTITUTION THROUGH THE JULY REVOLUTION TO THE STORMING OF THE MAIN POLICE STATION IN FRANKFURT: POLITICAL CONDITIONS IN GERMANY

In January 1834, Heinrich Marx was caught up in a political affair that reveals a bit about his political views; Karl, not yet sixteen, might have experienced it with awareness. In order to understand the political relevance of the events in Trier depicted in the next section, it is important to deal extensively with political developments between 1815 and 1834. These developments also constitute the background for some of the debates and conflicts addressed in the following chapters.

In the last years of Napoleonic rule, discontent grew increasingly in the German territories ruled by France and the states dependent upon France. Due to constant wars, tax burdens rose, borne by the population, and an increasing number of young men were forced into the French army. More than ever, the French were seen as occupiers, and a German national consciousness became widespread. The Anti-Napoleonic Wars of 1813–15 were glorified as "wars of liberation" and supported by a large portion of the population. The declaration of war by Prussia in 1813 against a France that had already been weakened by the Russian campaign was accompanied by a call by the Prussian king, Friedrich Wilhelm III, "To My People," in which he asked "Prussians and Germans" for support for his struggle against Napoleon. This call had great resonance. The Prussian army was expanded by a newly created home guard (*Landwehr*), a sort of citizen militia. In addition, voluntary associations of riflemen arose. The most famous was the *Freikorps* of Major Adolph von Lützow (1772–1834), which many students and men of letters joined. One of its members was also the young poet Theodor Körner (1791–1813), who enthusiastically celebrated the Freikorps in a poem that would later become very popular, "Lützow's Wild Hunt." Körner himself died in battle, which made his fame even greater.

After Napoleon's defeat, a large portion of the German population expected from their princes more political freedoms and a greater voice. In the edict of May 22, 1815, Friedrich Wilhelm III raised the prospect of a constitution and the convocation of an all-Prussian representation, which henceforth was considered the "promise of a constitution" (*Verfassungsversprechen*) (see Koselleck 1967: 214ff., 286; Clark 2007: 340).

In Weimar, ruled by Goethe's liberal friend, the Grand Duke Karl-August (1757–1828), a constitution was introduced in 1816, which among other things stipulated a far-reaching freedom of the press. The southern German states also obtained constitutions. In 1818 in Bavaria, a constitution was introduced with a "second chamber" elected according to census suffrage (in the first chamber, the nobility and clergy were represented). In the same year, Baden also obtained a constitution, as well as a politically influential "second chamber," no longer elected on the basis of estates. In 1819, there followed a constitution in the Kingdom of Württemberg and in 1820 one in the Grand Duchy of Hesse. In Prussia, however, the promise of a constitution was not redeemed. Conservative circles won the upper hand, and the king no longer wanted to hear anything about a constitution, which caused persistent discontent among the liberal bourgeoisie. The German Confederation, founded at the Congress of Vienna, which took the place of the dissolved German Empire, was in no way a precursor to a German nation-state, but rather a confederation of states through which German princes primarily sought to secure their own rule.

Resistance arose against this development, the most radical representatives of which were the "*Burschenschaften*," a political youth movement emerging from students politicized during the "wars of liberation." The *Turnerbewegung* (roughly, a gymnastics movement) founded by Friedrich Ludwig Jahn (1778–1852) in 1811 also aimed in a similar direction. Physical training, including the fencing practiced by many members of the Burschenschaften, was basically an act of pre-military training. The simple gray gymnastics clothing and the use of the familiar second person (*Du*) were expressions of a bourgeois equality aiming at transcending different social strata as well as the diverse intra-German borders. These nationalist movements were not fundamentally anti-monarchist, but they placed the unity of "the nation" above monarchist and princely dynasties.

With the Wartburg Festival, which took place at the indulgence of the Grand Duke of Weimar on October 18, 1817, at the Wartburg castle near Eisenach, and in which hundreds of students participated, the Burschenschaften organized a large political event that was without precedent in Germany. The festival was intended to commemorate a double anniversary: the 300th anniversary of Martin Luther's 95 Theses, and thus the beginning of the Reformation, as well as the fourth anniversary of the Battle of the Nations (*Völkerschlacht*) in Leipzig, at which Napoleon was decisively defeated. Both events were regarded by the Burschenschaften as milestones of German liberation: from Roman-Papal foreign domination on the one hand, and French foreign domination on the other. A highlight of this festival was the burning of the insignia of the Prussian, Hessian, and Austrian armed forces—not dynastic rule, but a German nation-state was the goal—as well as "un-German" writings. Among these texts were dramas by the poet August von Kotzebue (1761–1819), who had attacked the Burschenschaften and Turnerbewegung as hotbeds of revolution and was regarded as an agent of the Russian tsar, and "The Germano Mania," in which the Jewish publicist Saul Ascher (1767–1822) opposed the increasing hostility to Jews within the national movement. Primarily under the influence of Jakob Friedrich Fries and his students, folkish anti-Semitism had become an important component of the nationalism of the Burschenschaften (Hubmann 1997: 191ff.). The only explicitly non-anti-Semitic current was that around a student of Hegel from Heidelberg, Friedrich Wilhelm Carové (1789–1852), who openly advocated admitting Jews to the Burschenschaften (ibid.: 188n150). After the Wartburg Festival, the Burschenschaften were banned in Prussia, which did not prevent them from gaining followers.

A year and a half after the Wartburg Festival, on March 23, 1819, August von Kotzebue (1761–1819) was murdered by theology student and Burschenschaft member Karl Ludwig Sand (1795–1820). This served as a pretext for the German Confederation to issue the "Karlsbad Decrees," which were intended to combat national and liberal tendencies. Such ideas were now considered "sedition" (*Volksverhetzung*) and their originators dangerous "demagogues." Students and professors were more closely monitored, nationally or liberally inclined professors were banned from employment, and public gymnastics grounds were closed. For newspapers and printed works not exceeding twenty printed sheets (320 pages), prior censorship was introduced (Geisthövel 2008: 20ff.).

Prussian reform policies implemented after the defeat of 1806 now came to a definite end. Wilhelm von Humboldt was dismissed from all state offices due to his criticism of the Karlsbad Decrees (Gall 2011: 333ff.). However, the Prussian government had problems imposing its policies of repression in the courts. Not because the courts sympathized with the liberal and national ideas of those being persecuted, but because many judges insisted upon adhering to legal provisions. They did not wish to penalize sentiments, but rather crimes that had actually occurred (Hodenberg 1996: 243ff.).

E. T. A. Hoffmann (1776–1822) satirically described the spirit of incipient repression in his fairy tale "Master Flea" (1822). Hoffmann, today known primarily as a poet of the Romantic movement, was, as a councilor of the court of Justice in Berlin from 1819 to 1821, a member of the Immediate Commission for the Investigation of Associations of High Treason and Other Dangerous Activities (*Immediat-Kommission zur Ermittlung hochver-räterischer Verbindungen und anderer gefährlicher Umtriebe*), was confronted with appalling prosecutions. The hero of his fairy tale is accused of kidnapping a "distinguished lady." Responding to the objection that no kidnapping has occurred, the investigating privy councilor, Knarrpanti, a caricature of the Berlin police commissioner Karl von Kamptz (1769–1849), answers that "once the culprit had been identified, the crime would follow automatically. Even if the principal charge could not be proved, owing to the obduracy of the accused, only a shallow and superficial judge would be incapable of introducing issues into the enquiry that would blemish the accused some-how and justify his arrest" (Hoffmann 1992: 298). On the basis of the accusation of quoting from trial documents, "Master Flea" was censored, and disciplinary proceedings against Hoffmann initiated. Hoffmann died in 1822, before these proceedings were concluded. His fairy tale was first published in uncensored form in 1908.

Long after the southern German states had obtained constitutions and representative bodies with certain democratic rights, the "Provincial Estates" (*Provinzialstände*) were established in Prussia in 1823. These were estate-based bodies limited to individual provinces, representing the nobility, cities, and rural communities. Only those owning land could vote. These provincial *Landtage* (state assemblies) were not intended as parliamentary representation; there was no real say involved. They were supposed to merely advise provincial governments, as quiescently as possible.

In large parts of the population, disappointment reigned regarding the broken promise of a constitution by the Prussian King and authoritarian policies. Political assemblies were banned and political statements in newspapers were censored. Under these conditions, developments abroad, of which one could speak more openly about than the political conditions in Germany, were followed with great interest. In particular, the Greek struggle for independence against the Ottoman Empire was regarded with great sympathy. Since the second half of the eighteenth century, in Germany in particular, ancient Greece was stylized as the lone summit of "classical" art, and through Prussian educational reforms, importance had been placed upon the preoccupation with Greek antiquity at the gymnasium. Furthermore, ancient Athens was regarded as a refuge of freedom and democracy. Conservatives and liberals were united in their enthusiasm for ancient Greece, philhellenism was widespread among educated people, and was expressed in practical support for the Greek struggle for independence.[42] The Prussian king and his government viewed such endeavours with suspicion; they feared agitators everywhere and distrusted in particular the population in the Rhenish province newly obtained in 1815.

In this repressive epoch of restoration, the Paris July Revolution of 1830 hit like a bolt of lightning out of the blue. These days, this revolution, which took place between the "great" French Revolution of 1789 and the European Revolutions of 1848–49 has largely disappeared from public awareness. For contemporaries, however, it was an enormously important event. The French king, Charles X (1757–1836), had exploited the weakness of the Ottoman Empire and conquered Algiers in 1830.[43] After this military success, in July of 1830, he dissolved parliament, tightened census suffrage, and restricted freedom of the press even further. In Paris, protests occurred, which ultimately culminated in barricade fights. After three days, Charles X had to abdicate the throne and flee to Great Britain. In Eugène Delacroix's most famous painting, *Liberty Leading the People*, this event is glorified: the bare-breasted Marianne, leading the people, holds the tricolor banned by the Bourbons and wears a Jacobin cap. But, in reality, radical, Jacobin-oriented forces were not able to prevail in France. The politically moderate grand bourgeoisie accomplished having Louis Philippe of Orleans (1773–1850), a distant cousin of Charles, crowned as king. Louis Philippe came to terms with the parliament and went down in history as the "bourgeois king." However, it was quickly revealed that he was only concerned with the interests of a part of the grand

---

42. Philhellenism was not just limited to Germany. Lord Byron, the famous English poet, participated in the liberation struggle and died in 1824 in Greece. After an intervention by the European great powers England, France, and Russia, a small Greek state was created in 1830. In 1832, the Bavarian Prince Otto became the first king of Greece.

43. In the years following, France conquered all of Algeria, which first achieved independence in 1962, after disastrous French colonial rule and the extremely brutal Algerian War lasting eight years (see: Schmid 2006).

bourgeoisie. Strikes and workers' uprisings, such as the uprisings of the silk weavers of Lyon in the years 1831 and 1834, were brutally suppressed.[44] The corrupt policies of Louis-Philippe and his myrmidons were caricatured by Honoré Daumier (1808–1879) in countless periodicals – the great era of political caricature began, as well as its persecution by the government (see NGBK 1974).

The German public was kept up to date on French developments by Ludwig Börne (1786–1837), with his *Letters from Paris* (1832–34), as well as by Heinrich Heine's series of articles, initially published in the Augsburg *Allgemeine Zeitung* and then as a book, *Französische Zustände* (French Conditions) (Heine 1832). After interventions by Friedrich von Gentz (1764–1832), for a long time a close collaborator of the Austrian state chancellor, Clemens Wenceslaus von Metternich (1773–1859), who was still the head of German reaction, Heine's articles were no longer allowed to be published starting in mid-1832: they were too critical in their analytical acuity. Heinrich Heine (1797–1856) was not only an important poet; in his essays and polemics, he also showed himself to be a clear-sighted analyst of society. We will see later that the young Marx, who befriended Heine in Paris in 1844, was also influenced by him with regard to theory.

Although the July Revolution of 1830 had neither the importance nor the repercussions of the French Revolution of 1789, it made clear that one had to reckon with revolutionary uprisings, and that these could have a certain level of success. For monarchs and princes, the July Revolution represented a terrible case of déjà-vu, to which they reacted with increased repression and surveillance. In the Rhenish province, the district administrator, Heinrich Schnabel (1778–1853), on behalf of the Prussian interior ministry,

---

44. Twenty years later, Marx accurately characterized the results of the July Revolution in *The Class Struggles in France*: "It was not the French bourgeoisie that ruled under Louis Philippe, but one faction of it: bankers, stock-exchange kings, railway kings, owners of coal and iron mines and forests, a part of the landed proprietors associated with them—the so-called *finance aristocracy*. It sat on the throne, it dictated laws in the Chambers, it distributed public offices, from cabinet portfolios to tobacco bureau posts. The *industrial bourgeoisie* proper formed part of the official opposition, that is, it was represented only as a minority in the Chambers. . . . The petty bourgeoisie of all gradations, and the peasantry also, were completely excluded from political power. . . . Owing to its financial straits, the July monarchy was dependent from the beginning on the big bourgeoisie, and its dependence on the big bourgeoisie was the inexhaustible source of increasing financial straits. . . . The July monarchy was nothing but a joint-stock company for the exploitation of France's national wealth, the dividends of which were divided among ministers, Chambers, 240,000 voters and their adherents. Louis Philippe was the director of this company" (MECW 10: 48ff.).

constructed a spy system that for a decade monitored not only the population, but also the local public agencies (see Hansen 1906: 1: 219ff).

For many oppositionists, the July Revolution was a source of hope, and a
revolutionary impulse emanated from it that seized other parts of Europe. In
1830, after being separated from the Netherlands, Belgium became an independent state with a relatively liberal, constitutional monarchy. In the mid-
1840s, this liberal Belgium would also become a place of refuge for Marx.
In the Papal States, which at the time encompassed a large section of Italy,
and in a few other Italian states, there was unrest. In November of 1830, an
uprising by Polish officers against Russian rule began in Warsaw, which was
only successfully suppressed in September of 1831. This uprising sparked an
enthusiasm for Poland in liberal circles in Germany and France that lasted for
years. The defeated Polish armed forces, which crossed Germany into French
exile, were celebrated enthusiastically along the way. Even in England, which
was untouched by the revolutionary upheavals, not everything remained the
same. In 1832, it had its first great electoral reform: the number of eligible
voters was expanded and electoral districts rearranged, which had long-term
effects upon the strength of political parties.

In Germany, there were numerous instances of unrest at a local level. In
Saxony and above all in the Electorate of Hesse, it was the extreme poverty of
sections of the population that led to social unrest. The constitutional opposition used this social pressure and was able to push through constitutions
in both states. After protest actions at the beginning of the 1830s, Hannover
and Braunschweig also obtained constitutions. However, in the two largest
German states, Prussia and Austria, nothing changed.

With a certain delay, the revolutionary wave also took hold of southern
and southwest Germany. In Baden and Bavaria, after elections, there were
oppositional majorities in the parliaments, which intensified political conflicts. Censorship was increased, although this was not accepted without
resistance by journalists and publishers who achieved some spectacular
successes in the courts. In order to implement freedom of the press, the
"German Fatherland Association to Support the Free Press" was founded
in 1832, which was decisively involved in the organization of the Hambach
Festival that took place from May 27 to 30 in the ruins of Hambach Castle.
Announced as a public festival—political assemblies were forbidden—it
was the first mass political rally in Germany, in which 20,000 to30,000 people participated.[45] Many well-known citizens of Trier, such as the merchants

---

45. On the Hambach Festival and the subsequent wave of repression, see Wehler 2008: 2:
363–69.

Lautz and Cetto, were also present (Böse 1951: 8n41). Demands were raised for freedom of assembly, expression, and the press, civil rights, and the national unity of Germany. As a symbol of these demands, the black-red-golden tricolor was used for the first time in large numbers (these colors were worn by the Lützow Freikorps mentioned above as a mark of identification). Representatives of the Burschenschaften demanded the creation of a provisional government and the beginning of an armed uprising, which was rejected, however, as futile.

The German Confederation reacted with massive repression against the speakers and organizers of the Hambach Festival. Many were indicted, and many fled abroad. In Trier, the most well-known victim was the Burschenschaft member (and later lawyer) Johann August Messerich (1806–1876) from Bitburg. He was jailed in 1834 in Trier and sentenced to thirteen years' imprisonment, but was released in 1839 (Trierer Biographisches Lexikon: 294). These events, attracting attention, were probably no secret to sixteen-year-old Karl.[46]

The repression following the Hambach Festival led to further radicalization. In Frankfurt, student groups planned to storm the seat of the Bundestag, the permanent federal diet of the German Confederation as well as both police stations, arm themselves, then take ownership of the treasury of the German Confederation and take the emissaries of the German state as prisoners. They hoped that these events would lead to the beginning of a general German revolution. On April 3, 1833, the "Frankfurter Wachensturm" was carried out by about fifty people, primarily members of the Burschenschaften. The young Karl Schapper (1812–1870) also participated; Marx would later work with him in the League of the Just. However, the entire project was betrayed and failed at the outset, though the action earned the Burschenschaften much sympathy from the population. The German Confederation reacted with years of persecution. Up to 1842, investigations were carried out against 2,000 suspects, many of whom emigrated to the United States (Geisthövel 2008: 38).

Georg Büchner (1813–1837), who was nineteen at the time, today regarded as one of the most important German poets, assessed the Frankfurt events accurately in a letter to his family: "If anything is to help us in our times, it is *force*. We know what to expect from our princes. Everything they've

---

46. Marx would later befriend Messerich. A letter Marx received in 1864 from his brother-in-law Johann Jacob Conradi refers to "your close friend Messerich" (MEGA III/12: 493). But it is improbable that this friendship already existed in 1834, since Messerich was twelve years older than Marx and had studied since 1829 in Bonn and Heidelberg.

authorized was wrested from them by necessity . . . our estates are a parody of common sense . . . the young people are accused of the use of force. But are we not in a permanent state of force? . . . What do you refer to as a *condition of legality*? A *law* that makes beasts of drudgery of the great mass of citizens in order to satisfy the unnatural wants of an insignificant and spoiled minority? And this law, supported by raw military force and the dumb cleverness of its agents, this law is an *eternal, raw force*, committed against right and common sense, and I will struggle against it wherever I can with *mouth* and *hand*." But Büchner was skeptical with regard to the chances for a revolutionary uprising. He continues: "if I have taken no part in what has happened and will take *no part* in what might happen, this is not due to disapproval, nor fear, but rather because at the current point in time, I regard any revolutionary movement as a futile endeavor and don't share the illusions of those who see the Germans as a people who fight for their rights" (Büchner 1988: 278).

In the same year, Büchner participated in the founding in Gießen of the secret "Society for Human Rights." In 1834, he composed the first—and until the *Communist Manifesto* of 1848, most important—manifesto of social revolution in Germany, "The Hessian Courier." There, he not only formulated the battle cry that would later become famous, "Peace to the cottages! War on the palaces!" but also supported his critique with facts and figures that proved the exploitation of the people and the waste of the ruling class. A revolution carried out by the people was to be prepared not by individual actions such as the Frankfurter Wachensturm, but through enlightenment and critique. Büchner expected nothing from the liberals: "the relation between the poor and the rich is the only revolutionary element in the world," he wrote to Gutzkow in 1835 (Büchner 1988: 303). However, the group around Büchner that had distributed "The Hessian Courier" was betrayed, and Büchner had to flee to Strasbourg. Friedrich Ludwig Weidig (1791–1837), the most important head of the group alongside Büchner, was arrested in 1835 and was repeatedly subject to bad mistreatment by the investigating magistrate. He died in jail in 1837, supposedly by suicide. Only a few days earlier, the twenty-three-year-old Büchner had died of typhoid fever in Zurich.

THE TRIER CASINO AFFAIR OF 1834 AND HEINRICH MARX'S POLITICAL VIEWS

In Trier as well, poor economic development, the king's unkept promise of a constitution, and the imperious behavior of the Prussian military led in the 1820s to increasing dissatisfaction with Prussian rule. The July

Revolution in Paris had given a boost to liberal tendencies. Höfele (1939: 28) quotes a government report that mentions "anonymous appeals," lively debates, and booksellers offering "laudatory" accounts of the Paris events. In an anonymous letter delivered in September of 1830 to the directorates of the casino societies of multiple Rhenish cities, under the heading "The State Constitution Lives," demands were raised for a constitution, reforms, and a far-reaching separation of the Rhineland from Old Prussia (Monz 1973: 126; Höfele 1939: 30). Such a critique was not just the concern of marginal groups or individuals, but was widespread as well among the bourgeoisie and urban officials. The district president of Trier even suspected that the letter was "a concoction of the judiciary" (Monz 1973: 127). In October of 1830, the district president complained to Mayor Haw that municipal officials were providing disparaging opinions "on domestic and foreign political subjects" in full view of the public (ibid.: 129). When the city administration hosted a banquet to honor the retiring city commander, General Lieutenant von Ryssel, on December 29, 1830, only seventy-nine out of the 278 invited guests accepted the invitation (ibid.: 131).

The Prussian government distrusted the Rhenish population, fearing they might seek annexation by France. Smaller, more symbolic acts of criticism were also noted, very precisely; for example, in August of 1832, during a banquet honoring the retiring president of the commercial court, which Mayor Haw of Trier also attended, eight toasts were made, but none to the well-being of the king (ibid.: 132, 193).

The degree to which the government was dissatisfied with a large part of the Trier district court is indicated by an ordinance of the justice minister von Kamptz from January 26, 1833, in which the Trier judiciary is accused of not prosecuting political machinations consistently enough, of granting too much freedom to political detainees, and of accepting statements by the accused without confirming whether they corresponded to the truth (ibid.: 138).

The Casino Society, originally founded to make possible an unforced conviviality, developed after 1830 into a center of oppositional thought, which is not surprising if one considers that liberal tendencies critical of Prussia were present not least in the upper bourgeoisie, among public officials, lawyers, merchants, doctors, etc., that is, precisely in those strata to which most of the members of the Casino Society belonged. These oppositional tendencies found clear expression in multiple events of the year 1834.

On January 12, 1834, there was a celebratory banquet to honor the returning Trier delegates to the Rhenish provincial diet. It was initiated by about forty citizens, who had elected an organizational committee of five, to which both Heinrich Marx and the above-mentioned judiciary council, Schlink, with whom he was friends, belonged. Not only the Trier press, but also Cologne newspapers reported on it, since such a banquet honoring the delegates was unusual, and 160 people took part in it. Since political assemblies were forbidden, in southern Germany people had begun organizing banquets as substitutes. This custom was new in Prussia.[47]

Heinrich Marx played an important role in the organizational committee, as can be seen by the fact that he gave the welcoming speech, which was followed by further speeches.[48] When one reads Heinrich Marx's speech today, at first glance it appears rather harmless and even "deferential."[49] He thanks the returning delegates for the work they've done and the king for the creation of the provincial diet. But if one examines this speech a bit more and situates it within the context of the language regime of the time, it becomes clear that it formulates a decisive critique of the prevailing political conditions.[50]

The public reception for the delegates and the arrangement of a festive banquet to honor them was already an oppositional act. From the viewpoint of the king and the government, the members of the estate assemblies were not elected to represent the interests of the people. They were elected in order to function as advisers to the royal government. They were therefore not responsible to their voters, but to the king. With the reception by their voters and public praise for their work, however, they were treated as representatives of the people, exactly what the king *did not* want.

Heinrich Marx's speech also began with a small but clear affront to the king: he is not thanked first; rather, the representatives of the city are. He subsequently thanks the king for "the first institution of popular representation." But an institution of popular representation is what the estates assembly was not supposed to be! In speaking as well of the "first" institution, Heinrich Marx implies that further institutions are to follow, a clear reference to the

---

47. On this form of oppositional culture, to which among other things singing also belonged, see Brophy (2007).

48. All the speeches are printed in Schöncke (1993: 226ff.).

49. This is the judgment, for example, of McLellan (1973: 4) who only pays attention to a single sentence praising the Prussian king.

50. Künzli (1966: 43) takes this speech as proof of Heinrich Marx's "opportunist subservience," which "wraps up" everything oppositional "in the wadding of a cowardly conformism." Following Künzli, Raddatz (1975: 17) sees a "mixture of servility, adoring worship of the monarchy, and yet a cunning distance" at work. Both authors not only ignore the tone that was usual for that time with regard to the monarch (I noted above that even a toast not made to the king was officially noted by the government), they also spare themselves a more exact analysis of the speech. Sperber (2013) doesn't even mention this speech.

convocation of an all-Prussian diet, desired by many citizens. The observation that the monarch had established the assembly "so that truth can ascend to the steps of his throne" because "where justice sits enthroned, truth must also find a point of entry" is also not without a critical barb: the monarch needed the assembly in order to hear the truth, and only by hearing the truth could he rule justly. This means conversely that plans to abolish the provincial diets would prevent the monarch from hearing the truth, so that a just government would no longer be possible.

In this speech, Heinrich Marx does not take a republican or fundamentally anti-monarchist position; he still hopes for an improvement of political conditions "from above," by an enlightened monarch. But he expresses his criticism very clearly within the framework of the linguistic regime of the time, and as the reaction of the Minister of Justice von Kamptz made clear, the government had very much understood the criticism and regarded it as dangerous. Von Kamptz wrote: "The city of Trier has provided the first example that the lunchtime societies of private persons brought together through subscription have taken it upon themselves in an ignorant and unauthorized way to observe and take to task the proceedings—and indeed even the principles and votes and the behavior of individual members—of an assembly responsible to His Royal Majesty the King, and at the very most only to him. It is already the case that the great majority of deputies to the diet do not regard themselves as German deputies to the diet on the basis of estates, but rather as representatives of the people, and are strengthened in this madness by the public when they, as in England, receive and hold speeches in taverns concerning their service in the diet and the dangers and plans threatening the diet that they have averted, receiving the civic crown from the guests" (quoted in Monz 1973: 135).

The reception for the delegates was not the only event to reveal the oppositional attitude of the Casino members. Two weeks later, on January 25, the founding day of the Casino Society, a well-attended dinner took place there. There was drinking, and at a late hour, when most of the guests had already left, there was singing—in French. An army captain stationed in Trier reported to his division general that various participants in the event, among them Heinrich Marx as well as Johann Gerhard Schneemann, one of young Karl's teachers, had begun to hold speeches and sing revolutionary songs, including "La Marseillaise." Also present was Robert Schleicher (1806–1846), the family doctor of the Westphalen family (Monz 1973: 326) and later a friend of Karl and Jenny. The army captain continued to note that things did not just remain at singing. A cloth with the colors of the French tricolor and a depiction of a memorial to the fallen fighters of the

July Revolution was also displayed, whereupon the lawyer Brixius remarked: "If we had not experienced the French July Revolution, we'd have to eat grass now like cattle." The captain allegedly heard all of this through the window while passing by the Casino. The division general forwarded the report to the district president, and Brixius was ultimately charged with high treason. However, the Trier district court acquitted him on December 15, 1834, since there was an absence of the intention of high treason. The interior minister then appealed the decision, but the appeals court in Cologne confirmed the acquittal on July 18th, 1835, with the argument that what had occurred was not decorous, but did not violate any criminal code (ibid.: 135ff.).

A further occurrence also shows the oppositional mood of many Casino members. When in June 1834 the senior civil servant Schmeltzer spoke in the Casino about his life's reminiscences and in doing so condemned the Jacobins, "he was 'razzed' and mocked" (ibid.: 137). Apparently, because of all these occurrences, great pressure was exerted upon the Casino Society, so that it dissolved itself on July 6, 1834. However, it was re-founded in August (ibid.; also Schmidt 1955: 31ff.).

Due to these incidents, the Prussian government not only distrusted the population of Trier, but Mayor Wilhelm Haw increasingly drew its attention. Already in 1832, the district president of Trier had noted an "inclination to the Francophone" on the part of Haw. Haw attempted to portray the singing of revolutionary songs on January 25 as harmless and caused by excessive alcohol consumption. At the same time, he criticized the behavior of the district president and the division general in this affair; this critique brought disciplinary proceedings. On August 2, he was even stripped of his leadership of the city police. The government regarded him as so suspicious that they kept him under surveillance when he traveled to Brussels in 1838 in order to enroll his son at the Ecole de Commerce. Ultimately, things came to a conflict in 1839 regarding the rights of the city vis-à-vis the district administration, in the course of which considerable pressure was exerted upon Haw until he finally announced his resignation because he no longer saw himself as able to represent the interests of the citizens.[51]

All these events make clear that in the 1830s, enlightened and liberal attitudes were widespread, especially among members of the judiciary and

---

51. This conflict is depicted in detail by Monz (1973: 193ff.). In the years following, liberal and republican tendencies in Trier were even more considerable. In the 1840s, the *Trierische Zeitung* took relatively "left" positions, and during the elections to the national assembly in 1848, Trier was the only Rhenish city that elected exclusively leftist republicans as representatives (Monz 1973: 207).

Mayor Haw. Heinrich Marx had many friends and acquaintances in these circles; he even represented the mayor in court. The fact that Heinrich Marx was elected to the organizing committee for the reception of the Trier delegates and held the welcoming address shows how well regarded he was in these critical circles. Measured in terms of conditions at the time, his talk was courageous. It showed that Heinrich Marx professed his critical attitude even in public. It must be assumed that the young Karl Marx consciously took notice of these events and his father's critical attitude.

However, Heinrich Marx was often characterized as a Prussian patriot. Old Edgar von Westphalen had already spoken of Heinrich Marx as a "Patriot und Protestant à la Lessing" in a letter to Engels (quoted in Gemkow 2008: 507n33) and Mehring also writes that he was a "Prussian patriot," adding "though not in the humdrum sense the word has today" but rather in terms of "having an honest belief in the 'Old Fritzian'[52] enlightenment" (Mehring 1962: 2). Some authors copy the part about the "Prussian patriot" but leave out the specification.

Patriotic feelings were supposedly recognizable in a letter that Heinrich Marx wrote to Karl on March 2, 1837. His literary son Karl had apparently communicated to him his desire to enter the public sphere by writing a drama. The father advised his son against drama as a debut, saying that the danger of failure was too great. He recommends an ode on a turning point in Prussian history, the Battle of Waterloo, at which much was at stake for Prussia. "If executed in a patriotic and German spirit with depth of feeling, such an ode would itself be sufficient to lay the foundation for a reputation, to establish a name." Thus, in the case of this recommendation, the main focus is not on Heinrich's own political view, but rather the consideration of how his son could make a name for himself. But Heinrich also adds a justification for being "enthusiastic" about this moment in history. The fact that Heinrich Marx felt he had to justify this reveals that Prussian patriotism was not a matter of course for him. And how does he justify this enthusiasm? A victory for Napoleon "would have imposed eternal fetters on mankind and especially on the human mind. Only today's two-faced liberals can deify a Napoleon. And in truth under his rule not a single person would have dared to think aloud what is being written daily and without interference throughout Germany, and especially in Prussia. And anyone who has studied the history of Napoleon and what he understood by the absurd expression of ideology can rejoice greatly and with a clear conscience at his downfall and the victory of Prussia" (MECW 1: 673).

---

52. What is meant there is the Enlightenment promoted by "Old Fritz," that is, the Prussian king Friedrich II (1712–1786).

It's noteworthy that what Heinrich Marx holds against Napoleon the most is his way of dealing with "ideologues." In the 1790s, Destutt de Tracy (1754–1836) coined the term "ideology" to describe a science of ideas and perceptions. It was a project of the Enlightenment that analyzed human thoughts in an empirical manner and criticized the various forms of obscurantism— that is, the "obscuring" of the world, springing from superstition or the dogmatic clinging to tradition. Politically, Destutt de Tracy and his pupils were moderate republicans. For them, intellectual and civil liberties were the most important achievements of the revolution. The young, aspiring Napoleon had initially sought the support of these respected "ideologues." To the extent that he became an autocratic-despotic ruler, and on his path to the imperial throne sought the support of the Catholic Church, the relationship deteriorated. He was not interested in independent research into topics having to do with politics or moral philosophy that an opposition to his rule could build upon. Ultimately, the "ideologues" served him as scapegoats who were made responsible for everything bad that befell France since the revolution. The negative connotation that the word *ideology* still has today goes back to Napoleon's hounding of the "ideologues."[53] So it was precisely Napoleon's anti-Enlightenment, illiberal side that Heinrich Marx criticized, and in light of this side, he preferred Prussian victory. So Heinrich Marx was anything but an uncritical lover of Prussia.[54]

In his final text as well, a draft written in 1838 intended as a contribution to the "*Kölner Kirchenstreit*" (Cologne church conflict, sometimes referred to as the "Cologne Muddle" or *Kölner Wirren*), to which Karl had made some corrections (MEGA IV/1: 379–80), Heinrich Marx took the side of Prussia. The occasion of the Cologne conflict was the question of the religious education of children whose parents belonged to different religions. According to Prussian law, the religion of children was determined by the religion of the father. But the Catholic Church, which was dominant in the Rhineland, demanded that before a marriage a bride should promise to raise the children as Catholics, so that children of all "mixed marriages" would be raised Catholic. The archbishop of Cologne, Clemens August Droste zu Vischering (1773–1845), who had taken office in 1836, advocated the Catholic position uncompromisingly. A few months before, he had taken a position against *Hermesianism*, the doctrine of the theology professor Georg Hermes (1775–1831), who had come

---

53. On the conflict between Napoleon and the "ideologues," see Barth (1945: 13–31).

54. Künzli (1966: 45) writes with regard to this letter of an "enthusiasm for Prussia that had to be kept alive with so much humiliating subservience," but he doesn't address in the slightest *why* Heinrich Marx preferred Prussia's victory.

out of the Catholic Enlightenment. Overstepping his authority, the arch-bishop prohibited Catholic theology students at the university from attend-ing corresponding lectures. At the high point of the conflict over mixed mar-riages, the government arrested the bishop in November of 1837 and placed him under house arrest, which made him a martyr in conservative Catholic circles and generated strong anti-Prussian sentiment.

The harsh approach of the Prussian government was due not only to the fact that religion played a large role in everyday life and that the Prussian state understood itself to be a Protestant state. Equally important was the fact that the pope, as ruler of the Papal States, which at the time encompassed large swathes of Italy, also constituted a secular power, one closely allied with Catholic France, and the relationship between Prussia and France was still tense. Furthermore, after the Revolution of 1830, in Belgium, a Catholic and liberal state had come about that the Prussian state feared could become an attractive model for the Rhineland.

The arrest of the bishop led to numerous public statements. This conflict also had an important significance for the political formation of the Young Hegelians (see chapter three). In his brief draft, Heinrich Marx justifies the approach of the Prussian government as a defense against the political dan-ger emanating from an aggressive Catholicism.[55]

In both cases—the praise of Prussia's victory over Napoleon as well as his statement on the Cologne church conflict—Heinrich Marx showed him-self to be not at all a blind proponent of the Prussian authoritarian state. He took the side of the Prussian state where he regarded it (whether rightly or wrongly) as a defender of enlightenment and liberality.

THE FATHERLY FRIEND JOHANN LUDWIG VON WESTPHALEN

As Eleanor Marx emphasized in her biographical sketch, Karl Marx in his youth was strongly stimulated intellectually not only by his father, but also by his future father-in-law, Johann Ludwig von Westphalen. Heinrich Marx and Ludwig von Westphalen had a friendly relationship over the course

---

55. The conflict continued up to 1842, when it ended with a compromise under the new Prussian king, Friedrich Wilhelm IV, who made far-reaching compromises with the Catholic Church. This "Cologne Muddle" was anything but a provincial farce. It functioned as a catalyst for the development of political Catholicism in Germany, which ultimately led in 1870 to the founding of the Catholic Centre Party. This party played an important role in the Kaiserreich and during the Weimar Republic. The Centre Party lost its significance with the founding of the CDU as an inter-denominational Christian political party after the Second World War.

of many years. There were multiple points of contact: both were members of the small Protestant congregation in Trier as well as the Casino Society. Furthermore, it's quite possible that the lawyer Marx in the course of his legal proceedings came into contact professionally with the government official Westphalen. For various reasons, both could have initially stood somewhat outside Trier's society of Catholic dignitaries: Heinrich Marx as a Jew baptized as a Protestant, and Ludwig von Westphalen having moved to Trier as a Protestant, Prussian official. This might have also had an effect in bringing the two together. However, it's unclear how and when the relationship between the two fathers began. Rather improbable is the story peddled by Wheen (1999: 19) without citing a source,[56] according to which the five-year-old Jenny first saw her later husband when he was an infant during a visit by her father to the Marx household. If this story were true, then this friendly relationship would have had to exist as early as 1819. But when Heinrich Marx's children were baptized in 1824, Ludwig von Westphalen was not among the godparents, which could be expected if there had already been a close friendship at that time.

Family Background

The von Westphalen family was not an old Prussian noble family.[57] Ludwig's father was born in 1724 under the still-bourgeois name Christian Philip Westphal.[58] He studied law at the universities at Helmstedt and Halle; after

---

56. This story is also found—likewise without a source, but with the additional information that little Karl was being breastfed at that moment—in the Jenny Marx biography by Peters (1984: 26).

57. They are not related to the Westphalian noble family of the same name (see Adelslexikon Bk. 16: 135).

58. The most important sources on the life of Philip Westphal are found in the texts of his grandson, Ferdinand von Westphalen (1859, 1866), on which Franz Mehring's study (1892) is also based. Further information on Philip and his son Ludwig is provided by the comprehensive appendix in Krosigk (1975). The author of this book, Lutz Graf Schwerin von Krosigk (1887–1977), was a grandson of Jenny's stepsister, Lisette. In 1932, he was named finance minister of Germany by chancellor von Papen, a position he also held throughout the entirety of the Nazi period. After the war, he was convicted as a war criminal, among other things, because of plundering Jewish property through the revenue offices, but he received amnesty in 1951. The most recent research on the Westphalen family is found in Gemkow (2008) and Limmroth (2014).

that, he accompanied a Herr von Spiegel on a trip through Europe, which at the time was a part of the educational canon of rich nobles. In 1751, he became secretary to Duke Ferdinand von Braunschweig (1721–1792), who was three years older and the brother of the reigning duke as well as a Prussian officer. It seems he soon had a close relationship of mutual trust with Ferdinand.

For both, their great chance came with the beginning of the Seven Years' War (1756–63). Prussia was allied with England, which also ruled Hanover in personal union, against France, Austria, and Russia. At the wish of the English king, George II, Ferdinand was named commander-in-chief of the English-Hanoverian-Hessian armed forces in the western part of Germany by the Prussian king, Friedrich II. His job consisted primarily in securing the western flank. Whereas Friedrich attempted in the east to deal with the Russian and Austrian forces, Ferdinand was supposed to keep the French troops in check to the extent of preventing them from intervening in the war in the East. However, the French armed troops were usually twice as numerous as those commanded by Ferdinand. Furthermore, the French army was under united leadership, whereas Ferdinand's army resulted from a coalition and was thus dependent upon different princes. Despite the numerical inferiority of his own troops, Ferdinand inflicted multiple bitter defeats upon the French. Philip Westphal, although not a soldier himself, was the strategist who contributed decisively to these victories (see the detailed presentation in Mediger 2011). Other than that of secretary, he did not have any official position, but as made clear by the abundance of surviving papers, he not only functioned as a de facto chief of staff, he also organized the provisioning of the armed forces and conducted the entirety of the duke's correspondence. That a person of a bourgeois background had such a position of trust within the military was, as Franz Mehring (1892: 406) correctly emphasizes, unique. The king of England also honored Westphal by granting him the title of "adjutant general" of the English armed forces.

Philip Westphal met Jeannie Wishart de Pittarow (1742–1811), his future wife and eighteen years his junior, in a military camp. She was visiting her sister, who was married to an English general. Her ancestors descended from old Scottish nobility. An ancestor of her father's, George Wishart, was burned at the stake in 1547 in the struggle to introduce the Reformation in Scotland. Archibald Campbell, 9th Earl of Argyll (1629–1685), an ancestor of her mother's, led the (failed) rebellion against the English king James II, and was beheaded in Edinburgh. Later, Jeannie wrote a history of her ancestors, which her son Ludwig translated. Every one of his children received a copy of this translation (Krosigk 1975: 170). Jenny—and through her, Karl—was also informed about this line of ancestors.[59]

Probably in order to allow Jeannie a wedding befitting her social status, Philip Westphal took on a title of nobility in 1764 that Ferdinand obtained for him. Philip Westphal became Philip Edler von Westphalen. He married Jeannie in 1765. After the war, he left the service of the duke and lived as a landowner, first in what is now Lower Saxony, then in Mecklenburg, where he died on September 21, 1792. He was not able to complete his plan to write a history of Ferdinand's military campaigns. It was his grandson, Ludwig's oldest son Ferdinand, who became the Prussian interior minister, who issued this work posthumously in 1859, supplementing it with some biographical information on the Westphalen family.

Profession and Political Attitudes

Philip and Jeannie had four sons. Ludwig, who was born on July 11, 1770, in Bornum near Braunschweig, was their youngest son and the only one who founded a family and had children. He studied law at the University of Göttingen, which at the time was one of the most important in Germany. Among his academic instructors were, according to the obituary by his son Ferdinand (1842), Gustav Hugo (1764–1844), one of the founders of the German Historical School of Jurisprudence (which Karl Marx later engaged with critically); the famous publicist and historian August von Schlözer (1735–1809), who on the occasion of the final Swiss witch trial in 1782 coined the phrase "judicial murder"; as well as Georg Christoph Lichtenberg (1742–1799), famous today primarily for his aphorisms. Ludwig began as an assessor in 1794 but left the civil service at his own wish in 1798. He bought an estate and tried his luck at agriculture. In the same year, he married Elisabeth (Lisette) Luise Wilhelmine Albertine von Veltheim, who was eight years younger. He had four children with her: Ferdinand was born in 1799, Louise (Lisette) in 1800, Karl in 1803, and Franziska in 1807. In 1807, at the age of only twenty-nine, Elisabeth died, so that Ludwig was a widower at the age of thirty-seven with four children. The daughters moved in with relatives of their mother, while the sons stayed with Ludwig. That was not at all unusual at the time, since sons usually left the household early on, while daughters usually lived with their parents until marriage. Ludwig's household was led by his mother Jeannie, who died in 1811. His second wife, Caroline Heubel, who was born in 1779, was not from a noble family, but rather came

---

59. In "Herr Vogt" (1860), Marx refers in one passage to this ancestor of his wife (MECW 17: 33).

from an upscale family of civil servants from Thuringia (on the Heubel family, see Limmroth 2014: 28–34). Ludwig had three children with her: Jenny was born in 1814, Laura in 1817 (but died in 1822), and Edgar in 1819.[60]

Very positive descriptions of Ludwig by both wives have been passed down. His first wife characterized him as being "of a very English ['angelic' is what is meant]—gentleness of character, rare kindheartedness, and an always constant emotional state" (quoted in Monz 1973: 330). In a letter from December 21, 1826, to her cousin, his second wife wrote: "Fate has supplied me with a man to whom few can compare in terms of greatness of the soul and intellect. A delightful character through which I enjoy heaven on earth, we endure all the tempests of life together with love, because often fate has dragged on us harshly, we have endured many agonies, but having such a support as I do in him, my foot does not slip" (quoted in Monz 1973d: 22).

Ludwig was not very successful as a landowner and farmer. He had only purchased an estate in order to marry his first (noble) wife Elisabeth von Veltheim and offer her a life befitting her social status. Ultimately, Ludwig leased the property, which he had purchased largely on credit, and returned to the civil service in Braunschweig in 1804. The debts from his time as a landowner would burden him for some time.

After Prussia's defeat in 1806, Napoleon deposed the House of Welf in Hannover and Braunschweig and established the "Kingdom of Westphalia," which encompassed large parts of the current German states Lower Saxony and Hesse. He appointed his younger brother Jérôme as king. In 1807, Ludwig von Westphalen entered the service of this kingdom; he was initially General Secretary of the Prefecture in Halberstadt, and finally Sub-Prefect in Salzwedel. Like many others, Ludwig became an opponent of Napoleon because of the pressing tax burdens and constant recruitment that Napoleon required for every new war of conquest. Mehring (1892: 414) reports that Ludwig was even arrested in 1813 by Marshal Davoust. When in the same year Prussian rule in Salzwedel began, the government retained him as district administrator. In 1816, landowners once again obtained the right to elect the district administrator, and they used it to get rid of Ludwig von Westphalen. He was probably too liberal for them; furthermore, his second marriage to a "bourgeois" woman was not "befitting his social status" (see Krosigk 1975: 178).

The Prussian government ordered him thereupon to Trier. The government preferred to send more liberal officials to the newly acquired Rhineland,

---

60. Konrad von Krosigk (1973) provides valuable information about the children from the first marriage, particularly concerning Lisette and her relationships with Jenny and Edgar.

since it wanted to deal with the population there first in a cautious manner. With his son Karl from the first marriage, the two-year-old Jenny, his wife Caroline, and her by then seventy-five-year-old father, Ludwig relocated to Trier. Christiane, an unmarried sister of Caroline's, who cared for their frail mother, as well as the oldest son Ferdinand, who would soon take the Abitur exams, remained in Salzwedel. In Trier, Laura and Edgar were born. After the death of her mother, Christiane also moved to Trier, where she lived in Ludwig and Caroline's household until her death in 1842 (see Limmroth 2014: 41; Monz 1973: 329n64). From 1818 at the latest, two domestic servants were employed (Limmroth 2014: 42). Around 1828–29, Helena Demuth, who later kept house for Karl and Jenny, must have entered the Westphalen household; at least that's what Eleanor Marx reported to Wilhelm Liebknecht (see Liebknecht 1896/1908: 162).

In Trier, Ludwig von Westphalen became state councillor of the district government. This was a step down compared to his previous post as district administrator; however, at 1,800 talers, he received the highest annual salary of all government officials in comparable positions (Monz 1973: 331). But with this salary, he not only had to finance a household that encompassed six to seven people; he also had to service the debt from his purchases of land, though these pieces of land didn't bring in much revenue.[61]

In the meantime, in Berlin the conservative interior minister von Schuckmann (whose anti-Semitic attitude was mentioned above), was able to increasingly prevail against the liberal state chancellor, Karl August von Hardenberg (1750–1822), so that liberal sentiments among state officials were now rather suspect. Ludwig von Westphalen was not promoted any further; only in 1834—during his retirement—did he obtain the title of privy senior civil servant, *"Geheimer Regierungsrat."*[62]

In Trier, Ludwig von Westphalen was responsible among other things for the gendarmerie, prisons, charitable institutions, statistics, and the official journal. So he was directly confronted with all the social problems that existed there. In the evaluations of his superiors, he was on the one hand

---

61. In a letter from December 23/24, 1859, to Engels, Jenny Marx also mentions an annual life annuity that Heinrich, an older brother of her father, demanded be paid from the small widow's pension of her mother (MECW 40: 575). It's possible that Ludwig had his brother's share of his inheritance from their father paid out in exchange for a life annuity in order to finance a purchase of land.

62. Two or three years later, Ludwig also received a Prussian order of merit. The street directory for Trier from 1838 to 1840 referred to him as Knight of the Order of the Red Eagle, Fourth Class (Schöncke 1993: 876). The Order of the Red Eagle was the second-highest Prussian order, the Fourth was its lowest class.

praised for being an indefatigable worker and for being very knowledgeable; on the other hand, he was criticized for his statements that were supposedly too verbose and distracted from what was essential. In 1831, the district president of Trier proposed to the government in Berlin that Westphalen be retired—without the latter's knowledge. In the next year, he backed away from this proposal, since Westphalen applied for retirement due to a heavy and persistent "catarrh of the lungs." He then retired in 1834 (Monz 1973: 324ff.). After the "Casino Affair," the government was probably all right with a high-level official regarded as politically not completely trustworthy who was no longer in active service.

We learn something of Ludwig von Westphalen's political views from a letter that he sent on April 7, 1831, to the publisher Friedrich Perthes, a cousin of his wife (printed in its entirety in Monz 1973d). Perthes apparently wanted to be taught about the situation in Trier; after the July Revolution of 1830, there were all kinds of rumors about French "agitators" that had come to Germany and about German sympathizers of France who would allegedly call for overthrow. In this letter, Ludwig acknowledged Trier's economic problems, as well as complaints about "the onerous, almost unaffordable taxes" and the "great state of emergency really present in most areas" (ibid.: 18). A "special devotion to the Prussian state" had not yet evolved. But supposedly there was still trust in the government and "above all great respect and love for the most just of kings." An inclination toward France in Trier was found "only in the upper classes of bourgeois society, namely among lawyers, bankers, merchants, doctors, notaries, etc. The pupils at the gymnasiums and university students are also infected by this Francomania" (ibid.: 14, 15, 16).

Ludwig von Westphalen's own views are expressed most clearly in the passage that follows. Under contemporary political conditions, two irreconcilable principles were in conflict: "the old one of divine right and the new one of popular sovereignty." Regarding the convulsions emanating from this conflict, he writes: "Only *one* notion can ensure calm, namely that the dreams of republican do-gooders no longer fit a generation that has matured in the school of misfortune and of deeper meaning, and in this awareness I still gladly surrender myself—despite the threatening manifestations of a condition of anarchy in the fermenting west and south of Europe—to better hopes to which the enthusiasm of my youth was dedicated, that from the immeasurable world event that produced a general commotion for eight months [that is, the July Revolution in France and its consequences] and from the current confusion of an unhinged political world, *true* freedom, inseparably in league with order and reason, will emerge like a phoenix from the ashes" (ibid.:15).

What emerges from this letter is that Westphalen had a critical view of social conditions in Trier and recognized clearly that the Prussian tax system, which entailed a much heavier burden for the poorer strata than the earlier French system, led to further impoverishment. For another thing, the letter makes his fundamental political attitude clear. He distances himself from "republican do-gooders" but is not at all therefore an adherent of absolute monarchy. He only vaguely hints at what he regards as desirable: a "true freedom" in league with "order and reason." Since he hopes that this state of affairs might emerge from the turmoil of the July Revolution, in which the Bourbon king, Charles X, was deposed and the "citizen-king," Louis-Philippe, came to power, it's not hard to guess that hiding behind his hints is the suggestion of a constitutional monarchy. The fact that Ludwig Westphalen expresses himself so vaguely here might be due to the fear of spying and surveillance, which was particularly intense during the period after the July Revolution. This fear is expressed in the lines that his wife Caroline added to the letter: she asked her cousin to burn the letter after reading it (ibid.: 18).

How much Ludwig von Westphalen abhorred absolutism is made clear in a letter from his son Ferdinand, who had considerably more conservative views than his father. On November 31, 1830, Ferdinand reported to his brother-in-law Wilhelm von Flourencourt that a relative of his mother had been a guard officer of King Charles X and had remained an "ultra-Carlist" after the overthrow of 1830. He then wrote concerning his father, Ludwig: "This obstinate and petty clinging to outdated ideas and to a *worm-eaten* (iptissima verba!) dynasty including its camarilla of Jesuits and courtiers, and by a *young* man, was incomprehensible to my father" (quoted in Monz 1973d: 11).

Also fitting this critical attitude is the information passed down by Makim Kowalewsky (1851–1916). The Russian historian and sociologist lived for a while in London in the mid-1870s, where he frequently met with Marx and Engels (later, both studied Kovalevsky's work on Russian common land). In 1909, Kovalevsky published his reminiscences of Karl Marx. Among other things, Marx had told him that his father-in-law, Ludwig von Westphalen, was enthusiastic about the theories of Saint-Simon and was the first to speak to him (Kowalewski 1909: 355). Henri de Saint-Simon (1760–1825) regarded the "industrial class," among which he counted all who participated in the production of goods and services, as being the only productive class. Standing opposite to it was the parasitic and superfluous class of the nobility and the clergy, which was unfortunately the ruling class of the country. Saint-Simon rejected neither private property nor the capitalist mode of production, but given his fundamental critique of the nobility and the clergy, it's no wonder that he and his followers were regarded as dangerous subversives in both the France of the Bourbon Restoration as well as in Prussia.

It's not known how strongly Ludwig von Westphalen was actually influenced by Saint-Simon. But the enthusiastic dedication of Marx's dissertation emphasizes above all his receptiveness to everything new: "May everyone who doubts of the Idea be so fortunate as I, to be able to admire an old man who has the strength of youth, who greets every forward step of the times with the enthusiasm and the prudence of truth and who, with that profoundly convincing sun-bright idealism which alone knows the true word at whose call all the spirits of the world appear, never recoiled before the deep shadows of retrograde ghosts, before the often dark clouds of the times, but rather with godly energy and manly confident gaze saw through all veils the empyreum which burns at the heart of the world. You, *my fatherly friend*, were always a living argumentum ad oculos to me, that idealism is no figment of the imagination, but a truth."

Many of the conversations that Ludwig von Westphalen had with the young Karl may have been conducted during walks together through Trier's idyllic surroundings. In a deleted paragraph of this dedication, Marx had originally added that he hoped to be in Trier again soon and "to roam again at your side through our wonderfully picturesque mountains and forests" (MECW 1: 28).

KARL MARX AT GYMNASIUM

Alongside his parental home and contact with Ludwig von Westphalen, his attendance at gymnasium might have had the greatest influence upon the young Karl. Marx probably did not attend an elementary school, but rather received private lessons, so that at the age of twelve he could be enrolled directly in the third class of gymnasium.

The Prussian Education Reform

The Prussian gymnasium that the young Karl attended from 1830 on was a relatively new institution at the time. It no longer had much in common with the type of school predominant just thirty or forty years before.[63] Up until the late eighteenth century, Latin schools were predominant in Germany. In these schools, Latin grammar was practiced excessively, but not German grammar. A lot of theological material was also taught, since the teachers

---

63. On the development of the institution of the Prussian gymnasium, see Jeismann (1996), Kraul (1984).

were often young theologians who were waiting to be assigned their own parish. For them, teaching was burdensome transitional employment. Schools were frequently in poor condition, teachers poorly paid, and education insufficient. Obligatory requirements and teacher certification did not exist any more than did a mandatory curriculum. The first reform efforts were made at the end of the eighteenth century. With the Prussian Abitur regulations of 1788, the Abitur was supposed to become the precondition for admission to university. However, in an estate-based society, it was not possible to exclude the sons of the nobility from university studies based on poor school performance. In light of the French Revolution and the wars that followed, these early reform efforts petered out.

The forceful surge of reforms triggered by the Prussian defeat in 1806 led to a fundamental reorganization of educational institutions. Johann Gottlieb Fichte (1762–1814), Friedrich Schleiermacher (1768–1834), and Wilhelm von Humboldt (1867–1836) propagated their ideas of human development and education. They proceeded from the notion that the state, now guaranteeing personal freedom and equality before the law, required mature and educated citizens. In any case, the reformed state needed lots of well-educated officials.

Organizationally, obligatory training for teachers and therefore the profession of the gymnasium teacher, as something separate from teaching at an elementary school or at a *Bürgerschule,* was first created in 1810 with the certification edict for gymnasium teachers (Kraul 1984: 37). The Abitur regulations of 1812 did not yet make the Abitur the sole precondition for the transition to university, but the granting of stipends and later entry into the civil service were both tied to the Abitur. With set examination requirements, these regulations also contributed to the standardization of lessons. Prior to this, only a general reference framework existed, which individual schools filled in in quite varied ways. First, in 1834 there was a general curriculum for the Rhine province and then, in 1837, a mandatory curriculum for all Prussian gymnasiums, whereby the independent shaping of the curriculum by individual schools was abolished. With the Abitur regulations of 1834, which made the Prima (the final class of gymnasium) a two-year class (consisting of the *Unterprima* and *Oberprima*) in addition to the Sekunda, the Abitur was also made the obligatory precondition for admission to the universities.[64] The universities now no longer had the right to admit students on the basis of their own decisions or special exams. It was no longer one's

---

64. For which merely passing the Abitur was sufficient. The evaluation of individual subjects was done qualitatively, a grade point average did not yet exist.

social standing, but rather school performance that would count. "Education" finally became a vehicle for social advancement, while the content of education was increasingly standardized by the state.

Substantively, the Prussian education reforms were strongly influenced by those ideas that Friedrich Paulsen (1846–1908) would describe much later in his "History of Educational Instruction" (1885) as "new humanism." Whereas the old humanist lesson aimed at an "imitation of the ancients," the new humanism emerging in the late eighteenth century gives up "this intention as having been made antiquated by reality; through reading the ancient writers, it aims not at imitation of the Latin and the Greek, but rather to form judgment and taste, intellect and insight, and thus nurture the capacity for independent production in one's own language" (Paulsen 1885: 438). In doing so, Greek antiquity in particular, in connection with the notions of art history of Johann Joachim Winckelmann (1717–1768)—Marx would go on to engage with him during his second year of study (discussed in chapter 2)—was received in an idealized manner. In the new humanist conception of education, the study of old languages was to contribute to the development of "humanity," to a person who developed his or her powers of mind and feeling into a harmonic whole. In 1792, Wilhelm von Humboldt wrote in his "The Limits of State Action": "The true end of man, or that which is prescribed by the eternal and immutable dictates of reason, and not suggested by vague and transient desires, is the highest and most harmonious development of his powers to a complete and consistent whole." He also made clear the precondition of such an education: "Freedom is the first and indispensable condition which the possibility of such a development presupposes" (Humboldt 1792–1969: 16).[65] Schiller's letters, "On the Aesthetic Education of Man" (1795), also point in such a direction and became an important source for new humanist ideas about education.

Humboldt, who in 1809–10 directed the section of cultural affairs and education for the Prussian ministry of the interior, began to reform schools and universities in Prussia on the basis of the new humanism. Starting in 1807 in Bavaria as well, Friedrich Immanuel Niethammer (1766–1848), a lifelong friend and correspondent of Hegel's, started reforming the schools according to the new humanism. The school should no longer simply impart practical, useful knowledge, but rather also the "general shaping of human development," to be achieved primarily through engagement with the culture and

---

65. The text as a whole remained unpublished during Humboldt's lifetime, but part of it (including the quoted sentences) was published in 1792 in the *Neue Thalia* edited by Friedrich Schiller, which secured them the attention of an educated middle-class audience.

languages of antiquity. Ancient Greek now took its place alongside Latin, which had been taught for a long time, and one was expected to learn not only the grammar of both languages, but to engage with the classics of ancient philosophy, historiography, and literature. Language, philosophy, and art stood at the center of this conception of education. Reinhold Bernhard Jachmann (1767–1843) programmatically formulated the aim of this "education" in the *Archiv der Nationalbildung* that he published with Franz Passow: the educator must proceed "from the ideal of physically and mentally perfected humanity. . . . The pure aim of reason of humanity is therefore also the aim of pedagogy. What humanity should become, every single individual must also be educated toward. *You, like everyone else, should present the ideal of perfected humanity in yourself*" (Jachmann 1812: 5).

Humboldt and his fellow campaigners, who like Jachmann were assembled in the "scholarly deputation" of the ministry, did not think of education as something only for a social elite. In a report on the work of his section, Humboldt maintained: "There is absolutely certain knowledge that must be general, and even more a certain formation of attitude and of character that no one may lack. Everyone is obviously only a good craftsman, merchant, soldier, and businessman, when he is intrinsically, and without regard to his particular profession, a good, decent, and according to his status enlightened human being and citizen" (Humboldt 1809b: 205).

Wehler correctly emphasizes the ambivalence of the bourgeois concept of education at the beginning of the nineteenth century, when it was not only a battle cry against the privileges of the nobility and the propertied bourgeoisie, but also served as a means of segregation and defending one's social position against those "below" (Wehler 2008: 1: 215). However, it is precisely against this background that the emancipatory dimension of the conception advanced by Jachmann and Humboldt becomes clear: the gymnasium, which had already become an important institution of segregation from those "below"—and still is today—was conceived by Jachmann and Humboldt as a comprehensive school, as a school for all, proceeding from the assumption of a fundamental "perfectibility of human nature." Independent of the social classes that pupils came from, the perfectibility of human beings through education was pursued, whereby the "highest aim" according to which "human nature should be formed" lay "in the ideal of harmonically educated and perfected humanity" (Jachmann 1812: 7). One limit was not touched by this conception, however: that the gymnasium was to be a school exclusively *for boys* was so self-evident that it did not even have to be mentioned separately.

There was a world of difference, however, between the noble objective transcending class boundaries and the reality of Prussian gymnasiums. Nonetheless, not a few of the first generations of gymnasium teachers were influenced by these notions. The young Marx was instructed by such teachers, and as we will see, was strongly influenced by these ideas.

The gymnasium was never able to impose itself as a comprehensive school, but it soon enough offered the emerging educated middle class opportunities for advancement, through both the education obtained in gymnasium, as well as through the profession of the gymnasium teacher, the prestige of which increased considerably. Instead of becoming a school for all, after a few decades a gymnasium education served as a marker of distinction. Better school education also reflected practically in a shorter period of military service: whoever had concluded middle school or had reached the Obersekunda of gymnasium could, instead of fulfilling three years of military service, serve for the shorter and less stringent one-year voluntary service, which, however, also included the obligation of bearing the costs for one's weaponry and clothing, thus remaining reserved for the economically better-off strata. We will see in volume two that the young Friedrich Engels made use of this privilege—above all in order to spend at least a semester at the University of Berlin during his military service, since his father had refused him the chance to study.

The period of reaction setting in after the Karlsbad Decrees of 1819 brought considerable changes for the gymnasium. The new humanist educational impulses were curtailed, the perfectibility of the human being was robbed of its political edge and was limited more and more to inwardness and tended to mere aestheticism. The importance of the Greek element was reduced, since Greek antiquity had been idealized as a place of freedom. In the course of the nineteenth century, the humanist gymnasium had become a pedantic institution divorced from everyday life against which the reform pedagogy arising around 1890 would struggle. However, this frequently caricatured institution is in no way identical to the gymnasium of the early nineteenth century.

The Karlsbad Decrees not only limited freedom of the press and banned Burschenschaften as well as organized physical exercise, but the universities—and with them, the gymnasiums—became subject to strict surveillance. The behavior of teachers, whom it was assumed had significant influence upon the thought and action of their pupils, wasn't just regimented in terms of their official duties. Teachers were also supposed to serve as positive role models (in the sense of the Prussian state). Lessons were to serve only for the transmission of knowledge, not to discuss political events. A decree from October 30, 1819, thus states that no teacher "through the tendency of his lessons causes arrogant presumptuousness among the youth, as if they were entitled to their own judgment of current events and public affairs, and as if they were particularly qualified to intervene in the shaping of public life, or even to bring about a dreamed of better order of things" (Rönne 1855: 100). In history lessons, no comparisons with the immediate present were to be employed, and "all unnecessary argument and discussion with the youth" was to be "avoided, so that they learn early to follow compulsory laws without question, and submit willingly to the present authority." Teachers who did not adhere to this were to be removed from service (ibid.: 101).

Teachers were not only meant to monitor the behavior of their pupils at school; they were also to "collect inquiries in a suitable manner" on whether students "held contacts and meetings among themselves or with other young people" and to "investigate the purpose of these," and then report them to the director (quoted in Kraul 1984: 51). The director for his part was to monitor the teachers and register all findings in their personnel record. Directors were themselves monitored by the school councils and evaluated (ibid.). So teachers and directors were not only supposed to instruct and be moral role models, they were also supposed to function as extended arms of state surveillance and repression. If they attempted to withdraw from this assignment, they had to reckon with repressive measures.

The Trier Gymnasium and Its Teachers

The predecessor of the gymnasium in Trier was a Jesuit school founded in 1563. During the French period, the gymnasium was initially opened as a secondary school; from 1809–10 it obtained the name Collège de Trèves. When the Rhineland became part of Prussia as a consequence of the Congress of Vienna, the collège became the state Gymnasium zu Trier. The school first obtained the name mentioned in many biographies of Marx, Friedrich-Wilhelm-Gymnasium, in 1896 (see Gockel 1989: 8).

The school felt the increased surveillance in the wake of the Karlsbad Decrees. In 1819, teachers and pupils who had taken a trip to Bonn were accused of having met people there who were "notorious for their subversive principles, harmful to the common good" (report of the minister of police to the district government of Trier, July 28, 1819, quoted in Monz 1973: 146). At the end of the 1820s, there were many "Philhellenists" among the pupils who supported the Greek independence struggle (Groß 1956: 60). Nicolaevsky and Maenchen Helfen (1937: 13) report—without providing a source—that in 1833 a pupil was discovered to own a copy of the speeches from the Hambach Festival, and that in 1834 some pupils of the gymnasium had composed poems with a political tendency. In 1833, the district president of Trier reported to his superiors that among the pupils of the gymnasium "an ill spirit reigns, and many teachers intentionally support it" (according to the formulation in Monz 1973: 298). Böse (1951: 12) refers to a government report from 1834 "according to which teachers and pupils were suspected of demagogic machinations and secretly monitored."

The towering presence of the Trier gymnasium was its director of many years, Johann Hugo Wyttenbach (1767–1848). He was also an archaeologist and founder of the Trier city library. In 1804, Wyttenbach was already director of the French secondary school; he remained director of the gymnasium until 1846. His thinking was strongly influenced by the Enlightenment; in his earlier years, he was an adherent of the French Jacobins. He maintained his liberal and humanistic ethos even under Prussian rule.[66] Regarding his interactions with teachers and pupils, a rather critical report by the school inspector Schulze from the year 1818 states: "He lives in most friendly relations with all teachers, and he treats the students affectionately; one would only wish him more force, seriousness, stringency, and insistence" (quoted in Gross 1962: 27). When in 1846, at almost eighty years of age, he retired from the teaching profession, the *Trierische Zeitung* wrote: "What distinguished Director Wyttenbach in particular was his manner of dealing with young people. One spoke to him as if to a trusted friend, yet felt the great dignity. He inspired enthusiasm for everything great, noble, and good, and became young again in his interactions with the youth" (quoted in Gross 1962: 34).

As noted above, the directors of gymnasiums were not only supposed to see to orderly instruction, but also politically monitor the teachers subordinate to them and when appropriate to report them to the superior authorities. Instead, on multiple occasions Wyttenbach protected teachers who had been attacked, which earned him in 1833 the accusation from the supervisory authorities that he was too weak and "insufficiently decisive in his disposition" (quoted in Monz 1973: 172).

One year later, Wyttenbach seems to have intentionally undermined the cooperation with police authorities demanded of him. On October 2, 1834, the district president of Trier reported to the ministerial commission in Berlin that Wyttenbach was an educated as well as respectable man, without, apparently, the least amount of energy and authority and so little prudence that he shared

---

66. Monz (1973: 160–68), by means of Wyttenbach's publications over the course of five decades, provides an overview of his political and ethical views. Klupsch (2012) has published a biography of Wyttenbach; Wyttenbach's pedagogy, oriented toward Rousseau and the Enlightenment, is outlined in Klupsch (2013).

the report of the police administration that had been confidentially provided to him with the to some extent most ill-disposed teachers of the gymnasium, thus inducing a publication of this report, compromising the police (quoted in Gemkow 1999: 409n22). What the district president attributed to lack of prudence was the best possible defense of the teachers under surveillance, and one can assume that Wyttenbach took this step quite consciously.

For Wyttenbach, who had felt enthusiasm for classical antiquity early on, new humanist notions of education fell on especially fertile ground. He had an effect on his pupils especially through history lessons, which he taught himself to the higher grades of the gymnasium. According to Groß (1956: 148), starting with classical antiquity, "history lessons served him in placing feelings of responsibility and virtue into young hearts." Karl was also taught history at the Untersekunda and Obersekunda as well as Prima levels by Wyttenbach. Wyttenbach was most likely the preponderant influence upon the specific humanism expressed in Marx's Abitur examination papers.

When the young Karl started gymnasium in 1830, Wyttenbach was sixty-three years old. Most teachers were considerably younger, and as can be gleaned from the fragmentary information of the surviving records, at least a few of them had rather critical attitudes toward the reigning social and political conditions and were observed with distrust by the Prussian authorities.[67]

First and foremost to be named in this regard is Thomas Simon (1793–1869), who taught French to Karl at the Tertia level. He had long been active in providing relief to the poor and, as he said himself, had sufficient opportunity to "get to know the ills of social life in their true shape and often heartbreaking reality." He had "turned toward the concerns of the poor, neglected people," since as a teacher he had seen daily that "it was not the possession of cold, filthy, minted money that makes a human being a human being, but rather character, disposition, understanding, and empathy for the weal and woe of one's fellows" (quoted in Böse 1951: 11). In 1849, Simon was elected to the Prussian house of representatives, where he joined the left. His son, Ludwig Simon (1819–1872), also attended the gymnasium in Trier and took the Abitur exams a year after Karl. He was elected to the national assembly in 1848. As a result of his activities during the revolutionary years of 1848–49, the Prussian government brought multiple legal proceedings against him and convicted him *in absentia* to death, so that he had to emigrate to Switzerland.

---

67. On Marx's teachers, see Monz (1973: 169ff.) as well as the *Trierer Biographische Lexikon*. Monz (1973: 154ff.) also uses the school program to provide an overview of the material taught.

Heinrich Schwendler (1792–1847), who taught French to Marx at the Obersekunda and Prima levels, was suspected in 1833 by the Prussian government of being the author of an insurgent leaflet; he was accused of "poor character" and of "familiar relationships to all the fraudulent minds of the local city." In 1834, a ministerial commission warned of the "pernicious orientation" of Simon and Schwendler, and in 1835, the provincial school council regarded his dismissal as desirable, but could not find a sufficient reason (Monz 1973: 171, 178).

Johann Gerhard Schneeman (1796–1864) had studied classical philology, history, philosophy, and mathematics; he published numerous contributions on the archaeology of Trier. At the Tertia and Obersekunda levels, he taught Karl Latin and Greek. In 1834, Schneeman also participated in the singing of revolutionary songs at the Casino and was interrogated by the police as a result.

Even if Simon, Schwendler, and Scheeman hardly expressed their political views during lessons (if they had, their dismissal would have been a certainty), it is probable that they expressed their attitudes in their ways of dealing with the subject matter and through individual remarks during and outside of lessons. That likely further reinforced the critical view of political conditions that Karl was already familiar with through his father, as well as Ludwig von Westphalen.

Probably of a somewhat different nature was the influence of Johannes Steininger (1794–1874), who taught natural sciences and physics to Karl at the Untersekunda and Obersekunda levels as well as mathematics at the Obersekunda and Prima levels. Steininger had initially attended a seminary, but dropped out in 1813 and then studied mathematics, physics, and geology in Paris. As can be gleaned from the school program of 1817, he taught about the formation and decay of mountains and about "revolutions that not only change the surface of the earth, but redistribute organic matter and through which earlier plant and animal forms disappear while on the other hand new ones emerge" (quoted in Groß 1994: 88). With this teaching content, he stood in conflict with a Christianity based upon a literal understanding of the Bible. As the school inspector Lange disclosed in a report from 1827, Steininger had to ward off hostility from the clergy (ibid.). Ultimately, in 1834 the provincial schools council doubted his "patriotism" (*vaterländische Gesinnung*) because as a mathematician and physicist he had a special fondness for invoking the achievements of the French. In 1837, Steininger was denounced in an anonymous letter: it was alleged that for twenty years he had been shaking the foundations of Christianity in his lessons, "which causes some lads to lose their faith" (quoted in Monz 1973: 170). Steininger disputed this allegation. But it emerges from his defense that he taught about

the consequences research in the natural sciences had for a literal understanding of the Bible. Steininger claimed that whenever geological truths
appeared to contradict the Bible, he emphasized that this did not undermine
divine revelation.[68] Alongside impulses critical of religion, Marx (as Krüger
2000: 156 emphasizes) may have received from Steininger basic knowledge
of natural history and geological development that served him well in his
later studies of the natural sciences and his studies of geology in the 1870s.

Johann Abraham Küpper (1779–1850), a Protestant senior civil servant and school inspector for the district government in Trier and at the
same time pastor of the small Protestant congregation there, also taught
the Protestant religion class at the gymnasium, starting in November 1831.
Karl was taught by him for four years. Küpper saw Christianity as being
under attack by the Enlightenment and rationalism. With his rejection of
Voltaire and Kant, his lessons stood in opposition to Enlightenment views
that the young Karl became familiar with through his parents as well as
most of his teachers. For Küpper, true religiosity required recognizing
human sinfulness and the insight that human beings could not free themselves of this sinfulness on their own, but rather through a redeemer, Jesus
Christ (Henke 1973: 116ff.).

In contrast to most of the young Karl's teachers, Vitus Loers (1792–1862)
was extremely conservative, as well as very loyal to the church and state. He
also must have been rather authoritarian in his interactions with students.
For example, he had refused to teach a student who had grown a mustache
(Monz 1973: 176). Loers was a respected classical scholar, who had published
multiple essays and books.[69] He taught Karl Greek at the Obersekunda and
Prima levels, Latin as well at the Prima level, and occasionally German. In
1835, he was named the second director of the gymnasium. In 1833, the
Trier district president had proposed replacing Wyttenbach as director with
another person (ibid.: 172). But the authorities recoiled from the idea of forc-
ing the highly respected Wyttenbach into retirement against his will. They
therefore placed Loers at his side as co-director. It was obvious to all parties,
however, that the point was to take leadership of the gymnasium away from
the liberal Wyttenbach and place it in the hands of a person devoted to the

---

68. Ferdinand Meurin, who attended the gymnasium in Trier scarcely twenty years after
Marx, also noted in his memoirs that Steininger's lessons often passed into discussions that
"had the loosest connection to mathematics" (Meurin 1904: 148).
69. Meurin mentions the Roman authors Ovid (43 BC–17 AD) and Virgil (70–19 BC) as his
favorite poets (Meurin 1904: 138). Marx also had high regard these poets, as the references in
the first volume of *Capital* make clear.

Prussian state. On November 17, 1835, on the occasion of Loers's inaugura-
tion, a celebration took place, about which Heinrich Marx wrote to his son
Karl, who was studying in Bonn: "On the occasion of the celebration for Herr
Loers I found the position of good Herr Wyttenbach extremely painful. I
could have wept at the offence to this man, whose only failing is to be much
too kind-hearted. I did my best to show the high regard I have for him and,
among other things, I told him how devoted you are to him and that you
would have liked to compose a poem in his honour but had no time. That
made him very happy. Will you do me the favour of sending me a few verses
for him?" (MECW 1: 648).

From the same letter, we also learn that Karl and Heinrich Clemens were
the only pupils of the Abitur class who did not pay the usual farewell visit to
Loers (ibid.: 647). We don't know the reason, but it is reasonable to assume
that Karl explicitly did not wish to bid farewell to this reactionary teacher
and express gratitude for his lessons.

*The Abitur Examination Papers: First Glimpses of the Young Marx's
Intellectual Development*

In August of 1835, Karl Marx, along with thirty-one classmates, took the written Abitur examination. His Abitur examination papers are (except for two
poems of uncertain date; see chapter 2) his oldest known texts. Alongside a
translation from German into French, one from ancient Greek into German,
and one from German into Latin as well as a mathematics examination,[70]
three papers had to be written: a Latin paper, a religion paper, and a German
paper. In the case of these texts, it must be taken into consideration that they
do not necessarily reflect the opinions of the young Karl. One can assume
that, if not the exact topics of the papers, each of the topic areas were objects
of discussion in lessons and that the teachers had made the "correct" view of
each problem more or less clear.

For the Latin essay, the question posed was: "Does the reign of Augustus
deserve to be counted among the happier periods of the Roman Empire?"
Marx compared the era of Augustus with the early Republic and the

---

70. Raussen (1990) deals in depth with the mathematics exam. Since in the case of one
problem, the young Karl, despite using the wrong sign in the calculation, nonetheless jotted
down the right answer, and Edgar von Westphalen was the only one who chose a similar
calculation path, Raussen (1990: 229ff.) suspects that Karl copied this problem (not entirely
without mistakes) from Edgar.

period of Nero's imperial reign.[71] Compared to the latter, the period of Augustus's reign comes out considerably better. The comparison with the early Republic is not so unequivocal: Augustus was a mild ruler, but citizens lacked freedom. However, Karl gives Augustus credit for having gotten rid of the chaos caused by the civil war. Marx concludes that the state established by Augustus was the most appropriate under the given conditions. As the editors of MEGA emphasize, Marx's paper did not go beyond the considerations of his classmates; they mainly reproduce what was taught by Loers in lessons, attempting to bring it into passable Latin. Loers's evaluation, also formulated in Latin, turned out to be rather positive. It ended with the sentence: "Verum quam turpis litera!!!" (What shameful handwriting!!!) (MEGA I/1: 1212). That would not change in the future. From the Quarta until the Obersekunda, "penmanship" was also taught (Monz 1973: 158), but it didn't help Marx at all.

The religion paper had the topic "The union of believers with Christ according to John 15: 1–14, showing its basis and essence, its absolute necessity, and its effects." It was not a case of a problem to be discussed, but rather of the explanation and justification of a given statement using a section of the Gospel of John. Here as well the papers exhibit great commonality and probably repeat what was taught in lessons.[72] The young Karl emphasized that the reason for union with Christ is "our sinfully inclined nature, our wavering reason, our corrupted heart, our iniquity in the sight of God" (MECW 1: 637). If we are united with Christ, then we are virtuous "solely out of love for Him" (ibid.: 638), then we have "a heart which is open to love of mankind, to all that is noble, to all that is great, not out of ambition, not through a desire for fame, but only because of Christ" (ibid.: 639). These statements stand in the lineage of Karl's religion teacher Küpper's theological views as reconstructed by Henke, but they are missing a few aspects, such as the significance of the act of redemption by Christ. Küpper attests to Karl a "presentation rich in ideas, vivid and powerful," but maintains that "the essence of the union in question is not specified, the reason for it is comprehended only from *one* side, and its necessity is inadequately accounted for" (MEGA I/1: 1191). He evaluated Karl's classmates in a similarly critical way (Henke 1973: 125ff.). Marx's Abitur certificate states: "His knowledge of the Christian faith and morals is fairly clear

71. The Latin paper is published in MEGA I/1: 465–469; a German translation is in MEGA I/1: 1212–1215 and MEW 40: 595–597. The English translation is available in MECW 1: 639–642. The Latin essays of Marx's classmates have not been published.
72. Henke (1973: 127), who examined the religion papers and compared them with Küpper's views, arrives at this conclusion.

and well grounded; he knows also to some extent the history of the Christian Church." This sentence has little informative value, since it only formulates—largely verbatim—what is required of pupils as stipulated in the Abitur examination regulations of 1834 (Monz 1973: 313n84).

Whether the young Marx was a devout Christian at this time cannot be clarified on the basis of the religion paper, though it's rather clear he wrote exactly what was required to pass the examination. Compared to the German paper, which we will discuss shortly, one has the impression that he did not go about it with anywhere near the same level of engagement. The concluding section comes across as downright amusing, where Marx writes: "Therefore union with Christ bestows a joy which the Epicurean strives vainly to derive from his frivolous philosophy or the deeper thinker from the most hidden depths of knowledge" (MECW 1: 639). Whether Marx is just repeating the platitudes proclaimed by Küpper during lessons, or whether a trace of irony is already mixed into the formulation, cannot be decisively determined. In any case, just a few years later, his judgment on Epicurean philosophy will turn out to be quite different.

The most interesting document is the German paper, "Reflections of a Young Man on the Choice of a Profession." Here, the young Karl made an effort, both in terms of substance and style. The teacher correcting the exam, Hamacher, who had only been teaching for a short time (see MEGA I/1: 1198; Wyttenbach merely gave his signature), opined somewhat derogatorily in his evaluation that the writer succumbed "here as well to the error quite common to him of an excessive quest for a rare expression rich in imagery" (MEGA I/1: 1200). To modern readers, the paper might come across as a bit excessively impassioned, but one should take into consideration that during this period, texts were formulated in a much more passionate way than today, and that we're dealing with an enthusiastic seventeen-year-old.

Ever since Marx's German paper was published for the first time in 1925, it has occasioned numerous and in part far-reaching interpretations. The text was usually understood as the direct expression of the thoughts and feelings of the young Marx. Künzli (1966: 79ff.) and Hillmann (1966a: 214ff.) want to draw conclusions about psychological conflicts within the young Marx on the basis of this paper. A serious interpretation of this paper must first of all distinguish between Marx's original contribution to the text and that which can be regarded more as the result of the school lessons. This distinction is possible if one compares Marx's paper with the papers of his classmates. Monz (1973a) has published these papers in full, but they remain largely disregarded in the biographical literature.

Loers had temporarily taken over German lessons in the first half-year of the Prima level; in the second half-year they were taken over by Wilhelm Hamacher (1808–1875), newly arrived at the school. The rather general terms of the topic of the paper may have been, as Monz (1973: 302) suspects, a stop-gap solution. It had frequently been the subject of graduation speeches by Wyttenbach.[73] He had probably already dealt with it in a general manner in the classroom, as indicated by the similar basic structure of the papers written by both Marx and his classmates: the important biographical significance of the choice of profession is pointed out; the terrible consequences of the wrong choice; the danger of being blinded by the brilliant appearance of a profession; the necessity of precisely examining one's own inclinations and abilities is stated, and the recommendation is given to seek advice from experienced people (parents, relatives, teachers). Also appearing in multiple papers is the consideration that a profession should not only serve the one who takes it up, but other people as well, and that one becomes a useful member of society by doing something for the well-being of fellow human beings.

However, Marx's text is distinct from the others not only in its clear structure, but also in numerous special characteristics of its content. Right at the beginning, Marx places the question of choosing a profession in a broad, anthropological context, not addressed by any of his classmates: animals have a fixed sphere of activity; only human beings have a choice between various activities, and this particularity of human beings is the result of divine creation. The "Deity," according to Marx, gives humanity its general aim "of ennobling mankind and itself" and also "never leaves mortal man wholly without a guide; he speaks softly but with certainty" (MECW 1: 3). Marx mentions the "Deity" a total of five times, more frequently than his classmates, including those who had given "pastor" as their desired profession. Over half of those taking the exam did not mention God at all. The fact that Marx mentions the "Deity" so often and also refers positively to religion at the end of the paper, without these being essential to the topic, are strong indications that Marx was devout at the time. It's noteworthy that he does not speak of God, but rather—in a more distanced way—of the "Deity." In the religion paper, he mentions the Deity twice at the beginning, and subsequently refers to "God" five times, which is more in keeping with the usual Protestant usage. A sinfulness rooted in human nature, referred to in the religion paper, also no longer plays a role here. This could be an indication that the young Karl no longer assumed the personal God of Christianity, but rather tended toward the kind of Deism widespread during the Enlightenment: a belief in

---

73. Such as in the speech from 1832 (Wyttenbach 1847: 164).

a God who created the world is maintained, but this God is no longer conceived of in the concrete shapes implied by individual religions. Heinrich Marx's letter from November 1835 (MECW 1: 647) indicates that he adhered to such a conception.

In discussing the difficulties that arise in choosing a profession, Marx writes a sentence that in the literature has become the object of far-reaching interpretations: "But we cannot always attain the position to which we believe we are called; our relations[74] in society have to some extent already begun to be established before we are in a position to determine them" (MECW 1: 4). Other classmates also wrote of individual conditions and that one's profession must fit them. But none of them arrived at such a remarkable generalization that conditions determine us before we can determine them. Franz Mehring saw in this the "first germ of the materialist conception of history in unconscious anticipation" (Mehring 1913, IV: 366); others have more or less followed him (for example, Cornu 1954: 61). In contrast, the objection has been raised that the insight into the restricting effect of circumstances upon the individual is an insight of the eighteenth century (see Hillmann 1966: 39; Oiserman 1980: 51). Other more or less subtle interpretations of this passage can be found in the literature (for example, Thomas 1973). A much simpler explanation for this sentence appears plausible: Karl was reflecting upon his father's experience. Heinrich Marx had grown up in materially humble conditions and as a Jew, so that both material and legal limits were set to his choice of profession, and it cost him considerable strain to even partially overcome these limits. Heinrich Marx may have spoken with his son over the limiting circumstances of his youth while at the same time making clear that he, Karl, was subject to far fewer limitations.

Like most other examination candidates, Marx also emphasized how harmful the effects of choosing the wrong profession can be upon one's self. But whereas his classmates only wrote about the feeling of unhappiness, Karl went far beyond that. If we're not capable of fulfilling a profession, we must say to ourselves that we are "useless created beings." The consequence is "self-contempt." According to Marx, this is worse than—and sets in without—any rebuke from the outside world. Marx thus expresses more sharply and existentially than any of his classmates the consequences of failing due to one's own inability. At the same time, he makes clear that passing muster according to one's own judgment is far more important than praise or rebuke from others, an attitude that would also have an impact later in his life.

---

74. In German, *Verhältnisse.* —Trans.

If one has the opportunity to choose any desired profession, however, then there are three criteria for choosing which the young Karl cites: we should first of all choose the "profession" that "assures us the greatest worth," which second of all is based upon ideas whose truth we are convinced of, and which third of all offers the greatest possibilities "to work for mankind, and for ourselves to approach closer to the general aim for which every profession is but a means—perfection" (MECW 1: 7).

Concerning the first criterion, worth, Marx writes that it "is that which most of all uplifts a man," that it makes him "admired by the crowd and raised above it." In this desire to stand out from "the crowd," to be "raised above it," one hears a bourgeois elitism that the young Karl presupposes as a matter of course: he assumes that the great "crowd" cannot achieve the worth aspired to; it is only granted to a minority standing above the crowd. But which profession assures such worth? "But worth can be assured only by a profession in which we are not servile tools, but in which we act independently in our own sphere" (ibid.). With that, it's clear why the great "crowd" is excluded from the worth aspired to. With the possible exception of master craftsmen, traders, or independent farmers (whose dependence on the market is not yet a topic for Marx), no one in the lower classes—employed as domestic servants, day laborers, or in the newly arising factories—can "act independently."

Marx raises the question of a dignified profession for gymnasium graduates who can strive for careers as doctors, lawyers, or scholars, in which "acting independently" is paramount. Marx does not mention which professions he would exclude as without worth; however, one can think of two professional fields for gymnasium graduates where people might become "servile tools": the military and state administration. Both cases involve strict hierarchies, where the subordinate authority has to carry out the directions of the higher one, regardless of whether the person carrying them out regards them as correct and appropriate or not. Marx may have regarded such authoritarian structures as degrading.

It is similarly terrible for the young Karl if the profession that one seeks "is based on ideas that we later recognise to be false." Then the only remaining salvation is "self-deception" (ibid.: 8). Here it also remains an open question as to which activities he had in mind. Again, one thinks of the civil service, if for example the state is based upon a form of government that one considers wrong.

The final criterion—the "welfare of mankind" and "our own perfection"—Marx highlights as the most important; it must be the "chief guide" (ibid.). The notion that through one's profession, one should work for the welfare of society or humanity as a whole—"mankind" is mentioned a total of six times—was already part of Enlightenment thought. This thought is also found among many of Marx's classmates, so that one may assume it was part of the lesson. However, it is not further specified what is meant by "welfare."

The moment of one's "own perfection" was an important topos of the sophisticated bourgeois culture of the time. It played a central role in Schiller's *On the Aesthetic Education of Man* (1795–96), and it is the main theme in Goethe's *Wilhelm Meister's Apprenticeship* (1795–96). It was also a central point for the new humanist conception of education: education should aim to perfect individual human beings and therefore humanity as much as possible (see the programmatic formulation by Jachmann above). Even if one doesn't know whether Marx was familiar with the texts mentioned at the time of his Abitur exams, one can assume that the idea of one's own perfection and the improvement of humanity played an important role in Wyttenbach's German and History lessons. In his speech to graduates from 1834, he described the school as the institution in which young people are "educated in the sacred belief in progress and ennoblement" (Wyttenbach 1847: 175). We will later see that the aim of developing individual capabilities also plays a central role in Marx's various conceptions of communism.

One's own perfection was also mentioned as an aim, or at least hinted at, by other pupils. Thus, Franz Ludwig Blaise expected the right choice of profession "to benefit human society as a useful member to the best of one's abilities, and to provide for one's own ennoblement and that of one's fellow human beings, which is the final goal of all human endeavor" (Monz 1973a: 52). Edgar von Westphalen emphasized that one should promote "not only one's own happiness, but also that of the state and fellow human beings as much as an individual is capable of doing so" (ibid.: 49). Some pupils emphasized the conflict between one's own interest and benefit to the community, whereby they emphasize that one must also accept burdens in order to work for the welfare of society or the state. In contrast, Marx was the only pupil who disputed that there was such a relation of conflict at all, which he justifies anthropologically: "Man's nature is so constituted that he can attain his own perfection only by working for the perfection, for the good, of his fellow men. If he works only for himself, he may perhaps become a famous man of learning, a great sage, an excellent poet, but he can never be a perfect, truly great man" (MECW 1: 8).

Here, the difference from the religion paper becomes clear. There, striving for that which is noble and great is supposed to follow from union with Christ, but here there is no mention of such a union; "man's nature" is already sufficiently arranged.

With the position that one's own perfection not only goes hand-in-hand with work on behalf of the welfare of humanity, but also depends upon it, the young Marx went beyond the arguments of both his classmates as well as those of Wyttenbach. However, it's not accurate to say that he had thus already "left behind the bourgeois environment of many of his classmates," as Monz (1973: 309) does. In the Abitur paper, there is not the slightest indication that young Karl saw a conflict between working for the welfare of humanity and the bourgeois world. On the contrary. As was made clear by his wish to elevate himself above the crowd as a dignified human being, he did not call into question the given hierarchy of classes that completely denied the majority a "dignified" profession. He wanted to contribute to the welfare of humanity within the bourgeois world, as a member of the bourgeois elite.

Marx does not name any specific profession as being the best one to work for the welfare of humanity. In the sentence last quoted, he mentions numerous examples, but what's interesting is which—for a gymnasium graduate, obvious—professions he does not name: merchant, civil servant, officer, or lawyer (so also not the profession he sought to prepare for with his university studies). More obvious to Marx are clearly the man of learning, the sage, and the poet: if these would orient their activity toward the welfare of humanity, then a "truly great man" could be made of them. It can hardly be doubted that the young Marx strove to be one, according to the passionate final sentence of his paper: "If we have chosen the position in life in which we can most of all work for mankind, no burdens can bow us down, because they are sacrifices for the benefit of all; then we shall experience no petty, limited, selfish joy, but our happiness will belong to millions, our deeds will live on quietly but perpetually at work, and over our ashes will be shed the hot tears of noble people" (MECW 1: 8). Here, finally, recognition by others is mentioned—as an inevitable, if perhaps late consequence of action on behalf of humanity, bound by one's own guiding principles.

Oral exams took place in September. Of the thirty-two examination candidates, twenty-two ultimately passed (Monz 1973: 302). Monz attempted to translate the qualitative evaluations into the grading system common today, and arrives at the conclusion that Marx, along with another pupil, had the eighth-best Abitur, while Edgar von Westphalen, along with another pupil, came in at third place (ibid.: 298). In the Abitur certificate issued on September 24, Marx's "diligence" is noted: "He has good aptitudes, and in ancient languages, German, and history showed a very satisfactory diligence, in mathematics satisfactory, and in French only slight diligence" (MECW 1: 642). This does not sound like a consistently diligent model pupil. Regarding his handling of the Latin classics read during the lessons, it says that he

translated and explained the easier passages well even without preparation, and the difficult ones with some assistance, "especially those where the
difficulty consists not so much in the peculiarity of the language as in the
subject-matter and train of thought." The case was similar with Greek classics. At the end of the certificate, it's noted that the examining commission
discharged him "cherishing the hope that he will fulfill the favourable expectations which his aptitudes justify" (ibid.). What sounds like a standard formulation for better pupils might contain subtle assessments. Gemkow (1999:
411) reproduces the corresponding sentence from Edgar von Westphalen's
certificate, that "he will fulfill the good expectations which his aptitudes and
his hitherto demonstrated diligence justify." In the case of Edgar, who had a
better certificate than Marx, the expectations are not just "favourable,"[75] but
"good,"[76] and most important, his diligence is mentioned. This mention is
absent in Karl's case.

The graduation ceremony took place on September 27. In the different
classes, the best pupils in individual subjects were honored with a book
award; in addition there were commendations (Meurin 1904: 139). Two
commendations of Marx from earlier years are known: in 1832 in ancient
and modern languages and 1834 in German (Schöncke 1993: 836, 838).
From Marx's Abitur class, Jacob Fuxius made a speech in which he compared the death of Socrates with that of Seneca, "Comparatio mortis
Socratis ac L. A. Seneca," and another classmate, Heinrich von Notz, held
the valedictory address for the pupils. At the end came the annual graduation speech by Wyttenbach, whose subject this year was the connection
between lessons conveying knowledge and moral education (Monz 1973:
316ff.).

BONDS AND IMPETUSES

Family Life

According to everything we know, Karl Marx spent a rather carefree childhood and youth in Trier. He grew up in relatively affluent, educated middle-
class conditions. In terms of income, the Marx family did not belong to the
richest 1.2 percent, but was still part of the upper 10 percent of Trier households (see data from Herres 1990), and as a matter of course, service staff was
employed. That only one of nine children died at an early age speaks for the
care they must have received. There are no indications of greater conflicts in

---

75. *Günstige* —Trans.
76. *Schöne* —Trans.

the parental home or at school, nor of corporal punishment. Karl's relationship to his siblings also appears to have been harmonious, by and large. On the basis of the style of the surviving letters to the studying son, it's clear that the parents were frequently concerned and also didn't spare on admonitions, though they were anything but authoritarian.[77]

After the firstborn Mauritz David died at an early age, the parents' hopes were pinned entirely on Karl. He was a good pupil, intelligent and open-minded; one could assume of him that he would be successful at university and his future professional life, whereby in this period—before state social welfare systems—this was always bound up with the hope that a successful son would later financially support siblings and if necessary his parents in old age. In November of 1835, his father wrote to him: "I should like to see in you what perhaps I could have become, if I had come into the world with equally favourable prospects. You can fulfill or destroy my best hopes. It is perhaps both unfair and unwise to build one's best hopes on someone and so perhaps undermine one's own tranquility. But who else than nature is to blame if men who are otherwise not so weak are nevertheless weak fathers?" (MECW 1: 646).

This remark shows the high expectations placed upon Karl, and also that a certain pressure to fulfill these expectations burdened him. But it also becomes clear that his father dealt with these expectations in a somewhat reflective manner. It's clear to him that they are burdensome to his son and he admits this. This reflection upon one's own demeanor was at that time (and probably still today) not necessarily typical. When we encounter the young Engels in the next volume, we will find a very different type of father.

In any case, every effort was made to support Karl. Above all, in his father and later father-in-law, he had two mentally and politically interested adults who not only provided him with much encouragement, but who early on took him seriously as an interlocutor, which might have had an extremely advantageous effect upon his intellectual development. Even if his mother

---

77. An example: After Karl went to Bonn in October of 1835 to begin his studies, his father reprimanded him for not having written after more than three weeks, and his parents were greatly concerned: "That, unfortunately, only too strongly confirms the opinion, which I hold in spite of your many good qualities, that in your heart egoism is predominant." After an extensive letter by Karl, his father made clear in the next letter that he was very sorry for the strong reprimand: "Dear Karl, First of all, a few words about my letter, which may possibly have annoyed you. You know I don't pedantically insist on my authority and also admit to my child if I am wrong. I did actually tell you to write only after you had had a somewhat closer look around you. However, since it took so long, you ought to have taken my words less literally, especially as you know how anxious and worried your good mother is" (MECW 1: 645).

was not as uneducated as alleged in much of the literature, there are no indications that Karl had an intellectual relationship with her as strong as the one with his father.

Judaism

The fact that Karl Marx came from a Jewish family has led to a whole string of speculations. Thus, Rühle concludes from Marx's poor health, his Jewish heritage—which Marx, according to Rühle, regarded as a stigma for his entire life—and his position as the firstborn and only son of the family—which carried the burden of high expectations—is that Marx had an inferiority complex (Rühle 2011: 372ff.). It is definitely false that Marx was the firstborn and only son. That Marx's state of health was not especially good at an advanced age is correct. We lack any information on his health from the period of his youth. Rühle cannot offer a single piece of evidence for the assertion that Marx regarded his Jewish heritage as a stigma, but simply asserts that "racial origin could not be washed away by the waters of baptism" (Rühle 2011: 377). Rühle was obviously projecting the racial anti-Semitism familiar to him from the 1920s onto the first half of the nineteenth century. As discussed earlier in this chapter, one could, in fact, escape the anti-Jewish sentiment predominant in the early nineteenth century through baptism.

It has also been asserted that central concepts of Marx exhibit analogies to Jewish tradition. One example can be found in the work of Karl Löwith, who grasps Marx's conception of history as the expression of a "transparent messianism" and concludes that Marx was "a Jew of Old Testament stature" (Löwith 1949: 44). Gustav Mayer (1918) had already made a similar argument. Whether the alleged analogies exist has to be discussed on the basis of Marx's work. What is of interest here is the assumption that descent from Jewish parents would ensure that the young Marx was equipped with Jewish tradition and Jewish thought. Whereas Löwith and others simply assert this, Künzli (1966) and Massiczek (1968) have attempted to prove it in detail. These two authors stand in strong contradiction to each other in terms of their conclusions: Künzli's intention is to demonstrate that Karl Marx's Jewish heritage ultimately led to "Jewish self-hatred" and anti-Semitism, whereas Massiczek attempts to demonstrate that Marx's specific humanism can only be understood in terms of the traditions passed down to him on the basis of his Jewish heritage. Both have huge problems proving their conclusions on the basis of biographical facts. Ultimately, both of them can only assert. Künzli asserts that Heinrich Marx's baptism led to a break with his family and later to a traumatic conflict between Karl and his father, whom

Karl supposedly rejected as weak and opportunistic not only due to his baptism, but also because of his moderate political statements. Künzli cannot provide evidence for either claim, but he assures the reader again and again that it must have been so, and then draws further conclusions from Marx's supposed trauma. Massiczek assembles a lot of material concerning the special character of the Jewish family, the differing roles of mother and father, the special intimacy of relationships, and much more. Furthermore, he invokes psychological theories that are supposed to make clear how strongly a person is shaped by early childhood experiences. Since Massiczek assumes that every Jewish family bears the stamp of these special characteristics, he concludes without further ado or verification that the family of Karl Marx also possessed these characteristics and that Marx had thus been shaped in a way that was decisive for his later life. Leaning upon Massiczek's considerations, Monz also speaks of a parental "trauma" due to the baptism forced by the state, a trauma that supposedly surfaced for Karl again and again (Monz 1995: 137, 148).

Indeed, there is not a single indication that Jewish holidays were celebrated in Karl Marx's family or that the children otherwise had a Jewish upbringing. Heinrich Marx probably allowed himself to be baptized in 1819–20, shortly after Karl's birth. It was probably clear to him that his children would have to be baptized if he wanted to spare them any disadvantages. To baptize one's self and one's children but then raise them as Jewish, would have posed great problems for the children, since they would have to keep this upbringing secret. Such behavior could only be expected if the parents were strongly devout and wanted to pass on their Jewish faith to their children at any price. We don't know whether Karl's mother had a pronounced faith. As emerges from the already mentioned letter from Heinrich Marx to his son from November 1835, he had a rather Rationalist-Deist attitude. He believed in God but did not tend toward any particular religion. To that extent, it's improbable that a particularly Jewish upbringing, the observance of Jewish laws, or the celebration of Jewish holidays took place. It is just as unlikely that Protestant Christianity, to which the family had converted, played an especially large role in Karl Marx's upbringing.

None of this means that Judaism was not a topic in the Marx family. At the very latest, when the adolescent children noticed that their parents had Jewish relatives, but that they themselves weren't Jews, they would have asked why that was the case. It's also plausible that the thoughts and attitudes of the parents had been shaped by their Jewish background, and that this would be reflected in some statements and behavior. But there are no indications supporting the thesis that a special familial constellation arose therefrom.

Künzli, Massiczek, and Monz can only allege that descent from a Jewish family must have led to a strong Jewish influence. But even disregarding the lack of clues for such a strong influence, it needs to be taken into consideration that Jewish traditions were far from the only influences the parents were subject to. For Heinrich Marx's thought, as is made clear by many of his statements, the Enlightenment played a decisive role. Heinrich Marx was likely also somewhat familar with Kant's philosophy. In a letter to Karl, he mentions Kant's anthropology in passing (MECW 1: 648). This strong influence of Enlightenment thought probably made for a certain amount of alienation of Judaism. Within the upheavals that were experienced by Jewish communities at the beginning of the nineteenth century, such an act of distancing was not an isolated case.

Rather than a Jewish influence, there are clear indications (such as in the Abitur examination paper) for Enlightenment-humanist influences upon the young Marx. His father's views, those of the "fatherly friend" Ludwig von Westphalen, and those of numerous teachers at the gymnasium in Trier all operated in similar directions, so that there might have been mutual reinforcement.

Friends from Youth

It's known that the young Karl was friends with Edgar von Westphalen. How close the relationship of the two boys must have been is demonstrated by a hitherto unpublished letter from Edgar to Friedrich Engels composed three months after Marx's death. On June 15, 1883, Edgar wrote: "I can only speak to you in person about my relationship to Jenny and Marx. I grew up in Marx's house as a child. The elder Marx was a patriot and Protestant à la Lessing. I was always drawn to Emilie (Mrs. Conradi).[78] Pacati tempi" (quoted in Gemkow 2008: 507n33).

Nothing has been passed down directly concerning the young Karl's friendships, so that several biographers have concluded that Marx had no friends in his youth and grew up rather isolated. Thus Otto Rühle (2011: 13) suspected that Marx had experienced his Jewish heritage as a stigma in childhood, which had spurred him to a high level of intellectual achievement, through which, however, he was unable to gain friends.[79] Cornu (1954: 60)

---

78. Marx's sister Emilie, born in 1822, had married the hydraulic engineering official Johann Jacob Conradi.

79. As already mentioned, Karl was an above-average pupil, but not an excellent one. Considerably better in his accomplishments, and according to his Abitur certificate also more diligent, was Edgar von Westphalen.

also writes that Marx had "few friends among his classmates," and Francis Wheen (1999) even gave the first chapter of his biography, devoted to Marx's youth, the title "The Outsider." The notion that Marx as a school pupil might have had the position of an outsider is not absurd from the outset. Marx's later remark about the "country bumpkins" at the Trier gymnasium (letter to Engels, September 17, 1878, MECW 45: 322) is readily invoked as evidence that he did not have any close relationships to his classmates. However, it's not at all the case that Marx dismisses all his classmates as "country bumpkins"; the sentence continues that some classmates "were preparing to enter the seminary (Catholic) and most of them drawing stipends."[80]

Rühle and Wheen see in this alleged outsider role of the young Marx a first instance of intellectual conditioning. However, an array of evidence contradicts this notion of the outsider without friends. Marx retained the strong accent of his hometown for his entire life (see F. Kugelmann 1983: 253). He could hardly have gotten this accent from his parents, neither of whom grew up in Trier. It could have come from contact with the domestic servants, but it appears more probable that he acquired it through contact with other children, which means that he must have passed considerable time with them during his childhood. That also fits with what his daughter Eleanor reports, that Karl as a pupil was both popular (because he took part in all pranks) as well as feared because of his mocking verses. Such a characterization does not point to an outsider.

Karl was probably friends with his classmate Heinrich Balthasar Christian Clemens (1814–1852) during or toward the end of his school days. As mentioned earlier, Karl and Heinrich Clemens were the only pupils in the class who did not bid farewell to the reactionary Vitus Loers. Like Karl, Heinrich Clemens studied in Bonn in 1835–36; later, he became a notary in Saarlouis (MEGA III/1: 932). When Karl and Jenny married in Kreuznach in 1843, one of the witnesses was the notary candidate Heinrich Balthasar Christian Clemens. Given that the first names and the profession are the same, it's likely that it was Marx's former classmate (Monz 1973: 351). It's also quite possible that they had a school friendship that continued for a few years.

---

80. These farmers' sons were somewhat older; in Marx's Abitur class, the two oldest pupils were twenty-four and twenty-seven (Monz 1973: 299), were frequently worse in their performance at school than other pupils, and in their interactions not infrequently somewhat roughshod. They obtained church stipends and after school were educated at a seminary in order to be Catholic clergy. Ten of Marx's classmates would later become priests.

In multiple letters from Heinrich Marx, there are clues to further friends from Marx's youth. In a letter from February 3, 1837 (MECW 1: 669), he refers to "your friend Karl von Westphalen." This would be Edgar's stepbrother, who was born in 1803 and who died in 1840. In a total of three letters, there is mention of a Kleinerz, who is also referred to by Heinrich Marx as "your friend" (MECW 1: 654; further mentions, 663 and 669). Since Marx's father refers to him as "Dr. Kleinerz" (MECW 1: 669), he must have been, like Karl von Westphalen, somewhat older than Karl. It's not known who this Kleinerz was.[81] Heinrich Marx also mentions in the letter of February 3, 1837: "Herr von Notz told me that you would come here during the autumn vacation" (ibid.). This "Herr von Notz" was likely the father of Karl's classmate Heinrich von Notz. If this former classmate knew when Karl was coming back to visit Trier, there must have been contact between the two beyond their school years, which points to a school friendship.

Finally, in the 1850s, we find in Marx's writings a clue to an earlier acquaintance. When Engels wrote an article about the Crimean War mentioning a former Prussian officer named Grach serving on the Turkish side, Marx wrote to him (June 13, 1854) that this was "an acquaintance of mine from Trier; not one of your Prussian instructors, but a talented adventurer who went to Turkey as much as 19 or so years ago to seek his fortune" (MECW 39: 461). This was Friedrich Grach, born in 1812 in Trier (and who died in 1854).[82] If Grach had been in Turkey for nineteen years in 1854, that is, since 1835, then Marx must have known him during his school days.

Viktor Valdenaire (1812–1881) also comes into question as a possible school friend. In 1843, he provided the *Rheinische Zeitung* information concerning the Mosel, actively took part in the Revolution of 1848, visited Marx in London at the end of 1856, and, during the auctioning of Marx's late mother's wine collection, helped to obtain a better price by bidding (Conradi to Marx, March 12, 1864, MEGA III/12: 494). Valdenaire had taken the Abitur examination at the gymnasium in Trier in 1834, a year before Karl. He was the son of Nikolaus Valdenaire (1772–1849), who in 1834 was one

---

81. Kiehnbaum (2013) suspects that "Kleinerz" is a transcription error and that it must be Reinartz. He was able to track down a Reinartz who had studied medicine in Berlin, but this person had not yet obtained the title of Doctor at the time these letters were written. No indication of Marx being acquainted with a Reinartz has surfaced so far.

82. Grünberg (1925: 429) had already referred to this letter but mixed up the officer Friedrich Grach with Marx's classmate Emmerich Grach (which he then corrected in an addendum from 1926: 239). Auguste Cornu (1954: 60) also succumbed to the same mistake, when he wrote without citing a source that Marx had a closer acquaintance with Emmerich Grach.

of the four members of the Rhenish provincial diet who were honored at the same celebratory banquet at the Casino where Heinrich Marx gave the welcoming address. So, the fathers probably knew each other. It's possible that the friendship between Karl and Viktor began during their years at the gymnasium.

Besides Edgar, six people can already be identified from the few surviving sources with whom an early friendship was more or less probable. Furthermore, if it's true that Karl was elected one of the "presidents" of the Trier student corps during his second semester in Bonn (see chapter 2 for more), then this also speaks for him already having had friends and good acquaintances in Trier and was anything but the outsider that Wheen claims he was.

Writing Poetry, Fencing, Dancing

The invigorated political and social mood after the July Revolution also had literary effects. To this day, several young authors, most of whom began publishing in the early 1830s, are collected under the label "Young Germany." However, these authors didn't constitute a real group—it was the banning of their writings by the German Confederation in December of 1835 that made them into one.[83] The first literary and journalistic attempts by the young Friedrich Engels were also influenced by "Young Germany" (see volume 2). This invigorated literary mood also left traces in Trier. As mentioned earlier in the outline of the cultural life of the city were the poet Eduard Duller (1809–1853), who had emigrated from Vienna due to the conditions of censorship there, and the Silesian lieutenant who wrote poems, Friedrich von Sallet (1812–1843), who had been stationed in Trier since 1832, and who had been sentenced twice to confinement in a fortress due to his disrespectful verses. A circle (or *Kränzchen*, "garland," as it was described by Sallet; see Groß 1956: 135) of young people interested in theater and poetry formed around these two. Belonging to this circle were, among others, the son of Johann Hugo Wyttenbach, the painter Friedrich Anton Wyttenbach

---

83. On December 10, 1835, the German Bundestag in Frankfurt banned the printing and distribution of writings by the "Young Germany" authors. Explicitly named were Heinrich Heine, Karl Gutzkow, Heinrich Laube, Ludolph Wienbarg, and Theodor Mundt (Ludwig Börne, who is also counted among this current, was forgotten in haste). According to the justification of the ban, these writers "in literary works, accessible to all classes of readers," aimed "to attack Christianity in the most impudent manner, disparage the present social relations, and destroy all discipline and morality" (Miruss 1848: 397).

(1812–1845), as well as two younger teachers at the gymnasium, Nikolaus Saal and Franz Philipp Lavern (1805–1859) (Böse 1951: 12, Groß 1956: 135f.). In 1834–35, Laven edited the literary entertainment newspaper *Treviris*, which was published twice a week, in which alongside articles from many fields of knowledge, art, and technology, he also published his own poems as well as those of Sallet and other members of the literary circle (Groß 1956: 138). It is not known how long this circle existed. In 1834, Duller moved to Frankfurt am Main, where he published the magazine *Phönix*, the literary review of which was edited by Karl Gutzkow (1811–1878), an important representative of "Young Germany." An advanced publication of Büchner's revolutionary drama *Danton's Death* appeared in *Phönix* in 1835.[84]

Due to his age alone, the young Karl probably did not belong to the circle, but he might have been aware of its existence and interested in its debates, since he wrote poems in his school days. His sister Sophie, who collected some of his poems in her notebook, dates the oldest one to 1833 (MEGA I/1: 760ff.). It is possible that Karl knew some of the members of the circle personally, given that many of them were graduates of or teachers at the gymnasium in Trier. There is also a further indication. When, in 1843, shortly after Friedrich von Sallet's early death, there was a dispute in the press about his "Layman's Gospel," Marx, who was editor of the *Rheinische Zeitung* at the time, got involved in the debate. Although he regarded Sallet's religious views critically, he formulated an engaged defense of Sallet as a person, whereby he took aim not only at Sallet's critics at the *Rhein-Mosel Zeitung*, but also his halfhearted defenders at the *Trierische Zeitung*.[85] The background to this decisive advocacy could have been not only familiarity with Sallet's work, but acquaintance with him in Trier.

Another area of possible importance to the young Karl was gymnastics. In 1816–17, organized gymnastics had begun in Trier under the direction of Franz Heinrich Rumschöttel (1795–1853), a student of Jahn's (Schnitzler 1988). After the Karlsbad Decrees of 1819 and the ban on organized gymnastics, however, it had to be discontinued, and Rumschöttel was monitored

---

84. Büchner distanced himself from "Young Germany." He held Gutzkow in high regard, despite all their differences. "In his sphere, Gutzkow has courageously fought for freedom," wrote Büchner to his parents on January 1, 1836. Concerning his own relationship to "Young Germany," he informed them: "By the way, I personally do not belong to the so-called Young Germany, the literary party of Gutzkow and Heine. Only a complete misunderstanding of our social conditions could cause people to believe that through ephemeral literature, a complete reshaping of our religious and social ideas is possible" (Büchner 1988: 313),

85. Marx's article, "The Rhein- and Mosel-Zeitung as Grand Inquisitor," appeared on March 12, 1843, in the *Rheinische Zeitung* (MECW 1: 370).

for years. In 1831, Trier's Mayor Haw petitioned to reauthorize gymnas-tics, which the government approved. From 1834, possibly from 1832 (see Schnitzler 1993: 92), Rumschöttel again started organized gymnastics in Trier, in which not only school pupils, but also adults took part (ibid.: 97). In 1842, after the official lifting of the ban on gymnastics, Rumschöttel men-tions fencing for the first time in his gymnastics report. Schnitzler regards it as plausible that fencing, as an important part of Jahn's conception of gym-nastics, was part of Rumschöttel's gymnastics program from the very begin-ning and was simply not mentioned in official writings (ibid.: 100).

We don't know whether the young Marx participated in these gymnas-tics and fencing exercises. As a student in Bonn (and even later), he was an enthusiastic fencer (see the next chapter). It's possible that Karl had already learned fencing in Trier, in the gymnastics lessons directed by Rumschöttel. Furthermore, he had the opportunity not only to meet a few classmates, but also to make the acquaintance of young people who were a few years older than he; perhaps he met the above-mentioned Kleinerz and Grach there.

Finally, the young Marx must have been an enthusiastic dancer. If this weren't the case, his mother would have hardly given him the advice in the letter quoted earlier from February–March 1836 that he shouldn't dance as long he wasn't completely healthy (MECW 1: 652). The young Karl probably didn't first discover dancing in Bonn. Precisely in the educated middle class, as well as among the nobility, dancing was among the indispensable social qualifications of young adults, since at balls, such as those organized by the Trier Casino Society, one could casually meet partners "befitting one's own social class."

Experiences and Views of a Gymnasium Graduate

Widespread poverty was in evidence in Trier. Social conditions, the tax bur-den, and municipal measures for poor relief led repeatedly to public debates, and as the example of Ludwig Gall shows, also initial socialist sketches. The young Karl probably became familiar with the poverty of a large part of the population through his own observation. It might have been a subject of conversation with Ludwig von Westphalen, who dealt with social conditions professionally, as well as conversations in the Marx household. The pov-erty of clients might have played a role in some of the legal proceedings his father litigated. That the father's legal proceedings and experiences were the subject of discussion, and thus were part of the young Karl's field of experi-ence, is documented by a letter that Marx wrote to Engels on March 25, 1868 (MECW 42: 557), where he mentions such conversations.

When the July Revolution occurred in France in 1830, Karl was just twelve years old, an age at which sometimes one's first interest in political events awakens. The boy might have noticed the resulting excitement in Trier. The following period of political upheaval, the Hambach Festival of 1832, the Frankfurter Wachensturm of 1833, and the events at the Trier Casino in 1834, with the subsequent trial of the lawyer Brixius for high treason, were no doubt just as consciously witnessed by young Karl as the suspicions raised against teachers and classmates during his school days.

He might have discussed all of that with his father and Ludwig von Westphalen, both of whom had an enlightened, liberal attitude. They did not hold the poor responsible for poverty, but rather criticized social and political conditions. Both Heinrich Marx and Ludwig von Westphalen were critical of the authoritarian and unsocial policies of the Prussian government. They didn't have revolutionary attitudes, but they were advocates of far-reaching political and social reforms.

Somewhat more radical positions might have been advanced by some of Karl's teachers or the members of the literary circle around Duller and Sallet. In Karl's circle of friends, critical-liberal views were likely predominant. He shared with Heinrich Clemens an aversion to the reactionary teacher Loers. Viktor Valdenaire, who later supported the *Rheinische Zeitung* and participated in the Revolution of 1848, and who came from a liberal home, was probably also not exactly conservative as a youth. One gets an impression of the political views of Karl von Westphalen, with whom according to Heinrich's testimony Karl must have definitely enjoyed a friendly relationship, from a letter that Ferdinand's wife, Louise Florencourt, wrote in the year 1831 to her parents: Karl was full of "revolutionary zeal, against the current state of things in Prussia, which he furiously affirms, cannot remain so for very much longer" (quoted in Monz 1973: 336).

Both within his family and in his circle of friends, young Karl encountered a politically interested, enlightened-liberal milieu, within which he could discuss the social and political processes he observed. But no decisively political attitudes on his part are known to us. The fact that he refrained from a farewell visit to Loers might have been based upon a rejection of Loers's reactionary stance, but that doesn't say very much about the views that Marx held at this time. The only document from which we can extract a few clues is the Abitur examination paper on the subject of German. Three things can be taken from this text: First: Marx still believes in a, probably abstractly conceived, "Deity." Second: he rejects any form of servile submission as undignified but accepts as an inevitable fact that the great "crowd" of the lower classes must live in such an undignified way. Third: he nurtures the strong wish to work for "the welfare of mankind," without it being clear what this would concretely entail.

Cornu's (1954: 62) view that the Abitur paper expresses that Marx "had decisively taken a side in the great epochal struggle between reaction and democracy" seems to me exaggerated. The young Karl was surely an opponent of reaction, but so were adherents of an enlightened constitutional monarchy, such as his father or his future father-in-law.

More important than such largely speculative assignations is that Marx the secondary school graduate did not yet see politics as the field upon which he wanted to work for the "welfare of mankind." When Karl left his parents' home after the Abitur, much was still open. What interested him far more than politics were literature and art. An educated middle-class career as a lawyer or judge who engaged in literary activity on the side was just as much in the realm of possibility as the role of a politically engaged liberal professor at a university. What most likely appeared most sympathetic to Karl was a future as a poet whose poetry had effects upon society. The fact that he began to study law may have corresponded to his father's wish that he pursue a solid education. In any case, in the gymnasium graduate there is not yet an intimation of the future revolutionary, socialist theorist.

——— 2 ———

AWAKENING AND
FIRST CRISIS
1835–1838

In the winter semester of 1835–36, Marx began his studies in Bonn; one year later, he transferred to the University of Berlin, where he would remain for five years, far away from his fiancée, Jenny von Westphalen. In Bonn and Berlin, Marx studied law, but initially he was much more interested in literature. He wrote poems, fragments of a humorous novel, began a drama, and sought opportunities for publication. But in the summer of 1837, Marx began to doubt his notions of literature, and in the autumn of 1837, found himself in both an intellectual and emotional crisis. He had serious conflicts with his father about the course of his studies and his future. At the beginning of 1838, his father's health deteriorated; in May, shortly after a visit from his son, he died. Karl thus lost his most important familial contact.

Only a few texts have survived from Marx's time as a university student. The first (and only) surviving letter from this period is from November 10, 1837, when he had been living in Berlin for over a year. This piece of writing usually serves as a source for the issues that Marx was dealing with in his first year in Berlin. However, this letter also documents the crisis of the nineteen-year-old, an aspect that has been fairly ignored in the literature. Alongside this letter from Marx there exist some poems and literary attempts, most of which were written in the years 1835 and 1836 and the last few in the first half of 1837. The first surviving scholarly text by Marx is a doctoral thesis from the year 1841, only part of which has been passed down. Alongside university records, the main sources on the period in Bonn and the early Berlin period are the letters written to Karl by his father. Despite rather sparse sources, in many biographies one finds vivid depictions of Marx's student life, up to and including a duel in which he supposedly sustained a head injury. Many of these detailed depictions originate more in the imagination of the biographers than in the available facts.

INTERLUDE IN BONN

Scarcely three weeks after Karl had received his Abitur certificate at the graduation ceremony on September 27, 1835, he set out for Bonn to study law. He enrolled on October 17. On the registration form for lectures, he's listed as "Studiosus juris et cameralium" (Lange 1983: 186, 221). "Kameralistik," or cameralistics, was the term in the eighteenth and nineteenth centuries for the administrative and bookkeeping skills required of a high state official. Bonn was the obvious choice to study, as it offered the closest Prussian university. Eight of his classmates also began their studies in Bonn.[86] The exact date of his departure from Trier is not known, nor is his means of transport. It was probably the seventeen-year-old's first trip without his parents, maybe even his first trip that led beyond the immediate environs of Trier.

Student Life in the Early Nineteenth Century

Marx was a student for six years. There are serious differences between student life then and as it exists today. Perhaps the most noticeable back then was that there were no female students or professors; universities were purely male institutions and would remain so for quite a while. Whereas in Switzerland women could enroll at the University of Zurich beginning in the 1860s, it wasn't until the end of the nineteenth century that women were admitted as regular students to German universities. Prussia only allowed women to study universally starting in 1908. Another important difference, not only in terms of absolute numbers, but also as a percentage of the population, there were far fewer students than today. In 1840, there were barely 12,000 students in all of Germany, about 0.4 percent of the total population (Ringer 2004: 202). In contrast, German institutions of higher education in 2013 had about 2.6 million students, which is about 3.2 percent of the population. In other words, whereas in 1840 there was 1 student for every 250 inhabitants, the contemporary ratio is about 1 to 31. In contrast to today, the universities weren't mass operations, and a university degree almost always

---

86. These were Heinrich Clemens, Jakob Fuxius, Gustav von Horn, Emmerich Grach, Matthias Haag, Johan Baptist Müller, Karl Praetorius, and Ernst Pütz (Schöncke 1994: 247). A year later, Edgar von Westphalen also began studying in Bonn (Gemkow 1999: 411).

guaranteed a high professional status, although even in the nineteenth century there were instances of "academic gluts." The third most important difference is that to a much greater extent than today students were recruited from the propertied classes of the bourgeoisie and nobility. There were a few students from poorer artisan families, but hardly any from working-class families. The great majority likely came from the upper 10 or 15 percent of the population in terms of income. That students mostly came from prosperous families and could spend a lot of money, relatively speaking, made them an important economic factor in smaller university cities. Correspondingly, they were prized, but not necessarily beloved.

The concrete life circumstances of students were also different than those of today. Most students did not have their own apartments. Usually, they were tenants of small artisans, frequently also of widows. For the person renting out the room, this provided important supplementary income. Not infrequently, the student tenant had the best room in the home. Usually, the landlord or landlady also performed services, bought provisions, took care of the washing, and in part prepared meals for the students.[87] Students not only brought in money; on the basis of their family background and social interactions with professors, who normally belonged to the local upper class, they stood considerably higher in the social hierarchy than their landlords and landladies and the retailers and innkeepers they dealt with. They were usually treated with corresponding respect. Conversely, most students had grown up in households with service staff (in the household of Karl's parents, there had been two maids), and many had gotten used to behaving in a "lordly" way. Frequently, a certain academic arrogance was added to this: one felt far superior to the "philistines," that is, to normal citizens, artisans, and merchants, not to speak of the common people, the "rabble."

Since one could usually recognize people of "status" on the basis of their expensive clothing (they wanted to be recognized), it wasn't cheap for students to lead lives "befitting their social status." During the Bonn period, Karl's father complained about his high level of spending, and in Berlin, Karl was even sued for debts, as his leaving certificate noted (Lange 1983: 192). A good part of these expenditures were presumably for clothing. The frock coat he wore in the only picture from his time in Bonn probably wasn't cheap.

For most students, the beginning of studies was the first phase of life without direct parental control, which in the nineteenth century was exercised in a far more authoritarian manner than today. Thorough advantage was taken

---

87. On the living conditions of students in Bonn, see Dietz (1968: 232–36).

of this new freedom. In many cases, students caroused in taverns together until late in the evening, and sometimes concluded by walking the streets singing and causing an uproar. Every now and then, they engaged in skirmishes with other groups of students, and sometimes with residents of the city. If the residents wished to complain, or report students for unpaid bills or other miscellaneous damages, they had to contact the university. Students had, as a remnant of the feudal order, a special status. They were not subject to the general judicial system; special university magistrates had jurisdiction over them. Universities not only had their own jurisdiction, but with the so-called *Pedelle* (sometimes rendered in contemporary German as *Hausmeister*, or custodians, which is wrong, however, as applied to that period), they had their own small executive authority. The *Pedelle* were something like marshals and special constables. Evenings, they had to patrol the taverns and ensure that the students left at the hour of curfew, deal with rowdy students, and, when necessary, bring them before university judges. Frequently, university magistrates were rather lenient with students. In the 1830s, however, when students were judged to be politically suspect by the Prussian government after the Hambach Festival and the Frankfurter Wachensturm, the regime of university magistrates was tightened in many places. The Bonn university magistrate, Friedrich von Salomon (1790–1861), was known well beyond Bonn for his strictness. He earned the derisive nickname "Salamander" and was also caricatured as such (see the depiction in Gerhardt 1926: 75). Karl Marx also made his acquaintance in the case of a rather harmless affair.

The University and Studies in Bonn

In the middle of the 1830s, Bonn, with its barely 14,000 residents, was hardly bigger than Trier. However, it had a university with around 700 students (Höroldt 1968: 346), a considerable number at the time. The University of Bonn was not old. In the course of the Prussian education reforms, the universities of Berlin and Breslau were founded in 1810 and 1811, respectively; in 1818, the University of Bonn, named for the new Rhine province, followed.

Among the early professors in Bonn were some names that were well known in their time. Among them was the classicist and archaeologist Friedrich Gottlieb Welcker (1784–1868), who had participated as a volunteer in the anti-Napoleonic Wars. After the Karlsbad Decrees, he was arrested but was able to continue his teaching activities. His brother was the noted liberal constitutional law expert, Carl Theodor Welcker (1790–1869), who taught in Freiburg and who, together with Karl von Rotteck (1775–1840), published the fifteen-volume "Lexicon of the State" between 1834 and 1842, a work famous in Germany in the nineteenth century and in which the political knowledge of the time was presented from a liberal perspective. In Prussia, this work was banned. The then well-known writer Ernst Moritz Arndt (1769–1860), whose ardent nationalism went hand-in-hand with a deeply felt hatred for the French and Jews, became a professor in Bonn in 1818. However, in 1820, he was suspended after the Karlsbad Decrees (discussed below) and first rehabilitated in 1840 by King Friedrich Wilhelm IV after the latter's ascension to the throne, so that he could teach again. During the entire period of his suspension, he retained his place of residence and was regarded by the students with great awe, as the jurist Karl Schorn (1898: 68), who studied in Bonn from the winter semester 1836/37, reports in his memoirs. Also appointed as a professor in 1818 was August Wilhelm Schlegel (1767–1829), who, along with his brother Friedrich Schlegel (1772–1829), was one of the founders of German Romanticism and a celebrity in this time.

According to his Certificate of Release from 1836, Karl enrolled at the University of Bonn under the name "Carl Heinrich Marx" (MECW 1: 657). We don't know whether he chose the middle name Heinrich to honor his father, or whether he simply thought "Carl Marx" was too prosaic. After his studies, he never returned to using this addition.

In Bonn, Karl initially lived at the same house as Christian Hermann Wienenbrügge and Wilhelm Kewenig—two graduates of the gymnasium in Trier who had taken the Abitur examination a year before Marx (Schöncke 1994: 247; Gockel 1989: 30).

After Karl arrived in Bonn in the middle of October, he at first did not get in touch with his parents. On November 8, his father wrote him an angry letter: he had been gone for three weeks and they still had not received any message from him (MECW 1: 645). For Karl, these three weeks, probably the first he had ever spent not under the watchful eyes of his parents, likely went by in a flash. In a response letter that has not survived, Marx described the new circumstances of his life. He had quickly befriended Wienenbrügge, describing him very positively. At least, his father congratulated him in the next letter for having "found a friend, and a very worthy friend" at the "important initial stage of your career" (ibid.: 646). Wienenbrügge was still fondly remembered at the gymnasium in Trier; Heinrich Marx had been congratulated for Wienenbrügge being a friend of his son (ibid.: 647).

Christian Hermann Wienenbrügge, born in 1813, studied philosophy and philology in Bonn. During the first semester, according to the enrollment lists, he and Marx attended a few seminars together.[88] One can well imagine that Marx was initially impressed by Wienenbrügge, who was five years older and certainly better read. However, the friendship seems to have cooled off rather quickly. In the next semester, Karl moved (Gockel 1989: 30). He lived in the same house as his classmate from Trier, Emmerich Grach (Schöncke 1994: 251), and there was no longer any mention of Wienenbrügge.[89]

In a letter from Karl's mother, we learn something about the usual conditions of cleanliness of the time. She demands that Karl not only make sure that his room is scrubbed weekly (by the landlords, apparently), but that he should also "have a weekly scrub with sponge and soap" (MECW 1: 649).

In his first semester, Marx plunged into his studies with complete élan. He wrote to his father that he had enrolled in nine lecture courses, so that his father cautioned him to not to take on too much (MECW 1: 646). According to the registration form, Marx had indeed paid for nine courses—back then, one had to pay tuition, and the professor had to attest at the end of the semester that the course had been attended successfully—however, three courses were crossed out again. Marx was probably so infrequently in attendance that he couldn't hope for an attestation of "present" (Bodsch 2012: 15).

The Certificate of Release of 1836 (MECW 1: 657ff.) notes with corresponding appraisals for the winter semester of 1835–36 that Marx had attended three courses of the faculty of law regularly: "The Encyclopedia of Jurisprudence" with Eduard Puggé (1802–1836) (graded "very diligent and attentive"); "Institutions" with Eduard Böcking (1802–1870) ("very diligent and with constant attention"); and "History of Roman Law" with Ferdinand Walter (1794–1879) ("ditto"). Furthermore, he attended three courses of the faculty of philosophy: "Mythology of the Greeks and Romans" with the already mentioned Friedrich Gottlieb Welcker ("with excellent diligence and attentiveness"); "History of Modern Art" with Eduard d'Alton (1772–1840) ("diligent and attentive"); and finally "Questions about Homer" with August Wilhelm von Schlegel ("diligent and attentive").

In the summer semester of 1836, Marx registered again for more courses than he attended (Bodsch 2012: 17). In the Certificate of Release, only four courses are noted with attestations: "History of German Law" with Ferdinand Walter ("diligent"); "European International Law" and "Natural Right," with Puggé, which "could not be testified owing to the sudden death of Professor

---

88. The enrollment lists for the courses attended by Marx were evaluated by Deckert (1966).
89. Wienenbrügge studied from 1837 to 1840 at the Trier seminary and was ordained a priest in 1841. He died in 1851 (Lexikon Westfälischer Autorinnen und Autoren).

Puggé,"[90] and another course with Schlegel, "Elegiacs of Propertius" ("diligent and attentive").

Marx studied law, but he didn't only attend courses on law. That one not only studied a major subject, but also attended courses on completely different subjects, was not at all unusual in the nineteenth century.[91] Back then, attending a university still had something to do with education. The usual practice today in Germany of testing the results of one's learning with exams in which knowledge learned by rote is interrogated would have probably been rejected as absurd.

With the six courses in law he attended in Bonn, Marx had already established a solid foundation in law. In the process, his understanding of legal theory probably obtained its first unique stamp. Both the young Puggé, three of whose courses Marx had attended, as well as Böcking, had studied in Berlin with Friedrich Carl von Savigny (1779–1861) (on Böcking, see Lenz 1910: 2.1: 384). Both were adherents of the German "Historical School of Law" founded by Gustav von Hugo (1764–1844) and Savigny. This school criticized the transhistorical doctrine of natural law and emphasized the historical conditionality of law, whereby Savigny saw the development of law as being rooted in the "spirit of the people" (*Volksgeist*), which cannot be altered by a legislator going by principles of natural law. Ferdinand Walter, the third legal expert whose lectures Marx had attended, had studied with Anton Friedrich Thibaut (1772–1840), an opponent of Savigny, but as he wrote in his memoirs the sharp conflicts over method between schools of jurisprudence did not interest him (Walter 1865: 110). So Marx had become familiar with two representatives of the "historical school," but none of their critics. We will return to the historical school within the context of Marx's time at the University of Berlin, where he studied under Savigny.

In the faculty of philosophy, August Wilhelm Schlegel was the only instructor from whom Marx took more than one course. Marx's later friend Heinrich Heine (1797–1856), who had studied in Bonn in 1819/20, had already made fun of Schlegel's vanity. Schlegel appeared at lectures always dressed in accordance with the latest Parisian fashion, wearing glacé leather gloves, accompanied by a servant clad in livery who brought silver candlesticks and stood next to the lectern and to take care of the candles (Heine 1835: 418). But Schlegel must have still impressed his listeners. As Emanuel Geibel (who we

---

90. Puggé, an unhappy widower and the father of two small children, hanged himself in his study. The fact that his death was a suicide was initially covered up (Bodsch 2012: 17, 26).

91. In present-day Germany, university studies usually only involve courses for the subject of one's major. —Trans.

will discuss shortly) emphasizes, he found in the "man of advanced age a still quick-witted, deft, and astute man" (in 1835, Schlegel was sixty-eight) (Geibel 1909: 34). Marx must have also been impressed by Schlegel. Not only does his attendance of two courses indicate this; four decades later, when he was in Karlsbad for a spa treatment and a local newspaper reported on the famous guest in its feuilleton section (*Der Sprudel*, September 19, 1875), Marx fondly recalled these lecture courses. In conversation, according to the article, "Marx share[d] copiously from the rich, well-ordered treasure of his memories." Among these was also that "while Romanticism was still singing its last free forest song,[92] when he was a black-curled, enthusiastic journeyman, he sat at the feet of A. W. Schlegel" (quoted in Kisch 1983: 75).

In the winter of 1835–36, perhaps during the Christmas holidays, Marx took a trip to Holland. Since his mother asked him in a letter from February–March of 1836 how he had liked her "native city" (MECW 1: 652), his journey must have taken him to Nimwegen. Martin Presburg, his mother's brother, still lived there; their parents were already deceased. In the summer of 1835, Karl's sister Sophie had visited their Dutch relatives and had stayed in Maastricht, Lüttich, Aachen, Nimwegen, and Zaltbommel.[93] It's possible that Karl made a similar trip. In the letter from February–March 1836, however, his parents are astonished that he only told them about this trip retrospectively, and his father asks with concern: "You haven't eked out your existence by cadging, I hope" (MECW 1: 651).[94] Apparently, the son had very quickly gotten used to acting completely independently from his parents.

The Literature Circle

Marx's parents' letter from February–March 1836 offers the only contemporary evidence of fondness concerning two memberships of Marx's. Heinrich

---

92. An obvious allusion to one of Heine's most popular books, *Atta Troll*. In the final chapter, the book itself becomes the subject (Heine 1887: 325):

> Ah! perchance it is the last free
> forest-song of the Romantic;
> In the daytime's wild confusion
> Will it sadly die away.

93. This information comes from entries in her poetry album (Gielkens 1999: 364).
94. In the original German, the sentence is "Du hast Dich doch hoffentlich nicht mit Fechten durchgeschlagen?" (MEGA III/1: 294). The German word *Fechten* (fencing) in this case does not refer to a fight with swords or daggers, but rather the begging of itinerant journeymen. This meaning for *Fechten* had been widespread in Germany since the seventeenth century (Duden Herkunftswörterbuch, 2007: 208).

Marx wrote: "Your little circle appeals to me, as you may well believe, much more than ale-house gatherings" (MECW 1: 650). That this circle was a poetic circle is suggested by the rest of the letter, where Heinrich Marx agrees with his son that he should wait a while before publishing his own literary works.

On the basis of police records—which are not verified—Nicolayevsky and Maenchen-Helfen (1933: 34; and 1937: 19) stated that the founders of the "association of poets" were "the student Fenner von Fenneberg, one of the most active revolutionaries in 1848–49, first in Vienna and then in Baden, and Biermann from Trier," who had been accused when he was a gymnasium pupil of having written "subversive poems." This is apparently Johann Michael Birmann, who had completed his Abitur in 1832 at the gymnasium in Trier and who was the target of an investigation for writing political poems (see Monz 1973: 128, 133).[95] The Police had allegedly monitored the circle, which had not led to any results. Bodsch (2012: 22) points out that Fenneberg and Birmann studied at the University of Bonn only until the summer semester of 1835. They left before Marx arrived, so could not have been members of this circle at the same time as Marx. Apart from that, it's unclear whether the circle founded by Fenneberg and Birmann continued to exist after their departure, and if so, whether it was the same one frequented by Marx. In any case, there is no evidence.

A further source on this circle are the memoirs of Moriz Carrière (1817–1895), who had studied in Göttingen starting in 1836 and later taught art history in Munich. Among his friends in Göttingen were Karl Ludwig Bernays (1815–1876), who worked with Marx in the 1840s in Paris, as well as the poet and historian of literature Theodor Creizenach (1818–1877). Carrière noted, concerning his circle of friends: "We exchanged letters with Bonn, where Geibel, Karl Marx, later a famous agitator and sharp thinker, and Karl Grün had an association of poets, and competed with each other to write poems. . . . We planned an almanac of muses that was to publish the best poems of Göttingen and Gießen, with contributions from Bonn" (Carrière 1914: 167).

On the basis of this statement, the circle in Bonn with Marx, Geibel, and Grün as members is accepted as fact in many biographies of Marx. In light of

---

95. Birmann is also named, without a source, as the co-founder of the poetry circle in the MEGA (III/1: 725). Also without providing a source, Cornu (1954: 66) names Biedermann (instead of Birmann) as well as Fenner von Fennersleben (instead of Fenner von Fenneberg) as the founders, and has thus caused some confusion in the biographical literature. Karl Biedermann (1812–1901) was a Burschenschaft member and later delegate to the Reichstag for the National-Liberal Party. However, he never studied in Bonn. Deckert (1966: 42) had already pointed out that Cornu mixed up the two names.

the later development of its alleged members—Emanuel Geibel (1815–1884) would go on to become a conservative contemplative poet, highly regarded by the Prussian royal house, and Karl Grün (1817–1887) would become one of the most important representatives of "True Socialism," which Marx heavily criticized—the composition of this Bonn circle is remarkable, so it's worth taking a closer look.

From the enrollment list from the winter semester of 1835–36, it can be gleaned that Geibel, Grün, and Marx all sat in Schlegel's course on Homer (Deckert 1966: 42), but other than Carrière's remark, there is no further indication that the three had ever belonged to a common circle. None of the three ever mentioned this circle. Karl Grün, who like Marx had enrolled at Bonn in October of 1835 (Schöncke 1994: 242), had at least spoken of Marx in a letter to Moses Hess from September 1845 as "an old university friend" (Hess 1959: 138). But since Grün, like Marx, started studying in Berlin in 1837, it's not clear whether this university friendship had begun in Bonn, or in Berlin.

Even more questionable is the membership of Emanuel Geibel, as Decker (1966: 43) has noted. Geibel left Bonn at the beginning of 1836, so he only spent a single semester in common with Marx. In Berlin as well, he and Marx were both enrolled at the university at the same time for a while. However, nowhere in Marx's writing is there a mention of Geibel, nor did Geibel ever mention Marx or even a poetry circle in Bonn. Geibel's letters to his mother (Geibel 1909) depict in great detail his stay in Bonn. Along with many details about the university and the living situation, we learn intimately all the people Geibel had visited, and the impressions he had of his conversation partners. Not a single detail is left out. It's not plausible that he would have failed to mention, of all things, a poetry circle in which he had participated. From Berlin, looking back at his time in Bonn, he wrote: "There, I was almost completely on my own" (Geibel 1909: 56). Carrière likely made a mistake in his memoirs,[96] which were published decades later, especially since he had not participated himself in the Bonn circle. Furthermore, Carrière's statements are questionable with regard to the time frame: Geibel left Bonn at the beginning of 1836, Marx in the summer of 1836. As Carrière states, Oppenheim and Creizenach came to Göttingen in the autumn of 1836, and through these two he got to know Bernays. According to Hirsch (2002: 32), Bernays had first enrolled at Göttingen in April of 1837. The circle in Göttingen that Carrière mentions could therefore only have been formed after Geibel and Marx had already left Bonn. Thus who corresponded and competed with

---

96. The publisher Diehl states they were written between 1874 and 1879 (Carrière 1914: 135).

whom is unclear. Marx might have been a member of a literary circle in Bonn in 1835–36, but it's rather improbable that Karl Grün and Emanuel Geibel were also members.

Tavern Life and an Alleged Duel

Things look a bit better with respect to information on the "ale-house"[97] mentioned by Heinrich Marx. After the July Revolution of 1830, not only had the long-forbidden Burschenschaften been persecuted, but also the rather unpolitical student corps. This persecution appears to have been particularly intense in Bonn.[98] Heinrich Bürgers (1820–1878), who studied in Bonn shortly after Marx and later worked closely with him for a short time, remarked in his memoirs from 1876 concerning the situation after the persecution: "Everything narrowed down to tavern life in the corps associations, which were actually banned and stood under the strict surveillance of the curator and university magistrates as a tolerated nuisance" (quoted in Kliem 1970: 68).

When Marx arrived in Bonn, student life had already become largely apolitical. It either took place in "table societies," loose associations of students from the same hometown or region, or in the more formally organized student corps. There were three table societies in Bonn at the time: the Trier, Cologne, and Aachen. There were also three corps in 1835, the Rhenania, the Guestphalia, and the Borussia; the Saxonia was founded in 1836 (quoted in Kaupp 1995: 142). The "ale-house" referred to by Marx's father was probably the Trier table society, which in 1838, after Marx left Bonn, became the Corps Palatia. The Trier table society was devoted extensively to fencing. From the corps chronicle of the Palatia from the year 1899, one learns about its predecessors: "At the head of the Trier society stood five presidents, who alternated weekly within the presidium at the tavern evenings. Visiting the common fencing hall was obligatory" (Palatia 1899: xi). The Marx chronicle published by Czobel in 1934 states, with reference to a letter from Prof. Dr. F. Lenz, relying upon the records of the Palatia corps, that Marx had been "one of the five presidents" of the Trier society in the summer semester of 1836 (Czobel 1934: 3).[99]

For a long time, the only known picture of Marx in his youth was from a drawing made in 1836, which shows the Trier table society in front of the

---

97. German: *Kneipe*, meaning "tavern," "pub," "bar."
98. See Höroldt (1968a: 100) and more extensively Gerhardt (1926: 58–78).
99. Gerhardt also writes in his history of the Bonn corps that Karl Marx had belonged to the "executive" of the Trier society in the year 1836 (Gerhardt 1926: 101).

guesthouse Weißes Ross[100] in Godesberg. This drawing is a typical semester picture of a tavern society (many such pictures are printed in Gerhardt) (1926). These pictures were commissioned works. Usually, the students were portrayed against a landscape, and frequently their heads were drawn on a previously drawn figure, so that those depicted did not all have to be present at the same time. On the basis of this drawing, prints were then made and sold to the students depicted (see Bodsch 2012: 20).

A lithograph of the picture of the Trier table society still existed in the 1920s in the Palatia corps house. According to Gerhardt (1926: 441n226), in 1890 the names of the people depicted, among them Karl Marx, were noted on the back of the print by a judicial council, Schneider, who had been senate president in Cologne. Schneider also identified five of Marx's classmates from the Abitur (Fuxius, Praetorius, v. Horn, Clemens, and Pütz, see Gerhardt 1926: 442). From a perusal of university records, Bodsch (2012: 21) was able to establish that in the winter semester of 1836/37, a Friedrich Schneider from Mayen had enrolled at the University of Bonn; this is probably the judicial council named by Gerhardt. However, Schneider could not have known Marx, since he had already left Bonn. Identifying numerous people after fifty years is also not very plausible, so that it's not at all certain that we're dealing with a picture of the young Karl Marx. But Schneider could have had an already labeled print of the drawing, from which he merely copied the names. In any case, the picture allegedly of Marx fits very well with the description of the "black-curled" lad referred to in the *Karlsbader Zeitung* article cited above. Within the Palatia corps, the prominent member of the Trier table society was fondly commemorated. The corps chronicle published in 1913 states the following concerning the picture: "One person standing there in the picture with elegant restraint—and appearing to represent the elegance of the association as the only one in a lace-up frock coat—was Karl Marx" (Palatia 1913: 11).

According to Schneider, Heinrich Rosbach (1814-1879) is also depicted in the drawing. He studied medicine in Bonn from 1832 and settled in Trier as a doctor in 1840. He was also an enthusiastic painter. According to family tradition, one of his drawings shows the young Karl Marx in Bonn. It was donated to the Stadtmuseum Simeonstift in Trier in 2017.

The young Karl Marx no doubt enjoyed fencing with his pals and didn't always go home quietly. In his Certificate of Release, a one-day sentence of detention "for disturbing the peace by rowdiness and drunkenness at night" is recorded (MECW 1: 658), issued by the above-mentioned university

---

100. The White Steed. —Trans.

magistrate Friedrich von Salomon. According to the detention book, Marx had to report to serve the sentence on the morning of June 16 at 10 a.m.; it lasted until the same hour of the next day (Bodsch 2012: 21). That the university "detention cell" was a rather "merry prison" is described by Schorn (1898: 62): "The prisoners were allowed to receive visitors, who almost never failed, with wine and beer and card games," which, however, entailed considerable service costs. In addition, there were expenses for a lunch obtained from the guesthouse and decent bed sheets, so that Schorn concludes: "The detention sentences were essentially sentences levied against the purses of parents." That student life could indeed be expensive is also proven by Heinrich Bürgers in his reminiscences. There he states that it did not make a good impression during tavern evenings if one spoke in an "educated" way; a "'beer convention' was immediately convened, and the culprit had to pay the fine in the price of beer" (quoted in Kliem 1970: 68).

Heinrich Marx's letters often deal with his son's expenditures; Karl needed too much money, and it wasn't evident what he was spending the money on, since Karl only made vague statements. In any case, he probably had some expenditures for clothing "befitting his station" and for books.[101] Ultimately, Karl must have made some kind of confession. An undated letter from his father, written in either May or June of 1836, states: "Dear Karl, your letter, which I received only on the 7th, has strengthened my belief in the uprightness, frankness, and loyalty of your character, which means more to me than the money" (MECW 1: 653). However, it appears that Karl had not yet confessed to everything. Two years later, in a letter from February 10, 1838, Heinrich wrote that he gave "full credit" to Karl's "morality," and adds: "In the first year of your legal career I gave you irrefutable proof of this by not even demanding an explanation in regard to a very obscure matter, even though it was very problematic" (MECW 1: 692). And in the letter before that from 1837, Heinrich Marx, referring to the Bonn period, describes his son as "a wild ringleader of wild young fellows" (MECW 1: 688) (probably a reference to Karl being one of the presidents of the Trier table society) and reminds him of his "wild goings-on in Bonn" (MECW 1: 689). This could also be an explanation for the expenditure of large sums of money: penalties at the beer convention, "service costs" as president of the Trier table society, which meant he now and then paid for a round of beer for all present, expenses for *Paukzeug* (fencing equipment), and maybe expenses for student pranks, where the damage had to be paid for afterwards.

---

101. In his father's letter from February/March 1836, mention is made of the purchase of many books (MECW 1: 650).

In Heinrich's letter to Karl from May–June 1836, there's a remark that has occasioned much speculation in the literature: "And is duelling then so closely interwoven with philosophy? It is respect for, indeed fear of, opinion. And what kind of opinion? Not exactly always of the better kind, and yet!!! Everywhere man has so little consistency.—Do not let this inclination, and if not inclination, this craze, take root. You could in the end deprive yourself and your parents of the finest hopes that life offers" (MECW 1: 653).

On the basis of this letter, the majority of biographers assume that Marx had been in a duel in 1836. Today, when one hears of a duel in the nineteenth century, one thinks perhaps of a duel with pistols at the crack of dawn. If Marx had really participated in a duel, it was likely not a pistol duel, which was uncommon among students. More probably, it was one of the student fencing duels that began in the eighteenth century between the members of the various student associations and out of which emerged the "Mensurs," conducted according to strict rules. In these fencing duels, the outcome was not decisive, but rather that one had accepted the duel. That Marx liked fencing can be gleaned from his letter of November 10, 1837, where he assures his father of his intention "no longer to practice tricks of swordsmanship" (MECW 1: 18). However, even later Marx was still an enthusiastic fencer. Wilhelm Liebknecht (1896/1908: 105) reports that in London in the 1850s he and Marx had frequently visited a "fencing salon" operated by a French emigrant, where one could practice fencing and pistol shooting, and where Marx had liked to fence.

In some biographies, Marx's supposed duel is associated with conflicts between the various student groups. Gerhardt (1926: 102ff.) reports on conflicts between the Borussia corps and the Trier table society, which had not yet constituted a corps. However, Gerhardt focuses on the year 1837, when Marx was no longer in Bonn,[102] and besides, the conflict had consisted in the fact that students who were members of corps did *not* accept duel challenges from students who were not members of corps, since they regarded them as "incapable of giving satisfaction."

The possible duel is also readily associated with another matter. On Marx's Certificate of Release from Bonn from August 22, 1836, it is noted that he was accused of "carrying prohibited weapons in Cologne. The investigation is still pending" (MECW 1: 658). What these weapons were is not stated in the certificate, and it's also not said whether these weapons were connected to a

---

102. Kaupp (1995: 144) writes about conflicts in the winter of 1835–36 but does not specify any sources.

duel. Though that hasn't prevented a number of biographers from indulging in wild speculation.[103]

For a few decades now, more has been known about the Cologne incident, but none of this information has found its way into the biographies published thus far. The records of the University of Berlin magistrate reveal that the "royal superior procurator" of Cologne finally charged Marx in May 1838 (when he had long since started studying in Berlin). Marx had allegedly carried a sword cane, and during a dispute, one of his companions injured a bystander with it. Marx was sentenced to a penalty of 20 thalers (Kossack 1978: 105). So the Cologne incident had nothing to do with a duel; rather, it belongs to the category of a street brawl, where nothing is known about the background.

Regarding the alleged duel, the only conclusion that can be reached from the letter from Marx's father quoted above is that Marx justified dueling by constructing a parallel to philosophical argumentation. Perhaps he meant that, just as one must argumentatively defend against attacks upon one's philosophical position, one must defend against attacks upon one's honor with a duel, an attitude that would have indeed fit with the attitudes prevalent among students at the time. In any case, Marx did not maintain his positive attitude toward duels. When in 1858, Ferdinand Lassalle (1825–1864) was challenged to a duel and asked Marx for advice, he stated his fundamental opposition (MECW 40: 322).

---

103. Whereas Nicolaevsky and Maenchen-Helfen (1933) still do not provide any details on the duel, they write in their book, published four years later (1937: 20), that Marx had dueled in August 1836 with a Borussia corps member and sustained an injury above the left eye. Cornu (1954: 67) also reports this, but here the injury is over the right eye. In terms of the specified time, this story is not plausible. If there had been a duel, then it must have happened before Heinrich Marx's response letter. If Karl had first announced it, then his father would have hardly restricted himself to general admonitions; rather, he would have attempted to stop Karl. Furthermore, there is no evidence for Karl having a duel injury. The letter that Prof. Lenz—relying upon the records of Palatia concerning Marx's time in Bonn, sent to Moscow, and from which Nicolaevsky, Maenchen-Helfen, and Cornu also received their information—merely indicates that the Trier member Fuxius sustained an eye injury while fencing (the letter is partially reprinted in Schöncke 1994: 243). Cornu's unsubstantiated claim was frequently cited, however; Raddatz (1975: 24) mentions it and in the study by Kaupp (1995: 150) on Marx's time as a member of a student association and fencer, it also plays an important role. Raddatz apparently insinuates that the "forbidden weapon" must have been a pistol and asserts without further ado that Marx had dueled in Cologne with pistols. In the case of Wheen (1999: 16), the duel story is adorned with an entire bouquet of products of the imagination: the Borussians had allegedly forced other students to kneel and swear fealty to the Prussian nobility; in order to defend himself, Marx supposedly procured a pistol and ultimately accepted a challenge to a duel. There is not a single piece of evidence for any of this.

In a letter to the university dated July 1, 1836, Heinrich Marx wrote that "I not only grant my son Karl Marx permission, but it is my will that he should enter the University of Berlin next term" (MECW 1: 655). This has frequently led to the conclusion that Heinrich Marx wanted to end his son's wild goings-on in Berlin—detention due to drunkenness, excessive spending, a possible duel—and send him to the more strictly controlled environment of Berlin (see, for example, Cornu 1954: 67; McLellan 1973: 13; Gabriel 2011: 23; or Sperber 2013: 39). If one considers the tone of his letters, then it's hard to imagine that Heinrich Marx put his foot down and sent his son to Berlin against his will. The assumption of a fatherly command at the end of the summer semester overlooks the fact that the transfer to Bonn had long been planned. In the letter written in February or beginning of March, Heinrich writes that if the natural sciences were so badly taught in Bonn, then "you will indeed do better to attend these courses in Berlin" (MECW 1: 650). If the transfer to Berlin is mentioned so casually, then the decision for Berlin must have already been made before February–March 1836. In his father's previous letter from November 1835 the topic wasn't raised, so again we can assume that the transfer had been planned from the beginning of Marx's studies. Karl would spend the first year in Bonn, which was nearer and cheaper, and then transfer to Berlin, in order to end his studies at the leading Prussian university.

JENNY VON WESTPHALEN

Before Karl relocated to Berlin, he moved back to Trier, where he supposedly, as claimed overwhelmingly in the biographical literature, became secretly engaged to Jenny von Westphalen.

Childhood and Youth

Jenny was born on February 12, 1814, in Salzwedel and christened Johanna Bertha Julie Jenny. She was the first child of Ludwig von Westphalen and his second wife, Caroline. The name she went by, Jenny, is reminiscent of that of her grandmother, Jeannie Wishart. However, Jenny never got to know her grandmother, who died in 1811. Jenny probably also didn't have any memories of Salzwedel. When she was two years old, her parents moved to Trier, where the Prussian government had transferred her father. In Trier, Jenny grew up with her stepbrother Carl, born in 1803, her sister Laura, born in 1817 (but who died in 1822), and her brother Edgar, born in 1819. A sister of her mother's also lived in the household. There were also service personnel, a matter of course for the upscale bourgeoisie. From 1818 at the latest, two maidservants are verifiable (Limmroth 2014: 42).

As mentioned in chapter 1, Ludwig Westphalen had, with 1,800 talers, the highest annual salary of all government officials in a comparable position, but he not only had to provide for a large household, he also had to pay the debt on earlier land purchases and pay a lifelong annuity to his older brother Heinrich. The financial situation was frequently tense, so that the prospect of a large inheritance was a cause of considerable excitement within the family for some time in the 1820s. However, this inheritance never came (Monz 1973d: 20).

Jenny had a close relationship to her younger brother Edgar for her entire life, though her relationships to her step-siblings, the children of Ludwig von Westphalen's first marriage, varied. Her relationship to Carl, who came along to Trier and with whom she grew up, appears to have been good, up to his early death in 1840. And Karl Marx was a friend of his.

Jenny's relationship with Ferdinand, the oldest child from her father's first marriage, was sometimes difficult.[104] In 1816, when the family moved to Trier, Ferdinand stayed in Salzwedel to finish his Abitur. After that, he began studies in Halle. In 1819, he made a first visit to Trier, and everything seems to have proceeded harmoniously. During his second visit in 1820, he appears to have taken a somewhat negative attitude toward his stepmother, "whose education and aptitude was so completely different from his," referring to his father, Ludwig. In particular, he criticized the manner of her parenting: "The mother's guiding principle was to allow the children their own wills—they were praised by her, one could say, to their faces, even when they played stupid pranks" (memoirs quoted by Gemkow 2008: 511).

When Lisette, Ludwig's oldest daughter, married Adolph von Krosigk in 1821, Ludwig and Carl traveled to Hohenerxleben, but not his wife, Caroline, or her seven-year-old daughter Jenny. The fact that only Ludwig and Carl attended the wedding can be gleaned from the description of Lisette's life written by her daughter Anna (see Krosigk 1973: 50). Limmroth (2014: 49) mentions a reference by Gemkow to an unpublished letter, which reveals that it was the expressed wish of Ferdinand that Caroline and Jenny not be invited.

Ferdinand's bourgeois stepmother appears to have become increasingly embarrassing to him. In a letter from December 1, 1829, to his fiancée, Louise von Flourencourt, he describes her as a "repugnant person" (quoted in

---

104. It appears that Jenny got to know her stepsisters Lisette and Franziska—who after their mother's death had gone to live with her relatives—later on. As emerges from Ferdinand's memoirs, partially published by Heinrich Gemkow, Ferdinand came to visit Trier in 1834 along with Franziska (Gemkow 2008: 512). Whether Jenny ever met Lisette is not known.

Gemkow 2008: 511). Caroline, in contrast, remained benevolent toward him and still wrote him letters up until his death in 1856.[105] Ferdinand, who had a noteworthy career after his father's death and became the Prussian interior minister during the "period of reaction" after the defeat of the Revolution of 1848–49, appears to have still regarded her as a blemish. When in 1859 he published the papers of his grandfather on the campaigns of Duke Ferdinand during the Seven Years' War and introduced them with a brief family history, his father's second marriage and the children issuing from it are not mentioned.[106] What might have added to his aversion to his bourgeois stepmother in the meantime was that her daughter had married Karl Marx, who was regarded in Prussia after the Revolution of 1848–49 as a dangerous subversive, an unpleasant fact for a conservative interior minister.

It is not known whether Jenny attended a school. The gymnasium that her brother Edgar had attended with Karl Marx was, as usual for those times, a boys' school. It's possible that Jenny attended one of the schools in Trier for daughters of the upper class (Monz 1973: 344). In any case, her mother was very satisfied with Jenny's development. On February 9, 1827, she wrote to her cousin, the publisher and bookseller Friedrich Perthes: "My oldest daughter Jenny will be 13 years old on Monday, and I may say, beautiful in both soul and body, she is our true joy in the household" (Monz 1973d: 23).

In her parents' home, Jenny obtained an education that was far beyond the usual for women at the time, even in bourgeois circles. From a letter that Carl von Westphalen wrote to his brother Ferdinand on February 11, 1836 (printed in Gemkow 2008: 514), we learn that Jenny later took English lessons with a language teacher named Thornton, who did not, however, speak any German, only French, so that translations from English to French were practiced. Jenny also read many French books in a reading circle. Carl reports further that Ludwig von Westphalen, when he came home from the Casino in the evenings, provided an overview of news from the newspapers. Her father probably had at least as great an influence upon Jenny's intellectual development as upon Karl Marx's. He inspired in both an enthusiasm for Shakespeare that would last for the rest of their lives, and he probably contributed to their developing an alert regard for political and social conditions. Krosigk (1957: 709) reports that in the 1830s, Jenny had positioned herself on the side of "Young Germany," the group of writers whose works had been banned in December of 1835 by the German Bundestag. Even if

---

105. Ferdinand told this to Jenny in a letter from July 25, 1856 (Hecker/Limmroth 2014: 211).
106. This omission bothered Jenny enormously. See her letter from December 23–24, 1859, to Friedrich Engels (MECW 40: 575).

there is no further evidence for this assertion,[107] it appears plausible, considering the rest of the information we have about Jenny.

At the age of sixteen or seventeen, daughters of the upper classes usually attended a ball for the first time, and were thus introduced to "high society" and the marriage market. That was also the case for Jenny, and she must have made an impressive appearance. Despite having been absent from Trier for twenty years, she was remembered as the "queen of the ball."[108] With her brown hair, brown eyes, and dainty figure, she corresponded to the beauty ideal of the time, which promised good chances on the marriage market, despite a small dowry. A beautiful appearance and modesty were decisive criteria for young women to fulfill. A portrait painting, probably made in the year 1832, shows her in a green, almost shoulderless dress with a broad décolletage, which like her hairstyle corresponded to the fashion of the Biedermeier period. The green dress is contrasted with a long dark band worn around her neck. Angela Limmroth (2014: 257) points out that it is very probably a lorgnon band. The lorgnon, a small reading glass, was a popular fashion accessory at the time, and it also indicated erudition.[109]

Fitting with this picture, Jenny's stepbrother Ferdinand wrote in 1834 on the occasion of a visit: "Jenny was equipped with the charms of youth,

---

107. Lutz Graf Schwerin von Krosigk, a grandson of Jenny's stepsister Lisette, based this upon family letters that were lost during or shortly after the Second World War.

108. On December 15, 1863, Karl Marx wrote from Trier to Jenny in London that he was asked daily about "the most beautiful girl in Trier" and "the queen of the ball" (MECW 41: 499).

109. We know nothing about the painter of this picture. After the death of Jenny's mother, Caroline, Ferdinand mentions in a letter to Jenny the portrait of her that hung in her parents' home, but without any further detail (July 27, 1856, Hecker/Limmroth 2014: 213). Laura, the second-oldest daughter of Karl and Jenny, wrote on January 8, 1909, to John Spargo, who prepared the first large biography of Marx, that she possessed an oil painting depicting her mother at the age of eighteen, and that she would send him a photograph of this painting (MEJ Bd. 8: 304). The photo was then printed in Spargo's book (Spargo 1912: 40). If Laura's statement concerning Jenny's age is correct, the portrait must have been painted in 1832. In 1957, a great-grandchild of Jenny's sold the painting to the German Democratic Republic. There is also a second oil painting, that supposedly depicts the young Jenny. In that one, she isn't wearing the lorgnon band, but rather a red coral necklace and matching red earrings. This second picture was given to the Marx-Engels-Lenin Institute in Moscow by one of Jenny's grandchildren in 1948. Although the two women depicted indeed resemble each other, it cannot be ruled out that they are two different people. Limmroth raises doubts about the identification of the second painting: since portraits were costly, it's unlikely that the von Westphalen family could afford a second portrait of Jenny within such a short period of time. In addition, one finds no mention of a second portrait in either letters of the family or in any memoirs (Limmroth 2014: 261n26).

beautiful girl, expressive countenance, superior to most of her peers through her bright mind and energetic character traits" (quoted in Gemkow 2008: 512).

Unsurprisingly, Jenny did not lack admirers. We know from Ferdinand's memoirs as well as the letters of Ferdinand and his wife, Louise, evaluated by Monz (1973d) that in 1831, as a seventeen-year-old, Jenny got engaged to the second lieutenant Karl von Pannewitz (1803–1856) who was eleven years older and stationed with his regiment in Trier (Monz 1973d: 29). However, Jenny must have quickly recognized that he didn't suit her. After a short time, they canceled the engagement. A letter from Louise shows that it was a "lack of knowledge, a sense for it" (quoted in Monz 1973d: 30) that so disturbed Jenny.[110] In 1831, Pannewitz was transferred to another city; Jenny probably never saw him again. In this period, engagements and marriages were important family matters in which parents usually had a decisive voice. But apparently, both the engagement as well as its cancellation were decisions made solely by Jenny, which speaks to the "energetic character" Ferdinand referred to, but also to the liberal attitude of her parents.

Engagement to Karl

Karl Marx had known Jenny's brother Edgar at least since 1830, when they both entered the third class of gymnasium. They must have become friends quickly: as mentioned in chapter 1, the older Edgar spent much time in his youth in Marx's house (Gemkow 2008: 507n33). If Ludwig von Westphalen discussed literature and politics during his long walks with Edgar and Karl, which Karl recalled in the dedication of his dissertation, then Jenny was probably present at times. Jenny later wrote regarding her relationship to Edgar: "He was the ideal of my childhood and youth, my dear, only companion. I was attached to him with my entire soul" (letter from May 25, 1865, Hecker/Limmroth 2014: 372).

In the first years of the friendship between Karl and Edgar, the age difference relative to Jenny likely played a large role. When Jenny briefly got engaged at the age of seventeen in 1831, Karl was thirteen. A few years later, however, the age difference was less important. In the biographical literature on Karl as well as Jenny, the predominant opinion is that both secretly got engaged in the summer or autumn of 1836. Angelika Limmroth writes in what is up to now the most diligent biography of Jenny Marx that after Karl

---

110. On the reactions to the engagement and its cancellation, see Krosigk (1975: 26ff.) and Limmroth (2014: 53).

had spent a year in Bonn and returned to Trier in the summer of 1836, "it hit both of them like a bolt of lightning: their youth friendship became a stormy love" (Limmroth 2014: 60). The MEGA (III/1: 729) also states that the engagement occurred during the "autumn vacation of 1836." That Karl and Jenny got engaged in autumn of 1836 at the latest is obvious. From the autumn of 1836, Jenny and the engagement are mentioned in Heinrich Marx's letters (he was let in on the secret). Many times, Heinrich admonishes his son that considering the responsibility he had taken on, he must finish quickly with his studies.

It can be doubted, however, whether the engagement really *first* occurred in summer–autumn of 1836. The only statement made by Karl Marx concerning the moment of his engagement is found in a letter to Arnold Ruge from March 13, 1843: "I have been engaged for more than seven years" (MECW 1: 399). If Karl Marx had then been engaged for over seven years in March of 1843, then the engagement must have happened before March of 1836. Provided that Karl and Jenny did not meet secretly after Karl's departure from Trier, the engagement must have happened in September or October of 1835. Two statements by Eleanor also lead to this determination of date. In her reminiscences of her father published in 1895, she wrote: "As children, Karl and Jenny played together. As a young man and a young woman—he was 17, she was 21—they became engaged. And like Jacob and Rachel, Marx waited on Jenny for 7 years, before he took her home"[111] (E. Marx 1895: 249). On February 12, 1836, Jenny turned twenty-two. If she had gotten engaged to Marx at the age of twenty-one, then this must have happened before February of 1836. If the engagement had occurred in October of 1835, shortly before Karl's departure from Trier, then at the wedding in June of 1843, eight years had not yet elapsed from the time of engagement, and the statement that the engagement had lasted seven years would still be correct. In another statement of Eleanor's, published two years later, she refers to the seventeen-year-old Marx being engaged, which was accepted by his parents when he turned eighteen (E. Marx 1897–98: 237).

If it is not the case that all the direct statements made by Karl Marx and Eleanor concerning the moment of engagement are false, then Karl and Jenny

---

111. As reported in the first Book of Moses, Jacob, the son of Isaac and grandson of Abraham, loved Rachel. But Rachel's father, Laban, demanded that before getting married, Jacob would have to work for him for seven years, which he did. During the wedding night, however, Laban substituted his older and less beautiful daughter Leah for Rachel. In order to still win Rachel, Jacob had to work for Laban for another seven years, and then had two wives. Karl was at least spared the additional seven years.

must have been secretly engaged for a year in the summer of 1836. It appears plausible that the engagement occurred in the barely three weeks between the oral Abitur examinations and Karl's departure from Trier. The tension accompanying the examinations was over, and the time was approaching when the two childhood friends would have to be separated for a longer time. Both were probably unsure of how the other's feelings would develop: perhaps Jenny, who was at her most marriageable age, would meet a young man during one of the winter balls; perhaps Karl would encounter another woman in the unfamiliar city. The impending farewell might have scared them and led to a secret engagement.

We don't know if Karl and Jenny had the opportunity during the first year of secretly exchanging letters. It can no longer be determined whether even Karl's trip to Holland in the winter of 1835–36, which we know about because of statements made in his parents' letters, served to accommodate a secret meeting with Jenny. In the summer of 1836, in any case, for the first time they were together again for a few weeks[112] and could consider the state of their love. Not only were both a year older; when Karl left Trier in 1835, he was a recent secondary school graduate, and Jenny was already a young woman. The year in Bonn had probably made him a more independent young man, who now came across differently to Jenny. In any case, their relationship appears to have become more intense during this summer. When Marx passed over the previous year in review in that famous letter to his father from November 10, 1837, he wrote concerning his departure from Trier in October of 1836: "When I left you, a new world had come into existence for me, that of love" (MECW 1: 11). The first person let in on this secret (or who found out coincidentally) was Karl's father. According to Eleanor's report, it must have led to "rather heavy scenes." "My father," Eleanor writes about Marx, "used to say he was a veritable furious Roland" (E. Marx 1897/98: 238).[113] As emerges from the letters of Heinrich Marx, however, he must have accepted the engagement rather quickly and kept the secret from Jenny's parents.

It is understandable that Karl and Jenny initially kept their engagement secret, though it went considerably against the conventions of the time. The problem was not, as one still reads, that a large social gap existed between

---

112. His father's letter from March 19, 1836, mentions Karl visiting soon (MECW 1: 653). If he spent Easter of 1836 in Trier, it would have only been for a few days, so as not to miss any courses.

113. *Orlando Furioso* (the furious or raging Roland) is a famous epic poem by Ludovico Ariosto (1474–1533), which takes place during the time of Charlemagne and contains a

Karl and Jenny's families or the fact that Karl came from what was originally a Jewish family.[114] Religion probably played the least role. Converted Jews, particularly when they belonged to the upper classes, were quickly socially accepted in the period before the rise of racist anti-Semitism.[115] The fact that Jenny's father was a nobleman, whereas Karl came from a non-noble family, was also not too important. The noble status of the Westphalens was not very old, it was a case of service nobility (*Dienstadel*); Ludwig was not at all a "baron," and he had himself married a "bourgeois" woman in his second marriage. On the other hand, Heinrich Marx was one of the most well-respected citizens of Trier. The social position of both fathers was rather similar. With regard to the wealth of both families, the Westphalens were the ones with problems. After Ludwig requested retirement for health reasons in 1834, he obtained a modest retirement pension of 1,125 talers annually, as well as a minimal amount of interest from a Scottish inheritance (Gemkow 2008: 513), whereas Heinrich Marx earned about 1,500 talers annually (Herres 1990: 197).

Things were different with regard to the age difference between Karl and Jenny and Karl's unsettled professional future. The image of the bourgeois family of this time was unambiguous: the man was supposed to provide the money necessary to keep a home at the level befitting his social station by practicing a respected profession; the woman was to keep house and raise the children. It was therefore usual within the bourgeoisie that men, if they didn't come from a very wealthy family, first started looking for wives at the age of twenty-five or later, that is, when they had finished their education and had a profession that could support a family (see Hausen 1988). The husband was therefore usually six or seven years older than the wife. Even an age difference of ten years or more was not uncommon. For the twenty-one-year-old Jenny, therefore, a twenty-seven- or twenty-eight-year-old lawyer, merchant, officer, or civil servant would have been the socially proper marriage candidate, but not a seventeen- or eighteen-year-old student. Marx entailed a double social risk. For one thing, it wasn't known when (and if) he would graduate university, and how things would then look for his career chances.

---

multitude of fantastic adventures, such as a trip to the moon.

114. For example, in Wheen's (2002: 29) biography: "It may seem surprising that a twenty-year-old princess of the Prussian ruling class—the daughter of Baron Ludwig von Westphalen—should have fallen for a bourgeois Jewish scallywag."

115. One of the most famous examples is Friedrich Julius Stahl (1802–1861), who advanced to become one of the prominent thinkers of Prussian conservatism and become the Prussian legal adviser to the monarch (Kronsyndikus) under Friedrich Wilhelm IV.

For another thing, there was the danger in the case of an eighteen-year-old lad that his first love might not endure for so long. If Karl were to cancel the engagement after three or four years, it wouldn't have any great influence upon his own marriage prospects. Jenny's, however, would have worsened considerably. It might sound odd from a contemporary perspective, but in her mid-twenties, she would have already been far beyond the best age for marriage. At the beginning of the nineteenth century, the majority of bourgeois women married between the ages of seventeen and twenty-two (Hausen 1988: 96).

Heinrich Marx perhaps saw the problem more clearly than his son. On December 28, he wrote to Karl in Berlin: "I have spoken with Jenny and I should have liked to be able to set her mind at rest completely. I did all I could but it is not possible to argue everything away. She still does not know how her parents will take the relationship. Nor is the judgment of relatives and the world a trifling matter. . . . She is making a priceless sacrifice for you. She is showing a self-denial which can only be fully appreciated in the light of cold reason. Woe to you, if ever in your life you could forget this!" (MECW 1: 664). Despite many tempests as well as some marital problems, Karl and Jenny held firmly to each other, and throughout the next forty-five years until Jenny's death. They had a first ally in Heinrich Marx.

THE FIRST YEAR IN BERLIN

When Karl departed Trier for Berlin in October of 1836, he could not make use of a railroad; he had to take a "post wagon" pulled by horses. The trip lasted five to seven days and was expensive: besides about 20 talers for the carriage, overnight stays and catering during the trip also had to be paid for (see Miller/Sawadzki 1956: 14, 213). Travelers had to cross multiple borders between different German states. Thanks to the German Customs Union which started in 1834, the duties that had existed previously had been dropped. Before the construction of the railroad network, travel was extraordinarily expensive and time-consuming. For that reason, Karl's parents never visited him in Berlin, and during his time in Berlin, he probably only visited Trier once.

The City and the Young Karl's Rounds

Berlin was the first big city in which Marx lived. Berlin was then considerably smaller than it is today, both in terms of population and surface area. Many of today's Berlin districts were still independent towns until the beginning of the twentieth century. The horse-drawn carriage went from Potsdam to Berlin,through the municipalities of Zehlendorf, Steglitz, and Schöneberg, which at the time were not part of Berlin. Only the names of subway stations today that end in "*Tor*" (gate) commemorate what were then the borders of Berlin: Frankfurter Tor, Schlesisches Tor, Kottbusser Tor, Hallesches Tor, Oranienburger Tor. The old town wall with its gates still existed; however, the rapidly growing city was already expanding "at the gates." If about 265,000 people inhabited Berlin in 1834, by 1840 there were 329,000, a growth in population of almost 25 percent over six years. This enormous growth resulted solely from migration; infant mortality was so high that the established population did not increase. Despite this increase, there was still a considerable difference in population between Berlin and the other big European capitals: 2.2 million people lived in London (1831), 900,000 in Paris (1836).[116]

When Marx arrived, Berlin was transforming itself from a provincial royal seat into an industrial city. The number of small workshops employing merely one or two journeymen had declined. At the same time, new workshops and large industrial enterprises (they were considered "large" if they had fifty employees) arose with a proletariat living under bad conditions, recruited from impoverished artisan families and rural migrants. On the basis of location—the Spree crossed an old trade route that led from Aachen to Königsberg—Berlin had always been a commercial city, but not a very rich one.

In the center of the city stood the massive city palace of the Hohenzollern, a not particularly sightly Baroque building, which was constructed in the seventeenth and early eighteenth centuries. Besides this, there were a number of urban palaces belonging to the Prussian nobility. In the urban population, civil servants and officers set the tone. Within the city, rich and poor lived close together, often in the same buildings, but strictly separated: "worthy people" lived on the ground floor, in the "*bel-etage*" (the first upper floor), and the "*Obergeschoß*" (the second upper floor). Poorer people lived in the cellar or on a further upper floor. The very poorest had a hovel under

---

116. Lots of information on the Berlin of the 1830s and 1840s can be found in the second volume of the Berlin stories of Adolf Streckfuß (1886). Special information on the 1830s is provided in the Conversation Handbook published by Freiherr von Zedlitz (1834). A critical depiction of both everyday life, as well as political life, in Berlin in the first half of the 1840s is provided by Friedrich Sass (1846) and Ernst Dronke (1846). The latter was convicted of lèse-majesté because of his book; in 1848, he was part of the editorial board of the *Neue Rheinische Zeitung* along with Marx. Focusing especially on Marx's life in Berlin are Miller/Sawadzki (1956) and Kliem (1988).

a staircase or lived in the attic. What is today referred to as a "Berliner Altbauwohnung," large apartments with high ceilings in five-story buildings, did not exist in Marx's time. Most of today's "Altbauten" were built at the end of the nineteenth and beginning of the twentieth century. The typical three-story residential buildings of Marx's time were torn down to build them. Buildings that are well-known today didn't exist when Marx was studying in Berlin: the Rotes Rathaus, Berlin's city hall, emerged around thirty years after Marx's stay, the Berlin Cathedral appeared at the end of the nineteenth century. When Marx came to Berlin, many streets were not even paved. The gas lighting operated by an English firm since 1826 existed for the larger streets and squares; the old oil lighting had to suffice everywhere else. Starting at 10 p.m., night watchmen moved through the streets with pikes and hounds.

The Berlin "corner men" (*Eckensteher*) had become known in all of Germany; these were commissionaires licensed by the police who stood at corners and waited on instructions. The farce *Eckensteher Nante im Verhör* (The Corner Man Nante under Interrogation) by Friedrich Beckmann (1803–1866) had its premiere in 1833 and was frequently performed, making Nante (based on Ferdinand Stump, a real person) the epitome of popular Berlin humor.

As the residence of the Prussian king, Berlin not only had numerous governmental and administrative offices, but also a diverse cultural life. There was an opera established by Friedrich II (the Staatsoper, which still exists today); a royal capella (the predecessor of today's Staatskapelle Berlin) with numerous violinists and cellists, which was able to perform operas and symphonies; a ballet; a playhouse encompassing about 1,400 people; as well as numerous public and private theaters. Here, the young Marx experienced the famous actor Karl Seydelmann (1793–1843), who left a lasting impression upon him. Wilhelm Liebknecht reports that in London, the Marx family often discussed literature during Sunday outings and fondly declaimed from the works of Dante Alighieri and Shakespeare. When Marx was "in the highest of high spirits, he represented Seydelmann as Mephisto. He adored Seidelmann, whom he had seen and heard in Berlin as a student, and *Faust* was his favourite German poem" (Liebknecht 1896/1908: 131).

Alongside the *Allgemeine Preußische Staatszeitung* published by the government since 1819 (called the *Allgemeine Preußische Zeitung* from 1843 on), there were two newspapers that had been published daily since the 1820s: the *Vossische Zeitung* (actually the *Königlich privilegierte Berlinische Zeitung von Staats- und gelehrten Sachen* but usually referred to by the name of its earlier owner), and the *Spenersche Zeitung*. After the Karlsbad Decrees, they were subject to strict censorship, which was intensified in the 1830s after the

Hambach Festival. As a result, both of these newspapers had become largely apolitical in the 1830s (Salomon 1906: 261ff., 355).

Whoever wanted to be politically informed had to read foreign, primarily French, newspapers, which was as good as impossible for the poorer strata. The politically interested bourgeoisie were drawn to the Berlin confectioneries where there were not only baked goods, but also various German and foreign newspapers. One came to be informed and to discuss. The audience of the various confectioneries varied considerably, both in terms of social situations as well as political attitudes. The confectioneries for the lowest strata of the bourgeoisie only had a few newspapers on offer, while those catering to the more upscale strata offered a selection of German and foreign newspapers. Across from the Stadtschloss, there was the confectionery Josty, a meeting point for merchants and stock market speculators; higher-level public officials could also be seen here. In Kranzler on Unter den Linden, rich aristocratic dandies and guard lieutenants tried to outdo each other in their snobbery. Conservatives of various stripes met in the confectionery Spargnapani, also on Unter den Linden. In contrast, literati, artists, and the more or less radical critics of existing conditions could be found in the café Stehely on Gendarmenmarkt. Friedrich Saß (1846: 52ff.) in his description of some of the Berlin confectioneries characterized some of the well-known visitors of Stehely, such as Eduard Meyen, Johann Caspar Schmidt (a.k.a. Max Stirner), or Adolf Rutenberg, all acquaintances of Karl Marx. One can assume that as a student Marx was also a frequent guest of Stehely. Saß does not mention him; when he wrote his book, Marx had not been living in Berlin for quite a while.

The affluent bourgeoisie and the nobility were not reliant upon the confectioneries; they met in salons, such as that of Rahel Varnhagen (1771–1833) or in the various table societies (usually reserved for men), such as the Deutsche Tischgesellschaft (which had an emphatically anti-Semitic attitude; even converted Jews were denied membership) founded by Achim von Arnim (1781–1831), or the Gesetzlose Gesellschaft (Lawless Society; the name derives from the idea that this society did not issue any rules of conviviality), which still exists today. In the table societies, talks were held and discussed during a common meal.

In the winter of 1836–37, when Marx took up his studies in Berlin, the "Laube affair" was kicking up a lot of dust. Heinrich Laube (1806–1884), one of the "Junges Deutschland" writers, and a friend of Karl Gutzkow, had always written critically about the Prussian royal house and the Russian tsars allied with it, was arrested in 1834 for such criticisms and had already spent many months in custody. At the instigation of Gustav Adolf von Tzschoppes (1794–1842), one of the members of the commission against demagogic activity and notorious for his prosecutorial enthusiasm, the Berlin Superior Court of Justice (Kammergericht) tried the case and ultimately sentenced Laube at the end of 1836 to seven years of imprisonment because he had criticized the Prussian king and the Russian tsar—and because he had been a member of a Burschenschaft in the 1820s. However, in 1837, Laube's high-ranking advocates managed to achieve a reduction of the sentence to eighteen months, as well as permission to serve the sentence on the estate of the Prince von Pückler-Muskau (Laube 1875: 351ff., Houben 1906).

Marx's first years of study in Berlin coincided with the final years of the reign of the Prussian king, Friedrich Wilhelm III, who had sat on the throne since 1797. At the beginning of his reign, he was quite popular, since he appeared modest, put an end to the keeping of court mistresses that was usual in the eighteenth century, and exhibited an almost bourgeois family life with his wife, Luise. However, because of the broken promise of a constitution and his increasingly reactionary policies, he became more and more unpopular, which stoked distrust of the population on the part of the government. In the 1820s and 1830s, even the smallest oppositional impulse (or what was regarded as such) was subject to surveillance and prosecution. When the king could have celebrated his forty-year jubilee in October 1837, any public celebration was waived, because protests and disruptions were feared. The hopes of large parts of the population were directed toward his son, since his aversion to his father's military monarchy was known. It was expected that he would finally transform Prussia into a liberal state with bourgeois liberties; however, these hopes were crushed soon after his ascension to the throne in 1840.

WHEN THE EIGHTEEN-YEAR-OLD MARX arrived in Berlin in October of 1836, he probably had a few letters of recommendation from his father in tow. Such letters, written by parents, close relatives, or friends of the parents and addressed to acquaintances or business associates, were supposed to make access to higher social circles in a strange city easier for a young student. They paid visits, delivered the letters of recommendation, and were then invited to further visits and celebrations, at which they could get to know more or less important people. Not infrequently, close connections were made to some of the families to whom the letters of recommendation were addressed, and these reported on the young man's further development to his parents.

His father's letters reveal that Karl made initial visits to multiple Berlin jurists (letter of November 9, 1836, MECW 1: 661). Among them were a few who indeed had important positions: the privy auditor council (Geheime Revisionsrat) Johann Peter Esser (1786–1856), and the privy superior auditor council (Geheime Oberrevisionsrat) Franz Ludwig Jaehnigen (1801–1866) sat in the presidium of the Rhenish Appellate and Cassation Court, the highest court for the "Rhenish law" that was still valid in the Rhineland provinces and based upon the Code Civil introduced by Napoleon. Both had previously been active in the district court of Trier; Heinrich Marx probably knew them from this time. Another acquaintance of Marx's father, Privy Councilor Meurin, who Karl also visited, was connected to this district court: he was the director of the exchequer.

Two further members of the Rhenish Appellate Court, Friedrich Karl von Savigny and August Wilhelm Heffter, taught at the university. In the winter semester of 1836–37, Karl Marx attended a lecture course of Savigny's, and three of Heffter's in the summer semester of 1837. There was a pending case against Heinrich Marx at this Rhenish Appellate Court. The municipality of Irsch, which had been represented by Heinrich Marx in 1832, had sued him for exceeding his mandate. This suit was dismissed by the district court of Trier on February 7, 1833, but accepted on June 12, 1833, by the appellate court of Cologne. Heinrich Marx thereupon filed an application to dismiss with the Berlin Appellate Court (MEGA III/1: 729). The matter was still sitting there in the winter of 1836 and was not progressing. That's why Heinrich Marx gave his son the task of inquiring about the state of the proceedings to Judicial Council Reinhard, who represented him before the court, as well as to Judicial Council Sandt, the attorney of the counterparty (letter of November 9, 1836, MECW 1: 662). When nothing was decided ten months later, Heinrich asked his son to see Reinhard and request that he speed up the matter, the outcome having become of secondary importance: "Win or lose, I have cares enough and should like to have this worry off my mind at least" (letter of September 16, 1837, MECW 1: 682). But everything was already underway, since only a few days later, on September 23, there was a judgment: the Cologne judgment was "scrapped," that is to say, the decision was in favor of Heinrich Marx (MEGA III/1: 729).

When Heinrich Marx brokered contact between Karl and Berlin jurists, he not only had his own legal proceedings in mind, but above all his son's professional advancement. As emerges from his letter of November 9, Jaehnigen and Esser had expressed themselves positively about Karl (MECW 1: 661). Karl even seems to have had a closer relationship to the Jaehnigen family for a while, for when he became ill in the summer of 1837, Frau Jaehnigen wrote to Jenny multiple times (letter from Heinrich Marx of August 12, 1837, MECW 1: 676). However, Karl seems to have broken off contact, since his father points out with regard to Jaehnigen that Karl had "missed a lot" and that "perhaps you could have acted more wisely" (ibid.). What exactly happened, we don't know.

Of particular importance for Karl's later juridical career would have been the Privy Auditor Council Esser, who was also a member of the immediate justice examination commission. This commission had the task of examining those jurists who wished to be employed by the state justice councils (Landes-Justiz-Kollegien) or also by the larger lower courts throughout the kingdom (Kliem 1988: 31). But Karl resisted building his own career by making contacts (this is mentioned by his father, who notes his son's "strict principles," MECW 1: 661); his career wishes were not directed toward one in the judicial service (see below). However, Esser appears to have maintained his good opinion of Karl. As Marx reports in a letter from March 3, 1860, to Julius Weber (MECW 41: 101), Esser had offered Marx a job in the summer of 1843, after the *Rheinische Zeitung*, which Marx had directed, was banned.

Apart from these contacts brokered by his father, Karl does not seem to have initiated any relationships during the first months of his stay in Berlin. In the letter from November 1837, in which he looks back on his first year in Berlin, he writes: "After my arrival in Berlin, I broke off all hitherto existing connections, made visits rarely and unwillingly, and tried to immerse myself in science and art" (MECW 1: 11). It's not known what connections these were.

Hegel and the University of Berlin

At the beginning of the nineteenth century, there was no university in Berlin, even though it was the capital of the increasingly powerful kingdom of Prussia. Theologians and state officials were educated at the University of Frankfurt (Oder), and more prestigiously at the University of Halle. However, scientific research was being conducted in Berlin at the Academy of Sciences founded by Gottfried Wilhelm Leibniz in 1700. There had long been proposals to found a university in Berlin, but these only took concrete form after Prussia's defeat in 1806, when French troops occupied Halle and closed the university there. In the course of a wide-ranging process of reform that followed the defeat, the University of Berlin was founded in 1809, and officially started teaching activities in 1810. In 1828, it was named after the Prussian King Friedrich-Wilhelm. After the Second World War it obtained the name it has today, Humboldt University, in honor of the Humboldt brothers. The university was housed in the Prince Heinrich Palais, the building on Unter den Linden that still serves as its main building today.

Wilhelm von Humboldt (1767–1835), as leader of the directorate of culture and education, was involved decisively in the founding of the university. Important generators of ideas were the philosopher Johann Gottlieb Fichte (1762–1814) and the theologian Friedrich Schleiermacher (1768–1834). The founders wanted to make the university not only a center of scholarship, but also one of spiritual renewal. In 1811, Fichte became the first elected rector of the University of Berlin, which would soon assemble a faculty of excellent scholars. The organization of the university partially took up existing university subjects, but in part new university subjects were established, such as archaeology and comparative philology (see Baertschi/King 2009; Tenorth 2010). Medicine and the natural sciences were also well represented, so that the University of Berlin quickly gained in importance.

As in other places, in 1813 students in Berlin enthusiastically went to war in the anti-Napoleonic "Wars of Liberation" and were deeply disappointed by political developments after the victory. The Prussian king did not keep his promise of a constitution; instead of a liberal state, there came an authoritarian monarchy and, after the Karlsbad Decrees of 1819, repression, censorship, and spying were strongly expanded (see chapter 1). In Berlin, the surveillance of students was particularly strict.

Karl vom Stein zum Altenstein (1770–1840) played a central role in the early development of the University of Berlin. In 1817, he was named as the first Prussian minister of culture, retaining this office until his death. During his time in office, he fundamentally reformed the Prussian educational and school system. Among other things, in 1825 he expanded compulsory schooling to all of Prussia, and in 1834 introduced a uniform curriculum for the gymnasiums. After Humboldt's resignation in 1819 and the death of the state chancellor, Karl August von Hardenberg (1750–1822), Altenstein was the last reformer with a high-level position, but he had to defend himself against attacks from conservative circles, above all from the "crown prince party," that is, the friends of the crown prince and later king, Friedrich Wilhelm IV.

One important event, both for early Berlin university history as well as for intellectual life in Berlin, was the appointment of Georg Wilhelm Friedrich Hegel (1770–1831) to the professorial chair previously occupied by Fichte, who had died in 1814. As one of his first acts in office, Altenstein in December 1817 invited Hegel under rather favorable financial conditions to come to the University of Berlin. Hegel accepted and taught in Berlin from 1818 until his death.

That Altenstein made an effort to win Hegel right after assuming office was not only due to Hegel presenting himself as an important philosopher through his publications; in 1812–13 and 1816 his *Science of Logic* was published, and in 1817 the *Encyclopedia of the Philosophical Sciences*. On the one hand, Altenstein regarded philosophy as a leading field in the reform process, and on the other hand he regarded Hegel as a thinker whose starting point was enlightened, politically liberal notions, without appearing too provocative or even republican. To that extent, Hegel fit outstandingly with the Prussian reformers around Humboldt and Altenstein. Goethe, familiar with Hegel since Hegel's time in Jena, wrote on May 1, 1818, to the famous art collector Sulpiz Boisserée (1783–1854) concerning Hegel's appointment: "Minister Altenstein appears to want to acquire scholarly bodyguards" (Nicolin 1970: 173).[117]

Hegel was prepared to fulfill these expectations. In his inaugural address at the University of Berlin, he states with a view to the Prussian reforms: "And it is this state in particular, the state which has taken me into its midst, which, by virtue of its spiritual supremacy [*Übergewicht*], has raised itself to its [present] importance [*Gewicht*] in actuality and in the political realm, and has made itself the equal, in power and independence, of those states which may surpass it in external resources. Here, the cultivation and flowering of the sciences is one of the most essential moments—even of political life. In this university—as the central university—the center of all spiritual culture [*Geistesbildung*] and of all science and truth, namely philosophy, must also find its place and be treated with special care" (Hegel 1999: 182). According to Hegel's conception (and indeed Altenstein's), this special role of philosophy as the center of spiritual culture was to be completed primarily by Hegel's own philosophy.

However, Hegel was not welcomed from all quarters. Friedrich Schleiermacher would become his chief opponent, among other things preventing Hegel from being admitted to the Academy of Sciences. Despite such resistance, Hegel displayed expansive activity in Berlin. He attempted to philosophically penetrate an increasing number of fields of knowledge. The point was not to impose certain principles upon these fields "from outside," so to speak, but to uncover the formative and structuring principles in the objects themselves. The act of philosophical penetration that Hegel strove for thus presupposed enormous expertise in each field, regardless of whether one was dealing with politics or aesthetics; his philosophical reflections were therefore filled with all kinds of knowledge of reality. At the same time, he

---

117. Altenstein's policies, as well as Hegel's work at the University of Berlin, is dealt with in detail in volume 2.1 of the comprehensive *Geschichte der königlichen Friedrich-Wilhelms Universität zu Berlin* by Max Lenz (1910).

reflected upon the historical conditions of his philosophy: how had it become at all possible to think what he presented to the public? Which intellectual-conceptual preconditions had to be formed for that, and who formed them? Hegel very consciously placed his philosophy in a process of historical development. The universal as well as conclusive knowledge claims of his philosophy fascinated Hegel's contemporaries tremendously. His lectures were soon attended not only by students, but also by colleagues, state officials—the most prominent was probably Johannes Schulze (1786–1869), who was responsible for the universities in Altenstein's ministry—and educated citizens. This despite Hegel's less-than-attractive lecturing style. Heinrich Gustav Hotho (1802–1873), who had studied with Hegel, belonged to his circle of friends, and after Hegel's death published his *Lectures on Aesthetics*, describing his style of lecturing as follows: "He sat there tense and sullen, collapsed and with his head lowered, and leafed through the folio notebooks, searching as he spoke. . . . The constant throat clearing and coughing disturbed the entire flow of the talk, every sentence stood there isolated, and emerged with strain chopped and jumbled up," and all this "in broad Swabian dialect." Hotho continues that whoever was able to follow Hegel, however, "saw himself displaced into the strangest tension and fear. To what abyss was thought led down, to what endless antagonisms torn apart." Yet Hegel's conclusions were "so clear and exhaustive, of such simple truthfulness, that anyone capable of grasping it felt like he had invented and thought of it himself" (quoted in Nicolin 1970: 246, 248).

In Berlin, a Hegelian school began to take shape, with its own journal, the *Jahrbücher für wissenschaftliche Kritik*, that started publication in 1827. Altenstein and Schulze made every effort to support Hegel's students by appointing them to professorships and defending them against attacks. After Hegel's unexpected death—in 1831 he fell victim to the cholera rampant in Berlin—his students and friends, together with Hegel's widow, founded an "Association of Friends of the Immortalized," and quickly organized an edition of his works including previously unpublished lectures, the contents of which went well beyond his main works. Thus with this Association of Friends Edition (*Freundes-Vereins-Ausgabe*), which was published 1832–45, the *Philosophy of History*, the *Aesthetics*, and the *Philosophy of Religion* were published for the first time, which considerably increased the effect of Hegel's philosophy. When Marx arrived in Berlin in 1836, Hegelianism was one of the most influential currents in German philosophy, and Berlin was its center.

The young Marx was also not able to escape the impact of this philosophy: "I became ever more firmly bound to the modern world philosophy," he wrote his father in a letter from November 10, 1837. However, Marx did not only engage once with Hegel's work. During various times of his life, he did the same, and formulated critiques that by no means always had the same thrust.

To this day there has been controversial discussion over how strongly Marx was influenced by Hegel. Judging Marx's relationship to Hegel, however, cannot be conducted independently of how one evaluates Hegel's philosophy. Judgments of Hegel vary as widely as those concerning Marx, with widely divergent evaluations found by both Marxists as well as critics of Marx. Similar to the case of Marx, the discussion of Hegel in the last fifty years has profited considerably from the historical-critical edition of his works.[118] The image of Hegel predominant among the general public has, however, remained largely untouched by these debates. The same is the case for how the various Marx biographies deal with Hegel, generally drawing a rather simplistic picture of him. Usually, Hegel is regarded either as the one who first grasped the "dialectical" development of nature, history, and society, albeit in an "idealist" manner, that is, as the development and self-recognition of "spirit,"[119] or he is regarded as an unscientific metaphysician, who only perceived reality through the abstract templates of his philosophy of mind and thus provided an extremely distorted, useless picture. Correspondingly, Hegel's influence on Marx is evaluated in very different ways: by some as an important impetus in the formation of Marx's own investigations, by others as an enticement to unscientific speculation, which Marx—this is again subject to differing judgments—either succumbed to or did not.

Here, I will forgo a rushed outline of Hegel's philosophy of the sort that one encounters in many biographies of Marx, since usually such summaries promote misunderstandings.[120] I will deal more closely with individual elements of Hegel's philosophy when necessary to follow the development of Marx's work. Here, it should merely be made clear that a few of the widespread opinions of Hegel are more like preconceptions.

Engaging with Hegel isn't very easy: his characteristic linguistic style is foreign to us; the complex of philosophical and political problems that he was reacting to are no longer common currency; and not infrequently,

---

118. The publisher Meiner Verlag in Hamburg has been issuing a historical-critical edition of Hegel's works since 1968 under the title *Gesammelte Werke* (Collected Works).

119. *Geist*, sometimes translated as "mind"—Trans.

120. An overview of Hegel's works and creative periods is provided in the *Hegel-Handbuch* by Jaeschke (2003). The most recent biography is by Pinkard (2000).

Hegel only hints at the positions he criticizes and assumes that the reader is familiar with them. At first reading, Hegel's texts give the impression of not only being incomprehensible, but downright impenetrable. The notion of Hegel as a perhaps deep, but largely inaccessible philosopher is widespread. It's also supported by a painting that one can hardly avoid, even if one has engaged only superficially with Hegel, the portrait by the artist and restorer Johann Jakob Schlesinger (1792–1855), who knew Hegel well, shortly before Hegel's death in 1831. Without further objects such as books or manuscripts, Hegel is depicted against a dark red, almost black background, in a high-necked white shirt worn under a green coat with a brown fur collar. All of this serves only to frame the head, which stands fairly at the center of the picture, immediately drawing the attention of the viewer. Schlesinger's portrait appears to embellish nothing. It shows the sixty-one-year-old Hegel marked by effort, with noticeable bags under his slightly red eyes. His skin is in places droopy and wrinkled, his hair gray and thin. The few remaining strands of hair on his head fall forward, nestled closely to the head, where they insufficiently cover the bald forehead. The most expressive aspect of this portrait is Hegel's look: clear and concentrated. He is absolutely present. He looks sideways at the viewer without turning his head. This attitude has something doubting, skeptical about it, as if Hegel is considering whether he should really deal with this counterpart. Hegel appears inaccessible. He is occupied, concentrated upon his work.

The suggestive power of this popular portrait should not be underestimated.[121] Contrary to what the portrait suggests, Hegel was not at all a thinker lost in his own reveries, divorced from practical reality. In Jena, he had sired an illegitimate son, Ludwig Fischer (1807–1831), with his landlady Johanna Burkhardt (born Fischer). In 1811, Hegel married Marie von Tucher (1791–1855), who was twenty years younger. Besides a daughter who died shortly after childbirth, the couple had two sons, Karl (1813–1901) and Immanuel (1814–1891). Hegel was able to achieve an academic career only late in life. After finishing his studies of philosophy and Protestant theology, he initially worked as a private tutor in Bern and Frankfurt am Main, before doing his postdoctoral qualification in philosophy in Jena in 1801. But since

---

121. Jonathan Sperber, in whose Marx biography it is also printed, also appears to have succumbed to it. Regarding Kant and Hegel, he writes: "These two greatest figures of German idealism were both lifelong bachelors, married as it were to the ethereal world of philosophy" (Sperber 2013: 49). Kant was, in fact, a bachelor. Hegel was married and stood with both feet firmly on the ground.

he was only able to obtain a poorly paid, associate professorship there, in 1807 he took over the editorship of the *Bamberger Zeitung* and promptly had problems with censorship authorities. In 1808, he became rector of the Ägidiengymnasium in Nuremberg. In 1816 he first obtained a professorship, at the University of Heidelberg. In 1818, finally, he was appointed to the University of Berlin. Hegel was familiar with the requirements of practical life in every regard. In the appointment negotiations with Altenstein, one of the first things Hegel addressed was payments to the widow's insurance system, in order to provide for the financial security of his wife and children in the case of his death (letter to Altenstein, January 28, 1818, Hegel 1984: 379).

Also problematic is the classification, still used as if self-evident, of Hegel as a representative of German idealism. Hegel himself, as well as his contemporaries, would have reacted with considerable astonishment to such a classification. In 1840, under the entry for "Idealism" an encyclopedia classified the teachings of Johann Gottlieb Fichte as part of philosophical idealism, since he understood the external world, the "not-I,"[122] confronting the "I"[123] as being posited by the "I" whereby "I" does not refer to an individual self, but rather the ability to think inherent to each individual, which is why the positing of the "not-I" is not individual and arbitrary. Hegel's system, however, was explicitly excluded from idealism (*Allgemeines Deutsches Conversations-Lexicon*, vol. 5, 1840: 490).

Jaeschke (2000) has sketched out the genealogy of the term *German idealism*. In a less specific sense, the expression is already found in the early writings of Marx and Engels, *The Holy Family* (1845) and the (unpublished) "German Ideology" (1845–46), but in those works it still did not have much influence. It was first the neo-Kantian Friedrich Albert Lange (1828–1875) who, with his influential *History of Materialism* (1866), placed the term within the context of a conflict between "materialism" and "idealism." As a category in the history of philosophy it was established starting in 1880 by another neo-Kantian, Wilhelm Windelband (1848–1915), in the second volume of his *Geschichte der neueren Philosophie* (History of Modern Philosophy), which understood German Idealism to be a precursor of the German nation-state created by Bismarck. It was in the subsequent period that the concept was frequently confined to the triumvirate of Fichte, Schelling, and Hegel, whereby there were, Jaeschke (2000) continues, considerable problems in determining what was common to this German idealism. As a result, it can be stated that talk of German Idealism, which was to

122. *Nicht-Ich* —Trans.
123. *Ich* —Trans.

become self-evident, obscures the complexity of post-Kantian philosophy rather than illuminating it.[124]

Also stubbornly persistent is the notion that the "Prussian state philosopher" had, in his *Philosophy of Right* published in 1820, legitimized the Prussian monarchy, which had become increasingly authoritarian after the end of the reform period. This notion was advanced particularly aggressively in Rotter and Welcker's *Staats-Lexikon* from 1846.[125] The nationalist liberal Rudolf Haym (1821–1901) even wrote in his Hegel biography published in 1857—which had a lasting influence upon the image of Hegel in the latter half of the nineteenth century—of a "philosophy of restoration" (Haym 1857: 361). In the twentieth century, authors such as Popper considered Hegel as a precursor to Hitler (see Popper 1945, ch. 12).[126] Some Marxists as well, such as Cornu (1954: 78) or in the last few years Antonio Negri, who understands the author of the *Philosophy of Right* to be the "philosopher of the bourgeois and capitalist organization of labor" (Negri 2011: 37), follow in the lineage of Haym's critique of Hegel. Marx reacted rather indignantly to a similar statement by Wilhelm Liebknecht. On May 10, 1870, he wrote about it to Engels: "I had written to him that if, when he wrote about Hegel, he knew nothing better than to repeat the old Rotteck-Welcker muck, then he would do better to keep his mouth shut" (MECW 43: 511).

The early critique of Hegel had been ignited primarily by a sentence from the preface to the *Philosophy of Right*: "What is rational is actual; and what is actual is rational" (Hegel 1991: 20). This sentence was taken to be a philosophical justification of the existing Prussian state, which then spared the critique from having to take a closer look at the main text of the *Philosophy of Right*. The fact that Hegel noted in 1827, in the introduction to the second edition of his *Encyclopedia of the Philosophical Sciences* (Hegel 2010: 33) with regard to this preface, that he had already made a distinction in *The Science of Logic* between "actuality" and merely coincidental "existence," was simply ignored by his critics. If one takes this distinction into consideration, then the

---

124. The development of post-Kantian philosophy is presented in a differentiated way in Jaeschke/Arndt (2012).

125. See the articles "Hegelsche Philosophie und Schule" and "Hegel (Neu-hegelianer)," in the 2nd ed., vol. 6 (Scheidler 1846a, 1846b). There, all the usual arguments against Hegel of that time are listed, regardless of whether they fit together. The author, Karl Hermann Scheidler (1795-1866), was a founder of the original Burschenschaft in Jena in 1815 and a student of Jakob Friedrich Fries, who had been sharply attacked by Hegel.

126. Brief overviews of the varied reception of Hegel's *Philosophy of Right* are provided by Riedel (1975) and Schnädelbach (2000: 333–53). Ottmann (1977), even though some of his judgments are problematic, is far more extensive.

sentence criticized contains—instead of a justification of that which exists—
a threat against the existence of the unreasonable: no actuality belongs to it;
it must "collapse," as Hegel elaborated in the preface to his lectures held in
1818–19. There, Hegel argues, the state of law rests upon "the general spirit
of the people," but if "the spirit of the people ascends to a higher level, the
constitutional elements referring to an earlier level no longer hold; they must
collapse, and no power is able to keep them. Thus, philosophy recognizes
that only the rational is able to occur, even if individual external phenomena
may appear to resist it so strongly" (Nachschrift Homeyer, in Hegel 1973–74:
1:232). The late Engels as well, in *Ludwig Feuerbach and the End of Classical
German Philosophy* (1886), summarizes the contested sentence from the
preface in a rather critical sense, undermining that which exists, and laconi-
cally characterizes the history of its influence: "No philosophical proposition
has earned more gratitude from narrow-minded governments and wrath
from equally narrow-minded liberals" (MECW 26: 358).

If one considers the development of Hegel's political views, there are
noticeable transformations. The young Hegel was not only enthusiastic
about the French Revolution, showing republican tendencies; in a text written in 1796 or 1797, even anarchistic notes, critical of the state, can be heard:
"First—I want to show that there is no idea of the state because the *state* is
something *mechanical*, just as little as there is an idea of a *machine*. Only that
which is the object of *freedom* is called *idea*. We must therefore go beyond
the state!—Because every state must treat free human beings like mechanical
works; and it should not do that; therefore it should *cease*. . . . At the same
time I want to set forth the principles for a *history of a human race* here and
expose the whole miserable human work of state, constitution, government,
legislature—down to the skin" (Behler 1987: 161).[127] The older Hegel, in contrast, tended toward constitutional monarchy, which, however, was far from
existing in Prussia.

When Hegel wanted to publish his *Philosophy of Right* in 1819, universities
had lost their freedom from censorship in the wake of the Karlsbad Decrees,
and Hegel delayed publication. Very probably, he partially reworked the
manuscript. As Ilting (1973) has demonstrated by a comprehensive comparison of the lecture transcripts published by him, created both before and

---

127. This text was first published in 1917 under the title *The Oldest Systematic Program of
German Idealism*; it is based upon collective discussions between Schelling, Hölderlin, and
Hegel. In the Tübinger Stift, the study house of the Protestant state church of Württemberg,
these three figures, who would go on to become famous, studied together, for a while even
sharing a room.

after the publication of *The Philosophy of Right*, Hegel avoided a number of pointed formulations in the published text that appear in the lectures. Hegel apparently wanted to avoid providing any point of attack to the reaction. However, he maintained the liberal core of his views, that the state should make possible the freedom of the individual. Public court cases, trial by jury, freedom of the press—all of these liberal demands, which were far from being realized, or realized completely, in Prussia, can be found in Hegel's *Philosophy of Right*. Hegel found himself fighting on two fronts: he criticized both the nationalist, German-chauvinist circles around Jahn, Fries, and the Romantics (which had turned reactionary) as well as the restorative state doctrine of Karl Ludwig von Haller (1768–1854) and the conservatism of Gustav von Hugo and Savigny, the representatives of the German Historical School of Law.[128]

In his *Philosophy of Right*, Hegel deals with the new "civil society," a sphere located between that of the family on one side and that of the state on the other, and which did not exist in earlier social formations. His continuous theme is the possibility of *freedom* within this new constellation.[129] In his "Lectures on the Philosophy of History," Hegel conceived of "freedom" as the "final aim" of world history, "at which the process of the World's History has been continually aiming; and to which the sacrifices that have ever and anon been laid on the vast altar of the earth, through the long lapse of ages, have been offered" (Hegel 1956:19).

This orientation toward human freedom was not limited to theoretical discussions. As police records that were first evaluated in the twentieth century show, Hegel made every effort to support, financially as well as personally, those of his students and assistants who were persecuted and jailed as "demagogues" by the Prussian state (see d'Hondt 1973: 96ff.; Ilting 1973: 51ff.).

We will deal more in depth with Hegel's *Philosophy of Right* when we turn to the critique Marx formulated in his Kreuznach manuscript of 1843.

---

128. These multiple fronts, contemporary conflicts, and Hegel's Berlin "cultural politics" are discussed more extensively by Losurdo (1989). See also d'Hondt (1973), Pöggeler (1986), Klenner (1991: 143ff.), and Pinkard (2000: 418ff.).

129. This is recognized in many contributions to recent Hegel research, even if they come from different conditions. To name just two examples, that of Klaus Vieweg, who understands *The Philosophy of Right*, to which he provides an extensive commentary, as the "most theoretically substantial draft of a philosophy of free action in the modern era" (Vieweg 2012: 19) and Michael Quante, who sees in the *The Philosophy of Right* an "important and topical theory of personal autonomy and freedom of the will" (Quante 2011: 327). That *The Philosophy of Right* also allows for conclusions that go much further is made clear by Frank Ruda (2011) in the case of Hegel's dealing with the "rabble" (*Pöbel*). I will return to this in the second volume.

Savigny and Gans

The debates concerning Hegel's *Philosophy of Right* also influenced the young Marx's study of law in Berlin, probably without this being clear to him initially. At the faculty of law at the University of Berlin, Friedrich Carl von Savigny (1779–1861), the most important representative of the historical school of law, and Eduard Gans (1797–1839), the most important Hegelian, stood irreconcilably opposed to one another, both theoretically and personally.

Savigny had taught at the University of Berlin from its founding. He had the trust of the Prussian king, and taught law to the crown prince. Even more than Gustav von Hugo, Savigny was the actual founder of the historical school of law. The school took on clear contours primarily through the "codification debate" in the year 1814 and the founding of the *Zeitschrift für geschichtliche Rechtswissenschaft* (Journal of Historical Legal Studies) in 1815. After codes of law had been adopted in numerous European states that were influenced by natural law (such as the Code Civil in France in 1804 or the "Allgemeines Bürgerliches Gesetzbuch" in Austria in 1812), and the legal fragmentation was seen as detrimental to further development, Anton Friedrich Justus Thibaut (1772–1840), a leading teacher of civil law, in his essay "On the Necessity of a General Civil Law for Germany" ("Ueber die Nothwendigkeit eines allgemeinen bürgerlichen Rechts für Deutschland," 1814) raised the demand for a unified German system of law in the domains of civil law and criminal and procedural law, building upon the experiences of previous codifications. It was obvious that such a standardization of law would promote the unification of Germany and, to the extent unification would occur on the basis of natural law, would tend toward liberal legislation. Both were vehemently fought by the aristocratic-conservative side.

With his text "The Calling of Our Time for Legislation and Jurisprudence" ("Vom Beruf unserer Zeit für Gesetzgebung und Rechtswissenschaft," 1814), and the introductory text "On the Purpose of this Journal" (1815) in the first issue of the *Zeitschrift für geschichtliche Rechtswissenschaft*, Savigny delivered a decisive critique of Thibaut. Savigny doubted whether law could simply be created without further ado by legislators. Against this, he emphasized the historical, traditional character of law, which just like language was rooted in the history and customs of a people, the "spirit of the people," and could not simply be arbitrarily formed by legislators. Savigny thus contested that "our time" was "calling for legislation." Instead, all legal material should be traced back to its historical roots, in order to systematically arrange it in the whole ensemble of law. Roman law played a central role for both. For one thing, Savigny wanted to prove that Roman law had been valid throughout the entirety of the Middle Ages, whereby the point wasn't the existence of corresponding records or formal application, but rather its correspondence to the spirit of the people. For another thing, Roman law was to provide the clear terminology and system for the ordering of law.

Savigny's appeal to the "spirit of the people" does not at all imply any kind of democratic tendencies: the people are not able to recognize the juridical spirit of the people; only trained jurists are capable of doing so. However, the spirit of the people is not simply given in the sources; it requires interpretation. For this difficult act, as Hannah Steinke emphasizes, Savigny "could ultimately only offer the trained feeling of the researcher, but not a methodologically clarified research operation. . . . It is the paradox of the method of the historical school that precisely the objective validity or non-validity of legal clauses is to be found by means of trained feeling" (Steinke 2010: 113). This "paradox," however, makes understandable how the German historical school of law was able to furnish conservative legal content with the nimbus of objectivity.

With his historical research focused upon the German Middle Ages, Savigny also took up motifs of Late Romanticism, which had become conservative. He maintained close personal relationships to important representatives of late Romanticism. His wife, Kunigunde, was a sister of Clemens Brentano (1778–1842), and Savigny had been a friend for many years of Achim von Arnim (1781–1831), the husband of the famous Bettina von Arnim (1785–1859), another sister of Brentano's, to whom we will return.

Since Roman law was so decisive for Savigny, the Pandects—a collection of thematically ordered legal codes from the works of various Roman legal scholars going back to the time of the emperor Justinian (482–565)—played a central role for him. He offered regular lectures on the subject that were widely known and were also attended by Karl Marx.

The "legal science" that Savigny strove for was supposed to recognize the true concepts of law, developed over the course of the history of a people in an organic process. A codification, according to Savigny, is first possible when the historical development of law has reached a certain summit. But then it would be superfluous, since it would no longer yield any progress. Savigny advanced these positions with a great deal of erudition, an exact line of thought, and a style extraordinarily impressive to his contemporaries. In primarily juridical circles, he was downright venerated. In 1850, Bethmann-Hollweg dedicated his Festschrift for the fifty-year celebration of Savigny's doctorate to "the prince of German teachers of law." The historical school of law also dominated German jurisprudence for decades after Savigny's death in 1861, which contributed to the fact that toward the end of the nineteenth century a book of civil law was first developed for the German Empire; it went into effect on January 1, 1900. In the twentieth century as well, Savigny was admired across broad swathes of German jurisprudence as an extraordinary legal scholar, whereby his anti-Semitism was either ignored or trivialized for a long time.[130]

To summarize, Savigny's arguments were at their core directed against the emancipatory impulse of the Enlightenment, that people could take control of and shape their social relations and therefore their legal relations. In contrast, Savigny defended maintaining traditional law as well as the relations of domination legitimized by such law. However, Savigny and the historical school of law cannot be reduced to this conservative aspect. Hermann Klenner has emphasized that Savigny's orientation toward "pure" Roman law, which, *inter alia*, encompassed the first comprehensive legal ordering of an economy of commodity exchange, also contributed to driving back the feudal hybrid law then dominant in Germany and developing a civil law compatible with capitalist commodity production (Klenner 1991: 105).

Hegel's *Philosophy of Right* stands in sharp contrast to the conceptions of the historical school of law. Right at the beginning, in §3, the school is criticized fundamentally on the basis of a textbook by Gustav Hugo. Hegel accuses it of mixing up the explanation and comprehension of law with the history of its emergence (Hegel 1991: 30). Hegel does not mention Savigny anywhere by name, but he writes in §211, in a passage clearly aimed at Savigny's position in the codification debate, "To deny a civilized nation, or the legal profession within it, the ability to draw up a legal code would be among the greatest insults one could offer to either" (Hegel 1991: 242).

The main burden of conducting the debate was not, however, borne by

---

130. This anti-Semitism was not expressed for the first time in his debate with Eduard Gans. In his essay "Stimmen für und wider neue Gesetzbücher" (Voices For and Against New Codes of Law) from 1816, he referred to the legal equality of Jews and Christians as "badly applied humanity" and maintained "in their inner essence, the Jews are and remain aliens to us" (Savigny 1816: 181). In the case of the Jewish medical student Joseph Brogi, who in 1811–12 was first harassed by his non-Jewish classmates, and then beaten when he attempted to defend himself, so that he officially complained to Fichte as the rector of the University of Berlin, Savigny also showed his Christian anti-Judaism. Against Fichte's will, the court of honor of the university condemned not only the attackers, but also Brogi. Fichte refused to enforce the judgment, and requested that the government relieve him of his position as rector in February of 1812. Savigny justified the condemnation of Brogi by declaring that his "custom" (that is, he was Jewish and not Christian) was the occasion of the conflict. Fichte was dismissed as rector, and Savigny became his successor (on the case of Brogi, see Lenz 1910: 1: 410ff.; concerning Savigny's role in particular, see Henne/Kretschmann 2002).

Hegel himself, but rather by his "student" Eduard Gans (1797–1839).[131] The widespread use of the word *student* is not quite correct, since Gans had never been among Hegel's students. He came from a formerly prosperous Berlin Jewish family, which, during the turmoil of French occupation, had lost most of its property. Gans had studied law and in 1819 obtained his doctorate in Heidelberg under Thibaut—in Prussia at this time it was almost impossible for Jews to obtain doctorates. After his doctorate, he returned to Berlin and, through reading Hegel's writings, above all the *Philosophy of Right*, became a "Hegelian" (Gans 1824: xxxix). He quickly gained access to the circle of friends and students of Hegel and in 1826 played a decisive role in the founding of the *Jahrbücher für wissenschaftliche Kritik*, which started publication in 1827.

In Berlin, Gans attempted to become a professor starting in 1820, pinning his hopes upon the Emancipation Decree of 1812, which, while excluding Jews from the civil service did allow them to take teaching positions, to the extent that they had the necessary qualifications. However, in two reports (printed in Lenz 1910: 4:448ff.), the faculty of law cast doubt upon Gans's professional qualifications, whereby the first report raised the question as to whether Gans's Jewish faith was a barrier to employment. The driving force behind this rejection was Savigny. Above all, his vote, presented to the faculty during the second report in which he deals extensively with the question of whether a faculty of law could employ Jewish professors, is full of anti-Semitic stereotypes (first published by Klenner/Oberndorf 1993). Ultimately, the king decided the case. Through an order of the cabinet from August 18, 1822 (printed in Braun 1997: 70), he repealed the stipulation of the edict of 1812 that granted Jews access to academic office and explicitly declared that Gans could not be employed as an associate professor. This "Lex Gans" attracted a great deal of public attention (Braun 1997: 56–74).

Gans now concentrated upon working upon his major work of jurisprudence, *Inheritance Law in Its World-Historical Development*. In it, he attempted, on the basis of Hegel's *Philosophy of Right*, a universal legal history of inheritance law. The structure of the work already constituted an implicit critique of the historical school of law, which only related legal history to a single or a small group of peoples. Gans, in contrast, emphasizes in the preface to the first volume (1824) that legal history must necessarily be universal history, since exclusive importance belongs to no people and no historical

---

131. In contrast to Savigny, Gans was ignored for a long time by research. In what follows, I rely alongside the older, but still sole biography by Reissner (1965), upon Waszek (1991), and the works of Braun (1997; 2005; 2011). On the discussion of Gans, see Blänkner et al. (2002).

period: "Every people is only considered to the extent that it stands at the level of development following from the concepts" (Gans 1824: xxxi). In the preface to the second volume, published in 1825, he accused the historical school not of doing too much, but rather too little actual history. With regard to Roman law, it conducted thoughtless trifles and made the coincidental and unimportant its object. Under the influence of the historical school, jurisprudence had succumbed to "disgraceful thoughtlessness" by "expelling everything philosophical" (Gans 1825: VIIf.). Gans could hardly have expressed his opposition to Savigny and the historical school of law more pointedly and polemically.

In 1819, Gans still belonged among the co-founders of the Association for the Culture and Scholarship of Jews (Vereins für Cultur und Wissenschaft der Juden) and functioned as its president from 1821 to 1824 (see Reissner 1965: 59ff.; Braun 2011: xi). But he soon had to bury his hopes of participating in the development of the Prussian state as a Jew after his experiences at the University of Berlin. In December of 1825, he allowed himself to be baptized.[132] This removed the formal barrier to becoming a professor, but a professorship would have foundered upon the resistance of the faculty. Altenstein, however, who regarded Gans as a comrade-in-arms in the struggle against conservatism, made him an associate professor in March of 1826 without Gans having to fulfill a postdoctoral qualification, which was possible without the faculty's assent. At the end of 1828 he accomplished something still greater when the king appointed Gans to a full professorship. Altenstein had waited for a favorable moment to propose the appointment: the crown prince, who was completely on Savigny's side, was on a trip abroad, and the king's advisers were silent because, shortly before, they had managed to push through the appointment of the conservative theologian Ernst Wilhelm Hengstenberg (1802–1869) as a professor (we will return to him in the next chapter). Savigny, who regarded Gans's appointment as a personal affront, demonstratively withdrew from all faculty business and only held his lectures (Braun 2011: xix; Braun 1997: 75–90).

By 1827, Gans had taken over Hegel's lectures on the philosophy of law. He supplemented them not only with professional juridical knowledge, but also prefixed them with a philosophical-historical introduction and at the end outlined a universal history of law, thus confronting the historical school at the historical level within the lesson.[133] Beyond that, he drew the

---

132. In the previous chapter, I quoted a statement from Gans where he expresses his own assessment of this baptism.

133. This remarkable lecture, which Gans delivered under the title "Natural Law or the

relevant political consequences, dealt with the question of a constitution, and discussed the competencies of the estates assemblies or the necessity of a political opposition. He thus went far beyond what he found in Hegel's work (see Riedel 1967; Lucas 2002; Braun 2005: xxi; Sgro' 2013: 26ff.). Gans attracted some attention with this lecture. Arnold Ruge (1802–1880) shares the following anecdote in his memoirs: "One day, Hegel was a guest at the table of the crown prince. 'It's a scandal,' said the royal host, 'that the professor Gans is making republicans out of all of our students. His lectures on your philosophy of law, Herr Professor, are always attended by hundreds and it's sufficiently well known that he gives your presentation a completely liberal, even republican tinge. Why don't you deliver the lecture yourself?' Hegel did not contradict this account, apologized, said he had no knowledge of what Gans was presenting, and committed to giving his own lecture on his philosophy of law next semester" (Ruge 1867: 431). Ruge does not name a source for this account. We don't know whether this conversation occurred as presented, but it's possible. In any case, during the winter semester of 1831–32, Hegel again took up his lecture on the philosophy of law, but he died during the second week of the semester.

It became clear after Hegel's sudden death that Gans played a decisive role within the Hegelian school. Gans not only wrote the obituary for Hegel in the *Allgemeine Preußische Staatszeitung* (printed in Nicolin 1970: 490–496); for the "Association of Friends Edition," he also edited two key political texts, the *Philosophy of Right* (1833) and the *Lectures on the Philosophy of History* (1837). Furthermore, Gans was supposed to write the official Hegel biography, so to speak, which was prevented, however, by his early death, as noted by Karl Rosenkranz (1805–1879), who then took over this task, in the preface (Rosenkranz 1844: xvi).

Gans supplemented the *Philosophy of Right* with "additions," marked as such, from lecture notes. These additions were frequently more politically pointed than the published text of the first edition. In his preface, Gans highlighted the liberal content of Hegel's *Philosophy of Right* and defended him against the accusation of having philosophically legitimized the Restoration. It was the edition published by Gans that was referred to in the reception of the *Philosophy of Right* well into the twentieth century; Marx also used this edition.[134]

Philosophy of Law in Connection with Universal History" ("Naturrecht oder Rechtsphilosophie in Verbindung mit Universalgeschichte") in the 1830s as well as each winter semester, was reconstructed by Braun with the aid of various lecture notes. See Gans (2005).

134. In his edition of the *Philosophy of Right* published in 1955, Johannes Hoffmeister

Alongside his academic lectures, Gans also held public lectures, for example on "The History of the Last 50 Years," that is, history since the French Revolution, which were met with extraordinary interest. As Lenz (1910: 2.1: 495) states, these lectures attracted audiences of more than nine hundred "from all social backgrounds." Here as well, Gans aroused displeasure at the highest level. Altenstein, the minister of culture, was told by a cabinet colleague that a lecture announced for the winter semester 1833–34 on the history of Napoleon "would appear offensive to his majesty" (quoted in Braun 2011: xxvi). Gans canceled the lecture. But he did not give up. Starting in the summer of 1832, Gans held a lecture on "European Constitutional Law, and German in Particular" and one starting in 1834 on "International Law," both topics that made it easy to address topical political questions (ibid.: xxvii).

That Gans in his lectures gladly went to the limits of what could be expressed in Prussia is made clear by the writer Heinrich Laube (mentioned above) in his reminiscences of Gans: "Often, a sentence on the most captious topic began in a frighteningly bold manner; everything was listened to silently by both concerned friend and lurking enemy, in the expectation that the limit of convenience would be transgressed, but the extraordinary rhetorical fencer parried the thrust so skillfully that everything was done, and he was just as covered at the end of the sentence as at the beginning" (1841: 127).

A book that had been announced by a publisher, "The History of the Last 50 Years," could no longer be published due to Gans's early death, and the manuscript was lost (Braun 2011: xxxvi). However, another book was published in the summer of 1836, shortly before Marx came to Berlin: *Rückblicke auf Personen und Zustände* (A Look Back on Personages and Conditions). There, Gans dealt among other things with Saint-Simonism, which he had become acquainted with during his stays in Paris in 1825 and 1830. Prepared by Hegel's analysis of civil society in the *Philosophy of Right* and his own insights into the industrial conditions of England, which he had gained during a longer trip to England in 1831, Gans arrived not only at a critique of Saint-Simon's authoritarian social utopia, but also at a remarkable insight

---

dispensed completely with these additions, since he regarded them as falsifying. However, as can be seen from the publication of the complete lecture transcripts by Ilting (1973–74), this is not at all the case. In the *Gesammelte Werke*, which is supposed to be a historical-critical edition, the additions are also omitted. In the edition of Hegel's works by the publishing house Suhrkamp, the additions are retained. The version of Gans's edition issued by Hermann Klenner in 1981 (thus with the additions) is still the best student edition, due to the extensive annotations (Hegel 1821a).

into the history and present class relations that went far beyond Hegel:[135] "They [the Saint-Simonists] have correctly noted that slavery is still not over, that it was formally abolished, but materially present in the most complete shape. Just as previously master and slave, later the patrician and plebeian, then the feudal lord and vassal confronted one another, now the idle one and the worker do. One visits the factories of England, and one finds hundreds of men and women who are emaciated and miserable, who sacrifice their health, their enjoyment of life in the service of another merely in order to maintain themselves in this impoverished condition. Is that not called slavery, when one exploits a human being like an animal, even when he would otherwise be free to die of hunger?" (Gans 1836: 99).

Cornu (1954: 81n86) had already emphasized the possible influence of these insights on Marx, and Braun (2011: xxxiv) calls attention to how much the second sentence of this quotation recalls the beginning of the *Communist Manifesto*: "Freeman and slave, patrician and plebeian, lord and serf, guild-master and journeyman, in a word, oppressor and oppressed, stood in constant opposition to one another" (MECW 6:482).[136] We don't know whether Marx had read Gans's book. But since he had attended his lectures, Gans being at the center of public attention, and being a voracious reader, it's quite possible Marx knew the book. At the end of the 1830s, he was still lacking the economic knowledge to fully understand the scope of Gans's considerations; but the notion that bourgeois society, with regard to the exploitation of working people, was far less distinct from pre-bourgeois societies than generally assumed by liberals, probably fell on fertile soil in Marx's case.

Gans was also directly politically engaged, such as in the case of the

---

135. See Waszek (1988). On the relationship between Hegelianism and Saint-Simonism, see the contributions in Schmidt am Busch et al. (2007).
136. Cornu (1954: 80) sees Gans as close to "socialism" or demanding a "socialist organization of labor." In doing so, he refers to a sentence that follows shortly after the one quoted above. Gans regards the workers after the abolition of guilds as "emerging from the domination of the masters and succumbing to the domination of the factory owners" and answers the question as to whether there is any means against this with "Absolutely. It is free corporation, it is socialization" (Gans 1836: 101). As emerges from the context, this does not mean a socialist socialization of the means of production, but rather something more like a form of early trade union organization (see vgl. Waszek 1988: 359; 2006: 38ff.). Hans Stein (1936: 20ff.) makes clear that as a reaction to pauperism, social policy debates in Western Europe from the 1830s on were dominated by thoughts of "association" (also referred to as "socialization" or "the organization of labor"). This meant all forms of benevolent societies, pension institutions, land settlement societies, or credit unions intended to improve the situation of the poor, albeit capitalist society.

"Göttingen Seven," which created a huge stir in Germany. In 1837, due to different regulations for succession to the throne, the personal union between Great Britain and the Kingdom of Hanover, existing since 1714, came to an end: Victoria, who was just eighteen years old, was crowned queen of the United Kingdom of Great Britain and Northern Ireland, which she remained until her death in 1901—the Victorian era, unbeknownst to anyone, began. In Hannover, Ernst August (1771–1851) ascended to the throne and abolished the relatively liberal constitution of 1833. When seven professors from Göttingen, among them Jacob and Wilhelm Grimm, protested against this, they were dismissed and some of them were even expelled from the country. In Germany, there was broad solidarity with them, expressed among other things in donations. Gans was also engaged in Berlin on behalf of such fundraising, which, once again, attracted the suspicion of the government. We know from Karl August Varnhagen von Ense (1785–1858)[137] that Gans cleverly extricated himself from the affair by making use of the surveillance of his position, which he could assume almost with certainty: "In a letter sent by post to Marquise Arconati, Professor Gans expressed himself in such a manner concerning his fundraising on behalf of the Göttingen professors that the authorities should become informed of the matter as he desired. A couple of days ago, Minister von Rochow said to privy councilor Boeckh, the current rector of the local university, [that] they now knew exactly how things were, Gans had done something displeasing, but in such a way that they had nothing on him, and then reported it in Gans's own words!" (Varnhagen von Ense 1994: 261).

Gans's esteem on the part of the students at the University of Berlin is made clear by another occurrence noted by Varnhagen. On March 22, 1838, around six hundred students held a birthday serenade in front of Gans's residence. In doing so, they celebrated not only Gans, but also the Göttingen Seven. Coincidentally, living in the same apartment house was the same privy councilor, Tzschoppe, who distinguished himself by prosecuting all those alleged to have held oppositional views (for example, the poet Heinrich Laube; see

---

137. Varnhagen was the husband of Rahel Varnhagen, mentioned in the previous chapter. For his merits as an officer in the anti-Napoleonic Wars, in 1814 he received the decoration Pour le Mérite from the Prussian king, the highest decoration for bravery in Prussia, and subsequently became a Prussian diplomat. Only five years after his decoration, he was dismissed due to "democratic tendencies." Varnhagen was acquainted with a large part of the political and cultural elite of Prussia. In his diary entries, which span from 1819 to 1858, he recorded numerous conversations and background information concerning events in Prussian politics and culture (on Varnhagen, see Greiling 1993).

above). When Tzschoppe showed himself at his window, a student shouted a "Pereat!" at him (May he perish!) (Varnhagen von Ense 1994: 262). A "*Vivat*" for the Göttingen Seven and a "*Pereat*" for a Prussian official was a scandal; the police as well as the university magistrates investigated, and Gans once again had to explain himself (Streckfuß 1886: 2:791; Braun 1997: 190–94).

Gans was not to survive this incident for long. On May 5, 1839, the twenty-first birthday of Karl Marx, he died from the results of a stroke. In the previous winter semester, Gans had once again held a lecture series aimed at a larger audience: "The History of the Period from the Peace of Westphalia onward, with special consideration of Constitutional and International Law."[138] The lectures were extraordinarily well attended (Braun 2011: xxviii) and likely engaged with numerous political questions. In his memoirs, the mineralogist Karl Cäsar von Leonhard (1779–1862) reports on a meeting with Gans in Dresden in 1833 and also mentions—without providing a source—Gans's supposed "last words" at the lectern. It's quite possible it was the final sentence of this lecture series: "The history of the modern period is that of a great revolution. In the past, the nobility made revolutions, or the privileged in general [England's 'Glorious Revolution' of 1688]; then the French upheaval [French Revolution of 1789] had been created by the aristocracy of the third estate, with the help of the people, meaning the poor people, the rabble. But a third revolution will be made by this rabble, the entire great mass of those without privilege and property; when it occurs, the world will shake" (Leonhard 1856: 214).

Juridical and Non-Juridical Studies of Young Marx

On October 22, 1836, Karl Marx enrolled at the University of Berlin. That information is given in his "leaving certificate" from March 30, 1841 (MECW 1: 703). At the time, 1,700 were enrolled at the University of Berlin; with over 500 students, the faculty of law was the largest. Berlin thus counted more than double as many students as Bonn, but there were twenty times as many inhabitants. The share of students in the total population was small; they therefore did not play as large an economic role as in smaller university towns. The intensive surveillance of the students and their far lesser importance to the city also had an influence upon the character of student life.

---

138. Perhaps what the physician and poet Max Ring (1817–1901), who studied in Berlin from 1838 to1840, disclosed in his *Memoirs* refers to this lecture: "Triumphantly, the original servant of the free-thinking professor, old Feige, reported to us: 'This year, we'll read about the French Revolution with a bang!'" (Ring 1898: 128).

Ludwig Feuerbach (1804–1872), who had studied in Berlin in the 1820s, wrote on July 6, 1824, to his father: "Nobody thinks about drinking sessions, duels, or group trips at all here; at no other university does such a general diligence predominate, such a sense for something more elevated than student stories, such a striving toward science, such calm and quiet"; the University of Berlin was a veritable "workhouse" (Feuerbach, 17:48).

In Marx's leaving certificate, the lectures Marx attended, including evaluations, are listed. In the winter semester of 1836–37 he attended "Pandects" by Friedrich Carl von Savigny (graded "diligent"), "Criminal Law" by Eduard Gans ("exceptionally diligent"), and "Anthropology" by Henrik Steffens ("diligent"). In the summer semester of 1837, there were three different lecture series by August Wilhelm Heffter: "Ecclesiastical Law," "Common German Civil Procedure," and "Prussian Civil Procedure," which were all graded with "diligent" (MECW 1: 703).

Since Marx had attended a lecture on the history of Roman law in Bonn, attendance at Savigny's Pandect lectures was not mandatory. Perhaps Marx did not want to miss the luminary lecturing on his most well-known field. Marx completed criminal law by Eduard Gans, but did not attend his classic lectures on natural law and universal legal history. Probably Marx wasn't very familiar with the name Gans when he arrived in Berlin, and he had already attended lectures on natural law in Bonn by Savigny's student Puggé.

Henrik Steffens (1773–1845) advocated a philosophy of nature strongly influenced by Friedrich Wilhelm Joseph Schelling (1775–1854). In his speculative anthropology, he conceived of human beings as a unity of mind and nature, as microcosmic representatives of the universe (Liebmann 1893). Due to Steffens's lectures, Marx probably engaged with Schelling's work.

Regarding August Wilhelm Heffter (1796–1880), Lenz writes that he was initially strongly influenced by Savigny but took an independent position with regard to other students of Savigny and moved closer to Hegel's philosophy (Lenz 1910: 2.1: 498). It's unclear what the last assertion is based upon. Heffter was a practical jurist. Before he obtained—without a doctorate—his first professorship in Bonn, he was an associate judge in Düsseldorf. He had taught in Berlin since 1833 and was also, as noted above, a member of the Rhenish Appellate Court (Lauchert 1880). The fact that he did not clearly take the side of Savigny in the conflict between Savigny and Gans does not mean he moved closer to Hegel's philosophy. In his publications and courses, he dealt less with the philosophy of law and more with practical legal problems, as is made clear by the title of the lectures attended by Marx.

In Berlin, Marx did not take up his studies as enthusiastically as he had in Bonn—there, he had completed six courses in the first semester, and four in the second. But he soon worked on his own elaborations of legal theory. He must have sent an initial text, or at least longer expositions, in a letter to his father in December of 1836, since his father answered on December 28: "Your views on law are not without truth, but are very likely to arouse storms if made into a system, and are you not aware how violent storms are among the learned? If what gives offense in this matter itself cannot be entirely eliminated, at least the form must be conciliatory and agreeable" (MECW 1: 665).

But these first considerations were just the beginning of an enormous productivity, about which we are informed in his longer letter from November 10, 1837, which is the only preserved letter from his time as a student. Looking back, Marx writes. "I had to study law and above all felt the urge to wrestle with philosophy" (MECW 1: 11). He attempted to resolve this quandary by, on the one hand, engaging with legal literature and among other things translating the first two books of the Pandect, and, on the other hand, trying to "elaborate a philosophy of law . . . a work of almost 300 pages [Bogen]." With the term Bogen, it's unlikely that Marx meant a print sheet of sixteen pages, but rather single pages (possibly leaves written on both sides), which still constitutes an enormous output of writing. As an introduction, he had "prefaced this with some metaphysical propositions" (MECW 1: 12). The choice of words suggests the influence of Kant, who had published his philosophy of law in 1797 under the title *The Metaphysics of Morals*, the first part of which was titled "Metaphysical Elements of Justice." By "metaphysical propositions," Marx likely meant nothing more than a philosophical introduction. This was followed by "the philosophy of law, that is to say, according to my views at the time, an examination of the development of ideas in positive Roman law" (ibid.). This attempt at systematization oriented toward Roman law shows the influence of Savigny, to whom Marx refers in the next paragraph, when he writes that he "shares with" him the "error" of separating the form and content of jurisprudence. Marx outlines the attempted classification of law for his father, but then breaks off and explains, full of self-criticism: "The whole thing is replete with tripartite divisions, it is written with tedious prolixity, and the Roman concepts are misused in the most barbaric fashion in order to force them into my system. . . . At the end of the section on material private law, I saw the falsity of the whole thing, the basic plan of which borders on that of Kant, but deviates wholly from it in the execution." As a result, it became clear to him that "there could be no headway without philosophy." And what did he do? He "drafted a new system of metaphysical principles, but at the conclusion of it I was once more compelled to recognize that it was wrong, like all my previous efforts" (MECW 1: 17). Marx does not appear to have undertaken any further attempts at formulating a philosophy of law.

The works of jurisprudence that Marx finished in his first semester or shortly afterward are strongly influenced by Kant and Savigny. Marx undertook attempts at a systematization of law, but he recognized how superficial and formal they remained. Hegel's *Philosophy of Right* does not appear to have played a role in either their elaboration or the critique thereof. In the letter, a Hegelian critique can be heard, but this is a retrospective assessment, formulated *after* the transition to Hegel's philosophy. In the biographical literature since Mehring (1962: 10), it has been repeatedly asserted that Eduard Gans was the most important university teacher for Marx, but there is no indication at all that Marx had been lastingly influenced by Gans during this first semester. In the next two semesters, he did not attend any of Gans's courses, and in his letter to his father, Gans is not even mentioned once. It was first in the summer semester of 1838 that he completed "Prussian Law" with Gans.[139] In the summer semester of 1837, Marx attended the three courses by Heffter mentioned above, and in the winter semester of 1837–38 he attended only a single course, "Criminal Legal Procedure," again with Heffter ("diligent").

Young Marx was not, however, exhausted by the legal studies of his first year in Berlin. Along with his attempts at poetry, he managed a massive reading workload. "In the course of this work I adopted the habit of making extracts from all the books I read." Marx maintained this habit until the end of his life; in the MEGA, the surviving extracts (along with those of Engels, the volume of which is much smaller, however) would fill a total of thirty-one volumes. Marx made extracts of "Lessing's Laokoön, Solger's Erwin, Winckelmann's history of art, Luden's German history. . . . At the same time I translated Tacitus' Germania, and Ovid's Tristia, and began to learn English and Italian by myself, i.e., out of grammars, but I have not yet got anywhere with this. I also read Klein's criminal law and his annals, and all the most recent literature, but this last only by the way" (MECW 1: 17).

---

139. Cornu (1954: 82) writes that Marx had deeply felt the influence of Gans; Kliem refers to Gans as "the most important legal and philosophical teacher of Karl Marx" (Kliem 1988: 16, emphasis in original), and that with Gans's death, Marx had lost his "mentor" (ibid.: 52). Sperber (2013: 60) speculates that Marx's life would have taken a different course if Gans had not died in 1839. But other than the two attended lecture series, with a space of eighteen months between them, and the above-mentioned similarities between the *Look Back on Personages and Conditions* and the beginning of the *Communist Manifesto* (whereby it's not certain if and above all when Marx read the *Look Back*), there is no evidence for this strong influence by Gans. Later as well, there are no mentions by Marx of Gans, neither in his letters nor in his texts, that would indicate a special relationship.

Marx's habit of passing time by reading authors of classical antiquity in their original languages and sometimes translating them, was maintained in later years. Nothing remains of the Tacitus translation; in the work *Germania*, the Roman historian Tacitus (58–120) had presented the culture of the Germanic peoples as an antithesis to what he regarded as a corrupt and decadent Roman society. A loose translation, in verse, of the first elegy of Ovid's *Tristia* is contained in the collection of poems that Marx gave to his father as a birthday present in 1837 (MECW 1: 531–632). In *Tristia*, Ovid (43 BCE–17 AD), who was banished to the Black Sea by Emperor Augustus, laments his loneliness.

Nothing remains of the early extracts. However, the titles named are very revealing. The *Geschichte des Teutschen Volkes* by Heinrich Luden (1778–1847) that Marx mentions was published between 1825 and 1837 in twelve volumes. It was the newest work of German history on the market in 1837. In 1841, Luden was a member of the philosophical faculty of the University of Jena, from which Marx obtained his doctorate.

Particularly interesting are the three titles of art theory that Marx names first. The works of Winckelmann and Lessing belonged at the time to the canon of members of the educated middle classes with an interest in art. In *Laocoön: An Essay on the Limits of Painting and Poetry* (1766), Gotthold Ephraim Lessing (1729–1781) had criticized Winckelmann's interpretation of the famous *Laocoön* group of sculptures in the Vatican Museum, in doing so emphasizing the fundamental differences in the possibilities of depiction of the visual arts (painting, sculpture) and poetry.

Johann Joachim Winckelmann's (1717–1768) two-volume *History of Ancient Art* (1764) had an enormous influence upon the reception of ancient Greek art in Germany, which was presented by Winckelmann as an unattainable ideal. Even twenty years later, one finds echoes of this reading in Marx's work. In the "Introduction," written in 1857 for the planned *Critique of Political Economy*, Marx presupposes Winckelmann's idea of Greek art as an unattainable ideal but poses the question as to why this is the case today: "But the difficulty lies not in understanding that Greek art and epic poetry are bound up with certain forms of social development. The difficulty is that they still give us aesthetic pleasure and are in certain respects regarded as a standard and unattainable model" (MECW 28: 47).

Somewhat surprising is the reading of *Erwin* by Karl Wilhelm Ferdinand Solger (1780–1819), a treatise of art theory conceived in the form of a dialogue that hardly received any attention. Below, we will return to Solger and the possible importance he held for Marx.

Literary Attempts

During his time at school, Karl had written poems. The oldest surviving one (about Charlemagne) is from the year 1833 (MEGA I/1: 760ff.). During German lessons, pupils were instructed to write poems themselves; limiting lessons to mere analysis was a later development.[140] His friend Edgar also wrote poems; a poem of his from the year 1830 when he was eleven has even survived (Gemkow 1999: 407). Within the bourgeoisie, writing poetry was far more usual and widespread than it is today. An educated person was supposed to be able to produce a couple of simple verses in order to recite them at a celebration or dedicate them to an esteemed person.

Young Karl, however, wanted more. The volume of surviving works alone, written in only about two years (1835–1837) is remarkable. In the MEGA, they comprise about 300 printed pages, and by no means has everything been preserved. Karl revised his poems, attempted to improve them, and experimented with different genres. There exists the fragment of a humorous novel as well as parts of a drama.

It's quite possible that as an Abitur student, young Karl envisioned a career as a poet rather than as a jurist. In a letter from February–March 1836, when Karl was at the end of his first semester in Bonn, his father wrote: "You do well to wait before going into print." So Marx was at that point thinking about publication. His father, a man who thought practically, was skeptical. He continued: "A poet, a writer, must nowadays have the calling to provide something sound if he wants to appear in public. . . . I tell you frankly, I am profoundly pleased at your aptitudes and I expect much from them, but it would grieve me to see you make your appearance as an ordinary poetaster" (MECW 1: 650). Karl must have assured his father that he would not publish anything without his judgment. In any case, his father thanked him for that, although he didn't seem completely convinced that Karl will keep that promise (MECW 1: 651). He turned out to be right: only a few months later, Karl must have tried to publish his work without presenting it to his father beforehand. The latter reacted calmly; he simply wished to be included in the "negotiations conducted" (MECW 1: 654). However, the plan came to nothing.

---

140. As emerges from the school program of the gymnasium in Trier, German lessons at the Quarta level (1831–32) were concerned, *inter alia*, with "prosody and meter" in the Untersekunda (1832–33) with "Style. Exercises in storytelling, description, short poems" (Große 2011: 355n5). It's possible that this first poem was written in the context of German class.

In the next few months, his father did not remain skeptical of Karl's plans for publication. In a letter from March 2, 1837, he considers what would be an appropriate first work that might bring Karl success with the public (MECW 1: 672). Heinrich Marx obviously wanted to support his son, even if the latter took a path different from the one he wanted.

However, a few months later, in a letter from November 10, 1837, Karl delivered a scathing critique of his own poetry. As a consequence, he burned his recently written outlines and announced his attention to "give them up completely" (MECW 1: 19). What remained were notebooks that he had given to Jenny and his father as presents. As we know from his daughter Laura, in later years these poems were for Marx merely an occasion for merriment. To Franz Mehring, to whom Laura had loaned albums with poems by Marx as he was preparing an edition of posthumous writings by Marx, Engels, and Lassalle, she wrote: "I must tell you that my father treated these verses very disrespectfully; whenever my parents spoke of them, they laughed heartily about these follies of youth" (Mehring 1902: 25).

Mehring, who had also written works of literary history, denied that Marx's poems had any literary value and did not include any of them in his edition of posthumous works; in the introduction he merely quoted a few verses under the heading "The Fanciful Poet."[141] In his biography of Marx, he didn't even do that. Mehring saw this act of passing over the literary attempts as justified since Marx had not published any of his poems (which is not true; see below) and he had deceived himself "about the nullity of these creations for only a few months." Marx, according to Mehring, "lacked the creative genius of the poet, who creates a world out of nothing" (Mehring 1902: 26, 27).

Both of Mehring's judgments, according to which Marx's poems have no aesthetic value, and that Marx had abandoned his attempts at poetry because he had recognized his own lack of talent, have been taken up largely uncritically in most of the biographical literature. Even in the more comprehensive Marx biographies, these poems are regarded largely as a curiosity not worthy of a more comprehensive engagement.[142]

---

141. Mehring had taken this formulation from a letter by Heinrich Marx (MECW 1: 668).

142. So it is in the newer Marx biographies as well. Concerning these writings from youth, Sperber writes, "The less said, the better," to which he adheres (Sperber 2013: 49). Neffe is similar, devoting a six-line paragraph to the "failed poet" (Neffe 2017: 61). Stedman Jones quotes a few poems, but only to make clear how insignificant they are; he sees them exclusively as a result of "Karl's infatuation with the idea of himself as a poet" (Stedman Jones 2016: 67). Künzli (1966: 148ff.) deals more extensively with the poems, but only to prop up his adventurous thesis of Marx's "Jewish self-hatred." Even outside of the biographical literature, Marx's attempts at poetry have met with a rather low level of interest. Due to their topics,

In the further course of this section, it will become clear that for various reasons, considerable doubt is appropriate with regard to Mehring's judgments. First of all, it must be kept in mind that Mehring was only familiar with part of Marx's (surviving) poems. These have been passed down in two different collections. One is three albums that Karl put together as a Christmas present for Jenny in October–November 1836. Mehring would have been able to look at these three albums, which were preserved by Marx's daughter Laura. The second collection is an extensive book that Marx gave to his father as a present for his sixtieth birthday in April of 1837. There, a few of the poems from the albums for Jenny are also incorporated; the others were written after those, in early 1837. Furthermore, this book also contains a fragment of the above-mentioned humorous novel *Scorpion and Felix* and the play *Oulanem*. Some of the new poems are qualitatively different from the earlier ones; they also aren't judged completely negatively by Marx in his letter from November 1837; he had "caught sight of the glittering realm of true poetry like a distant fairy palace" (MECW 1: 17). This book was first discovered in the 1920s during the preparation of the first MEGA, when Mehring was no longer alive. That means that Mehring was not able to take note of the progress Marx had made. The three albums that were available to Mehring had initially disappeared after Laura's death, however, so that it was not possible to publish their content in the first MEGA. This led to the paradoxical situation that until the publication of the second MEGA, Mehring's withering judgment was known, but not the poems to which it referred. On the other hand, poems and fragments were available that were largely unknown to Mehring. Several authors who uncritically adopted Mehring's judgments did not even notice this discrepancy.

In the 1950s, the three albums that Mehring had seen turned up again in the estate of Edgar Longuet (1879–1950), a grandson of Marx. Thus, in the second MEGA both collections—the three albums for Jenny from the year 1836 and the one for Marx's father from 1837—could be published together for the first time. Furthermore, there is an album put together by Karl's sister Sophie containing poems written from 1835 to 1836, as well as parts of her notebook, in which even older poems are found.

"Marx and literature," Lifschitz (1960: 41–48), Demetz (1969: 52–62), and Prawer (1976: 11–25) deal somewhat more extensively with Marx's poems, but Demetz and Prawer agree completely, and Lifschitz agrees for the most part, with Mehring's judgment. Independent of Mehring's judgment, among others Hillmann (1966: 49–72), Rose (1978), Wessell (1979), and Mah (1986; 1987: 154–70) deal with Marx's literary attempts.

In the next section, I will deal more extensively with Marx's literary attempts. For one thing, poetry constituted an important initial orientation for the young Marx, and for another, Marx's turn away from poetry was not at all, as Mehring assumed, due to a recognition by Marx of his own lack of talent. His reasons for this turning away are completely different, and may indeed contain the key to solving a further problem of the young Marx's intellectual development, namely his transition toward Hegel's philosophy.

Marx's poems can be easily associated with Romanticism. The contemporary, colloquial usage of "romantic" (gushing-idealistic, oriented toward an unrealistic harmony) must be distinguished from the *literary Romanticism* meant here, which lasted from the end of the eighteenth century through the middle of the nineteenth. And we should not conflate the latter with the *political Romanticism* of the early nineteenth century (with Adam Müller 1779–1829, as its main representative). The characterization of literary Romanticism is contested. There is widespread agreement that a large role is given to subjectivity, that Romanticism is concerned with the world of feelings, inner experience, the (unrealizable) longing for an ineffable other, that it expresses suffering in a world that is too rational and businesslike, and that it frequently makes use of a distancing, ironic attitude, a "romantic irony." It's also undeniable that in *Late Romanticism,* tendencies toward glorifying the Middle Ages and Catholicism were at work, and many Romanticists in this phase tended toward politically conservative positions. However, the character of Romanticism as a whole, its relationship to the Enlightenment, and in particular its political content have been interpreted in very different ways in the last 180 years.

The "Young Germany" movement had already seen in Romanticism primarily something Catholic and backwards, a critique that finds its initial culmination point in Heinrich Heine's *The Romantic School* (1836). This critique was continued in the *Hallische Jahrbücher* of Theodor Echtermayer (1805–1844) and Arnold Ruge (1802–1880), with their manifesto "Protestantism and Romanticism" (1839–40). The *Hallische Jahrbücher* were something like the "central organ" of the Young Hegelians—we will return to them in the next chapter. Liberal historians of literature also saw in Romanticism primarily a countermovement to the rationalism of the Enlightenment. Rudolf Haym in his work, *The Romantic School* (1870), which was just as influential as his Hegel biography of 1857 mentioned above, points in this direction. He identifies Romanticism largely with political reaction. Early Marxist literary studies, particularly in the case of Franz Mehring, were strongly influenced by this view of Romanticism as an ultimately politically reactionary current. For that reason, Mehring was invested in making clear that Marx had such brief contact with Romanticism that it was inconsequential to his further development.

In the early twentieth century, (German) Romanticism was increasingly placed in a German chauvinist, nationalist framework—and celebrated. This interpretation was also predominant under Nazism and led to a considerable discrediting of Romanticism. Not a few, primarily Anglophone, authors after the Second World War saw in the German tendency toward (anti-modern and anti-rationalist) Romanticism an element that contributed to the rise of the Nazis (see Craig 1982: 207ff.). Against the background of this negative image of Romanticism, some critics of Marx attempted to prove that his work was also strongly influenced by Romanticism (such as Kux 1967) or even contained conservative elements (Levin 1974).

Since the 1960s, however, progressive and modern aspects of Romanticism have been highlighted, such as the thematization of the unconscious or the identity of the individual, which had become problematic. Above all, Ernst Behler, publisher of the critical edition of the works of Friedrich Schlegel, emphasized the rational and Enlightenment potential of early Romanticism (Behler 1992). In connection with these debates, in the last few decades there has been an increasing tendency to distinguish between a progressive Early Romanticism, interpreted as a veritable second Enlightenment, and an increasingly conservative Late Romanticism.[143] Now, Romantic content in Marx's work can be evaluated positively (see for example Behler 1978; Röder 1982). I will return later to the question of the extent to which Romantic motifs continued to have an effect on Marx's work, for example in the *Economic-Philosophical Manuscripts* of 1844. Here, the focus is only on his attempts at poetry.

The albums for Jenny—the first two are captioned with "Book of Love" and the third with "Book of Songs"—are devoted to Karl's love for her. He draws strength from this relationship, but at the same time fears losing her. In the first poem, "Die zwei Himmel" (or "The Two Skies/Heavens"), he writes at the end (MEGA I/1: 485): "If you break the bond, I will plummet / the flood envelops me, the grave swallows me / both heavens have been submerged / and the bleeding soul has withered away."[144]

In "Human Pride," the euphoric element has won the upper hand. Everything appears to be possible, everything can be achieved, indeed Karl feels "Like unto a God":

---

143. On the current state of the debate concerning the political content of Romanticism, see the two collections by Ries (2012) and Dreyer/Ries (2014).

144. Brichst Du das Band, so stürz' ich hinab / Mich umhüllt die Fluth, mich verschlingt das Grab / Es haben beide Himmel sich untergetauchet / und die blutende Seele verhauchet.

Jenny! Do I dare avow
That in love we have exchanged our Souls,
That as one they throb and glow,
And that through their waves one current rolls?

Then the gauntlet do I fling
Scornful in the World's wide-open face
Down the giant She-Dwarf, whimpering,
Plunges, cannot crush my happiness.

Like unto a God I dare,
Through that ruined realm in triumph roam.
Every word is Deed and Fire,
And my bosom like the Maker's own. (MECW 1: 586)

In a poem written later, found in the second album,[145] Karl is no longer so exuberantly euphoric; rather, he reflects upon his own temperament and striving. Since this poem (MECW 1: 525) probably expresses Marx's self-image from that period, it is reproduced more extensively here:

FEELINGS

Never can I do in peace
That with which my Soul's obsessed,
Never take things at my ease;
I must press on without rest.

. . . .

Heaven I would comprehend,
I would draw the world to me;
Loving, hating, I intend
That my star shine brilliantly.

All things I would strive to win,
All the blessings Gods impart,

---

145. Marx had dated the first album "at the end of Autumn"; the second "November" 1836 (MEGA I/1: 479, 525).

Grasp all knowledge deep within,
Plumb the depths of Song and Art.

. . . .

So it rolls from year to year,
From the Nothing to the All,
From the Cradle to the Bier,
Endless Rise and endless Fall.

. . . .

Therefore let us risk our all,
Never resting, never tiring;
Not in silence dismal, dull,
Without action or desiring;

Not in brooding introspection
Bowed beneath a yoke of pain,
So that yearning, dream and action
Unfulfilled to us remain.

Whereas in the first verses Marx deals with his restless nature, his desire to comprehend everything, emphasizing "knowledge" and "song and art," in the last verses he takes up themes he had addressed in his Abitur essay: the refusal to force oneself into a yoke, and the striving to do great things, or at least to try.

The belief in individual power, and above all in the special role of the artist, are components of the Romantic understanding of art by which Marx was obviously strongly influenced. In the ballad "Siren Song" (MECW 1: 545), the youth is able to resist the temptations of the sirens precisely because he feels a longing that the sirens can never know:

You lack the bosom's beat,
The heart's life-giving heat,
The soul's high flight so free.

. . . .

> You shall not captivate
> Me, nor my love, nor hate,
> Nor yet my yearning's glow.

The object of this "yearning" is not defined. The yearning is just the unlimited romantic longing by means of which the self can grasp itself.

Other examples clarify that the imagery of Marx's poems and ballads originated in the Romantic cosmos, which he had been familiar with since his youth. At school, Marx probably did not get to know very many Romantic poems. Both of the readers for the lower and upper classes of the Trier gymnasium primarily present authors belonging to the Enlightenment and Weimar Classicism. There was a lot of Schiller, but only a little Goethe and hardly any Romanticists (Große 2011: 352). However, as his daughter Eleanor reports, Marx's first love for the Romantic school was awakened rather early by Ludwig von Wesphalen (E. Marx; https://www.marxists.org/archive/eleanor-marx/1883/06/karl-marx.htm).

The poems, particularly those in the albums intended for Jenny, leave a lot to be desired in formal terms. That many of them have a somewhat clumsy and awkward effect should not be surprising given that the author was only eighteen. Mehring's criticism of the technical inadequacy of Marx's verses is, then, justified: "To say it in one sentence: they're formless in every sense of the word. Even the technique of the verse is completely stuck in a raw condition; if the time of their writing had not already been firmly established, one would never guess that they were written a year after Platen's death,[146] nine years after Heine's book of songs. But nothing of their content suggests that either. It consists of Romantic harp tones: a song of elves, a song of gnomes . . . not even the valiant knight is missing who commits many heroic deeds in a foreign land and returns home just at the moment when the unfaithful bride is striding toward the altar with another" (Mehring 1902: 26).

Although not everything that Mehring writes is wrong, but even in the case of the early poems, the only ones he knew of, his perspective remains superficial. It's true that not even the valiant knight is missing, but how does the ballad "Lucinda" end? The knight kills himself with his dagger in front of the assembled wedding party, and his faithless bride Lucinda takes the dagger and slits her own wrists. And that's not all: whereas the maid manages to take the dagger from her and save her life, the bloodstained Lucinda descends, crying, into madness (MECW 1: 570). What Marx delivers here as well as in a few other

---

146. This is a reference to the poet August Graf von Platen (1795–1835).

poems tends toward what would later be called Black Romanticism. Yet poems such as "Der Wilden Brautgesang" (The Bride Song of the Wild One) (MEGA I/1: 505ff.) or "Die Zerißne" (Distraught) (MECW 1: 582ff.) cannot be reduced to merely causing pleasant shudders among the audience. Whereas the main current of German Romanticism had long since departed from the rebelliousness of Early Romanticism, with its sympathies for the French Revolution, and made its peace with social and political conditions by means of glorifying the Middle Ages, Catholicism, and the nobility, there is not the slightest trace of such glorification in Marx's works. In the poems named, Marx emphasizes distress, doubt, and despair, and without the conciliatory gesture of offering a solution that would thus weaken what is depicted.

In the later poems, the concentration and strength of expression demonstrates clear progress. In "Des Verzweifelnden Gebet" (The Invocation of One in Despair) (MECW 1: 563), Marx no longer needs multiple pages to lend expression to despair and the defiant rebellion growing out of it. The two poems published in 1841 in the magazine *Athenäum* under the title "Wild Songs"—both originate in the album from 1837—are in this regard perhaps the best; they even received a positive review (see MEGA I/1: 1258). The poem "The Fiddler" (MECW 1: 22) concerns a man who carries a fiddle and saber, who plays so that "the soul's cry" is carried "down to Hell." He disputes having received this art from God:

> That art God neither wants nor wists,
> It leaps to the brain from Hell's black mists.

He states that "with Satan [he] [had] struck [his] deal" and is now bound to him:

> He chalks the signs, beats time for me,
> I play the death march fast and free.

He makes a Faustian bargain with the devil that cannot be canceled; the Fiddler must play "Till bowstrings break my heart outright."

The second poem, "Nocturnal Love," deals with the nocturnal death of a lover. We learn nothing of the circumstances and causes; everything is concentrated upon the moment of pain, which in its brevity has an unsettling effect (MECW 1: 23).

Marx not only improved his lyricism, he also experimented with the repertoire of his depiction. In this final album from 1837, we also find short humorous poems and mocking epigrams—among others, one about Hegel, which I will address in the next section—*Scorpion and Felix*, the fragment of a comic novel, and finally parts of a fantastical drama with the title *Oulanem*.

As the editor of the first MEGA, David Riazanov, noted, *Oulanem* was supposed to be one of those "tragedies of fate" fashionable at the time, "for from the beginning, an enigma rules over all persons and their mutual relationships" (Rjazanov 1929: XV). However, it is not clear from the fragment how Marx intended to solve this enigma.

Riazanov had also pointed out that *Scorpion and Felix* stylistically leaned strongly on *Tristram Shandy* by Laurence Sterne, and also took up influences from E. T. A. Hoffmann's "The Devil's Elixirs." In this fragment of a novel, focused upon the master tailor Merten, his son Scorpion, the journeyman Felix, and the cook Grethe, everything goes haywire. The compiled fragment begins with chapter 10; whether previous chapters were planned appears questionable to me, since fragmentation can be used as a stylistic means, for example by E. T. A. Hoffman in "The Life and Opinions of the Tomcat Murr." The chapter begins as follows:

Now follows, as we promised in the previous chapter, the proof that the aforesaid sum of 25 talers is the personal property of the dear Lord.

They are without a master! Sublime thought, no mortal power owns them, yet the lofty power that sails above the clouds embraces the All, including therefore the aforesfaid 25 talers; with its wings woven from day and night, from sun and stars, from towering mountains and endless sands, which resound as with harmonies and the rushing of the waterfall, it brushes where no mortal hand can reach, including therefore the aforesaid 25 talers, and—but I can say no more, my inmost being is stirred, I contemplate the All and myself and the aforesaid 25 talers, what substance in these three words, their standpoint is infinity, their tinkle is angelic music, they recall the Last Judgment and the state exchequer, for—it was Grethe, the cook, whom Scorpion, stirred by the tales of his friend Felix, carried away by his flame-winged melody, overpowered by his vigorous youthful emotion, presses to his heart, sensing a fairy within her. (MECW 1: 616)

It continues in this breathless style, jumping from topic to topic. Reading it, one has the impression that Marx was attempting to wittily amalgamate all the philosophical, literary, philological, and other knowledge he possessed at the time.

It's obvious that the young Karl was experimenting, stylistically and thematically; he was searching. That the literary products of a nineteen-year-old don't at all approach those of a Heinrich Heine should not be surprising. But one cannot deny that the young Karl had a certain potential; a literary career could not have been excluded as a possibility. Some of Marx's last poems were in any case a bit more interesting than the "reminiscences softened in sugar water" of his (supposed) friend from Bonn, Emanuel Geibel,[147] who, starting in the early 1840s, catered to the tastes of the bourgeoisie as well as the Prussian monarch, and became one of the most famous German poets in the nineteenth century, but was then quickly forgotten.

Regardless of how one judges the quality of Marx's poetry, he himself did not mention any lack of poetic talent. On the contrary, in a letter to his father, he expresses his annoyance over Adelbert Chamisso (1781–1838), the famous poet had rejected publishing Marx's poems in his almanac (MECW 1: 19). Furthermore, Marx could not have regarded all his poems as being "null," as Mehring assumed, otherwise, he would not have taken the opportunity in 1841 of publishing two of them.

THE FIRST INTELLECTUAL CRISIS: THE TURN AWAY FROM POETRY AND TRANSITION TO HEGEL'S PHILOSOPHY

From his letter to his father of November 1837, we learn which studies Karl had been dealing with in the previous months. He also shares two important changes with his father: he had given up his attempts at writing poetry, and he had associated himself with Hegelian philosophy. In the biographical literature, both these points are constantly reported upon, but their causes are not rigorously traced. Regarding the abandonment of poetry, Mehring's view is taken to be that Marx recognized he did not have any talent as a poet. In treating the transition to Hegelian philosophy, frequently the mere fact is reported, or the cause is seen in the discussions in the "Doctor's Club" that Marx mentions in his letter. This disregards that Marx had connected with this Doctor's Club *after* he had made the fundamental decision in favor of Hegel's philosophy. That the causes for Marx's turn toward Hegel's philosophy are not traced more thoroughly is all the more astounding given that this is one of the most momentous turns of the young Marx. His confrontation with Hegel's work would last over the next few decades, and it is undisputed

---

147. This characterization of Geibel's poems comes from Wilhelm Schulz (1797–1860), a friend of Georg Büchner. He used it in his review of Büchner's *Nachgelassene Schriften* (Posthumous Writings) published in 1851 (Grab 1985: 51). As an author of an economic study, *Die Bewegung der Produktion* (The Movement of Production, 1843), he provided an important stimulus for Marx (for a biography of Schulz, see Grab 1987).

that this confrontation influenced Marx's work, even if there is heavy debate concerning the nature and extent of this influence. Even in the newer biographies, which claim to contextualize Marx within the nineteenth century, the transition to Hegelian philosophy is merely asserted (Sperber 2013: 49; Stedman Jones 2016: 82).

Auguste Cornu is among the few who at least attempted an explanation for Marx's turn to Hegel's philosophy. First, Cornu mentions Eduard Gans, claiming he had contributed much to "winning Marx for Hegelian philosophy" (Cornu 1954: 82).[148] But as we saw, it is not evident that Gans actually had such an influence; in the letter to Marx's father, he is not mentioned. This does not mean that Gans had no influence on Marx, but rather that he became important after Marx had associated himself with Hegelian philosophy. Cornu's second argument is also not very convincing: "The intellectual crisis that Marx went through at the time was indeed essentially brought about by the fact that in his decisive turn toward the liberal-democratic movement, he could no longer be content with the Romantic worldview, which corresponded to a reactionary political and social attitude." Marx had sought a "concrete worldview" and found it in "Hegel's philosophy" (Cornu 1954.: 95). Apart from the fact that Cornu had already seen Marx as standing on the side of the democrats in his Abitur examination essay in the subject of German (ibid: 62), there is no indication that Marx's decision in favor of Hegel's philosophy was based upon a prior political turn. When should such a turn have occurred, and what might have caused it?[149]

Why Did Marx Give Up His Attempts at Poetry?

The only information concerning this question is found in the November 1837 letter. Concerning the poems composed for Jenny in 1836, Marx writes that these were "purely idealistic": "My heaven, my art, became a world beyond, as remote as my love. Everything real became hazy and what is hazy

---

148. Breckman (1999: 259ff.) also sees the cause for Marx's turn to Hegel's philosophy in Gans's alleged influence and Marx's critical engagement with legal theory.

149. Hillmann also criticizes Cornu, but his own explanation for Marx's transition toward Hegel's philosophy is similar: the backward conditions of Berlin had the effect of a cold shower upon the student from the progressive Rhineland, so the questions arising in response could no longer be clarified with the tools of Romanticism (Hillmann 1966: 73). Marx had turned to Hegelian philosophy because he no longer understood the world (ibid.: 82). But if Marx had such problems with understanding social and political conditions (there is no evidence for this), why did he turn to Hegel's philosophy and not, for example, the historical school of law? What was the decisive factor in favor of Hegel?

has no definite outlines. All the poems of the first three volumes I sent to Jenny are marked by attacks on our times, diffuse and inchoate expressions of feeling, nothing natural, everything built out of moonshine, complete opposition between what is and what ought to be, rhetorical reflections instead of poetic thoughts.... The whole extent of a longing that has no bounds finds expression there in many different forms and makes the poetic 'composition' into 'diffusion'" (MECW 1: 11). The main accusation Marx raises against his own work is that it was "purely idealistic." This is obviously not meant in the philosophical sense, but in the colloquial sense of that which should be *ideally* so, from which the "opposition between what is and what ought to be" mentioned in the letter arises. The concentration upon the "ought" also explains the lamented distance from reality, the lack of the "natural."

Marx also accuses the poems he sent to his father in April 1837 for his sixtieth birthday of "idealism." *Scorpion and Felix* is characterized by "forced humor" and *Oulanem* is "an unsuccessful, fantastic drama." Finally, this idealism was transformed into "mere formal art, mostly without objects that inspire it and without any impassioned train of thought." Yet there was a glimmer of hope in the poems: "And yet these last poems are the only ones in which suddenly, as if by a magic touch—oh, the touch was at first a shattering blow—I caught sight of the glittering realm of true poetry like a distant fairy palace, and all my creations crumbled into nothing" (MECW 1: 17).

This statement was taken by Mehring and many others as proof that Marx had recognized his lack of poetic talent and had therefore abandoned his attempts at poetry. But he does not refer to "talent" here, but rather to "true poetry," which is not completely absent and of which there were at least flashes. Nonetheless, Marx abandoned his literary attempts; the flash of "true poetry" did not contribute to encouraging him. In the letter to his father, he writes rather dramatically: "A curtain had fallen, my holy of holies was rent asunder, and new gods had to be installed." (ibid.: 18).

But in what did this "holy of holies" consist? McLellan puts forward the thesis: "In general Marx's first contact with Berlin University brought about a great change in the views he had expressed in his school-leaving essay. No longer was he inspired by the thought of the service of humanity and concerned to fit himself into a place where he might best be able to sacrifice himself for this noble ideal; his poems of 1837, on the contrary, reveal a cult of the isolated genius and an introverted concern for the development of his own personality apart from the rest of humanity" (McLellan 1973: 41).[150]

---

150. Hillmann had made a similar argument: "Instead of devotion to humanity, we find the elevation of oneself above humans" (Hillmann 1966: 58). However, Hillmann is also unable

But the case is not so simple. It was made clear in the poems for Jenny that Marx was not entirely free of the influence of the subjectivism of Romanticism. But an exclusively introverted interest in one's own ego does not necessarily follow from that. In the epigrams of 1837, Marx begins to take up socially relevant debates. He defends Goethe and Schiller against the attacks of religious philistinism (Epigrams V and VI, MECW 1: 577, 578); and he criticizes the passivity of the Germans:

> In its armchair, stupid and dumb,
> The German public watches it come. (Epigram I, MECW 1: 575)

And, dripping with sarcasm, he remarks upon the political hopes arising after the defeat of Napoleon, but which the Germans then quickly abandoned:

> They were all smitten by deep remorse.
> Too much has happened at once, it's plain.
> We'll have to behave ourselves again.
> The rest it were better to print and bind,
> And buyers will not be hard to find. (Epigram III, MECW 1: 577)

But Marx's other poetic attempts also do not at all have to be placed in opposition to the goals he stated in the Abitur essay. There, Marx had named work on behalf of "the welfare of mankind" as the main criterion for choosing a profession; only then could one achieve one's own perfection (MECW 1: 7). These notions are compatible with a poetry embedded in a philosophical-political conception aiming at an improvement of human relations. What he criticized in the letter as "idealism" after turning away from poetry appears to be precisely such a conception: improving the world and humanity by means of art, by, poetically, contrasting the bad "is" with the better "ought."

In his letters "On the Aesthetic Education of Man," Friedrich Schiller had expressed considerations from which Marx could have proceeded. However, stylistically and in its pictorial language, Marx's poetry was oriented much more towards early Romanticism than to Schiller; it's more plausible that it was there he sought a political-philosophical conception for his poems.

---

to measure all of Marx's poetic attempts by the same yardstick, which is why he is forced to distinguish between Romantic and non-Romantic poems (ibid.: 66–70). He regards as non-Romantic that which stands in opposition to the Catholic-reactionary content of Late Romanticism; in other words, Romanticism is reduced to the reactionary tendencies of Late Romanticism.

Ideas critical of society were prevalent in early Romanticism. Art was not just regarded as a higher form of knowledge; for example, Friedrich Schlegel's Aethenaeum fragments or the works of Novalis attributed to art the potential to change the world through poeticizing society. Thus, in the well-known Fragment 216, Schlegel presupposes the connections between politics, philosophy, and art as completely self-evident: "The French Revolution, Fichte's philosophy, and Goethe's Meister are the greatest tendencies of the age." With "progressive, universal poetry," he formulates in Fragment 116 a program for connecting art, philosophy, and life: "Romantic poetry is a progressive, universal poetry. Its aim isn't merely to reunite all the separate species of poetry and put poetry in touch with philosophy and rhetoric. It tries to and should mix and fuse poetry and prose, inspiration and criticism, the poetry of art and the poetry of nature; and make poetry lively and sociable, and life and society poetical" (Schlegel 1991: 31). Aiming in a similar direction, Novalis (Friedrich von Hardenberg, 1772–1801) writes: "The world must be romanticized. In that way, one finds its original sense. Romanticizing is nothing other than a qualitative raising of power. In this operation, the lower self is identified with a better self" (Novalis 1797–98: 384). We don't know the extent to which the young Marx appropriated early Romanticism's concepts on art theory. But it's plausible that with his intensive interest in art and in light of how well known the texts of Schlegel and Novalis were, that he came into contact with these notions and was influenced by them.

When, in his letter to his father, Marx accuses his own poems of "idealism," the "complete opposition between what is and what ought to be" (MECW 1: 11), then he is taking aim precisely at this supposed potential of art to change the world, which he now doubts. So the point is not primarily any kind of lack of craft or thematic deficits of his poetry—deficits hardly surprising in the case of a nineteen-year-old author—but rather what he believed he could achieve for humanity with his art. But if the connection between poetry and work on behalf of humanity could no longer be maintained, if it dissolved into "idealism," then Marx, to the extent that the imperative formulated in his Abitur essay was still valid, could no longer become a poet, irrespective of the question of talent.

Marx's turn away from an envisaged career as a poet was thus far more than simply the abandonment of an earlier career wish; it was the abandonment of a certain conception of reality and the possible critique thereof, and thus the abandonment of everything that had hitherto given him moral and political orientation in the broadest sense. But why did Marx, in the middle of 1837, suddenly criticize as "idealism" that aesthetic-moral conception that had been the "holy of holies" during the last two years? What had happened?

Hegel's Critique of the Romantics and Marx's Transition to Hegel's Philosophy

Whatever Marx's notions of art theory might have looked like individually, they must have encountered a devastating critique in the year 1837. In his November letter, he describes how he reacted to this critique, but he does not explicitly say what the origin of this critique was. However, this can be deduced. In accusing his own poetry of "idealism," the confrontation of reality with an abstract "ought," he repeats a central point of critique that Hegel had formulated against Romantic art.[151]

It is probable that Marx encountered this critique in the course of the spring, before he went over to Hegelian philosophy. Marx says that, before the summer, he "had read fragments of Hegel's philosophy, the grotesque craggy melody of which did not appeal to me" (MECW 1: 18). The "grotesque craggy melody" probably refers to the level of abstraction of Hegel's argumentation. His epigram on Hegel, which could only have been written at the beginning of April at the latest, since it was included in the album given to his father in April for his birthday, suggests that he was familiar with at least the beginning of Hegel's *Science of Logic*, and was not very enthusiastic. One line of the epigram states: "Now you know all, since I've said plenty of nothing to you!" (MECW 1: 576), the "I" here is Hegel. The *Science of Logic* begins with the consideration that pure being (being as such, not the determinate being of something) encompasses *everything*, but is merely "indeterminate immediacy," thus does not have a determination and therefore no specific content: "There is nothing to be intuited in it," this being "is in fact nothing" (Hegel 2010: 59). In the quoted line, Marx remains at this unity of being and nothing, so that the unity appears rather absurd. But for Hegel, this unity serves to obtain his next and more important category: the truth of this unity, he continues, is not that being and nothing are "without distinction," but rather "this *movement* of the immediate vanishing of the one into the other: *becoming*" (Hegel 2010: 60).

---

151. That which Hegel refers to in his "Aesthetics" as "Romantic art" encompasses far more than what is today referred to as Romanticism; it includes all Christian art of the Middle Ages. However, there is also a decisive critique of those authors who are considered Romantics today. In the literature, Hegel's critique of Romanticism is not addressed very often. Alongside the short commentary by Emanuel Hirsh (1924) on the section on morality in the *Phenomenology of Spirit*, Otto Pöggeler's dissertation, published in 1956, must be mentioned in particular. Pöggeler's dissertation not only distinguishes between different dimensions of Hegel's critique of Romanticism, but also makes clear how this critique arises from his conception of substance and subjectivity (Pöggeler 1999). This is not the place to follow up on such distinctions, or the question of whether Hegel's critique of the Romantics was on target. The concern here is solely with making clear that the young Marx was struck by this critique.

Marx probably also read fragments of other texts by Hegel during this period. It appears plausible that he engaged with Hegel's most famous work—which at the same time constitutes a sort of introduction to the entire system—*The Phenomenology of Spirit*. There, he might have been especially interested in those passages that he could relate to his understanding of art and morality. In the section "Spirit that is certain of itself. Morality," Hegel formulated a critique of the "beautiful soul" which can also be read as a fundamental critique of Romanticism. In *On Grace and Dignity* (1793), Schiller had used this term in a positive sense; it is "in a beautiful soul, that sensuousness and reason, duty and inclination harmonize" (Schiller 1985: 368). In Goethe's work, the term starts to become ambivalent. In *Wilhelm Meister's Apprenticeship*, under the title "Confessions of a Beautiful Soul," a first-person narrator describes her life and education, which ultimately leads her to the pietist Moravians (the Herrnhuthers). But at the end, Goethe has the niece of this narrator make the observation: "Perhaps too much employment with her own thoughts, and withal a moral and religious scrupulosity, prevented her from being to the world what, in other circumstances, she might have become" (Goethe 1907: 207). Finally, in Hegel's work there is a devastating critique of the beautiful soul.

Hegel regards the "beautiful soul" as a consciousness concentrated upon itself, which lives in constant "dread of besmirching the splendour of its inner being by action and an existence. And, in order to preserve the purity of its heart, it flees from contact with the actual world" (Hegel 1977: 400). Hegel derives this seeking and longing which is typical for Romanticism from the unresolved contradiction of "the 'beautiful soul' lacking an *actual* existence," which wishes to maintain its pure self, but stands before the necessity "to externalize itself," that is, to act in reality. The beautiful soul, as the consciousness of this contradiction, "wastes itself in yearning and pines away in consumption" (Hegel 1977: 406). If one thinks, on the one hand, of the activist impulse contained in the poem "Feelings" quoted above, and, on the other hand, of the "yearning's glow" in "Siren Song," which allows the youth to escape the siren but the object of which is completely unclear, then it becomes clear that Marx must have felt struck by such a critique. His criticism of "idealism" in the letter to his father is an abridged version of Hegel's critique of the beautiful soul: it does not take the plunge into reality, although it claims to, but rather merely contrasts reality with an abstract "ought."

Whereas the critique of Romanticism remained implicit in the "Phenomenology," Hegel explicitly criticized the Romantics in his Berlin "Lectures on Aesthetics." The fact that Marx definitely took notice of this critique is proven by a later work. In "The Great Men of the Exile" (1852), an unpublished work by Marx and Engels, they state that "Romanticism" had been "demolished philosophically by Hegel in his Aesthetik" (MECW 11: 265). The first volume of these lectures, which were issued posthumously by Heinrich Gustav Hotho, was first published in 1835. In Marx's "Hegel Epigram" from 1837, the *Aesthetics* is the only work of Hegel's mentioned by name. The final verse can be taken as a clue that Marx had not yet read the *Aesthetics* but planned to:

> Forgive us epigrammatists
> For singing songs with nasty twists.
> In Hegel we're all so completely submerged,
> But with his *Aesthetics* we've yet to be purged.
> (MECW 1: 577)

In the introduction to the *Aesthetics*, Hegel criticizes Romantic irony, which was emphasized in particular by Friedrich Schlegel. Behind this all-encompassing and -dissolving irony, Hegel sees an artistic ego that "looks down from his high rank on all other men" from "this standpoint of divine genius. . . . This is the general meaning of the divine irony of genius, as this concentration of the ego into itself, for which all bonds are snapped and which can live only in the bliss of self-enjoyment" (Hegel 1975: 66). Whereas Friedrich Schlegel and Ludwig Tieck are explicitly criticized in the paragraphs that follow, Hegel excludes from this critique Ferdinand Solger, for whom irony was also the highest principle of art: "Solger was not content, like the others, with superficial philosophical culture; on the contrary; his genuinely speculative[152] inmost need impelled him to plumb the depths of the philosophical Idea." However, Solger only grasped the philosophical idea in a one-sided manner, Hegel continues, and his early death made further development impossible (Hegel 1975: 68).

Karl Wilhelm Ferdinand Solger (1780–1819) had been since 1811 a professor of philosophy at the University of Berlin. He greeted Hegel's appointment to Berlin enthusiastically and invited him to collaborate (see his letter to Hegel, May 1818, Hegel, Briefe 2: 189). Solger, who was also a close friend of the poet Ludwig Tieck (1773–1853), found himself in terms of aesthetics somewhere between Schelling, who was close to the Romantics, and Hegel (on Solger, see Henckmann 1970; Schulte 2001). However, his main work, *Erwin: Four Dialogues on Beauty and Art* (*Erwin: Vier Gespräche über das*

---

152. By "speculation," Hegel means comprehending recognition and not, as is today the case, assumption that is less sound.

Schöne und die Kunst, 1815) had hardly any reception, which might have been due in part to the unusual dialogic form. To that extent, it's notable that in Marx's letter to his father, he also mentions Solger's *Erwin* alongside Lessing's *Laocoön* and Winckelmann's *History of Art*, both of which were well-known classics at the time (MECW 1: 17). It's possible that Marx first had his attention drawn to Solger by the mention in Hegel's *Aesthetics*, and perhaps he read Solger because he attempted to find philosophical arguments against Hegel's critique of Romanticism.

Thus, there are indications that Marx engaged with Hegel's critique of Romanticism, and that it was this critique that so strongly unsettled him that he had to give up his notion to work on behalf of the welfare of humanity by means of art. The effect of Hegel's critique of Romanticism would probably have been strengthened if Marx had taken note of other passages of the *Phenomenology*. Under the heading "Virtue and the Way of the World," Hegel writes: "Thus the 'way of the world' triumphs over what, in opposition to it, constitutes virtue.... However, it does not triumph over something real but over the creation of distinctions that are no distinctions; it glories in this pompous talk about doing what is best for humanity. . . . Ideal entities and purposes of this kind are empty, ineffectual words which lift up the heart but leave reason unsatisfied, which edify, but raise no edifice; declamations which specifically declare merely this: that the individual who professes to act for such noble ends and who deals in such fine phrases is in his own eyes an excellent creature" (Hegel 1977: 233). The young Karl, who wanted so much to serve the welfare of humanity yet didn't have much to say about what the welfare of humanity would look like, might have felt personally addressed here.

Hegel's critique of Romanticism was enough to destroy Marx's earlier notions about art ("A curtain had fallen, my holy of holies was rent asunder," MECW 1: 18), but it was not yet clear which conceptions the young Marx would now orient toward. The return to the pre-Romantic, simple rationalism of the Enlightenment was in any case blocked, since Romanticism was criticized precisely on the point that it had in common with the Enlightenment the rigid opposition between "is" and "ought." Marx also did not immediately adopt Hegel's philosophy. Initially, he attempted to work out his own conception.

Immediately after the sentence about his holy of holies being rent asunder, Marx writes: "From the idealism which, by the way, I had compared and nourished with the idealism of Kant and Fichte, I arrived at the point of seeking the idea in reality itself" (MECW 1: 18). Marx thus moved closer to Hegel's path toward knowledge of reality, as formulated at the end of the second part of the *Logic*. Concerning the "idea," which as the "adequate concept"

Hegel distinguishes from the mere "representation" of a thing (Hegel 2010: 670), he maintains that "we must not regard it as just a *goal* which is to be approximated but remains a kind of *beyond*; we must rather regard everything as *being* actual only to the extent that it has the idea in it and expresses it. It is not just that the subject matter, the objective and the subjective world, *ought* to be in principle *congruent* with the idea; the two are themselves rather the congruence of concept and reality; a reality that does not correspond to the concept is mere *appearance*, something subjective, accidental, arbitrary, something which is not the truth" (Hegel 2010: 671). What Hegel examines is precisely not an abstract realm of ideas beyond the real world. Rather, what he describes as an "idea" is knowledge of a real object, its necessary determinations as distinct from its merely coincidental properties. In the "Hegel Epigram," Marx still made fun of Hegel's claim of grasping real relations. There, he writes mockingly about this realism:

> Kant and Fichte soar to heavens blue
> Seeking for some distant land,
> I [Hegel] but seek to grasp profound and true
> That which—in the street I find. (MECW 1: 577)

Now Marx was also taking this path, though he initially sought an alternative to Hegel's philosophy: "I wrote a dialogue of about 24 pages: 'Cleanthes, or the Starting Point and Necessary Continuation of Philosophy.' Here art and science, which had become completely divorced from each other, were to some extent united, and like a vigorous traveler I set about the task itself, a philosophical-dialectical account of divinity, as it manifests itself as the idea-in-itself, as religion, as nature, and as history. My last proposition was the beginning of the Hegelian system. And this work, for which I had acquainted myself to some extent with natural science, Schelling, and history, which had caused me to rack my brains endlessly, and which is written so *concinné*[153] (since it was actually intended to be a new logic) that now even I myself can hardly recapture my thinking about it, this work, my dearest child, reared by moonlight, like a false siren delivers me into the arms of the enemy" (MECW 1: 18).

This text, which Marx put so much into, has not survived. However, a few things can be taken from Marx's description. That Marx chose the form of dialogue might be due to the influence of Solger. The namesake of his dialogue, Cleanthes (331–232 BC), was a Greek philosopher, a student of Zeno

153. Corrected translation, since *concinné* (elegantly, delicately) is not included in the MECW text. —Trans..

of Citium (332–262 BCE), the founder of the Stoic school.[154] Among other of Cleanthes' works, a hymn to Zeus has survived, which praises Zeus as a world soul. This was probably the reason that Marx used Cleanthes for the title and probably as the central figure of the dialogue. He fits the pantheist content outlined by Marx: God is manifest in nature and history and is therefore conceived not as a *person* beyond the terrestrial world, but rather as a world soul. It might be surprising that Marx centered his text on the unification of "art and knowledge" upon a "philosophical-dialectical account of divinity." But if one considers that Hegel in the *Phenomenology* conceived of art, religion, and philosophy as the central stages (both historically and systematically) of humanity's understanding of the world and itself, then what Marx writes about his dialogue is a clear indication that he was working through Hegel's conception. This strengthens my suspicion that Marx had been shaken by Hegel's critique of Romanticism. Marx wanted to confront "the enemy" with the aid of Schelling, and maybe Solger as well. But this project missed its aim: Marx's own considerations increasingly brought him into the proximity of Hegel's philosophy, driving him "into the arms of the enemy." This undesired result caused all kinds of chagrin for Marx: "For some days my vexation made me quite incapable of thinking; I ran about madly in the garden by the dirty water of the Spree, which 'washes souls and dilutes the tea'" (ibid.).[155]

But before Marx could engage more intensively with this disliked philosophy, he initially conducted "positive studies." In the letter, alongside Savigny's *Ownership*, he lists writings ranging from Feuerbach (the jurist Paul Johann Anselm von Feuerbach, 1775–1833, who was the father of the philosopher Ludwig Feuerbach, 1804–1872), and Grolman's "criminal law" to works on the Pandect as well as on civil procedure and canon law (MECW 1: 19). Thematically, this reading list overlaps to a great extent with the material of the lectures on law from the first two semesters in Berlin.

But Marx's general interests also weren't short-changed: "Then I translated in part Aristotle's *Rhetoric*, read *De Augmentis Scientiarum* of the famous Bacon of Verulam, spent a good deal of time on Reimarus, to whose book

---

154. Stoicism was a philosophical school that proceeded from the assumption that the world was animated by a divine reason (Logos) and that everything that occurs was subject to a comprehensive causality, whereby it was unclear whether and to what extent there was human freedom. Through control of their passions, individual people should achieve self-sufficiency (Autarkeia) and unshakable equanimity (Ataraxia), which would allow one to best endure the ups and downs of life. The expression "stoic calm" originates in this Ataraxia.

155. With the last quotation, Marx was showing that he had already read his Heine ("Die Nordsee," "Frieden"; *Heine Werke,* 3: 187).

on the artistic instincts of animals I applied my mind with delight" (ibid.). Bacon of Verulam is better known today as Francis Bacon (1561–1626). His most famous work is the *Novum Organum Scientarium* (1620), in which he defends a natural science that works empirically against a view of nature based upon preconceived dogmas. The work mentioned by Marx, *De Dignitate et augmentis scientiarum* (1623), attempts to provide an encyclopedic overview of the fields of knowledge, as well as to outline future fields of research in the natural sciences. In *The Holy Family* (1845), Marx writes concerning Bacon that he was the "real progenitor of *English materialism* and all *modern experimental* science" (MECW 4: 128). When he adds that in Bacon's work, "materialism still holds back within itself in a naive way the germs of a many-sided development. On the one hand, matter, surrounded by a sensuous, poetic glamour, seems to attract man's whole entity by winning smiles" (ibid.), then this estimation probably originates in his reading of *De augmentis*, since Bacon's *Novum Organon* (which Marx was probably also familiar with in 1845) is rather dry.

Hermann Samuel Reimarus (1694–1768) is known primarily for his posthumously published deistic critique of the Bible and religion (discussed in chapter 3). In his book *Allgemeine Betrachtungen über die Triebe der Thiere, hauptsächlich über ihre Kunsttriebe* (General Observations on the Instincts of Animals, Primarily Concerning Their Skills, 1760), the word *Kunst* is used primarily in its old meaning of skill or proficiency (the way one speaks in contemporary German of cooking as *Kochkunst*), and the focus is on where animals' skills come from, for example, the ability of bees to construct complex honeycombs. In the eighteenth century, two competing notions about animals were predominant: either they were considered as soulless automatons, following René Descartes (1596–1650), who attributed the ability to think solely to humans, or they had limited thinking abilities, with which they could process external impressions and learn their skills. Reimarus, who like Descartes also believed that only humans possessed understanding, attributed the skills of animals to innate drives necessary to their survival. Even without understanding, they were thus far more than mere automatons. With his theory of instincts, Reimarus was a predecessor of modern animal psychology, but his work was quickly forgotten in the nineteenth century (on Reimarus's contributions, see Mayr 1982; Kempski 1982). This text appears to have left a lasting impression upon Marx. The distinction he makes in the first volume of *Capital* between "those first instinctive forms of labor which remain on the animal level" and the specifically human labor process takes up Reimarus's considerations: "A spider conducts operations which resemble those of the weaver, and a bee would put many a human architect to shame by the construction of its honeycomb cells. But what distinguishes the worst architect from the best of bees is that the architect builds the cell in his mind before he constructs it in wax" (Marx 1976: 284).

Presumably, due to these conflicts and efforts "and as the result of nagging annoyance at having had to make an idol of a view that I hated" (MECW 1: 19), Marx fell ill. It's not clear what this illness was, though nervous exhaustion seems likely. A doctor advised him to go to the countryside, "and so it was that for the first time I traversed the whole length of the city to the gate and went to Stralow" (MECW 1: 18). Stralau (as it is currently named) now belongs to the borough of Friedrichshain in Berlin. During Marx's time, it was a fishing village before the gates of Berlin. It was most well known for the Stralauer Fischzug, the biggest and most popular folk festival of Berlin, which was always celebrated on August 24 (Zedlitz 1834: 753). Here, Marx first experienced a large folk festival, with a crowd of tens of thousands.

The stay in Stralau didn't just strengthen Marx physically; he had also made a fundamental decision concerning his attempts at poetry: "When I got better I burned all the poems and outlines of stories, etc." (MECW 1: 19). Furthermore, he had begun to systematically study Hegel: "While I was ill I got to know Hegel from beginning to end, together with most of his disciples. Through a number of meetings with friends in Stralow I came across a Doctor's Club, which includes some university lecturers and my most intimate Berlin friend, Dr. Rutenberg. In controversy here, many conflicting views were expressed, and I became ever more firmly bound to the modern world philosophy from which I had thought to escape" (ibid.).

Here, Marx mentions the Doctor's Club, which cannot be left out of any biography. In the next chapter, we will deal with it. Here, it's important to note that Marx first joined this Doctor's Club *after* his transition to Hegel's philosophy. The Doctor's Club was thus not the cause of this transition; rather, it merely strengthened the transition that had already occurred.

CONFLICTS WITH JENNY AND MARX'S FATHER

Marx's November 1837 letter to his father documents one of the first critical upheavals in the life of the nineteen-year-old: his departure from the aesthetic-political notions of Romanticism, which included not only leaving behind his envisaged career as a writer, but also those notions that had hitherto offered Karl an orientation in life. Although it was primarily an intellectual crisis, it also had emotional and, as Marx's ailments suggest, psychosomatic consequences.

The intellectual crisis was not the only shock in the young Marx's life. His relationship to Jenny was not free of crisis-ridden aggravations. During his trip to Berlin, Karl felt possessed by "a passionately yearning and hopeless love" (MECW 1: 11). As we can see in some of his poems, his love for Jenny was a source of great strength for Karl, but fears of loss arose again and again. These fears are hardly surprising, since familial resistance had to be reckoned with as soon as the relationship became known. Furthermore, Karl and Jenny had to live separately for a very long time, and letters, which took about a week to be delivered, were their only means of communication. Apparently, Karl insisted at the beginning of 1837 upon no longer keeping the relationship secret from Jenny's parents (see the letter from Heinrich Marx from March 2, 1837, MECW 1: 671). Jenny's parents probably found out about the engagement in the spring of 1837, since from that point on the secrecy of the relationship is no longer a topic in letters from Marx's father. In a letter from September 16, 1837, Heinrich Marx mentions that he would not show Karl's most recent letter to the Westphalens, which can only mean that it had become usual to read Karl's letters in both families.

The fear of rejection by Jenny's parents was apparently unfounded. In January of 1838, Ludwig von Westphalen wrote a long letter to his son Ferdinand, in which he referred to Karl as a "splendid fourth son" (Gemkow 2008: 517) and praised him in the highest of tones, so that he not only accepted Jenny's decision, but explicitly endorsed it: "And so for my part, I don't have the slightest doubt anymore in the quality of her choice, since I regard both as made for each other, and that they will be a very happy married couple, even if perhaps first after 5 or more years" (ibid.: 519). Ludwig von Westphalen would prove to be right about the five years until marriage.

The fact that he praised Karl so was an expression not only his high esteem but also an indication that Ferdinand regarded this relationship with mistrust—an attitude that was probably also predominant among other members of the Westphalen family, and in light of the risk that Jenny took (see section 2 of this chapter) was also not entirely unfounded.

Karl's worries did not end with the end of the secretiveness, however. His father repeatedly warned him not to forget that with his early engagement, he had taken on a great responsibility, which he must now face. His father was plagued by doubt: "Is your heart in accord with your head, your talents? Has it room for the earthly but gentler sentiments which in this vale of sorrow are so essentially consoling for a man of feeling? And since that heart is obviously animated and governed by a demon not granted to all men, is that demon heavenly or Faustian? Will you ever—and that is not the least painful doubt of my heart—will you ever be capable of truly human, domestic happiness?" (MECW 1: 670). That which Heinrich shared so candidly as his concerns (with the obvious ulterior motive of having an educative effect upon Karl) was then quickly transformed during disputes into an accusation. Thus, he wrote on August 12, 1837: "I do you justice in many matters, but I cannot entirely rid myself of the thought that you are not free from a little more egoism than is necessary for self-preservation" (MECW 1: 674). We don't know what preceded this, since not only are Karl's letters missing, the prior letter from Heinrich has also not survived. A few lines later, he writes: "But to abandon oneself to grief at the slightest storm, to lay bare a shattered heart and break the heart of our beloved ones at every suffering, do you call that poetry?" And finally, the admonition follows: "Quite soon you will and must be the father of a family. But neither honour nor wealth nor fame will make your wife and children happy; you alone can do that, your better self, your love, your tender behaviour, the putting behind you of stormy idiosyncrasies, of violent outbreaks of passion, of morbid sensitivity, etc., etc., etc." (ibid: 675).

Alongside the fear that Karl could be possessed by a "Faustian" demon that would make a normal family life impossible, Heinrich also formulated two more concrete complaints: that Karl was too sensitive and even laid bare his shattered heart and that Karl was too quick-tempered, which fits Eleanor's remark quoted above that at the time "he was a veritable furious Roland" (E. Marx 1897–98: 238).

Jenny was also a cause of concern to Karl. In the course of the summer, she fell ill for a longer period of time; we don't know the cause. When her health finally improved, she didn't want to write to Karl. "She has somehow got the idea that it is unnecessary to write, or some other obscure idea about it that she may hold, she has also a touch of genius," wrote Heinrich Marx on September 16, 1837, to Karl. Almost desperately he implored his son: "She is devoted to you body and soul, and you must never forget it, at her age she is making a sacrifice for you that ordinary girls would certainly not be capable of. So if she has the idea of not being willing or able to write, in God's name let it pass" (MECW 1: 682).

But Karl did not let it pass. At the end of September or beginning of October 1837 he must have written a letter that caused great concern to his mother as well as Jenny's parents. We only have indirect knowledge of this letter, from the response letter of his father from November 17, 1837. In the MEGA (III/1: 736) as well as in many contributions to Marx's biography, this letter from Heinrich is regarded as a response to Karl's letter from November 10. But this is not plausible for reasons of both time and content. Karl dated his letter November 10; at the end he writes that "it is almost 4 o'clock, the candle has burnt itself out" (MECW 1: 21), so he first ended the letter on the morning of November 11. In the case that he sent it on November 11 (to the extent this was possible, since the postal service did not run every day between Berlin and Trier), it could have just barely arrived in Trier on November 16 or 17. But if the letter had been sent after November 11, then Marx's father could not have received it on November 17.

That Heinrich Marx writes on November 17 that the last letter from Karl was "without form or content, a torn fragment saying nothing" does not fit at all with his son's letter from November 10: in any case, it was not "without content" or "saying nothing." The concluding characterization also doesn't fit: "I received a letter of bits and fragments, and, what is much worse, an embittered letter. Frankly speaking, my dear Karl, I do not like this modern word, which all weaklings use to cloak their feelings when they quarrel with the world" (MECW 1: 684). Heinrich reminds Karl of the love of his parents and that he has won a girl's love, and that he is envied. "Yet the first untoward event, the first disappointed wish, evokes embitterment! Is that strength? Is that a manly character?" (ibid.). This is obviously not about the letter from November 10, in which Karl does not bemoan an unfulfilled wish. The following two paragraphs in his letter disclose what wish Heinrich had in mind. Heinrich accuses his son of having agreed that he "would be satisfied with assurances for the future" (ibid.), but of not keeping to this. But "Your good mother … sounded the alarm, and the all too good parents of your Jenny could hardly wait for the moment when the poor, wounded heart would be consoled, and the recipe is undoubtedly already in your hands, if a defective address has not caused the epistle to go astray" (ibid.: 685).

This is obviously about Jenny's refusal to write, mentioned in Heinrich's letter from September 12–14. Karl felt torn because Jenny did not write to him. The united effort of his mother and Jenny's parents then succeeded, however, in moving Jenny to write. As emerges from the sentence just quoted, Heinrich did not yet know for sure whether Karl had already received Jenny's letter. But Karl had confirmed exactly that in his letter from November 10; he had read Jenny's letter "twelve times already" (MECW 1: 21). So Heinrich's letter from November 17 cannot be the response to Karl's letter from November 10; it is the answer to a lost letter, in which Karl must have described his inner turmoil.

A permanent topic in the letters from Karl's father were Karl's professional prospects, which became increasingly unclear. By studying law, he could become a lawyer, strive for a judgeship, or take on an administrative position. But Karl did not want any of this, as his father noted with a lightly resigned undertone: "Such a career, however, seemed not to your liking and I confess that, infected by your precocious views, I applauded you when you took academic teaching as your goal, whether in law or philosophy" (MECW 1: 679). Marx must have expressed the desire to become a professor in 1836 or at the beginning of 1837, since the letter from his father from February 3 mentions it (ibid.: 668).

Also in 1837, Karl pursued yet a further project: founding a journal of theater criticism. We find out about this for the first time in the letter from his father of August 12–14, 1837: "The plan you have outlined is fine, and if properly executed, well fitted to become a lasting monument of literature. But great difficulties are piling up in the way, particularly because of the self-ishness of those who are offended, and of the fact that there is no man of outstanding critical reputation to be at the head" (MECW 1: 676). The letter of September 16 makes clear that the journal would not be concerned with literary criticism in general, but rather "dramatic criticism" (MECW 1: 680). From the perspective of today, such a project might look rather harmless. Keep in mind that in a time before the invention of film, radio, and television, theater was a central medium not only of entertainment, but also of political-social education. In Berlin in particular, theater was heavily sponsored and supported. Friedrich Wilhelm III liked going to the theater; however, he had extremely conservative taste. One can imagine how the critical discussion of performances cherished by the king, and praise for pieces that were rejected by conservatives, could quickly become a political matter.

In November as well, Marx still kept to his plan; it even seemed to take on concrete shape. In the letter of November 10, he informed his father that he had already written to the bookseller Wigand,[156] and that "all the aesthetic celebrities of the Hegelian school have promised their collaboration through the help of university lecturer Bauer, who plays a big role among them, and of my colleague Dr. Rutenberg" (MECW 1: 20). Some discussion of Bruno Bauer (1809–1882) and Adolf Rutenberg (1808–1869) is in the next chapter, but not of the planned journal: it was never published.

On December 9, Heinrich Marx wrote the response to Karl's letter of November 10, and it turned out to be rather harsh, at least if one bears in mind the style of the earlier letters. His letter is an outright reckoning with Karl's conduct. In order to understand this, one has to make clear the context in which Karl's letter was written.

During his stay at the health spa in Bad Ems, Heinrich wrote on August 20,

---

156. Otto Wigand (1795–1870) was a bookseller and publisher in Leipzig. He published authors of the Young Germany movement and later some important Young Hegelians. Engels's first major work, *The Condition of the Working Class in England* (1845) was also published by Wigand.

Karl Marx in Bonn, ca. 1835/1836; drawing by Heinrich Rosbach,
Stadtmuseum Simeonstift, Trier

Karl Marx; drawing by Hellmut
Bach (1953) after the group
picture of Trier students

The Parochialstraße in Berlin; painting
by von Eduard Gärtner 1831

Group picture of the Trier students in Bonn, 1836 (from Monz)

Ludwig von Westphalen
(from Monz)

Georg Friedrich Wilhelm Hegel;
painting by Jakob Schlesinger, 1831

Jenny von Westphalen with lorgnon, ca. 1832

Hugo Wyttenbach; painting by Johann Anton Ramboux,
1829, Stadtmuseum Simeonstift, Trier

Bruno Bauer

Arnold Ruge

Eduard Gans

1837, to Karl: "If you have leisure and write to me, I shall be glad if you will draw up for me a concise plan of the positive legal studies that you have gone through this year" (MECW 1: 678). Marx's father would have liked to have had a brief report on his studies, especially with regard to how long Karl's studies would still take, since the usual three years were already over. Karl's next letter did not contain such a report, so his father wrote on September 16, 1837, that he awaited a "sequel" (MECW 1: 679). Instead of this sequel, in October there is the "embittered" letter that Heinrich Marx answered on November 17. Finally, in November, Karl's letter arrived. What interested his father the most, however, namely which courses Marx attended and how his studies were to proceed, does not emerge from the letter. Instead, Karl describes studies and drafts that ultimately had no tangible result, other than that Karl turned toward Hegel's philosophy.

Already, the beginning of the letter must have been a challenge for the rather sober and pragmatically oriented father: "Dear Father, There are moments in one's life which are like frontier posts marking the completion of a period but at the same time clearly indicating a new direction. At such a moment of transition we feel compelled to view the past and the present with the eagle eye of thought in order to become conscious of our real position. Indeed, world history itself likes to look back in this way and take stock, which often gives it the appearance of retrogression or stagnation, whereas it is merely, as it were, sitting back in an armchair in order to understand itself and mentally grasp its own activity, that of the mind" (MECW 1: 10). His father would have liked a simple report on Marx's studies, but the son can think of no better comparison for his "looking back" than the course of world history!

Karl continues: "At such moments, however, a person becomes lyrical, for every metamorphosis is partly a swan song, partly the overture to a great new poem" (ibid.). His father probably was not very pleased with such passionate statements. For us, however, it is of interest that the nineteen-year-old Karl was very aware that in 1837 a deep break in his intellectual development had occurred. On this break, the rest of the letter, which has been cited frequently above, is informative, but to his father it didn't mean very much.

In Heinrich's response from December 9, one notes the effort he makes to remain dispassionate despite his annoyance. He reminds Karl of his obligations toward his parents, toward his fiancée and her parents, who consented to the unusual and for their own child dangerous relationship. And herein lay Heinrich Marx's greatest concern: "For, in truth, thousands of parents would have refused their consent. And in moments of gloom your own father almost wishes they had done so, for the welfare of this angelic girl is all too dear to my heart; truly I love her like a daughter, and it is for that very reason that I am so anxious for her happiness" (ibid.: 688).

One notes how much pent-up annoyance Heinrich Marx must have had when he answers the rhetorical question of how Karl had fulfilled his obligations: "God's grief!!! Disorderliness, musty excursions into all departments of knowledge, musty brooding under a gloomy oil-lamp; running wild in a scholar's dressing-gown and with unkempt hair instead of running wild over a glass of beer," obviously a reference to the period in Bonn, "unsociable withdrawal with neglect of all decorum and even of all consideration for the *father*," that is, Karl had apparently ceased contact with the families he had been introduced to by his father's recommendations. Heinrich Marx notices his own increasing excitement and his hurting of Karl: "I am almost overwhelmed by the feeling that I am hurting you," but now he must say it: "I must and will say that you have caused your parents much vexation and little or no joy. Hardly were your wild goings-on in Bonn over, hardly were your old sins wiped out—and they were truly manifold—when, to our dismay, the pangs of love set in . . . But what were the fruits we harvested? . . . On several occasions we were without a letter for months, and the last time was when you knew Eduard was ill,[157] mother suffering and I myself not well, and moreover cholera was raging in Berlin; and as if that did not even call for an apology, your next letter contained not a single word about it" (ibid.: 689). Finally, Heinrich comes to the topic of money, and can only express himself through bitter irony: "As if we were men of wealth, my Herr Son disposed in one year of almost 700 talers contrary to all agreement, contrary to all usage, whereas the richest spend less than 500. And why? I do him the justice of saying that he is no rake, no squanderer. But how can a man who every week or two discovers a new system and has to tear up old works laboriously arrived at, how can he, I ask, worry about trifles? How can he submit to the pettiness of order?" (ibid.: 690).

Heinrich mentions in this passage two people who had apparently reported to him about Karl in the past. It's possible that the accusation of "running wild in a scholar's dressing-gown" did not originate merely in Heinrich's imagination, but in such reports. "Narrow-minded persons like G. R. and Evers may be worried about that, but they are common fellows. True, in their simplicity these men try to digest the lectures, even if only the words, and to procure themselves patrons and friends here and there . . . whereas my hardworking talented Karl spends wretched nights awake, weakens his mind and

---

157. Karl's youngest brother Eduard fell ill with tuberculosis. At age eleven Eduard died on December 14, just a few days after his father's letter (Schöncke 1993: 820).

body by serious study . . . but what he builds today he destroys tomorrow" (ibid.). It was probably Karl who had described these students as "narrow-minded" and "simple," which his father now takes up with total sarcasm. They could not be identified by those working on the MEGA. Kliem found out that in 1837, two brothers, Gustav and Friedrich Evers, were enrolled at the University of Berlin. They were from Warnburg in West Prussia, but their father had become a commissioner of justice in Trier (Kliem 1988: 23). It's understandable that Heinrich Marx was happy to receive any report about his son. But to claim, as Kliem does, that Heinrich had his son observed (ibid.: 24) seems a bit exaggerated.

Finally, Heinrich mentions Karl's neglected siblings: "I must add, too, the complaints of your brothers and sisters. From your letters, one can hardly see that you have any brothers or sisters; as for the good Sophie, who has suffered so much for you and Jenny and is so lavish in her devotion to you, you do not think of her when you do not need her" (MECW 1: 691).

In order to properly order all this annoyance on the part of Heinrich Marx, one has to be clear about the implicit familial contract that existed at that time—in the absence of health or retirement insurance. For Karl to study for many years meant an enormous financial burden for the family. At the beginning of the 1830s, Heinrich Marx's annual income was 1,500 talers (Herres 1990: 197). In 1837, Heinrich suffered for months from a bad cough, so that he ultimately made a trip to a health spa. He probably couldn't work as much as he had in the past, so that his income was probably a bit smaller than the 1,500 talers. If Karl had used up 700 talers in the previous year, that would have been about half the annual income of the ten-member family, from which doctors' and medicine bills for Heinrich and Eduard had to be paid and from which savings for old age had to be taken. Even if Karl had spent less than 700 talers, the family would not have been able to sustain this in the long run. The enormous expenditures for his studies came with expectations that Karl would study purposefully and take up a well-paid profession, so that in the future he could support his parents, but above all his siblings if this proved to be necessary. In an earlier letter, Heinrich had once formulated this expectation ironically: "The hope that you might some day be a support for your brothers and sisters is an idea too beautiful and too attractive for a good-natured heart for me to want to deprive you of it" (MECW 1: 651).

His father's letter must have been quite a shock to Karl. The inner struggles that he wished to make clear to his father, the turn away from poetry and toward Hegel's philosophy, and above all, what this meant to him, a completely new orientation in the world had apparently not been understood at all. Heinrich could only see that his gifted son was wasting his talents in completely fruitless fields, and that his studies were not leading to an end. This was a situation that many young people are repeatedly confronted with: their parents cannot understand that the young do not think and act within a system of coordinates that they themselves view as completely natural.

But his father's lack of understanding was not all. Karl's father also accused him of ignoring his parents and his siblings, who all found themselves in a difficult situation due to the illnesses of his brother and father, and of not sharing in their suffering, an accusation that was apparently accurate, and which left young Karl, as we shall soon see, feeling stricken.

The effect emanating from his father's letter was strengthened by another one: as emerges from the letter that Ludwig von Westphalen wrote in January 1838 to his son Ferdinand, Jenny had also written a letter to Karl in December 1837 that levied accusations similar to those formulated by Heinrich Marx. This letter was written without Jenny knowing of it. According to Ludwig, the two letters appeared to Karl to be an act of collusion, which "deeply offended and shook" him, so that he succumbed to a "nervous disease." But he recovered quickly and reacted with a "splendid, exquisite treasure, a veritable flood of long-desired letters from him to me and Mom, to his esteemed father and splendid mother, all of his siblings, and his adored Jenny, as well as wonderful poems to her" (Gemkow 2008: 518).

With all of these letters and poems, all of which have been lost, Karl attempted to heal the wounds he had inflicted, and he appears to have been more or less successful.[158] Not only did Ludwig von Westphalen praise him in the highest terms; his father also showed himself to be reasonably pleased with his son. He did complain that Karl did not address the issue of money, but he assured him of his fatherly love and praised him: "Your latest decision is worthy of the highest praise and well considered, wise and commendable, and if you carry out what you have promised, it will probably bear the best fruits. And rest assured that it is not only you who are making a big sacrifice. The same applies to all of us, but reason must triumph" (MECW 1: 692). We don't know what decision this was. The editors of the MEGA volume suspect that Marx wanted to forgo his Easter visit, even though Heinrich Marx had allowed this visit in his letter from December 9 (MEGA III/1: 738). But measured against the amount of his father's praise, forgoing the visit seems to be a bit too little. It appears more

---

158. The "apparent lack of real interest in the condition of his family" that Stedman Jones (2017: 58) claims to discern is not so clear, at least if one considers the available sources.

plausible that Karl had announced far more, at the very least to conclude his studies quickly, maybe even that he would not visit Trier before the conclusion of his studies. This would explain Heinrich's remark that Karl would not be the only one making a sacrifice, since the family and Jenny would also have to do without him.

Heinrich Marx wrote the letter just quoted on February 10, 1838, after he had been sick in bed for two months and was still very weak. It is the last letter from Heinrich to Karl that has been passed down to us. On February 15–16, his mother wrote him that his father's condition was slowly improving but that he was only able to add a greeting; he was too weak for anything else. However, he does appear to have recovered somewhat shortly before his death, given that he wrote the text on the "Cologne Muddle" (see MEGA IV/1: 379) mentioned in the last chapter. Since he refers to literature that was first published at the beginning of 1838, the conclusion of the MEGA editors that he had written the text in March or April is plausible.

Shortly before Heinrich's death, Karl was in Trier once more. From a fragment of a letter from Jenny, we know that Karl departed from Trier on May 7 and that his father died on May 10 (MEGA III/1: 331). Maybe Karl spent Easter in Trier (Easter Sunday fell on April 15, his father's birthday) and then stayed a bit longer; perhaps his mother or Jenny informed him of his father's deteriorating condition and Karl made the trip in order to see him one last time. We don't know anything about the course of this visit, other than that there was a hefty and mutually hurtful conflict between Karl and Jenny—the fragment from Jenny's letter makes a reference to this. However, it's not clear what it was about.[159]

The death of his father was an important rupture in the life of young Marx.[160] Not only did he have a strong emotional connection to his father; he also respected his authority. The constant admonitions might have annoyed Karl, but he took them seriously, as the "flood of letters" from December

---

159. Referring to Heinrich Marx's letter from December 9, Neffe (2017: 66) writes: "The death [of Heinrich] was preceded by a complete falling out." And concerning Karl's visit: "It is not known whether a reconciliation occurred, or what it looked like." In light of the letter from February 10 just quoted, and the cooperative work on the text concerning the Cologne Muddle—Neffe takes notice of neither—one can hardly speak of a "falling out."

160. That Karl did not attend his father's funeral has been tidily embellished by the imaginative Francis Wheen (1999: 29): "Karl did not attend the funeral. The journey from Berlin would be too long, he explained, and he had more important things to do." The use of indirect speech by Wheen suggests that this last sentence was a statement by Karl. In fact, there is no such statement provided by any source. However, it was not invented by Wheen; he copied it, like the story about the duel, without attribution from Payne (1968: 55). It was simply impossible

1837 mentioned by Ludwig von Westphalen makes clear. His father was a strong pillar for Karl, which probably first became clear to Karl after his death. Neither his mother nor Ludwig von Westphalen could take his place: the young Marx was on his own in a completely new way.

---

for Marx to attend his father's funeral due to the logistics of travel. For the trip from Trier to Berlin, the stagecoach, which carried both people as well as letters, needed five to seven days; and it did not make the trip every day. Between the mailing of a letter announcing the death and Karl's arrival in Trier, there would have been at least twelve to fourteen days. In Trier during the early summer, there would have been little possibility of preserving Heinrich Marx's body for such a long time. The proof that Marx was deeply affected by his father's death emerges from a letter written by Ferdinand von Westphalen to his wife. There he reports that his brother Edgar, who had also begun his studies in Berlin, had written a "very nice letter" to Karl's mother "about the disclosure of news of the death to young Marx," which Ludwig von Westphalen read to the family (Gemkow 2008: 520). Ferdinand's choice of words, "disclosure of news of the death" (Eröffnung der Todesbotschaft) suggests that Karl did not find out about the death from a letter, but rather that his mother, Henriette, or possibly Jenny had written to Edgar and asked him to personally share the news of the death with Karl, precisely because they knew how attached Karl was to his father.

3

THE PHILOSOPHY OF RELIGION, THE BEGINNINGS OF YOUNG HEGELIANISM, AND MARX'S DISSERTATION PROJECTS 1838–1841

From the first two years of Marx's studies (1835–37), the sources available to us are his father's letters, Karl's extensive letter from November 10, 1837, as well as the surviving attempts at poetry. For the period from the end of 1837 until the end of 1840, the availability of sources is considerably worse. From Marx, only a short letter to Adolf Rutenberg has survived; otherwise, there are few letters to Marx. Beyond that, there exist excerpts from the years 1839 and 1840 that were made within the context of Marx's planned dissertation. Since so little is known about Marx's life from 1838 to 1840, these years are gladly passed over in biographies and studies of his work. Frequently, the depictions leap from Marx's letter from November 1837, where he explains his turn to Hegel's philosophy, to his finished dissertation in 1841.

But the years 1837–41 were important for Marx's intellectual development. First, his appropriation of Hegel's philosophy, which had begun in 1837 but was far from concluded, occurred in a specific period of transition. In the second half of the 1830s, Hegel's reputation had, on the one hand, reached its high point due to the Association of Friends edition of his works and lectures, and, on the other, the Hegelian school began to differentiate itself. This chapter will discuss the extent to which the image of a split between politically conservative "Old Hegelians" and radical "Young Hegelians" is accurate. In any case, Hegelianism was subject to increasingly strong attacks by conservatives, and with the death of the liberal minister of culture, Altenstein, in the year 1840, it also lost its institutional backing. Second, Marx began to occupy himself more intensely in the years after 1837 with a topic that is not examined in many accounts: the philosophy of religion. In the late 1830s, this was a highly political topic in Prussia. The split in the Hegelian school also began with controversies surrounding the philosophy of religion.

The relationship between Marx and Bruno Bauer also has to be considered against this background. In those years, Bauer was connected to Marx not only through an intense personal friendship, but also through considerable proximity in terms of subject matter and politics. Between 1836 and 1839, Bauer consummated a breathtaking development from the "right" to the "left." We will discuss what Marx's possible share in this development was, and in turn how Marx was influenced by Bauer.

Toward the end of the 1830s and above all after the royal succession of 1840 and the disappointment that followed when the new king did not bring the liberal reforms that had been hoped for, "Young Hegelian" authors developed increasingly radical positions, "bolder," wrote Friedrich Engels in 1851, "than hitherto it had been the fate of German ears to hear expounded." Furthermore, they "attempted to restore to glory the memory of the heroes of the first French Revolution," which was frowned upon in Germany at the time (MECW 11: 15).[161] Looking back, Marx wrote in January 1859, also for the *New York Daily Tribune*, about this phase: "The middle class, still too weak to venture upon active movements, felt themselves compelled to march in the rear of the theoretical army led by Hegel's disciples against the religion, the ideas and the politics of the old world. In no former period was philosophical criticism so bold, so powerful and so popular as in the first eight years of the rule of Frederick William IV, who desired to supplant the 'shallow' rationalism, introduced into Prussia by Frederick II, by medieval mysticism. The power of philosophy during that period was entirely owing to the practical weakness of the bourgeoisie; as they could not assault the

---

161. The quote is taken from a series of articles in the *New York Daily Tribune* about Germany, published in German after Engels's death under the title "Revolution and Counter-Revolution in Germany." In the *Tribune*, Marx was named as the author, but letters indicate that Engels wrote the articles, since Marx didn't have the time.

antiquated institutions in fact, they must yield precedence to the bold idealists who assaulted them in the region of thought" (MECW 16: 169).

These political and theoretical contexts have to be considered when dealing with the further development of Marx. However, here we will follow only the Young Hegelian debates and the intellectual development of Marx's friend Bruno Bauer up to 1840–41, since the aim of this chapter is to reconstruct the discursive background of Marx's last years at university and in particular his dissertation, written in 1840–41.

MARX'S LIFE IN BERLIN, 1838–41

Before tracing Marx's intellectual development, let us turn our attention to the circumstances of his life at the time, that is, to the extent they are made clear by the few available sources.

Edgar von Westphalen and Werner von Veltheim

Whereas Marx, as he disclosed in his letter from November 10, 1837, spent his first year in Berlin largely in seclusion, his life must have changed strongly from the late summer of 1837 on. During the summer, he had not only joined the Doctor's Club mentioned in the letter to his father; his school friend Edgar von Westphalen had also moved to Berlin. After his Abitur examination, Edgar did not immediately begin university studies, but instead spent a year at home. It is possible that his parents did not want to allow the sixteen-year-old to move to a strange city on his own. In 1836–37, he studied law for two semesters in Bonn before enrolling at the University of Berlin on November 3, 1837 (Gemkow 1999: 416). In Bonn, Edgar, who during his school years was assiduous, reserved, and perhaps even a bit shy, appears to have developed into an outgoing young man who valued the merry side of student life. In any case, he participated in the preparations for founding the Corps Palatia (ibid.: 309), the student association that emerged from the Trier table society to which Marx had belonged. In Berlin, Karl and Edgar then appear to have both accepted invitations and participated in dances and balls. As Ludwig von Westphalen communicated to his son Ferdinand in 1838, "high and low," "but especially female company" liked Edgar (ibid.: 414). Since there were no women at the university, this observation probably referred to such festivities.

In Berlin, Edgar joined up with Werner von Veltheim (1817–1855), with whom, as is made clear by the enrollment lists, he attended a few lectures (Kliem 1988: 47). Werner's father, Franz von Veltheim (1785–1839), was a brother of Elisabeth von Veltheim, the first wife of Ludwig von Westphalen. Werner started studying law in Berlin in the summer semester of 1837 (Gemkow 1977: 18). When he visited Lisette—Edgar's pietistic half sister whom Adolph von Krosigk had married in 1821 (see chapter 2)—in Hohenerxleben during the Easter of 1838, Edgar accompanied him. In Hohenerxleben, Werner got to know Lisette's barely fourteen-year-old daughter Margarete, whom he married in 1842. After Werner's early death, another daughter of Lisette, Anna, wrote a biographical portrait of him based upon letters and diaries, that was published in an edition with a small print run without specifying the year (Krosigk, A.: n.d.). From this biographical portrait, it becomes clear that Werner, like Edgar, had a plan to emigrate to America (ibid. 17). Unlike Edgar, however, he never followed through; instead, he took over his parents' estate in Ostrau near Halle. Anna's portrait also shows that Werner oscillated for a long time between the views, considered radical, of David Friedrich Strauß, Bruno Bauer, and Ludwig Feuerbach, on the one hand, and the pietist-conservative notions of the Krosigk family, on the other (ibid.: 118). To some extent, the influence of the young Karl Marx on his interest in radical thought probably played a role. In a letter of Werner's that is probably from the first half of 1839,[162] he writes: "There is once again a great revolution with me. I found Marx with Edgar, and the former, with his philosophical sophistry and word construction, swept away my calm for several days. I was finally able to once again clarify things within myself" (ibid.: 39).

During the summer semester of 1838, Edgar and Werner even lived in the same house (Gemkow 1977: 19). Until his early death in 1855, Werner remained a good friend to Edgar, even supporting him financially during his multiple attempts to emigrate to the United States (Krosigk, A., n.d.: 123, 143, 174, 188, 211). Marx also received a loan from Werner von Veltheim in 1851, when he was having an extremely hard time financially in London. Veltheim noted in his diary: "Marx, the notorious one, asked me for a loan of 30 pounds sterling. He's a communist; if his writings were applied, I would lose property and family; he has my cousin Jenny Westphalen as a wife, is an acquaintance from university, is in need—I sent him 15 pounds sterling through Lorenz Meyer in Hamburg" (Krosigk, A., n.d.: 189).

After Karl had attended only a single lecture course in the winter semester of 1837/38, he took up his studies in the summer semester of 1838, after the death of his father, with more energy. However, among the three courses he

---

162. The quotations from letters and diaries used by Anna von Krosigk are not dated, but her presentation is divided into individual years.

attended, only one was in law: "Prussian law" with Eduard Gans ("exception-ally diligent"). The other two courses were "Logic" ("extremely diligent") with Georg Andreas Gabler (1786–1853), the friend and follower of Hegel, who proved, however, mediocre,[163] and "Geography" ("taken") with Carl Ritter (1779–1859). Together with Alexander von Humboldt, Ritter is considered a founder of scientific geography. Ritter conceived of geography as the unity of topographical conditions, history, and ethnography, and in doing so left far behind the merely statistically oriented study of states of the eighteenth century (see Lindgren 2003).

In the summer of 1838, Karl and Edgar must have interacted socially a lot. In August, both were reported for "excessive behavior on the street" (Straßenexzess) and admonished by the university magistrate. There were more such reports concerning Edgar in April and August 1839 (Gemkow 1999: 421). In the winter semester of 1838–39, Karl and Edgar shared a dwelling (Gemkow 1977: 19). With the summer semester of 1839, Edgar von Westphalen ended his studies in Berlin; he had the then-usual three years of university under his belt. He probably then returned to Trier (Gemkow 1999: 422).

For the winter semester of 1838–39, there is just a single course taken, "Inheritance Law" (graded "diligent") with the Savigny student Adolf Friedrich Rudorff (1803–1873). After that, Marx participated in only two courses. In the summer semester of 1839 he attended—along with Bruno Bauer (1809–1882), with whom he had developed a close friendship—a course on Isaiah ("attended"),[164] and in the winter semester of 1840/41 one on the Greek dramatist Euripides ("diligent") taught by Carl Eduard Geppert (1811–1881), a student of the well-known philologist and archaeologist August Boeckh (1785–1867).[165] In the winter semester of 1839–40 and in the summer semester of 1840, Marx did not take any more courses.

---

163. Lenz (1910: 2.1: 483) writes about him: "He himself confirmed the expectations placed in the Christian character of his philosophy, indeed . . . apart from that, he disappointed all who made an effort on his behalf, the gentlemen in the ministry just as much as his colleagues at the university, and not least the students. He was really nothing but a schoolmaster, who performed the sport of arguing in Latin with a dozen pupils about Hegel's dialectic. . . . He never went beyond apologetic on behalf of Hegel and Christian dogmatics."

164. Isaiah was an Old Testament prophet who predicted the appearance of the Messiah, which the Christians applied to Jesus. According to the course catalog for the summer semester of 1839, the title of the course was "The Prophecies of Isaiah."

165. According to the course catalog for the winter semester of 1840–41, the course on Euripides dealt with the play Ion, about the legendary founding father of the Ionians.

The course with Rudorff in the winter semester of 1838–39 was Marx's last course on law; with it, he effectively ended his study of that discipline. When he wrote a good twenty years later in the preface to the *Contribution to the Critique of Political Economy*, "Although jurisprudence was my special study, I pursued it as a subject subordinated to philosophy and history" (MECW 29: 261), it was not entirely accurate. Marx did not take an exam in law, but with the six courses in law in Bonn and the eight in Berlin, he obtained a reasonably solid (theoretical) education in law, measured according to the standards of the time. By contrast, there are only two philosophical courses in the narrower sense, with Steffens on anthropology in the summer semester of 1837 and with Gabler on (Hegel's) logic in the summer semester of 1838, but not one course on history. Marx conducted his study of philosophy and history primarily outside the lecture halls.

In the literature, the fact that Marx had solid training in law is frequently overlooked or underestimated.[166] But Marx's knowledge of law left behind clear traces in his work. Directly legal arguments are found in a few of his articles for the *Rheinische Zeitung*, but his *Critique of Hegel's Philosophy of Right* from 1843 and some passages in *Capital* also demonstrate Marx's legal knowledge. And last but not least, in February of 1849 in Cologne, Marx successfully pleaded before the court twice when the *Neue Rheinische Zeitung* was charged with insulting a magistrate and in a further trial for inciting rebellion.

Marx's Relationship with Jenny and with His Mother

The conflict between Karl and Jenny discussed in chapter 2 (letter from Jenny to Karl after the death of Heinrich Marx, MEGA III/1: 331) was apparently resolved quickly. In the summer, Jenny accompanied her half-brother Karl to a spa treatment in Niederbronn in Alsace (details of this trip are in Monz 1990); from there, she wrote a letter to Karl on June 24, 1838 (MEGA III/1: 332) in which this conflict is no longer mentioned. Rather, she writes about her sorrow over the death of Heinrich Marx, to whom, as we know from his letters, she had a close connection: "I still can't get my bearings, still can't bear the thought of an irreplaceable loss with calm and composure; everything appears so cloudy to me, so ominous, the whole future so dark." Just a year ago, she had taken a trip to Kürenz with him: "We were both completely alone and for two or three hours, conversed about the most important matters of life, the most noble, most current interests, religion and love. He spoke

---

166. Important exceptions are Kelley (1978) and Klenner (1984).

splendid, exquisite words, golden lessons in my heart, spoke to me with such a love, a cordiality, an intimacy, that only a soul as rich as his is capable of. My heart faithfully returned it, this love, and will preserve it forever!" But this reminiscence also couldn't chase away her depressed mood: "Nonetheless, I don't wish to have him back in this world of sorrow; no, I bless, I envy his fate; I rejoice in the blessed calm he enjoys in the arms of his God, rejoice that he no longer struggles, no longer suffers, that he has found the rich reward in the next world for his beautiful life!" (MEGA III/1: 332). This last sentence makes clear that at this time Jenny believed in an afterlife, although a certain distance resonates in the phrase "in the arms of his God."

A second letter from this trip has been preserved, which Jenny wrote to her mother. There, she goes into detail about spa life and describes with a sharp eye the characteristics of the people she met. Among others, she met two young Protestant theologians who had studied in Göttingen and Berlin. She informed her mother of the professors whose lectures they had attended: Dahlmann, the Brothers Grimm, Ewald, Schleiermacher, Gans, Hegel, and Strauß (Monz 1990: 248). That Jenny so casually mentions these names suggests that they were known both to her and her mother, that they had also spoken of these people at home. In the case of Dahlmann, the Brothers Grimm, and Ewald, this isn't so surprising. These were among the "Göttingen Seven," and their fate was a heavily discussed topic in all of Germany. Hegel, Schleiermacher, Strauß, and Gans were also familiar names in more educated circles, but the fact that Jenny mentions them so casually probably goes back to her correspondence with Karl. He probably had reported upon his transition to Hegelian philosophy not only to his father, but also to Jenny. It's quite possible that he also reported to her, since she felt increasingly trapped in Trier,[167] about the content of the lectures he attended and the discussions in the Doctor's Club.

Before Edgar left Berlin permanently in the summer of 1839, he forwarded a letter from Jenny to Karl, which has only been handed down as a fragment.[168] From the fragment, it emerges that there had once again been conflict between Karl and Jenny. Karl had apparently accused Jenny in a previous letter of no longer loving him, since she had met with another man,

---

167. In her letter from Niederbronn, Jenny refers to Trier as the "place of sorrow, the old nest of pastors with its miniature humanity" (MEGA III/1: 332).

168. The letter fragment does not contain a date. In the MEGA (III/1: 337) and the MECW (1: 695), 1839–1840 is given as a time period. Since, in a postscript, Jenny asks her brother to forward the letter to Karl (MEGA III/1: 744), it must have been written before Edgar's departure from Berlin, thus in the spring or summer of 1839.

which had been reported to him from Trier. What exactly happened cannot be determined. However, it is clear that both young people weren't sure of the love of the other. For Karl, the smallest hints were enough to start doubting Jenny's love. In the letter, she accuses him multiple times of not trusting her enough. But Jenny also had doubts about the permanence of Karl's love: "That I am not capable of retaining your present romantic youthful love, I have known from the beginning" (MECW 1: 695). In light of the long period of separation of the two lovers, which in the meantime had become longer than the time they had shared together as a couple in love in Trier, this insecurity is not surprising. It's also not surprising that Jenny sometimes took refuge in fantasy worlds: "So, sweetheart, since your last letter I have tortured myself with the fear that for my sake you could become embroiled in a quarrel and then in a duel. Day and night I saw you wounded, bleeding and ill, and, Karl, to tell you the whole truth, I was not altogether unhappy in this thought: for I vividly imagined that you had lost your right hand, and, Karl, I was in a state of rapture, of bliss, because of that. You see, sweetheart, I thought that in that case I could really become quite indispensable to you, you would then always keep me with you and love me. I also thought that then I could write down all your dear, heavenly ideas and be really useful to you" (MECW 1: 696). Jenny's wish would be fulfilled, although a hand injury wasn't necessary: Marx's handwriting was so unreadable that Jenny would later have to copy some texts so that they could be submitted to a publisher.[169]

In the year 1839, Karl also prepared a collection of folksongs, "for my sweet little Jenny of my heart" (such is the dedication, MEGA I/1: 775), consisting primarily of love lyrics and a few joke songs, but also of a few serious texts. In doing so, he was following the interest recently awakened by Romanticism in folk poems, which were seen as evidence of an original and authentic spirit. An important source for his collection was the one published in four volumes by Friedrich Karl von Erlach in 1834/35, *Die Volkslieder der Deutschen* (Folk Songs of the Germans). However, Marx also took non-German folksongs

---

169. In the upper strata of society, it was not unusual for a man to challenge another man to a duel if he had supposedly come too close to his fiancée, Kliem (1988: 54) suspects that behind Jenny's duel fantasy was a canceled duel in connection with a man she was seen with in Trier: the man was supposedly her former fiancé Karl von Pannewitz, who had visited the Westphalens. Werner von Veltheim, who knew of this, supposedly committed an intentional indiscretion toward Karl as revenge for his intellectual superiority. A duel between Werner and Karl was supposedly prevented. However, Kliem provides no source for either Pannewitz's visit or for the requested duel. It's mere speculation that something like that could have happened, without any factual indicator, which, however, does not prevent Sperber (2013: 45) from presenting it as a fact, with reference to Kliem.

into consideration, in doing so resorting among other sources to Herder's *Stimmen der Völker in Liedern* (Voices of the People in Songs) and works by Lord Byron (on the sources, see MEGA I/1: 1263). Marx dates the collection "Berlin. 1839." There is no indication whether he gave it as a present to Jenny on February 12 for her twenty-fifth birthday, or for Christmas. It is also possible that it was a conciliatory gift after a fight.

That many details of Marx's life in Berlin are unknown to us is made clear by a letter from Marx's mother, Henriette, that she wrote to him on May 29, 1840. A few sentences are partially unintelligible, since the paper was damaged, which led to lost text. But much of it is unintelligible because of references to familiar events that are not further explained. It's clear that after the death of her husband, Henriette felt she was treated poorly by the Westphalen family: "Six weeks after your lovely dear father was taken from us, nobody from Westphalen's family made an appearance to us, no consolation, no friendliness came from that side, it was like they had never seen us—at the time H. Schlink hadn't committed any misdeed—Jenny once came every 4–5 weeks and then she just complained and moaned, afterward H.S. traveled to Berlin and the unhappy story came from your side, now pride and vanity were injured [. . .] now I was blamed for everything, I hadn't presented the matter properly . . . " (MEGA III/1: 347).

"H. Schlink" and "H.S." probably refer to district court councilor Johann Heinrich Schlink, the friend of Heinrich Marx who was made, after Heinrich's death, the legal guardian of the Marx children who were still minors. We don't know what this "misdeed" was. Later in the letter, Henriette writes: "H.S. says it was far from his intentions to insult a lady who was universally liked and respected" (ibid.: 348). Apparently the Westphalen family felt insulted by a statement by Schlink.

It's also not clear what the "unhappy story from your side," that is, from Karl's side, was. Was it conflicts with Jenny that her parents had found out about? That may be what's being referred to in the remark that their pride and vanity were offended and that they blamed Marx's mother for "not presenting the matter properly." Perhaps it was Karl's mother who had stoked his jealousy by mentioning Jenny's social interactions with other men, which he then reacted to with statements that the Westphalen family took as insults. But these are all guesses. The only thing that can be taken with certainty from the letter is that there had been a quarrel between the Westphalen family and Marx's mother that began after Heinrich Marx's death and hadn't been completely ended two years later, when the letter was written.

Marx's sister Sophie also felt neglected by her brother. Thus, a brief letter from her from the beginning of 1841 ends with the sentence: "I would have shared a lot about my own matters with a loyal, loving brother, but this is fine too" (MEGA III/1: 351). But in the same letter, she wrote that he should depart for Trier as quickly as possible and that she would send him money if he needed it.

Financial Problems

With the death of his father, the financial situation of the student Marx also changed. His father had complained multiple times about the high level of his son's expenses, but consistently supported him as best he could. After Heinrich's death, the only income remaining to the family was interest upon a few securities and private loans, as well as income from the agriculture use of their land in Kürenz and from their shares in a vineyard in Mertesdorf. The estate inventory evaluated by Monz indicates that alongside interest-free loans, there were promissory notes in the amount of 6,900 talers, with an interest rate of 5 percent. Accordingly, there were returns on interest in the amount of 345 talers annually. The value of the agricultural land and the shares in the vineyard were given as 1,500 and 3,000 talers respectively (a detailed statement of assets can be found in Monz 1973: 272–82). If one assumes that the average earnings here were somewhat above the usual interest rate of 5 percent, then this yields a further income in the amount of 250–350 talers, so that the total annual income would have ranged from 600 to 700 talers, less than half of the 1,500 talers that Heinrich Marx had earned in 1830 (see chapter 1). It's possible that Henriette Marx improved upon this income by renting out rooms, which was then a widespread method for widows to increase their income, but there is no direct evidence. In any case, financial support for the student son must have been considerably less. During the allocation of Heinrich Marx's estate, which was first conducted on June 23, 1841, Karl Marx confirmed that in the years 1838, 1839, and 1840 he had received a total of 1,111 talers from his mother, which were reckoned against his share of the inheritance (Monz 1973: 284). That means that he had an average of 370 talers a year at his disposal during these three years, with which he could have only gotten by with difficulty.

The fact that during the winter semester of 1838–39 Marx had attended only one of the courses, which weren't exactly cheap, was possibly due to his financial problems, which apparently intensified during that winter: at the university court, multiple complaints brought against him by creditors were pending. From the university records, which are partially still available, these complaints were compiled by Kossack (1978); they convey a dramatic picture of Karl's financial difficulties: "At the beginning of September 1838, the master tailor Kremling demanded 40 talers and two and a half groschen for the manufacture of articles of clothing. Marx acknowledged the debt and promised payment on October 1 and November 1. At the beginning of October of 1838, the master tailor Selle brought the claim of 41 talers, 10 groschen for the manufacture of outer garments. The claim was acknowledged and payment was promised in monthly installments of 10 talers. At the same time, Kremling in turn brought a claim of 30 talers, which was registered with the note 'execution still pending.' Since enforcement was carried out fruitlessly, Marx and Kremling reached a settlement for the payment of the contract. In the middle of November 1838, Selle made a request for enforcement for the claim of 10 talers. This sum was collected from Marx. At the end of January 1839, the merchant Habel demanded the sum of 15 talers for cloth, which Marx acknowledged, promising payment on April 1. Since enforcement was carried out fruitlessly, the two came to an agreement to cover the debt. At the same time, Selle demanded the amount of 31 talers, 10 groschen. Since enforcement also failed in this case, the parties reached a settlement. In the middle of February 1839 the bookseller Eysenhart turned to the university court with an enforcement request in the amount of 48 talers and four groschen. In this case as well, the collection proceedings are identified as still in progress (Kossack 1978: 106).

The demanded claims show that expenses for clothing played an important role. This was not due to any vanity on Marx's part. At the time, appropriate clothing played a far more important role as a mark of distinction. It could open or close doors; without the correct clothing, one couldn't go out socially. A brief letter to Adolf Rutenberg from October 10, 1838, is also concerned with clothing. In a familiar tone, Marx excuses his breaking an engagement with the lack of appropriate clothing.[170] It would be forty years until the Swiss poet Gottfried Keller (1819–1890) could caricature the prominent significance of the right clothing in his well-known novella, *Clothes Make People*.

On the basis of a letter from his mother Henriette from October 22, 1838, we know that she sent Karl 160 talers for his doctoral tuition fees (MEGA III/1: 334). At this point in time, Marx had not begun working on his dissertation. That he needed money for the doctoral tuition fees was probably a white lie in order to cover his most important expenses. However, Marx probably planned to write his doctoral dissertation quickly. The first excerpts related to it date from the beginning of 1839, and the bill of the bookseller Eysenhardt that came before the university magistrate was probably based

---

170. This letter is not contained in the MECW nor in the MEGA. It was first published by Martin Hundt (1994).

upon the purchase by Marx a few months earlier of books that he needed for his dissertation.

In Berlin, the young Karl was able to marvel at the latest technological developments. In September of 1839, the first daguerreotypes were exhibited. Just a few days later, the making of daguerreotypes was offered, at a rather high price, however (Kliem 1988: 14). Marx probably could not afford to have a daguerreotype made of himself to send to Jenny. But another pleasure was within the realm of his possibilities. In 1838–39, a railway line from Berlin to Zehlendorf and Potsdam was built, and on October 29, 1839, regular travel operations began on the 27-kilometer line; four trains traveled in both directions daily. Railway travel was an attraction. Tickets had to be purchased a day before in a Berlin bookstore; a third-class trip cost 10 silver groschen (Kliem 1988: 14). It's quite possible that Marx purchased a trip, maybe in the company of a few friends.

Friends from the "Doctorklubb": Rutenberg, Köppen, Bauer

The young Karl found the friends most important to his intellectual development in the Doctor's Club, mentioned in the letter to his father from November 1837. There, he received the stimulation for his historical and philosophical studies that was lacking in the seminars at the University of Berlin. This "doctor's club" was probably a loose discussion circle. We don't know when it first began and who exactly was associated with it. However, one cannot relate all reports on philosophical discussion circles in Berlin at this time to the Doctor's Club—there was more than one such circle.[171] The only list of members is found in a letter from Bruno Bauer to Marx from December 11, 1839: "Greet Köppen, Rutenberg and Althaus and whoever you see from the club" (MEGA III/1: 336).[172]

---

171. Max Ring, for example, who came to Berlin in 1838, speaks in his *Memoirs* (1898: 113–17) of a circle of doctors and older students that met on certain days of the week to discuss their own work, but also "Hegel's philosophy with great enthusiasm." He names numerous members (Carrière, Oppenheim, the Behr brothers, Benary), but none we know with certainty belonged to the "Doctorklubb" in which Marx participated.

172. Marx's letter to his father and this letter from Bauer to Marx are the only two sources available on the Doctorklubb. Stedman Jones (2016: 65), as well as Breckman (1999: 260), simply assume as a matter of course that Eduard Gans also belonged to the club, but there is no evidence for this. Apart from lack of evidence, such a membership does not appear plausible: Gans wasn't interested in the questions of philosophy of religion that were so important to Bauer and he did not participate in the corresponding debates of the 1830s. Furthermore, Gans was something like a star intellectual who traveled in successful academic circles. It's not

When the nineteen-year-old Karl first ran into the club in 1837, Althaus was thirty-one, Köppen and Rutenberg were twenty-nine, and Bauer was twenty-eight. They were initially far superior to Karl in terms of knowledge. It's remarkable and speaks for his intellectual abilities that the young Karl was accepted so quickly in this circle.

Karl Heinrich Althaus (1806–1886) had obtained his doctorate in Halle in 1837 and postdoctoral qualification in philosophy in Berlin in 1838. From then on, he taught at the University of Berlin, initially as a lecturer, then from 1859 as an associate professor (Gerhardt et al. 1999: 119), without figuring prominently in any way. He was definitely the most colorless among those named here, and there is no indication of any intensive contact with Marx. Things look much different with regard to Rutenberg, Köppen, and, above all, Bruno Bauer.

Adolph Friedrich Rutenberg (1808–1869) had attended the Friedrich Wilhelm Gymnasium in Berlin, together with Bruno Bauer, and afterward studied theology and philosophy at the University of Berlin.[173] He had taught geography and history at the Royal Cadet School in Berlin (Bunzel et al. 2006: 62). The cadet schools were secondary schools that prepared their pupils for an officer's career in the army.

In the letter to his father, Karl described Rutenberg as "my most intimate Berlin friend." He had also introduced Karl to the Doctor's Club (MECW 1: 19). When in December of 1838, Rutenberg celebrated the birth of his daughter Agathe with a party, to which, as Agathe wrote in her memoirs, only men were invited (Nalli-Rutenberg 1912: 13), Karl was probably also invited. Whether he was at the party, or whether he declined due to his money problems, we do not know.

In 1840, Rutenberg was dismissed as a teacher from the cadet school; officially it was for drunkenness, but a few critical journal articles he wrote appear to be the real reason for the dismissal (Klutentreter 1966: 61). Rutenberg was the only Young Hegelian who had been asked by Karl Theodor Welcker to collaborate on the liberal *Staats-Lexikon*. Among other things, he wrote the article "Poland" for volume 12, published in 1841, and the article "Radical, Radicalism" for volume 13 (1842). In the year 1842, he initially took over the leadership of the newly founded *Rheinische Zeitung*, and later was succeeded by Marx.

---

impossible to say he participated in a discussion circle of students and (with the exception of Bauer) unknown younger lecturers; however, it is rather improbable.

173. On Rutenberg's biography, see the information provided by his daughter Agathe (Nalli-Rutenberg 1912) as well as Lambrecht (1993).

Karl Friedrich Köppen (1808–1863)[174] was also a close friend of Marx. He had studied theology from 1827 to 1831 at the University of Berlin and had been a teacher at the Realschule in Dorotheenstadt[175] since 1833. He was interested primarily in history and mythology. In 1837, he published his first book, *A Literary Introduction to Norse Mythology* (*Literarische Einleitung in die nordische Mythologie*). It's quite possible that the incorporation and the selection of the three "Finnish Runes"[176] with which Marx concludes his collection of folksongs for Jenny is due to advice from Köppen (on this, see Kunze 1955).

Köppen also intervened in the increasingly critical debates conducted at the end of the 1830s about Hegel's *Philosophy of Right*. Whereas some liberals accused Hegel of mystifying the Prussian state with his book (see chapter 2), conservatives argued the opposite in the 1830s. In 1839, Karl Ernst Schubarth (1796–1861), who had already criticized Hegel's conception of the state in 1829, published a brochure with the programmatic title "On the Incompatiblity of Hegel's Doctrine of the State with the Highest Life Principle and Developmental Principle of the Prussian State" ("Über die Unvereinbarkeit der Hegelschen Staatslehre mit dem obersten Lebens- und Entwicklungsprinzip des Preußischen Staates"). Schubarth accused Hegel of wanting to transform Prussia into a constitutional monarchy. In the *Telegraph für Deutschland*, published by Karl Gutzkow in Hamburg, in which the young Engels also published, Köppen answered with an article in which he not only lampooned Schubarth's narrow-mindedness with much wit; he also declared, far more explicitly than had ever been done before, that Hegel was a constitutionalist. "Is the Prussian state called upon to become a constitutional one? Hegel answered the question, indirectly at least, with 'yes'" (Köppen 1839: 282). Schubarth's attempt to co-opt Friedrich II for his position of a "personal" state, that is, bound to the person of the king, was decisively rejected by Köppen. "It's about time to elaborate in detail the great king's views on the state, the church, and religion" (ibid.: 283), Köppen remarks at the end of his essay, and that's precisely what he set out to do in his book, *Friedrich the Great and His Adversaries: A Celebration* (*Friedrich der Große und seine Widersacher: Eine Jubelschrift*). Köppen used the 100th anniversary of Friedrich's ascension to the throne as an occasion to celebrate his enlightened spirit, which in Prussia at the time had a

---

174. On Köppen's biography, see Hirsch (1955a) and Pepperle (2003).

175. A historical neighborhood in Berlin, now part of what is now the borough of Mitte. —Trans.

176. In Finnish, *Rune* does not mean a type of character as it does in Germanic languages, but rather a song or carol (Kunze 1955: 58 n. 1).

subversive content. To "properly understand" this text, Mehring (1902: 35) writes, "one has to realize that at the time of its writing, the commemoration of Old Fritz served as the bone of contention for everything in the Prussian state that pushed backwards." Köppen's text was enthusiastically received by the Young Hegelians, since at the time they regarded the Reformation, the enlightened absolutism of Friedrich II, and the Stein-Hardenberg reforms as constituting progressive traditions that one had to link up with in the present. Arnold Ruge devoted an enthusiastic review to Köppen's book in the *Hallische Jahrbücher* (Ruge 1840). But Köppen was not the only one who became famous through this piece of writing; it was "dedicated to my friend Karl Heinrich Marx from Trier." For the first time, the name Karl Marx became known to a broader public.

In the *Hallische Jahrbücher* of 1841 and 1842, there are contributions by Köppen dealing with the University of Berlin. In particular, its luminaries of history, Friedrich von Raumer (1781–1873) and Leopold von Ranke (1795–1886), were dissected with a sharp scalpel (for more detail, see Pepperle 2003: 24ff.). All things considered, these texts by Köppen show him to be a critical and polemically witty, pointed historian, from which the young Marx surely could have learned a lot not just in terms of content, but also of style.

His close friendship with Marx—in 1889, Engels still called Köppen "a special friend of Marx's" (letter to Max Hildebrand, October 22, 1889, MECW 48: 393). This is not just indicated by the dedication mentioned. Also revealing is a letter from Köppen to Marx written in a gushing, self-mocking tone. On June 3, 1841, shortly after Marx had departed Berlin, Köppen wrote that as a result of separation from Marx, which had now "lasted more than a week," he "had melancholy and lacked for your presence daily." The strong role that Marx had in discussions is made clear in this statement: "Ever since my worthy hereafter is on the other side of the Rhine, I've started to once again gradually become this-worldly. I once again have, so to speak, thoughts that I've thought on my own, whereas previously all of my thoughts didn't come from afar; namely from the Schützenstraße, or on it." Marx's final dwelling in Berlin was on the Schützenstraße. The impression that Marx had left behind was obviously tremendous: "You are a storehouse of thoughts, a workhouse, or, to say it in Berlinisch, an ox head [*Ochsenkopf*] of ideas" (MEGA III/1: 360).[177]

---

177. This formulation was "Berlinisch" to the extent that the workhouse at Berlin Alexanderplatz was described as the "ox head" in popular parlance: It was the former house of the butcher's guild, and an earlier building of this guild had been adorned with an ox head (Miller/ Sawadski 1956: 218).

Köppen, in contrast to many other leftists, did not consummate a nationalist or reactionary turn after the defeat of the Revolution of 1848, and was the only one of Marx's Berlin friends with whom he still had basic substantive commonalities. After Marx visited him in 1861, he wrote to Engels on May 10, 1861: "While in Berlin I also went to see Friedrich Koppen. I found him still very much as he always was. Only he's grown stouter, and 'grizzled.' I went out to spend an evening in a pub with him twice and it was a real treat for me" (MECW 41: 286, corrected translation).

The most important friend from Marx's time in Berlin was surely Bruno Bauer (1809–1882). In the letter to his father from November 1837, he writes respectfully of "university lecturer Bauer" (MECW 1: 20). That both would soon become close friends emerges clearly from Bauer's letters to Marx. Thus Bauer writes at the beginning of April 1841 from Bonn: "I have enough cheering up, gaiety, etc. here, I've also done enough of what's called laughing, but never again like in Berlin when I merely crossed the street with you" (MEGA III/1: 356). Others also noticed the closeness between Marx and Bauer. In a letter from January 20, 1840, Bruno reminded his brother Edgar of a shared excursion: "I'm just thinking about how Adolph [Rutenberg] took you aside that night at Tegel lake and pointed to me and M. as brooders" (Bauer 1844a: 33). That intense personal contact was also documented not least by the fact that even after Bauer's departure from Berlin, Marx visited his parents in Charlottenburg[178] (see Edgar to Bruno Bauer, March 22, 1840, in Bauer 1844a: 55). But Marx was connected to Bruno Bauer not only by friendship but by great proximity in theoretical questions. Bauer was, as far as we know, the only one of his Berlin friends with whom he planned a joint publication, as well as the joint editorship of a journal (I will return to this).

Bruno Bauer was the son of a porcelain painter who was well-read and took care to provide a good school education to his children.[179] Bruno had attended the Friedrich Wilhelm Gymnasium in Berlin and studied theology at the University of Berlin from 1828 to 1832. Among the theologians, the Hegelian Philipp Marheineke (1780–1846) was particularly important. Bauer not only attended Hegel's lectures, he also caused a furor as a student. In 1829, Hegel held a prize competition for the faculty of philosophy on Immanuel Kant's aesthetics. Bauer submitted a contribution in which he analyzed Kant's aesthetics with the categories of Hegel's philosophy (Bauer 1829) and won, after having been a student for only a year (Eberlein 2009:

178. An independent city near Berlin but now a neighborhood in Berlin. —Trans.
179. For the biography of Bruno Bauer, see Hertz-Eichenrode (1959), Eberlein (2009), and the materials in Barnikol (1972).

27). Just how quickly and precisely Bauer grasped Hegel's philosophy is also made clear in that his transcriptions of Hegel's lectures on aesthetics from his second semester were used by Heinrich Gustav Hotho in his edition of *Aesthetics*.

In 1834, Bauer did his postdoctoral qualification in theology; until 1839, he was a lecturer at the University of Berlin. In his courses, he dealt primarily with the Old Testament. The seminar on the prophet Isaiah which Marx had attended in the summer semester of 1839 also falls in this time period. For the winter semester of 1839–40, Bauer transferred to the University of Bonn, on Altenstein's recommendation. The first surviving letters from Bauer to Marx date from the Bonn period; the letters from Marx to Bauer have not survived.

The writer Max Ring mentions in his memoirs (Ring 1898: 119) that Bruno Bauer socialized in the salon of Bettina von Arnim (1785–1859). Bettina was a sister of the poet Clemens Brentano (1778–1842); she was married to another Romantic poet, Achim von Arnim (1781–1831). After his death, she published his works and also stepped more and more into the public light herself. In 1835, three years after Goethe's death, she published *Goethe's Correspondence with a Child* (*Goethes Briefwechsel mit einem Kinde*). This book, which made Bettina famous and had a great influence upon the contemporary image of Goethe, contained the correspondence she had with Goethe, not as a child, but as a woman in her early twenties. However, Bettina strongly revised the letters. In 1843, under the title *This Book Belongs to the King* (*Dieses Buch gehört dem König*), she published a critical depiction of the living conditions of the poor in Berlin which caused quite a stir; in Bavaria, the book was even banned.

In the 1830s and 1840s, Bettina operated a widely known salon, in which personalities from politics, science, and culture rubbed shoulders. It has been claimed several times that Marx also visited this salon.[180] However, he is never mentioned in any of the accounts of it, and Bruno Bauer could not have introduced him. Bettina had asked Varnhagen to invite Bauer; she wanted to meet him, which Varnhagen noted in his diary on October 1, 1841 (Varnhagen 1863: 341). At this point in time, Marx had left Berlin months before. Karl also wasn't exactly among Bettina's admirers. In the collection

---

180. For example, Cornu (1954: 100) or Krosigk (1975: 41). In the film *The Young Karl Marx* (dir. Raoul Peck, France/Belgium/Germany 2017), Marx says about the first meeting between himself and Engels that it occurred in Bettina von Arnim's salon, where they discussed communism. But when Engels began his military service in Berlin in October 1841, Marx had already left the city and communism was not an issue then for either Marx or Engels.

of poems he gave to his father as a birthday present, there is a satirical poem about her under the title "Romanticism à la mode" (MECW 1: 541).

Marx not only kept in contact with Bruno Bauer; he also must have been in touch—especially after Bruno's departure—with his brother Edgar Bauer (1820–1886), who was eleven years younger and began studying theology in Berlin in 1838 (see Edgar to Bruno Bauer, February 11, 1841, Bauer 1844a: 123f).

In 1840–41, Marx also associated with a circle of literati flocking around Karl Riedel (1804–1878) and Eduard Meyen (1812–1870),[181] who together published the weekly *Athenäum: Zeitschrift für das gebildete Deutschland* (Athenaeum: A Journal for the Educated Germany) starting in January of 1841. In a letter from March 20, 1841, Meyen lists the members of this circle: "We have a literature club that meets every evening in a cozy pub. Belonging to it is everyone you know among our acquaintances: Eichler, Mügge, Buhl etc. then Riedel, Cornelius, Ferrand, Arthur Müller, Carrière, Friedrich Reinarz, Marx (aus Trier), Köppen etc. We often pub until late at night" (MEJ 1 1978: 341).[182]

How intensive these contacts were, and how often those named actually participated in the meetings, we don't know. One can guess that the circle fluctuated. It is not mentioned at all by Carrière (1914) in his memoirs. Marx at least had a somewhat closer relationship to Meyen, since he's referred to multiple times in his letters. As noted in the last chapter, two poems by Marx were published in *Athenäum* in January 1841 under the title "Wild Songs"— his first published texts. Under his pseudonym Friedrich Oswald, the young Engels also published in *Athenäum*. At the end of 1841, this journal was banned.

---

181. Karl Riedel had studied theology and was a pastor in various cities in Franconia. In 1839, he quit his activity as a pastor and went to Berlin. Eduard Meyen had studied philosophy and philology and obtained his doctorate in 1835 in Berlin; in 1838–39 he was editor of the Berlin *Literarische Zeitung* (some further information on Meyer can be found in Bunzel et al. 2006: 53–57).

182. Ludwig Eichler (1814–1870) was a liberal-minded writer and translator, Theodor Mügge (1802–1861) was part of the editorship of various journals; he wrote primarily adventure novels. Ludwig Buhl (1814–1882) was a writer and translator. In 1837, he received his doctorate under the Hegel student Carl Michelet and published a book on *Hegel's Doctrine of the State*. Wilhelm Cornelius (1809–?) was a writer, editor, and bookseller; in 1832 he had given a speech at the Hambach Festival. Eduard Ferrand was a pseudonym of Eduard Schulz (1813–1842); a lyricist, he was friends with the poet Friedrich von Sallet, who had lived in Trier while Marx attended gymnasium (see chapter 1). The historian of art and philosophy Moriz Carrière was mentioned in the second chapter.

It's very probable that Marx had many more acquaintances, possibly even close friends, about whom we know nothing. In the letter quoted above from June 3, 1841, Köppen mentions a Lieutenant Giersberg who had just come by and who had received a letter from Marx just eight days previous (MEGA III/1: 362). The editors of the MEGA volume identified a law student named Giersberg in Berlin and speculate that he is the Lieutenant Giersberg stationed in Münster in the 1840s (ibid.: 938). Further details about him are not known. But Marx must have been on familiar terms with him, since after his departure from Berlin, he sent him a letter even before sending one to Köppen.

Political Developments in Prussia

In terms of foreign policy, the years between 1839 and 1840 were exciting ones for Prussia. In Egypt, which was formally under the rule of the Ottoman Empire, the strong viceroy Muhammed Ali Pasha (circa 1770–1849) rose up against the Turkish sultan Mahmud II (1785–1839). He was supported by the French government under Adolphe Thiers (1797–1877), who wanted to strengthen French influence in the Mediterranean. Russia, Austria, Prussia, and England, all of which feared a disintegration of the Ottoman Empire with uncontrollable developments, supported the Turkish sultan, so that Muhammed Ali Pasha had to withdraw to Egypt, where he could continue acting as viceroy. In France, this prompted great public outrage, since the old anti-Napoleonic coalition had once again turned against France. To distract from his defeat in this "Orient crisis," Thiers made territorial demands to the German Confederation. France wanted to regain the areas on the left bank of the Rhine that had been lost at the Congress of Vienna in 1815; the Rhine was to form the border between Germany and France. This "Rhine crisis" triggered strong nationalist emotions in both France and Germany, reflected correspondingly in poems and songs. After Thiers's resignation in October 1840, the situation was defused under Foreign Minister François Guizot (1787–1874), but the wave of nationalist literature continued. Hoffmann von Fallersleben (1798–1874), the originator not only of nationalist, but also numerous anti-Semitic poems, composed in August 1841 the *Lied der Deutschen* to a melody by Joseph Haydn:

> Deutschland, Deutschland über alles,
> Über alles in der Welt,
> Wenn es stets zu Schutz und Trutze
> Brüderlich zusammenhält,

von der Maas bis an die Memel,
von der Etsch bis an den Belt –
Deutschland, Deutschland über alles,
Über alles in der Welt!

Germany, Germany above all,
above all in the world,
When, for protection and defense,
it always stands together brotherly,
From the Meuse to the Nieman,
From the Adige to the Belt,
Germany, Germany above all,
above all in the world!

This is no longer about France and the Rhine, but about a strong Germany, beyond the many individual states ruled by dynasties, which saw nationalism as a threat. The Prussian government reacted by revoking Hoffmann's professorship in Breslau. After the First World War, *Lied der Deutschen* was declared to be the German national anthem, after the Second World War it remained that of the Federal Republic of Germany; however, now one was only supposed to sing the third verse, which was concerned not with the greatness of Germany, but rather with freedom and justice.

In terms of domestic policy, the Prussian reform process pushed for by the government after the defeat against Napoleon in 1806 came to its definite end. After the Congress of Vienna, it already ran up against the increasingly strong resistance of conservatives, and with the death of state chancellor Hardenberg, it largely came to a standstill. Solely in the areas of school and educational policy was Altenstein able to continue to act as minister of culture for barely two decades and, in alliance with the Hegelian school, defend a sort of liberal thought.

The exponent of this Hegelian liberalism, known far beyond Prussia, was Eduard Gans. He died on May 5, 1839, at the age of forty-two. In 1838, Gans had suffered a light stroke; on May 1, 1839, two severe strokes followed, from which he was no longer able to recover (Reissner 1965: 159). The news of Gans dying moved parts of the bourgeoisie strongly, made clear in an anecdote from Varnhagen von Ense: "In the well-known wine house at Luther's and Wegener's, there was this incident yesterday: somebody entered, and stated the news that Prince Wilhelm, son of the king, was recovering; 'Oh what,' a merchant cried out, 'such a person could die ten times, what's the point! But if you could tell us that Gans is coming back, that would be worth it! Such a man can't be found again. There's no lack of princes!" (Varnhagen von Ense 1994: 269). The young Friedrich Engels as well, who at the time was training as a merchant in Bremen, asked his school friends who were studying in Berlin: "Were you not with Gans's body? Why aren't you writing anything about this?" In the next letter, he then shows satisfaction that they participated in the funeral (MEGA III/1: 140, 155).

This funeral, which took place on May 8, was a demonstration by liberal Berlin: "All of educated and liberal Berlin accompanied the body on foot in an incalculable procession to the cemetery in front of Oranienburger Tor, where Gans rests near his famous teacher Hegel. Among the mourners, one spotted all the notables of the Residenz, without party distinction, at their head the 70-year-old minister for culture von Altenstein and the aged president of the court of appeal, Grolman, even though Gans was unpopular in the high and highest circles due to his decisive liberalism" (Ring 1898: 127). With Gans's death, Germany had not only lost a strong liberal voice; within the academic field of jurisprudence, the conservatism of the Savigny school could now impose itself with considerably more ease, since its most competent opponent was no longer present.

Almost exactly a year after Gans, on May 14, 1840, the last of the generation of reformers still holding an important office, Minister of Culture Altenstein, died. With him, as would soon become apparent, the Hegelian school at the universities lost its most important backer.

Three weeks later, on June 6, 1840, the Prussian king Friedrich Wilhelm III, who had ruled for forty-three years, also died. Great hopes from different parts of the population, particularly liberals, were directed at the new king, Friedrich Wilhelm IV. He also initially appeared to fulfill these hopes. He reappointed Ernst Moritz Arndt, who had been dismissed during the "demagogue persecution," to his professorship in Bonn; the Brothers Grimm, who had belonged to the Göttingen Seven and lost their professorships, were appointed to the University of Berlin; and in the course of an amnesty, many who had been convicted for political reasons were freed from prison. On the basis of somewhat ambiguous statements, there was even speculation that Friedrich Wilhelm IV would finally introduce the constitution that had been promised on May 22, 1815.

However, the enthusiasm present in large parts of the population yielded rather quickly to general disappointment. In October 1840, Friedrich Wilhelm IV made clear that he was not considering establishing a constitution or a Prussian parliament that went beyond the provincial estate assemblies.

Also in October, the once liberal Johann Albrecht Friedrich Eichhorn (1779–1856) was appointed minister of culture. Soon after, the former Hessian minister, Ludwig Hassenpflug (1794–1862), who made a name for himself in Hesse with the annulment of the constitution there and was hated by liberals throughout Germany, was appointed to the highest Prussian court. At the University of Berlin, the occupation of Gans's professorial chair would be a special affront: the arch-conservative Friedrich Julius Stahl (1802–1861) was appointed as Gans's successor. When he began his first lecture on November 26, 1840, with sharp attacks on Hegel and Gans, he was booed by the students; there were tumultuous scenes (Streckfuß 1886: 879).

The initially anonymously published text *Four Questions Answered by an East Prussian* (*Vier Fragen beantwortet von einem Ostpreußen*) from the beginning of 1841 caused a sensation in Germany. With a sharpness that was previously unheard of, the text demanded the participation of the people in politics and declared that "what the estates had so far requested as a favour [the establishment of a Landtag], now had the proven right to claim" (Jacoby 1841: 47). The text had been banned in March 1841 by the German Confederation, but that didn't do anything to alter its popularity. The Königsberg physician Johann Jacoby (1805–1877), who soon revealed himself as the text's author in a letter to the king, was charged with treason and finally acquitted by the Berlin Court of Appeal in 1843 after several legal disputes.

The appointment of Friedrich Wilhelm Joseph Schelling (1775–1854) to the University of Berlin was also completely in keeping with the conservative line. This friend from Hegel's youth had developed in a decidedly conservative direction. Now, Schelling was to come to Berlin in order to, in the words of the king, counter the "dragon's seed of Hegelian pantheism" (quoted in Lenz 1910: 2.2: 10). Schelling followed this call and began his lectures in November 1841. (I will return in the second volume of this work to the conflicts surrounding Schelling's lecture, which was also attended by the young Friedrich Engels.)

THE CRITIQUE OF RELIGION IN THE EIGHTEENTH AND EARLY NINETEENTH CENTURY

In the late 1830s in Prussia, there were heavy controversies concerning the philosophy of religion that had a strong political component. Within the framework of these debates, the fundamental conflicts within the Hegelian school were revealed, leading it to split into different wings. Disputes over the state and politics followed, leading to an increasing radicalization of the Young Hegelians. Bruno Bauer, Marx's closest friend during this time, played an important role in these debates: not only through his writings, but also because the Prussian minister of culture, Eichhorn—Altenstein's successor—ultimately withdrew his authorization to teach theology, which caused a stir among the public. Marx was hardly a presence in these conflicts. But they constituted the contemporary background against which his early political and philosophical conceptions were formed.

In order to understand the relevance of debates in the 1830s over theology and the philosophy of religion, one has to make clear the specific relation between politics and religion in Prussia. Today, in most countries where Christianity plays a significant role, the church is more or less separate from the state. It receives, to varying degrees, money from state coffers or tax privileges, but most states stay out of questions within the church, whether of a theological or personal/political nature. In turn, while Christian churches attempt to influence political decisions, usually concerning the legal regulation of abortion, divorce, and same-sex partnerships, they do so as—in some countries very powerful—interest groups. In a narrower sense, theological controversies find hardly any resonance in the broader public, and even within the church such questions are discussed only in small circles.

In Prussia in the early nineteenth century, things looked different. Not only because the overwhelming majority of the population belonged to a Christian church and religion had much greater significance in everyday life than it does today, but also because Prussia understood itself to be a "Christian state." That is, the great majority of the population adhered to Christian belief and basic moral concepts were shaped by Christianity. In this general sense, one could characterize all European states outside of the Ottoman Empire as "Christian." What was meant was something far more concrete: Christianity, in its Protestant variant, was regarded as a central foundation of the Prussian state, which is why it received special promotion—but also special control— by the state. The Prussian King was—not just formally—the head of the Protestant regional church (*Landeskirche*). Pastors and professors of theology were not only paid by the state; they were state officials, monitored by superintendents deployed by the state and dismissed in cases of insubordination. The government had an influence not only upon the staffing of the church, but also on internal church questions. Thus, the Prussian king, Friedrich Wilhelm III, attempted, with state authority, to impose the unification of both large Protestant churches, the Lutheran and Reformed denominations. Catholics, who were usually a minority outside of the Rhine provinces, were regarded with a certain distrust by the Prussian state, since it wasn't clear how strongly they followed the Pope politically; until 1870 he was not only head of the Church but a secular ruler allied with France. Due to the tight integration of Protestant Christianity and the Prussian state, the theological debates on Protestantism had direct political relevance and were followed attentively by the public. So when critical intellectuals dealt with theological questions, it was not at all an evasion of political debate.[183] This critique began long before Ludwig Feuerbach's *The Essence of Christianity* was published in the year 1841, a work that is usually the focus of concentration when dealing with the role of religion in the intellectual development of the young Marx. For Marx as well, the confrontation with the critique of religion did not first begin with Feuerbach, but rather with the controversies around Hegel's philosophy of religion in the 1830s. In order to understand these debates, we first have to consider the upheavals experienced by the Christian religion in general, and above all Protestant theology, in the late eighteenth century.

Today, it's seen that these upheavals were not a consequence of isolated thought processes, but rather the result of a new understanding of nature, as well as the natural sciences beginning with Galileo and Newton. Further, these changes in thought are embedded in the social, economic, and political upheavals that led to early capitalist relations. Debates today usually revolve around the manner of this embedding, the degree of dependence of discursive processes upon non-discursive ones, etc. I do not address such problems, because in this volume I am concerned merely with a few theoretical results of this development, primarily in the area of theology, which play an important role in the conflicts in the first half of the nineteenth century.[184]

---

183. Cornu (1954: 126) suggests such a view when he writes that "it was less dangerous" for the Young Hegelians to attack "first the Christian religion and then the state." Probably inspired by Cornu, Neffe (2017: 75) states that "under the strict censorship rules in Germany, hardly any room for political critique" remained. "To express itself at all, it had to hide. The most effective way to denounce the reigning conditions was found by the young atheists of the Doctor's Club—who addressed each other with 'your godlessness'—in the critique of religion." Apart from wanting to find out how this author knows how the members of the Doctor's Club addressed each other, the notion that the critique of the state was "hidden" behind the critique of religion assumes that the critique of the state already existed and was merely not stated openly. The later, radical critique of the state was the result of a learning process, for which the theological debates played an important role. The field of the critique of religion was by no means without danger, as the ban on the writings of Young Germany demonstrates. Among other things, the ban used their attacks on religion as justification. Strauß, Feuerbach, and Bauer paid for their critical interventions by being excluded from the university for the rest of their lives.

184. The following cannot be concerned with providing a representative overview of the development of the theological debates; primarily, the problematics into which the Hegelian philosophy of religion intervened in the 1820s and 1830s will be outlined. Encyclopedic presentations of the development of Protestant theology in the eighteenth and nineteenth centuries in Germany can be found in the multi-volume works of Hirsch (1949–1954) and Rohls (1997). I have used primarily the latter for the following overview.

Apart from the debates still to be dealt with in this chapter, however, these conflicts are relevant to the concept of materialism, which will be discussed in the second volume.

"Natural Theology" and the Critique of
Faith in Revelation

As early as the so-called Middle Ages, attempts were made to prove the existence of God by purely rational means. The most famous are the proofs of God by Anselm of Canterbury (1033–1109) and Thomas Aquinas (1225–1274). Rationalist philosophers of the early modern period such as René Descartes (1596–1650) also attempted to derive God's existence as well as his fundamental properties purely from rational arguments. The statements thus obtained were dubbed "natural theology."

Baruch de Spinoza (1632–1677) occupies a special position in this context. He discarded the doctrine asserted by Descartes of there being two substances, one material (res extensa—or extended substance) and one mental (res cogitans—thinking substance): if substance was that which could only exist of itself and be understood only of itself, then there could only be a single substance. This substance could also not stand opposite a creator, since it would then no longer be the only substance. Rather, this single substance was God. So Spinoza rejected a personal God existing outside the world; rather, God is present in being. God is the cause of things, but God is not free to create them or not; creating things is part of divine essence. Starting in the eighteenth century, the notion identifying God with existence was referred to as pantheism, and it was frequently equated with atheism by those who believed in a personal God. The accusation of atheism was also raised against Spinoza.

"Natural theology" that adhered to a personal creator God argued independently of any revelation but was not directed against belief in revelation. The student of Leibniz, Christian Wolff (1679–1754), who was important to philosophical discussions in Germany in the eighteenth century, saw in revelation insights that were necessary for humanity, but which could not be obtained in a natural manner (that is, by rational means). Revelation for him was not opposed to reason, but rather beyond reason.

Similar to natural theology, English deism, which was strongly influenced by the Enlightenment, also attempted to arrive at knowledge of God by purely rational means. In the case of John Locke (1632–1704), this was still paired with the acceptance of Christian revelation. However, this was soon subject to critique. Thus Thomas Woolston (1668–1733) advanced the notion that the miracles of Jesus and his resurrection were not to be taken literally but allegorically—which was not at all possible given the contradictory nature of the reports on the miracles. Due to this conception, he was sentenced to prison in 1729 for blasphemy. Finally, David Hume (1711–1776), from a radical empiricist standpoint, criticized both rationalism and thus the possibility of rational knowledge of God as well as belief in revelation. He regarded the miracles that were supposed to prove the truth of Christian revelation as being in contradiction to natural law. Since the acceptance of natural law is based upon multiple experiences, and miracles and revelation upon the testimony of a few people, it's more probable that these people were mistaken or deceived.

English deism, which assumed the existence of a creator God, but denied that this God directly intervened in the course of the world or revealed himself directly to human beings, had a strong influence upon the French Enlightenment. Voltaire (1694–1789), who had sharply criticized the Church and Christian dogma, still held to the notion of a supreme being whose eternal moral laws are owed obedience by humanity, whereby the observance of these moral laws benefits human beings to the extent that they guarantee a tolerable coexistence. In the case of Paul-Henri Thiry d'Holbach (1723–1789), whose engagement with the natural sciences led him to a materialist and deterministic understanding of nature, the confrontation with deism culminated in an explicitly atheistic position. He attempted to refute the rationalist proofs of God's existence and interpreted religion as the result of insufficient human knowledge of nature, human fear, and conscious manipulation by clerics. He only dared to publish his main work, the *System of Nature* (1770), which Marx also cited in his dissertation manuscript in 1841, under a pseudonym.

In Germany, the Enlightenment promoted a critique of the Bible that made use of historical-critical methods: the same methods of philological investigation applied to other historical texts were applied to biblical texts. In the case of Johann Salomo Semler (1725–1791), this led to the conception that the canon of the New Testament could not be the result of divine inspiration (the fact that there had originally been different lists of canonical scripture in different congregations already contradicted this). Rather, the canon was an item that had grown historically, so that the texts could also contain contradictions and mistakes. Furthermore, Semler made a fundamental distinction between the Old and New Testaments: he regarded them as the results of two different religions. With Christianity, he tried to separate its core, a series of spiritual-moral propositions, from its contemporary accouterments. Among the latter, he counted not only the belief in the devil and demons, but also the notion of the messiah transferred onto Jesus. In neology, that is, the new version of Protestant theology influenced by enlightenment, this historical-critical view of the Bible was continued. As a result central dogmas—from the idea of original sin through the doctrine of the Trinity up to Jesus's nature as both God and man—were questioned, and Christianity was understood primarily as an ethics.

Reimarus, Lessing, and the "Fragments Controversy"

Neology and the historical-critical reading of the Bible had provoked criticism by the old-Protestant orthodoxy. However, the most important theological dispute in Germany in the eighteenth century was ignited by the posthumously published texts of Hermann Samuel Reimarus (1694–1768) who was already mentioned in the last chapter because of his book on the artistic instincts of animals. During his lifetime, the Hamburg Orientalist had only made his mark in the field of religion with a deist text, *Treatise on the Most Noble Truths of Religion* (*Abhandlungen von den vornehmsten Wahrheiten der Religion*, 1754), in which he wished to refute atheism and say something about the existence and properties of God in a purely rational manner. Since Reimarus avoided an open critique of belief in revelation (a critique of the belief in miracles was only carefully hinted at), and the properties of God he identified converged with many elements of Lutheran dogma, the text enjoyed the approval of Lutheran orthodoxy.[185] In contrast, his *Apology or Protective Brief for Rational Worshipers of God* (*Apologie oder Schutzschrift für die vernünftigen Verehrer Gottes*), on which he had worked from the middle of the 1730s until his death, constitutes the most comprehensive text-critical examination of the Bible to date. Reimarus justified his undertaking by the fact that we have no direct knowledge of Christian revelation, that revealed scripture has been handed down by humans, so that the possibility of error and fraud exists. As a criterion of verification, he wishes to use "natural religion," that is, what people can say about God on the basis of pure reason. In his examination of both the Old and New Testaments, however, the concern is not only compatibility with "natural religion." Reimarus used both the contradictions within the texts as well as those between different texts, criticized obviously implausible representations, and pointed out Jewish linguistic customs and conceptual worlds that give certain terms like "son of God" or the invocation of God as "father" different meanings than those attributed to them

---

185. See Klein (2009: 262ff.). Dietrich Klein's book is the most comprehensive engagement in German with Reimarus's theological work.

by Christian dogma. From his extensive discussion, Reimarus concluded that Jesus was not at all both God and human and also not the founder of a new religion. Rather, he advocated for a renewal of Judaism. The "Kingdom of God" that Jesus was striving for in the near future was nothing other than the reestablishment of Jewish rule in Palestine. Regarding the story of the resurrection, the reports in the Gospels were so contradictory that they couldn't be true at all. Reimarus concluded that the story of the resurrection was a conscious deception by disappointed disciples, as a means of coping with the defeat of the political project for which they had been striving.

Reimarus, who only showed the various drafts of his text to close friends, made no attempts to publish it. He would have certainly lost his position as professor at the academic gymnasium in Hamburg, and probably would have been tried in court. Gottfried Ephraim Lessing (1729–1781), who had been a librarian since 1770 at the ducal library in Wolfenbüttel, first published the total of seven pieces of text from the *Apology* between 1770 and 1778 as *Fragments by an Anonymous Writer*. By presenting the texts as the manuscript of an unknown author discovered in the library, he not only protected Reimarus's family, but could also get around the censorship, since he enjoyed freedom from censorship for the publication of library manuscripts. That Reimarus is the author of the fragments was definitively confirmed at the beginning of the nineteenth century, when a more comprehensive excerpt from the *Apology* was published. The *Apology* was published in complete form in 1972, more than two hundred years after its writing.

The publication of the fragments ignited a fierce controversy, the most important protagonists of which were the Hamburg pastor Johann Melchior Goeze (1717–1786) and Lessing. Goeze attacked the anonymous author and Lessing as his editor from the standpoint of Lutheran orthodoxy; Lessing defended Reimarus, without, however, promoting the same position. Reimarus and orthodoxy were both in agreement that the truth of the Christian religion could only be guaranteed by the truth of the Bible as divine revelation. Whereas orthodoxy wished to maintain both, Reimarus disputed the historical truth of the Bible and as a consequence the truth of Christianity, so that he ultimately held to a purely deistic notion of God. Lessing, in contrast, separated the letter of the Bible (and thus belief in biblical literalism) from Christianity, which led him to the statement that "contingent truths of history can never become the proof of necessary truths of reason" (Lessing 2005: 85). If Christianity were actually true, then its truth must be accessible as an inner truth independent of all historical events, whether or not they contain miracles. This thought would also play a central role in Hegel's philosophy of religion.

Since the "fragments controversy" was conducted with rising intensity and made increasingly big waves, in 1778 the Duke of Braunschweig-Wolfenbüttel revoked Lessing's freedom from censorship for library manuscripts, so that he was not able to publish any further fragments. At the same time, he banned Lessing from publishing on topics having to do with religion, so that he could no longer express himself within the "fragments controversy." Condemned to silence on the terrain of theology, Lessing answered on the terrain of the literary: in 1779, he published *Nathan the Wise*. Lessing's most famous drama propagated religious tolerance and found no essential differences between the three great monotheistic religions (Judaism, Christianity, and Islam). It memorialized his friend Moses Mendelssohn, the most important representative of the Jewish Enlightenment, in the form of the character Nathan; the views presented in this drama are partially a result of the "fragments controversy."

Lessing, who died just two years after the publication of *Nathan*, provided occasion after his death for a fierce philosophical controversy. He had confessed to being a Spinozist to Friedrich Heinrich Jacobi (1743–1819), which Jacobi disclosed after Lessing's death in his book on Spinoza (Jacobi 1785). This book, in which Jacobi criticized rationalism and wished to demonstrate in particular that Spinoza's pantheism leads necessarily to atheism ignited a debate that has gone down in the history of philosophy as the "pantheism controversy," and which had the effect that once again Spinoza was debated in Germany. A good eighty years later, in the afterword to the second edition of *Capital*, Marx hints at this debate when remarking "mediocre epigones who now talk large in educated German circles began to take pleasure in treating Hegel in the same way as the good Moses Mendelssohn treated Spinoza in Lessing's time, namely as a 'dead dog.'" (Marx 1976: 102).[186] From the parallel that Marx constructs, one can conclude that he valued Spinoza just as highly as he did Hegel. That is remarkable, since explicit references to Spinoza in Marx's work are rather rare, albeit consistently positive.

For Protestant theology in Germany, the "fragments controversy" was a profound rupture. Reimarus had not only rebutted individual reports of

---

186. The reference to Mendelssohn wasn't quite right. As indicated in his letter from June 27, 1870; to Kugelmann, Marx was of the opinion that Mendelssohn himself had written to Lessing that Spinoza was a dead dog (see MECW 43: 528). But it was Lessing who had expressed himself critically to Jacobi: "People still talk about Spinoza as if talking about a dead dog" (Jacobi 1785: 32). Hegel also quoted Lessing's observation in 1827 in the preface to the second edition of the *Encyclopedia* (Hegel 2010: 14) when he defended himself against attacks from the conservative-religious side.

miracles; rather, his critique aimed at asserting that biblical texts were anything but evidence of divine inspiration. The naive dogmatism, which concluded that the canonical scriptures were directly true on the basis of their divine inspiration, was fundamentally called into question. There was now no way around a historical-critical consideration of the Bible, which in the nineteenth century made possible comprehensive research into the life of Jesus according to historical-critical standards (see the classical presentation by Albert Schweitzer, beginning with Reimarus). Reimarus's *Apology* also had an influence reaching far beyond inner-theological debates. Thus Karl Gutzkow, in his 1835 novel *Wally, die Zweiflerin* (Wally, the Doubter), has his protagonist read Reimarus's text, which strengthens her religious doubt. It was this novel that provided the occasion for the ban on the writings of the Young Germany group, because they supposedly attacked religion and destroyed all morality.

Kant's Separation of Belief and Knowledge

Against the background of Reimarus's critique of belief in revelation and a historical-critical dissection of the Bible, those who wished to hold on to both central motifs of the Enlightenment as well as Christianity, justifying the latter in terms of pure reason—that is, independent of any revelation—had to gain enormous importance. Precisely such rational justifications for God's existence—such as the "ontological" proof of God, which from our notion of a perfect being concludes that it exists, since it would otherwise not be perfect—were, only a few years after the fragments controversy, subjected to a devastating critique by Immanuel Kant (1724–1804). In his dissertation, Marx would deal with this critique and curtail it in one aspect.

In his *Critique of Pure Reason* (1781), Kant made clear that what can be known by "pure reason," that is, mere thought independent of any experience, is limited to two areas: to formal sciences like geometry and arithmetic (which for their part ground in the forms of intuition, namely space and time), and to the fundamental apparatus of categories with which all experiential knowledge is structured, such as quality, quantity, causality, etc. Neither in the formal sciences nor in this categorical apparatus did Kant see a conscious creation by human beings (which could also be changed); rather, for him they were the expression of the structures of human intuition and human understanding. These structures could be recognized by human reason, insofar as the latter inquired into the "conditions of possibility" of experiential knowledge, which is exactly what Kant undertook in his *Critique of Pure Reason*. Traditional metaphysical statements, such as those concerning

the presence of human free will, the existence of God, and the immortality of the soul thus do not refer to objects of experience—they cannot be
investigated with the means of empirical sciences—nor do they belong to the
apparatus of categories of understanding. Thus, they also cannot be objects
of pure reason. They are objects of thought, but they are not accessible to
scientific *knowledge*. Kant does not conclude that they are therefore superfluous. God, free will, and an immortal soul cannot be proved scientifically, but
they are necessary "regulative ideas" that serve our orientation in the world.

Kant further followed this way of treating religious questions, which is only
briefly outlined in the *Critique of Pure Reason*, in his justification of moral
philosophy in the *Groundwork of the Metaphysics of Morals* (1785) and the
Critique of Practical Reason (1788). An act is only moral, according to Kant, if
it is determined by moral law, thus following obligation. However, the requirement that moral law be objective and universally valid does not entail any specific content. Moral law merely says that one's own guiding principles have
to be generalizable. Kant's famous "categorical imperative" is therefore: "Act
only in accordance with that maxim through which you can at the same time
wish that it become a universal law" (Kant 1997: 31). Now, Kant wanted to
demonstrate further that it was a necessary law for rational beings. As distinct
from mere things, which only have a relative purpose, namely as a means for
something else, a rational being, having a will, "exists as an end in itself, not
merely as a means to be used by this or that will at its discretion" (ibid.: 37).
Therefore, the categorical imperative can also be formulated as follows: "So act
that you use humanity, whether in your own person or in the person of any
other, always at the same time as an end, never merely as a means" (ibid.: 38).

Four years before the French Revolution, Kant had thus found a classical formulation for the anti-feudal/bourgeois conception of equality: every
human being is to be treated equally as an end in itself. However, Kant did
not raise the question of which social relations prevent this. Just sixty years
later, in the *Contribution to the Critique of Hegel's Philosophy of Law*, the
young Marx placed at the center of focus exactly that which Kant left out, and
formulated the "categorical imperative to overthrow all relations in which
man is a debased, enslaved, forsaken, despicable being" (MECW 3: 182).

Proceeding from moral law, Kant constructs freedom of will, the immortality of the soul, and the existence of God as *postulates* of "practical" reason
(meaning directed toward action and its moral conditions). In doing so, he
made use of, to put it briefly, the following considerations. Since moral law
includes a "should" (the categorical imperative), we must conclude a "can,"
and thus postulate human free will. The correspondence of the will with
moral law is an endless task; it assumes an endless perfection, so that we

must conclude from it an endless duration of the moral subject, thus the immortality of the soul. Since perfected virtue can only be thought of with bliss as its consequence, but no entity other than God is capable of guaranteeing this bliss, we are forced to postulate the existence of God.

Whereas the strict separation of belief and knowledge undertaken in the *Critique of Pure Reason*, and therefore the critique of all "natural theology," displayed great persuasive power, this was not the case to the same extent for the postulates grounded in Kant's moral philosophy. The part of Kant's philosophy that displaced religion from the domain of knowledge developed a far greater influence than the part that attempted to conquer new terrain for religion in moral philosophy.

Further discussion led to the conception advanced by Friedrich Karl Forberg (1770–1848) that the existence of God does not at all have to be necessarily postulated, a position branded immediately as "atheistic." Forberg had published his text in 1798 in the *Philosophisches Journal* edited by Fichte and Niethammer. Fichte, who did not share Forberg's position but stated in the debate that the "moral order" is "the true belief" and promoted a notion of God that was no longer that of the personal God, was soon drawn into the vortex of this "atheism dispute." He was indicted for the spread of atheist ideas and had to give up his professorship in Jena in 1799.[187] Although Fichte again obtained a professorship in Erlangen in 1805 and was appointed to the newly founded University of Berlin in 1810, the atheism dispute had made clear that the suspicion of promoting atheist positions was still sufficient to endanger one's academic existence. Fear of such a danger also played a role for Hegel in the 1820s.

Supernaturalism, Theological Rationalism, and Schleiermacher's Theology of Feeling

In the period after Kant, two currents in German Protestantism stood opposed to each other: supernaturalism and (theological) rationalism. Supernaturalism saw supernatural, divine revelation as the foundation of religion. This revelation was found in the Bible. But instead of merely asserting, as earlier Lutheran orthodoxy did, that biblical texts were divinely inspired, it saw its task as proving the historical credibility of the Bible, which was really a way of posing the task that shows the influence of the Enlightenment.

The most important representative of early supernaturalism was the

---

187. On the prehistory of the atheism dispute and its placement in the development of post-Kantian philosophy, see Jaeschke/Arndt (2012: 131–61).

Tübingen theologian Gottlob Christian Storr (1746–1805). In dealing with Kant-oriented fundamental critiques of the belief in revelation, he relied upon the results of Kant's philosophy: if knowledge is confined to the world of experience, and theoretical reason cannot say anything about supernatural objects, then it also cannot be used to reject revelation. Storr agreed with Kant that practical reason forces us to postulate the supernatural (the existence of God and the immortality of the soul). He is thus able to conclude that biblical doctrine cannot be refuted by theoretical reason, whereas it agrees with practical reason. So it's only a matter of establishing whether the texts of the Gospels are credible. Storr therefore attempts to prove that the texts of the New Testament actually originate with the apostles. The divine authority of Jesus that they attested Storr saw confirmed in the latter's moral way of life and performance of miracles, so that the character of the text as revelation is also guaranteed.

In Tübingen in the early 1790s, Storr was one of the theological teachers of Schelling, Hölderlin, and Hegel, all of whom, under the influence of Kant's philosophy and the enormous impression of the French Revolution, nonetheless had no sympathy for his supernaturalism (Pinkard 2000: 35ff.). Probably stimulated by these discussions, in 1793 Hegel started composing his first theological drafts, in which a number of extremely critical remarks on traditional Christianity can be found. In a letter to Schelling from April 16, 1795, he states in summary: "Religion and politics have joined hands in the same underhanded game. The former has taught what despotism willed: contempt for the human race, its incapacity for any good whatsoever, its incapacity to be something on its own" (Hegel 1984: 35). In 1795, Hegel even wrote a *Life of Jesus* that summarized the reports from the Gospels, but left out all stories of miracles, including the resurrection. However, these drafts, first published in 1907 by Hermann Nöhl, had no influence upon the debates of the nineteenth century.

Schelling's first publications also arose against the background of the debate between Kantian criticism and supernaturalism. Both his text on the *I* (Schelling 1980a) and his *Philosophical Letters on Dogmatism and Criticism* (Schelling 1980b) were quoted by Marx in 1841 in his doctoral dissertation.

Opposed to supernaturalism was theological rationalism. It did not contest revelation; however, it regarded reason as the guiding principle for the credibility of the content of revelation. The most important representative of this rationalism was Heinrich Eberhard Gottlob Paulus (1761–1851), who had been a professor at the University of Heidelberg since 1811. Paulus assumed that the scriptures of the Bible were based upon true events, but he attempted to free them of anything miraculous. According to Paulus, the evangelists testified to what they had actually seen, but since they did not know the natural foundations of what they observed, they believed in God's direct intervention. Paulus attempted to find a rational explanation for every apparent miracle. Thus, he understood the resurrection of Jesus as a recovery from an apparent death; the real death of Jesus occurred later without witnesses, so that the disciples glorified their last encounter with him as his heavenly ascension. Paulus also did not understand Jesus's death as a sacrifice for humankind's sins. Rather, the crucifixion stands for Jesus remaining true to his convictions to the last.

Like many representatives of theological rationalism, Paulus also tended toward liberal ideas and criticized the Restoration that set in in the 1820s. This led to a quarrel with Hegel, with whom he'd had friendly relations during his time in Heidelberg. Paulus saw in Hegel's *Philosophy of Right* a justification of the Restoration in Prussia. In a review (Paulus 1821), he sharply attacked Hegel, who resented this, since he could assume that Paulus of all people should know him better.

In spite of all antagonisms, both supernaturalism and rationalism maintained that faith was based upon certain tenets. Opposed to this was the theology of feeling, with its most important exponent, Friedrich Schleiermacher (1768–1834): it based belief not upon understanding but upon feelings. Schleiermacher (1821/22) distinguished self-activity by humans from mere receptivity, the mere receptiveness for other things. Whereas the feelings involved with self-activity are based in a feeling of freedom, the feelings that accompany receptivity are based in a feeling of dependence. Our consciousness of being-in-the-world is therefore always connected to feelings of freedom *and* dependence. We cannot have a feeling of unconditional and complete (*schlechthinniger*) freedom because for one thing our self-activity is always directed toward an object that exhibits its own properties, and for another, because we do not completely posit our self-activity on our own; it does not originate completely with us. Schleiermacher concluded that with the negation of a feeling of complete freedom, there is a feeling of complete dependence. However, the other upon which we are dependent cannot be the world, since we have a partial feeling of freedom with regard to it. But if that on which we are absolutely dependent is not the world, then it must be God. Therefore, our relationship to God, our complete dependence upon him, is shown by our own feelings.

For Schleiermacher, Christianity was determined by Jesus as a figure of redemption, whereby he oriented to the Gospel of John, which he regarded as the direct testimony of the apostle. If the historical figure Jesus is the redeemer, then he does not himself require any redemption, so that he is distinct from all human beings. Schleiermacher therefore understands the appearance of Jesus as divine revelation. Nothing supernatural is necessary for that. Like the rationalists, Schleiermacher also sought rational explanations for the miracles and the resurrection, which he also regarded as a recovery from an apparent death. The actual "miracle" for Schleiermacher was Jesus's spiritual influence. For Protestant theology hardly any other theologian of the nineteenth century had as great a significance, in the twentieth century as well, as Schleiermacher.

HEGEL'S PHILOSOPHY OF RELIGION AND THE DEBATES OF THE 1830s

The previous outline should make clear how strongly the belief in revelation—at least at the philosophical level—was shaken by the theological debates of the 18th century. Supernaturalism and theological rationalism offered less-than-convincing solutions. Schleiermacher's theology of feeling showed one way out, but only by giving up the claim to a rational knowledge of religion.

The Relation between Religion and Philosophy in Hegel's Work

Hegel was not willing to accede to such a shift in terrain. He did not dispute that religion was connected with feelings, but he maintained that feelings say nothing about the truth content of what is felt.[188] Hegel wanted to overcome this split between belief and knowledge brought about by the Enlightenment, without curtailing the possibility of rational knowledge—even on the terrain of religion. Knowledge of God was not only integrated into Hegel's philosophical system; in a certain way, it was the highest aim of his philosophy. But the question arose quickly as to whether this philosophically recognized God still had anything to do with the personal God of Christianity. Hegel's philosophical defense of Christianity was a critique of the customary form of Christianity, which brought him hostility from

---

188. In a preface to an 1822 piece of writing on the philosophy of religion by his Heidelberg student and friend Hermann Friedrich Wilhelm Hinrichs (1794–1861), Hegel subjected Schleiermacher's conception, without referring to it by name, to a devastating criticism: "If feeling is supposed to be the fundamental determination of the essence of humankind, then humankind is equated to animals. . . . If religion in human beings is based only on a feeling, then it truly has no better purpose than the *feeling of dependence*, and thus the dog would be the best Christian, since he holds it most strongly and lives primarily within this feeling. The dog also has feelings of redemption, when its hunger is satisfied by a bone" (Hegel 1822: 58; emphasis in original).

opposing sides: for orthodox theologians, Hegel's philosophy of religion was too critical of religion, whereas later the critics of religion accused him of having adapted too much to religion.

Hegel determined the relation between religion and philosophy at a fundamental level in his *Phenomenology of Spirit*, which he outlined in the third and concluding section of the *Encyclopedia of the Philosophical Sciences*. Hegel understood by the term "spirit"[189] not simply an endowment, but rather something active, constituting relationships, the essence of which was freedom. Hegel distinguished between subjective, objective, and absolute spirit. "Subjective spirit" can be understood as a form of interiority (consciousness, will) on the part of individual human beings, directed at something external and non-spiritual/mental.[190] "Objective spirit" refers to an "objective" social reality, created by individuals, but at the same time standing above them. Its manifestations are right (*das Recht*), morality (*die Moralität*), and ethical life (*Sittlichkeit*) in family, civil society, and the state. "Absolute spirit" is spirit that refers to itself, spirit that has spirit as its object and recognizes itself as spirit. Spirit relating to other things can occur in fundamentally three ways: as the *sensory intuition* of an individual object, as *representation* located in time and space; as *conceptual thought* (*begreifendes Denken*) that produces concepts. For all three of these types of relationship, Hegel identifies a field upon which spirit relates to itself in its relationship to others. For sensory intuition, this field is *art*, the contemplation of the beautiful;[191] for representation, the field is *religion*; and for conceptually aimed thought, *philosophy*. The following discusses only the interrelation between religion and philosophy in Hegel's work.

Hegel emphasized that religion and philosophy had the same content, but the content is presented in different ways: religion with the help of representations and images, and philosophy with the help of the concept. Within religions, there is a constant distrust of images, including the prohibition of images, but religious representations have such images as their foundation. The Bible's God is imagined as a person acting in space and time, and in particular God's incarnation is narrated as a sensory, historical story—as the history of Jesus. Hegel opposed this by saying that God can only be adequately

---

189. German *Geist*, meaning both "mind" and "spirit." —Trans.

190. *nicht-Geistiges* —Trans.

191. Underlying these considerations is a conception of art very distant from that of the contemporary world. For Hegel, the creation of the beautiful is the depiction of the absolute (or said religiously, the depiction of God). Thus, Hegel can place art in a continuum with religion and philosophy, to the extent that all three, albeit in different ways, aim for the Absolute.

grasped in the form of thought; religious representations are only a step in that direction. In that sense, the historical critique of Christian tradition, for example the question of whether miracles actually occurred, plays no role for Hegel. But that also means that Hegel, when he speaks of the substantive identity of Christianity and philosophy, does not mean the content of a naive, pious Christianity, but a Christianity that has already been reflected upon theologically.

Far more extensively than in the *Encyclopedia*, Hegel dealt with religion within the framework of his *Lectures on the Philosophy of Religion*, which he delivered multiple times in the 1820s. These lectures were first published in 1832 within the scope of the "Association of Friends" edition. Philosophy of religion is enlightenment concerning what religion actually is; that is to say, according to its concept. Religion for Hegel was "the self-consciousness of God" (Hegel 1988: 177). By self-consciousness, Hegel meant a consciousness of the self that can only come about in a mediated way by the relation to something else. This other, standing opposite to the infinite consciousness of God, is the finite consciousness of humans. "God is self-consciousness; he knows himself in a consciousness that is distinct from him," and that is finite, human consciousness. "Finite consciousness knows God only to the extent that God knows himself in it; thus God is spirit, indeed the spirit of his community" (Hegel 1988: 392).

For Hegel, God and man are not two independent subjects that can either enter into a relationship or not. For Hegel, God and man are mutually interdependent. Spirit is something active that creates relationships. God as spirit is precisely this activity of going outside of oneself, of revealing oneself, of manifesting oneself. But this revelation requires another spirit to which it is revealed, and which can accept this revelation, that is, man as God's likeness. Religion is thus not only a relation of finite man to God, but also that of God to man: "We have here, therefore, the religion of the manifestation of God, since God knows himself in finite spirit" (ibid.). Only through the relation to finite man as his other can God relate to himself. And that is just as essential for God as for man.

This mutual relationship between God and man is also a matter for other religions, but, according to Hegel, only Christianity makes this relationship its own object. Christianity is therefore for Hegel the "absolute religion." Hegel interprets the doctrine of the Trinity as a visual conception of this mutual relationship: God the father produces the son and his creation of the world in which the son becomes the God-Man and brings humanity divine revelation, so that God can think himself in the consciousness of human beings. The son returns to the father, but the divine spirit is now the spirit of the community. That means the story of son, father, and holy spirit, the three that are in fact one, is the vivid presentation of the outlined philosophical concept of God, where God is spirit knowing himself in his other.[192]

Hegel's religious-philosophical conceptions were attacked early on as "pantheistic." Hegel vehemently denied this attribution, but he based his rejection on a specific concept of pantheism, namely that all things without exception are regarded as divine (see Encyclopaedia §573). However, the question is justified as to whether this philosophically recognized God, for whom the self-relationship is so essential that he cannot be any God at all without the world and humans, still has to do with the Christian God. That which many Christians regard as essential is criticized by Hegel as mere "representation" and is dropped from the philosophical reconstruction.

In the preceding outline of Hegel's views, I have relied upon the *Encyclopaedia* and the *Philosophy of Religion*. But an adequate discussion of the relation between religion and philosophy in Hegel's work would have to begin with the *Science of Logic*, at the end of which stands the "absolute idea." The limited aim of my outline, making the debates of the 1830s understandable, justifies this omission. One remark about the *Logic* appears to be necessary, however. It's often claimed that in the *Logic*, the study of the determinations of thought, Hegel wished to depict God's thoughts before the creation of the world. Sometimes this statement is placed in quotation marks, creating the impression that it's a quote from Hegel. If thoughts are attributed to God, then God is conceived of as a thinking person. In the introduction to the *Logic*, however, on which the claim above is based, Hegel formulates something else. After stating "Logic is to be understood as the system of pure reason, as the realm of pure thought" and emphasizing "*This realm is truth unveiled, truth as it is in and for itself,*" he adds: "It can therefore be said that this content is *the exposition of God as he is in his eternal essence before the creation of nature and of a finite spirit*" (Hegel 2010: 29). So Hegel did not present the "thoughts" of God, but rather the "essence" of God "before the creation" of the world, and all that with the distancing addition that "it can" (*man kann*) be stated that way (see Jaeschke 2003: 253). If, as argued in the *Philosophy of Religion*, God requires the world in order to relate to himself, so that he can be absolute spirit, then God is not at all possible "before the creation" of the world. The existence of a God existing before the creation

---

192. A cursory version of this interpretation of the doctrine of the Trinity is found in §§ 564–571 of the *Encyclopedia* and more extensively in the third part of the *Lectures on the Philosophy of Religion*.

of the world, however, is a central *representation*[193] of the Christian religion. Hegel's sentence can then be understood as a somewhat reluctantly given answer as to what remains of this representation at the level of the concept: the categories of logic, for these are also true if the world doesn't exist. However, this truth is not thought by anyone, also not by God, and Hegel does not claim this anywhere.

Hegel claimed to have reconciled religion with the state of science, thus overcoming the divide between belief and knowledge. He presented himself as the better theologian, rescuing what the theologians had in part already abandoned.[194] However, in the 1820s, Hegel still feared the accusation of atheism;[195] to that extent, it was still in his interest to present himself as an orthodox Protestant. So, for example, on July 3, 1826, he wrote to August Tholuck: "I am a Lutheran, and through philosophy have been at once completely confirmed in Lutheranism" (Hegel 1984: 520). It was not at all a coincidence that he emphasized his Lutheranism to the pietistic Tholuck. This effort also explains Hegel's positive reference to the *Aphorisms on Non-Knowledge and Absolute Knowledge in Relation to the Christian Creed* (*Aphorismen über Nichtwissen und absolutes Wissen im Verhältnis zum christlichen Glaubensbekenntnis*, 1829) by the higher regional court councilor of Naumburg, Carl Friedrich Göschel (1781–1861). Göschel had attempted, from a Protestant-conservative standpoint, to prove the compatibility of Hegel's philosophy and Christianity, which Hegel, in light of the increasing attacks on his philosophy, gratefully accepted (see Jaeschke 2003: 300ff.).[196]

That Hegel's philosophy of religion was subject to increasingly sharp

---

193. *Vorstellung*, a "notion." —Trans..

194. Against theologians who "complain against philosophy for its destructive tendency," Hegel objected that they "no longer possess any of the content that is subject to possible destruction" (Hegel 1988: 81), since as a result of the debates of the eighteenth century, they had de facto abandoned even important dogmas, such as the doctrine of the Trinity.

195. See the draft letter to Creuzer, May 1821 (Hegel 1984: 467).

196. In the twentieth century as well, it remained controversial whether Hegel's philosophy of religion was more a critique or a rescue of Christianity. Karl Löwith (1964), who strongly emphasizes the ambiguous character of Hegel's philosophy of religion, ultimately situates it on the side of the destruction of religion, whereas the famous Protestant theologian Wolfhart Pannenberg (1976: 184), sees in it "the high point so far of the conceptual clarification of the doctrine of the Trinity with regard to the relationship between unity and Trinity," and Christof Gestrich (1989: 190ff.), also a Protestant theologian, sees in Hegel the defender of the Christian religion that Hegel presented himself as. A brief summary of the ambiguities of Hegel's philosophy, giving rise to such different interpretations, is found in Siep (2015: 22–25).

attacks over the course of the 1820s also had to do with a reversal in the intellectual climate. Prussia's reform period had been over since the early 1820s. The increasing conservatism was supported by Protestant orthodoxy and increasingly strong pietism, which focused upon the piety of the individual. Schelling too, who started teaching again in Munich in 1827, fit in well on this front, since he was now defining his philosophy as "Christian philosophy": philosophy was to find its basis in Christianity and not, as with Hegel, attempt to deduce Christianity from its concept at all. For all of them, Hegel's philosophy of religion, with its scientific claims, was a red flag.

This reversal also made itself felt within the theological faculty of the University of Berlin. In 1826, Ernst Wilhelm Hengstenberg (1802–1869), who was close to pietism, obtained an associate professorship for the study of the Old Testament, which was turned into a full professorship in 1828 against Altenstein's resistance. Along with August Tholuck (1799–1877), also a Pietist, who taught at the University of Halle, and Ernst Ludwig von Gerlach (1795–1877), who soon became one of the most important Prussian conservatives, Hengstenberg founded the *Evangelische Kirchenzeitung* in 1827, which developed into the leading organ of early Prussian conservatism (on Hengstenberg, see Lenz 1910: 2.1: 327–48; Hachtmann 2016).

The influence of Hegel's philosophy of religion upon Protestant theology remained limited. Among academically established theologians, it was primarily Carl Daub (1765–1836), a professor in Heidelberg since 1795, and Philipp Konrad Marheineke (1780–1846), a professor at the University of Berlin since 1811, who turned to Hegel's conception after both had initially been influenced by Schelling. Marheineke was also the editor of Hegel's *Lectures on the Philosophy of Religion* in the Association of Friends edition. Wilhelm Vatke (1802–1882), initially a lecturer in Berlin and from 1837 a professor for the Old Testament, was also a Hegelian. In the 1830s, Ferdinand Christian Baur (1792–1860), who taught theology in Tübingen and applied the historical-critical method to researching the New Testament and early Christianity, also oriented toward Hegelian philosophy. Hegel's philosophy of religion also had a great influence upon the next generation of radical critics of religion: David Friedrich Strauß, Bruno Bauer, and Ludwig Feuerbach were all students of Hegel.

David Friedrich Strauß and the Split of the Hegelian School

The fiercest controversies about Hegel's philosophy of religion began in the

1830s.[197] An early piece of writing by Ludwig Feuerbach (1804–1872), who would play an important role in the debates of the 1840s, constitutes the overture for the coming storm. In 1823–24, Feuerbach had begun studying theology under Carl Daub and thereby got to know the Hegelian school. This prompted him to switch subjects: he went to Berlin to study philosophy with Hegel. In 1828, he obtained his doctorate at the University of Erlangen; as a stipendiary of the Bavarian king, he had to conclude his studies at a Bavarian university. His debut work, *Thoughts on Death and Immortality* (1830), published shortly after the July Revolution and quickly banned, was strongly influenced by Hegel's philosophy of religion. Feuerbach rejected both the notion of a personal God as well as that of personal immortality. The latter, according to Feuerbach, is merely egotistical wishful thinking. Instead of adhering to such wishful thinking, man, in awareness of the finite nature of his existence, finds his way to a new, "essential" life. The text was published anonymously and as a result of the ban only slightly influential, and when Feuerbach was identified as the author in Erlangen, it led to him having to give up his activity as a lecturer.[198]

The topics addressed by Feuerbach also remained an important object of controversy in the following years. Critics of Hegelian philosophy accused it of not being compatible with Christian conceptions of an immortal soul and a personal God, which was repudiated by representatives of the Hegelian school like Carl Friedrich Göschel.[199]

An independent position that played an important role in the debates of the 1830s was developed by the so-called speculative theists[200] such as Christian

---

197. The contributions of Hegel's students are dealt with extensively in Sass (1963); the debate as a whole is dealt with in Jaeschke (1986: 361–436).

198. See Winiger (2011: 65). An exhaustive and updated interpretation of this early writing by Feuerbach is provided by Grandt (2006: 43–60).

199. Whereas Hegel explicitly rejected pantheistic conceptions, in his works he avoided statements on the immortality of the soul. A story circulated by Heinrich Heine, however, suggests that Hegel had only ridicule for such notions: "We [Heine and Hegel] stood one evening at the window, and I gushed about the stars, the residence of the blessed. But the master growled: 'the stars are only a luminous leprosy in the sky!' 'For God's sake!,' I cried, 'so there's no happy place up above to reward virtue after death?' He looked at me mockingly: 'So you want to have tip money for performing your duties in life, for caring for your sick mother, for not letting your brother starve and not poisoning your enemies?'" (quoted in Nicolin 1970: 235).

200. As distinct from deism, "theism" assumed that God was not only the creator of the world, but also had a continuous relationship to the world and, in particular, had revealed himself to humankind.

Hermann Weisse (1801–1866), Immanuel Hermann Fichte (1796–1879), and Karl Philipp Fischer (1807–1885). They took up elements of Hegel's philosophy, but criticized that their claim of philosophically grounding the content of Christianity was not redeemed. This was particularly the case for the existence of a personal God and the immortality of the soul. Therefore, a speculative theology of their own was necessary.[201]

The book *The Life of Jesus, Critically Examined*, by David Friedrich Strauß (1808–1874) and published in 1835, became the most important point of contention in the 1830s and a rupture in the theology of the nineteenth century. Strauß had studied theology in Tübingen and had also already studied Hegel's work there. To deepen his studies of Hegel's philosophy, he went to Berlin in November 1831, but was only able to attend Hegel's lectures for a week, since Hegel died of cholera on November 14. But his stay in Berlin was not in vain; before Strauß returned to Tübingen, he joined Wilhelm Vatke for the rest of the semester. Vatke, who was preparing a historical critique of the Old Testament, which was published in the same year as Strauß's *The Life of Jesus* but caused far less excitement. It was probably Vatke who introduced Strauß to the concept of mythos that would become central to *The Life of Jesus*.[202] Once again back in Tübingen, Strauß held lectures on philosophy with a Hegelian orientation at the theological seminary. On the side, he worked on his book.

The influence of this comprehensive work—it encompassed two volumes with a total of almost 1,500 pages—went far beyond the academic circles of philosophers and theologians; it was discussed well into broad swathes of the educated bourgeoisie.[203] What was so exciting about it? In contrast to some other theological contributions, the work's basic statement could be grasped easily: what the Gospels reported concerning Jesus were not historical events but the result of myth formation that began in the early Christian congregations. Despite all controversies, neither the supernaturalists nor the (theological) rationalists had called into question the historical character of the biblical narrative, but that's exactly what Strauß did, and that was the scandal.

In contrast to Reimarus, who interpreted the story of the resurrection as an act of conscious deception on the part of the disciples, Strauß's concern was not with any such intentional manipulation. Strauß understood the

---

201. Speculative not in the contemporary sense of a poorly founded presumption, but rather in the sense of comprehending recognition.

202. See Sandberger (1972: 152), who has examined in detail Strauß's development between 1830 and 1837.

203. On the widespread impact of Strauß and reactions to him, also from the Catholic side, see Courth (1980).

reports of miracles and the story of the resurrection as the result of the emergence through oral tradition of "history-like forms (Einkleidungen) of early Christian ideas (Ideen), formulated in sagas without conscious intention in the poetic process" (Stepelevich 1997: 33). However, this myth formation followed certain tendencies: the person Jesus was increasingly idealized and his life was adjusted to the passages of the Old Testament that were interpreted as prophecies of the messiah (Strauß 1835: 1: 72).[204]

The interpretation of Bible stories as myths wasn't completely new, but before Strauß it was confined to the Old Testament and only a few passages of the New Testament. What was new was the consistent application of this interpretation to central events described in the Gospels.

With *The Life of Jesus*, Strauß's aim was not a critique of Christianity. He distinguished between the life of Jesus and Jesus's preaching. He did not intend to call the latter into question. Already in the preface to his work, Strauß emphasized: "The author is aware that the essence of the Christian faith is perfectly independent of his criticism. The supernatural birth of Christ, his miracles, his resurrection and ascension, remain eternal truths, whatever doubts may be cast on their reality as historical facts" (Stepelevich 1997: 22).

The certainty that he could hold on to "eternal truths," even if they weren't "historical facts," was taken from Hegel's philosophy, which distinguished between religious representations and their conceptual reconstruction, whereby only the latter, and not historical events, could demonstrate the truth of the content of religion. For Hegel and most theologians oriented to Hegel, the distinction between representation and concept justified their disinterest in historical criticism. This criticism was perceived as a limited, rationalist position. However, the distinction between representation and concept could also be radicalized in such a way that it would be completely irrelevant whether religious representations had any kind of historical events at their foundation. This is precisely the path taken by Strauß.

What was new was the conclusion drawn at the end of his deliberations, that the properties attributed in legendary form to Jesus as a God-man, namely of being the incarnation of the unity of man and God, could not accrue to any individual human being, but only to humanity as a whole in its development (Strauß 1835: 2: 734). In light of the restorative tendencies of the time, this thought had considerable explosive political power. In 1833, Friedrich Julius Stahl (1802–1861) published the second part of his *Philosophy of Right*, in which, referring to Schelling's "Christian" philosophy, he justified absolute

---

204. Whereby the Old Testament messiah was supposed to be a future king of the Jews; the Apostle Paul was the first to expand this role to the redeemer of humanity.

monarchy by analogy to the rule of God. But if this God is not incarnated in an individual God-man, but only in the entire human species, then Stahl's justification of absolute monarchy was invalid.

Strauß's book led to a flood of angry critiques and replies. Shortly after the publication of the first volume, Strauß lost his teaching position at the Tübinger Stift and was transferred to a Gymnasium. When in 1839 he finally obtained a professorship at the University of Zurich, this led to such massive protests, primarily by the rural population, that Strauß was retired before he even began to hold lectures. Strauß did not receive any further appointments.[205]

It's clear why Strauß would be attacked by supernaturalists, theological rationalists, and the conservative Lutherans around Hengstenberg's *Evangelische Kirchenzeitung*. But representatives of the Hegelian school also criticized Strauß harshly. In that case, the fact that Strauß served the conservative opponents of the Hegelian school as a prime example for the ominous consequences of this philosophy played a role. Those Hegelians seeking a balance between Hegel's philosophy and Protestantism had to therefore make clear that Strauß could not rightly appeal to Hegel.

In the *Streitschriften (Polemics)* published in 1837, Strauß dealt extensively with his critics from the Hegelian school. With regard to Christology, Strauß distinguished between a Hegelian "right," a Hegelian "center," and a Hegelian "left." He regarded the position on the historicity of the Gospels as the central criterion for this division, either with the idea of the story of the Gospels accepted as historical fact, or only a part of it, or the idea that the history of the Gospels is not confirmed as historical fact, neither as a whole nor in part (Strauß 1837: 95). Whoever took the first position (Göschel, Gabler, Bauer) was counted as part of the Hegelian right by Strauß, those taking the second position as part of the center (here, Strauß names Rosenkranz), and whoever took the third position was counted as part of the Hegelian left. Strauß continued that at the moment he was the only one to take this left position, to the extent that he could be counted a part of the Hegelian school at all. Strauß did not remain the only "left" Hegelian, however. In the meantime, it has even become common to date the split of the Hegelian school to the debates around Strauß's *Life of Jesus*.

Strauß's division wasn't just taken up positively in the review of his

---

205. Quite contrary to this condemnation in his time is the importance conceded to Strauß in contemporary theology. Theißen/Merz (1998: 4), authors of the most widely used (Protestant) textbook on the life of Jesus in Germany today, state with regard to Strauß: "Scholarship can never go back before its basic thesis of the mythical transformation of the Jesus tradition."

Streitschriften in the *Hallische Jahrbücher* (Ruge 1838d: 1910). Carl Ludwig Michelet (1801–1893) also quoted it approvingly in the second volume of his *History of the Last Systems of Philosophy in Germany from Kant to Hegel* (*Geschichte der letzten Systeme der Philosophie in Deutschland von Kant bis Hegel*), published in 1838. Michelet's word had weight. He had been a student and friend of Hegel, and for the Association of Friends edition he had edited Hegel's *Lectures on the History of Philosophy* from 1833 to 1836. Michelet made Strauß's division prominent, even if one could not fail to notice a certain irony in his case. For example, he proposed an alliance of the center with the left, in order to achieve a majority. He regarded himself, Gans, and Vatke as being part of the left (Michelet 1838: 659).

THE BEGINNINGS OF YOUNG HEGELIANISM

The distinction Strauß noticed in the Hegelian school between right and left Hegelians, on the basis of controversies concerning the philosophy of religion, is usually identified with another distinction, that between "Old Hegelians" and "Young Hegelians." The Old Hegelians are regarded as conservative (and therefore as part of the right), the Young Hegelians as progressive to revolutionary (and therefore left). Today, the descriptions Right and Left and Old and Young Hegelian, respectively, are widely regarded as synonyms. It has become just as usual to attribute to Marx and Engels a more or less pronounced Young Hegelian phase. However, in the literature, there are great difficulties in substantively defining Old/Right Hegelianism and Young/Left Hegelianism, and demarcating them from each other in terms of personnel. The first is usually achieved only at a general level, and in the latter, there is hardly a consensus. It's therefore not sufficient to trace the emergence of Young Hegelianism; one also has to discuss how sensible these divisions are in the first place.

Arnold Ruge and the Founding of the Hallische Jahrbücher

For the oppositional currents in Prussia, but also in Germany as a whole, the *Hallische Jahrbücher for deutsche Wissenschaft und Kunst* played a decisive role between 1838 and the beginning of 1843.[206] For the currents referred to

---

206. The democratic publisher Ernst Keil wrote shortly after the outbreak of the Revolution of 1848 in the journal *Der Leuchtturm*: "These yearbooks had the most tremendous effect upon the scientific youth. They were the *revolution* on the terrain of knowledge and ideas. Without this revolution, we would not have had the March Days" (quoted in Hundt 2010b:

as Young Hegelianism, this was the most important publishing organ. The central figure of the *Hallische Jahrbücher* was Arnold Ruge (1802–1880), who had founded it with Theodor Echtermeyer (1805–1844). Ruge, through both his editorship of the *Jahrbücher* as well as his own articles, soon become one of the most important people in oppositional journalism in Germany. In order to escape Prussian censorship, in 1841 Ruge moved the editorial board to Dresden in Saxony and renamed the publication *Deutsche Jahrbücher für Wissenschaft und Kunst.* At the beginning of 1843, the publication was also banned in Saxony. After the end of the *Jahrbücher*, Ruge attempted a continuation and founded, together with Karl Marx, the *Deutsch-Französische Jahrbücher*, of which, however, only a single double issue was published. For a few months, there was close collaboration between Ruge and Marx, which ended in the summer of 1844. The great respect that both initially had for each other soon turned into mutual contempt. During the Revolution of 1848, Ruge belonged to the left and after the defeat of the revolution had to go into exile in England, just like Marx and Engels. In the 1860s, he supported (as many other former "48ers" did) Bismarck's project of the unification of the empire. In 1868, he read Marx's *Capital* and expressed himself enthusiastically concerning this "epoch-making work" (Ruge to Steinthal, January 25, 1869, MECW 43: 542). It's worth examining this dazzling personality in greater detail.

Arnold Ruge was born on the island of Rügen, the son of an estate manager.[207] He began studying theology in 1821 at the University of Halle, but after a short time switched to philosophy. Besides Halle, he also studied in Jena and Heidelberg and was active in Burschenschaften in both cities. Ruge also joined the secret "Jünglingsbund" (youth association) which was founded at the suggestion of the radical Burschenschaftler, Karl Follen (1796–1840). Follen had participated in the founding of various radical student associations in 1814–1816, out of which the Burschenschaften had developed; he was strongly influenced by the nationalist conceptions of Jakob Friedrich Fries and called for "tyrannicide." From the Jünglingsbund, he hoped for revolutionary actions against the German states, which had become increasingly repressive after the Carlsbad Decrees. The goal was supposed to be a united, republican-democratic Germany. However, before the Jünglingsbund could

---

2). In his *History of German Newspaper Publishing*, Ludwig Salomon referred to the *Hallische Jahrbücher* as Germany's "most important periodical" at the time (Salomon 1906: 495).

207. In a letter to Karl Rosenkranz from October 2, 1839 (contained in Hundt 2010a: 407–11), Ruge provides information on his life up to that point. Also largely autobiographical are the four volumes published from 1862 to 1867, *Aus früherer Zeit* (From Earlier Times). On Ruge's life up to 1837, see also Walter (1995: 68–88) as well as Reinalter (2010).

become active in any form (it's doubtful whether it ever could have), it was denounced, and many of its members jailed. Follen had been forced to emigrate to the United States before that; Ruge was arrested at the beginning of 1824 and sentenced to fourteen years of imprisonment in a fortress. In 1827, the sentences for the convicted members of the Jünglingsbund were reduced, so that Ruge was released on January 1, 1830.

Imprisonment had in no way broken Ruge; he had confronted the strains with great force of will and enthusiasm. During his imprisonment, he had the opportunity to study ancient authors, which strongly changed his political notions. "I longed for Fries when I did not yet know Plato, and for Hegel since tasting the Platonic dialectic and the objective movement that he sets in motion," he wrote in a letter to Rosenkranz (Hundt 2010a: 410). Instead of the strongly anti-French nationalism of the Burschenschaften, he now advanced an ideal of freedom and the dignity of the citizen oriented toward models from antiquity, above all Athenian democracy (Walter 1995: 75–77).

After his release from prison, Ruge obtained his doctorate in 1830 in Jena with a dissertation on the Roman satirical poet Juvenal. At the end of 1831, he obtained his postdoctoral qualification in Halle with a work on Plato's aesthetics. In Halle, he also connected with a number of instructors of about the same age, who were more or less influenced by Hegel's philosophy, among them Karl Rosenkranz (1805–1879), Heinrich Leo (1799–1878), Hermann Friedrich Wilhelm Hinrichs (1794–1861), Karl Moritz Fleischer (1809–1876), Adolf Stahr (1805–1876), and, above all, Ernst Theodor Echtermeyer, who (according to Ruge) had the idea of founding the *Hallische Jahrbücher*.[208]

Ruge had to hold back with political statements at this time. He had submitted a request for rehabilitation to the government, so that after his imprisonment he could work as a lecturer, which was a civil service position. For that reason, his first articles in the *Blättern für literarische Unterhaltung* published by Brockhaus, in which he spoke out for freedom of the press, a constitution, and a government in the sense of the majority of people's representatives, were published anonymously (Pepperle 1978: 38).

In 1831, Ruge married Luise Düffer, a wealthy heiress, which provided him with a certain level of material independence. But his young wife died in 1833, causing Ruge to largely withdraw "in order to calmly wander out for 2 years into the newly discovered land of the new spirit," that of Hegelian

---

208. Echtermeyer dealt primarily with aesthetics and literary history. His collection of samples of German poetry published in 1836, which was divided into eras, was repeatedly republished and expanded. Up to the end of the twentieth century, it remained a standard work for German lessons in German schools (for Echtermeyer's biography, see Hundt 2012).

philosophy, which he now studied in-depth: "I first emancipated myself to philosophical freedom with the *Logic*, which I read twice," he writes in the letter to Rosenkranz (Hundt 2010a: 410).

But his appropriation of Hegel's philosophy did not cause him to join up uncritically with the Hegelian school. Ruge formulated a programmatic distance in his article "Unsere gelehrte kritische Journalistik" (Our Educated Critical Journalism), which was published on August 11 and 12, 1837, in the *Blätter für literarische Unterhaltung*. In an overview of the various "educated" journals, he asked, regarding the Old-Hegelian Society, which published the *Jahrbuch für wissenschaftliche Kritik*, whether "with Old Hegelian principles, one is still keeping up with the movement." It was a rhetorical question. The question had been answered by the fact that the Berlin *Jahrbücher* had so decisively opposed Strauß's *Life of Jesus* with Bruno Bauer's review of it, and Ruge's critical review of a book by the conservative Hegelian Johann Eduard Erdmann (1805–1892) had been rejected by the *Jahrbücher*.[209] But Ruge wasn't the only one who doubted the *Jahrbücher*. Eduard Gans, a co-founder and still a member of the editorial board, had written a year before: "The *Jahrbücher für wissenschaftliche Kritik* have however not remained what they were initially supposed to be, but rather have completely changed their character. Instead of standing above scholarship as an organ of discussion and cohesion, they simply follow it, like every other literary newspaper" (Gans 1836: 253).

In the essay quoted, Ruge concludes from his critique that "a further perfection of educated journalism would be that of addressing the spiritual life of the present in such a way that its history would be spiritually reborn, whereby the essential standpoint that the Berlin *Jahrbücher* has achieved through the principle of spirit should not be lost, but rather set into the correct movement, and not by old, stale authorities" (Ruge 1837: 910). A younger generation was to overcome the tendencies toward ossification of the Hegelian school, without dispensing with its achievements.

That was not a vague wish for a distant future. The preparations for a new publication, which was supposed to fulfill exactly that which Ruge demanded in his article, had long since begun.[210] On August 10, 1837, a day before the

---

209. See Graf (1978: 391ff.). That the emergence of the *Hallische Jahrbücher* was due primarily to Ruge's rejection by the *Jahrbücher für wissenschaftliche Kritik* and the shattering of his hopes for a university career, as Graf suggests, seems somewhat simplified. But even if that was the case, the success of the *Hallische Jahrbücher* is a clear indication that there was a demand for such a journal among critical intellectuals.

210. The emergence of the *Hallische Jahrbücher* is dealt with extensively in Pepperle (1978: 32ff.), Walter (1995: 101ff.), and Senk (2007: 47ff.). An overview of working methods, the

first part of his article was published, Ruge announced in a letter to Adolf Stahr that he would soon send him "a lithographic request to found a new literary newspaper." And, considerably more boisterous than in the *Blättern*, Ruge wrote: "A heroic society has come together and we don't want to wait for the old ones, i.e. allow them to die naturally; rather, they have to be killed while still alive, exterminated in a literary way" (Hundt 2010a: 3).

In the autumn of 1837, Ruge traveled through Germany in order to win supporters for the new project. It was the period when the Göttingen Seven protested against the annulment of the constitution in the kingdom of Hanover and were then dismissed by King Ernst August. The wave of outrage that followed also helped the new publication. One hundred and fifty-nine more or less well-known academics pledged their collaboration, though far from all of them actually provided contributions (Senk 2007: 52). David Friedrich Strauß was also won over, who now had at his disposal an important journal for defending his theological views (see Graf 1978: 460ff.). On January 1, 1838, the first issue was published by the liberal Leipzig publisher Otto Wigand (1795–1870), to whom Marx had once written concerning his planned journal of theater criticism. The new publication was edited by Arnold Ruge and Theodor Echtermeyer.

The term *Jahrbücher* today usually has associations of an annually published periodical. The *Hallische Jahrbücher*, in contrast, was a sheet published on six workdays each week. The word "sheet" is to be taken literally. Each edition consisted of a large sheet folded twice so that each number consisted of four printed pages. The content primarily consisted of book reviews, as was usual for "educated" papers of the time. However, characterizations of contemporary poets and scholars as well as discussions of the faculties of individual universities were also found in the *Hallische Jahrbücher*, something completely new in the publication landscape (Hundt 2010b: 31). Individual articles often spanned two, three, sometimes even four or more issues, whereby each issue contained not just one, but two or three articles, which were then continued the next day. The reviews often presented the contents of the books being reviewed far more extensively than is usual today, before praising or criticizing them. Frequently, debates were conducted in the form of such reviews and the responses to them.

---

correspondents, and the influence of the *Jahrbücher* is provided by Hundt (2010b) on the basis of the "editorial correspondence" he has published (Hundt 2010a).

The Dispute between Leo and Ruge

As noted in chapter 1, the arrest of the Cologne archbishop, Clemens August Droste zu Vischering (1773–1845), in November of 1837 caused a considerable stir and generated a plethora of polemics. Whereas according to Prussian law, the children of mixed-religion marriages were to acquire the religion of the father, Droste zu Vischering wanted to make marriages between Catholic women and Protestant men dependent upon the Catholic bride guaranteeing in writing that the children would be raised Catholic. This would thus abolish the principle of equal treatment of both Christian denominations: in all Protestant-Catholic marriages, the children would be raised Catholic. In the Catholic Rhineland, to which Prussia had sent many Protestant administrative civil servants and members of the military, who then frequently married Catholic women, such a rule would have as its consequence that many children of these pillars of the Prussian (Protestant) state would be Catholics.

Joseph Görres (1776–1848), a Catholic writer who had taught at the University of Munich since 1827, published *Athanasius*, a polemic fiercely critical of Prussia, in January of 1838. The title was supposed to draw a parallel between Vischering and Athanasius (ca. 300–372), the patriarch of Alexandria, who was embroiled in fierce conflicts with the Roman rulers. *Athanasius* quickly became the most influential piece of anti-Prussian writing, which went through four editions in 1838 alone.

A number of authors responded to Görres; numerous contributions were also published in the *Hallische Jahrbücher*, all of which took the side of Prussia and interpreted the conflict as a necessary defense against the arrogance of a reactionary Catholicism. The historian Heinrich Leo (1799–1878) also composed a response, his *Letter to Görres (Sendschreiben an Görres)*. Leo, a professor in Halle since 1830, had studied philosophy in the 1820s under Hegel and belonged to his broader circle of friends. In Halle, he had contact with Arnold Ruge, who initially wanted to win him over to collaborating on the *Jahrbücher*, for which he provided reviews. However, in the middle of the 1830s, Leo had moved in a strongly conservative and pietist-orthodox direction. Leo defended the Prussian government, but in his critique of Görres, he also criticized (Protestant) rationalism in that it had "fallen" from the Reformation, "like Judas from the Lord" (Leo 1838a: 124). In certain respects, Leo regarded the Catholic Church as a model. Protestantism "lacks," Leo wrote to the Catholic Görres, "what you have, the discipline and strict order of the Church" (ibid.: 54). And finally, Leo polemicized against a "liberal revolutionary" party in Prussia that supposedly made "worn-out commonplaces" into the basis of "superficial doctrines" (ibid.: 128).

In an extensive review of the *Letter* in the *Hallische Jahrbücher*, Ruge settled accounts with Leo. Against his attempt to introduce Catholic discipline and strictness into Protestantism, Ruge emphasized that the "reality of divine grace . . . the exclusivity of Christianity was entrusted not to the priests, nor the saints, nor the pietists, but rather to spirit in its free development"(Ruge 1838b: 1186). On this basis, Ruge accused Leo of a "completely unfree and corrupted conception of the Reformation" (ibid.: 1190). Completely in the tradition of Hegel, Ruge saw in the reformation a breakthrough in freedom of the spirit. From this perspective, then, both Leo and Görres were men of reaction, rising up "1) against the justification of reason, therefore crying out against Enlightenment and rationalism, 2) they rise up against the German Reformation, both in its principles and its formation, contemporary religious-political life in Prussia . . . , 3) they rise up against the justification of recent history, i.e. against the French Revolution and the state formations arising from it, namely the systems of centralization, civil service, and administration, and shout about liberalism and revolution" (ibid.: 1183). Ruge saw the Enlightenment, Protestantism, and the French Revolution as a triad holding up the modern state, a triad to be defended against "reaction."

How much Ruge's critique of Leo was appreciated by progressive intellectuals is indicated by a letter from Gans to Ruge from July 15, 1838. Gans wrote that he had long wanted to express his "deepest and most sincere thanks" to Ruge for the manner "in which you have poked the wasp's nest. We've known Leo here for years; he's a Hallerian [follower of the conservative jurist Karl Ludwig von Haller], and could just as well be anything else according to his convictions, since he has none" (Hundt 2010a: 176).[211]

It did not take long for Leo to reply to Ruge. In the preface to the second edition of his *Letter*, he turned against Ruge and his "Young Hegelian philosophy" with a harsh tone: he protested "against everything that Dr. Ruge and his consorts call science; for those who whore after it deny the God of Abraham and his incarnate son, replacing them with a 'free spirit' which is a bubble in which the prince of the abyss finds himself in" (Leo 1838a: VI). Leo emphasized that he did not wish to dispute Hegel's Christianity, but rather that of the "Young Hegelian gang" (ibid.: xiii). On the soil cultivated by Hegel, this had grown as a "desolate weed" (ibid.: xv). Leo's position was supported by an article in the Berlin *Politisches Wochenblatt*, an extremely conservative

---

211. Gans, who died in May 1839, could not make any contributions for the *Hallische Jahrbücher*. However, he provided an important impetus for the political critique of the Young Hegelians (see Magdanz 2002; Waszek 2015).

periodical founded in 1831, as its prospectus states, "to oppose revolution in all of its shapes" (quoted in Salomon 1906: 476). The liberal ideas streaming into the country from France after the July Revolution were to be quelled. This paper, which had a certain influence upon the crown prince, warned with an anonymous article that the Young Hegelians were striving for a revolution, and that the government should therefore keep an eye on them, a barely veiled demand to ban the *Hallische Jahrbücher*.

Ruge responded in his essay, "Die Denunciation der Hallischen Jahrbücher." He accused Leo of "being a dilettante in the matter of denunciation," since he was not able to explain "how the harmful Hegelians deviate from the harmless ones" (Ruge 1838c: 1430). Against the accusation of the *Politisches Wochenblatt*, Ruge defended himself and the *Hallische Jahrbücher* with two arguments. For one thing, the task of science, and hence of the *Jahrbücher*, consisted in "recognizing spirit, thus religion and the state as well, as it is and has become, not how it will or should be" (ibid.: 1433). For another thing, a revolution is "not made" by an individual; rather, "when it occurs, this violence of development is historically necessary. But if development is not stopped or obstructed, on the contrary, if the state has the principle of reform, as in Prussia, then there is no necessity, indeed not even a possibility, of revolution" (ibid.: 1437).

The high estimation of Prussia was not just tactically motivated. Ruge and his companions regarded the Prussian state as a state of Enlightenment and reform, even if this wasn't the line of the current government. One simply had to remind Prussia of its own characteristics to summon a change in political direction; at the time, this was the widespread belief on the part of critical intellectuals. This was also confirmed by Ruge in retrospect when he wrote "that neither theological philosophy [the Hegelian philosophy of religion] nor the conception of Prussia as the Protestant, that is to say, for us, philosophical state, was hypocrisy and pure pretense; rather, we were truly enraptured by Hegel and the scientific freedom of men such as Altenstein, and had to first have our own school and experiences. But that went rather quickly" (Ruge 1867: 484).

Leo also continued the dispute. In his brochure "Die Hegelingen," he presented a collection of text excerpts that were supposed to prove that the "Young Hegelian party" disputed the existence of a personal God and his incarnation in Christ, instead preaching atheism, and that it denied the immortality of the soul, thus promoting a religion exclusively of this world. All of this was supposedly clothed in Christianity, thereby deceiving people (Leo 1838b: 4ff.). Leo received support from an anonymous article in Hengstenberg's *Evangelische Kirchenzeitung*, in which a good, right side of the Hegelian school was distinguished from a dangerous, revolutionary side, that of the Young Hegelians (see Bunzel et al. 2006: 18). The latter were thus, as in the article from the *Politisches Wochenblatt*, branded as subversive.

The Expansion of the Combat Zone: Ludwig Feuerbach's
First Critiques of Hegel, the Manifesto Against Romanticism, and the First
Open Critique of Prussia

The dispute between Ruge and Leo led to a number of further publications by various authors.[212] Thus, Eduard Meyen published a brochure, "Heinrich Leo, der verhallerte Pietist,"[213] a reference to the conservative legal scholar Karl Ludwig von Haller (1768–1854), who had converted to Catholicism. As a result of the debate, direct attacks by conservatives on Hegel's *Philosophy of Right* also multiplied. Schubarth's critique of Hegel (Schubarth 1839) and the response of the friend of the young Marx, Karl Friedrich Köppen (1839), were already mentioned in the first part of this chapter.

Ludwig Feuerbach also participated in the debate in 1839. As noted above, after the publication of *Thoughts on Death and Immortality*, Feuerbach no longer had a chance of obtaining a professorship at a German university. However, his beloved, Bertha Löw (1803–1883), whom he married in 1837, was the co-owner of a small porcelain factory in the village of Bruckberg in Bavaria, so that she was able to secure the family a modest livelihood and Feuerbach an existence as an independent scholar. Alongside works in the history of philosophy, Feuerbach had dealt in two comprehensive and extremely critical reviews with Friedrich Julius Stahl's *Philosophy of Right*, as well as with the Kantian critic of Hegel, Carl Friedrich Bachmann (1785–1855). The review of Stahl showed that Feuerbach was not the unpolitical thinker that he is even today sometimes regarded as (see Breckmann 1999: 109ff.). In December of 1838, Feuerbach had published a rather polemical article in the *Hallische Jahrbücher*, "On The Critique of Positive Philosophy" (Feuerbach 1838), in which he fiercely criticized the "positive" philosophy, often drifting into the religious, around the *Zeitschrift für Philosophie und spekulative Theologie* founded by Immanuel Fichte in 1837, and in particular its notion of a personal God. Now, he offered Ruge the article "The True Viewpoint from Which the Leo-Hegelian Dispute Must Be Evaluated."[214] Ruge was

---

212. Pepperle (1978: 238n79) lists the most important of these contributions.
213. The German verb *verhallen* means "to fade away" or "to die away." The play on words consists in combining this with von Haller's name. —Trans.
214. Due to this title, reference is frequently made to the "Leo-Hegelian" dispute, but initially

enthusiastic about the text and made sure it was published quickly. After both parts were, on March 11 and 12, 1839, further publication was stopped by the censors. It was the first time that an article of the *Hallische Jahrbücher* did not receive permission to publish. A few months later, Feuerbach published the entire article in Baden as an independent brochure under the title "On Philosophy and Christianity in Relation to the Accusation Made Against Hegelian Philosophy of Being Non-Christian" (Feuerbach 1839a).

As the biographer of Feuerbach, Josef Winiger (2011: 127), emphasizes, Feuerbach argued in a far more radical way than Ruge had done previously. For Feuerbach the "true viewpoint" for evaluating the conflict was no longer the antagonism between Protestantism and Catholicism, but rather between science and religion. The accusation that Hegelian philosophy was un-Christian Feuerbach rejected as not only false but nonsensical. There could be no Christian philosophy, anymore than there could be a Christian mathematics or Christian mineralogy. Science and religion were not comparable, since science had thought as its foundation, whereas religion had feeling and fantasy as its basis (Feuerbach 1839a: 232). In the preface written for the brochure, this point was sharpened into a fundamental critique of the Hegelian philosophy of religion. According to Feuerbach, if it is asserted that philosophy and religion have the same content and only differ in form, then "the inessential is made essential, and the essential is made inessential. It is precisely fantasy and feeling that constitute the *essence* of religion—not the content as such" (ibid.: 220). In the next paragraph, Feuerbach categorically maintains: "Fantasy is the *subjective* intellectual activity that depicts things as they correspond to feeling; reason is the *objective* intellectual activity that depicts things as they are, without regard for the needs of feeling" (ibid.: 221). The sublation of religion in philosophy for which Hegel strove was thus obsolete. Religion could only be the object of critique for philosophy, a program that Feuerbach then carried out in his *Essence of Christianity* (1841).

In 1839, not only Hegel's philosophy of religion, but also the Hegelian system as a whole was subjected by Feuerbach to a fundamental critique. In a total of nine issues of the *Hallische Jahrbücher*, "Toward a Critique of Hegel's Philosophy" was published between August 20 and September 9, 1839 (Feuerbach 1839b, in *Stepelevich* 1983). Initially, Feuerbach attacked notions that he did not ascribe directly to Hegel, but to Hegel's students, namely that Hegel's philosophy was an absolute philosophy, a philosophy in which the

---

it was a dispute between Leo and Ruge. However, it was not a mere personal conflict; in the background stood the question as to what direction Prussia's future development should take, and that's exactly why this dispute made such waves.

idea of philosophy would be realized absolutely. Feuerbach countered this: "Is it at all possible that a species realizes itself in one individual, art as such in one artist, and philosophy as such in one philosopher?" (*Stepelevich* 1983: 97). Hegel's philosophy was, like any other philosophy, bound to the conditions of its time; it was not without presupposition (ibid.: 99). But Feuerbach not only criticized the fiction of the beginning of Hegel's system being without presuppositions; he also emphasized that the system itself could only be the presentation for another, who is to be convinced through the medium of language. Yet Hegel abstracts from this dialogic character of philosophy (ibid.: 103). And finally, Hegel's philosophy is also subject to a reproach that must be made of all of modern philosophy since Descartes and Spinoza, namely that of "an unmediated break with sensuous perceptions" (ibid.: 113). Feuerbach thus indicates a few points of his later critique of Hegel that were so extraordinarily important for Marx in 1843. In 1839, however, his essay remained largely ignored. The Young Hegelians had not yet come so far that they could deal with such a fundamental critique of Hegel.

Also rather ignored was the book *Prolegomena to a Historiosophy*, published in 1838 by the Polish Count August von Cieszkowski (1814–1894). A review was published in the *Hallische Jahrbücher* (Frauenstädt 1839), but this confined itself largely to Cieszkowski's critique of Hegel's teachings on the ages of the world as developed in his *Lectures on the Philosophy of History*. Cieszkowski replaced Hegel's Oriental, Greek, Roman, and Christian-Germanic ages with Antiquity, the Christian-Germanic age as its antithesis, and the future as synthesis, the discernment of which was his primary concern. He considered the fact that Hegel did not deal with the future in his philosophy of history, as its greatest shortcoming. Cieszkowski was not concerned with the prediction of individual events, but rather with insight into "the essence of progress as such" (Cieszkowski 1838: 11). That recognizing the future would require philosophical reflection of the act, since the act produces the future, did not yet play any role in the early reception, contrary to what Cornu (1954: 130ff.) suggests. It was in the 1840s that these considerations first appear to have had an influence on the Young Hegelians, albeit in a more subterranean manner than through direct reference (on the early reception, see Senk 2007: 132ff.). Stuke (1963: 255) claims that Marx's analysis in the early 1840s was "dependent" upon Cieszkowski. However, Marx does not appear to have read Cieszkowski in 1838 or later; in a letter to Engels from January 12, 1881, he remarks: ". . . the said count etc. [Cieszkowski] did in fact once call on me in Paris (at the time of the *Deutsch-Französische Jahrbücher*), and such was the impression he made on me that I neither wanted nor would have been able to read anything whatever of his contriving" (MECW 46: 177). The context of this letter concerned the later economic writings of Cieskowski; if Marx had known of his "Historiosophy," he certainly would not have denied himself a comment upon it.

Ruge and Echtermeyer undertook an expansion of the combat zone in another respect. Between October 1839 and March 1840, the article "Protestantism and Romanticism: Toward an Understanding of the Period and Its Antagonisms, A Manifesto." ("Der Protestantismus und die Romantik: Zur Verständigung über die Zeit und ihre Gegensätze") was published. Contemporary conflicts were interpreted as "obstruction on the part of depressed spirits made anxious by dark emotions against the recently initiated last phase of the Reformation, *the free formation of our spiritual reality*" (Ruge/Echtermeyer 1839–40: 1953). The darkness and depression of these spirits arose from their being rooted in Romanticism. Ruge and Echtermeyer gave a pointed outline of the intellectual and cultural development of Germany, contrasting Romanticism as Catholic and hostile to the Enlightenment with Protestantism. The latter, at least where it was free of Catholic and reactionary elements, stood for reason, freedom of thought, and Enlightenment. This "principle of the Reformation" could be rediscovered "in its highest theoretical presentation and formation in the newest philosophy" (obviously meaning Hegel's) (ibid.: 1961). With the juxtaposition of Reformation, Enlightenment, and Hegel's philosophy on one side and Catholicism, Romanticism, and conservative thought on the other, Ruge and Echtermeyer took up central arguments from both Heinrich Heine's critique of Romanticism (Heine 1836) as well as his *On the History of Religion and Philosophy in Germany* (Heine 2007).[215] However, they did not mention

---

215. In his text on Feuerbach, Engels impressively pointed out the insight into the revolutionary character of Hegel's philosophy that Heinrich Heine had achieved in his *On the History of Religion and Philosophy in Germany*, written in 1833: "Just as in France in the eighteenth century, so in Germany in the nineteenth, a philosophical revolution ushered in the political collapse. But how different the two looked! The French were in open combat against all official science, against the Church and often also against the State; their writings were printed across the frontier, in Holland or England, while they themselves were often in jeopardy of imprisonment in the Bastille. On the other hand, the Germans were professors, State-appointed instructors of youth; their writings were recognised textbooks, and the system that rounded off the whole development—the Hegelian system—was even raised, as it were, to the rank of a royal Prussian philosophy of State! Was it possible that a revolution could hide behind these professors, behind their obscure, pedantic phrases, their ponderous, wearisome periods? Were not precisely those people who were then regarded as the representatives of the revolution, the liberals, the bitterest opponents of this befuddling philosophy? But what neither governments nor liberals saw was seen at least by one man as early as 1833, and this man was none other than Heinrich Heine" (MECW 26: 357).

RELIGION, HEGELIANISM, AND MARX'S DISSERTATION   263

Heine. At this time, Ruge behaved rather negatively toward Heine; he regarded him as unserious and "frivolous."[216] It was a few years later, in exile in Paris, that he learned to value Heine (see Ruge 1846: Bd.1: 143; on the relationship of the Young Hegelians to Heine, Windfuhr 1981: 561ff.).[217] In contrast to Heine, Ruge and Echtermeyer expanded the concept of Romanticism: counting its predecessors, it was supposed to stretch from 1770 to the present of 1840. Young Germany and "Neo-Schellingianism" were understood as the most recent manifestations of Romanticism (Ruge/Echtermeyer 1839/40: 511), and the Old Hegelians as well, who were accused of behaving "theoretically harmlessly" and showed themselves to be "Hegelians with the Romantic plait" (ibid.: 512). Here it becomes clear that the critique by Ruge and Echtermeyer was aimed primarily at the present. This was also referred to in the indications of philosophy becoming practicals, sprinkled into the last part of the text, published in 1840, stating with regard to a new praxis, "This praxis is a new system, the absolute lust for action of the liberated spirit; the reformatory enthusiasm which seizes our fellow world everywhere, is not content with Hegelian contemplation" (ibid.: 417).

The aesthetic critique of Romanticism by Ruge and Echtermeyer was schematic and undifferentiated in many points, a fact that did not remain

---

216. Lambrecht (2002: 117) suspects that Ruge's hostility to Jews was the reason for his hostility to Heine. In Ruge's correspondence, there are numerous remarks hostile to Jews, mainly directed at people with whom he had fallen out. However, he had dedicated a volume of his collected works to the Jewish physician Johann Jacoby, the author of the *Four Questions*, and during the Revolution of 1848, in the periodical *Reform*, he criticized anti-Semitic tendencies in the parliament in session at the Paulskirche (see Walter 1995: 202–5).

217. At the beginning of the 1850s, in their unpublished work "The Great Men of the Exile," Marx and Engels expressed themselves disparagingly toward Ruge. Concerning the *Hallische Jahrbücher*, they wrote that Ruge's "ambition was to print the works of others and in so doing, to derive material advantage and also to quarry literary sustenance for the effusions of his own brain." Ruge's critique of Romanticism is also understood in this way. They continue that Ruge "fought valiantly against Romanticism because it had long since been demolished philosophically by Hegel in his *Aesthetik* and by Heine from the point of view of literature in *Die romantische Schule*" (MECW 11: 265). These remarks not only fail to do justice to the *Hallische Jahrbücher*; they also completely omit the political context of Ruge's critique of Romanticism. Marx and Engels's statements must be seen in the context of the fiercely conducted disputes in emigrant circles, in which Ruge had made some absurd accusations against Marx and Engels. As the quotations at the beginning of this chapter demonstrate, however, in calmer moments Marx and Engels arrived at considerably more balanced assessments. Ruge is not explicitly named in these quotes, but he was the central figure of the philosophical critique that Marx and Engels praise so highly.

hidden from their comrades-in-arms.[218] Nonetheless, it did not miss its aim of placing the resistance against conservative-reactionary tendencies on a broader historical foundation. Ruge and Echtermeyer in the "Manifesto" did not reach the level of radicalism that Feuerbach demonstrated in the contributions discussed above, but they promoted their critique with a far greater vehemence and level of detail than Feuerbach, so that their public influence was correspondingly greater.

The "Manifesto" exhibits a consistently positive reference to Prussia. But before its complete publication, the article "Karl Streckfuß and Prussianism" was published in the *Hallische Jahrbücher* in November of 1839, openly attacking Prussia for the first time, correspondingly causing a stir. Regarding the author, it merely stated "by a Württemberger," and many contemporaries suspected Strauß as the writer. But in fact, the article was written by Arnold Ruge (see Ruge 1867: 488).

The Prussian senior government council named in the title, Karl Streckfuß, had attempted to prove in his book that Prussia did not need the constitution that had been demanded for a long time. The book by Streckfuß is of no further importance; it merely served as occasion for Ruge to formulate his critique of Prussia, which had become far more fundamental in the meantime. It had become clear that the old image of Prussia as a free and Enlightenment-minded state could no longer be maintained. In his dispute with Leo, the Prussian state had positioned itself on the side of his opponents: Ruge, as a lecturer at the University of Halle, was even forbidden from attacking professors personally, which caused him to leave the university (ibid.: 487). In the Hannover constitutional conflict, Prussia had taken the side of the King of Hannover, who had abolished the constitution, thus igniting the protest of the Göttingen Seven celebrated throughout Germany. Censorship had also been intensified; there wasn't much left of the "free spirit."

Ruge's article on Streckfuß bears witness to a fundamental change in perspective. What was previously seen as a temporary deviation from the proper path was now considered Prussia's new path: with the Carlsbad Decrees, with press censorship and the revised city ordinance of 1831 (which in important questions subordinated the cities to the government), Prussia had

---

218. See, for example, the letter from Eduard Meyen to Arnold Ruge from May 20, 1840: "Honestly, you're taking your polemic against Romanticism too far, because you're becoming fanatical. Fight Romanticism and its wrong direction as much as you want, but don't kill Romanticism for us, the world of feelings" (Hundt 2010a: 549). Bunzel (2003) deals in a differentiated manner with Ruge and Echtermeyer's critique of Romanticism.

abandoned the enlightened Protestant "principle of the free spirit that cannot be patronized" (Ruge 1839: 2097). Provocatively for a state that understood itself to be Protestant, Ruge formulated, *"Prussia as a state is still Catholic*, absolute monarchy is politically completely the same as what Catholicism is religiously" (ibid.: 2100). In contrast, the "Württemberger" argued: "We non-Prussian Germans are even Protestant even in the state; we don't believe in anything in which we do not have the most vibrant share of spirit. . . . That's why we cannot tolerate the absolute state, for we cannot stand that the state deprives us of the absolute . . . We must have a share in it theoretically with full public self-confidence, and practically with the freest representation, for the spirit which is in possession of the absolute (and hence also of the absolute state) is Protestantism" (ibid.: 2100).

It was obvious that the "freest representation" of the citizens in the state derived from Protestantism could claim validity not just for "non-Prussian Germans," but also for Prussian Germans. In other words, Ruge demanded not only freedom of the press, but also democratic state relations, if initially only by appealing to Protestantism.[219]

With Ruge's Streckfuß article, a new stage of the critique of Prussia was reached at the end of 1839. In the *Hallische Jahrbücher* of the years 1840 and 1841, further arguments were made on this basis (for a more detailed analysis, see Senk 2007: 164ff.). A last, great attempt to remind Prussia of its enlightened past was the book by Karl Friedrich Köppen on Friedrich II, already mentioned at the beginning of the chapter, which was enthusiastically celebrated in the *Hallische Jahrbücher.*

Ruge formulated his critique in an increasingly direct manner, albeit frequently in the form of reviews, disguised as accounts of other authors. Thus he took up the topic of democracy in a discussion of the works of the scholar and poet Wilhelm Heinse (1746–1803). With his epistolary novel *Ardinghello* published in 1786/87, Heinse had made the Italian Renaissance popular in Germany. As a consequence of Heinse's conception of the state, wrote Ruge, a *"state of human beings who are worthy of the name,* perfect for all and everyone, must basically always be a democracy"; and he added that philosophy had since achieved much, since the presentation of the state as "constitutional self-government" was its work (Ruge 1840a: 1691).

At the end of 1840, Ruge arrived at a critique of Hegel that wasn't as radical

---

219. The affirmative reference to Protestantism was explicitly abandoned by Ruge in 1842, when in two articles he criticized both the "Manifesto" against Romanticism and the Streckfuß article in this regard (Ruge 1842a, 1842b). Ruge thus retraced what Feuerbach and Bauer had achieved between 1840 and 1841 on the terrain of the critique of religion.

as that formulated by Feuerbach in 1839, but had clear philosophical consequences. Ruge accused Hegel's *Philosophy of Right* of "accommodation
and inconsistency." Because Hegel recognized obsolete political institutions as necessary, he constructed the state "according to the pattern of past
existences," instead of "criticizing the contemporary ones and then allow-
ing the demands and formation of its near future or, if you will, its present
and reality spring from this critique" (Ruge 1840c: 2131). Ruge thus accused
Hegel of confusing the historical existence of the state with its rational reality. However, that was not the same accusation made by liberals when they
charged Hegel with having justified the Prussian restoration. The historical
existence that Hegel had mixed up with reality, according to Ruge, were "the
institutions of Old England" (ibid.: 2331). Regardless of this criticism, however, Ruge conceded to Hegel that "even the immense accommodation of
his natural law was still permeated with the correct and driving principle of
development" (ibid.: 2332). A few months later, Marx would criticize this
accommodation thesis in his doctoral dissertation as inadequate.

Not only did the *Hallische Jahrbücher* become increasingly radical; they
also encountered great resonance on the part of the educated strata. A somewhat bizarre example of this is shared by Martin Hundt (2000: 15): after the
first volume of the four-volume *History of France in the Age of Revolution*
(*Geschichte Frankreichs im Revolutionszeitalter*) had been published, its
author, Wilhelm Wachsmuth (1784–1866), who at the same time was also
censor of the *Hallische Jahrbücher*, sent a copy to Arnold Ruge and wrote in
the accompanying letter that it meant a lot to him to give Ruge "proof of my
sincere esteem and, wherever possible, to make amends for that which I have
had to do directly against your wishes and mine" (Hundt 2010a: 616). In the
summer of 1843, Marx was to make excerpts of the first two volumes of this
thorough work (MEGA IV/2: 163–74).

Since the death of Minister of Culture Altenstein in 1840, the *Hallische
Jahrbücher* no longer had any advocates in the higher ranks of the Prussian
state. It was only a matter of time before they would clash with the conservative Friedrich Wilhelm IV, with his orientation to Christian-Romantic
notions, who had also ascended to the throne in 1840. At the direct instigation of the king, in March 1841 the Prussian government demanded that
the printing of the *Hallische Jahrbücher* be moved from Leipzig in Saxony
to Halle in Prussia, in order to place it under Prussian censorship (Mayer
1913: 23). At that, Ruge moved to Dresden in Saxony, continued to print in
Leipzig, and on July 2,1841, changed the title of the publication to *Deutsche
Jahrbücher für Wissenschaft und Kunst*.

RELIGION, HEGELIANISM, AND MARX'S DISSERTATION 267

*Interim Consideration: Is the Juxtaposition of Old Hegelianism and Young
Hegelianism Merely a Construct in the History of Philosophy?*

In the preceding sections, we discussed how after the publication of Strauß's
Life of Jesus, a Young Hegelian current formed, primarily around the *Hallische
Jahrbücher*. We have followed these debates up to 1840–41, the period in which
Marx was preparing his dissertation. They constitute an important element of
the intellectual and political background against which Marx moved. Before
assigning the young Marx, as is usual, to the "Young Hegelians," we will consider in what sense we can speak of Young Hegelianism and Old Hegelianism.

The description became prominent during the dispute between Ruge
and Leo. In 1837, Ruge had spoken of the "Old Hegelian principle" of the
Berlin *Jahrbücher für wissenschaftliche Kritik* as being no longer adequate to
the demands of the time, without characterizing this principle more exactly
(Ruge 1837: 910); from 1838 on, Leo used "Young Hegelian" as a derogatory
term of attack. After initial resistance—Eduard Meyen (1839: 35) wrote in
his critique of Leo that "the difference between Young and Old Hegelianism"
was "nonsense"; he had dedicated his book "to all students of Hegel"—talk
of Young Hegelians prevailed as the self-description of a group of primarily
young authors. Thus, in the article from December 1840 quoted above, Ruge
wrote of the Young Hegelians (Ruge 1840c: 2330, 2331, 2342) and the Young
Hegelian philosophy (ibid.: 2340). In January of 1841, this designation was
used by the young Friedrich Engels as a matter of course (MECW 2: 144). In
contrast, there does not seem to be a usage of "Old Hegelianism" with similarly positive connotations.

In almost all the recent literature dealing with Young Hegelianism or
the young Marx, it is assumed that in the course of the 1830s, a split of
the Hegelian school into right and left wings occurred (whereby the terms
"right" and "left" are used in the general political sense, and not in the religious-philosophical meaning chosen by Strauß). As a rule, as already mentioned, the "Right Hegelians" are equated to the "Old Hegelians" and the
"Left Hegelians" to the "Young Hegelians," the first being conservative, the
latter progressive to revolutionary.

In the nineteenth century, the Young Hegelians, if one dealt with them
at all, were regarded as philosophically rather insignificant, such as in the
History of Philosophy by Johann Eduard Erdmann (1896), who was a conservative Hegelian. However, when there was a reawakening of interest in
Hegel at the beginning of the twentieth century, and Marx's early writings
began to be published in the 1920s, interest in Young Hegelianism increased.
In 1930, Willy Moog produced the most differentiated presentation of the

development of the Hegelian school up to that point, and in 1941, Karl Löwith published his study *From Hegel to Nietzsche*, which became quite influential with its rather pointed juxtaposition of Old and Young Hegelians. Marx's relationship to the Young Hegelians was first examined more comprehensively by Cornu (1934) and Hook (1936).

For a long time, and especially from the Marxist side, Young Hegelianism was perceived merely as a predecessor and source of keywords for Marx and Engels. Not infrequently, it was considered, right from the start, from the perspective of the critique formulated by Marx and Engels in 1844 in *The Holy Family* and 1845–46 in *The German Ideology*. The extent to which the critique formulated there, primarily of Bruno Bauer and Max Stirner, was accurate with regard to "Young Hegelianism as such," and the extent to which this critique was dependent upon the temporal and conflict relations of its emergence, was not even raised as a question in many contributions.

Starting in the 1960s, the discussion intensified, and original texts were increasingly published.[220] However, the discussion of Young Hegelianism concentrated primarily on a few well-known figures such as Bruno Bauer, Ludwig Feuerbach, or Max Stirner; Old Hegelianism was hardly a topic. In the 1990s a broader discussion of Young Hegelianism began, which was no longer limited to the famous names, and which no longer considered Young Hegelianism from the perspective of its relationship to the development of Marx and Engels.[221] Detailed knowledge increased enormously, not just concerning individual protagonists but the network of discourse in which they acted; however, what constituted the substance of Young Hegelianism (or Left Hegelianism), and who belonged to it, was not clarified.

The demarcation of personnel between "Young" and "Old" Hegelianism

---

220. Already in 1962, the text collections *Die Hegelsche Linke*, edited by Karl Löwith, and *Die Hegelsche Rechte*, edited by Hermann Lübbe, were published. In 1968, with *Feldzüge der reinen Kritik* (Campaigns of Pure Critique), Hans Martin Sass edited a collection of essays by Bruno Bauer. In 1971, a reprint of the *Hallische* and *Deutsche Jahrbücher* was published with a long introduction by Ingrid Pepperle, and in 1985, Heinz and Ingrid Pepperle published the nearly 1,000-page, large-scale collection *Die Hegelsche Linke: Dokumente zu Philosophie und Politik im deutschen Vormärz*.

221. For the German-speaking world, the series *Forschungen zum Junghegelianismus* published by Lars Lambrecht and Konrad Feilchenfeldt since 1996, with 22 volumes published so far, is particularly worth mentioning. Already before that, in a brief outline, Goldschmidt had critically illuminated the view of Bruno Bauer in research on Marx (Goldschmidt 1987). Outside of Germany, the discussion has also intensified; see for example Breckmann (1999), Moggach (2003, 2006), Tomba (2005), Leopold (2007). Lauermann (2011) has presented a research report on the Bauer literature.

has been contested ever since the first text collections were published in the early 1960s. Löwith had incorporated the Danish theologian and philosopher Sören Kierkegaard (1813–1855) into the Hegelian left, for which there is really no good reason. In the Hegelian right, Lübbe had presented Michelet and Gans, two authors who tended more to the left. His judgment that the Hegelian right was not as conservative as is always claimed, but rather had a politically liberal orientation (Lübbe 1962: 8, 10), was not just supported by these two rather left representatives, but also by the fact that Lübbe did not consider the two most conservative Hegelians of the 1830s—Göschel and Gabler.

Just as one could not agree over the last fifty years on a clear demarcation of personnel, it was also not possible to reach a consensus about the substantive characteristics or even the duration of influence of Old and Young Hegelianism.[222] Many Marxist contributions were oriented toward the assessment provided by Friedrich Engels in *Ludwig Feuerbach and the End of Classical German Philosophy*. Engels distinguished in Hegel's case between the *dialectical method*, which proceeds from an uninterrupted process of becoming, that "dissolves all conceptions of final, absolute truth and of absolute states of humanity corresponding to it," thus having a revolutionary character, from Hegel's *system*, which "in accordance with traditional requirements . . . must conclude with some sort of absolute truth" (MECW 26: 360), and was therefore conservative, necessarily suffocating the revolutionary side. The right-left split of the school was explained by Engels by reference to precisely this difference between system and method: "Whoever placed the emphasis on the Hegelian system could be fairly conservative in both spheres [religion and politics]; whoever regarded the dialectical method as the main thing could belong to the most extreme opposition, both in religion and politics" (MECW 26: 363).

This interpretation was probably confirmed by the statements of, for example, Ruge, who emphasized the importance of Hegel's method. On the occasion of the discussion of a book on Hegel's philosophy, Ruge writes: "The method cannot be avoided, that it, once recognized, leaves no way out, neither beside it nor beyond; which is to say, the acquisition of development

---

222. Moser (2003: 50ff.) exhaustively lists the contradictory judgments in the literature and the various discrepancies of the thesis of a split. But then he arrives, himself, at a barely modified division, which he distinguishes between "moderates" and "radicals" within both the right and the left, whereby he understands the radicals to be "schismatics": the left "schismatics" discarding Hegel as reactionary, the right "schismatics" discarding him as revolutionary (ibid.: 67ff.).

itself cannot be given up again, once it has been made, and the development, the increasingly deep version of truth in its own form, is the only departure that remains with a philosophy whose principle is precisely that of development" (Ruge 1838a: 780).

But what Ruge emphasizes here is merely the idea of development. This plays an important role for Hegel, but when dealing with "method," Hegel discusses far more than just "development." If we take this into consideration, then it's doubtful that we can undertake a clear separation between method and system in Hegel's work. The introduction to the *Phenomenology of Spirit*, is a well-argued plea against the possibility of an independent discussion of method (Hegel 1977: 46ff.). When Hegel engages in more differentiated considerations of method, such as at the end of the *Science of Logic*, these presuppose the systematic argumentation, and therefore cannot be separated from the system.

The circumstances addressed by Engels seem to be due to the simple fact that conservatives, and not just the Hegelian ones, are interested in maintaining things as they are, and that leftists wish to change things and are therefore interested in development. This general difference, however, cannot be equated without further ado to an interest in *either* the system *or* the method.

It can hardly be disputed that in the conflicts of the 1830s, the religious and political positions of Hegelians became differentiated from one another. It also cannot be disputed that there were clear front lines drawn between progressive Hegelians such as Ruge or Feuerbach on one side and pietist-orthodox Protestants such as Hengstenberg and conservative authors like Leo on the other. But it's quite an exaggeration to say that the Hegelian school had split into two hostile schools—a right-wing "Old" Hegelian one and a left-wing "Young" Hegelian.

One cannot really speak of an Old Hegelian "school." Among the older Hegelians, there were a few, such as Göschel, Erdmann, Hinrichs, and Gabler, who had a strong conservative orientation both religiously and politically, but they did not constitute a coherent school. The majority of older members, such as Michelet, Rosenkranz, Hotho, Marheineke, and Vatke, were politically liberal. Michelet, Rosenkranz, and Vatke also contributed to the *Hallische Jahrbücher*. Gans was unambiguously of the left, and had promised Ruge to contribute to the *Jahrbücher* (letter of April 22, 1839, Hundt 2010a: 313), but died before he was able to do so.

In the case of the younger Hegelians, it's not quite so easy to answer the question of whether one can speak of a school. Attitudes with regard to the two central fields of conflict of religion and politics were not always similar. Thus Strauß advocated a "left" position in the philosophy of religion, whereas he remained moderate politically. However, the *Hallische Jahrbücher*, over a period of many years, constituted an important point of reference for younger authors who considered themselves critical, and as the editorial correspondence of the *Hallische* (and later *Deutsche*) *Jahrbücher* published by Hundt (2010a) shows, Ruge made an effort at organized intervention, in that he spoke to collaborators and set topics in a focused manner. Far more strongly than one could say for the Berlin *Jahrbücher für wissenschaftliche Kritik* with regard to the Old Hegelians, the *Hallische Jahrbücher* constituted a focal point for a Young Hegelian current for a few years.

In determining the substantive core of this current, however, there are considerable problems. In a comprehensive study, Wolfgang Eßbach attempted to outline the "Sociology of a Group of Intellectuals" (the subtitle of his book *The Young Hegelians*, published in 1988). He arrived at the result that the Young Hegelians represented multiple types of groups: a *philosophical school*, a *political party*, a *journalistic bohème*, and an *atheist sect*. Eßbach's work, which was richer in material than any previous study of the Young Hegelians, yielded a plethora of important insights, but it also made clear that general statements about "the" Young Hegelians are hardly possible, whereby Eßbach had even limited the object of his investigation to the "Prussian" Young Hegelians, so that, *inter alia*, the at times very important Southern German representatives, such as Strauß, remained excluded. Above all, however, the four types of groups do not play a role at the same time, and it's not always the same people who stand at their respective centers. The group types named by Eßbach are found at different times in different groupings.

The problems arising with regard to the substantive determination, demarcation of personnel, and duration of Young Hegelianism were exhaustively listed by Martin Hundt in the year 2000. However, he did not wish to depart from the understanding of the Young Hegelians as "an ultimately united movement in the end" (Hundt 2000: 13). Hundt understood the Young Hegelian movement as the "end" of the classical German philosophy that had begun with Kant, which still saw philosophy, theology, science, and art as constituting a unity. According to Hundt, Young Hegelianism was "the final historical manifestation of this unity" (ibid.: 18). Although this may be correct, it only establishes the commonality between Young Hegelianism and classical German philosophy, but not its own specific achievement. Fifteen years later, Hundt had to state in an encyclopedia entry on "Left Hegelianism" (used synonymously with "Young Hegelianism"), that it could "not be clearly demarcated either in terms of content or personnel" (Hundt 2015: 1169). In 2013, Lars Lambrecht answered the question "Who *are* the Young Hegelians?" by saying they were "a product of twentieth-century research" (Lambrecht 2013: 175). He ultimately left open the question "Who were the Young Hegelians?" (the title of the essay), were they more than just a construct of research into the history of philosophy?

In light of this discussion, it appears appropriate not to speak in a naive sense of Young Hegelianism and Young Hegelians, as if the meaning of these terms were self-evident, but rather to proceed more cautiously than has often been the case in the biographical literature on Marx. At least, we should make clear the sense in which we are using these terms. Even if the relations aren't as clear as with the Old Hegelians, for whom it is not appropriate to speak of a "school," it nonetheless also appears questionable to proceed from the assumption of the existence of a "school" without further ado. It might be more sensible to speak of a "Young Hegelian discourse," using the categories of analysis developed by Michel Foucault in his *Archaeology of Knowledge* (1972). In a brief outline, Urs Lindner (2013: 52ff.) has made such an attempt.

From the end of the 1830s, a broad current, which, proceeding from Hegelian philosophy, arrived at a critical consideration of religion and politics. However, the dimensions of this critique are very different. For some important protagonists, the critique of religion and politics leads to a fundamental critique of their point of departure, that is, Hegel's philosophy; this was to be—again, in different ways—"overcome."

But it remains difficult to specify a common substantive core of Young Hegelianism. These difficulties are frequently attributed to the fact that none of the Young Hegelians produced a large, systematic work. They expressed themselves primarily through reviews, polemics, and writings on current topics. The lack of "great works" was not just because most Young Hegelians did not obtain professorships.[223] The deeper reason why there was no "great" Young Hegelian work indeed appears to be the frequently emphasized dynamic of the Young Hegelian movement.[224] It was a movement in constant transition. In the case of most of its representatives, in the course of the late 1830s and early 1840s, a radicalization of their critique of religion and/or politics occurred. For more than a few, the critique of religion resulted in atheistic positions (with differing accents) and the initially rather

---

223. The reasons for this were not just political. At the end of the 1830s, there was the first "academic glut" in Prussia. The universities that were quickly growing or being established in the first third of the nineteenth century had produced more graduates, primarily in the subjects of philosophy, theology, and law, than the state could use (see Briese 2013).

224. For the almost nine years between the middle of 1835 and beginning of 1843, Bunzel, Hundt, and Lambrecht (2006: 19ff.) distinguish between five great phases of the development of the Young Hegelian movement. On average, that's less than two years per phase.

cautious critique of Prussia ultimately led in the case of many to demands for democratic and republican conditions; in the case of some, it led to communist views.

The point of departure of the Young Hegelians in Hegel and their early critiques of religion and politics demonstrate a number of commonalities. But the transitions ignited by these critiques no longer traverse common checkpoints; instead the transitions aimed in different theoretical and political directions. That's why it's so difficult to determine the content of Young Hegelianism as such, because beyond the critiques, there is hardly any shared substantive core. This should in no way diminish the intellectual achievements of individual Young Hegelian authors. It's just that these intellectual achievements, which diverged in the 1840s, can no longer be integrated into a Young Hegelian theoretical core. But if there was no such core, then we also cannot precisely determine who belonged to the Young Hegelians and who no longer did. The problem frequently discussed, especially from the Marxist side, of when and under what circumstances Marx and Engels transitioned from "Young Hegelian-idealist" positions to "materialist" positions then presents itself in a different way, one that I will return to in the second volume.

BAUER AND MARX

With the beginning of the controversy around Strauß's *Life of Jesus*, Bruno Bauer (1809–1882) also achieved some fame. In the *Jahrbücher für wissenschaftliche Kritik*, the organ of the Hegelian school without competition, Bauer published an extremely critical two-part review in 1835–36, defending the historicity of the Gospels. Corresponding to the division that Strauß undertook in 1837 in his *Streitschriften*, Bauer thus belonged to the right (in terms of the philosophy of religion).

However, Bauer did not remain at this position. Within a few years, he passed Strauß on the left in terms of the philosophy of religion: the Gospels were not just a myth arising in the early Christian congregations; they were literary products of their writers, according to his later thesis. Furthermore, the once orthodox Protestant transformed into a decisive atheist, and Bauer also became increasingly radical politically. Finally, in 1842, his permission to teach theology was withdrawn. The period in which Bauer radicalized so enormously, 1838–41, was the period of his most intense friendship with Marx. The biographical literature usually contents itself with noting that in his dissertation finished in 1841 Marx more or less adopted Bauer's theory of self-consciousness. The question of whether there was recipocral influence between Bauer and Marx is usually dealt with as minimally as the question of what connected the two during their close friendship lasting five years.

Bruno Bauer's Speculative Theology (1834–1839)

In the year 1834, Bauer took his licentiate exam (which corresponded to a doctorate) at the theological faculty of the University of Berlin. As an exception, this exam was also recognized as a postdoctoral qualification, so that he obtained permission to teach theology (Barnikol 1972: 22). Until 1839, as a lecturer he offered numerous courses, primarily on topics having to do with the Old Testament. Bauer's theological conceptions were initially in line with those of his theological teacher, Konrad Philipp Marheineke, who used Hegel's philosophy as philosophical justification for the content of biblical tradition. But whereas Hegel only justified the Christian religion broadly, that is, sublated the abstractly conceived content of the religion in philosophy but criticized the beliefs of the religion as an inadequate conception of this content, Bauer endeavored to justify it in detail, in particular the supernatural parts of tradition. Thus, in a review written in 1834 in somewhat difficult to understand Hegelian jargon, he formulated: "Science [*Wissenschaft*, Hegel's philosophy] has achieved . . . that the miracles of Christ . . . are known as the equally necessary self-exposition [*Selbstdarstellung*] of the personality of Christ as are the teachings [Christian dogma]" (Bauer 1834: 200). That means that "science" says, according to Bauer, that Christ's personality cannot present itself other than through miracles.

For David Friedrich Strauß, the philosophical justification of central elements of Christian belief had opened up the possibility of subjecting to a radical critique the *religious form* of testimony to this content—that it was supposed to be based on *historical* (and supernatural) events—while still adhering to Christianity. Bruno Bauer, in contrast, wanted a philosophical justification of the historical events, including their supernatural components, not just for history's sake, but for the sake of the idea that is supposed to appear in history. Correspondingly, his critique of Strauß was fundamental. In his review of *The Life of Jesus*, Bauer accused him of a lack of philosophical understanding: "He [Strauß] believes that the question of whether the necessity of its historical manifestation does not lie in the idea itself is overcome by the difficulties adhering to the reports of the Gospels, at the same time destroying the possibility of sacred history" (Bauer 1835–36: 888).

Bauer tried to demonstrate how to overcome these difficulties with the virgin birth of Jesus, of all things. Human nature alone could not bring about the unity of human and divine nature manifest in Jesus; it could only contribute to it through its own "receptivity." On this basis, Bauer concluded by means of an idiosyncratic gender discourse: "Because in woman, or more specifically in the virgin," receptivity to the spirit is "available in an immediate way," and because "man's activity is always one whose consequence is the limitation of the result," Jesus, who was "unlimited," must have been sired by the Holy Spirit. Physiological objections are not the point: "The physiological perspective is sublated in the theological" (Bauer 1835–36: 897).

To theologists with a rationalist orientation and non-conservative Hegelians, the effect of this argument, as Strauß made rather clear in his *Streitschriften*, was rather amusing. In contrast, conservative Hegelians like Göschel could live rather well with such arguments, and Hengstenberg's *Evangelische Kirchenzeitung* also praised Bauer. However, unlike Hengstenberg, Bauer's primary concern was not rescuing the supernatural element of the Bible stories. Bauer saw it as an important achievement of Hegelian philosophy that it had "understood spirit in its manifestation." Exactly this inner connection between spirit and its manifestation, that spirit must manifest, and can only be grasped in its manifestation, is what Strauß missed. Bauer continues in the passage quoted: "The critique [articulated by Strauß] also connects spirit and historical manifestation, but only through a loose, supplementary 'also.'" Strauß failed to understand the "absolute content" as the "driving force" of the production of historical events (Bauer 1835–36: 904). Thus, Bauer's following theological program is shown in a nutshell: the development of divine spirit is traced by the development of revelation.

Bauer was esteemed primarily by the Hegelian theologian Philipp Konrad Marheineke. The latter probably had a background supportive role when Bauer founded the *Zeitschrift für spekulative Theologie* in 1836 (Hertz-Eichenrode 1959: 16), which operated within the framework of the conservative Hegelian theology. The journal managed to reach three volumes but was only published from the middle of 1836 to the beginning of 1838, with a total of six issues (ibid.: 15ff.). According to Mehlhausen, the publication was canceled for economic reasons; it did not even sell a hundred copies (Mehlhausen 1999: 191).

Two years later, Bauer only had irony left for his own role at that time. After Hegel's death, his disciples had gathered "in the realm of ideas," and their "dreams . . . of the time of perfection seemed to have already come true, when the lightning of reflection [Strauß's *Life of Jesus*] entered the realm of bliss and troubled the dream. So little was one prepared for the blow that the Berlin scientific critique [the *Jahrbücher für wissenschaftliche Kritik*] confronted Strauß's book with a reviewer [Bauer] who, still in a blissful dream, spoke of the unity of the dream and immediate reality, or rather of the world and empirical consciousness, and even wanted to continue his dream in a special journal" (Bauer 1840a: 2).

What is addressed by Bauer mockingly as the dream of unity of the idea and immediate reality, the unity of spirit with its historical manifestation, marked the difference both to pietists and adherents of conservative orthodoxy who wished to justify biblical history because it was handed down through tradition and was considered the source of faith. This unity also marked the difference to Strauß, who, with reference to the speculative reconstruction of the idea, thought the historical process did not matter. For the early Bauer, however, the development of the idea had to show itself in history.

What this approach means in the field of the philosophy of religion can be seen in Bauer's first large work, which he presented in 1838. As the first part of a *Critique of Revelation*, Bauer published his two-volume *The Religion of the Old Testament in the Historical Development of Its Principles*. In a comprehensive introduction, Bauer outlines the idea of revelation. God reveals himself in concrete events, which are perceived with the senses and translated into religious representations by the human beings who receive his revelation. Revelation is therefore not a unified act but a historical process, with the biblical texts as an expression of different stages of this—contradictory—process. As Bauer explained, it is a contradiction against God's infinite essence if God "sets a limited content as the manifestation of his infinite purpose at the individual stages of revelation" (Bauer 1838a: Bd.1: xxiv). The "critique" that Bauer strove for was supposed to explain these contradictions with the help of a speculative concept of religion based upon Hegel's philosophy of religion. That is, what appears as a contradiction in the historical development of revelation was supposed to be shown as a necessary step toward the complete understanding of religion. With this conception of revelation and history, Bauer believed himself to be in a superior position to both a merely "faithful theology" that wished to maintain "the positive" (tradition along with its contradictions), as well as in a critique that "merely cunningly seizes and destroys" the positive (Bauer 1838a: 2: ix).[225]

Whereas in his *Critique of the History of Revelation*, Bauer sought to merely apply the principles of Hegel's philosophy of religion, in the same year he had begun to recognize, in his discussion of Strauß's *Streitschriften* and not least under its influence, that a further development of these principles was necessary. Bauer stated that "the master had left his school of

---

225. The early development of Bauer's theological thought is dealt with extensively in Mehlhausen (1965) and Lämmermann (1979), and considerably shorter but sharpened to striking points in Kanda (2003: 100ff.) and Lehmkühler (2010).

the philosophy of religion—despite all its admirable riches—in such a form that makes the further inner development through the principle necessary" (Bauer 1838b: 836).

At the same time, Bauer defended his own position with increasing determination. As editor of the *Zeitschrift für spekulative Theologie*, he had acted quite moderately. He had hoped that the various currents of Protestant theology would see that each of their approaches was justified, but valid only in a limited sense, a limitation that had been overcome in Hegelian speculative theology. Now he began to have increasingly fierce debates with those who opposed his positions. This critique was initially expressed in reviews: at the beginning of 1839, it led to the publication of a book that was directed against Ernst Wilhelm Hengstenberg of all people, who at the time was the most influential Berlin theologian. The title itself was a provocation: *Herr Dr. Hengstenberg: Critical Letters on the Antagonism of the Law and the Gospel* (*Kritische Briefe über den Gegensatz des Gesetzes und des Evangeliums*). No less provocative was the form: the book consisted of letters that Bruno Bauer had written to his younger brother Edgar, who wanted to study theology. So, it wasn't a professional theological debate; the intent instead was to demonstrate to philosophical laymen how wrong Hengstenberg's views were.

The main point of contention was the relation between the Old and New Testaments. Whereas Bauer, from his developmental-historical approach, made a fundamental distinction between both, Hengstenberg saw the Old Testament as containing essential elements of Christianity, so that for him the Old and New Testaments constituted a unified revelation. Bauer accused Hengstenberg of "shortsighted theological apologetics" (Bauer 1839: 2). He unsparingly showed how unfounded many of Hengstenberg's Christian interpretations of the Old Testament were, and how this at the same time flattened out the specificity of the New Testament. Whereas the Old Testament was dominated by the Mosaic Law, but legal consciousness was servant's consciousness, on the basis of which a theocracy was erected, Bauer grasped the Christianity of the New Testament, in the tradition of Hegel, as a religion of freedom.

It was clear to Bauer what the critique of the influential Hengstenberg, who was known for his relentless and denunciatory manner of fighting opponents, would mean for himself. Bauer wrote that he knew very well that "whoever attacks Dr. Hengstenberg, whoever even dares to deviate from the statutes of this scribe, isn't just putting the hand in the fire, but running into it alive" (ibid.: 3).

Bauer's text was a fierce attack on a reactionary theologian, an attack that robbed Bauer of his chances for a career in Berlin, but it was an attack that still came from the perspective of the same conservative, speculative theology with which he had criticized Strauß. He had not, therefore, as is sometimes claimed (for example, Pepperle 1978: 67), gone over to "left" positions in the philosophy of religion. It's therefore no wonder that in the autumn of 1839, Bauer was still placed by Arnold Ruge alongside Göschel and Erdmann (see Ruge to Rosenkranz, October 2, 1839, Hundt 2010a: 410).

Atheism and Critique of the Gospels (1839–1841)

Bauer had the good will of Minister of Culture Altenstein in Berlin but he could no longer appoint Bauer to a professorship. That would have been too great an affront against Hengstenberg. Altenstein, therefore, recommended to Bauer that he go to Bonn as a lecturer, where an (associate) professorship in theology had become available. If Bauer didn't ruin things with his colleagues in Bonn, Altenstein could appoint him to this professorship. For Altenstein, who was still interested in promoting Hegelian philosophy, appointing Bauer in Bonn would have been a good fit, because there weren't any Hegelians there, neither among the philosophers nor the theologians. Among the theologians, the spirit of Schleiermacher was dominant, primarily represented by Karl Immanuel Nitzsch (1787–1868). After the summer semester of 1839, the semester that Karl Marx attended Bauer's seminar on Isaiah, Bauer departed for Bonn.

Formally, the theological faculty at the University of Bonn had to approve Bauer's transfer. No one wanted to oppose Altenstein's recommendation, but Bauer was met with distrust. Bruno Bauer's letters to his brother Edgar bear witness to this (Bauer 1844a). However, in Bonn, Bauer found enough time for further work. Marheineke had tasked him with preparing the second, expanded edition of Hegel's *Lectures on the Philosophy of Religion*, which was published in 1840. Alongside this, Bauer worked on his *Critique of the Gospel History of John* (*Kritik der evangelischen Geschichte des Johannes*) as well as *The Protestant State Church of Prussia and Science* (*Die evangelische Landeskirche Preußens und die Wissenschaft*). In the latter, published in the early summer of 1840, shortly after the death of Friedrich Wilhelm III, Bauer vehemently argued that the Prussian state should not allow itself to be instrumentalized by the church hierarchy in its struggle against science: "The hierarchical madness which regards the state as its executioner's assistant, has up to now maintained itself in the Protestant church. . . . Recent science is destined to endure these latest attacks by the Protestant hierarchy, and it rejoices in the task that history has set for it, and which it alone can solve" (Bauer 1840a: 6). Bauer did not expect from the state—and by state, Bauer meant the new king, Friedrich Wilhelm IV—that it would take the side of science; it would be enough if it would remain "a spectator to the struggle" (ibid.: 7). But science would remain consistently on the side of the state.

With this text, Bauer, similar to Feuerbach a year before, traced current conflicts back to a fundamental level. If for Feuerbach it was the antagonism between philosophy and religion, for Bauer it was the conflict between the church hierarchy and science. At the same time, Bauer, as quoted above, made a critique of his own earlier conceptions of the "unity of the idea and immediate reality." With this text, Bauer made public that he had moved to the "left," both in terms of the philosophy of religion and in the general political sense. The fact that his book was published by Otto Wigand, the publisher of most Young Hegelians, was consistent. His text was received positively by the Young Hegelians (see C. M. Wolf to Ruge, September 22, 1840, Hundt 2010: 587) and reviewed with extreme praise by Ruge in the *Hallische Jahrbücher* (Ruge 1840b). At the end of 1840, Ruge and Bauer were in contact with each other; starting in 1841, Bauer contributed to the *Jahrbücher*. Bauer had arrived, albeit rather late, at the Young Hegelians.

In the late summer of 1840, Bauer's *Critique of the Gospel History of John* was published, which was to constitute the prelude to an ever more radical critique of religion. Bauer did not publish the critique of the Gospel of John as a continuation of his *Critique of the History of Revelation*; he did not continue the latter after the first part on the Old Testament. As a reason, Bauer stated in the preface to his new book that "the history of Jewish consciousness as it developed after the conclusion of the canon [the Old Testament] until Jesus's appearance" was "still unknown territory" (Bauer 1840a: v). The deeper reason for not continuing his earlier work was probably not this lack of historical material, but rather that Bauer, as he had made clear in *The Protestant State Church and Science*, no longer held to the theoretical preconditions from which the earlier book proceeded, namely the "unity of idea and reality." Bauer's new project consisted in extracting the historical core of the history of Jesus from the Gospels and to distinguish it from that which was merely a later addition. He thus moved closer to the text-critical method used by David Friedrich Strauß, which he had previously rejected.

Bauer began his investigation with the Gospel of John, which both stylistically and in terms of content has a unique position with respect to the

three other Gospels. The result of Bauer's book was devastating for previous apologetics: an investigation of the given places and times, as well as the
logical (or rather illogical) coherence of the presentation, made clear that
the fourth evangelist was not giving his own or someone else's observations;
rather, it was a later reflection upon earlier events. This "reflection is a weak,
albeit abundantly proliferating climbing plant, which is capable of covering
a trunk, but not of forming its own" (ibid.: 101). The Gospel of John, according to Bauer's conclusion, is not a historical report, but rather a free artistic
creation by the evangelist.[226] In his "concluding remark," Bauer noted: "We
have not found a single atom that would have eluded the work of reflection of
the fourth evangelist" (Bauer 1840b: 405). Therefore, this gospel is no source
for a historical revelatory event; the event is presupposed and processed in a
literary way. When Bauer wrote in some interim observations under the title
"Point of Rest" ("Ruhepunkt"): "Whereas previous apologetics could only
flourish as long as the general view of history was a poor one ... in our time
the process now occurs in which the self-consciousness of absolute spirit will
complete and conclude the memory of its historical revelation," and when
he emphasized that critique is "the pure being with itself [Beisichseyn] of
Christian self-consciousness, which wishes to finally be at home with itself
[bei sich selbst seyn] also in terms of the given, the positive, and in the particular gospel records" (ibid.: 183), then that is formally correct. But the
substantive implications of the statement only become apparent if one takes
into consideration what can be said about the "historical revelation" or the
"Gospel records": namely, nothing on the basis of the Gospel of John.

In fact, Bauer's attitude toward theology and religion had changed radically when he was preparing his book on the Gospel of John in 1839–40. This
emerges from his correspondence with Edgar, which he published in 1844.
The original letters have not survived, and the possibility cannot be excluded
that Bauer retroactively made the formulations more pointed.[227] However,
the statements, I will discuss below are quite plausible; they also fit with letters to Marx written shortly afterward. The censors took offense at them,
however, and they are not contained in Bauer (1844a). It was as a result of
legal proceedings brought by Bauer that he was able to publish the incrimi-
nated passages retroactively in the Allgemeine Literatur-Zeitung, of which he
was editor (Bauer 1844b).

In a letter from December 29, 1839, Edgar informed Bruno of his decision

---

226. Strauß had already suspected that at least "the discourses of Jesus in the fourth Gospel are
to a great extent the free compositions of the Evangelist" (Strauß 1835/1892: 376).
227. Kanda (2003: 117f.) gives a plausible example for such a probable retroactive sharpening.

to give up studying theology and switch to history. As a reason, he stated: "It's impossible for me to remain an honest theologian, since I'm losing all faith" (Bauer 1844b: 40). In his January 5, 1840, response, Bruno congratulated his brother for evading the "Megaera" of theology. He explained his own further occupation with it as follows: "I'm already stuck in it, and the struggle has eaten its way too far into me for me to be able to separate myself from it. I've become so fused with theology that I only do to myself what I do to theology; meaning I wash myself clean of refuse by cleaning up in theology. When I'm finished, I'll be pure" (Bauer 1844b: 41).[228]

But Bruno Bauer was concerned not just with a critique of theology, but also with belief. On January 20, 1840, Bruno wrote to his brother about a letter he had received from their father. The father had reported on a conflict with Edgar, in the course of which his son had said to him, "Bruno also believes in nothing," which Bruno did not dispute (Bauer 1844a: 31). Apparently, Bruno Bauer had not only arrived at a radical critique of theology, but also at atheist positions. This does not appear to have been new information for Edgar in January of 1840; probably Bruno had already spoken to Edgar a few months earlier. However, one may assume that in the case of a person who had first been a believer, the process of detaching from faith takes somewhat longer. To that extent, the autumn of 1839 merely marked the endpoint of this development. Bauer's transition to atheism must have occurred before January 1840, in any case. This chronological order is relevant to the extent that it clarifies that Bauer's atheist turn occurred prior to, and independently of, his critique of the Gospels. In the literature, this is not always distinguished; sometimes Bauer's atheism is understood to be a consequence of his examination of the Gospels (such as in Lehmkühler 2010: 55). Conversely, the critique of the Gospels was not a consequence of Bauer's atheism: completely independent of one's own belief, one can pursue the question of whether the texts of the Gospels allow for conclusions regarding the historical Jesus.

After a year in Bonn without a permanent appointment, Bauer's financial situation, which even in Berlin had not been particularly good, had become precarious, so that he presented himself to the Ministry of Culture regarding the promised Bonn professorship. Altenstein had died in May of 1840, and the provisional director of the ministry, Adalbert von Ladenberg (1798–1855), wanted to appoint Bauer to the professorship in Bonn, which was still free. In a submission to the new minister, Eichhorn, the faculty spoke out against

228. Instead of the two last sentences, the censored version states: "I will first be able to finish when I've gone through all turns" (Bauer 1844a: 30).

an appointment of Bauer; they preferred Gottfried Kinkel (1815–1882), at this time also a lecturer in Bonn.[229] Minister of Culture Eichhorn, to whom Bauer personally presented himself in the autumn of 1840, recommended that Bauer remain in Berlin and write a (neutral) work on church history. The ministry, according to Eichhorn, would support it with a contribution. But Bruno Bauer wanted to keep teaching and returned to Bonn.

Bauer did not publish a neutral work on the history of the church. He was far too driven by the question of what could be said about the historical Jesus and his sermons. Consequently he now turned to the Gospels of Matthew, Luke, and Mark, the "synoptic Gospels." These three evangelists are referred to as "synoptics" because their Gospels exhibit great overlap, and in the eighteenth century "synopses," that is to say, parallel compilations of the three texts, that addressed commonalities and differences.[230] In the spring of 1841, the first volume of Bauer's *Critique of the Gospel History of the Synoptics* (*Kritik der evangelischen Geschichte der Synoptiker*) was published.

Here as well, Bauer's investigation of the texts of the Gospels led to the result that they were not based upon direct knowledge concerning the historical Jesus, but were instead products of the "self-consciousness" of the evangelists. Bauer had used this term in his critique of the Gospel of John; now he endeavored to specify it: "Self-consciousness, in this creative activity, does not behave as a pure, isolated 'I' and does not create and form out of its immediate subjectivity . . . self-consciousness has . . . stood in a tension with its substance [here: the spirit of the congregation], was fecundated by it, and driven to its activity" (Bauer 1841a: 69). In the course of his argument, further refinements are found. The bearers of self-consciousness are individual people, but only to the extent that this particularity "is no longer the point of an exclusive individuality," but rather "carries within it the determination of the universal." Self-consciousness, one may summarize, "is no longer a single I, but rather the universality, in which the I is raised above its immediacy" (Bauer 1841a: 221).

With this concept of self-consciousness, Bauer clearly differs from Hegel's concept of self-consciousness. Hegel had determined self-consciousness within the framework of his investigation of subjective spirit: in self-consciousness, the self relates to itself by relating to another (*Encyclopedia*,

229. Kinkel would still play an important role in the Revolution of 1848. During his subsequent exile in London, he was one of the exiles that Marx dealt with extremely critically and polemically.
230. These synopses are not to be mistaken with the "Gospel harmonies" circulating since late antiquity. In these, a new text is created on the basis of the four Gospels, with the intention of taking into consideration all available information about Jesus.

§436).[231] Over the course of the year 1841, this concept of self-conscious-ness in Bauer's work would be further expanded, becoming central for his *Trumpet of the Last Judgment* (Stepelevich 1985: 177ff.).

Since my primary concern in this chapter is with Bauer's influence upon Marx's dissertation, I will not follow his further development. Marx was probably familiar with the concept of self-consciousness as used in the cri-tique of the synoptics. Even if we don't know whether Marx obtained a copy of Bauer's book, one may assume that when Bauer spent a few weeks in Berlin in the autumn of 1840, he discussed it with Marx.

The Religious Development and Studies in the Philosophy of Religion of the Young Marx

His Abitur essay from 1835 demonstrates that the seventeen-year-old Marx still believed in a God. From the preface to his dissertation from March 1841, in contrast, it becomes evident that he now took a decidedly atheist position. Prometheus, who in Aeschylus's tragedy of the same name is quoted as say-ing "I hate all the gods," was regarded by Marx as "the most eminent saint and martyr in the philosophical calendar" (MECW 1: 31).

We don't know exactly why Marx became an atheist. However, the assump-tion suggests itself that he must have started having first doubts about his faith shortly after the Abitur. This emerges from a letter that his father wrote to him on November 18, 1835 (the brackets indicate missing text as result of damage to the paper): "That you will continue to be good morally, I really do not doubt. But a great support for morality is pure faith in God. You know that I am any-thing but a fanatic. But this faith is a real requirement of man sooner or later, and there are moments in life when even the atheist is involuntarily drawn to worship the Almighty. And it is common [. . .] for what Newton, Locke and Leibniz believed, everyone can [. . .] submit to" (MECW 1: 647). This para-graph has no relationship to what precedes it, so it must refer to a letter from Karl that has not survived. But as a reply, this paragraph only makes sense if Karl had expressed doubt about his belief in God in his previous letter.

For the period that directly followed, there are no direct statements by Marx concerning his faith, but a rejection of the belief in God can be read from his attempts at poetry in 1836–37. Precisely in this, they differ from late Romanticism, which had made a turn toward Christianity. The motif of being caught by God's grace or of finding relief in faith in God does not

---

231. For example, in the relation of recognition: "I confirm myself in that I am recognized by another self."

appear in a single one of Marx's poems. On the contrary, in the first album of poems, which he sent to Jenny for the Christmas of 1836, Marx describes despair and hopelessness, for which even faith in God can no longer do anything. Thus, in the poem "The Pale Maiden," the figure that gives the poem its title falls in love with a passing knight who doesn't even notice her. In her despair, no faith can help her. Before killing herself, she explains:

> Thus Heaven I've forfeited,
> I know it full well.
> My soul, once true to God,
> Is chosen for Hell. (MECW 1: 613)

Things are similar in "Der Wilden Brautgesang" (The Bride Song of the Wild One), which deals with a maiden who does not wish to marry the man her family has selected for her:

> And I am chained,
> forever to the rough man,
> No God mildly saves me,
> From slavery and exile. (MEGA I/1: 507)

When, inwardly broken, she finally agrees to the marriage, the closing verses comment:

> And the mountains lean proudly,
> and the sky laughs golden,
> because it doesn't know human longing,
> it calmly rejoices in its splendor.
>
> Buds swell, blossoms are resplendent,
> for nothing great has happened,
> a soul enveloped by death,
> and a heart lapses mutely. (MEGA I/1: 510)

Consolation or redemption, according to the message, are not to be expected from God. In the second album, the tone is sharpened. In "Song to the Stars," one finds the following verse:

> Alas, your light is never
> More than aethereally rare.

> No divine being ever
> Cast into you his fire. (MECW 1: 608)

God is not even metaphorically in the world. The "Invocation of One in Despair" deals with the defiant rebellion against a God who "has snatched from me my all" (MECW 1: 563). God appears here as an opponent with whom one must take up the struggle.

In "The Last Judgment" (subtitled "A Jest"), religious notions of a life after death are only the target of mockery:

> Ah! that life of all the dead,
> Hallelujahs that I hear,
> Make my hair stand on my head,
> And my soul is sick with fear. (MECW 1: 572)

And why was he so afraid of this life of the dead? Because it's so boring:

> God Eternal we must praise,
> Endless hallelujahs whine,
> Endless hymns of glory raise,
> Know no more delight or pain. (MECW 1: 573)

In the fragment of the novel *Scorpion and Felix*, there is also only scorn and mockery for religious subjects, such as the trinity of the Christian God (MECW 1: 628).

These poems, which were written before April 1837, make clear that Marx no longer believed in the "Deity" who, as he wrote in his Abitur essay, "never leaves mortal man wholly without a guide; he speaks softly but with certainty" (MECW 1: 3). In his lost dialogue *Cleanthes*, which he mentioned in the letter to his father, Marx must have experimented with a pantheistic notion borrowed from the early Schelling. God is conceived not as a person, but as an impersonal world soul that would have to be developed in a "philosophical-dialectical" manner (MECW 1: 18). We don't know for how long or how strongly Marx remained captive to such pantheistic notions.

Marx's parents had converted to Protestantism, but there is no indication that they had developed a closer relationship to Christian belief and Protestantism. As emerges from the letter from Marx's father quoted above, his religious beliefs were more deistic; he became a Protestant in order to keep his job as a lawyer. It is, therefore, probable that the young Karl never had an emotional relationship to Protestantism, either through family or congregational life. Hence, his parting with Christian religious belief—in contrast with the young Friedrich Engels—was probably easy.[232]

The transition to atheism did not lead to either Bauer or Marx ceasing to deal with topics related to the philosophy of religion. This is well known in Bauer's case, but it's less known that Marx had plans between 1838 and 1841 to write multiple contributions on the philosophy of religion. Nothing came of these plans, so that today one usually doesn't think of the philosophy of religion as one of Marx's fields of work. Yet we know that Marx must have engaged with it intensively, so it's no curiosity that he attended Bauer's seminar on Isaiah in the summer semester of 1839; rather, it's part of a large-scale engagement with questions of the philosophy of religion, which at this time definitely had a political significance.

Marx's publication plans with regard to philosophy of religion emerge primarily from the letters that Bauer sent from Bonn to Marx; the letters from Marx to Bauer have not survived.[233] In the letter from March 1, 1840, Bauer asks: "What's going on with your farce: Fischer vapulans [this chastised

---

232. The early development of Marx's religious notions has thus far hardly been investigated. Walter Sens suspects without further justification that "Marx, already in the summer of 1839 at the beginning of his preparations [for the doctoral dissertation] had taken this atheist position" (Sens 1935: 35). Johannes Kadenbach also sees in Marx's poetry an initial critique of religion, but one that was relativized through the transition to Hegel's philosophy. This transition had supposedly issued from Marx's desire "for a monist integrated view of spirit" (but where this desire came from is not explained), and Hegel's "monism affirms God as total being" (Kadenbach 1970: 45). Hegel's philosophy had conveyed a new understanding of religion to Marx, with a God immanent to the world (ibid.: 46ff.). Marx, under the influence of Bruno Bauer, first developed a new understanding of Hegel and religion corresponding more or less to that found in Bauer's *Trumpet of the Last Judgment* (ibid.: 55ff.). Kadenbach assumes that the Christian-religious interpretation of Hegel, which was already controversial in Marx's time, to be the only one possible. But he further assumes that in transitioning to Hegel's philosophy, Marx also drew these religious conclusions, without being able to produce any evidence for them. Ruedi Waser concludes, primarily on the basis of Marx's father's letters as well as his poetry, that the young Marx was an "agnostic," and that this agnosticism had made it hard for Marx in 1837 to go over to Hegel's philosophy (Waser 1994: 23, 25). However, Waser does not argue why Marx was an agnostic in 1836–37 and not an atheist. Agnostics are characterized in general by a certain leniency toward religion, since they can't exclude the possibility that religious notions have a kernel of truth. There is no sign of such leniency in Marx's poetry. If Marx's agnosticism (or atheism) was supposed to be the great hindrance to Marx's transition to Hegel's philosophy, then it's completely incomprehensible why Marx in his dialogue *Cleanthes* sought support against Hegel in the work of Schelling, of all people. See Marx's letter to his father, November 10, 1837 (MECW 1: 18).

233. Not all of Bauer's letters have survived. In the second surviving letter, of March 1, 1840, he writes: "How often have I written to you already—and you remain silent!" (MEGA III/1: 340).

Fischer]?" (MEGA III/1: 341). This is obviously a reference to Karl Philipp Fischer (1807–1885), who belonged to the speculative theists. In 1839, he had published *The Idea of Divinity*, in which he had asserted the personhood of God and the immortality of the soul against the pantheism attributed to Hegel. It's possible that Marx's "Logical Lucubrations" (night work; a metaphor for intensive studies), which Bauer mentions in his letter of December 11, 1839, were connected to this (MEGA III/1: 336). Since the speculative theists referred to Hegel's *Logic*, but promoted an independent theology not sublated in philosophy, a critique of this current had to start with its understanding of *Logic*.

Bauer's letter from March 30, 1840, notes two of Marx's projects. For one, "Anzeige der Rel. Phil." (MEGA III/1: 343), referring to a review of the second edition of Hegel's *Lectures on the Philosophy of Religion*, considerably revised by Bauer. For another, Bauer, who saw Marx as a future lecturer in philosophy at Bonn, wrote: "If you didn't want to read about Hermesianism next winter, I would have undertaken it. But it goes without saying and doesn't need to be mentioned: you must read about it; you must, because you have long borne yourself with a word on this matter. It will cause a tremendous sensation" (MEGA III/1: 344). Georg Hermes (1775–1831), a Catholic theologian at the University of Bonn, had attempted to reconcile Catholic dogmatism with the Enlightenment. The Prussian government had supported Hermesianism, but Pope Gregor XVI had placed Hermes's writings on the index of banned books. As a consequence, the Archbishop of Cologne, Droste zu Vischering—before his conflict over mixed-confessional marriages—forbade Catholic students of theology to attend lectures about Hermesianism. That Marx's engagement with Hermesianism would cause a "tremendous sensation" could only mean that Marx wanted to fundamentally criticize this doctrine, which was met with some sympathy in Protestant Prussia.

Marx also planned to publish a book on Hermesianism and had asked Bauer to make contact with a publisher in Bonn. On July 25, 1840, Bauer wrote to him that he couldn't use the letter that Marx had provided to send to the publisher; Marx had apparently taken quite the wrong tone: "You can write to your laundress like that, but not to a publisher you're first hoping to win" (MEGA III/1: 349). With the help of a lecturer who was a friend, Bauer found another publisher who was interested in the book. It's not known, however, whether a contract was made. Marx must have pursued this project at least until 1841. On February 23, 1841, Eduard Meyen said in a letter to Ruge that Marx wanted to "write a brochure on Hermes" and therefore was out of the question as a collaborator on the *Hallische Jahrbücher* (Hundt 2010a: 693). At the beginning of 1841, Marx must have been thinking about a critique of Feuerbach (Bauer

KARL MARX AND THE BIRTH OF MODERN SOCIETY

to Marx, April 12, 1841, MEGA II/1: 358). The only work of Feuerbach's that comes into question at all as an object of critique is his brochure published in 1839, "On Philosophy and Christianity in Relation to the Accusation Made Against Hegelian Philosophy of Being Non-Christian."

In letters to Arnold Ruge in 1842, Marx announced a work on "Religion and Art" multiple times, originally planned as a contribution to the continuation of Bauer's *Trumpet*, but which would then be published independently and apparently continued to expand (Marx to Ruge, March 5, 1842, MECW 1: 382). Thus, on March 20, 1842, Marx informed Ruge: "In the article itself I necessarily had to speak about the general essence of religion; in doing so I come into conflict with Feuerbach to a certain extent, a conflict concerning not the principle, but the conception of it. In any case religion does not gain from it" (MECW 1: 386).

So, from the beginning of 1840 until the spring of 1842, Marx had planned at least five publications concerning the philosophy of religion. In the case of all five, nothing was published, and it's not known how far Marx had gone in working on them. Corresponding manuscripts have not survived. The only publication on questions related to the philosophy of religion was a brief text in the *Deutsche Jahrbücher* in November of 1842. In it, Marx defended Bruno Bauer's text on the synoptics against attacks by the philologist Otto Friedrich Gruppe (1804–1876), an early collaborator of the *Hallische Jahrbücher*, who had switched over to reactionary positions. An article by Marx on the "Cologne Church Conflict" that was supposed to appear in the *Rheinische Zeitung* but was canceled by the censors, probably at least touched upon questions of the philosophy of religion. According to Marx, in a letter from July 9, 1842, to Arnold Ruge, he had "shown in this article how the defenders of the state adopted a clerical standpoint, and the defenders of the church a state standpoint" (MECW 1: 389).

Even if Marx's studies in the philosophy of religion were not reflected in independent publications, they did not remain without effect. In all of Marx's work, in particular in *Capital*, there are numerous quotations and allusions to the Bible as well as references to theological topics.[234] Marx's familiarity with these topics was not simply the result of a good general education, which was far more shaped by religion than it would be today. It is probable that this comprehensive knowledge is due to the studies in the philosophy of religion that Marx conducted between 1838 and 1842.

---

234. Reinhard Buchbinder's dissertation (1976) provides information concerning the extraordinary number of Bible quotations, biblical allusions, and theological comparisons in

Marx's Friendship with Bauer

From 1837 to 1842, Bruno Bauer was Karl Marx's closest friend and con-versely, Karl Marx, alongside Bauer's brother Edgar, was probably the most important person for Bruno Bauer. The emotional side of the relationship is hinted at in Bauer's letters. In a letter to Marx of April 1841, Bauer wrote that he had never laughed as much in Bonn, "like in Berlin when I merely crossed the street with you" (MEGA III/1: 356). Bauer had begun the previ-ous letter from March 31, 1841, with the sentence: "If things went according to my wishes, I would have long since written to your bride" (ibid.: 354). Apparently, Marx had demanded that Bauer write to Jenny and then admon-ished him when this still hadn't happened. Marx evidently wanted to bring the two people who were most important to him into direct contact with each other. Others had also noticed the close friendship between Marx and Bauer. Eduard Meyer characterized Marx as "Bruno Bauer's intimate friend" (letter to Ruge, January 14, 1841, Hundt 2010: 654).

Bauer and Marx also had plans for collaborative publications in 1841; they even wanted to publish a periodical together (on that, more below). Furthermore, there was a plan that after receiving his doctorate Marx should come to Bonn to do his postdoctoral qualification, so that Bauer and Marx could teach together in Bonn and stand up to theological and political reac-tion. In the earliest surviving letter to Marx from December 11, 1839, Bauer wrote: "Just make sure you come and read in the summer" (MEGA III/1: 335), meaning that Bauer expected that Marx would be able to hold lectures in Bonn for the summer semester of 1840. At the time, Marx was far from finished with his dissertation. in a letter from March 1, 1840, Bauer states: "Finally, put an end to your procrastination and your dilatory treatment of nonsense and a mere farce such as the exam. If only you were first here, and we could talk about more than paper can bear" (ibid.: 341). And so it contin-ued in the letters that followed.

The background of this continued urging we find not least in Bauer's con-stantly stated view that with the collision of the church and science, a politi-cal and social crisis of historical dimensions would arise. On March 1, he wrote: "The time is becoming increasingly terrible and more beautiful. . . . Everywhere, the emergence of the most decisive antagonisms and the futile Chinese police system that wishes to cover them up and only contributes to strengthening them. Finally, philosophy, which in this Chinese oppression[235]

---

the work of Marx and Engels.

235. That Bauer speaks of the "Chinese police system" and characterizes Prussian conditions

will emancipate itself and lead the struggle, whereas the state, in its blindness, will hand over the reins!" (ibid.: 341). On April 5, 1840, Bauer informed Marx: "The catastrophe will be terrible, profound, and I'd almost like to say, it will be greater and more tremendous than the one with which Christianity entered into the world. . . . What's coming is too certain to be unsure for even a moment. . . . The enemy powers have now moved so close that one blow will decide" (ibid.: 346).

It would be interesting to know how Marx reacted to these expectations on the part of Bauer. Apparently, he did not contradict him, since in Bauer's letters there is no attempt to convince a doubtful Marx.[236] Bauer wanted Marx, as the companion he obviously trusted the most, at his side for the coming struggles. "Come to Bonn," Bauer wrote on March 31, 1841, "this nest will maybe soon become the object of general attention and we can bring about the crisis here at its most important moments" (ibid.: 354).

What did Marx and Bauer find so attractive in each other that they developed such an intense relationship? Both had sharp minds and were able to deal with an enormous amount of reading in a short period of time; both were immensely interested in the political and intellectual developments of their time. But that wasn't all. Bauer pursued his own concept with admirable consistency. He was not only intellectually consistent, not recoiling from any conclusion; he was also politically consistent, without much regard for his situation, as his critique of Hengstenberg showed. The young Marx, whose "strict principles" his father had quickly perceived (ibid.: 300), was probably deeply impressed in both regards. At least a few aspects of his notion of "critique" were probably formed by the relationship with Bruno Bauer, notions to which Marx still adhered after things had come to a break between the two at the end of 1842. Not only did he write in the *Deutsch-Französische Jahrbücher* that what was now important was "ruthless criticism of all that exists, ruthless both in the sense of not being afraid of the results it arrives at and in the sense of being just as little afraid of conflict with the powers that be" (MECW 3: 142). More than forty years later, Marx, occasioned by a proposal brought to him and Engels

---

as "Chinese oppression" is probably an allusion to the depiction of China in Hegel's *Lectures on the Philosophy of History*, where the Chinese state is portrayed as a despotic system of rule by the emperor (Hegel 1956: 116–138).

236. When we look at the 1850s, we will get to know a similarly excited attitude on the part of Marx, but on the basis of a completely different theoretical foundation. With the next economic crisis, he expected a massive shock to the capitalist system and a renewed revolutionary wave—until the crisis of 1857–58 taught him better.

to found a scientific socialist journal with people whose abilities he didn't trust, formulated: "In such company ruthlessness—the prime requirement in all criticism—becomes impossible" (Marx to Friedrich Engels, July 18, 1877, MECW 45: 242).

But the young Marx also had something to offer. His early atheism might be an explanation for why he was recognized so quickly in the Doctor's Club, whose members, as far as we know, were all considerably older than Marx and initially possessed much more philosophical knowledge. He surely also made an impression with his quick comprehension and reading workload. But that he was also quickly accepted as someone from whom the older ones could learn—which emerges from Köppen's letter to Marx from June 3, 1841, quoted at the beginning of this chapter—could have also been due to the unself-consciousness with which Marx advocated atheist positions. The other members of the club came from Protestant families, and not only Bauer but also Köppen and Rutenberg had initially started out studying theology. They were all far more strongly rooted in the Christian-Protestant world of belief than Marx ever was. In the case of a strong religious bond, parting from faith is not only an intellectual problem but also an emotional one. The young Marx did not have such an emotional attachment to faith, and his poems suggest that in the club discussions he treated not just theology but also religion rather disrespectfully.

When Marx joined the Doctor's Club in the summer of 1837, it had been exactly a year and a half since Bruno Bauer had defended the virgin birth of Jesus, and he was still the editor of a conservative theological publication. It's improbable that Bauer was then an atheist. But then it couldn't have been Bauer who brought Marx to atheism, as for example McLellan suggests (1973: 41); rather, it could have been the other way around, that Marx was the one who led his friend Bauer to atheism in the years 1838 and 1839, or at least encouraged him on his path to atheism. This would also fit the finding cited above that Bauer had already become an atheist before his critique of the Gospels.

In 1840–41, Bauer and Marx planned to publish a journal together. The earliest reference to this journal is found in Bauer's letter to Marx from March 28, 1841. However, Bauer and Marx must have come to an agreement on this early on, perhaps during Bauer's visit to Berlin in the autumn of 1840. In any case, in his letter, Bauer assumed the familiarity of the plan for a journal: "This summer, the journal has to happen. . . . It's unbearable. The Berlin claptrap [meaning Berlin's *Jahrbücher für Wissenschaftliche Kritik*] and the dullness of the *Hallische Jahrbücher* . . . is coming increasingly to light. . . . The terrorism of the true theory must clear the field." This "true theory" could only be provided by a few, since for Bauer it was clear that "we can only admit a few collaborators" (MEGA III/1: 353).[237]

The title of the journal isn't given in Bauer's letters, but Ruge mentioned the plan for it in a letter to Adolf Stahr from September 8, 1841: "It will be a Journal of Atheism (explicitly)" (Hundt 2010a: 826). This was not a mere characterization by Ruge, but the actual planned title, as confirmed by a report of the *Mannheimer Abendzeitung* from February 28, 1843: "Dr. Marx . . . is a friend of Bruno Bauer, with whom he had earlier wished to publish a philosophical-theological journal in Bonn which was supposed to be based on the standpoints of Bauer's critique of the Gospels and bear the title "Archiv des Atheismus'" (MEGA III/1: 751). Although the journal was never founded, what was expected of it was described by Georg Jung (1814–1886), one of the co-founders of the *Rheinische Zeitung*, in October 1841 in a letter to Arnold Ruge: "Dr. Marx, Dr. Bauer, and L. Feuerbach are associating with each other around a theological-philosophical journal; then may all the angels flock around the old Lord God and may he have mercy upon himself, for these three will certainly throw him out of his heaven and hang a trial around his neck, to boot; Marx at least calls the Christian religion one of the most immoral; by the way, he is, despite being a rather desperate revolutionary, one of the sharpest minds I know" (Hundt 2010a: 852).

MARX'S DISSERTATION PROJECTS

Today, if one takes to hand a doctoral dissertation in medicine or in one of the natural sciences, it's usually a rather thin work dealing with a narrowly delimited special problem. Things look different in the humanities and social sciences, where dissertations are typically extensive and sometimes constitute a substantial contribution to the discussion in the respective field. But this wasn't always the case in Germany. Only in the late 1950s, when degrees below the level of doctorate were introduced in Germany that also required a written assignment did the scope and quality of doctoral dissertations increase considerably. Up until then, one could still obtain a doctorate in the humanities and social sciences with a non-extensive work that was dedicated to a secondary, special problem. In the case of many scholars of the nineteenth century, the dissertation is their least interesting work. To that extent, Bruno Bauer's urging mentioned in the last section that Marx should

---

237. The journal project is also briefly mentioned in Bauer's letter from April 12, 1841 (MEGA III/1: 358).

end the "farce" quickly is understandable. At the time, one wrote a doctoral dissertation in a few months. The truly independent scholarly work began not with a dissertation, but afterward.

If we take these circumstances into consideration, then it's not self-evident that after scarcely three and a half years of studying, Marx would require such a long time to prepare his dissertation on the "Difference between the Democritean and Epicurean Philosophy of Nature." The first excerpts on this topic come from the beginning of 1839, but Marx submitted his dissertation over two years later, in April 1841. One of the reasons for the long time it took was that Marx did not exclusively occupy himself with his dissertation. As we have just seen, he also occupied himself intensively with topics having to do with the philosophy of religion, whereby he planned not only to publish individual articles, but also an entire book (on Hermesianism). Another reason was that Marx approached his dissertation considerably more thoroughly than was usual back then. Even if Marx did not take a stand with regard to all points that interested him, the dissertation from 1841 provides important insight into the philosophical positions he had reached in the four years since his turn to Hegel's philosophy in 1837.[238]

Marx's Studies in the History of Philosophy and His First Dissertation Project (1839–1840)

As we know from a letter from Marx's mother (MEGA III/1: 334), in October of 1838 she sent him money for the doctoral fees. He probably used this money to pay his living costs, but he must have had concrete plans for his dissertation at this time. At the beginning of 1839, the first excerpts were made, which Marx titled "Notebooks on Epicurean Philosophy." By the spring of 1840, he had produced a total of seven such notebooks. Apparently he had decided upon Epicurus as a topic for his dissertation at the end of 1838. When exactly, and above all, why Marx chose Epicurean philosophy as a topic we don't know; no statement by him on this has survived. However, we will soon see that the selection of this topic is not surprising.

Marx's view of the history of philosophy was strongly influenced by Hegel's *Lectures on the History of Philosophy*, published between 1833 and 1836. In

---

238. For a long time, Marx's dissertation was rather neglected in the literature; it's only in the last few years that it has encountered increased interest, but this has sometimes been accompanied by a certain amount of overestimation. For Browning (2000: 132), Marx's later explanation of capital follows the course set here. Levine (2012: 119) sees in it the program of a materialist critique of what exists, and Eichler (2015: 25) sees it as a "key" to Marx's work as a whole.

the foreword to his dissertation, Marx wrote that "the history of philosophy can in general be dated" from Hegel's "admirably great and bold plan"
(MECW 1: 30). Hegel did not understand the history of philosophy simply
as a sequence of more or less arbitrary doctrines; rather, he attempted to
uncover an inner coherence and explained that "the historical succession of
the systems of philosophy is the same as the succession in the logical deriva-
tion of the idea's conceptual determinations. My contention is that, by strip-
ping away from the basic concepts of the systems appearing in the history of
philosophy whatever pertains to their external configuration, to their application to particular concerns, and the like, we are left with the different stages
of determination of the idea itself in its logical concepts" (Hegel 2009: 176).[239]
What initially sounds like a strong parallel between the development of the
history of philosophy and conceptual-logical development is thus immediately constrained. One must "know how to discern these pure concepts
within what the historical shape contains. The temporal sequence in history
also differs in one respect from the sequence in the order of the concepts,
although showing in detail what this involves would lead us too far afield
from our purpose" (ibid.).[240] However, Hegel certainly attempted to grasp
the philosophical systems at a general, categorical level. Thus, for him, the
post-Aristotelian philosophers of Stoicism, Epicureanism, and Skepticism
are philosophies of "self-consciousness"; they attempted "to gain the freedom
of self-consciousness through thought" (HW 19: 401).[241]

These three philosophies emerged at a time of decline for the Greek polis.
With the gigantic empire of Alexander (356–323 BCE) and the still colossal
successor empires into which the Alexandrian empire dissolved, the man-
ageable world of the polis was no longer the center of the world for Greek
thought, and free (male) citizens deciding upon the political fate of their

239. As noted in chapter 2, Hegel's concern is not with a realm of ideas distinct from the real
world. The idea for him is the unity of the concept of a thing and its objectivity (see Hegel
2010: 671). The "logical concepts" of the idea spoken of here are the fundamental categories of
philosophical knowledge of reality developed in the *Science of Logic*.
240. In his analysis of Hegel's concept of the history of philosophy, Fulda (2007) has pointed
out that it aims far less at a parallel to "logic" than is often imputed to Hegel, which becomes
clear not least from the fact that Hegel's actual presentation of the history of philosophy
precisely does not seek a parallel to the conceptual logical development in his *Science of Logic*.
241. This passage is omitted in the translation of the second volume of *Hegel's History of Philosophy*
by Robert F. Brown, which concludes the second part on "Dogmatic and Skeptical Philosophy" with
the sentence beginning "This may be enough about Skepticism. . . ." (Hegel 2006: 316), omitting
the subsequent passages where this quotation is found. The citation for the original passage in the
Hegel Werke published by Suhrkamp Verlag is therefore used here. —Trans.

commonwealth was a thing of the past. Philosophical interest was now directed more than before toward practical life management on the part of the individual, and Stoicism, Epicureanism, and Skepticism provided support in different ways. Here, too, what Hegel stated in the preface to the *Philosophy of Right* was demonstrated: "Philosophy is its own time comprehended in thoughts" (Hegel 1991: 21).

Hegel's characterization of these schools as philosophies of "self-consciousness"—which already amounts to a valorization with regard to the history of philosophy in Hegel's time, a history that only saw Epigonism and Eclecticism in these three systems—must have attracted the attention of the Young Hegelians, since the concept of self-consciousness played a central role in the debates over Hegel's philosophy of religion. For Bruno Bauer, with whom Marx was in close contact, the term acquired central importance in 1840–41. Friedrich Köppen as well, in his book on Frederick the Great, which was dedicated to Marx, pointed to Stoicism, Epicureanism, and Skepticism as sources of Friedrich's philosophical conception, whereby Köppen saw a parallel between the Enlightenment of the eighteenth century and the Epicureans as the "Enlighteners of antiquity" (Köppen 1840: 157). In the preface to his dissertation, Marx mentions the treatment of these philosophers in "the essay of my friend Köppen" (MECW 1: 30).

What spoke in particular for an engagement with Epicurus was his pronounced critical attitude toward religion. Epicurus did not dispute the existence of the gods; however, he assumed that they lived in their own world and were completely uninterested in the world of humans. Human worship of the gods, cults of sacrifice, etc., was thus regarded as unpleasant superstition. This attitude, along with the emphasis upon a sensual (but not, as is often assumed, excessively so) life, made Epicurus hated among the religious and conservatives of antiquity.[242]

It's doubtful whether Marx from the outset had in mind as the topic for his dissertation a comparison of the philosophies of nature of Epicurus (ca. 341–ca. 271 BCE) and Democritus (460–370 BCE). In the *Notebooks on Epicurean Philosophy*, the fifth notebook deals somewhat extensively with Democritus, and in the seventh notebook, Marx writes: "Epicurus's philosophy of nature is basically Democritean" (MECW 1: 504); there is no talk of a fundamental "difference." The notebooks give the impression that Marx was primarily interested in a systematic reconstruction of Epicurus's philosophy. A hint he made in a letter to Ferdinand Lassalle from May 31, 1858, points in this

---

242. Kimmich (1993) provides an overview of the reception of Epicurean philosophy from antiquity into the twentieth century.

direction. Lassalle had sent Marx his book on Heraclitus (ca. 520–ca. 460 BC) and asked for his opinion. In his reply, Marx says that he had once written a similar work on Epicurus, "namely the portrayal of a complete system from fragments" (MECW 40: 316).

Of the numerous writings of Epicurus, in Marx's time the only ones known were three letters and a collection of quotations that Diogenes Laertius (ca. third C. BCE) had passed down in his popular work *On the Lives and Opinions of Eminent Philosophers*. The situation doesn't look much better today as far as sources go. In the papyrus rolls from Herculaneum, a city buried by the outbreak of Vesuvius in 79 AD, nine fragments from Epicurus's writings were found (Marx made use of the first of these fragments), and in 1888, a further collection of Epicurus's teaching was found in the Vatican library in a medieval manuscript, which, however, did not provide any essential new insights. In Marx's time, there was no separate collection of ancient sources on Epicurus; he had to make one himself.[243] Other than the main ancient sources used by Hegel—alongside Diogenes Laertius, mainly Sextus Empiricus (second C.) and Plutarch (ca. 45–125)—Marx relied upon the poem *De rerum natura* (*On the Nature of Things*) by Lucretius (ca. 95–55 BC), an enthusiastic follower of Epicurus whom Hegel had not used and that Marx initially underestimated: "It goes without saying that but little use can be made of Lucretius," he noted in the first sentence of his Lucretius excerpt (MECW 1: 466). But Marx soon changed his estimation and emphasized "how infinitely more philosophically Lucretius grasps Epicurus than does Plutarch" (MECW 1: 469).[244] It was while reading Lucretius that Marx first realized the enormous significance of the "declination" of the movement of atoms (the deviation from a straight line); it was "one of the most profound conclusions, and it is based on the very essence of the Epicurean philosophy" (ibid.: 472). This point would also be extremely important for his dissertation.

Excerpts of these main sources fill the first five notebooks on Epicurean philosophy. Notebooks 6 and 7 contained supplementary excerpts from the

243. Currently, one of the best collection of texts and commentaries is found in the volume edited by Long and Sedley in 1987, which along with Epicurean philosophy also deals with Stoicism and Skepticism (Long/Sedley 2000).
244. One hundred and seventy years after Marx had realized Lucretius's importance, Stephen Greenblatt (2012) vividly described the rediscovery of Lucretius's poem in 1417 and its influence on the Renaissance, making Lucretius known to a wider public. A new translation into German and extensive commentary on *De rerum natura* was subsequently presented by Klaus Binder (Lukrez 2014).

works of other authors that only occasionally mention Epicurus, such as Cicero (106–43 BCE), Seneca (ca. 4 BCE–65 AD) or Stobaeus (fifth C.). The excerpts were frequently interrupted by Marx's sometimes longer remarks, in which he attempted to clarify the relation of Epicurean philosophy to the development of Greek philosophy as a whole, as well as to its opponents (above all Plutarch).

Probably in the first half of 1840, about the same time as the last notebook on Epicurean philosophy, or immediately afterward, Marx made an excerpt of parts of Aristotle's text *On the Soul* that also included extensive translations. The MEGA editors do not see any concrete occasion for this excerpt, but rather attribute it to Marx's general interest in Aristotle (MEGA IV/1: 733.). But since Marx had been preparing a dissertation for over a year and would have had an interest in concluding his studies quickly if for no other reason than financial ones, it's not plausible that he made such a comprehensive excerpt for no concrete reason.

One interesting hypothesis, which can explain not only the creation of this excerpt, was developed by the Jena classical philologist Günther Schmidt. Using references and allusions from the *Notebooks on Epicurean Philosophy*, Schmidt demonstrated that Marx already possessed thorough knowledge of other works by Aristotle, namely the *Physics*, the *Metaphysics*, and the text *On Generation and Corruption* (Schmidt 1980: 264–66). So the excerpts from the text *On the Soul* do not stand alone; rather, they complete an intensive study of Aristotle's central works. And there Schmidt drew a direct connection to Marx's dissertation project: his plausible hypothesis is that Marx initially endeavored to make a direct comparison between Epicurus's philosophy and that of Aristotle (ibid.: 266). It has frequently been pointed out that Marx's dissertation is not just concerned with a comparison of the philosophies of Epicurus and Democritus, but also with the relation between the philosophy of Epicurus and that of Aristotle (Cornu 1954: 167ff.; Sannwald 1957: 49ff.), but Schmidt goes a step further by determining that this comparison is not just background but is the original project of Marx's dissertation.

Schmidt sees a longer comment that Marx makes in the fifth notebook, after concluding his Lucretius excerpt (MECW 1: 490–93), as the first draft of an introduction for this initial dissertation project.[245] Since Marx also did a test translation into Latin of a paragraph of this comment, Schmidt concludes

---

245. In the Marx-Engels-Werke edition (MEW) of the notebooks and in MECW, the sequence of notebooks 5 and 6 is switched. These editions thus do not make clear that notebooks 1–5 reflect an initial phase of work, at the end of which comes the Lucretius excerpt, followed by the conceptual comment that Schmidt regards as the draft of an introduction.

that Marx wanted to submit this dissertation in Berlin, where a Latin paper was required (Schmidt 1980: 280–83).

The text Schmidt discusses is extraordinarily dense. It announces Marx's intention: "As in the history of philosophy there are nodal points which raise philosophy in itself to concretion, apprehend abstract principles in a totality, and thus break off the rectilinear process, so also there are moments when philosophy turns its eyes to the external world, and no longer apprehends it, but, as a practical person, weaves, as it were, intrigues with the world, emerges from the transparent kingdom of Amenthes and throws itself on the breast of the worldly Siren. That is the carnival of philosophy, whether it disguises itself as a dog like the Cynic, in priestly vestments like the Alexandrian,[246] or in fragrant spring array like the Epicurean. It is essential that philosophy should then wear character masks. . . .[247] But as Prometheus, having stolen fire from heaven, begins to build houses and to settle upon the earth, so philosophy, expanded to be the whole world, turns against the world of appearance. The same now with the philosophy of Hegel" (MECW 1: 491).

With the talk of "nodal points" by which philosophy is raised to concretion, Marx directly ties into Hegel, who wrote that in the history of philosophy, "Nodal points such as this must arise in the line of progression of philosophical development, because the truth is concrete" (Hegel 2006: 182). Hegel saw such a "node" of the concrete in the philosophy of Plato (427–347 BCE). Marx establishes that not only are there such nodal points, but also "moments" in which the entire mode of philosophy changes; it turns to the external world in a "comprehending" way, but as a "practical person." Philosophy costumes itself as a practical person; it is its "carnival."[248] However, this turn to the world is not an affirmative one; philosophy turns "against" the appearing world, as Hegel's philosophy now does. Marx thus establishes a link to contemporary conflicts, in which Feuerbach, Ruge, and Bauer, each in his own way, criticized Hegel's philosophy, but also deployed it against the appearing world, namely against the religious and philosophical conditions in Prussia.

---

246. Cynicism argued for a philosophy of frugality, which was frequently equated to a "dog's life." In Marx's time "Alexandrians" referred to the various Neo-Platonic currents whose representatives at times acted like priests of an occult doctrine.

247. Here, Marx uses the term "character mask" in its original meaning in theatrical language, referring to a specific character type (the farmer, the merchant, the scholar, etc.). In *Capital*, Marx will use this term with a new meaning.

248. That Marx thinks, of all things, of the "carnival" as a metaphor is probably a consequence of his background in the Catholic Rhineland, with a long carnival tradition. In Protestant Berlin, where Marx wrote these lines, carnival still had not established itself, nor has it even today.

Marx writes at the end of this text that it's important for the "historian of philosophy" that "this turnabout of philosophy, its transubstantiation into flesh and blood, varies according to the determination which a philosophy total and concrete in itself bears as its birthmark," so that "reasoning back from the determinate character of this turnabout, we can form a conclusion concerning the immanent determination and the world-historical character of the process of development of a philosophy." Marx brings this deliberation to the decisive point that allows him to speak in the first person for the first time in this text: "Since I hold that the attitude of the Epicurean philosophy is such a form of Greek philosophy [that is, a product of the turnabout characterized], may this also be my justification if, instead of presenting moments out of the preceding Greek philosophies as conditions of the life of the Epicurean philosophy, I reason back from the latter to draw conclusions about the former and thus let it itself formulate its own particular position" (MECW 1: 493).

But this project of reasoning, from Epicurean philosophy to the particular character of Greek philosophy, which expressed an emphatic difference to Hegel's conception, was not tackled by Marx. Notebooks 6 and 7 continue with excerpts on Epicurus, and at the end of notebook 7, Marx states with some surprise: "It is of substantial significance that the cycle of the three Greek philosophical systems, which complete pure Greek philosophy, the Epicurean, the Stoic and the Sceptic, take over their main elements from the past as they were already there. . . . And yet these systems are original and form a whole" (MECW 1: 504).

Marx must have engaged intensively with Stoicism and Skepticism in the period that followed. This is not just suggested by the foreword to his dissertation. There, he refers to his dissertation as "the preliminary to a larger work in which I shall present in detail the cycle of Epicurean, Stoic and Sceptic philosophy in their relation to the whole of Greek speculation. . . . These systems are the key to the true history of Greek philosophy" (MECW 1: 19). In the 1845–46 manuscript *Saint Max* as well, which belongs to the bundle of *The German Ideology*, Marx and Engels dealt in detail within the context of their critique of Max Stirner with his treatment of these three systems (MECW 5: 138–43). It's improbable that Engels contributed the knowledge on Stoicism and Skepticism. During his one year in Berlin, he occupied himself primarily with Schelling, Hegel, and the critique of the New Testament. It's more plausible that besides the Aristotle excerpts that haven't survived, there were also notebooks on Stoicism and Skepticism that perished.

The only surviving works from that time until the completion of his dissertation are excerpts from various works by Leibniz, from Hume's *A Treatise on Human Nature*, from Spinoza's *Tractatus theologico-politicus*, and from a book by Rosenkranz about Kant, all of which probably date from the beginning of 1841 (MEGA IV/1: 183–288). Along with the Aristotle excerpt, they are referred to as the "Berlin Notebooks." A quotation from the Hume excerpt was incorporated into the foreword of the dissertation, and Leibniz is briefly mentioned in two passages of the text, but otherwise these excerpts have no connection to it. They also do not contain any remarks by Marx; they are a pure collection of material. Perhaps they were intended to serve as preparation for an oral doctoral examination in Berlin. Bauer had written to Marx on March 30, 1840, that he had heard that oral exams in Berlin always revolved "around Aristotle, Spinoza, Leibniz—nothing else" (MEGA III/1: 342).

Probably dating from 1840 is a fragment on Plutarch (MECW 1: 74–76), which in the first MEGA and in the MEW and MECW editions was erroneously regarded as a fragment of the lost appendix to the dissertation. Like the surviving dissertation manuscript, this fragment was not written in Marx's own hand. However, the handwriting for this fragment is not identical to that of the copyist of the dissertation manuscript and parts of the Spinoza excerpt (MEGA IV/1: 726). That means that in the years 1840/41 Marx employed at least two copyists. Who they were, we don't know.

Also unanswered is the question of when and why Marx decided upon the topic of his dissertation, the "difference" between the philosophies of nature of Epicurus and Democritus. In the notebooks, such a difference is not yet emphasized. Taubert/Labuske (1977: 705) suspect that between the notebooks and the start of work on the dissertation manuscript, there was a further stage of researching sources, from which, however, no excerpts have survived.

The Dissertation Manuscript

On April 6, 1841, Marx sent his dissertation, *The Difference between the Democritean and Epicurean Philosophy of Nature*, to the faculty of philosophy at the University of Jena (MECW 1: 379). (I will discuss in the final section of this chapter why he did his doctorate at Jena and not in Berlin.) Apparently Marx prepared his dissertation for publication, but it did not come to that. In 1902 sections of the dissertation were published as part of the edition of the literary estates of Marx, Engels, and Lassalle procured by Mehring. A complete version of the surviving manuscript, which encompasses only a part of the dissertation, was published by David Riazanov in 1927 in the first MEGA; the edition in the MEW and many translations is based upon that one. But it was only with the publication for the second MEGA in 1976 that a number of deciphering errors and the erroneous ordering of the Plutarch fragment could be eliminated (on the edition history, see Blank 2017).

RELIGION, HEGELIANISM, AND MARX'S DISSERTATION   301

The publication of Marx's dissertation was consequently impeded. The rule common in Germany today that a dissertation has to be published only took hold later in the nineteenth century. The copy that Marx sent to Jena is lost. After the Second World War, Marx's doctoral records were found in Jena, but not his dissertation. What has survived is merely an incomplete copy by an unknown scribe. However, it's not certain whether this copy, intended as a print template, is identical with the copy submitted in Jena. It's probably not the case that Marx sent the title page to Jena, on which the title "Doctor of Philosophy" is written under the author's name, nor the foreword dated March 1841, which contains not only a clear confession of atheism, but mention of the completed doctorate, since Marx still wanted to receive a doctorate from the university. Whether there are changes to the text cannot be verified, but it would be quite plausible. With the submitted dissertation, Marx wished to obtain a doctorate at a university that he previously had had nothing to do with. Since he was not necessarily looking for a political confrontation from which he could gain nothing, this would be all too understandable.[249] The case is different with the publication of the work; there, the point would have been public impact.

According to the table of contents, the dissertation encompassed two parts: "Difference between the Democritean and Epicurean Philosophy of Nature in General" and "Difference between the Democritean and Epicurean Philosophy of Nature in Detail," as well as an appendix, "Critique of Plutarch's Polemic Against the Theology of Epicurus" (MECW 1: 32). From the first part, the last two subsections are missing; however, the notes on the missing sections are available. The second part has survived completely. The text of the appendix is entirely missing, but here again the notes on the first half of the appendix (noticeable by the subheadings in the notes section) are available.

In the case of the missing parts, the question arises of whether the scribe copied them and they were subsequently lost, or whether they were not available for him to copy, because Marx still wanted to revise them. One can at least presume the latter with regard to the missing passages of the first part. The scribe numbered the pages of the first part but did not number the pages of the second part. In the case that the scribe had begun with the copy of the second part before he was finished with the first part, the matter can be explained simply: the scribe wanted to wait for the pagination of the second part until he knew how many pages the first part encompassed.

The surviving notes of the missing parts of the text also exhibit a peculiarity.

---

249. Bauer also cautioned him against including Aeschylus's verse on Prometheus, "I hate all the gods," in the dissertation. Letter from April 12, 1841 (MEGA III/1: 357).

In the main text, Marx had usually reproduced statements by ancient authors in German, either directly or summarized in his own formulations. In the notes, he not only provided sources, but also the original quotations in Greek or Latin. Only for the missing sections are there notes that deviate from this. Among them are two comments, each with a length of multiple pages, which refer to contemporary debates over Hegel's philosophy as well as to Schelling and the proofs for the existence of God (MECW 1: 84–87, 102–5). It's possible the text to which these notes refer had already gone beyond the discussion of Greek philosophy, and Marx wanted to further develop it for publication, and thus he did not give these parts of the text to the copyist.

Atoms and Self-Consciousness

"Greek philosophy seems to have met with something with which a good tragedy is not supposed to meet, namely, a dull ending. The objective history of philosophy in Greece seems to come to an end with Aristotle, Greek philosophy's Alexander of Macedon. . . . Epicureans, Stoics and Sceptics are regarded as an almost improper addition bearing no relation to its powerful premises" (MECW 1: 34). Thus begins the first part of Marx's dissertation. As in the notebooks and the foreword, Marx opposes the underestimation of post-Aristotelian philosophy. He presents his dissertation as the first example of evidence for his thesis, whereby he emphasizes that it's not an easy task, since "it is an old and entrenched prejudice to identify Democritean and Epicurean physics, so that Epicurus's modifications are seen as only arbitrary vagaries" (ibid.: 36).

Democritus and Epicurus were both "atomists"; they proceeded from the assumption that the world was built out of the smallest particles, "atoms" (translated literally: the "indivisible"), and in Marx's day, Epicurus was seen merely as an epigone of Democritus with regard to atomic theory. To that extent, it's not accurate, as Marx writes in his foreword, that he had solved "a heretofore unsolved problem" (ibid.: 29); it was not seen as a problem, and certainly not as an unsolved one. To that extent, with his work Marx was breaking new ground in the history of philosophy.

If one speaks of atoms today, one thinks of atom bombs and atomic power plants. In the case of both, tremendous energy is released by splitting the nuclei of atoms. It's part of general education today to know that atoms consist of a positively charged nucleus and a negatively charged shell. And whoever is a little interested in physics also knows that the "elementary particles" of which atoms consist are not indivisible; they can transform into each other. The objects that we call "atoms" today are missing the property expressed in the name, that of indivisibility. Greek atomism is distinct from modern physics not just in terms of the content of the term atom, but also in terms of method. The ancient conception that the world consists of atoms moving through an otherwise empty space was not the result of experimental studies; it was one of two possible answers to the question of whether materials are infinitely divisible, or whether they are composed of the smallest indivisible bodies. Aristotle among others criticized atomic theory. In Marx's time, atomic physics in the modern sense did not yet exist; however, chemistry, since the beginning of the nineteenth century, had assumed that chemical elements consist of similar atoms. Only toward the end of the nineteenth century did it become clear through experiment that these atoms are not compact, but rather possess an inner structure.

We must distinguish two different levels of argument in Marx's dissertation. On the one hand, Marx argues purely in terms of the history of philosophy. Relying upon numerous sources, he confronts the conceptions of Democritus and Epicurus. On the other hand, he interprets Epicurus' conceptions using his own categories, stemming from Hegel—above all essence, appearance, and self-consciousness. It is not simply an application of these categories, but a free usage that builds a bridge between the theory of atoms and the discussion of the position of human beings in society. Here it is made clear what Marx meant when he wrote to Lassalle on December 21, 1857, that he had conducted his study of Epicurus "for [political][250] rather than philosophical reasons" (MECW 40: 226).

The first part of the dissertation concerns the difference between the Democritean and Epicurean philosophies of nature "in general." Marx shows that Democritus and Epicurus both proceed from the existence of atoms and their movement in empty space, but otherwise have completely different views. Regarding the question of the *truth and certainty* of human knowledge, one finds, according to Marx, a contradiction with Democritus, to the extent that, on the one hand, he ascribes truth to phenomena, but, on the other hand, also claims that the truth only exists in the hidden— and that can only mean, not in phenomena, since these are not hidden. Epicurus, in contrast, holds to the perception of the senses as the incontrovertible criterion of truth. This difference in their theoretical judgments corresponds to a difference in their *scientific practice*. Democritus is dissatisfied with philosophical reflection; he constantly explores new fields of knowledge and makes countless journeys in order to gather new knowledge. However, Epicurus is satisfied with philosophy and has contempt for

---

250. Due to damage to the paper, there is a loss of text in this letter. The word "political" is a plausible addition of the editors.

"positive sciences." The most important difference for Marx is their positions toward determinism. Whereas Democritus sees the world as ruled by *necessity* and dismisses chance as a human fiction, Epicurus disputes the necessity of what occurs and emphasizes that some things depend upon *chance*, while others depend upon our *arbitrariness*. Marx points out the consequences of this rejection of necessity for individual humans with a quote from Epicurus cited by Seneca: "It is a misfortune to live in necessity, but to live in necessity is not a necessity. On all sides many short and easy paths to freedom are open" (MECW 1: 43).

In explaining individual phenomena Epicurus thus does not claim a particular explanation; instead he regards everything as possible to the extent it does not contradict the perception of the senses. Epicurus emphasizes ataraxy (contentedness, peace of mind) as the aim of knowledge, which Marx sharpens to a point: "Epicurus confesses finally that his method of explaining aims only at the *ataraxy of self-consciousness, not at knowledge of nature in and for itself*" (MECW 1: 45), a difference that's about to become important.

In the second part of the dissertation, Marx turns to the "declination" of atomic movement. Democritus knew only two types of atomic movement: falling in a straight line and repulsion of the atoms. Epicurus introduces declination as the third type of atomic movement, a small deviation from falling in a straight line, a deviation that itself has no cause.

Marx interprets Epicurus so that with the fall in a straight line, he depicted the movement of a dependent body, which expressed the "materiality" of atoms. With declination, in contrast, the movement of an independent body not subordinate to necessity is depicted; this movement expresses the "form-determination" of atoms (ibid.: 48).

According to Marx, Lucretius was the only one among the ancient writers who understood the meaning of declination, stating he "is correct when he maintains that the declination breaks the fati foedera [the bonds of fate]" (ibid.: 49). Only on the basis of the declination of atomic movement can Epicurus dispute Democritus's deterministic view of the world,[251] and, this is the important point for Marx, only on the basis of the rejection of determinism is freedom possible. The declination of atomic movement is for Marx "not

251. For this reason, a few modern authors (Long/Sedley 2000: 60; Euringer 2003: 40) have constructed a connection between Epicurus's theory with the uncertainty principle of quantum mechanics. However, the relationship is similarly superficial, as the theory of atoms is. Epicurus consequently thinks that the material world is not deterministic to its end: if we regard the operation of non-material quantities as superstition, then indeterminacy must have a basis in the properties of the smallest building blocks of the material world, and this is

a particular determination which appears accidentally in Epicurean physics. On the contrary, the law it expresses goes through the whole Epicurean philosophy" (ibid.: 50).

How this "swerve" (*Ausbeugen*, Marx's German translation of declination) asserts itself is hinted at by the following paragraph: "The entire Epicurean philosophy swerves away from the restrictive mode of being wherever the concept of abstract individuality, self-sufficiency and negation of all relation to other things must be represented in its existence. The purpose of action is to be found therefore in abstracting, swerving away from pain and confusion, in ataraxy. Hence the good is the flight from evil, pleasure the swerving away from suffering. Finally, where abstract individuality appears in its highest freedom and independence, in its totality, there it follows that the being which is swerved away from, is *all being, for this reason, the gods swerve away from the world*, do not bother with it and live outside it" (ibid.: 50).

Marx sees in the question concerning the properties of atoms a difference between Democritus and Epicurus as important as that of declination. Marx interprets the sources in such a way that Democritus does not attribute any properties to atoms, and the properties of the world of appearances emerges from the different combinations of atoms (ibid.: 55). In contrast, Epicurus maintains, on the one hand, that the invariable atoms cannot possess any properties, since properties are variable, but, on the other hand, it is a necessary consequence to attach various properties to atoms, since the many atoms that repel each other must also be different. Marx sharpens this contradiction with the categories of Hegel's *Logic*: "Through the qualities the atom acquires an existence which contradicts its concept; it is assumed as an *externalised being different from its essence*" (ibid.: 54).

This contradiction between essence and existence, between form and material is, for Marx, in the case of the Epicurean atom, an inevitable, necessary contradiction: "Through the quality the atom is alienated from its concept, but at the same time is perfected in its construction. It is from repulsion and the ensuing conglomerations of the qualified atoms that the world of appearance now emerges. In this transition from the world of essence to the world of appearance, the contradiction in the concept of the atom clearly reaches its harshest realisation. For the atom is conceptually the absolute, essential form of nature. *This absolute form has now been degraded to absolute matter, to the formless substrate of the world of appearance*" (ibid.: 61). Marx thus expresses what he regards as a consequence of the Epicurean conception

---

expressed with the declination of atomic movement occurring without cause.

of the atom but he does not formulate his own natural philosophy, and certainly not any "dialectical atomism" as Schafer (2003: 129ff.) imputes to him.

Hegel had in his *Science of Logic* not simply juxtaposed essence and appearance; the section "Appearance" begins with the programmatic sentence "Essence must appear" (Hegel 2010: 418). And "Actuality" is "the unity of essence and concrete existence"; in it "shapeless essence and unstable appearance . . . have their truth" (Hegel 2010: 465). However, Hegel discusses the relation of being, essence, appearance, and actuality on a fundamental categorical level. Marx's argument operates on a different level. He uses the conceptual network crafted by Hegel to examine the inner logic of Epicurus's deliberations on atoms. As can be gleaned from the correspondence, Marx engaged intensively with Hegel's *Logic* in the years 1840–41. In the first (surviving) letter from Bauer to Marx, he writes of Marx's "logical lucubrations," which must have been referring to weaknesses in Hegel's doctrine of essence: "If you could work afresh on essence," wrote Bauer (December 11, 1839, MEGA III/1: 336). The fact that in later letters, both Bauer and Köppen assumed Marx wanted to write a treatise against Trendelenburg (March 31 and June 3, 1841, ibid.: 354, 361) also suggests an engagement with the *Logic*. Friedrich Adolf Trendelenburg (1802–1872) was from 1833 an associate professor and from 1837 an ordinary professor of philosophy at the University of Berlin. In 1840, he had published his *Logical Investigations*, in which among other things he had dealt critically with Hegel's *Logic* and understanding of science.

Behind Marx's application of Hegel's categories stood an intensive engagement with Hegel's *Logic*. However, that which we find in the dissertation is not Marx's own theory on the relation of essence and appearance, but rather the reconstruction of the inner logic of a foreign theory by means of Hegel's categories.[252]

Many years later, in his manuscripts on the critique of political economy, Marx again deployed the language of an essence standing opposite to appearance, which was frequently understood as a reference to a sort of hidden world, a reference that was regarded by critics as a relapse into pre-scientific metaphysics and by adherents as a higher form of knowledge. Against this, Marx's dissertation makes clear that his consideration of the relation

---

252. Fenves (1986) also emphasizes the importance of the discussion of the relation between essence and appearance in Marx's dissertation. However, he sees in the difference between Democritus and Epicurus examined by Marx merely a masked juxtaposition of the views represented by Kant and Hegel, whereby Kant is supposed to stand for empirical science and Hegel for its rejection—a rather unconvincing construct overall. More interesting is McIvor's

between essence and appearance, even in this early period, was considerably more complex than such simplifying conceptions assume.

Yet, in his dissertation, Marx doesn't just bring categories of Hegel's *Logic* into play, but also that of "self-consciousness." He thus sees, as did Epicurus, repulsion as a consequence of declination. It is the only way that abstract-individual atoms can relate to one another. Marx thus draws the conclusion: *"Repulsion is the first form of self-consciousness."* To the extent the atom refers to itself, in that it refers (through repulsion) to other atoms, repulsion has the general shape of self-consciousness—"It corresponds therefore to that self-consciousness which conceives itself as immediate-being, as abstractly individual" (MECW 1: 52). The fact that Epicurus saw the "covenant" in politics and "friendship" in the social sphere as the "highest good," Marx thus interprets as dealing with "more concrete forms of the repulsion" (MECW 1: 53).

Later, Marx writes that the atom is the "natural form of abstract, individual self-consciousness" (ibid.: 65). He quite obviously uses the Epicurean atom here as a metaphor for social relations based upon the interrelation of isolated individuals. A further statement on the atom also has to be seen against this background. Since the atom "presupposed as abstractly individual and complete, cannot actualise itself as the idealising and pervading power," Marx concludes that "abstract individuality is freedom from being, not freedom in being" (ibid.: 62). What does that mean? Human existence is relationship, interaction between humans. If human beings exist as "abstract individuality," then they have no relationship as human beings to each other; they are thus "free" of human existence.

With "self-consciousness" as an interpretive grid, Marx attempts in the final section of the second part of his dissertation to clarify an apparent anomaly in Epicurus's natural philosophy: his treatment of "meteors," whereby Epicurus's usage of the term refers to all celestial phenomena. Whereas in the entirety of Greek philosophy, heavenly bodies and their movements were seen as eternal and immutable, Epicurus disputes precisely that. Aristotle had already pointed out that humans tend to connect the immortal with the eternal, and therefore believed the immortal gods would have their seat in

---

(2008) attempt to discern in the way Marx uses Hegel's categories a certain affinity with more recent interpretations of Hegel, above all those of Robert Pippin and Terry Pinkard, who have caused something of a stir in the English-speaking world by rejecting long-held predominant notions about Hegel as a metaphysicist who fell behind Kant. Finelli (2016) deals extensively with Marx's dissertation. In the second volume, I will discuss his thesis that the writings of the young Marx can be interpreted as an attempt at a—failed—"patricide" against the intellectual father Hegel.

eternal heaven. For Epicurus, the greatest confusion of the soul arises from such a belief: "Aristotle reproached the ancients for their belief that heaven required the support of Atlas. . . ."[253] Epicurus, on the other hand, blames those who believe that man needs heaven. He finds the Atlas by whom heaven is supported in human stupidity and superstition" (ibid.: 68). Epicurus thus did not justify his rejection of prevailing notions about heavenly bodies on the basis of empirical insights, but on the basis of the effects of these notions: with them, one would throw oneself into the arms of myth and superstition (that of astrology). Marx makes the statement more pointedly: "Since eternity of the heavenly bodies would disturb the ataraxy of self-consciousness, it is a necessary, a stringent consequence that they are not eternal" (ibid.: 70).

But this priority of the ataraxy of self-consciousness is for Marx not yet the whole point of Epicurus' argument. Epicurus presented atoms as the immutable, independent building blocks of the world. The eternal heavenly bodies, which unlike dependent bodies do not move in a straight line but like independent bodies in a curved orbit, are, according to Marx, "the atoms become real" (ibid.: 70). But instead of celebrating this result, Epicurus "feels that here his previous categories break down, that the method of his theory becomes different" (ibid.: 71). What has happened?

Epicurus' entire philosophy of nature, according to Marx, is traversed by the contradiction between essence and existence, between form and matter. In the heavenly bodies, this contradiction is extinguished, the antagonistic moments are reconciled. With this reconciliation, matter ceases "to be affirmation of abstract self-consciousness" (ibid.). On the basis of the reconciliation of matter and form, matter in the heavenly bodies has ceased to be "abstract individuality"; it is now "universality." Marx concludes: "In the meteors, therefore, abstract-individual self-consciousness is met by its contradiction, shining in its materialised form, the universal which has become existence and nature. Hence it recognises in the meteors its deadly enemy, and it [abstract-individual self-consciousness] ascribes to them, as Epicurus does, all the anxiety and confusion of men. Indeed, the anxiety and dissolution of the abstract-individual is precisely the universal" (ibid.).

The meteors thus do not disturb the ataraxy of self-consciousness; rather, they disturb the "ataraxy of abstract-individual self-consciousness." Epicurus's concentration upon abstract-individual self-consciousness has an enormous disadvantage, since "all true and real science is done away with [aufgehoben] inasmuch as individuality does not rule within the nature of

---

253. According to the legend, Atlas, a brother of Prometheus, had to hold up the firmament at its westernmost point.

things themselves," but everything is also done away with that which "is tran-scendentally related to human consciousness and therefore belongs to the imagining mind" (such as religion and superstition). These transcendental powers are subordinated to "abstract-universal self-consciousness," that self-consciousness that grasps itself as part of a divine universality. Marx there-fore arrives at the judgment that Epicurus is "the greatest representative of Greek Enlightenment" (ibid.: 73).[254]

Establishing Epicurus as a representative of Enlightenment against the prevailing philosophical doctrine, including that of Hegel, and thus reha-bilitating his critique of religion, was probably for Marx the most politically important result of his work. In the final paragraph, he summarizes the yield for the history of philosophy of the comparison of the philosophies of nature of Democritus and Epicurus: "In *Epicurus*, therefore, *atomistics* with all its contradictions has been carried through and completed as *the natural sci-ence of self- consciousness*. This self-consciousness under the form of abstract individuality is an absolute principle. Epicurus has thus carried atomistics to its final conclusion, which is its dissolution and conscious opposition to the universal. For *Democritus*, on the other hand, the *atom* is only *the gen-eral objective expression of the empirical investigation of nature as a whole*" (MECW 1: 73).

God and Immortality

According to the table of contents, the appendix to Marx's dissertation, "Critique of Plutarch's Polemic Against the Theology of Epicurus," was sup-posed to encompass two main parts, "I. The Relationship of Man to God" and "II. Individual Immortality" (MECW 1: 33). Notes and sources exist only for the first part, which is made clear by the subheadings incorporated into the notes section. Since there were still empty pages in the notebook containing these notes, one can assume that the notes for the second part of the appendix were not lost but were not made available to the copyist.

---

254. Despite this positive evaluation, one can hardly say, as for example Burns (2000: 22) or Baronovitch (1992) do, that Marx identifies with Epicurus's position. The critique of merely abstract-individual self-consciousness as Epicurus's starting point is too clear. For Baronovitch, this identification also serves to accuse Marx of "moral hypocrisy." Since Epicurus urged his followers to obey the law, but the laws of this time were based upon the existence of slavery, Epicurus had supposedly approved of slavery. And now Marx was invoking Epicurus (Baronovitch 1992: 165ff.). The attempt has often been made to attribute an intellectual responsibility on Marx's part for the atrocities of Stalinism. But accusing him of responsibility for ancient slavery by way of Epicurus is a true innovation.

That Marx during the process of copying or shortly thereafter worked on the appendix is made clear by the fact that the last footnote to the first part of the appendix (and therefore the last surviving footnote of the entire text) was not written by the copyist, but rather by Marx. But if the appendix was not yet finished, then it was also not submitted with the dissertation. In terms of content, this would not have been a problem, since the appendix contributes nothing to the philosophical-historical topic of the work and the question regarding the difference between the Epicurean and Democritean philosophies of nature.

In the foreword, which was probably also not sent to Jena, Marx characterizes Plutarch's polemic as "representative of an espèce [species], in that it most strikingly presents in itself the relation of the theologising intellect to philosophy" (ibid.: 30), which makes clear that Marx saw parallels to the theologically motivated attacks on Hegel's philosophy in the 1830s. Marx leaves no doubt about his own position in this dispute; he does not consider it possible, as Hegel claimed, to mediate between philosophy and religion: "Philosophy makes no secret of it. The confession of Prometheus: 'In simple words, I hate the pack of gods,' is its own confession, its own aphorism against all heavenly and earthly gods . . ." (MECW 1: 30). How Marx wished to argue in the appendix emerges from the third of his *Notebooks on Epicurean Philosophy*, where he deals extensively with Plutarch's critique of the theological notions of Epicurus.

Whereas Epicurus understands human beings' fear of God to be something bad, which Marx affirms in one of the notes in the appendix with corresponding quotations from Holbach's *The System of Nature* (MECW 1: 102), Plutarch argues that this fear protects humans from committing evil. Marx retorts in the third notebook: "What is then the essence of the empirically evil? That the individual shuts himself off from his eternal nature in his empirical nature; but is that not the same as to shut his eternal nature out of himself, to apprehend it in the form of persistent isolation in self, in the form of the empirical, and hence to consider it as an empirical god outside self? . . . In this relation God is merely what is common to all the consequences that empirical evil actions can have" (MECW 1: 448). This makes clear that Marx's critique of religion points in a similar direction to that published by Feuerbach in the spring of 1841 in *The Essence of Christianity*: the essence of God is merely the externalized, autonomized essence of man. That is not to say that Marx had already anticipated Feuerbach's critique. That which Feuerbach had clearly worked through and reflected upon in many of its consequences is a mere inkling for Marx. What Marx is concerned with here is not the elaboration of the implied concept of God, but rather the proof that Plutarch doesn't say anything other than what Epicurus states without any reference to God: "Do not act unjustly, so as not to go in continual fear of being punished" (MECW 1: 449).

In a longer note to the first part of the appendix (it is the final footnote of the manuscript in Marx's handwriting), Marx deals with the proofs of God. First, apparently in agreement he quotes from the early writings of Schelling, who in the meantime had become a Christian reactionary: "But he is not a *weak* intellect who does not know an objective God, but he who *wants* to know one." Marx comments: "Herr Schelling should at any rate be advised to give again some thought to his first writings" (ibid.: 103).

For the proofs of God, Marx takes the ontological proof already criticized by Kant as an example. This proof states that one can conclude from the idea of a perfect being its existence, since without existence, this being cannot be thought to be perfect. Marx sees two possibilities here: either this proof of God is a "hollow tautology," since "that which I conceive for myself is a real concept for me," so that with this proof, the existence of every God in which I believe can be proved. This consideration is not sophistry: "Did not the ancient Moloch reign? Was not the Delphic Apollo a real power in the life of the Greeks? Kant's critique means nothing in this respect" (ibid.: 104). Why? If an act of imagination is widely shared, then this act of imagination becomes a social power. However, the inverse is also the case: if one brought a foreign god to Greece, one would be shown that this god does not exist. Marx concludes: "That which a particular country is for particular alien gods, the country of reason is for God in general, a region in which he ceases to exist" (MECW 1: 104). In the "country of reason" as well, one could just as little prove the existence of God as refute it, Kant was right to that extent. But social behavior would have changed, God would no longer be a universally shared notion, and to that extent he would cease to exist. With this deliberation, Marx stands on the threshold of a discussion of religion that is no longer merely epistemological, but social, and he addresses for the first time the idea of a rationally arranged world. However, neither are pursued. Instead, Marx considers the second possibility: "Such proofs are proofs of the existence of essential human self-consciousness . . . take for example the ontological proof. Which being is immediate when made the subject of thought? Self-consciousness. Taken in this sense all proofs of the existence of God are proofs of his nonexistence" (MECW 1: 104).

In the third notebook, there's also a critique of Plutarch's belief in immortality, which was supposed to constitute the second part of the appendix. Plutarch's most important argument is the fear of death, from which a striving for an eternal existence, independent of its content, results. Marx counters this by noting that Epicurus advanced the same doctrine of immortality, but that he was consistent enough to call the matter by its name, "to say that the animate returns to the atomistic form" (MECW 1: 455); that is, the soul dissolves into individual atoms, and only they have an eternal existence.

Plutarch is not only inferior to Epicurus argumentatively; he doesn't even know what he is doing, because he constantly affirms Epicurus where he wants to refute him. Marx can therefore summarize: "Plutarch everywhere says something else than what he means to say and at bottom also means something else than what he says. That is in general the relationship of common consciousness to philosophical consciousness." (MECW 1: 457)

Political-Philosophical Determination of Position

It's been frequently discussed whether Marx in his dissertation "still" promoted philosophical idealism or "already" endorsed materialism. Underlying such questions is the notion that there is a well-defined idealistic continent and an equally well-defined materialist continent, and that the young Marx, as if on a ferry, moved from one continent to the other, so that one can constantly check how far he'd already come. For Marx himself, these questions play no role in the dissertation.[255] Instead of introducing a provisional and to some extent arbitrary concept of materialism against which the dissertation is measured, it appears more sensible to wait until we come to the point at which Marx himself explicitly promotes materialist positions. Only then does it become possible to reconstruct his understanding of materialism and retrospectively pursue the question of when it emerged.

Marx made no attempt to locate himself within the relationship between idealism and materialism, but he took a decisive position regarding the disputes conducted in 1839–40 concerning Hegel's philosophy. Marx, himself, had had no chance anymore of becoming an orthodox Hegelian; he came too late for that. His reception of Hegel beginning in 1837 developed in the middle of a critical discussion about Hegel. However, as we shall soon see, Marx tried to distance himself from the various factions critical of Hegel.

As depicted in this chapter, the Young Hegelian authors, Arnold Ruge first and foremost, criticized a subjective "accommodation" by Hegel of political conditions. Marx deals with this accusation in a longer footnote referring to the final section of the first part of the dissertation, which hasn't survived. It's possible that in those passages not handed down Marx addressed the

---

255. Kondylis (1987: 25) correctly points out that Epicurus's materialism was important to Marx not in an ontological sense of the priority of matter or mind, but primarily as an argument against religion.

difference between Epicurus's consciousness and what his philosophy actually expressed. Corresponding observations are found in the seventh notebook (MECW 1: 505); and in 1858, Marx wrote to Lassalle that he was still convinced that Epicurus's "complete system" was "only implicitly present in his work, not consciously as a system" (MECW 40: 316). In the seventh notebook, there is also an initial determination of the relation between the personality of the philosopher and the history of philosophy: "Philosophical historiography is not concerned either with comprehending the personality, be it even the spiritual personality of the philosopher as, in a manner of speaking, the focus and the image of his system. . . . Its concern is to distinguish in each system the determinations themselves, the actual crystallisations pervading the whole system, from the proofs, the justifications in argument, the self-presentation of the philosophers as they know themselves. . . . This *critical element* in the presentation of a philosophy which has its place in history is absolutely indispensable in order scientifically to expound a system in connection with its historical existence" (MECW 1: 506).

Evidently on this basis, Marx—in a footnote of the dissertation—criticizes as philosophically insufficient the thesis that Hegel had adapted his philosophy to political conditions: "Also in relation to Hegel it is mere ignorance on the part of his pupils, when they explain one or the other determination of his system by his desire for accommodation and the like, hence, in one word, explain it in terms of *morality.*" What matters to Marx is something quite different from such a moral accusation: "It is quite thinkable for a philosopher to fall into one or another apparent inconsistency through some sort of accommodation; he himself may be conscious of it. But what he is not conscious of, is the possibility that this apparent accommodation has its deepest roots in an inadequacy or in an inadequate formulation of his principle itself. Suppose therefore that a philosopher has really accommodated himself, then his pupils must explain from his *inner essential consciousness* that which *for him himself* had the form of *an exoteric consciousness.* In this way, that which appears as progress of conscience is at the same time progress of knowledge" (MECW 1: 84).

At least with regard to the methodical starting point for the critique of Hegel, of looking for the possibility of accommodation in the system itself, Marx was far ahead of Ruge and approached the level that Feuerbach (1839b) had already reached, without copying it. Feuerbach had not yet formulated the methodological basis of his critique as clearly as Marx does here. However, the implementation of the critique of Hegel in terms of content was far more advanced in Feuerbach's work than in Marx's.

Marx did not remain standing at this methodological reflection. He attempted to order the development of the Hegelian school in a general

schema, the rough structure of which he had already outlined in the notebooks. There, Marx argued in the passages that Ernst Günther Schmidt identified as the introduction to the initial dissertation project, that philosophy,
which had become a closed totality, must also turn outward again, toward
the world (MECW 1: 491). This transition is now conceived as a "transition
from discipline to freedom" and is provided with an extraordinarily bold, not
to say foolhardy generalization: "It is a psychological law that the theoretical
mind, once liberated in itself, turns into practical energy, and, leaving the
shadowy empire of Amenthes as *will* turns itself against the reality of the
world existing without it." But what leads to this "practical energy"? "But
the practice of philosophy is itself *theoretical*. It is the *critique* that measures
the individual existence by the essence, the particular reality by the Idea"
(MECW 1: 85).

Many interpreters (for example Z. B. Kondylis 1987: 19, 80n17) heard the
voice of Bruno Bauer in this. Bauer had written to Marx: "Theory is now
the strongest praxis, and we cannot at all predict in what great sense it will
become practical" (MEGA III/1: 355). However, this sentence stems from
Bauer's letter of March 31, 1841, when Marx had probably long since written his footnote. Above all, Bauer speaks of "now" being when this is the
case, whereas Marx speaks in a generalizing way of "the" practice of philosophy and adds: "But this immediate realisation of philosophy is in its deepest essence afflicted with contradictions" (MECW 1: 85). So Marx does not
speak of his own praxis, his own dealings with philosophy, as Bauer does;
Marx is still describing the activity of "the theoretical mind, once liberated in
itself." And here he sees the contradiction in the turn to the world that makes
philosophical reflection impossible: "As the world becomes philosophical,
philosophy also becomes worldly, that its realisation is also its loss, that what
it struggles against on the outside is its own inner deficiency" (ibid.).

But this contradiction is only the "objective" side of the matter; it also has a
"subjective" side. For the "intellectual carriers," the "individual self-consciousness" of the process applies: "Their liberation of the world from un-philosophy
is at the same time their own liberation from the philosophy" (ibid.).

Marx sees this "duality of philosophical self-consciousness" at work in
two sides "utterly opposed" to each other, the "liberal party" on one side
and "positive philosophy" on the other: "The act of the first side is critique,
hence precisely that turning-toward-the-outside of philosophy; the act of the
second is the attempt to philosophise, hence the turning-in-toward-itself of
philosophy. This second side knows that the inadequacy is immanent in philosophy, while the first understands it as inadequacy of the world which has
to be made philosophical" (ibid.: 86).

In juxtaposing the liberal party and positive philosophy, Marx refers to the development of post-Hegelian philosophy. In this respect, it's remarkable that he does not get involved with the distinction between "left" and "right" Hegelians introduced by Strauß in his *Streitschriften* from 1837, nor with the one arising in the dispute between Leo and Ruge between "Old" and "Young" Hegelians. In the 1830s and 1840s in Germany, "liberal" was synonymous with opposition against the authoritarian state and with the demand for a constitution and parliament. When Marx speaks here of the "liberal party," he doesn't just have the Young Hegelian authors in mind, which is assumed in a large part of the literature. These Young Hegelians are certainly also meant, but Marx sorts them into a broader spectrum. It's possible that he regarded the division into Old and Young Hegelians as suspect, since people like Michelet and Rosenkranz stood on the liberal side.

Marx probably saw as representatives of "positive philosophy" those groups that Michelet, in his *History of the Last Systems*, described as "pseudo-Hegelians"; alongside Franz von Baader (1765–1841), who developed a strongly religious philosophy, are primarily the "speculative theists" such as Christian Hermann Weiße, Immanuel Fichte, and Karl Philipp Fischer, who partially referred to Hegel, but mainly wanted to go beyond him theologically. In his presentation, Michelet emphasizes that they connected to "positive" revelation and sought a "positive surplus" with regard to Hegel (Michelet 1838: 632, 646). Feuerbach had subjected this current to a devastating critique with his article "Toward a Critique of Positive Philosophy," while at the same time introducing the term "positive philosophy" (Feuerbach 1838).[256] As already noted in this chapter, Marx had engaged in greater detail with at least Fischer (see the letter from Bauer from March 1, 1840, MEGA III/1: 341).

Marx criticized both parties, regarding them as standing in a sort of mirror image relationship to each other, with both misunderstanding their own actions: "Each of these parties does exactly what the other one wants to do and what it itself does not want to do." (MECW 1: 86). What does that mean? The liberal party that wishes to turn toward the world clings to philosophy, it continues to philosophize, even when referring to the "world," that is, to political conditions. Positive philosophy, in contrast, which wished to

---

256. Breckman (1999: 266ff.) is of the opinion that Marx was already strongly influenced by Feuerbach at the time of his dissertation. It's probable that Marx knew Feuerbach's article on "positive philosophy." But the further correspondences that Breckman believes to have made out appear to be very speculative. Long before Breckman, Breuer (1954: 67ff.) had also claimed that Feuerbach, through his text *Death and Immortality* (it's not clear if Marx had ever seen a copy), had a lasting influence on Marx's dissertation. Also similar: Bockmühl (1961: 120ff.).

philosophize, lost philosophy, and not to theology, but rather—according to the accusation Feuerbach made of it—to "the madness of religious fanaticism, which regards itself alone as being in possession of the only true God, the only beatifying idea" (Feuerbach 1838: 2337). For Marx, this results in a qualitative difference between the two parties: "The first, however, is, despite its inner contradiction, conscious of both its principle in general and its goal. In the second party the inversion [*Verkehrtheit*], we may well say the madness [*Verrücktheit*], appears as such. As to the content: only the liberal party achieves real progress, because it is the party of the concept" (MECW 1: 86).

If we regard the Young Hegelians, as expounded upon in this chapter, not as a school but rather as a current initially emanating from Hegel that radicalized itself both philosophically and politically, then dissolved in the 1840s before it was able to form its own paradigm, then Bauer and Marx undoubtedly belonged to this current in 1841. But if we apply a narrower concept of Young Hegelianism, it becomes difficult to classify Marx as part of it. In any case, it's remarkable that in his analysis of the political-philosophical conflicts, Marx does not count himself on the Young Hegelian side. Bauer's statements in his correspondence with Marx also match this distance. Arnold Ruge is regarded with a certain sympathy, but a considerable measure of critique already resonates in his and Bauer's plans to found their own journal. That idea expressed the fact that the *Hallische Jahrbücher* were no longer enough for Bauer and Marx, and if the new journal would have succeeded, that would have been a serious blow for Ruge (see in particular Bauer's letter from March 31, 1841, MEGA III/1: 354).

In the literature, the question has been much discussed whether Marx borrowed his concept of self-consciousness from Bauer or whether there were already initial differences between them.[257] What seems more fundamental, however, is the question of what made the concept of self-consciousness so attractive for both Bauer and Marx. In the late 1830s, Hegel's philosophy was regarded by many Young Hegelians as, on the one hand, too self-contained, not open enough to new, above all political, dynamics, and, on the other, a surplus of the general was seen in it; the subjective individual played a subordinate role. Despite all critique, however, Hegel's

---

257. McLellan (1973: 21ff.) and Rosen (1977: 148ff.) are prominent representatives of the view that Bauer had a strong influence on Marx's dissertation. Stedman Jones (2016: 92) also accepts the thesis that it was Bauer's concept of self-consciousness that Marx used in the dissertation. In contrast, Cornu (1954: 163) and Thom (1986: 114) highlight the independence of Marx with regard to Bauer's "more individualistic" position. However, both Cornu and Thom have the tendency to view Bauer from the perspective Marx formulated in *The Holy Family*, that is,

philosophy was not to be discarded; it still served as a guideline. The concept of self-consciousness, which was part of the debate in any event, due to the dispute over Hegel's philosophy of religion, appeared to offer a way out. It displaced absolute spirit, with its theological ambiguities, from its central position and enabled the individual to understand, but not as a *mere* individual, but rather as an individual *to the extent that it shared in the universal*, as explicated by Bauer in the first volume of his text on the synoptics (Bauer 1841a: 221). In that regard, the philosophy of self-consciousness was, in 1840–41, at least not a regression into Fichte's philosophy of the "I," but rather an initial attempt at post-Hegelian Enlightenment. What drove history was not the movement of an abstract-universal reason; its motor was transferred directly to human beings themselves. The pathos of Marx's foreword to the dissertation, the reference to Prometheus, and the demand to recognize self-consciousness as "the highest divinity" (MECW 1: 262) make clear what a radical step he saw in this reference to human beings by means of self-consciousness. However, the human being grasped in terms of the concept of self-consciousness still remained largely abstract; self-consciousness was merely the first step in this post-Hegelian Enlightenment. In the next volume, we will see how Feuerbach, Stirner, and finally Marx and Engels would proceed further in this direction and accuse each other of still remaining imprisoned in abstract philosophy.

Why Jena?

Marx had studied since 1836 in Berlin, but he submitted his dissertation to the University of Jena, which he had never attended and which he also did not visit for the doctoral exam procedure. Marx earned his doctorate *in absentia*. There are no statements about the reasons that led him to do so; we are forced to reply upon conjecture.

On the basis of the preface being dated "March 1841," we can assume

---

Bauer expounds Hegel from "Fichte's point of view" (MECW 4: 139). Whether this applies to the Bauer of 1844 we will have to discuss; in any case, it does not apply to the Bauer of 1840–41. Waser (1994) as well, who disputes Bauer's overwhelming influence on Marx, bases himself on a sometimes idiosyncratic interpretation of Bauer's writings. In my book *The Science of Value*, first published in 1991, I also assumed that Marx had adopted the conception of self-consciousness from Bauer (Heinrich 2017: 90), a position that now appears questionable. One cannot allow oneself to be deceived by the triumphalist tone of Marx's foreword; the use of the term *self-consciousness* in the dissertation is considerably more cautious than the foreword leads one to expect. I will discuss the differences between Marx and Bauer in the second volume, in dealing with Bauer's *Trumpet*.

that Marx had finished his dissertation in March of 1841 or shortly before. Whether he had attempted to obtain his doctorate in Berlin is not known. If he had attempted it, he must have known that he had been ex-matriculated on December 3, 1840. This emerges from the university registry (see Kliem 1988: 60). Marx had enrolled at the University of Berlin in October of 1836 and according to university statutes "academic citizenship" ended after four years (ibid.: 61) unless one applied for an extension, which Marx had obviously not done. Marx was probably not aware that he had been ex-matriculated for many months in March of 1841. However, this ex-matriculation was not a problem: in exchange for paying a fee of five talers total, he could have reenrolled. A doctorate in Berlin would have been possible.

It has been speculated repeatedly that Marx did not wish to obtain his doctorate in Berlin because, after the royal succession, Hegelianism was no longer well received in Prussia and Marx would have encountered professors who would have been hostile to a dissertation with an orientation to Hegel (for example, Cornu 1954: 182; Thom 1986: 109; Kanda 2010: 156). This deliberation is not very convincing. In the spring of 1841, nothing had changed as far as the composition of the faculty of philosophy, and Marx could have stuck to Gabler, Hegel's successor, which Bruno Bauer had already recommended to him in March of 1840 (MEGA III/1: 342). Furthermore, Marx had not yet emerged publicly; his doctorate would not have been a political issue attracting greater attention.

What appears more plausible than these political considerations are the purely practical reasons that spoke for Jena and against Berlin. In Jena, the doctoral tuition fees were considerably lower than in Berlin, and Marx had little money. Further, there were the exam conditions in Berlin: Marx would have had to translate his dissertation into Latin. The oral examination would have been conducted at least partially in Latin and would have required some preparation time. After Marx had finished his dissertation considerably later than planned, he probably did not want to wait even longer for the exam. His family and Jenny also appear to have grown impatient. Bruno Bauer's remark in a letter from March 31, 1841, hints at that: "If only I could be in Trier to present the matter to your people" (MEGA III/1: 354). That Marx was primarily concerned with a speedy conclusion to the process also emerges in a letter to Oskar Ludwig Bernhard Wolff (1799–1851), who taught contemporary literature in Jena. Marx requested that he should ask for a quick transmission of the doctoral diploma (MECW 1: 380).[258]

---

258. Since the letter is rather formal, Marx does not appear to have been closely acquainted with Wolff. How the contact with Wolff came about, we don't know. Some further information

One could obtain a doctorate at the philosophical faculty of the University of Jena, as one could at a few other German universities, without an oral examination "in absentia." However, this obtained in Jena merely for the title of "doctor of philosophy," and not for the more highly rated title of a "doctor of philosophy and master of the liberal arts" (*Doctor der Philosophie und Magister der Freyen Künste*) for which Marx had apparently striven. See the communication from the dean, Bachmann, from April 13, 1841 (Lange et al. 1983: 201f.).

The "in absentia" doctorate was originally conceived for candidates who were already working or had already submitted a scholarly work and wished to retroactively obtain a doctor title. When, toward the end of the eighteenth century, smaller universities experienced financial difficulties, "in absentia" doctorates increasingly became a source of income for professors. Apart from a few celebrities at the major universities, most professors received a relatively small salary. They were therefore reliant upon lecture fees paid by their students, who were not numerous at small universities, and upon the doctoral fees. However, cases of abuse also increased with "in absentia" doctorates, so that over the course of the nineteenth century, mistrust of this type of doctorate increased and it was gradually abolished (see Rasche 2007).

With regard to the duration of the process, Marx would not be disappointed. On April 6, he sent his dissertation along with cover letter, certificates, and curriculum vitae to the dean of the philosophical faculty, Carl Friedrich Bachmann (1784–1865), and his doctoral diploma was issued on April 15. On April 13, Bachmann had written to his faculty colleagues that "in Herr Carl Heinrich Marx from Trier" he was presenting "a very worthy candidate"; his work testified "to intelligence and perspicacity as much as to erudition, for which reason I regard the candidate as preeminently worthy" (MECW 1: 705). Through their signatures, his colleagues immediately declared their approval of the doctorate, so that Bachmann was able to record a "fiat promotio" (he should be graduated) for Marx on the same day in the dean's registry (Lange et al. 1983: 200).

Among the faculty were, among others, the historian Heinrich Luden (1778–1847), whose work of history Marx had studied in 1837, as well as Jakob Friedrich Fries (1773–1843), who twenty years before had contributed strongly to the then-emerging *Völkisch* anti-Semitism and was a declared opponent of Hegel's philosophy. It's improbable that the members of the faculty had subjected Marx's work to a thorough examination on April 13; more

---

on Wolff, as well as on the situation at the University of Jena during this time, is found in Bauer/Pester (2012).

likely they relied upon the dean's judgment. However, it's quite possible that a member of the faculty took Marx's dissertation home for closer study and did not give it back, which would explain its absence from the university records. Possible candidates in particular would be the two representatives of classical philology, Ferdinand Gotthelf Hand (1786–1851) and Heinrich Carl Abraham Eichstätt (1771–1848), and maybe the philosopher Ernst Christian Gottlieb Reinhold (1793–1855).

Probably the only one who looked at the dissertation in detail was the dean, Bachmann. He had emerged a few years earlier as a vehement critic of Hegel. Ludwig Feuerbach had confronted him in a detailed review. We do not know whether Bachmann noticed the Hegelian references of the dissertation, since he made no statements on the substance of the work. However, Schmidt (1977: 284) points out that Bachmann's evaluation "eminently worthy" (*vorzüglich würdig*) was extraordinarily good: other dissertations from the summer semester of 1841 were accepted with evaluations such as "meets requirements" or "worthy." One may assume that in examining the dissertation, Bachmann primarily made sure that the faculty would not discredit itself by accepting an obviously inadequate work. Even a superficial review would reveal rather quickly that this would not be the case with Marx's work, that it was based on a detailed study of the sources and an original argument. To conclude from the merely superficial examination of Marx's dissertation that it was of low quality, as for example Rasche (2007: 322) suggests, is an obvious logical error. It's possible that a bad work could be accepted in the case of a superficial examination, but it in no way follows that every superficially examined work must therefore have been bad.

The doctoral diploma written in Latin that Marx received is a nice example of late-feudal, hierarchical presentation. The invocation of God is followed in decreasing type size by the names of Emperor Ferdinand I, who in 1557 granted the privilege of founding a university, the current Grand Duke of Saxony, Weimar and Eisenach, Karl Friedrich, who formally functioned as the "Rector Magnificentissimus" of the university, the "Prorector Magnificus" (the actual university rector) Ernst Reinhold, and the Dean of the Faculty of Philosophy, Carl Friedrich Bachmann, whereby the last two were listed with all academic titles and memberships in scholarly societies. Finally, and in the smallest type, there followed the name of the doctoral recipient.[259]

---

259. The doctoral diploma is reproduced in MECW 1: 702. A German translation is printed in Lange u.a. (1983: 204).

Marx probably didn't care what the diploma looked like. He had finally finished his studies. A good month after he had received his diploma, he departed Berlin at the end of May 1841—for Trier.[260]

---

260. It emerges from Köppen's letter of June 3, 1841, that Marx had departed more than a week earlier (MEGA III/1: 360).

How Is Biographical Writing Possible Today? On the Methodology of a Marx Biography

The life of a person is something different than a biography written by that person or by somebody else. A biography is only capable of conveying an incomplete picture of a life, since the available sources are more or less fragmentary. Biographical presentation is never independent of the interests of the author, his or her personal views, and views conditioned by the times in which the author lives. And beyond that, what one expects of a biography, what counts as a good or adequate biography, has changed again and again. Therefore, the question of how biographical writing is possible and meaningful today is anything but trivial.

CRITIQUE OF TRADITIONAL BIOGRAPHY

In 1930, Siegfried Kracauer characterized what was then a boom period of biographical writing as a "new bourgeois art form." He considered it as an expression of the flight of the bourgeoisie from the dissolution of the supposedly autonomous individual and the fracture points in the social system. Although this dissolution led in literature to the "crisis of the novel," a place of retreat for the articulation of the individual was found in biography, since here, the objectivity of representation appeared to be guaranteed by the historical importance of what was represented. Nonetheless, for Kracauer, the end of biographical writing had not been reached. In the essay, he highlighted Trotsky's biographical work, which, unlike the flood of fashionable biographies, was not concerned with evading knowledge of the contemporary situation, but rather with revealing it. A few years later, Kracauer himself presented a biography that went far beyond a mere description of a life,

Jacques Offenbach and the Paris of His Time (1937), a work he introduced in the preface as a "social biography."

What Kracauer had in view with his critique was the surge of *biographical belles lettres*. This kind of writing still enjoys uninterrupted popularity today. With more or less substantiated knowledge of the person being portrayed and his or her era, and enriched with a few psychological schemata, an image is crafted that usually claims to reveal the "essence" of the subject as well as the reasons for his success or failure. The available sources are usually used very selectively, and the image presented, whether positive or negative, is not called into question by contradictory material. The sources used are eagerly supplemented by the empathy of the writers and the writers' ability to "put" themselves "in the place" of the person being portrayed. Not infrequently, the subject's inner life is described in such detail and in such a lively manner, it was as if the biographer had conducted conversations with the person lasting hours. Correspondingly, many of the statements of such biographies are simply not verifiable. Often, because the presentation is supposed to be "reader-friendly," readers are spared exact references to sources, and the literature used is merely named in a literature list. One can no longer distinguish between what results from the "compassion" of the biographer and from a plausible or less plausible interpretation of the sources.

The following is not concerned with *belles lettres* forms of biographical writing, but rather with *scholarly* biographies. Biography has existed as a literary genre since antiquity; scholarly biography based upon documented and critically evaluated sources first took shape at the beginning of the nineteenth century. Whereas in antiquity and the Middle Ages, biographies were primarily collections of the "deeds" of the person portrayed, whereby sources were dealt with rather uncritically, this changed during the period of the Enlightenment. Alongside deeds, the inner development of the person also entered the picture; the question was pursued as to which personal qualities made these deeds possible. Goethe went a step further by conceiving of the developmental history of the person not only as something internal, but as historically conditioned. As he wrote in the preface to his autobiographical reflections, *Poetry and Truth*, he described "the main object of biography": "To exhibit the man in relation to the features of his time, and to show to what extent they have opposed or favored his progress; what view of mankind and the world he has formed from them, and how far he himself, if an artist, poet, or author, may externally reflect them." From this dependence upon temporal conditions, Goethe concludes that "any person born ten years earlier or later would have been quite a different being, both as regards his own culture and his influence on others" (Goethe 2008: 57).

The beginning of scholarly biography coincided in Germany with the rise of those historical-scientific tendencies that are referred to collectively as "historicism." It was assumed that human actions were determined by ideas accepted or posited by individuals. Ideas were regarded as the driving force of historical development. Within this framework, an outstanding role was played by those great men who, according to a famous statement by the historian Heinrich von Treitschke (1834–1896), "made history."[1] Thus the biographies of these men (and a few women) acquired an important value, since they served to "understand" the efficacy of the central ideas that determined the actions of these great historical personages. Wilhelm Dilthey (1833–1911), who strove for a systematic justification of the humanities based on historicism, gave biography a central position for historical knowledge. He saw the "fundamental cell of history" (Dilthey 2002: 265) in the course of a life. He formulated a hermeneutic requirement for biographers: to "relive" the ideas and impetuses of the subject by "empathizing," and therefore to "understand." What an individual could do for himself—reflect upon the course of his own life, understand his own realization of purposes from which his "life course" (ibid.: 267) emerges—was to be transferred to another course of life; biography then would emerge as a "literary form of understanding other lives" (ibid.: 266).

A large part of the biographical literature of the twentieth century was characterized by such notions, though this was not always clear to individual biographers. This also applies to the biographies of the labor movement beginning in the early twentieth century: the Marx biography (1918–1962) by Franz Mehring and Gustav Mayer's two-volume biography of Engels (1919–1932) contrasted the "greats" of bourgeois history writing with the "greats" of the labor movement, and made use of methodological instruments similar to those of bourgeois historians.

Traditional biography experienced a fundamental critique in the twentieth century, fed by various sources. In France, in the historical sciences the "Annales" school established itself in the 1930s (named after the journal founded by Lucien Febvre and Marc Bloch), which not only turned toward economic and social history and worked with quantitative methods, but also directed its interest toward long-term developmental processes. Against such a background, biographies strongly declined in significance. After the Second World War, a similar development became evident in West Germany. The understanding of history there, which for a long time had been oriented toward historicism, was called into question by conceptions oriented toward structural and social history. In contrast to the determining role of great historical personalities, the importance of structural factors was stressed. Programmatically, history was conceived in the "Bielefeld School" founded by Hans-Ulrich Wehler as "historical social science." Instead of assuming that individuals autonomously give meaning to their activity, the dependence of individuals upon their social environment was given primacy. Thus, the importance of biographical research was also called into question. Biographies were still published, but they could no longer claim a central role for historical knowledge. Starting in the 1970s in West Germany, a crisis of biography was diagnosed alongside the crisis of historical science (see Oelkers 1973; Schulze 1978).

In the German Democratic Republic (GDR, or East Germany) as well, the biographical genre was long regarded with skepticism, since not individuals, but rather classes, were viewed as the bearers of the historical process. Within Marxism-Leninism (not just in the GDR), social structure and the individual were frequently juxtaposed in an unmediated way. On the one hand, a strong structural determinism was promoted under the label "historical materialism," which hardly allowed room for individual activity beyond the collective subjects of "class" and "party." On the other hand, the founding fathers Marx, Engels, and Lenin were regarded as preeminent shining lights, whose individual genius ultimately outshone all social conditionality. A real mediation of conditioning social structures and individual thought and action was only achieved insufficiently in the depiction of these shining lights, as well as their political opponents. Jean-Paul Sartre criticized the rhetorical mediation of social relations with the life and thought of thinkers and artists within Marxism (Sartre 1964: 49), and with his five-volume biography of the young Flaubert (Sartre 1971–72), opposed it with an admittedly—in terms of scope—extreme alternative. The wide-ranging double biography of Marx and Engels presented by Cornu (a Frenchman teaching in the GDR) constituted an important exception, but no one attempted to continue it (it only goes up to 1846).

Parallel to the tendencies critical of biography within the field of history, within literary studies a debate about the "death of the author" arose following works by Roland Barthes (1967) and Michel Foucault (1969). If in structuralist and post-structuralist perspectives, authors no longer played a special role in the understanding of a particular work, then this also meant that important insights could no longer be expected from biography.

Most provocative was the fundamental critique of the possibility of biographical writing formulated in 1986 by Pierre Bourdieu in his essay "The Biographical Illusion." He criticized both talk of a "subject" that is held together by anything more than a proper name, as well as talk of a "life story," and concluded: "Trying to understand a life as a unique and self-sufficient series of successive events (sufficient unto itself), and without ties other than the association to a 'subject' whose constancy is probably just that of a proper name, is nearly as absurd as trying to make sense out of a subway route without taking into account the network structure, that is, the matrix of objective relations between the different stations" (Bourdieu 1986: 215).

With Bourdieu's contribution, the fundamental critique of scholarly biography reached its climax, but also its end. It could not be overlooked that the ignorance of that "matrix of objective relations" alleged by Bourdieu was an immense exaggeration. Many years earlier, Goethe had referred to that matrix in the preface to *Poetry and Truth* quoted above when he placed the person "in relation to the features of his time." In a similar manner, Dilthey explained that the "task of the biographer" was "to understand the productive nexus through which an individual is determined by his milieu and reacts to it" (Dilthey 2002: 265). The question now was, in what manner were the individual and those "objective relations" of the "features of his time" and "productive nexus" mediated with one another.

THE DEBATE CONCERNING "NEW BIOGRAPHY"

In the (West) German discussions, there was increasing dissatisfaction with the manner of writing history aligned merely with structural theory or quantitative statistics. Just as unsatisfactory was the reduction of human behavior to the operation of certain factors and social situations. Furthermore, new research directions formed, such as writing the history of everyday life, which, *inter alia*, turned to the biography of "ordinary" people. Overall, biography attained a higher status, but now as a sociohistorically and epistemologically reflective enterprise that explicitly set itself apart from traditional, historicist biography. Jacques Le Goff (1989) noted a similar development in France, and in the GDR, the publication of the first volume of Ernst Engelberg's biography of Bismarck (1985) marked the new status of biography.

In the debates conducted since (see, among others, Gestrich 1988; Engelberg/Schleier 1990; Klein 2002; Bödeker 2003), traditional biography was accused of proceeding in an unreflective manner based on a set of problematic assumptions:

1. The individual portrayed is conceived of as a self-contained self, as "a homo clausus" that gives meaning to his actions in an autonomous process.[2]
2. The biographer achieves understanding of this process of giving meaning through empathy and reexperience.
3. The form of presentation, mostly following the style of realist narration of the nineteenth century, assumes, with its stringent development, a

coherence and not infrequently a teleology to the course of a life, which is created by the act of narration, instead of being a depiction of real life.
4. The biographer takes the position of an omniscient narrator who recognizes the truth and wishes to present it, but does not possess any specific interests and perspectives that would have an effect upon the presentation.

Against this, it was argued that biography enlightened by social science and communication theory must proceed from fundamentally different assumptions:

1. The individual should not be conceived as a self-contained, autonomous subject; rather the subject should be brought back into society, considered in its social relations.
2. Giving meaning is not the autonomous act of an individual, but rather the result of a process of communication. Not empathy and reexperience, but rather the exact analysis of the conditions of this communication process will lead to the understanding of this meaning.
3. The presentation should not, by means of form, assume a coherence and teleology regarding the course of a life. Room for maneuver that can be exploited in different ways and, above all, the ruptures of a life, should be placed front and center.
4. The biographer writes from a specific perspective and, in that a process of selection and ordering has taken place according to this perspective, has a share in the construction of what is presented.

Before I take up these objections in the next point and discuss their significance for a biography of Marx, the response by representatives of a more traditional way of doing biography must be addressed. These anti-critiques weren't just formulated in various contributions. The comprehensive study by Olaf Hähner (1999) of the historical development of biography can be read as an implicit defense of at least a part of historicist biography.[3]

Hähner distinguishes in the case of historical biography between a "syntagmatic" biography, in which the effect of a (usually famous) person upon his or her historical environment stands in the foreground, and a "paradigmatic" biography, in which a (usually lesser known) person stands as an example for the conditions of the time. With this distinction, the different intentions of biographies are accounted for, but here we can ask to what extent such a distinction can be maintained, since the conditions of the time are also reflected in the well-known person.

Hähner divides the biography of German historicism into three phases that generated three specific types of biography. Hähner locates an "idealist historicism" in the first half of the nineteenth century. He refers to it as "idealist" on the basis of the influence of the idealist philosophy of history: history is grasped as the effect of driving intellectual forces (ibid.: 108). Johann Gustav Droysen (1808–1884), who studied under Hegel, draws from this the conclusion that the development of the person depicted should be largely ignored—for one thing because the historian lacks the competence, and for another because that isn't the point. What is decisive for the historian is not how specific notions developed within the individual, but rather how the individual became active proceeding from these ideas and influenced the course of history (ibid.: 112ff.). Leopold von Ranke (1795–1886) also saw the individual as a sort of executor of great historical ideas; however, more than Droysen, he emphasized the individual power and original contribution of the individual, and thus developed a stronger interest in the individual's educational history. The personal is not important for its own sake, but rather as a moment of history. Out of scattered statements by Ranke, Hähner reconstructs a "blueprint" of an "integrative" historical biography: "It has two prehistories to narrate, namely the development of the individual, called *biographical prehistory* in the following, and the development of general historical relations (*monographic prehistory*). Both prehistories converge upon the point 'where individual force meets the global relation' and the individual carries out historically significant behavior for the first time (*point of integration*). Here, both independent magnitudes grow together to a certain extent and biography expands into history (*bio-monographic history of activity*), in that with the historically eminent activity of the individual, individual and general history is narrated at the same time" (ibid.: 125).

Hähner locates the second phase between the revolutions of 1848–49 and the founding of the German Empire, the phase of "political historicism." An important part of German historical scholarship became political and dedicated itself to "Prussia's German calling," that is, a unification of Germany led by Prussia. Treitschke and, in turn, Droysen belonged to the representatives of this current. Biographies now had an immediate political purpose: they were to present the people portrayed as moral and political role models who did the right thing in critical situations. With this new orientation toward character, interest in the subject's individual development also increased.

With the founding of the empire in 1871, the aims of political historicism had been fulfilled. It was now superfluous and, according to Hähner, made a place for a "scientific historicism" that conducted fundamental controversies concerning the character of science. Among other things, a central role for historical science was attributed to "understanding," contrasting it to the causal "explanation" of the natural sciences. In this phase, biography was not just central to writing history. Now, according to Hähner, an integrative historical biography had finally developed: both the general course of history was taken into consideration, often leading to far-reaching monographical insertions, as well as the individual aspect, which occurred by means of empathetic understanding. Dilthey placed the latter at the center of his considerations mentioned above. Hähner's presentation makes clear that he also sees in the fully developed integrative historical biography an ideal form that is still valid today.

Dilthey's ideas, which came in for particularly fierce criticism in the newer debates, were explicitly defended by Hans-Christof Kraus (2007). The notion that Dilthey and traditional biography had proceeded from the assumption of a "homo clausus" was, according to Kraus, a completely overdrawn caricature. Beyond such considerations, Kraus argued that the "new" biography does not contain much that is new. Dilthey also examined the interaction between the person portrayed and the social environment. What was problematic was merely a tendency to cover up ruptures in the history of a life, as suggested by Dilthey's concept of the "life course." Hagiographic tendencies were to be rejected. Kraus then names multiple requirements for a modern political biography (ibid.: 328ff.). First, it must place the individual life within the respective nexuses; both the social "impressions" upon the individual as well as the repercussions of his or her actions must be grasped. Second, the individually shaped "way of life" must be reconstructed and analyzed. Third, in addition to the connecting threads, the ruptures of the course of a life must be analyzed; self-stylizations and historical legends must be uncovered. Fourth, a political biography especially must be concerned with the precise investigation of the respective historical-political "scopes for action"; motives and guiding interests must be ordered within the nexus of the historical process.

With Kraus's contribution, the phase of vehement debates appears to have come to an end. Since then, syntheses dominate the debate, which amount to listing numerous aspects to be considered. The contributions of Ullrich (2007) and Lässig (2009) also align with this synthesizing trend, attempting to summarize in a few points what constitutes a good biography. Whereas in Kraus's case an objectivist point of view of the person portrayed is still predominant, Ullrich and Lässig go beyond that. Both emphasize that the history of the tradition and reception of the person portrayed must be taken into consideration, and that the perspective of the biographer must be made clear. This at least recognizes that access to the person being dealt with is not independent of the history of their transmission and certainly not independent of the interests and perspectives of the writer.[4]

CONSEQUENCES FOR A BIOGRAPHY OF MARX

From the debates outlined here, considerations can be developed on all four levels referred to above: those that are relevant for biographical writing and in particular for a biography of Marx.

Person and Society

Dilthey emphasized that the course of a life is a "nexus in which the individual receives influences from the historical world" and in turn exerts an influence upon it (Dilthey 2002: 266), and that the task of the biographer is to understand this "nexus" (ibid.: 265). Even if the "homo clausus" that Dilthey's conception is accused of is an exaggeration, two fundamental objections to Dilthey's views are appropriate.

First, the channels of influence upon the individual and the individual's influence upon society are for Dilthey primarily mental; he emphasizes "religion, art, the state" and "science" (ibid.: 265, 266). But what constitutes a person begins in childhood, and does not proceed over purely cognitive paths. Family relationships, school experiences (beyond the pure transmission of knowledge), and experiences in the social space play an equally important role. For a Marx biography, this means that it's not enough to take the respective political and economic situation as a background in order to then consider the intellectual influences from philosophy, economics, and political theory and specify how these influences were implemented in his own theoretical thinking and practical activity. The respective conditions of life must be considered in a comprehensive sense (as limiting as well as enabling) in order to get an idea of how social and cognitive experiences can be processed, what is socially shaped, and how and to what extent an individual self-will could be and was developed at all.

The process of the constitution of the person addressed should not be mixed up with a deep psychological character study. Quite apart from the internal problems of psychoanalytical theory formation, its transhistorical application is not self-evident. There are a few interesting attempts, such as Erik Erikson's (1958) examination of the identity crisis of the young Martin Luther (on the theoretical foundations, see Erikson 1966). In the case of Karl Marx as well, the personal crisis of the year 1837 perhaps could be understood as such an identity crisis. However, we know far too few details of the circumstances of Marx's life and early personality development to make such an assumption with any degree of certainty. An initial and to some extent careful attempt to integrate an in-depth psychological analysis into his biography of Marx was undertaken by Otto Rühle (2011), who had been strongly influenced by the work of Alfred Adler. But here it was soon shown how much such an enterprise is forced to rely upon mere speculation, not knowing many details of Marx's early life. A downright dissuasive example of psychological interpretation is Künzli's "psychography" of Karl Marx (1966). Rather hastily, Künzli formulates theses on Marx's psyche, but instead of then attempting to present sound evidence for these theses, he repeatedly works with suggestive questions of the type "can we really imagine that this occurrence had no influence?" What is initially formulated as an assumption based on such a question then emerges in the next chapter as an established fact, which becomes the basis for further assumptions, which are then soon also treated as facts. In a similar manner, wild speculations are piled upon each other by Pilgrim (1990). Seigel (1978) argues more carefully in his search for "Marx's Fate." In contrast, Andreas Wildt's (2002) attempt to determine Marx's personality from the imagery of the letter to his father from 1837 and the early poems says more about the powers of association of the author than about Marx.

Second, without further problematization, Dilthey separates the "historical world" on one side from the "individual" on the other and lets both "act" and "react" upon each other. But relations aren't that clear; a mutual process of constitution takes place. The "historical world" contributes essentially to what constitutes the individual, who can only experience this constitution in actions, communications, and relations, whereby it also affects the "historical world." This means that "acting" and "reacting" occur simultaneously in most cases, albeit with different degrees of consequences at different times. In many biographies, however, this "acting" upon the individual and the individual's "reaction" in society are temporally separated. In other words, the person is formed by external influences, then this finished person reacts in the external world and experiences success or setbacks. In the case of Hähner, this separation is even elevated to a structural principle of biography: following the "biographical prehistory" comes the "point of integration," that is, the point at which the individual's effect upon the historical process begins. The question is what provides the standard by which this point of integration is determined. In Hähner's case, it appears to be the public perception of the person portrayed, which does not necessarily mean contemporary perception, but later perception on the basis of the consequences of the person portrayed having come to light. In Sperber's Marx biography, this point appears to have come in 1848. According to the table of contents, the "shaping" lasts until 1847, the "struggle" starts in 1848, without, however, any attempt by Sperber to justify the dates of this distinction. If one has even a rough overview of the course of Marx's life, it quickly becomes clear that it's difficult to determine such a *point* of integration. In Marx's case, starting with his work on the *Rheinische Zeitung* to the *Neue Rheinische Zeitung* up to his de facto leadership of the First International, there is a continuous increase in public perception and efficacy, which is repeatedly interrupted by periods of public indifference. His most famous works today, the *Communist Manifesto* of 1848 and the first volume of *Capital* published in 1867, were hardly noticed at the time of publication. Their reception (and fame) comes later. Marx became really well-known in Europe in 1871 through *The Civil War in France*, his analysis of the Paris Commune.

Thus, with Marx, we not only have the problem of determining an exact "point of integration" in the historical process, we have the problem of knowing when the "shaping" of his person was concluded. With the end of his studies in Berlin? Or after the ban of the *Rheinische Zeitung* and Marx's attempt in Kreuznach to understand the failure of his earlier political concepts? With the exile in Paris and Brussels and the role Marx strove for and achieved in the "Communist League"? Or was this shaping accomplished in the early 1850s, when Marx processed the defeat of the Revolutions of 1848-49, took leave from the exile cliques, and it dawned on him how much research he'd need to do to write a "critique of political economy"? The conditions of Marx's life, as well as the possibilities for his political and scientific intervention, had changed radically multiple times during his life. Marx reacted with an enormous willingness to learn and call into question the views he had gained so far. The shaping of the person and impact upon the social process can be neither temporally separated in Marx's case nor limited to specific periods of time.

That which we usually attempt to hold on to as a "person" is neither a simple, clearly delineated entity nor a mere illusion; it is the continuous result of a network of effects. These effects are not only changeable in time; they are at least in part the result of the actions of the person being considered. The impact of these effects constituting the person may decrease over time in the case of many people, so that we get the impression that the shaping of the person is concluded at a certain point. Whether and to what extent this process finds a conclusion should be an element of research and not merely an assumption by the biographer. Perhaps Marx the *person* proves to be a constant and unfinished process of constitution.

Life and Work, Meanings, and Scopes of Action

Over the last 150 years, Marx has been one of the most politically influential figures worldwide. He achieved this influence not through his role in struggles on the barricades or by captivating speeches. He obtained his influence primarily through his writings, having an impact both during his lifetime and after. For this reason, it's questionable when most biographies of Marx address his work superficially. The content of this work had a decisive importance for Marx's life: often, new insights contributed to alienating Marx from old friends while he sought new alliances. Without studying the development of his work, many aspects of Marx's life cannot be understood. Conversely, the constantly occurring interruptions and new approaches in his work cannot be completely understood without the turns in the course of Marx's life.

In examining both (political) activity as well as the results of the theoretical work, it must be kept in mind that its "meaning" is not determined solely by the actor or writer, but is the result of a common, social process of action and communication. Consideration of the work can therefore not be limited to recounting important results or stating the contents; it must be concerned with the (constantly interrupted and ruptured) *production process* as well as the intended and actual *effect* of this work. But the effect of that time has to be distinguished from that of today: some of today's most famous works by Marx (such as his early writings or the *Grundrisse*) were first published decades after his death, whereas many of his journalistic works, some of which made huge waves, are barely known today. And some texts published during his lifetime, such as the *Communist Manifesto* or the *18th Brumaire* remained largely unknown for several years.

If we consider the influence of Marx's texts, a distinction emphasized by the British historian Quentin Skinner proves useful. Contrary to traditional conceptions, Skinner did not see in the classical works of political philosophy contributions concerning fundamental political ideas, but rather saw interventions in specific political conflicts and debates, which have to be reconstructed. Skinner, therefore, distinguishes between the *semantic meaning* of a text, that is, the content of a text, its central statements, and the text as a *speech act*, that is, the text as a maneuver within a specific situation (Skinner 2009: 8ff.). Skinner emphasizes that what is important is not only what is said, but how it is acted out in saying it.

Marx's works are also interventions in specific conflicts and problem situations and must be analyzed as such. However, one must go beyond Skinner's orientation toward the intention of the author. Skinner recognizes that a complex political or socio-theoretical text usually contains more levels of semantic meaning than intended by the author. But in the case of the speech act, he maintains that the intention of the author is the decisive factor (ibid.:

25, 82ff.). It is precisely within the context of a biography that the intention of the person portrayed—to the extent that this intention can in fact be ascertained—constitutes an extremely important factor, but what is unintentional, at the levels of both the semantic and the speech act, cannot be disregarded.

It's also problematic that Skinner does not wish to concede any meaning to the works considered beyond the intentions of the author. "Any statement is inescapably the embodiment of a particular intention on a particular occasion, addressed to the solution of a particular problem, and is thus specific to its context in a way that it can only be naive to try to transcend.... The classic texts are concerned with their own questions and not with ours" (Skinner 2002: 88). Skinner's critique of a completely timeless conception of political philosophy is certainly justified. However, the fact that a text was written within a specific situation is not sufficient justification for the claim that this text cannot still reach beyond the situation of its emergence. That's especially the case when, as in the case of Marx, the basic conditions under which the text arose are not so fundamentally different from our current conditions. Even if all of Marx's texts stand within the disputes of their time, sometimes quite directly as polemical interventions, other times rather indirectly, the extent they reach beyond this context must be examined.

However, the intentionality that Skinner stresses, to the extent that it can be ascertained, must be considered more critically than he does. In his investigation of the *Archaeology of Knowledge*, Michel Foucault (1969–72) highlighted that the objects of science are not given by themselves; rather, they are discursively formed. The intention to say this or that occurs within an already existing discursive formation that not only affects the objects but the concepts, the modalities of expressions, and the strategies in the choice of theoretical entry points. These formations, even if they are initially given, are not immutable. In further studies, Foucault examined the relation between knowledge, truth, and power, the "politics of truth," which is concerned with the truth of individual statements, but also with the alteration of the fixed— discursively as well as non-discursively, in institutions and practices—orders of the "production" of truth. With this, a framework is defined that is not always obvious, within which every intentionality occurs.

In order to analyze Marx's actions and works as interventions, it's necessary to examine the social and political conditions, the respective possibilities of articulation and their regulation, the horizon of meaning of actors, and the available scopes of action. In doing so, apparently self-evident matters have to be looked at: at the time, what was a "newspaper" or a "party"? Each intervention also has to be seen in its totality. Belonging to a text is not only its content, but also its style, its rhetoric, whereby one must distinguish

336

what is temporal and what Marx's specific share is. Meanings, horizons of meaning, and scopes of action that we think we spot in earlier situations are due to a *contemporary* perspective. However, this can differ considerably from earlier perspectives. For example, the perspective Marx had of Hegel's philosophy in the year 1840 or of political economy in 1845 is a completely different one from our perspective today. We not only know how far philosophical and economic-theoretical thought has developed, but today, on the basis of more textual evidence, we know more details about the formation of the philosophical and economic theories of Marx's time than he did. And last but not least, our own perspective is influenced by the knowledge of Marx's further development and his engagement with philosophy and economics. So we have to distinguish between that which we know today about Hegel or Ricardo and that which Marx knew or was able to know. Where Marx's perspective is not immediately given to us, what constituted the semantics of philosophy, economics, communism, etc. for Marx must be worked out first.

Form of Presentation, Ruptures, and Contingencies of the Life Story

A chronologically oriented presentation always runs the danger of being read as a novel of personal development, interrupted by inserted analyses of social and discursive conditions. Understood as a novel of personal development, the presentation quickly acquires a teleological tendency. The factual course of events appears more or less inevitable: what happens, had to happen. That history is an open process applies not only to large-scale history but to individual life stories. Instead of narrating history as a constantly progressing maturation and convergence upon a goal (possibly in the variant that Marx was always right in every dispute), we must first determine the contingencies and ruptures due to external conditions as well as options for action to be used in different ways.

A special variant of the teleological presentation consists in seeking early reasons for later developments. The insinuation is made that only one possibility for development was given. Thus Neffe (2017: 52) believes that Marx had already received "a mission for life" in Trier and that a decisive "setting of the course" had occurred in Berlin (ibid.: 58). Marx ran into Hegel's philosophy and, Neffe continues, "without Hegel, no Marx" (ibid.: 73). However, in the case of Marx, there was not only his reception of Hegel in Berlin but his critique of Hegel in the mid-1840s and (at least) a renewed, differently positioned reception of Hegel at the end of the 1850s. Marx's relationship to Hegel was not fixed by his first encounter with Hegel's philosophy, nor was his further development.

But the teleological danger doesn't just exist with regard to Marx, it also exists for the depiction of the "side figures," the friends and adversaries of Marx. In the case of friends who then became adversaries, their history is often told backwards: the friendship is given little space, the break and its reasons are emphasized, frequently only from Marx's perspective. Marx's later perspective is thus superimposed upon the entire depiction of the corresponding figure. Why Bruno Bauer was Marx's closest friend over several years or why Marx initially held Proudhon in high esteem, for example, cannot be made clear by such an approach.

Furthermore, it's important not just to consider what we know but also what we don't know. In some places, more exact knowledge is missing—not only concerning Marx's drives and apprehensions, but what he did, when, and where. Even when such non-knowledge isn't replaced by biographical fictions, mentioned in the Introduction, when it's simply passed over, it allows the presentation to appear more coherent and complete than it actually is. For that reason, not only knowledge, but also non-knowledge must be clearly emphasized.

Historical Exactness and the Perspectivist Character of Every Biography

The importance of working precisely with sources was stressed in the Introduction. What is gathered from sources should be clearly distinguished from the conjectures of the biographer. What a source says might be disputed in an individual case, but then it is necessary to disclose this dispute. However, what is not such a dispute is, for example, the question of whether a certain name is mentioned in a letter, or whether the biographer merely supposes that in the case of a specific statement it must be an allusion to a certain person. Such distinctions must be made clear in the presentation.

Even if one deals meticulously with the sources and the presentation dispenses with all biographical fictions, an unambiguous, objective depiction of the person does not result. In writing a biography, one must select from the available sources, and the selected material must be evaluated and arranged. Some connections are emphasized, while others are placed in the background. Through that, every biography acquires a constructive character dependent upon the perspective of the biographer. This standpoint cannot be reduced to the consciously taken political perspective. If this is unambiguous and leads to a positive or negative exaggeration of the person portrayed, which is the case for many Marx biographies, then this is relatively easy to perceive through the reading. If one takes to hand the Marx biography of the British historian Edward Hallet Carr, *Karl Marx. A Study in Fanaticism* (1934), the

title itself makes clear what one can expect.[5] It's more difficult when prefer-
ences are not so openly bared, when positive, as well as negative, praise and
critique slip into the narrative. Then a balance and objectivity is suggested to
readers that allows them to accept the judgment of the biographer, since they
do not notice that it is a judgment.

In addition to the consciously adopted perspective of the biographer,
there is also a *situational historical* perspective (which by no means must
always lead to the same consequences for all writers in the same situation).
Every biography is written during a certain time period, when certain historical experiences have taken place, for example, the rise and fall of the
Soviet Union. This temporal situation will lead to different ways of processing it; for example, the question of whether the Soviet Union rightly
or wrongly invoked Marx is answered differently with the existence of the
history of the Soviet Union. A completely different experiential space is
available in the year 2018 than for example in the year 1918, when Franz
Mehring's Marx biography was published. The perspective consciously
adopted by the biographer is overlaid by a perspective that owes its existence to the (subjectively differential) processing of the respective historical
situation, and which the biographer is frequently not aware of to the same
extent: other plausibilities are present, other questions become important,
other connections are established.

But the perspectivist dependence of the presentation does not just relate
to the person portrayed. When one asks about the relationship of the young
Marx to Hegel's philosophy or Romantic poetry, one must take into consideration that the philosophy of Hegel or Romantic poetry are by no means
given quantities. A two-hundred-year-old history of reception enters into
our contemporary notions about Hegel or Romanticism and yields not just
differing, but in part opposed, conceptions about Hegel and Romanticism.
Whether Romanticism is understood as a conservative, anti-Enlightenment
tendency or a partially progressive one, whether Hegel is regarded as a conservative philosopher glorifying Prussia or as someone who defended liberal
values and whose philosophy contained a subversive potential with regard to
the Prussian state, all of this has considerable influence on any discussion of
the relationship between Marx and Romanticism or the philosophy of Hegel.
Marx biographers usually do not reflect upon the fact that their evaluations
are not self-evident but rather the result of a specific processing of the history of tradition and reception. For that reason, in a few passages I've briefly
outlined the history of the reception of important works or tendencies.

What is said here about biography, that it's not the "objective" reproduc-
tion of a given occurrence but rather a perspectivist depiction, is valid for

historical topics in general, and was also reflected upon in the field of history in its critical engagement with historicism, which largely still assumed the possibility of such an objective presentation. Perhaps the most radical position was advanced by Hayden White (1973), who understood the writing of history to be an essentially poetic act. What the historian presents as explanation is determined primarily by his narrative strategy, which White decodes using poetic categories, such as Romance, Tragedy, Comedy, and Satire. It should not be disputed that narrative strategies play a role—to varying extents, among the different authors—and in the corresponding passages, I will engage with White's conceptions of Hegel and Marx in this regard. The statement, however, that historical explanations at their core can be reduced to such narrative structures no doubt overextends the argument.

A more appropriate understanding of the unavoidable perspectivity of historical depiction is provided by the considerations that Hans-Georg Gadamer places at the center of his theory of understanding in *Truth and Method* (1960/2013). Against Schleiermacher and Dilthey, Gadamer emphasizes that underlying our understanding is not direct access to a text, but rather that every act of understanding is inserted into an "event of tradition." The interpreter always has a prior understanding of the object (Gadamer speaks of "prejudices," though this is not meant pejoratively) that emerges from the transmission. In his dispute with Habermas, Gadamer vehemently opposed the allegation that he understood transmission as purely cultural: "It seems altogether absurd that the concrete factors of work and dominance should be seen as lying outside the scope of hermeneutics. What else are the prejudices with which hermeneutical reflection concerns itself? Where else shall they originate if not in work and dominance?" (Gadamer 1967: 284).

Understanding for Gadamer is not merely retracing an already existing meaning, but the (inevitable) shaping of a meaning. This shaping is not to be mistaken for capriciousness or arbitrariness. "The anticipation of meaning that governs our understanding of a text is not an act of subjectivity, but proceeds from the commonality that binds us to the tradition." But neither the "commonality" nor the "tradition" is something static, or a given: "This commonality is constantly being formed in our relation to tradition. Tradition is not simply a permanent precondition; rather, we produce it ourselves inasmuch as we understand, participate in the evolution of tradition, and hence further determine it ourselves" (Gadamer 1960/2013: 305). We cannot leap out of the event of transmission, but we transform it, thus creating new conditions under which future acts of understanding occur.[6]

Completely independent of whether new material that could be relevant for the biography of Karl Marx is found, the unavoidable perspectivity of depiction and the never-ending history of reception and tradition ensures that there can never be such a thing as a final Marx biography. Every generation will develop a new perspective on the life and work of Marx under historically changed circumstances, which will then lead to a new Marx biography.

NOTES

1. "Men make history" (Treitschke 1879: 28). Almost forty years earlier, the British historian Thomas Carlyle (1795–1881) made an even more radical formulation: "The history of the world is but the Biography of great men" (Carlyle 1841: 47).
2. The term "homo clausus" used by critics originates with Norbert Elias, who used it in a somewhat different context (Elias 1969: IL).
3. The study of the history of biography presented by Scheuer (1979) is less fruitful for the debate on new biography. It was written before these debates started in the 1980s, and it aims more at discussing the relation between art and science on the basis of biography rather than determining the possibilities and limits of historical biography.
4. That this debate has taken a primarily compilatory character is made clear by two further publications from 2009: the *Handbook of Biography: Methods, Traditions, Theories,* ed. Christian Klein (2009), and the volume edited by Bernhard Fetz (2009), *The Biography: The Foundation of Its Theory,* which contrary to the announcement made in its title does not provide any theory, but rather collects possibilities and problems that have emerged within the biographical literature.
5. Carr later looked upon this biography extremely critically: "It was a foolish enterprise and produced a foolish book. I have refused all offers to reprint it as a paperback" (Carr 1980: xviii). However, it was quite efficacious and influenced, *inter alia,* Isaiah Berlin's Marx biography (Berlin 1939).
6. In the third part of *Truth and Method,* Gadamer then consummates a linguistic-ontological turn. Since all understanding (not just of texts) is embedded in language, but language is not simply a representation of something given, but the coming into language of meaning, Gadamer arrived at his famous dictum: "Being which can be understood is language" (ibid.: 490). However, the insights from the second part of *Truth and Method* outlined above are independent of this ontology.

Glossary of Names

Aeschylus (525–456 BCE) Greek tragedian

Altenstein, Karl vom Stein zum (1770–1840) Prussian reformer, from 1817 Prussia's first minister of culture

Althaus, Karl Heinrich (1806–1886) lecturer in philosophy in Berlin, member of the "Doctor's Club"

Alton, Eduard d' (1772–1840) art historian, professor under whom Karl Marx studied in Bonn

Anselm of Canterbury (1033–1109) theologian and philosopher

Aristotle (384–324 BCE) Greek philosopher

Arndt, Ernst Moritz (1769–1860) nationalist German writer and historian

Arnim, Achim von (1771–1831) Romantic movement writer, husband of Bettina von Arnim

Arnim, Bettina von (1785–1859) Romantic movement writer, sister of Clemens Brentano, wife of Achim von Arnim

Ascher, Saul (1767–1822) German-Jewish publicist [A "publicist" is a writer of opinion pieces and not a modern journalist.—*Trans.*]

Baader, Franz von (1765–1841) proponent of a strong religious philosophy

Bachmann, Karl Friedrich (1785–1855) professor of philosophy in Jena, critic of Hegel

Bacon, Francis (1561–1626) English philosopher and politician

Bauer, Bruno (1809–1882) theologian and philosopher, close friend of Marx from 1837 to 1842

Bauer, Edgar (1820–1886) publicist, brother of Bruno Bauer

Baur, Ferdinand Christian (1792–1860) Protestant theologian

Bernays, Karl Ludwig (1815–1876) publicist, worked with Marx in Paris

Bernkastel, Lion (ca. 1770–1840) family doctor to the Marx family in Trier

Biedermann, Karl (1812–1901) liberal publicist and politician

Birmann, Johann Michael, student of the Trier Gymnasium, took the Abitur examination in 1832

Bismarck, Otto von (1815–1898) prime minister of the Kingdom of Prussia 1862–1890, 1871–1890, at the same time imperial chancellor of the German Empire founded in 1871

Böcking, Eduard (1802–1870) jurist and historian, professor under whom Karl Marx studied in Bonn

Boeckh, August (1785–1867) philologist and archaeologist, professor in Berlin

Boiserée, Supliz (1783–1854) art collector and art historian, a friend of Goethe

Börne, Ludwig (1786–1837) journalist, literature and theater critic

Braunschweig, Ferdinand Herzog von
(1721–1792) general field marshal
in Prussian service during the Seven
Years' War

Brentano, Clemens (1778–1842)
Romantic poet, brother of Bettina
von Arnim

Brisack, Michle (1784–1860) wife of
Samuel Marx

Brogi, Joseph (1794–?) student at the
University of Berlin, attacked in
1812 by anti-Jewish students

Büchner, Georg (1814–1837) German
dramatist and revolutionary

Buhl, Ludwig (1814–1882) writer
and publicist, collaborator on the
Rheinische Zeitung

Bürgers, Heinrich (1820–1878) publi-
cist, collaborator on the *Rheinische
Zeitung* and member of the
Communist League

Burkhardt, Johanna (née Fischer)
(1778–?) mother of Hegel's out-of-
wedlock son Ludwig Fischer

Byron, George Lord (1788–1824)
English poet

Carlyle, Thomas (1795–1881) British
historian

Carové, Friedrich Wilhelm (1789–1852)
Burschenschaft member and student
of Hegel, publicist

Carrière, Moriz (1817–1895) writer,
philosopher, art historian

Chamisso, Adelbert von (1781–1838)
German poet and naturalist

Charles X (1757–1836) French king
1824–1830

Cicero, Marcus Tullius (106–45 BCE)
Roman politician and author

Cieszkowski, August von (1814–1894)
Polish economist and philosopher

Cleanthes (331–232 BCE) Stoicism
philosopher

Clemens, Heinrich (1814–1852) classmate of Karl Marx in Trier and witness to his marriage in Kreuznach

Cohen, Josef ben Gerson (ca. 1511–
1591) Jewish legal scholar, ancestor
of Karl Marx

Cornelius, Wilhelm (1809–?) poet and
publicist

Creizenach, Theodor (1818–1877) poet
and literary historian

Dante Alighieri (1265–1321) Italian
poet

Daub, Carl (1765–1836) Protestant
theologian

Daumier, Honoré (1808–1879) French
painter, sculptor, and caricaturist

Delacroix, Eugène (1798–1863) French
painter

Democritus (ca. 460–370 BCE) Greek
philosopher

Descartes, René (1596–1650) French
philosopher and mathematician

Destutt de Tracy, Antoine (1754–1836)
French philosopher and politician

Dilthey, Wilhelm (1833–1911)
Theologian and philosopher

Diogenes Laërtius (ca. third C.) writer of
a popular book about the lives and
doctrines of famous philosophers

Dohm, Christian Konrad Wilhelm von
(1751–1821) jurist and author of an
early text on Jewish emancipation

Droste zu Vischering, Clemens August
(1773–1845) Catholic archbishop of
Cologne

Droysen, Johann Gustav (1808–1884)
German historian

Duller, Eduard (1809–1853) German-
Austrian poet and publicist

Echtermeyer, Theodor (1805–1844)
teacher and literary historian,
founded the *Hallische Jahrbücher*
with Arnold Ruge

Eichhorn, Johann Albrecht Friedrich
(1779–1856) Prussian minister of
culture from 1840 to 1848

Eichler, Ludwig (1814–1870) German
writer, participant in the Revolution
of 1848

Engels, Friedrich (1820–1895) socialist, closest friend and comrade-in-arms of Karl Marx

Epicurus (ca. 341–ca. 271 BCE) Greek philosopher

Esser, Johann Peter (1786–1856) privy superior auditor councillor of the Rhenish Appeals Court and Court of Cassation of Berlin, acquaintance of Heinrich Marx

Erdmann, Johann Eduard (1805–1892) Philosopher, conservative Hegelian

Ernst August I (1771–1851) king of Hannover since 1837, dismissed the "Göttingen Seven"

Euripides (ca. 480–406 BCE) Greek tragedian

Evers, Gustav and Friedrich studied in Berlin, probably acquaintances of Karl Marx

Fenner von Fenneberg, Daniel (1820–1863) a leader of the revolt in the Palatinate region in 1849

Ferrand, Eduard (1813–1842) German lyricist

Feuerbach, Ludwig (1804–1872) philosopher, critic of Hegel and religion

Feuerbach, Paul Johann Anselm von (1775–1833) founder of modern German penal law, father of Ludwig Feuerbach

Fichte, Immanuel Hermann (1796–1879) philosopher and theologian, son of J. G. Fichte

Fichte, Johann Gottlieb (1762–1814) philosopher, first elected rector of the University of Berlin

Fischer, Karl Philipp (1807–1831) philosopher and theologian

Fischer, Ludwig (1807–1831) out-of-wedlock son of G. W. F. Hegel and Johanna Burckhardt

Fleischer, Karl Moritz (1809–1876) teacher, collaborator on the *Hallische Jahrbücher* and the *Rheinische Zeitung*

Florencourt, Louise von (1805–1861) wife of Ferdinand von Westphalen

Follen, Karl (1796–1840) radical Burschenschaft member

Forberg, Friedrich Karl (1770–1848) German philosopher and philologist

Fourier, Charles (1772–1837) French social theorist and early socialist

Friedrich II (1712–1786) Prussian king, 1740–1786

Friedrich Wilhelm III (1770–1840) grand-nephew of Friedrich II, Prussian king 1797–1840

Friedrich Wilhelm IV (1795–1861) son of Friedrich Wilhelm III, Prussian King 1840–1861

Fries, Jakob Friedrich (1773–1843) nationalist German philosopher, critic of Hegel, advocate of early, folkish anti-Semitism

Fuxius, Jakob (1818–1891) classmate of Marx in Bonn

Gabler, Georg Andreas (1786–1853) philosopher, student and successor to Hegel in Berlin

Gall, Ludwig (1791–1863) Trier inventor and writer of social reform texts

Gans, Eduard (1797–1839) publicist, Hegelian, professor of law under whom Karl Marx studied in Berlin

Geibel, Emanuel (1815–1884) lyricist, studied in Bonn and Berlin at about the same time as Marx

Gentz, Friedrich von (1764–1832) conservative politician, collaborator of Metternich

Geppert, Karl Eduard (1811–1881) classicist and historian under whom Karl Marx studied at the University of Berlin

Gerlach, Ernst Ludwig von (1795–1877) judge, conservative author, and politician

Giersberg (Lieutenant) acquaintance of Marx during his studies in Berlin

Goethe, Johann Wolfgang von (1759–1832) German poet and naturalist

Görres, Joseph (1776–1848) Catholic publicist

Göschel, Carl Friedrich (1781–1861) jurist and philosophical-theological writer

Goeze, Johann Melchior (1717–1786) Hamburg pastor

Grach, Emmerich took the Abitur exam with Marx

Grach, Friedrich (1812–1854) officer in the Turkish service, acquaintance of Karl Marx from Trier

Grimm, Jacob (1785–1863) and Wilhelm (1786–1859) the "Brothers Grimm," linguists and literary scholars, part of the "Göttingen Seven" dismissed by King Ernst August I

Gruppe, Otto Friedrich (1804–1876) philologist and publicist

Grün, Karl (1817–1887) journalist and socialist

Guizot, François (1787–1874) French foreign minister from 1840 to 1848

Gutzkow, Karl (1811–1878) dramatist and journalist, representative of Young Germany

Haller, Karl Ludwig von (1768–1854) conservative scholar of constitutional law

Hamacher, Wilhelm (1808–1875) teacher of Karl Marx at the Trier Gymnasium

Hardenberg, Friedrich von (see Novalis)

Hardenberg, Karl August von (1750–1822) Prussian reform politician, Prussian state chancellor, 1810–1822

Hassenpflug, Ludwig (1794–1862) conservative jurist, from 1840 judge at the highest Prussian court in Berlin

Haw, Wilhelm (1793–1862) mayor of Trier from 1818 to 1839

Haym, Rudolf (1821–1901) literary scholar, biographer of Hegel

Heffter, August Wilhelm (1796–1880) professor of law under whom Karl Marx studied in Berlin

Hegel, Georg Wilhelm Friedrich (1770–1831) philosopher, professor at the University of Berlin

Hegel, Immanuel (1814–1891) Prussian jurist, son of G. W. F. Hegel

Hegel, Karl (1813–1901) historian, son of G. W. F. Hegel

Heine, Heinrich (1797–1856) poet, journalist, and essayist. Friend of Karl Marx in Paris

Heinse, Wilhelm (1746–1803) poet and art historian

Hengstenberg, Ernst Wilhelm Theodor (1802–1869) Protestant theologian, professor at the University of Berlin, publisher of the *Evangelische Kirchenzeitung*

Heraclitus (ca. 520–ca. 460 BCE) Greek philosopher

Hermes, Georg (1775–1831) Catholic theologian and philosopher, professor in Bonn

Herz, Henriette (1764–1847) Berlin salon hostess for the early Romantic movement

Hess, Moses (1812–1875) German-Jewish philosopher and publicist, socialist, worked closely with Marx and Engels for a while

Heubel, Caroline (1779–1856) second wife of Ludwig von Westphalen, mother of Jenny von Westphalen

Hinrichs, Hermann Friedrich Wilhelm (1794–1861) theologian and philosopher, student of Hegel

Hoffmann, Ernst Theodor Amadeus (1776–1822) jurist, conductor, and Romantic writer

Hoffmann von Fallersleben, August Heinrich (1798–1874) poet and linguistic researcher

Holbach, Paul Henri Thierry d' (1723–1789) French philosopher and critic of religion

Hölderlin, Friedrich (1770–1843) lyricist, friend in youth of Hegel and Schelling

Homer (eighth/seventh C. BCE) Greek poet

Hommer, Josef von (1760–1835) from 1824, Catholic bishop of Trier

Hotho, Heinrich Gustav (1802–1873) philosopher and art historian, student of Hegel

Hugo, Gustav von (1764–1844) jurist, professor in Göttingen, founder of the German historical school of law

Humboldt, Alexander von (1769–1859) Prussian naturalist and explorer

Humboldt, Wilhelm von (1767–1835) Prussian politician, university reformer, and linguistics researcher

Hume, David (1711–1776) Scottish philosopher, economist, and historian

Isaiah (eighth C. BCE) Jewish prophet, active primarily between 740 and 701 BCE

Jachmann, Reinhold Bernhard (1767–1843) theologian and pedagogue, school reformer in Prussia

Jacobi, Friedrich Heinrich (1743–1819) merchant, jurist, and philosopher

Jacoby, Johann (1805–1877) German-Jewish physician and liberal publicist

Jaehnigen, Franz Ludwig (1801–1866) jurist, Privy Upper Revision Council in Berlin, acquaintance of Heinrich Marx

Jahn, Friedrich Ludwig (1778–1852) German pedagogue, founder of the gymnastics movement

Jung, Georg Gottlob (1814–1886) jurist, co-founder of the *Rheinische Zeitung*

Kamptz, Karl Albert von (1769–1849) judge, police director, Prussian justice minister 1832–1842

Kant, Immanuel (1724–1804) philosopher, professor in Königsberg

Karl August (1757–1828) grand duke of Weimar, friend of Goethe

Katzenellenbogen, Meir (ca. 1482–1565) Jewish scholar, rabbi of Padua and Genoa, ancestor of Karl Marx

Kierkegaard, Sören (1813–1855) Danish theologian, philosopher, and writer

Kinkel, Gottfried (1815–1882) Protestant theologian, art and literary historian

Kircheisen, Friedrich Leopold von (1749–1825) Prussian justice minister 1810–1825

Kleinerz acquaintance of the young Marx in Trier

Köppen, Karl Friedrich (1808–1863) teacher and historian, friend of Karl Marx

Körner, Theodor (1791–1813) German poet

Kotzebue, August von (1761–1819) German poet, murdered by Karl Ludwig Sand

Kowalewski, Maxim (1851–1916) Russian jurist and historian, acquaintance of Marx and Engels in London

Krosigk, Adolph von (1799–1856) husband of Lisette von Westphalen

Küpper, Johann Abraham (1779–1850) Lutheran pastor and religion teacher of Karl Marx at the Trier Gymnasium

Ladenberg, Adalbert von (1798–1855) jurist and Prussian politician

Laeis, Ernest Dominik (1788–1872) lawyer in Trier, friend of Heinrich Marx

Lafargue, Paul (1842–1911) French physician and socialist, married to Laura Marx

Lange, Friedrich Albert (1828–1875) philosopher and socialist

Lassalle, Ferdinand (1825–1864) writer and socialist politician

Laube, Heinrich (1806–1884) writer, member of the French National Assembly in 1848

Laven, Franz Philipp (1805–1859) teacher at the gymnasium in Trier and poet

Leibniz (Leibnitz), Gottfried Wilhelm (1646–1716) philosopher and mathematician

Leo, Heinrich (1799–1878) historian, professor in Halle, student of Hegel, later a critic of the Hegelian school

Leonhard, Karl Cäsar von (1779–1862) mineralogist

Lessing, Gotthold Ephraim (1729–1781) poet of the Enlightenment era

Lichtenberg, Georg Christoph (1742–1799) mathematician, naturalist, and author

Liebknecht, Wilhelm (1826–1900) journalist and socialist politician, friend of Marx and Engels

Locke, John (1632–1704) English philosopher

Loers, Vitus (1792–1862) teacher of Karl Marx at the Trier Gymnasium

Löw, Bertha (1803–1883) daughter of a porcelain manufacturer, married Ludwig Feuerbach in 1837

Louis Philippe of Orléans (1773–1850) king of France, 1830–1848

Löwenstamm, Moses Saul (1748–1815) rabbi, second husband of Chaje Lwow, grandmother of Karl Marx

Luden, Heinrich (1778–1847) historian, professor in Jena

Lucretius (circa 95–55 BCE) Roman poet and philosopher, follower of Epicurus

Luther, Martin (1483–1546) theologian, most important figure of the Reformation

Lützow, Adolph von (1772–1834) Prussian major and Freikorps commander

Lwów, Chaje (Levoff, Eva) (ca. 1757–1823) mother of Heinrich Marx, grandmother of Karl Marx

Lwów, Moses (?-1788) rabbi of Trier,

father of Chaje Lwów, great-grandfather of Karl Marx

Mahmud II (1785–1839) sultan of the Ottoman Empire from 1808

Marheineke, Phillip Konrad (1780–1846) Protestant theologian influenced by Hegel, professor at the University of Berlin

Maria Theresia (1717–1780) archduchess of Austria and Queen of Hungary from 1740

Marx, Eleanor (1855–1898) daughter of Karl Marx and Jenny von Westphalen

Marx, Emilie (1822–1888) sister of Karl Marx

Marx, Heinrich (1777–1838) lawyer, father of Karl Marx

Marx, Henriette (see **Presburg, Henriette**)

Marx, Laura (1845–1911) daughter of Karl Marx and Jenny von Westphalen, married to Paul Lafargue

Marx, Moses (1815–1894) son of Samuel Marx, cousin of Karl Marx

Marx, Samuel (1775–1827) rabbi of Trier from 1804, brother of Heinrich Marx

Marx, Sophie (1816–1886) sister of Karl Marx

Mendelssohn, Moses (1729–1786) German-Jewish philosopher, representative of the Jewish Enlightenment

Messerich, Johann August (1806–1876) lawyer from Trier, friend of Karl Marx

Metternich, Clemens Wenceslaus von (1773–1859) Austrian foreign minister from 1809, Austrian state chancellor, 1821–1848

Meurin finance official in Berlin, acquaintance of Heinrich Marx

Meyen, Eduard (1812–1870) publicist, Young Hegelian, acquaintance of Marx in Berlin, later national-liberal

Michelet, Karl Ludwig (1801–1893) philosopher, student of Hegel

Mordechai (Marx Levi) (ca. 1743–1804) rabbi of Trier, father of Heinrich Marx, grandfather of Karl Marx

Mügge, Theodor (1802–1861) author, writer of adventure novels

Müller, Adam (1779–1829) economist and state theorist, representative of political Romanticism

Muhammed Ali Pasha (ca.1770–1849) viceroy (governor) of Egypt

Mundt, Theodor (1808–1861) author and literary historian, belonged to "Young Germany" movement

Napoleon Bonaparte (1769–1821) French general, First Consul of the French Republic, 1799–1804, French emperor, 1804–1814

Niethammer, Friedrich Immanuel (1766–1848) philosopher and theologian

Nitzsch, Karl Immanuel (1787–1868) Protestant theologian in the tradition of Schleiermacher

Notz, Heinrich von (ca. 1818–1848) classmate of Karl Marx at the Trier Gymnasium, studied in Bonn and Berlin

Novalis (Friedrich von Hardenberg) (1772–1801) poet of early Romanticism and philosopher

Oswald, Friedrich pseudonym of Friedrich Engels

Ovid (Publius Ovidius Naso) (43 BCE-17 AD) Roman poet

Owen, Robert (1771–1858) British entrepreneur and early socialist

Pannewitz, Karl von (1803–1856) briefly engaged to Jenny von Westphalen

Paulsen, Friedrich (1846–1908) pedagogue and philosopher, professor in Berlin

Paulus, Heinrich Eberhard Gottlob (1761–1851) Lutheran theologian, professor in Heidelberg

Perthes, Friedrich Christoph (1772–1843) bookseller and publisher

Plato (427–347 BCE) Greek philosopher

Platen, August Graf von (1795–1835) German poet

Plutarch (46-ca. 125) Greek writer and philosopher

Presburg, Henriette (1788–1863) married to Heinrich Marx, mother of Karl Marx

Presburg, Isaac Heijmans (1747–1832) father of Henriette Presburg, father-in-law of Heinrich Marx

Puggé, Eduard (1802–1836) jurist, professor under whom Karl Marx studied in Bonn

Ranke, Leopold von (1795–1886) historian, professor at the University of Berlin

Reimarus, Hermann Samuel (1694–1768) Hamburg Orientalist and critic of religion

Riedel, Karl (1804–1878) writer and publicist, acquaintance of Marx in Berlin

Ring, Max (1817–1901) physician and poet

Ritter, Carl (1779–1859) geographer, University of Berlin professor under whom Karl Marx studied

Rosbach, Heinrich (1814–1879) fellow student of Marx in Bonn, later physician in Trier

Rosenkranz, Karl (1805–1879) German philosopher, student of Hegel

Rotteck, Karl von (1775–1840) liberal scholar of constitutional law, co-editor of the Staatslexikon

Rousseau, Jean-Jacques (1712–1778) French philosopher

Rudorff, Adolf August Friedrich (1803–1873) jurist, student of Savigny, University of Berlin professor under whom Karl Marx studied

Ruge, Arnold (1802–1880) publicist, Young Hegelian, for a while close collaborator of Marx, later a follower of Bismarck

Rühs, Friedrich (1781–1820) German historian, proponent of early folkish anti-Semitism

Rumschöttel, Franz Heinrich (1795–1853) organized gymnastics in Trier

Rutenberg, Adolf Friedrich (1808–1869) teacher, journalist, friend of Marx in Berlin

Saal, Nikolaus teacher at the Trier Gymnasium in the 1830s

Saint-Simon, Henri de (1760–1825) publicist, early socialist

Sallet, Friedrich von (1812–1842) writer, lived for a period in Trier

Salomon, Friedrich von (1790–1861) university magistrate in Berlin

Sand, Karl Ludwig (1795–1820) Burschenschaft member, murdered August von Kotzebue

Savigny, Friedrich Carl von (1779–1861) jurist, representative of the historical school of law, professor under whom Karl Marx studied at the University of Berlin

Schapper, Karl (1812–1870) participated in the Frankfurter Wachensturm, later member of the Communist League and the International Workingmen's Association

Scheidler, Karl Hermann (1795–1866) Burschenschaft member, jurist and philosopher, professor in Jena

Schelling, Friedrich Wilhelm Joseph (1775–1854) philosopher, early friend of Hölderlin and Hegel, from 1827 professor in Munich, from 1841 professor at University of Berlin

Schiller, Ernst von (1796–1841) son of Friedrich Schiller, judge in Trier for many years

Schiller, Friedrich (1759–1805) poet, physician, dramatist, and historian

Schlegel, August Wilhelm (1767–1845) historian of literature, translator and Indologist, important representative of Romanticism, professor under whom Marx studied in Bonn

Schlegel, Friedrich (1772–1829) poet, philosopher, Indologist, important representative of Romanticism

Schleicher, Robert (1806–1846) family doctor of the Westphalens in Trier

Schleiermacher, Friedrich (1768–1834) Lutheran theologian and philosopher, professor at the University of Berlin

Schlesinger, Jakob (1892–1855) painter and art restorer

Schlink, Johann Heinrich (1793–1863) lawyer in Trier, friend of Heinrich Marx

Schlözer, August von (1735–1809) historian and constitutional law scholar, professor in Göttingen

Schmalz, Theodor (1760–1809) jurist, founding rector of the University of Berlin

Schmidt, Johann Caspar (see **Stirner, Max**)

Schnabel, Heinrich (1778–1853) head district authority in the Rhine province

Schneemann, Johann Gerhard (1796–1864) teacher of Karl Marx at the Trier Gymnasium

Schubarth, Karl Ernst (1796–1861) teacher and conservative publicist

Schuckmann, Friedrich von (1755–1834) 1814–1830 Prussian interior minister

Schulz, Wilhelm (1797–1860) publicist, friend of Georg Büchner, member of the Frankfurt national assembly

Schulze, Johannes (1786–1869) senior government council in Altenstein's ministry, friend of Hegel

Schwendler, Heinrich (1792–1847) teacher of Karl Marx at Trier Gymnasium

Semler, Johann Salomo (1725–1791) Lutheran theologian

GLOSSARY OF NAMES

Seneca (ca. 4 BCE–65 AD) Roman philosopher of Stoicism and naturalist

Sethe, Christoph (1767–1855) Prussian jurist, judge in the Rhine provinces, later in Berlin

Sextus Empiricus (second C. BCE) physician and philosopher, representative of Skepticism

Seydelmann, Karl (1793–1843) important German actor

Shakespeare, William (1564–1616) English dramatist, poet, and actor

Simon, Ludwig (1819–1872) son of Thomas Simon, 1836 Abitur at the Trier Gymnasium, 1848 representative at the Frankfurt National Assembly

Simon, Thomas (1794–1869) teacher of Karl Marx at the Trier Gymnasium

Solger, Karl Wilhelm Ferdinand (1780–1819) philosopher and philologist, professor at the University of Berlin

Spinoza, Baruch de (1632–1677) Dutch philosopher

Stahl, Friedrich Julius (1802–1861) conservative scholar of constitutional law; as a professor, successor of Eduard Gans at the University of Berlin

Stahr, Adolph (1805–1876) teacher, collaborator on the *Hallische Jahrbücher*

Steffens, Henrik (1773–1845) Norwegian-German philosopher and naturalist, professor under whom Karl Marx studied at the University of Berlin

Steininger, Johannes (1794–1874) teacher of Karl Marx at the gymnasium in Trier

Sterne, Laurence (1713–1768) Irish-English author and pastor

Stirner, Max (Johann Caspar Schmidt) (1806–1856) philosopher and publicist, Young Hegelian

Stobaeus, Ioannes (fifth C. BCE) Greek philosopher

Storr, Gottlob Christian (1746–1805) Protestant theologian

Strauß, David Friedrich (1808–1874) Protestant theologian

Tacitus, Publius Cornelius (ca. 55–120) Roman historian

Thibaut, Anton Friedrich Justus (1772–1840) jurist, professor in Heidelberg

Thiers, Adolphe (1797–1877) French politician and historian

Tholuck, August (1799–1877) Protestant theologian close to Pietism

Thomas Aquinas (1225–1274) theologian and philosopher

Tieck, Ludwig (1773–1853) poet, translator, important representative of Romanticism

Treitschke, Heinrich von (1834–1896) German historian

Trendelenburg, Friedrich Adolf (1802–1872) German philosopher, critic of Hegel

Tucher, Marie von (1791–1855) wife of G. W. F. Hegel

Tzschoppe, Gustav Adolf (1793–1842) Prussian administrative jurist, member of the Commission Against Demagogic Machinations

Valdenaire, Nikolaus (1772–1849) member of the provincial Landtag of the Rhine province

Valdenaire, Viktor (1812–1881) son of Nikolaus Valdenaire, acquaintance of Karl Marx

Varnhagen von Ense, Karl August (1785–1858) writer and Prussian diplomat

Varnhagen von Ense, Rahel, née Levin (1771–1833) writer and Berlin salon hostess

Vatke, Wilhelm (1802–1882) Protestant theologian

Veltheim, Elisabeth (Lisette) von (1778–1807) first wife of Ludwig von Westphalen

Veltheim, Werner von (1817–1855)
relative of Elisabeth von Veltheim,
friend of Edgar von Westphalen

Victoria (1819–1901) queen of England,
1837–1901

Voltaire (François-Marie Arouet)
(1694–1789), French philosopher
and writer

Wachsmuth, Wilhelm (1784–1866)
historian, censor of the *Hallische
Jahrbücher*

Walter, Ferdinand (1794–1879) jurist,
professor under whom Karl Marx
studied in Bonn

Weber, Carl Maria von (1786–1826)
composer

Weidig, Friedrich Ludwig (1791–1837)
pastor, organized the distribution of
Georg Büchner's *Hessian Courier*

Weisse, Christian Hermann (1801–1866)
Protestant theologian

Welcker, Friedrich Gottlob (1784–1868)
classicist and archaeologist, professor under whom Karl Marx studied
in Bonn

Welcker, Karl Theodor (1790–1859)
liberal scholar of constitutional law,
professor in Freiburg, co-publisher of
the *Staatslexikon* founded in 1834

Westphalen, Edgar von (1819–1890)
brother of Jenny von Westphalen,
friend of Karl Marx

Westphalen, Elisabeth (Lisette) von
(1800–1863) half sister of Jenny von
Westphalen

Westphalen, Ferdinand von (1799–
1876), half brother of Jenny von
Westphalen, Prussian interior minister 1850–1858

Westphalen, Franziska von (1807–1896)
half sister of Jenny von Westphalen

Westphalen, Jenny von (1814-1881)
wife of Karl Marx

Westphalen, Karl Hans Werner von
(1803–1840) half brother of Jenny
von Westphalen, friend of Karl
Marx

Westphalen, Ludwig von (1770–1842)
father of Jenny von Westphalen

Westphalen, Philip von (1724–1792)
father of Ludwig von Westphalen

Wienbarg, Ludolph (1802–1872) writer,
belonged to Young Germany

Wienenbrügge, Christian Hermann
(1813–1851) student of philosophy
in Bonn, later pastor, acquaintance
of Marx

Wigand, Otto Friedrich (1795–1870)
publisher in Lepizig (Saxony) of
books by the Young Hegelians and
Engels's *Condition of the Working
Class in England* in 1845

Windelband, Wilhelm (1848–1915)
German philosopher and historian
of philosophy

Winckelmann, Johann Joachim
(1717–1768) archaeologist and art
historian

Wishart de Pittarow, Jeannie
(1742–1811) married to Philip von
Westphalen, mother of Ludwig von
Westphalen

Wolff, Christian (1679–1754) German
philosopher, student of Leibniz

Wolff, Oskar Ludwig Bernhard (1799–
1851) writer, historian of literature,
associate professor in Jena

Woolston, Thomas (1668–1733) English
theologian

Wyttenbach, Friedrich Anton
(1812–1845) son of Johann Hugo
Wyttenbach, painter

Wyttenbach, Johann Hugo (1767–1848)
director of the Trier Gymnasium,
teacher of Karl Marx

Karl Marx and his Siblings*

Heinrich Marx	**Henriette Presburg**
15.4.1777 – 10.5.1838	20.9.1788 – 30.11.1863
	∞
	20.9.1814

Mauritz	Sophie	Karl	Hermann	Henriette	Louise	Emilie	Caroline	Eduard
30.10.1815	13.11.1816	5.5.1818	12.8.1819	28.10.1820	14.11.1821	24.10.1822	30.7.1824	7.4.1826
15.4.1819	29.11.1886	14.3.1883	14.10.1842	3.1.1845	3.7.1893	24.10.1888	13.1.1847	14.12.1837
	∞∞ 12.7.1842	∞∞ 19.6.1843		∞∞ 3.9.1844	∞∞ 7.6.1853	∞∞ 22.10.1859		
	Robert	Jenny von		Theodor	Jan Carel	Jakob		
	Schmalhausen	Westphalen		Simons	Juta	Conradi		
	21.4.1817	12.2.1814		5.6.1813	23.3.1824	19.11.1821		
	1.11.1862	2.12.1881		9.2.1863	8.4.1886	28.4.1892		

*According to Monz (1973) and Schöncke (1993).

Heinrich Marx and his Siblings* (RT: Rabbi in Trier)

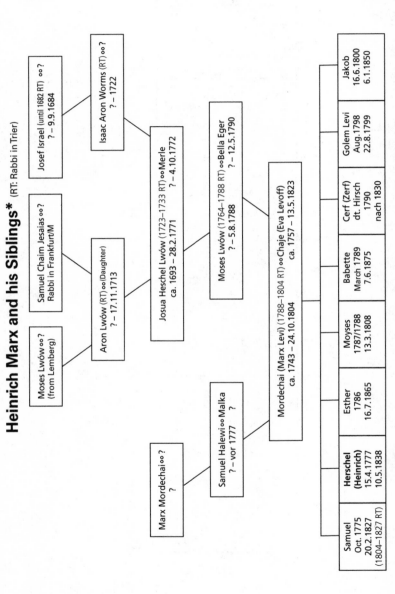

According to information in in Wachstein (1923), Horowitz (1928), Brilling (1958), and Schöncke (1993), Josua Heschel Lwów, great grandfather of Heinrich Marx, mentioned in a legal report that the two famous Jewish legal scholars, Josef ben Gerson Cohen (ca. 1511- 1.28.1591) and Meir Katzenellenbogen (ca. 1482 - 1.12.1565), were among his ancestors (Wachstein 1923: 284f.). Wachstein suspects that the first wife of Josua's father, Aron Lwów, (or even the wife of Aron's father, Moses Lwów) was a daughter of Moses Cohen (rabbi in Luck) and his wife Nessla, since Moses Cohn descended from Josef ben Gerson Cohen and Nessla descended from Meir Katzenellenbogen. On the basis of this surmise, Wachstein provides a family tree going all the way back to the 15th Century. However, Horowitz (1928: 487, fn. 2) was able to identify Aron's first wife as the daughter of the Frankfurt rabbi, Samuel Chaim Jesaias, so the first possibility must be discarded. Monz (1973: 222) then provides an expanded family tree, in which Aron's father, Moses Lwów, is married to this daughter of Moses Cohen and Nessla. However, there is no source for the wife of Aron's father; we do not know whether Moses Cohen and Nessla even had a daughter. The relationship to Gerson and Katzenellenbogen could also have come about by other means. That is why I have not reproduced this expanded family tree and limited myself to the ancestors known for certain.

Henriette Presburg and her Siblings*

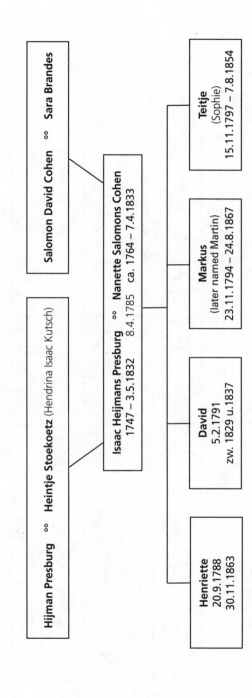

Hijman Presburg °° Heintje Stoekoetz (Hendrina Isaac Kutsch)

Salomon David Cohen °° Sara Brandes

Isaac Heijmans Presburg °° Nanette Salomons Cohen
1747 – 3.5.1832   8.4.1785   ca. 1764 – 7.4.1833

Henriette
20.9.1788
30.11.1863

David
5.2.1791
zw. 1829 u.1837

Markus
(later named Martin)
23.11.1794 – 24.8.1867

Teitje
(Sophie)
15.11.1797 – 7.8.1854

*Monz provides a more comprehensive family tree for Henriette's father, but it is based, in part, on speculation. Here, I have reproduced the ancestors that are known for certain.

Jenny von Westphalen and her Siblings*

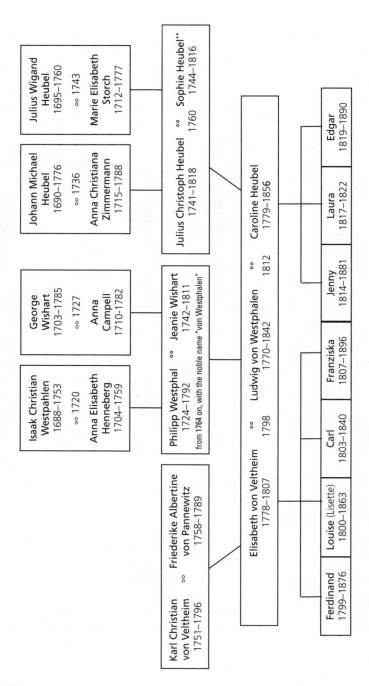

*According to Monz (1973) and Wilcke (1983: 764,777f.)).

**Sophie Heubel was a second cousin of her husband (Limmroth 2014: 31).

Bibliography

WORKS BY MARX AND ENGELS

Marx Engels Gesamtausgabe (MEGA) appearing since 1975 (Walter de Gruyter Verlag, Berlin).
Marx-Engels Collected Works (Lawrence and Wishart, London).
Marx, Karl (1973): *Grundrisse*, London: Penguin Books.
Marx, Karl (1976): *Capital Volume I*, London: Penguin Books.
Marx, Karl (1978): *Capital Volume II*, London: Penguin Books.
Marx, Karl (1981): *Capital Volume III*, London: Penguin Books.

Adelslexikon, 18 Bände (1972–2012), Limburg: Starke.
Adler, Georg (1887): *Zur Orientierung über Marx' Leben und Entwicklungsgang*, Anhang in: ders., Die Grundlagen der Karl Marxschen Kritik der bestehenden Volkswirtschaft, Tübingen (Nachdruck Hildesheim: Olms 1968) 226–290.
Allgemeines deutsches Conversations-Lexicon für die Gebildeten eines jeden Standes in 10 Bänden und 2 Supplements, Herausgegeben von einem Vereine Gelehrter (1839–1844), Leipzig: Gebrüder Reichenbach.
Ascher, Saul (1815): *Die Germanomanie. Skizze zu einem Zeitgemälde*, Berlin: Achenwall.
Bachmann, Karl Friedrich (1833): *Ueber Hegel's System und die Nothwendigkeit einer nochmaligen Umgestaltung der Philosophie*, Leipzig: Vogel.
Bachmann, Karl Friedrich (1835): *Anti-Hegel. Antwort an Herrn Professor Rosenkranz in Königsberg auf dessen Sendschreiben*, Jena: Cröker.
Baertschi, Annette M.; King, Colin G. (Hg.) (2009): *Die modernen Väter der Antike. Die Entwicklung der Altertumswissenschaften an Akademie und Universität im Berlin des 19. Jahrhunderts*, Berlin: Walter de Gruyter.
Barnikol, Ernst (1972): *Bruno Bauer. Studien und Materialien*. Aus dem Nachlaß ausgewählt und zusammengestellt von Peter Reimer und Hans-Martin Sass, Assen: Van Gorcum.
Baronovitch, Laurence (1992): "Karl Marx and Greek Philosophy: Some Explorations into the Themes of Intellectual Accomodation and Moral

Hypocrisy," in: McCarthy, George E. (Hg.): *Marx and Aristotle: Nineteenth Century German Social Theory and Classical Antiquity*, Lanham, MD: Rowman & Littlefield, 155–171.

Barth, Hans (1945): *Wahrheit und Ideologie*, Frankfurt/M.: Suhrkamp 1974.

Barthes, Roland (1968): "The Death of the Author," in: Leitch, Vincent et al. (eds.), *The Norton Anthology of Theory & Criticism*, New York: W.W. Norton and Company.

Bauer, Bruno (1829): *Über die Prinzipien des Schönen. Eine Preisschrift*, hrsg. von Douglas Moggach und W. Schultze, Berlin: Akademie Verlag 1996.

Bauer, Bruno (1834): [Rezension von] August Heydenreich, *Die eigenthümlichen Lehren des Christenthums rein biblisch dargestellt*. Erster Band, in: *Jahrbücher für wissenschaftliche Kritik*, 1834/II, 196–200.

Bauer, Bruno (1835/36): [Rezension von] David Friedrich Strauß, *Das Leben Jesu*, in: *Jahrbücher für wissenschaftliche Kritik*, 1835/II, 879–894, 897–912, 1836/I, 681–694, 697–704.

Bauer, Bruno (1838a): *Kritik der Geschichte der Offenbarung. Erster Theil: Die Religion des Alten Testaments in der geschichtlichen Entwickelung ihrer Principien*, 2 Bände, Berlin: Dümmler.

Bauer, Bruno (1838b): [Rezension von] David Friedrich Strauß, *Streitschriften zur Vertheidigung meiner Schrift über das Leben Jesu und zur Charakteristik der gegen wärtigen Theologie*, in: *Jahrbücher für wissenschaftliche Kritik*, 1838/I, 817–838.

Bauer, Bruno (1839): *Herr Dr. Hengstenberg. Kritische Briefe über den Gegensatz des Gesetzes und des Evangelium*, Berlin: Dümmler.

Bauer, Bruno (1840a): *Die evangelische Landeskirche Preußens und die Wissenschaft*, Leipzig: Otto Wigand.

Bauer, Bruno (1840b): *Kritik der evangelischen Geschichte des Johannes*, Bremen: Schünemann.

Bauer, Bruno (1841): *Kritik der evangelischen Geschichte der Synoptiker*. Erster Band, Leipzig: Wigand.

Bauer, Bruno (1844a): *Briefwechsel zwischen Bruno Bauer und Edgar Bauer während der Jahre 1839–1842 zwischen Bonn und Berlin*, Charlottenburg: Verlag von Egbert Bauer.

Bauer, Bruno (1844b): "Erkenntnis des Oberzensurgerichts in Betreff der zwei ersten Bogen des Briefwechsels zwischen Bruno und Edgar Bauer," in: *Allgemeine Literaturzeitung*. Monatsschrift hrsg. von Bruno Bauer, Heft 6, Mai 1844, 38–41.

Bauer, Joachim; Pester, Thomas (2012): "Promotion von Karl Marx an der Universität Jena 1841. Hintergründe und Folgen," in: Bodsch, Ingrid (Hg.), *Dr. Karl Marx. Vom Studium zur Promotion – Bonn, Berlin, Jena. Begleitbuch zur gleichnamigen Ausstellung des Stadtmuseum Bonn*, Bonn: Verlag Stadtmuseum, 47–82.

Bayly, Christopher (2004): *The Birth of the Modern World, 1780–1914*, Oxford: Blackwell.

Behler, Ernst (1978): "Nietzsche, Marx und die deutsche Frühromantik," in: Grimm, Reinhold; Hermand, Jost (Hrsg.), *Karl Marx und Friedrich Nietzsche. Acht Beiträge*, Königstein/Ts.: Athenäum.

Behler, Ernst (1987). *The Philosophy of German Idealism: Fichte, Jacobi, and Schelling*, London: Continuum.

Behler, Ernst (1992): *Frühromantik*, Berlin: Walter de Gruyter.

Beiträge zur Marx-Engels-Forschung Neue Folge. Sonderband 1: David Borisovic Rjazanov und die erste MEGA (1997), Hamburg: Argument.

Bentzel–Sternau, Karl Christian Ernst Graf von (1818): *Anti-Israel. Eine Vorlesung in der geheimen Akademie zum grünen Esel als Eintrittsrede gehalten*, in: Steiger, Johann Anselm (Hg.): *Karl Christian Ernst von Bentzel-Sternau, Anti-Israel. Eine projüdische Satire aus dem Jahre 1818. Nebst den antijüdischen Traktaten Friedrich Rühs' und Jakob Friedrich Fries' (1816)*, Heidelberg: Manutius 2004.

Berlin, Isaiah (1939/2013): *Karl Marx*, Princeton: Princeton University Press.

Bethmann–Hollweg, Moritz August von (1850): *Ueber die Germanen vor der Völkerwanderung. Festgabe dem Fürsten Deutscher Rechtslehrer Friedrich Carl von Savigny zur Jubelfeier des 31. Oktober 1850*, Bonn: Adolph Marcus.

Blank, Hans-Joachim (2017): "Zur Dissertation von Karl Marx. Über ihre Überlieferungs-, Editions- und Entstehungsgeschichte," in: *Beiträge zur Marx-Engels Forschung. Neue Folge* 2016/17, 225–254.

Blänkner, Reinhard; Göhler, Gerhard; Waszek, Norbert (Hg.) (2002): *Eduard Gans (1797–1839). Politischer Professor zwischen Restauration und Vormärz*, Leipzig: Leipziger Universitätsverlag.

Blumenberg, Werner (1962): *Karl Marx. Mit Selbstzeugnissen und Bilddokumenten*, Reinbek: Rowohlt.

Bockmühl, Klaus (1980): *Leiblichkeit und Gesellschaft. Studien zur Religionskritik und Anthropologie im Frühwerk von Ludwig Feuerbach und Karl Marx*, 2. Aufl., Gießen: Brunnen.

Bödeker, Hans Erich (2003): "Biographie. Annäherungen an den gegenwärtigen Forschungs- und Diskussionsstand," in: ders. (Hrsg.), *Biographie schreiben*, Göttingen: Wallstein, 9–63.

Bodsch, Ingrid (2012): "Marx und Bonn 1835/36 und 1841/42," in: dies. (Hg.), *Dr. Karl Marx. Vom Studium zur Promotion – Bonn, Berlin, Jena. Begleitbuch zur gleich namigen Ausstellung des Stadtmuseum Bonn*, Bonn: Verlag Stadtmuseum, 9–27.

Böning, Jürgen (2017): *Karl Marx in Hamburg. Der Produktionsprozess des «Kapital»*, Hamburg: VSA.

Börne, Ludwig (1832–34): *Briefe aus Paris*, in: ders., *Werke in zwei Bänden*, Bd. 2, 5–275, Berlin: Aufbau Verlag 1981.

Böse, Heinz–Günther (1951): *Ludwig Simon von Trier (1819–1872). Leben und Anschauungen eines rheinischen Achtundvierzigers*, Dissertation, Mainz.

Bourdieu, Pierre (1986): "The Biographical Illusion," in: Hemecker, Wilhelm and Edward Saunders (Eds.), *Biography in Theory: Key Texts with Commentaries*, Boston/Berlin: de Gruyter.

Braun, Johann (1997): *Judentum, Jurisprudenz und Philosophie. Bilder aus dem Leben des Juristen Eduard Gans (1797–1839)*, Baden–Baden: Nomos.

Braun, Johann (2005): "Einführung des Herausgebers," in: Eduard Gans, *Naturrecht und Universalgeschichte. Vorlesungen nach G.W.F. Hegel*. Herausgegeben und eingeleitet von Johann Braun, Tübingen: Mohr Siebeck, xix–lvii.

Braun, Johann (2011): Einleitung, in: *Eduard Gans, Briefe und Dokumente*, herausgegeben von Johann Braun, Tübingen: Mohr Siebeck.

Breckman, Warren (1999): *Marx, the Young Hegelians, and the Origins of Radical Social Theory*, Cambridge: Cambridge University Press.

Breuer, Karl Hugo (1954): *Der junge Marx. Sein Weg zum Kommunismus*, Inaugural–Dissertation an der philosophischen Fakultät der Universität Köln, Köln: Luthe–Druck.

Breuer, Mordechai (1996): "Frühe Neuzeit und Beginn der Moderne," in: Meyer, Michael A. (Hg.): *Deutsch-Jüdische Geschichte in der Neuzeit. Band I: Tradition und Aufklärung 1600–1780*, München: Beck, 85–247.

Briese, Olaf (2013): "Akademikerschwemme, Junghegelianismus als Jugendbewegung," in: Lambrecht, Lars (Hg.): *Umstürzende Gedanken. Radikale Theorie im Vorfeld der 1848er Revolution*, Frankfurt/M.: Peter Lang, 123–142.

Brilling, Bernhard (1958): "Beiträge zur Geschichte der Juden in Trier," in: *Trierisches Jahrbuch 1958*, Trier: Lintz, 46–50.

Brophy, James M. (2007): *Popular Culture and the Public Sphere in the Rhineland 1800–1850*, Cambridge: Cambridge University Press.

Büchner, Georg (1988): *Werke und Briefe. Münchner Ausgabe*, München: Hanser.

Browning, Gary K. (2000): "Marx's Doctoral Dissertation: The Development of a Hegelian Thesis," in: Burns, Tony; Fraser, Ian (eds.), *The Hegel-Marx Connection*, Houndmills: Macmillan, 131–145.

Buchbinder, Reinhard (1976): *Bibelzitate, Bibelanspielungen, Bibelparodien, theologische Vergleiche und bei Marx und Engels*, Berlin: Erich Schmidt Verlag.

Bunzel, Wolfgang (2003): "'Der Geschichte in die Hände arbeiten' Zur Romantikkonzeption der Junghegelianer," in: Bunzel, Wolfgang; Stein, Peter; Vaßen, Florian (Hg.), *Romantik und Vormärz* (Forum Vormärz Forschung, Vormärz Studien X), Bielefeld: Aisthesis, 313–338,.

Bunzel, Wolfgang; Hundt, Martin; Lambrecht, Lars (2006): *Zentrum und Peripherie. Arnold Ruges Korrespondenz mit Junghegelianern in Berlin*, Frankfurt/M.: Peter Lang.

Burns, Tony (2000): "Materialism in Ancient Greek Philosophy and in the Writings of the Young Marx," in: *Historical Materialism*, No. 7, 3–39.

Carlyle, Thomas (1841): *On Heroes, Hero-Worship and the Heroic in History*, London: Fraser.

Carr, Edward Hallett (1934): *Karl Marx. A Study in Fanaticism*, London: Dent.

Carr, Edward Hallett (1980): "An Autobiography," in: E. H. Carr: *A Critical Appraisal*, edited by Michael Cox, Houndmills: Palgrave 2000, xiii–xxii.

Carrière, Moriz (1914): *Lebenserinnerungen (1817–1847)*, hrsg. von Wilhelm Diehl, in: *Archiv für Hessische Geschichte und Altertumskunde*. N.F. Bd. X, H.2, Darmstadt.

Cieszkowski, August von (1838): *Prolegomena zur Historiosophie*, Berlin: Veit.

Clark, Christopher (2009): *Iron Kingdom: The Rise and Downfall of Prussia 1600–1947*, Cambridge, MA: Harvard University Press.

Clemens, Gabriele B. (2004): "Trier unter dem Hammer – die Nationalgüterverkäufe," in: Dühr, Elisabeth; Lehnert-Leven, Christl (Hg.):

Unter der Trikolore. Trier in Frankreich, Napoleon in Trier 1794–1814, Trier: Städtisches Museum Simeonsstift, 383–395.

Cornu, Auguste (1934): *Karl Marx, l'homme et l'oeuvre. De l'hegelianisme au materialism historique (1818-1845)*, Paris: Felix Alcan.

Cornu, Auguste (1954): *Karl Marx und Friedrich Engels. Leben und Werk. Band 1: 1818–1844*, Berlin: Aufbau Verlag.

Cornu, Auguste (1962): *Karl Marx und Friedrich Engels. Leben und Werk. Band 2: 1844–1845*, Berlin: Aufbau Verlag.

Cornu, Auguste (1968): *Karl Marx und Friedrich Engels. Leben und Werk. Band 3: 1845–1846*, Berlin: Aufbau Verlag.

Courth, Franz (1980): "Die Evangelienkritik des D. Fr. Strauß im Echo seiner Zeitgenossen. Zur Breitenwirkung seines Werkes," in: Georg Schwaiger (Hg.), *Historische Kritik in der Theologie. Beiträge zu ihrer Geschichte*, Göttingen: Vandenhoeck & Ruprecht.

Craig, Gordon A. (1982): *The Germans*, New York: Meridian.

Czóbel, Ernst (1934): *Karl Marx. Chronik seines Lebens in Einzeldaten*, Frankfurt/M.: Makol 1971.

Deckert, Helmut (1966): "Marx und seine Kommilitonen als Hörer Schlegels in Bonn. Zu einem Marx-Autograph der Sächsischen Landesbibliothek," in: *Festschrift zum 60. Geburtstag von Prof. Dr. phil. Hans Lülfing am 24. November 1966. 83. Beiheft zum Zentralblatt für Bibliothekswesen*, Leipzig: Bibliographisches Institut, 33–53.

Demetz, Peter (1969): *Marx, Engels und die Dichter. Ein Kapitel deutscher Literaturgeschichte*, Frankfurt/M.: Ullstein.

D'Hondt, Jacques (1973): *Hegel in seiner Zeit*, Berlin: Akademie Verlag.

Dietz, Josef (1968): "Bürger und Studenten," in: Höroldt, Dietrich (Hg.): *Stadt und Universität. Rückblick aus Anlaß der 150 Jahr-Feier der Universität Bonn. Bonner Geschichtsblätter Band 22*, Bonn, 215–266.

Dilthey, Wilhelm (2002): *The Formation of the Historical World in the Human Sciences*, Princeton and Oxford: Princeton University Press.

Dlubek, Rolf (1994): "Die Entstehung der zweiten Marx-Engels-Gesamtausgabe (MEGA) im Spannungsfeld von legitimatorischem Auftrag und editorischer Sorgfalt," in: *MEGA-Studien* 1994/1, 60–106.

Dohm, Christian Wilhelm (1781): *Ueber die bürgerliche Verbesserung der Juden*, Berlin: Nicolai.

Dowe, Dieter (1970): *Aktion und Organisation. Arbeiterbewegung, sozialistische und kommunistische Bewegung in der preußischen Rheinprovinz 1820–1852*, Hannover: Verlag für Literatur und Zeitgeschehen.

Dreyer, Michael; Ries, Klaus (Hg.) (2014): *Romantik und Freiheit. Wechselspiele zwischen Ästhetik und Politik*, Heidelberg: Universitätsverlag Winter.

Dronke, Ernst (1846): *Berlin*, Berlin: Rütten & Löning 1987.

Duden (2007): *Das Herkunftswörterbuch. Etymologie der deutschen Sprache*, 4. neubearbeitete Auflage, Mannheim: Duden.

Dühr, Elisabeth (Hg.) (1998): *«Der schlimmste Punkt der Provinz» Demokratische Revolution 1848/49 in Trier und Umgebung*, Trier: Städtisches Museum Simeonstift.

..

Eberlein, Hermann P. (2009): *Bruno Bauer: Vom Marx-Freund zum Antisemiten*, Berlin: Dietz.

Eichler, Martin (2015): *Von der Vernunft zum Wert. Die Grundlagen der ökonomischen Theorie von Karl Marx*, Bielefeld: transcript.

Elias, Norbert (1969): Über den Prozeß der Zivilisation, Bern: Francke.

Engelberg, Ernst (1985): *Bismarck. Band I: Urpreuße und Reichsgründer*, Berlin: Siedler 1998.

Engelberg, Ernst; Schleier, Hans (1990): "Geschichte und Theorie der historischen Biographie," in: *Zeitschrift für Geschichtsforschung*, Jg. 38, 195–217.

Engels, Friedrich: see works of Marx and Engels above.

Erikson, Erik H. (1958): *Der junge Mann Luther. Eine psychoanalytische und historische Studie*, Frankfurt/M.: Suhrkamp 2016.

Erikson, Erik H. (1966): *Identität und Lebenszyklus*, Frankfurt/M.: Suhrkamp.

Essbach, Wolfgang (1988): *Die Junghegelianer. Soziologie einer Intellektuellengruppe*, München: Fink.

Euringer, Martin (2003): *Epikur. Antike Lebensfreude in der Gegenwart*, Stuttgart: Kohlhammer.

Ewald, Johann Ludwig (1816): *Ideen, über die nöthige Organisation der Israeliten in Christlichen Staaten*. Herausgegeben und mit einem Nachwort versehen von Johann Anselm Steiger, Heidelberg: Manutius 1999.

Ewald, Johann Ludwig (1817): "Der Geist des Christenthums und des ächten deutschen Volksthums, dargestellt, gegen die Feinde der Israeliten," in: ders., *Projüdische Schriften aus den Jahren 1817 bis 1821*, herausgegeben von Johann Anselm Steiger, Heidelberg: Manutius 2000, 7–92.

Ewald, Johann Ludwig (1821): "Beantwortung der Fragen: Was sollten die Juden jetzt, und was sollte der Staat für sie thun?" in: ders., *Projüdische Schriften aus den Jahren 1817 bis 1821*, herausgegeben von Johann Anselm Steiger, Heidelberg: Manutius 2000, 111–139.

Fenves, Peter (1986): "Marx's Doctoral Thesis on two Greek Atomists and the Post–Kantian Interpretations," in: *Journal of the History of Ideas*, vol. 47, 433–452.

Fetz, Bernhard (Hg.) (2009): *Die Biographie. Zur Grundlegung ihrer Theorie*, Berlin: Walter de Gruyter.

Feuerbach, Ludwig (1830): *Gedanken über Tod und Unsterblichkeit*, in: ders., *Gesammelte Werke*, Bd.1, 177–515.

Feuerbach, Ludwig (1835a): *Kritik des Anti-Hegels. Eine Einleitung in das Studium der Philosophie*, in: ders., *Gesammelte Werke*, Bd.8, Berlin: Akademie Verlag 1989, 62–127.

Feuerbach, Ludwig (1835b): [Rezension von] Friedrich Julius Stahl, *Philosophie des Rechts nach geschichtlicher Ansicht*, in: ders., *Gesammelte Werke*, Bd. 8, Berlin: Akademie Verlag 1989, 24–43.

Feuerbach, Ludwig (1838): "Zur Kritik der positiven Philosophie," in: *Hallische Jahrbücher*, H. 289–293.

Feuerbach, Ludwig (1839a): Über Philosophie und Christentum in Beziehung auf den *der Hegelschen Philosophie gemachten Vorwurf der Unchristlichkeit*, in: ders., *Gesammelte Werke*, Bd. 8, 219–292.

Feuerbach, Ludwig (1839b): *Kritik der Hegelschen Philosophie*, in: *Hallische Jahrbücher*, Nr. 208–216.
Feuerbach, Ludwig (1841): *Das Wesen des Christentums*, in: ders., *Gesammelte Werke*, Bd. 5.
Feuerbach, Ludwig (1967–2004): *Gesammelte Werke*, 21 Bände, Herausgegeben von Werner Schuffenhauer, Berlin: Akademie Verlag.
Finelli, Roberto (2015): *A Failed Parracide. Hegel and the Young Marx*, Leiden: Brill.
Fischer, Karl Philipp (1839): *Die Idee der Gottheit. Ein Versuch, den Theismus speculativ zu begründen und zu entwickeln*, Stuttgart: Liesching.
Foucault, Michel (1982) *The Archeology of Knowledge*, New York: Vintage.
Foucault, Michel (1969): "What Is an Author?" in: Leitch, Vincent et al. (eds.), *The Norton Anthology of Theory and Criticism*, New York: W.W. Norton and Company.
Frauenstädt, Julius (1839): [Rezension von] August v. Cieszkowski, *Prolegomena zur Historiosophie*, in: *Hallische Jahrbücher* Nr. 60–61.
Friedenthal, Richard (1981): *Karl Marx. Sein Leben und seine Zeit*, München: Piper.
Fries, Jakob Friedrich (1816): *Ueber die Gefährdung des Wohlstandes und Charakters der Deutschen durch die Juden. Eine aus den Heidelberger Jahrbüchern für Litteratur besonders abgedruckte Recension der Schrift des Professors Rühs in Berlin: «Ueber die Ansprüche der Juden an das deutsche Bürgerrecht. Zweyter verbesserter Abdruck etc.»*, Heidelberg Mohr und Winter 1816 (wieder abgedruckt in Bentzel–Sternau 1818: 125–153).
Fulda, Hans Friedrich (2007): "Hegels These, dass die Aufeinanderfolge von philosophischen Systemen dieselbe sei wie die von Stufen logischer Gedankenentwicklung," in: Heidemann, Dietmar; Krijnen, Christian (Hrsg.), *Hegel und die Geschichte der Philosophie*, Darmstadt: Wissenschaftliche Buchgesellschaft, 4–14.
Gabriel, Mary (2011): *Love and Capital. Karl and Jenny Marx and the Birth of a Revolution*, New York: Little, Brown and Co.
Gadamer, Hans–Georg (1975/2013): *Truth and Method*, London: Bloomsbury.
Gadamer, Hans-Georg (1967): "Rhetoric, Hermeneutics, and the Critique of Ideology," in: Mueller-Vollmer, Kurt (Ed.) (1985): *The Hermeneutics Reader*, New York: Continuum.
Gall, Lothar (2011): *Wilhelm von Humboldt. Ein Preuße von Welt*, Berlin: Propyläen.
Gans, Eduard (1824): *Das Erbrecht in weltgeschichtlicher Entwicklung*. Band 1, Berlin: Maurer.
Gans, Eduard (1825): *Das Erbrecht in weltgeschichtlicher Entwicklung*. Band 2, Berlin: Maurer.
Gans, Eduard (1836): *Rückblicke auf Personen und Zustände. Neudruck.* Herausgegeben, kommentiert und mit einer Einleitung versehen von Norbert Waszek, Stuttgart: frommann-holzboog 1995.
Gans, Eduard (2005): *Naturrecht und Universalrechtsgeschichte. Vorlesungen nach G.W.F. Hegel.* Herausgegeben und eingeleitet von Johann Braun, Tübingen: Mohr Siebeck.

Geibel, Emmanuel (1909): *Jugendbriefe*, Berlin: Karl Curtius.

Geisthövel, Alexa (2008): *Restauration und Vormärz 1815–1847*, Paderborn: Schöningh.

Gemkow, Heinrich (1977): "Karl Marx und Edgar von Westphalen – Studiengefährten in Berlin," in: *Beiträge zur Marx-Engels-Forschung* 1, 15–22.

Gemkow, Heinrich (1978): "Nachträge zur Biographie der Studenten Karl Marx und Edgar von Westphalen," in: *Beiträge zur Marx-Engels-Forschung* 3, 143–146.

Gemkow, Heinrich (1999): Edgar von Westphalen. "Der ungewöhnliche Lebensweg des Schwagers von Karl Marx," in: *Jahrbuch für westdeutsche Landesgeschichte*, Band 25, 401–511.

Gemkow, Heinrich (2008): "Aus dem Leben einer rheinischen Familie im 19. Jahrhundert. Archivalische Funde zu den Familien Westphalen und Marx," in: *Jahrbuch für westdeutsche Landesgeschichte*, Band 34, 497–524.

Gerhardt, Hans (1926): *Hundert Jahre Bonner Corps. Die korporationsgeschichtliche Entwicklung des Bonner S.C. von 1819 bis 1918*, Frankfurt/M.: Verlag der Deutschen Corpszeitung.

Gerhardt, Volker; Mehring, Reinhard; Rindert, Jana (1999): *Berliner Geist. Eine Geschichte der Berliner Universitätsphilosophie bis 1946. Mit einem Ausblick auf die Gegenwart der Humboldt-Universität*, Berlin: Akademie Verlag.

Gerstenberger, Heide (2017): *Markt und Gewalt. Die Funktionsweise des historischen Kapitalismus*, Münster: Westfälisches Dampfboot.

Gestrich, Andreas (1988): "Einleitung: Sozialhistorische Biographieforschung," in: ders. u.a. (Hrsg.), *Biographie – sozialgeschichtlich. Sieben Beiträge*, Göttingen: Vandenhoek u. Ruprecht, 5–28.

Gestrich, Christoph (1989): *Das Erbe Hegels in der Systematischen Theologie an der Berliner Universität* im 19. Jahrhundert, in: Besier, Gerhard; Gestrich, Christoph (Hrsg.), 450 Jahre Evangelische Theologie in Berlin, Göttingen: Vandenhoeck & Ruprecht, 183–206.

Gielkens, Jan (1999): *Karl Marx und seine niederländischen Verwandten. Eine kommentierte Quellenedition*, aus dem Karl-Marx-Haus 50, Trier.

Gockel, Eberhard (1989): *Karl Marx in Bonn. Alte Adressen neu entdeckt*, Bonn.

Goethe, Johann Wolfgang von (1907): *Wilhelm Meister's Apprenticeship and Travels*, London: Chapman and Hall.

Goethe, Johann Wolfgang von (2008): *Poetry and Truth*. Auckland: The Floating Press.

Goethe, Johann Wolfgang von (1882): "Campaign in France 1792," in: Goethe, Johann Wolfgang von (1882): *Miscellaneous Travels of J.W. Goethe*, London: George Bell and Sons.

Goethe, Johann Wolfgang von (2000): *Werke in 14 Bänden*, herausgegeben von Erich Trunz (Hamburger Ausgabe), München: Deutscher Taschenbuch Verlag.

Goldschmidt, Werner (1987): "Bauer als Gegenstand der Marx-Forschung," in: *Marxistische Studien. Jahrbuch des IMSF 12* (I/1987), Frankfurt/M.: Institut für marxistische Studien, 68–81.

Görres, Joseph (1838): *Athanasius*, Regensburg: Manz.

Göschel, Karl Friedrich (1829): *Aphorismen über Nichtwissen und absolutes Wissen im Verhältnisse zur christlichen Glaubenserkenntniß. Ein Beytrag zum Verständnisse der Philosophie unser Zeit*, Berlin: Franklin.

Grab, Walter (1985): *Georg Büchner und die Revolution von 1848. Der Büchner Essay von Wilhelm Schulz aus dem Jahr 1851. Text und Kommentar*, Königstein/Ts.: Athenäum.

Grab, Walter (1987): *Dr. Wilhelm Schulz aus Darmstadt. Weggefährte von Georg Büchner und Inspirator von Karl Marx*, Frankfurt/Main: Büchergilde Gutenberg.

Graetz, Michael (1996): "Jüdische Aufklärung," in: Meyer, Michael A. (Hg.): *Deutsch-Jüdische Geschichte in der Neuzeit. Band I: Tradition und Aufklärung 1600–1780*, München: Beck, 251–359.

Graf, Friedrich Wilhelm (1978): "Friedrich Strauß und die Hallischen Jahrbücher," in: *Archiv für Kulturgeschichte*, Jg. 60, 383–430.

Grandt, Jens (2006): *Ludwig Feuerbach und die Welt des Glaubens*, Münster: Westfälisches Dampfboot.

Greenblatt, Stephen (2012): *The Swerve: How the World Became Modern*, New York: W.W. Norton and Company.

Greiling, Werner (1993): *Varnhagen von Ense. Lebensweg eines Liberalen*, Köln: Böhlau.

Gross, Guido (1956): *Trierer Geistesleben. Unter dem Einfluß von Aufklärung und Romantik (1750–1850)*, Trier: Lintz.

Gross, Guido (1962): "Geschichte des Friedrich-Wilhelm-Gymnasiums," in: Jakob Schwall (Hrsg.), *400 Jahre Friedrich-Wilhelm-Gymnasium Trier. Festschrift*, Trier: Paulinus Verlag, 7–73.

Gross, Guido (1994): "Johann Steininger (1794–1874). Erinnerungen an einen Trierer Pädagogen, Geologen und Historiker," in: *Neues Trierisches Jahrbuch*, Bd.34, 85–104.

Gross, Guido (1998): "Trier und die Trierer im Vormärz," in: Dühr, Elisabeth (Hg.): "Der schlimmste Punkt der Provinz" Demokratische Revolution 1848/49 in Trier und *Umgebung*, Trier: Städtisches Museum Simeonstift, 72–91.

Große, Wilhelm (2011): "«Ein deutsches Lesebuch für Gymnasialklassen» Oder: Was hielt Karl Marx im Deutschunterricht in Händen? Zum Deutschunterricht in der ersten Hälfte des 19. Jahrhunderts am Gymnasium in Trier," in: *Kurtrierisches Jahrbuch*, Jg. 51, 347–356.

Grünberg, Carl (1925): "Marx als Abiturient," in: *Archiv für die Geschichte des Sozialismus und der Arbeiterbewegung*, Jg. 11, 424–444.

Grünberg, Carl (1926): "Nachtrag zu: Marx als Abiturient," in: *Archiv für die Geschichte des Sozialismus und der Arbeiterbewegung*, Jg. 12, 239–240.

Gutzkow, Karl (1835): *Wally, die Zweiflerin*, Stuttgart: Reclam 1979.

Hachtmann, Rüdiger (2016): *Prediger wider alle demokratischen*, Teufel: Ernst.

Hengstenberg, Wilhelm (1802–1869), in: Schmidt, Walter (Hg.): *Akteure eines Umbruchs. Männer und Frauen der Revolution von 1848/49*, Band 5, Berlin: Fides, 129–180.

Hähner, Olaf (1999): *Historische Biographie. Die Entwicklung einer geschichtswissenschaftlichen Darstellungsform von der Antike bis ins 20. Jahrhundert*, Frankfurt/M.: Peter Lang.

Hansen, Joseph (1906): *Gustav von Mevissen. Ein rheinisches Lebensbild (1815–1899)*, 2 Bände, Berlin: Reimer.

Hausen, Karin (1988): ". . . eine Ulme für das schwanke Efeu." Ehepaare im deutschen Bildungsbürgertum," in: Frevert, Ute (Hg.): *Bürgerinnen und Bürger. Geschlechterverhältnisse im 19. Jahrhundert*, Göttingen: Vandenhoeck & Ruprecht, 85–117.

Haym, Rudolf (1857): *Hegel und seine Zeit. Vorlesungen über Entstehung und Entwicklung, Wesen und Werth der Hegel'schen Philosophie*, Berlin: Rudolf Gärtner.

Haym, Rudolf (1870): *Die romantische Schule. Ein Beitrag zur Geschichte des deutschen Geistes*, Berlin: Gaertner.

Hecker, Rolf (2000): "Erfolgreiche Kooperation. Das Frankfurter Institut für Sozialforschung und das Moskauer Marx-Engels-Institut (1924–1928)," in: *Beiträge zur Marx-Engels-Forschung. Neue Folge. Sonderband 2*, Hamburg: Argument Verlag, 9–118.

Hecker, Rolf (2001): "Fortsetzung und Ende der ersten MEGA zwischen Nationalsozialismus und Stalinismus (1931–1941)," in: *Beiträge zur Marx-Engels-Forschung. Neue Folge. Sonderband 3*, Hamburg: Argument Verlag, 181–311.

Hecker, Rolf; Limmroth, Angelika (Hg.) (2014): *Jenny Marx. Die Briefe*, Berlin: Dietz.

Hegel, Georg Wilhelm Friedrich (1975). *Aesthetics: Lectures on Fine Art. Volume I*, Oxford: Clarendon Press.

Hegel, Georg Wilhelm Friedrich (1991). *Elements of the Philosophy of Right*, Cambridge: Cambridge University Press.

Hegel, Georg Wilhelm Friedrich (2010). *Encyclopedia of the Philosophical Sciences in Basic Outline. Part I: Science of Logic*, Cambridge: Cambridge University Press.

Hegel, Georg Wilhelm Friedrich (1984). *Hegel: The Letters*, Bloomington: Indiana University Press.

Hegel, Georg Wilhelm Friedrich (2009). *Lectures on the History of Philosophy, 1825–6, Volume I*, Oxford: Oxford University Press.

Hegel, Georg Wilhelm Friedrich (2006). *Lectures on the History of Philosophy, 1825–6, Volume II*, Oxford: Oxford University Press.

Hegel, Georg Wilhelm Friedrich (1988). *Lectures on the Philosophy of Religion*, Berkeley and Los Angeles: University of California Press.

Hegel, Georg Wilhelm Friedrich (1977). *Phenomenology of Spirit*, Oxford: Oxford University Press.

Hegel, Georg Wilhelm Friedrich (1956). *The Philosophy of History*, Mineola, NY: Dover Publications.

Hegel, Georg Wilhelm Friedrich (1999). *Political Writings*, Cambridge: Cambridge University Press.

Hegel, Georg Wilhelm Friedrich (2010). *The Science of Logic*, Cambridge: Cambridge University Press.

Hegel, Georg Wilhelm Friedrich (1795): *Das Leben Jesu*, in: ders., *Frühe Studien und Entwürfe 1787–1800*, bearbeitet und kommentiert von Inge Gellert, Berlin: Akademie Verlag, 129–214.

Hegel, Georg Wilhelm Friedrich (1807): *Phänomenologie des Geistes*, in: ders., *Werke* Bd. 3, Frankfurt/M. Suhrkamp.

Hegel, Georg Wilhelm Friedrich (1812–16): *Wissenschaft der Logik*, in: ders., *Werke* Bde. 5–6, Frankfurt/M. Suhrkamp.

Hegel, Georg Wilhelm Friedrich (1818): *Konzept der Rede beim Antritt des philosophischen Lehramtes an der Universität Berlin*, in: ders., *Werke* Bd. 10, Frankfurt/M.: Suhrkamp, 399–417.

Hegel, Georg Wilhelm Friedrich (1821): *Grundlinien der Philosophie des Rechts*, in: ders., *Werke* Bd. 7, Frankfurt/M. Suhrkamp.

Hegel, Georg Wilhelm Friedrich (1821a): *Grundlinien der Philosophie des Rechts oder Naturrecht und Staatswissenschaft im Grundrisse*, nach der Ausgabe von Eduard Gans herausgegeben von Hermann Klenner, Berlin: Akademie Verlag 1981.

Hegel, Georg Wilhelm Friedrich (1822): *Vorrede zu Hinrichs' Religionsphilosophie*, in: ders., *Werke* Bd. 11, Frankfurt/M. Suhrkamp, 42–67.

Hegel, Georg Wilhelm Friedrich (1830): *Enzyklopädie der philosophischen Wissenschaften*, in: ders., *Werke* Bd. 8–10, Frankfurt/M. Suhrkamp.

Hegel, Georg Wilhelm Friedrich (1832): *Vorlesungen über die Philosophie der Religion*, in: ders., *Werke* Bde. 16–17, Frankfurt/M. Suhrkamp.

Hegel, Georg Wilhelm Friedrich (1833–36): *Vorlesungen über die Geschichte der Philosophie*, in: ders., *Werke* Bde. 18–20, Frankfurt/M. Suhrkamp.

Hegel, Georg Wilhelm Friedrich (1835–38): *Vorlesungen über die Ästhetik*, in: ders., *Werke* Bde. 13–15, Frankfurt/M. Suhrkamp.

Hegel, Georg Wilhelm Friedrich (1836): *Vorlesungen über die Philosophie der Geschichte*, in: ders., *Werke* Bd. 12, Frankfurt/M. Suhrkamp.

Hegel, Georg Wilhelm Friedrich (1952–1977): *Briefe von und an Hegel. 4 Bände*, Band 1–3 herausgegeben von Johannes Hoffmeister 1952–1954, Band 4 (in zwei Teilen) herausgegeben und völlig neu bearbeitet von Friedhelm Nicolin 1977, Hamburg: Meiner.

Hegel, Georg Wilhelm Friedrich (1973/74): *Vorlesungen über Rechtsphilosophie 1818–1831*. Edition und Kommentar in sechs Bänden [vier Bände sind erschienen] von Karl–Heinz Ilting, Stuttgart: frommann-holzboog, 1977.

Heil, Johannes (1997): " 'Antijudaismus» und «Antisemitismus.' Begriffe als Bedeutungsträger," in: *Jahrbuch für Antisemitismusforschung* 6, Frankfurt/M.: Campus, 92–114.

Heimers, Manfred (1988): "Trier als preußische Bezirkshauptstadt im Vormärz (1814–1848)," in: Düwell, Kurt; Irsigler, Franz (Hg.): *2000 Jahre Trier Bd. III: Trierin der Neuzeit*, Trier: Spee, 399–420.

Heine, Heinrich (1832): *Französische Zustände*, in: ders., *Sämtliche Schriften*, Bd. 5, 89–279.

Heine, Heinrich (2007). *On the History of Religion and Philosophy in Germany*, Cambridge: Cambridge University Press.

Heine, Heinrich (1836): *Die romantische Schule*, in: ders., *Sämtliche Werke*, Düsseldorfer Ausgabe, Bd.8/1, 121–249., Hamburg: Hoffmann und Campe, 1979.

Heine, Heinrich (1843): *Atta Troll. Ein Sommernachtstraum*, in: ders., *Sämtliche Schriften*, Bd. 7, 491–570.

Heine, Heinrich (1981): *Sämtliche Schriften in 12 Bänden*. von Klaus Briegleb, Frankfurt/M.: Ullstein.

Heinrich, Michael (2017): *Die Wissenschaft vom Wert. Die Marxsche Kritik der politischen* Ökonomie zwischen wissenschaftlicher Revolution und klassischer Tradition, 7. um ein Nachwort erweiterte Auflage, Münster: Westfälisches Dampfboot.

Henckmann, Wolfhart (1970): *Nachwort*, in: Solger (1815), München: Fink, 471a–541.

Henke, Manfred (1973): "Die Vereinigung der Gläubigen mit Christo nach Joh. 15, 1–14, in ihrem Grund und Wesen, in ihrer unbedingten Nothwendigkeit und in ihren Wirkungen dargestellt – Bemerkungen zum Religionsaufsatz von Karl Marx und seinen evangelischen Mitschülern in der Reifeprüfung," in: *Der unbekannte junge Marx. Neue Studien zur Entwicklung des Marxschen Denkens 1835–1847*, Frankfurt/M.: v. Haase & Köhler, 115–145.

Henne, Thomas; Kretschmann, Carsten (2002): "Carl von Savignys Antijudaismus und die «Nebenpolitik» der Berliner Universität gegen das preußische Emanzipationsedikt von 1812," in: *Jahrbuch für Universitätsgeschichte* 5, 217–225.

Herres, Jürgen (1990): "Cholera, Armut und eine «Zwangssteuer» 1830/32. Zur Sozialgeschichte Triers im Vormärz," in: *Kurtrierisches Jahrbuch* 30.Jg., 161–203.

Herres, Jürgen (1993): *Das Karl-Marx-Haus in Trier. 1727–heute*, Trier: Karl-Marx-Haus.

Hertz–Eichenrode, Dieter (1959): *Der Junghegelianer Bruno Bauer im Vormärz*, Inaugural–Dissertation zur Erlangung des Grades eines Doktors der Philosophie der Philosophischen Fakultät der Freien Universität Berlin, Berlin.

Hess, Moses (1959): *Briefwechsel*. Herausgegeben von Edmund Silberner, s–Gravenhage: Mouton.

Hillmann, Günther (1966): *Marx und Hegel. Von der Spekulation zur Dialektik*, Frankfurt/M.: Europäische Verlagsanstalt.

Hillmann, Günther (1966a): "Zum Verständnis der Texte," in: Karl Marx, *Texte zu Methode und Praxis I: Jugendschriften 1835–1841*, herausgegeben von Günther Hillmann, Reinbek: Rowohlt, 196–236.

Hirsch, Emanuel (1924): "Die Beisetzung der Romantiker in Hegels Phänomenologie. Ein Kommentar zu dem Abschnitte über die Moralität," in: Fulda, Hans Friedrich; Henrich, Dieter (Hrsg.), *Materialien zu Hegels Phänomenologie des Geistes*, Frankfurt/M.: Suhrkamp 1973, 245–275.

Hirsch, Emanuel (1949–54) (Hrsg.): *Geschichte der neuern evangelischen Theologie im Zusammenhang mit den allgemeinen Bewegungen des europäischen Denkens, 5 Bände*, Gütersloh: Mohn.

Hirsch, Helmut (1955): *Denker und Kämpfer. Gesammelte Beiträge zur Geschichte der Arbeiterbewegung*, Frankfurt/M.: Europäische Verlagsanstalt.

Hirsch, Helmut (1955a): *Karl Friedrich Köppen, der intimste Berliner Freund Marxens*, in: Hirsch (1955), 19–81.

Hirsch, Helmut (2002): *Freund von Heine, Marx/Engels und Lincoln. Eine Karl Ludwig Bernays Biographie*, Frankfurt/M.: Peter Lang.

Hodenberg, Christina von (1996): *Die Partei der Unparteiischen. Der Liberalismus der preußischen Richterschaft 1815–1848/49*, Göttingen: Vandenhoeck & Ruprecht.

Höhn, Gerhard (2004): *Heine Handbuch. Zeit – Person – Werk*, 3. Auflage, Stuttgart: Metzler.

Höfele, Karl Heinrich (1939): *Die Stadt Trier und der preußische Staat im Vormärz*, Inaugural–Dissertation an der J.W. Goethe Universität zu Frankfurt a.M., Frankfurt/M.

Hoffmann, E.T.A. (1815/16): *Die Elixiere des Teufels*, in: ders., *Sämtliche Werke in sechs Bänden*, Band 2.2, Frankfurt/M.: Deutscher Klassiker Verlag 1988, 9–352.

Hoffmann, E.T.A. (1819/21): *Lebens-Ansichten des Katers Murr nebst fragmentarischer Biographie des Kapellmeisters Johannes Kreisler in zufälligen Makulaturblättern*, in: ders., *Sämtliche Werke in sechs Bänden*, Band 5, Frankfurt/M.: Deutscher Klassiker Verlag 1992, 9–458.

Hoffmann, E.T.A. (1822): *Meister Floh. Ein Märchen in sieben Abenteuern zweier Freunde*, in: ders., Sämtliche Werke in sechs Bänden, Band 6, Frankfurt/M.: Deutscher Klassiker Verlag 2004, 303–467.

Holbach, Paul Henri Thierry d' (1770): *System der Natur oder von den Gesetzen der physischen und der moralischen Welt*, Frankfurt/M.: Suhrkamp 1978.

Hook, Sidney (1936): *From Hegel to Marx: Studies in the Intellectual Development of Karl Marx*, New York: Columbia University Press 1994.

Höroldt, Dietrich (1968a): "Stadt und Universität," in: ders. (Hg.), *Stadt und Universität. Rückblick aus Anlaß der 150 Jahr-Feier der Universität Bonn. Bonner Geschichtsblätter Band 22*, Bonn, 9–132.

Höroldt, Dietrich (Hg.) (1968): *Stadt und Universität. Rückblick aus Anlaß der 150 Jahr-Feier der Universität Bonn. Bonner Geschichtsblätter Band 22*, Bonn.

Horowitz, H. (1928): Die Familie Lwów, in: Monatsschrift für Geschichte und Wissenschaft des Judentums, 72.Jg., 487–499, Frankfurt/M.: J. Kaufmann.

Houben, Heinrich Hubert (1906): "Heinrich Laube," in: *Allgemeine Deutsche Biographie*, Bd. 51, Leipzig: Duncker & Humblot, 752–790.

Hubmann, Gerald (1997): *Ethische Überzeugung und politisches Handeln. Jakob Fries und die deutsche Tradition der Gesinnungsethik*, Heidelberg: Universitätsverlag C. Winter.

Hubmann, Gerald; Münkler, Herfried; Neuhaus, Manfred (2001): ". . . es kömmt drauf an sie zu verändern. Zur Wiederaufnahme der Marx-Engels-Gesamtausgabe (MEGA)," in: *Deutsche Zeitschrift für Philosophie* 49, Heft 2, 299–311.

Humboldt, Alexander von (2004): *Die Kosmos-Vorträge 1827/28 in der Berliner Singakademie*, Frankfurt/M.: Insel.

Humboldt, Wilhelm von (1792): *Ideen zu einem Versuch die Grenzen der Wirksamkeit des Staates zu bestimmen*, in: ders., *Gesammelte Schriften*, Bd. 1, Berlin: Behr 1903, 97–254.

Humboldt, Wilhelm von (1809a): Über den Entwurf zu einer neuen Constitution für *die Juden*, in: ders., *Gesammelte Schriften*, Bd. 10, Berlin: Behr 1903, 97–115.

Humboldt, Wilhelm von (1809b): *Bericht der Sektion des Kultus und des Unterrichts, Dezember 1809*, in: ders., *Gesammelte Schriften*, Bd. 10, Berlin: Behr 1903, 199–224.

Hundt, Martin (1994): "Marx an Adolf Friedrich Rutenberg. Ein unbekannter früher Brief," in: *MEGA-Studien* 1994/1, 148–154.

Hundt, Martin (2000): "Was war der Junghegelianismus?" in: *Sitzungsberichte der Leibniz-Sozietät*, Band 40, Heft 5, 5–32, Berlin.

Hundt, Martin (Hg.) (2010a): *Der Redaktionsbriefwechsel der Hallischen, Deutschen und Deutsch-Französischen Jahrbücher (1837–1844)*, Berlin: Akademie Verlag.

Hundt, Martin (2010b): "Junghegelianismus im Spiegel der Briefe," in: ders. (Hg.), *Der Redaktionsbriefwechsel der Hallischen, Deutschen und Deutsch-Französischen Jahrbücher (1837–1844)*, Apparat, 1–78.

Hundt, Martin (2012): *Theodor Echtermeyer (1805–1844). Biographie und Quellenteil mit unveröffentichten Texten*, Frankfurt/M.: Peter Lang.

Hundt, Martin (2015): "Stichwort: Linkshegelianismus," in: *Historisch-kritisches Wörterbuch des Marxismus*, Bd. 8.2, Hamburg: Argument.

Hunt, Tristram (2012): *Friedrich Engels. Der Mann, der den Marxismus erfand*, Berlin: Propyläen.

Hunt, Tristram (2009): *The Frock-Coated Communist: The Revolutionary Life of Friedrich Engels*, London: Allen Lane.

Ilting, Karl-Heinz (1973): "Einleitung: Die 'Rechtsphilosophie' von 1820 und Hegels Vorlesungen über Rechtsphilosophie," in: *Hegel (1973/74) Erster Band*, Stuttgart: frommann-holzboog; 23–126.

Ilting, Karl-Heinz (1974): "Einleitung des Herausgebers," in: *Hegel (1973/74). Dritter Band*, Stuttgart: frommann-holzboog; 37–86.

Ilting, Karl–Heinz (1974): "Einleitung des Herausgebers: Der exoterische und der esoterische Hegel (1824–1831)," in: *Hegel (1973/74). Vierter Band*, Stuttgart: frommann-holzboog; 45–66.

Jachmann, Reinhold Bernhard (1812): "Ideen zur Nations-Bildungslehre," in: *Archiv deutscher Nationsbildung*, 1. Bd., Berlin: Maurer, 1–45.

Jacobi, Friedrich Heinrich (1785): *Über die Lehre des Spinoza in Briefen an den Herrn Moses Mendelssohn*, Hamburg: Meiner 2000.

Jacoby, Johann (1841): *Vier Fragen beantwortet von einem Ostpreußen*, Mannheim: Hoff.

Jaeschke, Walter (1986): *Die Vernunft in der Religion. Studien zur Grundlegung der Religionsphilosophie Hegels*, Stuttgart: frommann-holzboog.

Jaeschke, Walter (2000): "Genealogie des Deutschen Idealismus. Konstitutionsgeschichtliche Bemerkungen in methodologischer Absicht," in: Arndt, Andreas; Jaeschke, Walter (Hg.): *Materialismus und Spiritualismus. Philosophie und Wissenschaften nach 1848*, Hamburg: Meiner, 219–234.

Jaeschke, Walter (2003): *Hegel Handbuch*, Stuttgart: Metzler.

Jaeschke, Walter; Arndt, Andreas (2012): *Die Klassische Deutsche Philosophie nach Kant. Systeme der reinen Vernunft und ihre Kritik 1785–1845*, München: Beck.

Jeismann, Karl-Ernst (1996): *Das preußische Gymnasium in Staat und Gesellschaft, 2 Bände*, Stuttgart: Klett–Cotta.

Jersch-Wenzel, Stefi (1996): "Rechtslage und Emanzipation," in: Meyer, Michael A.

(Hg.): *Deutsch-Jüdische Geschichte in der Neuzeit. Band II: Emanzipation und Akkulturation 1780–1871*, München: Beck, 15–56.

Kadenbach, Johannes (1970): *Das Religionsverständnis von Karl Marx*, München: Schöningh.

Kanda, Junji (2003): *Die Gleichzeitigkeit des Ungleichzeitigen und die Philosophie. Studien zum radikalen Hegelianismus im Vormärz*, Frankfurt/M.: Peter Lang.

Kanda, Junji (2010): "Bauer und die Promotion von Karl Marx," in: Kodalle, Klaus-M; Reitz, Tilman (Hg.): *Bruno Bauer (1809–1882). Ein 'Partisan des Weltgeistes?'* Würzburg: Königshausen & Neumann, 151–164.

Kant, Immanuel (1781): *Kritik der reinen Vernunft*, in: ders., *Werkausgabe* hrsg. von Wilhelm Weischedel, Bd. III/IV, Frankfurt/M.: Suhrkamp 1968.

Kant, Immanuel (1997). *Groundwork of the Metaphysics of Morals*, Cambridge: Cambridge University Press.

Kant, Immanuel (1785): *Grundlegung zur Metaphysik der Sitten*, in: ders., *Werkausgabe* hrsg. von Wilhelm Weischedel, Bd. VII, Frankfurt/M.: Suhrkamp 1968.

Kant, Immanuel (1788): *Kritik der praktischen Vernunft*, in: ders., *Werkausgabe* hrsg. von Wilhelm Weischedel, Bd. VII, Frankfurt/M.: Suhrkamp 1968.

Kant, Immanuel (1797): *Die Metaphysik der Sitten*, in: ders., *Werkausgabe* hrsg. von Wilhelm Weischedel, Bd. VIII, Frankfurt/M.: Suhrkamp 1968.

Kasper-Holtkotte, Cilli (1996): *Juden im Aufbruch. Zur Sozialgeschichte einer Minderheit im Saar-Mosel-Raum um 1800*, Hannover: Hahnsche Buchhandlung.

Kaupp, Peter (1995): "Marx als Waffenstudent. Burschenschafter an seinem Lebensweg," in: *Darstellungen und Quellen zur Geschichte der deutschen Einheitsbewegung im 19. und 20. Jahrhundert*, 15. Band, Heidelberg: Winter, 141–168.

Kelley, D.R (1978): "The Metaphysics of Law: An Essay on the Very Young Marx," in: *American Historical Review*, Vol. 83, No. 1, 350–367.

Kempski, Jürgen von (1982): "Samuel Reimarus als Ethologe," in: Reimarus (1760), 21–56.

Kentenich, Gottfried (1915): *Geschichte der Stadt Trier von ihrer Gründung bis zur Gegenwart. Denkschrift zum Hundertjährigen Jubiläum der Zugehörigkeit der Stadt zum Preussischen Staat*, Trier: Lintz.

Kiehnbaum, Erhard (2013): "Der unbekannte Freund oder: Wer war Kleinerz alias Richartz? Versuch einer biographischen Skizze," in: Lambrecht, Lars (Hg.): *Umstürzende Gedanken. Radikale Theorie im Vorfeld der 1848er Revolution*, Frankfurt/M.: Peter Lang, 191–210.

Kimmich, Dorothee (1993): *Epikureische Aufklärungen*, Darmstadt: Wissenschaftliche Buchgesellschaft.

Kisch, Egon Erwin (1983): *Karl Marx in Karlsbad*, Berlin und Weimar: Aufbau Verlag.

Klein, Christian (Hrsg) (2002): *Grundlagen der Biographik. Theorie und Praxis des biographischen Schreibens*, Stuttgart: Metzler.

Klein, Christian (Hrsg) (2009): *Handbuch Biographie: Methoden, Traditionen, Theorien*, Stuttgart: Metzler.

Klein, Dietrich (2009): *Hermann Samuel Reimarus (1694–1768). Das theologische Werk*, Tübingen: Mohr Siebeck.

Klenner, Hermann (1981): "Hegels Rechtsphilosophie in der Zeit," in: G.W.F. Hegel, *Grundlinien der Philosophie des Rechts oder Naturrecht und Staatswissenschaft im Grundrisse*, nach der Ausgabe von Eduard Gans herausgegeben von Hermann Klenner, Berlin: Akademie Verlag, 565–609.

Klenner, Hermann (1984): "Der Jurist Marx auf dem Wege zum Marxismus," in: ders, *Vom Recht der Natur zur Natur des Rechts*, Berlin: Akademie Verlag, 68–78.

Klenner, Hermann (1991): *Deutsche Rechtsphilosophie im 19. Jahrhundert. Essays*, Berlin: Akademie Verlag.

Klenner, Hermann; Oberkofler, Gerhard (1991): "Savigny-Voten über Eduard Gans nebst Chronologie und Bibliographie," in: *Topos*, H. 1, 123–148.

Kliem, Manfred (1970): *Karl Marx. Dokumente seines Lebens*, Leipzig: Reclam.

Kliem, Manfred (1988): *Karl Marx und die Berliner Universität 1836 bis 1841*, Berlin: Humboldt Universität.

Klupsch, Tina (2012): *Johann Hugo Wyttenbach. Eine historische Biographie*, Trier: Kliomedia.

Klupsch, Tina (2013): *Wyttenbach, der Pädagoge. In: Kurtrierisches Jahrbuch*, Jg. 53, 161–173.

Klutentreter, Wilhelm (1966): *Die Rheinische Zeitung von 1842/43*, Dortmund: Ruhfuss.

Kober, Adolf (1932): "Marx' Vater und das napoleonische Ausnahmegesetz gegen die Juden 1808," in: *Jahrbuch des Kölnischen Geschichtsvereins*, Jg. 14, 111–125.

Kondylis, Panajotis (1987): *Marx und die griechische Antike. Zwei Studien*, Heidelberg: Manutius

Köpke, Rudolf (1860): *Die Gründung der königlichen Friedrich-Wilhelms-Universität zu Berlin*, Berlin: Schade.

Köppen, Karl Friedrich (1837): *Literarische Einleitung in die nordische Mythologie*, Berlin: Bechtold und Hartje.

Köppen, Karl Friedrich (1839): "Über Schubarths Unvereinbarkeit der Hegelschen Lehre mit dem Preußischen Staate," in: Riedel, Manfred (Hrsg.): *Materialien zu Hegels Rechtsphilosophie*, Bd.1, Frankfurt/M.: Suhrkamp 1975, 276–284.

Köppen, Karl Friedrich (1840): *Friedrich der Große und seine Widersacher. Eine Jubel schrift*, in: Köppen (2003), Bd.1, 135–227.

Köppen, Karl Friedrich (2003): *Ausgewählte Schriften in zwei Bänden, herausgegeben von Heinz Pepperle*, Berlin: Akademie Verlag.

Koselleck, Reinhart (1967): *Preußen zwischen Reform und Revolution. Allgemeines Landrecht, Verwaltung und soziale Bewegung von 1791–1848*, Stuttgart: Klett, 2. Aufl. 1975.

Kossack, Heinz (1978): "Dokumente über die Studienzeit von Karl Marx an der Berliner Universität," in: *Beiträge zur Marx-Engels-Forschung* 2, 105–108.

Kowalewski, Maxim (1909): "Erinnerungen an Karl Marx," in: *Mohr und General. Erinnerungen an Marx und Engels*, Berlin: Dietz 1983, 343–364.

Kracauer, Siegfried (1930): "Biographie als neubürgerliche Kunstform," in: ders., *Das Ornament der Masse*, Frankfurt/M.: Suhrkamp 1970.

Kracauer, Siegfried (1937): *Jacques Offenbach und das Paris seiner Zeit*, Frankfurt/M.: Suhrkamp 1976.

Kraul, Margret (1984): *Das deutsche Gymnasium 1780–1980*, Frankfurt/M.: Suhrkamp.

Kraus, Hans Christof (2007): "Geschichte als Lebensgeschichte. Gegenwart und Zukunft der politischen Biographie," in: *Historische Zeitschrift*, Beiheft 44, 311–332.

Krosigk, Anna von (o.J.): *Werner von Veltheim. Eine Lebensgeschichte zum Leben. Aus Tagebüchern und Briefen*, Bernburg.

Krosigk, Konrad von (1973): "Ludwig von Westphalen und seine Kinder. Bruchstücke familiärer Überlieferungen," in: *Zur Persönlichkeit von Marx' Schwiegervater Johann Ludwig von Westphalen*, Schriften aus dem Karl-Marx-Haus Nr. 9, Trier, 43–79.

Krosigk, Lutz Graf Schwerin von (1957): *Die grosse Zeit des Feuers. Der Weg der deutschen Industrie. Band I*, Tübingen: Rainer Wunderlich Verlag.

Krosigk, Lutz Graf Schwerin von (1975): *Jenny Marx. Liebe und Leid im Schatten von Karl Marx*, Wuppertal: Staats-Verlag.

Krüger, Peter (2000): "Johann Steininger (1794–1874) – europaweit bekannter Geologe, Naturkundelehrer des Gymnasiasten Karl Marx," in: *Beiträge zur Marx-Engels-Forschung Neue Folge 2000*, 144–156.

Kugelmann, Franziska (1983): "Kleine Züge zu dem großen Charakerbild von Karl Marx," in: *Mohr und General. Erinnerungen an Marx und Engels*, Berlin: Dietz 1983, 252–285.

Kunze, Erich (1955): "Die drei finnischen Runen in der Volksliedersammlung des jungen Marx," in: *Deutsches Jahrbuch für Volkskunde*, Jg. 1, H. 1/2, 41–63.

Künzli, Arnold (1966): *Karl Marx. Eine Psychographie*, Wien: Europa.

Kux, Ernst (1967): *Karl Marx – Die revolutionäre Konfession*, Erlenbach–Zürich: Eugen Rentsch Verlag.

Lafargue, Paul (1890/91): "Karl Marx. Persönliche Erinnerungen," in: Mohr und General. Erinnerungen an Marx und Engels, Berlin: Dietz 1983, 286–312.

Lambrecht, Lars (1993): ". . . Mit der Heftigkeit der französischen Revolution von 1792 . . .? Zur Rezeption der französischen Revolution und der Philosophie Fichtes durch den Junghegelianer A.Rutenberg," in: Losurdo, Domenico (Hg.): *Rivoluzione francese e filosofica classica tedesca*, Urbino: QuattroVenti, 147–168.

Lambrecht, Lars (2002): "Ruge: Politisierung der Ästhetik?" in: Lambrecht, Lars; Tietz, Karl Ewald (Hg.): *Arnold Ruge (1802–1880). Beiträge zum 200. Geburtstag*, Frankfurt/M.: Peter Lang, 101–124.

Lämmermann, Godwin (1979): *Kritische Theologie und Theologiekritik. Die Genese der Religions-und Selbstbewußtseinstheorie Bruno Bauers*, München: Christian Kaiser Verlag.

Lange, Erhard; Schmidt, Ernst-Günther; Steiger, Günter, Taubert, Inge (Hg.) (1983): *Die Promotion von Karl Marx. Jena 1841. Eine Quellenedition*, Berlin: Dietz.

Lange, Friedrich Albert (1866): *Geschichte des Materialismus. 2 Bände*, Berlin: Suhrkamp 1974.

Lässig, Simone (2009): "Die historische Biographie auf neuen Wegen?" in: *Geschichte in Wissenschaft und Unterricht,* Jg. 10, 540–553.

Laube, Heinrich (1841): *Gans und Immermann,* in: *Gesammelte Werke* hrsg. von Heinrich Hubert Houben, Bd. 50, Leipzig: Hesse 1909, 98–164.

Laube, Heinrich (1875): *Erinnerungen 1810–1840,* in: *Gesammelte Werke* hrsg. von Heinrich Hubert Houben, Bd. 40, Leipzig: Hesse 1909.

Lauchert, Friedrich (1880): "August Wilhelm Heffter," in: *Allgemeine Deutsche Biographie,* Bd. 11, 250–254.

Lauermann, Manfred (2011): "Bauer nach zweihundert Jahren – ein Forschungsbericht," in: *Marx-Engels Jahrbuch 2010,* Berlin: Akademie Verlag, 163–176.

Laufner, Richard (1975): "Marx und die Regulierung der Steuerschulden der trierischen Judenschaft," in: Laufner, Richard; Rauch, Albert (Hg.): *Die Familie Marx und die Trierer Judenschaft,* Schriften aus dem Karl Marx Haus 14, Trier, 5–17.

Le Goff, Jacques (1989): "Wie schreibt man eine Biographie?" in: Braudel, Fernand u.a., *Der Historiker als Menschenfresser. Über den Beruf des Historikers,* Berlin: Wagenbach, 103–112.

Lehmkühler, Karsten (2010): "Offenbarung und Heilige Schrift bei Bauer," in: Kodalle, Klaus-M; Reitz, Tilman (Hg.): *Bruno Bauer (1809–1882). Ein "Partisan des Weltgeistes?"* Würzburg: Königshausen & Neumann, 47–62.

Lenz, Max (1910): *Geschichte der Königlichen Friedrich-Wilhelms-Universität zu Berlin,* 4 Bände, Halle: Verlag der Buchhandlung des Waisenhauses.

Leo, Heinrich (1838a): *Sendschreiben an J. Görres,* 2. Aufl., Halle: Anton.

Leo, Heinrich (1838b): *Die Hegelingen. Actenstücke und Belege zu der s.g. Denunciation der ewigen Wahrheit,* Halle: Anton.

Leonhard, Karl Cäsar von (1856): *Aus unserer Zeit in meinem Leben.* Zweiter Band, Stuttgart: Schweizerbart.

Leopold, David (2007): *The Young Karl Marx: German Philosophy, Modern Politics and Human Flourishing,* Cambridge: Cambridge University Press.

Lessing, Gotthold Ephraim (1777): "Über den Beweis des Geistes und der Kraft," in: ders., *Werke und Briefe,* Bd. 8, Frankfurt/M.: Deutscher Klassiker Verlag 1989, 437–446.

Lessing, Gotthold Ephraim (1779): *Nathan der Weise,* in: ders., *Werke und Briefe,* Bd. 9, Frankfurt/M.: Deutscher Klassiker Verlag 1993, 483–666.

Levin, Michael (1974): "Marxism and Romanticism: Marx's Debt to German Conservativism," in: *Political Studies,* Jg. 22, H. 4, 400–413.

Levine, Norman (2012): *Marx's Discourse with Hegel,* Houndmills: Palgrave Macmillan.

Lexikon Westfälischer Autorinnnen und Autoren 1750–1950, http://www.lwl.org/ literaturkommission/alex/index.php?id=00000002.

Liebknecht, Wilhelm (1908): *Karl Marx: Biographical Memoirs,* Chicago: Charles H. Kerr & Company.

Liebmann, Otto (1893): "Henrik Steffens," in: *Allgemeine Deutsche Biographie,* Bd. 35, Leipzig: Duncker & Humblot, 555–558.

Liedmann, Sven-Eric (2018): *A World to Win: The Life and Works of Karl Marx,*

London: Verso (expanded translation from the Swedish): *Karl Marx. En biografi*, Stockholm: Albert Bönniers 2015).

Lifschitz, Michail (1960): *Karl Marx und die Ästhetik*, Dresden: Verlag der Kunst.

Limmroth, Angelika (2014): *Jenny Marx. Die Biographie*, Berlin: Karl Dietz.

Lindgren, Uta (2003): "Carl Georg Ritter," in: *Neue Deutsche Biographie*, Band 21, Berlin: Duncker & Humblot, 655–656.

Lindner, Urs (2013): *Marx und die Philosophie. Wissenschaftlicher Realismus, ethischer Perfektionismus und kritische Sozialtheorie*, Stuttgart: Schmetterling.

Long, A. A.; Sedley, D. N. (2000): *Die hellenistischen Philosophen. Texte und Kommentare*, Stuttgart: Metzler.

Losurdo, Domenico (1989): *Hegel und das deutsche Erbe. Philosophie und nationale Frage zwischen Revolution und Reaktion*, Köln: Pahl-Rugenstein.

Löwith, Karl (1950): *Von Hegel zu Nietzsche. Der revolutionäre Bruch im Denken des neunzehnten Jahrhunderts*, Hamburg: Meiner 1995.

Löwith, Karl (1953): *Weltgeschichte und Heilsgeschehen. Die theologischen Voraussetzungen der Geschichtsphilosophie*, Stuttgart: Kohlhammer.

Löwith, Karl (1962): *Die Hegelsche Linke*, Stuttgart: Frommann.

Löwith, Karl (Hg.) (1962): "Aufhebung der christlichen Religion," in: Klaus Oehler, Richard Schaeffler (Hg.), *Einsichten. Gerhard Krüger zum 60. Geburtstag*, Frankfurt/Main: Klostermann, 156–203 (ebenfalls abgedruckt in Hegel–Studien, Beiheft 1 (1964), 193–236).

Lübbe, Hermann (Hg.) (1962): *Die Hegelsche Rechte*, Stuttgart: Frommann.

Lucas, Hans-Christian (2002): "Dieses Zukünftige wollen wir mit Ehrfurcht begrüßen – Bemerkungen zur Historisierung und Liberalisierung von Hegels Rechts- und Staatsbegriff durch Eduard Gans," in: Blänkner, Reinhard; Göhler, Gerhard; Waszek, Norbert (Hg.): Eduard Gans (1797–1839). *Politischer Professor zwischen Restauration und Vormärz*, Leipzig: Leipziger Universitätsverlag, 105–136.

Lucretius (2007): *The Nature of Things*, New York and London: Penguin Classics.

Magdanz, Edda (2002): "Gans' Stellung im Konstitutionsprozeß der junghegelianischen Bewegung," in: Blänkner, Reinhard; Göhler, Gerhard; Waszek, Norbert (Hg.): *Eduard Gans (1797–1839). Politischer Professor zwischen Restauration und Vormärz*, Leipzig: Leipziger Universitätsverlag, 177–206.

Mah, H.E (1986): "Karl Marx in Love: The Enlightenment, Romanticism and Hegelian Theory in the Young Marx," in: *History of European Ideas*, Vol. 7, No. 5, 489–507.

Mah, Harold (1987): *The End of Philosophy and the Origin of "Ideology": Karl Marx and the Crisis of the Young Hegelians*, Berkeley: University of California Press.

Mallmann, Lutwin (1987): *Französische Juristenausbildung im Rheinland 1794 bis 1814. Die Rechtsschule von Koblenz*, Köln: Böhlau.

Marx, Eleanor (1883): "Karl Marx (Erstveröffentlichung: Progress May 1883, 288–294, June 362–366)," in: Rjazanov, David (1928): *Karl Marx als Denker, Mensch und Revolutionär*, Frankfurt/M.: Makol 1971.

Marx, Eleanor (1895): "Karl Marx. Lose Blätter," in: *Mohr und General. Erinnerungen an Marx und Engels*, Berlin: Dietz 1983, 242–251.

Marx, Eleanor (1897/98): "Ein Brief des jungen Marx," in: *Mohr und General. Erinnerungen an Marx und Engels*, Berlin: Dietz 1983, 236–241.

Marx, Karl see works by Marx and Engels above.

Mayer, Gustav (1913): "Die Anfänge des politischen Radikalismus im vormärzlichen Preußen," in: ders., *Radikalismus, Sozialismus und bürgerliche Demokratie*, Frankfurt/M.: Suhrkamp; 1969, S. 7-107.

Massiczek, Albert (1968): *Der menschliche Mensch. Karl Marx' jüdischer Humanismus*, Wien: Europa Verlag.

Mayer, Gustav (1918): "Der Jude in Karl Marx," in: ders., *Aus der Welt des Sozialismus. Kleine historische Aufsätze*, Berlin: Weltgeist Bücher Verlagsgesellschaft 1927.

Mayer, Gustav (1919/32): *Der Friedrich Engels. Eine Biographie. 2 Bände*, Frankfurt/M.: Ullstein, 1975.

Mayr, Ernst (1982): "Geleitwort," in: Reimarus (1760), 9–18.

McIvor, Martin (2008): "The Young Marx and German Idealism: Revisiting the Doctoral Dissertation," in: *Journal of the History of Philosophy*, vol. 46(3), 395–419.

McLellan, David (1969): *The Young Hegelians and Karl Marx*, London: Palgrave Macmillan.

McLellan, David (1973/1995): *Karl Marx: A Biography*, London: Macmillan.

McLellan, David (1987): *Marxism and Religion*, New York: Harper & Row.

Mediger, Walther; Klingebiel, Thomas (2011): *Herzog Ferdinand von Braunschweig-Lüneburg und die alliierte Armee im Siebenjährigen Krieg (1757-1762)*, Hannover: Verlag Hahnsche Buchhandlung.

Mehlhausen, Joachim (1965): *Dialektik, Selbstbewusstsein und Offenbarung. Die Grundlagen der spekulativen Orthodoxie Bruno Bauers in ihrem Zusammenhang mit der Geschichte der theologischen Hegelschule dargestellt*, Dissertation, Bonn.

Mehlhausen, Joachim (1999): "Die religionsphilosophische Begründung der spekulativen Theologie Bruno Bauers," in: ders., *Vestigia Verbi. Aufsätze zur Geschichte der evangelischen Theologie*, Berlin: Walter de Gruyter, 188–220.

Mehring, Franz (1892): *Die von Westphalen*, in: ders., *Gesammelte Schriften* Bd. 6, Berlin: Dietz, 404–418.

Mehring, Franz (1902): *Aus dem literarischen Nachlass von Karl Marx, Friedrich Engels und Ferdinand Lassalle. Erster Band: Gesammelte Schriften von Karl Marx und Friedrich Engels 1841-1850*, Stuttgart: Dietz.

Mehring, Franz (1913): *Aus dem literarischen Nachlss von Karl Marx, Friedrich Engels und Ferdinand Lassalle. Vierter Band: Briefe von Ferdinand Lassalle an Karl Marx und Friedrich Engels 1849-1862*, 2. Auflage, Stuttgart: Dietz.

Mehring, Franz (1962): *Karl Marx: The Story of His Life*, Ann Arbor: University of Michigan Press.

Meier, Olga (Hrsg). (1983): *Die Töchter von Karl Marx. Unveröffentlichte Briefe*, Frankfurt/M.: Fischer.

MEJ1: Marx-Engels-Jahrbuch 1 (1978), Berlin: Dietz.

MEJ 8: Marx-Engels-Jahrbuch 8 (1985), Berlin: Dietz.

Meurin, Ferdinand (1904): *Plusquamperfektum. Erinnerungen und Plaudereien*, 2. Aufl., Coblenz: Schuth.

Meyen, Eduard (1839): *Heinrich Leo, der verhallerte Pietist. Ein Literaturbrief,* Leipzig: Otto Wigand.

Michelet, Karl Ludwig (1838): *Geschichte der letzten Systeme der Philosophie in Deutschland von Kant bis Hegel,* 2. Band, Berlin: Reprint: Hildesheim, Olms, 1967.

Miller, Sepp; Sawadzki, Bruno (o.J. [1956]): *Karl Marx in Berlin. Beiträge zur Biographie von Karl Marx,* Berlin: Das neue Berlin.

Miruss, Alexander (1848): *Diplomatisches Archiv für die Deutschen Bundesstaaten. Dritter Theil,* Leipzig: Renger'sche Buchhandlung.

Moggach, Douglas (2003): *The Philosophy and Politics of Bruno Bauer,* Cambridge: Cambridge University Press.

Moggach, Douglas (Hg.) (2006): *The New Hegelians: Politics and Philosophy in the Hegelian School,* Cambridge: Cambridge University Press.

Monz, Heinz (1973): *Karl Marx. Grundlagen der Entwicklung zu Leben und Werk,* Trier: NCO-Verlag.

Monz, Heinz (1973a): "Betrachtung eines Jünglings bei der Wahl eines Berufes – Der Deutschaufsatz von Karl Marx und seinen Mitschülern in der Reifeprüfung," in: *Der unbekannte junge Marx. Neue Studien zur Entwicklung des Marxschen Denkens 1835–1847,* Mainz: Hase & Köhler, 9–114.

Monz, Heinz (1973b): "Die jüdische Herkunft von Karl Marx," in: *Jahrbuch des Instituts für deutsche Geschichte,* Bd. 2, Tel Aviv, 173–197.

Monz, Heinz (1973c): "Marx und Heinrich Heine verwandt?" in: *Jahrbuch des Instituts für deutsche Geschichte,* Bd. 2, Tel Aviv, 199–207.

Monz, Heinz (1973d): "Anschauung und gesellschaftliche Stellung von Johann Ludwig von Westphalen," in: *Zur Persönlichkeit von Marx' Schwiegervater Johann Ludwig von Westphalen,* Schriften aus dem Karl-Marx-Haus Nr. 9, Trier.

Monz, Heinz (1979): *Ludwig Gall – Leben und Werk,* Trier: NCO-Verlag.

Monz, Heinz (1979a): "Advokatanwalt Heinrich Marx – Die Berufsausbildung eines Juristen im französischen Rheinland," in: *Jahrbuch des Instituts für deutsche Geschichte,* Bd. 8, Tel Aviv, 125–141.

Monz, Heinz (1981): "Funde zum Lebensweg von Karl Marx' Vater," in: *Osnabrücker Mitteilungen* 87, Meinders & Elstermann, 59–71.

Monz, Heinz (1990): Briefe aus Niederbronn (Elsaß). "Berichte der Jenny von Westphalen aus dem Jahre 1838 an Karl Marx in Berlin und ihre Mutter Caroline von Westphalen in Trier," in: *Kurtrierisches Jahrbuch,* 30. Jg., 237–252.

Monz, Heinz (1995): *Gerechtigkeit bei Karl Marx und in der Hebräischen Bibel.* Übereinstimmung, Fortführung und zeitgenössische Identifikation, Baden-Baden: Nomos.

Moog, Willy (1930): *Hegel und die Hegelsche Schule,* München: Reinhardt.

Moser, Matthias (2003): *Hegels Schüler C. L. Michelet: Recht und Geschichte jenseits der Schulteilung,* Berlin: Duncker & Humblot.

Müller, Michael (1988): "Die Stadt Trier unter französischer Herrschaft (1794–1814)," in: Düwell, Kurt; Irsigler, Franz (Hg.): *2000 Jahre Trier Bd. III: Trier in der Neuzeit*, Trier: Spee, 377–398.

Museum für Deutsche Geschichte (Hg.) (1986): *Karl Marx und Friedrich Engels. Ihr Leben und ihre Zeit*, 4. Aufl., Berlin: Dietz.

Nalli-Rutenberg, Agathe (1912): *Das alte Berlin, Jubiläumsausgabe*, Berlin: Curt Thiem.

Neffe, Jürgen (2017): *Marx. Der Unvollendete*, München: Bertelsmann.

Negri, Antonio (2011): "Rereading Hegel: The Philosopher of Right," in: Zizek, Slavoj u.a. (Hg.), *Hegel & the Infinite: Religion, Politics, and the Dialectic*, New York: Columbia University Press, 31–46.

Neue Gesellschaft für Bildende Kunst Berlin (NGBK) (Hg.) (1974): *Honoré Daumier und die ungelösten Probleme der bürgerlichen Gesellschaft*, Berlin.

Neuhaus, Manfred; Hubmann, Gerald (2011): "Halbzeit der MEGA: Bilanz und Perspektiven," in: *Z. Zeitschrift marxistische Erneuerung*, Nr. 85, März, 94–104.

Nicolaevsky, Boris; Maenchen-Helfen, Otto (1933): *Karl und Jenny Marx. Ein Lebensweg*, Berlin: Der Bücherkreis.

Nicolaevsky, Boris; Maenchen-Helfen, Otto (1937): *Karl Marx. Eine Biographie*, Frankfurt/Main: Fischer 1982.

Nicolin, Günther (Hg.) (1970): *Hegel in Berichten seiner Zeitgenossen*, Hamburg: Meiner.

Novalis (1797–1798): *Fragmente und Studien*, in: Novalis, *Werke*. Herausgegeben und kommentiert von Gerhard Schulz, München: C.H. Beck 1969, 375–413.

Oelkers, Jürgen (1974): "Biographik – Überlegungen zu einer unschuldigen Gattung," in: *Neue Politische Literatur*, Jg. 19, 296–309.

Oiserman, Teodor (1980): *Die Entstehung der marxistischen Philosophie*, Berlin: Dietz.

Osterhammel, Jürgen (2009): *Die Verwandlung der Welt. Eine Geschichte des 19. Jahrhunderts*, München: Beck.

Ottmann, Henning (1977): *Individuum und Gemeinschaft bei Hegel. Band I: Hegel im Spiegel der Interpretationen*, Berlin: Walter de Gruyter.

Padover, Saul K. (1978): *Karl Marx: An Intimate Biography*, New York: McGraw-Hill.

Palatia (1899): *Corps-Chronik der Palatia zu Bonn. Vom 10. August 1838 bis Dezember 1898*, J. F. Carthaus, Bonn.

Palatia (1913): *Pfälzer Leben und Treiben von 1838 bis 1913. Dritter Beitrag zur Korpschronik*. Überreicht bei der Feier des 75. Stiftungsfestes der Bonner Pfälzer am 14. 15. 16. Juli 1913.

Pannenberg, Wolfhart (1976): *Grundzüge der Christologie*, 5. Aufl., Gütersloh: Gütersloher Verlagshaus.

Paulsen, Friedrich (1885): *Geschichte des gelehrten Unterrichts auf den deutschen Schulen und Universitäten vom Ausgang des Mittelalters bis zur Gegenwart mit besonderer Rücksicht auf den klassischen Unterricht*, Leipzig: Veit.

Paulus, Heinrich Eberhard Gottlob (1821): Rezension von G.W.F. Hegel, *Grundlinien der Philosophie des Rechts*, in: Riedel, Manfred, *Materialien zu Hegels Rechtsphilosophie Bd.1*, Frankfurt/M.: Suhrkamp 1975, 53–66.

Payne, Robert (1968): *Marx*, London: W.H. Allen.

Pepperle, Heinz (2003): Einleitung, in: Köppen (2003) Bd. 1, 11–123.

Pepperle, Heinz; Pepperle, Ingrid (Hg.) (1985): *Die Hegelsche Linke. Dokumente zu Philosophie und Politik im deutschen Vormärz*, Leipzig: Reclam.

Pepperle, Ingrid (1971): "Einführung in die Hallischen und Deutschen Jahrbücher (1838–1843)," in: *Hallische Jahrbücher für Deutsche Wissenschaft und Kunst* (Reprint), Glashütten im Taunus: Auvermann: Detlev Auvermann, i–xl.

Pepperle, Ingrid (1978): *Junghegelianische Geschichtsphilosophie und Kunsttheorie*, Berlin: Akademie.

Peters, Heinz Frederick (1984): *Die rote Jenny. Ein Leben mit Karl Marx*, München: Kindler.

Pilgrim, Volker Ellis (1990): *Adieu Marx. Gewalt und Ausbeutung im Hause des Wort führers*, Reinbek: Rowohlt.

Pinkard, Terry (2000): *Hegel: A Biography*, Cambridge: Cambridge University Press.

Pöggeler, Otto (1986): "Begegnung mit Preußen," in: Lucas, Hans-Christian; Pöggeler, Otto (Hg.): *Hegels Rechtsphilosophie im Zusammenhang der europäischen Verfassungsgeschichte*, Stuttgart: frommann-holzboog, 311–351.

Pöggeler, Otto (1999): *Hegels Kritik der Romantik*, München: Wilhelm Fink Verlag.

Popper, Karl (1962/66): *The Open Society and Its Enemies*, Princeton: Princeton University Press.

Prawer, Siegbert S. (1976): *Karl Marx und die Weltliteratur*, München: Beck 1983.

Quante, Michael (2011): *Die Wirklichkeit des Geistes. Studien zu Hegel*, Frankfurt/M.: Suhrkamp.

Raddatz, Fritz J. (1975): *Karl Marx. Der Mensch und seine Lehre*, Hamburg: Hoffmann und Campe.

Rasche, Ulrich (2007): "Geschichte der Promotion in absentia. Eine Studie zum Modernisierungsprozess der deutschen Universitäten im 18. und 19. Jahrhundert," in: Rainer Christoph Schwinges (Hrsg.), *Examen, Titel, Promotionen. Akademisches und staatliches Qualifikationswesen vom 13. bis zum 21. Jahrhundert*, Basel: Schwabe, 275–351.

Rauch, Albert (1975): "Der Große Sanhedrin zu Paris und sein Einfluß auf die jüdische Familie Marx in Trier," in: Laufner, Richard; Rauch, Albert (Hg.): *Die Familie Marx und die Trierer Judenschaft*, Schriften aus dem Karl Marx Haus 14, Trier, 18–41.

Raussen, Bernd (1990): "Die mathematische Schriften Maturitätsprüfung im Jahre 1835 am Trierer Gymnasium. Zugleich ein Beitrag zur Karl Marx Forschung," in: *Kurtrierisches Jahrbuch*, 30. Jg., 205–236.

Reimarus, Hermann Samuel (1754): *Die vornehmsten Wahrheiten der natürlichen Religion in zehn Abhandlungen auf eine begreifliche Art erkläret und gerettet, 3. erw. Aufl. von 1766*, in: ders., *Gesammelte Schriften* Bd. I, Göttingen: Vandenhoeck & Ruprecht, 1985.

Reimarus, Hermann Samuel (1972): *Apologie oder Schutzschrift für die vernünftigen Verehrer Gottes, Im Auftrag der Joachim Jungius Gesellschaft herausgegeben von Gerhard Alexander*, Frankfurt/M.: Insel.

Reimarus, Hermann Samuel (1760): *Allgemeine Betrachtungen über die Triebe der Thiere, hauptsächlich über ihre Kunsttriebe*, Göttingen: Vandenhoeck & Ruprecht, 1982.

Reinalter, Helmut (2010): "Arnold Ruge, der Vormärz und die Revolution 1848/49," in: ders. (Hrsg.), *Die Junghegelianer. Aufklärung, Literatur, Religionskritik und politisches Denken*, Frankfurt/M.: Peter Lang 139-159.

Reinke, Andreas (2007): *Geschichte der Juden in Deutschland 1781–1933*, Darmstadt: Wissenschaftliche Buchgesellschaft.

Reissner, Hanns Günther (1965): *Eduard Gans. Ein Leben im Vormärz*, Tübingen: Mohr.

Riedel, Manfred (1967): "Hegel und Gans," in: Braun, Hermann; Riedel, Manfred (Hg.): *Natur und Geschichte. Karl Löwith zum 70. Geburtstag*, Stuttgart: Kohlhammer, 257–273.

Riedel, Manfred (1975): Einleitung, in: Riedel, Manfred (Hg.): *Materialien zu Hegels Rechtsphilosophie*, Frankfurt/M.: Suhrkamp, Bd. 1, 11–49.

Ries, Klaus (Hg.) (2012): *Romantik und Revolution. Zum politischen Reformpotential einer unpolitischen Bewegung*, Heidelberg: Universitätsverlag Winter.

Ring, Max (1898): *Erinnerungen*, Erster Band, Berlin: Concordia.

Ringer, Fritz (2004): "Die Zulassung zur Universität," in: Ruegg, Walter (Hrsg.), *Geschichte der Universität in Europa, Bd. III: Vom 19. Jahrhundert zum Zweiten Weltkrieg 1800–1945*, München: C.H. Beck, 199–226.

Rjazanov, David (1929): Einleitung, in: *Marx/Engels Gesamtausgabe*, Erste Abteilung, Band 1, Zweiter Halbband, Berlin: Marx-Engels-Verlag, ix–xlv.

Röder, Petra (1982): *Utopische Romantik, die verdrängte Tradition im Marxismus. Von der frühromantischen Poetologie zur marxistischen Gesellschaftstheorie*, Würzburg: Königshausen & Neumann.

Rohls, Jan (1997): *Protestantische Theologie der Neuzeit, 2 Bände*, Tübingen: Mohr Siebeck.

Rönne, Ludwig von (1855): *Die höhern Schulen und die Universitäten des Preußischen Staates*, Berlin: Veit.

Rose, Margaret A. (1978): *Reading the Young Marx and Engels: Poetry, Parody and the Censor*, London: Rowman and Littlefield.

Rosen, Zvi (1977): *Bruno Bauer and Karl Marx: The Influence of Bruno Bauer on Marx's Thought*, Den Haag: Martinus Nijhof.

Rosenkranz, Karl (1844): *Georg Wilhelm Friedrich Hegels Leben*, Darmstadt: Wissenschaftliche Buchgesellschaft 1977.

Ruda, Frank (2011): *Hegels Pöbel. Eine Untersuchung der «Grundlinien der Philosophie des Rechts»*, Konstanz: Konstanz University Press.

Ruge, Arnold (1837): "Unsere gelehrte kritische Journalistik," in: *Blätter für literarische Unterhaltung*, Nr. 223, Leipzig: Brockhaus, 905–907, Nr. 224, 909–910.

Ruge, Arnold (1838a): [Rezension von] Die Philosophie unserer Zeit. Apologie und Erläuterung des Hegel'schen Systems von Dr. Julius Schaller, in: *Hallische Jahrbücher* Nr. 97–98, Leipzig: Wigand.

Ruge, Arnold (1838b): [Rezension von] Sendschreiben an J. Görres von Heinrich Leo, in: *Hallische Jahrbücher* Nr. 147–151, Leipzig: Wigand.

Ruge, Arnold (1838c): "Die Denunciation der Hallischen Jahrbücher," in: *Hallische Jahrbücher* Nr. 179–180, Leipzig: Wigand.

Ruge, Arnold (1838d): [Rezension von] David Friedrich Strauß' *Streitschriften*, Drittes Heft, in: *Hallische Jahrbücher* Nr. 239–240, Leipzig: Wigand.

Ruge, Arnold (1839): "Karl Streckfuß und das Preußenthum," in: *Hallische Jahrbücher* Nr. 262–264, Leipzig: Wigand.

Ruge, Arnold (1840): [Rezension von] Friedrich Köppen, *Friedrich der Große und seine Widersacher. Eine Jubelschrift*, in: *Hallische Jahrbücher*, 125, Leipzig: Wigand.

Ruge, Arnold (1840a): [Rezension von] Wilhelm Heinse's *Sämmtliche Schriften*, in: *Hallische Jahrbücher*, Nr. 209–212, Leipzig: Wigand.

Ruge, Arnold (1840b): [Rezension von] *Die evangelische Landeskirche Preußens und die Wissenschaft*, in: *Hallische Jahrbücher* Nr. 229, Leipzig: Wigand.

Ruge, Arnold (1840c): "Politik und Philosophie," in: *Hallische Jahrbücher* Nr. 292–293, Leipzig: Wigand.

Ruge, Arnold (1842b): "Der christliche Staat. Gegen den Wirtemberger über das Preußenthum (*Hallische Jahrbücher* 1839)," in: *Deutsche Jahrbücher*, H. 267–268.

Ruge, Arnold (1842a): "Die wahre Romantik und der falsche Protestantismus, ein Gegenmanifest," in: *Deutsche Jahrbücher*, H. 169–171.

Ruge, Arnold (1846): *Zwei Jahre in Paris. Studien und Erinnerungen, 2 Bde., Reprographischer Nachdruck,* Hildesheim: Gerstenberg 1977.

Ruge, Arnold (1867): *Aus früherer Zeit*, Bd. 4, Berlin: Duncker.

Ruge, Arnold; Echtermeyer, Theodor; (1839/40): "Der Protestantismus und die Romantik: zur Verständigung über die Zeit und ihre Gegensätze. Ein Manifest," in: *Hallische Jahrbücher*, 1839: Nr. 245–251, 256–271, 301–310; 1840: Nr. 53–54, 63–65.

Rühle, Otto (2011): *Karl Marx: His Life and Work*, New York: Routledge.

Rühs, Friedrich (1816): *Ueber die Ansprüche der Juden an das deutsche Bürgerrecht. Zweiter verbesserter und erweiterter Abdruck. Mit einem Anhange über die Geschichte der Juden in Spanien*, Berlin: Realschulbuchhandlung.

Salomon, Ludwig (1906): *Geschichte des deutschen Zeitungswesens von den ersten Anfängen bis zur Wiederaufrichtung des Deutschen Reiches. Dritter Band: Das Zeitungswesen seit 1814*, Oldenburg: Schulzesche Hof–Buchhandlung.

Sandberger, Jörg F. (1972): *David Friedrich Strauß als theologischer Hegelianer*, Göttingen: Vandenhoeck & Ruprecht.

Sandmann, Nikolaus (1992): "Heinrich Marx. Jude, Freimaurer und Vater von Karl Marx – Anmerkungen zu einer überraschenden Entdeckung in der Nationalbibliothek Paris," in: *Humanität*, H. 5, 13–15.

Sandmann, Nikolaus (1993): "Französische Freimaurerlogen in Osnabrück während der napoleonischen Annexion," in: *Osnabrücker Mitteilungen*, Bd. 98, 127–159.

Sannwald, Rolf (1957): *Marx und die Antike*, Zürich: Polygraphischer Verlag.

Sartre, Jean-Paul (1964): *Marxismus und Existenzialismus. Versuch einer Methodik*, Reinbek: Rowohlt.

Sartre, Jean-Paul (1971/72): *Der Idiot der Familie. Gustave Flaubert 1821 bis 1857*, Reinbek: Rowohlt 1977–79.

Saß, Friedrich (1846): *Berlin in seiner neuesten Zeit und Entwicklung 1846*, Berlin: Frölich & Kaufmann 1983.

Sass, Hans-Martin (1963): *Untersuchungen zur Religionsphilosophie in der Hegelschule1830–1850*, Inaugural-Dissertation an der Philosophischen Fakultät der Westfälischen Wilhelms-Universität Münster.

Sass, Hans-Martin (Hg.) (1968): *Bruno Bauer, Feldzüge der reinen Kritik*, Frankfurt/M.: Suhrkamp.

Savigny, Friedrich Karl v. (1814): "Vom Beruf unsrer Zeit für Gesetzgebung und Rechtswissenschaft," in: Hattenhauer, Hans (Hg.): *Thibaut und Savigny. Ihre programmatischen Schriften*, 2. erw. Aufl. München: Vahlen 2002, 61–127.

Savigny, Friedrich Karl v. (1815): "Über den Zweck dieser Zeitschrift," in: Hattenhauer, Hans (Hg.): *Thibaut und Savigny. Ihre programmatischen Schriften*, 2. erw. Aufl., München: Vahlen 2002, 201–205.

Savigny, Friedrich Karl v. (1816): "Erste Beylage. Stimmen für und wider neue Gesetzbücher," in: Hattenhauer, Hans (Hg.): *Thibaut und Savigny. Ihre programmatischen Schriften*, 2. erw. Aufl., München: Vahlen 2002, 172–199.

Schafer, Paul M. (2003): "The Young Marx on Epicurus: Dialectical Atomism and Human Freedom," in: Gordon, Dane R.; Suits, David B. (eds.), *Epicurus: His Continuing Influence and Contemporary Relevance*, Rochester: Rochester Institute of Technology, Cary Graphics Arts Press, 127–138.

Scheidler, Karl Hermann (1846a): "Hegelsche Philosophie und Schule," in: *Das Staats-Lexikon, hrsg. von Carl von Rotteck und Carl Welcker*, zweite Auflage, Bd. 6, Altona: Hammerich, 606–629.

Scheidler, Karl Hermann (1846b): "Hegel (Neuhegelianer)," in: *Das Staats-Lexikon*, hrsg. von Carl von Rotteck und Carl Welcker, zweite Auflage, Bd. 6, Altona: Hammerich, 629–664.

Schelling, Friedrich Wilhelm Joseph (1980a): "The I as the Principle of Philosophy", in Schelling, *The Unconditional in Human Knowledge: Four Early Essays, 1794-1796*, Lewisburg: Bucknell University Press.

Scheuer, Helmut (1979): *Biographie. Studien zur Funktion und zum Wandel einer literarischen Gattung vom 18. Jahrhundert bis zur Gegenwart*, Stuttgart: J.B. Metzler.

Schiel, Hubert (1954): *Die Umwelt des jungen Karl Marx. Ein unbekanntes Auswanderungsgesuch von Karl Marx*, Trier: Jacob Lintz.

Schiller, Friedrich (1793): "Über Anmut und Würde," in: ders., *Sämtliche Werke*, Band 5, München: Deutscher Taschenbuch Verlag 2004, 433–488.

Schiller, Friedrich (1795/96): "Über die ästhetische Erziehung des Menschen" in einer *Reihe von Briefen*, in: ders., *Sämtliche Werke*, Band 5, München: Deutscher Taschenbuch Verlag 2004, 570–669.

Schiller, Friedrich (1988). *Friedrich Schiller, Poet of Freedom*, Washington, D.C. Schiller Institute.

Schlegel, Friedrich (1798): "Athenäums-Fragmente," in: ders., Athenäums»-Fragmente und *andere Schriften*, Stuttgart: Reclam 1978, 76–142.

Schleiermacher, Friedrich (1821/22): *Der christliche Glaube nach den Grundsätzen der evangelischen Kirche im Zusammenhang dargestellt*, 2 Bände, Berlin: Reimer.

Schmidt am Busch, Hans-Christoph; Siep, Ludwig; Thamer, Hans–Ulrich, et al. (Hg.) (2007): *Hegelianismus und Saint-Simonismus*, Paderborn: Mentis.

Schmidt, Ernst Günther (1977): "Neue Ausgaben der Doktordissertation von Karl Marx (MEGA I/1) und der Promotionsurkunde," in: *Philologus. Zeitschrift für klassische Philologie*, Jg. 121, 273–297.

Schmidt, Ernst Günther (1980): "MEGA 2 IV/1. Bemerkungen und Beobachtungen," in: *Klio*, Jg. 62, H. 2, 247–287.

Schmidt, Karl (1905): *Schillers Sohn Ernst. Eine Briefsammlung mit Einleitung*, Paderborn: Schöningh.

Schmidt, Peter Franz (1955): *Geschichte der Casino-Gesellschaft zu Trier*, Trier: Lintz.

Schnädelbach, Herbert (2000): *Hegels praktische Philosophie. Ein Kommentar der Texte in der Reihenfolge ihrer Entstehung*, Frankfurt/M.: Suhrkamp.

Schnitzler, Thomas (1988): "Die Anfänge des Trierer Turnens (1817–1820) in Zusammenhang der deutschen Einheits- und Verfassungsbewegung," in: *Kurtrierisches Jahrbuch* 28.Jg., 133–176.

Schnitzler, Thomas (1993): *Zwischen Restauration und Revolution. Das Trierer Turnen im Organisations- und Kommunikationssystem der nationalen Turnbewegung (1815–1852)*, Frankfurt/M.: Peter Lang.

Schöncke, Manfred (1993): *Karl und Heinrich Marx und ihre Geschwister*, Bonn: Pahl–Rugenstein Nachfolger.

Schöncke, Manfred (1994): "Ein fröhliches Jahr in Bonn? Was wir über Karl Marx' erstes Studienjahr wissen," in: *Beiträge zur Marx-Engels-Forschung Neue Folge 1994*, 239–255.

Schorn, Karl (1898): *Lebenserinnerungen. Erster Band (1818–1848)*, Bonn.

Schubarth, Karl Ernst (1839): "Über die Unvereinbarkeit der Hegelschen Staatslehre mit dem obersten Lebens- und Entwicklungsprinzip des Preußischen Staates," in: Riedel, Manfred (Hrsg.): *Materialien zu Hegels Rechtsphilosophie*, Bd.1, Frankfurt/M.: Suhrkamp 1975, 249–266.

Schubarth, Karl Ernst; Carganico, L. A. (1829): "Über Philosophie überhaupt und Hegels Encyclopädie der philosophischen Wissenschaften insbesondere," in: Riedel, Manfred (Hrsg.): *Materialien zu Hegels Rechtsphilosophie*, Bd.1, Frankfurt/M.: Suhrkamp 1975, 209–213.

Schulte, Paul (2001): *Solgers Schönheitslehre im Zusammenhang des deutschen Idealismus: Kant, Schiller, W. v. Humboldt, Schelling, Solger, Schleiermacher, Hegel*, Kassel: Kassel University Press.

Schulz, Wilhelm (1843): *Die Bewegung der Produktion. Eine geschichtlich-statistische Abhandlung*, Glashütten im Taunus: Auvermann 1974.

Schulze, Hagen (1978): "Biographie in der «Krise der Geschichtswissenschaft»," in: *Geschichte in Wissenschaft und Unterricht*, Jg. 29, 508–518.

Schweitzer, Albert (1906): *Geschichte der Leben-Jesu-Forschung*, Tübingen: J.C.B. Mohr (Paul Siebeck) 1984.

Seigel, Jerrold (1978): *Marx's Fate: The Shape of a Life*, Princeton: University Press.

Senk, Norman (2007): *Junghegelianisches Rechtsdenken. Die Staats-, Rechts- und Justizdiskussion der "Hallischen" und "Deutschen Jahrbücher" 1838–1843*, Paderborn: Mentis.

382 BIBLIOGRAPHY

Sens, Walter (1935): *Karl Marx. Seine irreligiöse Entwicklung und antichristliche Einstellung*, Halle: Akademischer Verlag Halle.

Sgro', Giovanni (2013): "«Aus dem einen Metalle der Freiheit errichtet». Zu Eduard Gans' Interpretation und Weiterentwicklung der Hegel'schen Rechtsphilosophie," in: Lambrecht, Lars (Hg.): *Umstürzende Gedanken. Radikale Theorie im Vorfeld der 1848er Revolution*, Frankfurt/M.: Lang, 21–37.

Siep, Ludwig (2015): "Säkularer Staat und religiöses Bewusstsein. Dilemmata in Hegels politischer Theologie," in: Quante, Michael; Mohseni, Amir (Hg.): *Die linken Hegelianer. Studien zum Verhältnis von Religion und Politik im Vormärz*, Paderborn: Wilhelm Fink Verlag, 9–27.

Skinner, Quentin (2009): *Visionen des Politischen*, Frankfurt/M.: Suhrkamp.

Solger, Karl Wilhelm Ferdinand (1815): *Erwin. Vier Gespräche über das Schöne und die Kunst. Mit einem Nachwort und Anmerkungen herausgegeben von Wolfhart Henckmann*, München: Fink 1971.

Sommer, Michael (2008): "Karl Marx in Hamburg," in: *Sozialismus*, Jg. 35, H. 1, 55–59.

Spargo, John (1923): *Karl Marx: His Life and Work*, New York: B.W. Huebsch.

Sperber, Jonathan (2013): *Karl Marx: A Nineteenth-Century Life*, New York: Liveright.

Sperl, Richard (2004): "Edition auf hohem Niveau." Zu den Grundsätzen der Marx-Engels-Gesamtausgabe, Hamburg: Argument.

Stahl, Friedrich Julius (1833): *Die Philosophie des Rechts nach geschichtlicher Darstellung. Zweyter Band: Christliche Rechts- und Staatslehre. Erste Abtheilung*, Heidelberg: J.C.B. Mohr.

Stedman Jones, Gareth (2016): *Karl Marx: Greatness and Illusion*, Cambridge, MA: Harvard University Press.

Stein, Hans (1932): "Der Übertritt der Familie Heinrich Marx zum evangelischen Christentum," in: *Jahrbuch des Kölnischen Geschichtsvereins*, Jg. 14, 126–129.

Stein, Hans (1936): "Pauperismus und Assoziation," in: *International Review of Social History*, Jg. 1, 1–120.

Steinke, Hannah (2010): "Die Begründung der Rechtswissenschaft seit 1810," in: Tenorth, Heinz-Elmar (Hg.): *Geschichte der Universität Unter den Linden. Band 4: Genese der Disziplinen. Die Konstitution der Universität*, Berlin: Akademie Verlag, 95–121.

Stepelevich, Lawrence S. (1997). *The Young Hegelians: An Anthology*, Atlantic Highlands, NJ: Humanities Press.

Sterne, Lawrence (1759–67): *Leben und Ansichten von Tristram Shandy, Gentleman*, Ins Deutsche übertragen und mit Anmerkungen von Michael Walter, Frankfurt/M.: Fischer Taschenbuch Verlag 2010.

Strauß, David Friedrich (1835): *Das Leben Jesu kritisch bearbeitet, 2 Bände, Nachdruck der Ausgabe Tübingen 1835*, Darmstadt: Wissenschaftliche Buchgesellschaft 2012.

Strauß, David Friedrich (1837): *Streitschriften zur Verteidigung meiner Schrift über das Leben Jesu und zur Charakteristik der gegenwärtigen Theologie*, 3 Hefte in einem Band, Tübingen: Osiander (Reprint: Hildesheim: Olms 1980).

Streckfuß, Adolf (1886): *500 Jahre Berliner Geschichte. Vom Fischerdorf zur Weltstadt*, 4. Aufl., 2 Bände, Berlin: Goldschmidt.

Stuke, Horst (1963): *Philosophie der Tat. Studien zur Verwirklichung der Philosophie bei den Junghegelianern und den Wahren Sozialisten*, Stuttgart: Klett.

Taubert, Inge; Labuske, Hansulrich (1977): "Neue Erkenntnisse über die früheste philosophische Entwicklung von Karl Marx," in: *Deutsche Zeitschrift für Philosophie*, Jg. 25, H. 6, 697–709.

Tenorth, Heinz-Elmar (2012): "Eine Universität zu Berlin – Vorgeschichte und Einrichtung," in: Tenorth, Heinz-Elmar (Hg.): *Geschichte der Universität Unter den Linden. Band 1: Gründung und Blütezeit der Universität zu Berlin 1810–1918*, Berlin: Akademie Verlag, 3–75.

Theißen, Gerd; Merz, Annette (2011): *Der historische Jesus. Ein Lehrbuch*, 4. Aufl., Göttingen: Vandenhoeck & Ruprecht.

Thibaut, Anton Friedrich Justus (1814): "Über die Notwendigkeit eines allgemeinen bürgerlichen Rechts in Deutschland," in: Hattenhauer, Hans (Hg.): *Thibaut und Savigny. Ihre programmatischen Schriften*, 2. erw. Aufl. München: Vahlen 2002, 37–59.

Thom, Martina (1986): *Dr. Karl Marx. Das Werden der neuen Weltanschauung 1835–43*, Berlin: Dietz.

Thomas, Rüdiger (1973): "Der unbekannte junge Marx (1835–1841)," in: *Der unbekannte junge Marx. Neue Studien zur Entwicklung des Marxschen Denkens 1835–1847*, Main: v. Haase & Köhler, 147–257.

Tomba, Massimiliano (2005): *Krise und Kritik bei Bruno Bauer. Kategorien des Politischen im nachhegelschen Denken*, Frankfurt/M.: Peter Lang.

Treitschke, Heinrich von (1879): *Deutsche Geschichte im Neunzehnten Jahrhundert*, Bd. 1, Leipzig: Hirzel. *Trierer Biographisches Lexikon* (2000), Trier: Wissenschaftlicher Verlag Trier.

Ullrich, Volker (2007): "Die schwierige Königsdisziplin," in: *Die Zeit*, Nr. 15, 4. April.

Varnhagen von Ense, Karl August (1863): *Tagebücher* Bd. 1, 2. Auflage, Leipzig: Brockhaus.

Varnhagen von Ense, Karl August (1994): *Tageblätter*, ders., *Werke*, Bd. 5, hrsg. v. Konrad Feilchenfeldt, Frankfurt/M.: Deutscher Klassiker Verlag.

Vieweg, Klaus (2012): *Das Denken der Freiheit. Hegels Grundlinien der Philosophie des Rechts*, München: Wilhelm Fink Verlag.

Wachstein, Bernhard (1923): "Die Abstammung von Karl Marx," in: Fischer, Josef (Hrsg.), *Festskrift i anledning af Professor David Simonsens 70-aarige fødselsdag*, Kopenhagen: Hertz, 277–289.

Walter, Ferdinand (1865): *Aus meinem Leben*, Bonn: Marcus.

Walter, Stephan (1995): *Demokratisches Denken zwischen Hegel und Marx. Die politische Philosophie Arnold Ruges: eine Studie zur Geschichte der Demokratie in Deutschland*, Düsseldorf: Droste.

Waser, Ruedi (1994): *Autonomie des Selbstbewusstseins. Eine Untersuchung zum Verhältnis von Bruno Bauer und Karl Marx (1835–1843)*, Tübingen: Francke.

Waszek, Norbert (1988): "Gans und die Armut: Von Hegel und Saint–Simon zu frühgewerkschaftlichen Forderungen," in: *Hegel-Jahrbuch* 1988, Bochum: Germinal, 355–363.

Waszek, Norbert (1991): *Eduard Gans (1797–1839). Hegelianer, Jude, Europäer. Texte und Dokumente*, Frankfurt/M.: Peter Lang.

Waszek, Norbert (2006): "Eduard Gans on Poverty and the Constitutional Debate," in: Moggach, Douglas (Hg.): *The New Hegelians: Politics and Philosophy in the Hegelian School*, Cambridge, MA: Cambridge University Press, 24–49.

Waszek, Norbert (2015): "Eduard Gans (1797–1839) der erste Links- oder Junghegelianer?" in: Quante, Michael; Mohseni, Amir (Hg.): *Die linken Hegelianer. Studienzum Verhältnis von Religion und Politik im Vormärz*, Paderborn: Wilhelm Fink Verlag, 29–51.

Wehler, Hans-Ulrich (2008): *Deutsche Gesellschaftsgeschichte. 5 Bände*, München: Beck.

Wessell, Leonard P. (1979): *Karl Marx, Romantic Irony, and the Proletariat: The Mythopoetic Origins of Marxism*, Baton Rouge: Louisiana State University Press.

Westphalen, Ferdinand von (1842): "Nekrolog auf Johann Ludwig von Westphalen," in: *Triersche Zeitung* Nr. 72 vom 15. März 1842, wiederabgedruckt in Schöncke (1993), 882–883.

Westphalen, Ferdinand von (1866): *Westphalen, der Secretär des Herzogs Ferdinand von Braunschweig-Lüneburg. Biographische Skizze*, Berlin: Verlag der Königlichen Geheimen Ober-Hofbuchdruckerei.

Westphalen, Ferdinand von (Hg.) (1859): *Philipp von Westphalen: Geschichte der Feldzüge Herzog Ferdinands von Braunschweig-Lüneburg, Band 1*, Berlin: Decker.

Wheen, Francis (1999): *Karl Marx*, London/New York: W. W. Norton.

White, Hayden (1973): *Metahistory. Die historische Einbildungskraft im 19. Jahrhundert in Europa*, Frankfurt/Main: Fischer 1991.

Wigand's Conversations–Lexikon. Für alle Stände. Von einer Gesellschaft deutscher Gelehrten bearbeitet, 15 Bände (1846–1852), Leipzig: Otto Wigand.

Wilcke, Gero von (1983): "Marx Trierer Verwandtschaftskreis. Zu seinem 100. Todestag," in: *Genealogie. Zeitschrift für deutsche Familienkunde*, Heft 12, 761–782.

Wildt, Andreas (2002): "Marx Persönlichkeit, seine frühesten Texte und die Moral der Militanz," in: *Deutsche Zeitschrift für Philosophie*, Jg. 50, H. 5, 693–711.

Windelband, Wilhelm (1880): *Die Geschichte der neueren Philosophie in ihrem Zusammenhange mit der allgemeinen Cultur und den besonderen Wissenschaften dargestellt, Band 2: Die Blüthezeit der deutschen Philosophie. Von Kant bis Hegel und Herbart*, Leipzig: Breitkopf und Härtel.

Windfuhr, Manfred (1981): Apparat, in: Heine, Heinrich, *Sämtliche Werke*, Düsseldorfer Ausgabe, Bd.8/2, Hamburg: Hoffmann und Campe.

Winiger, Josef (2011): *Ludwig Feuerbach. Denker der Menschlichkeit*, Darmstadt: Lambert Schneider.

Wyttenbach, Johann Hugo (1847): *Schulreden vom Jahre 1799 bis 1846*, Trier: Lintz.

Zedlitz, L. Freiherr von (1834): *Neuestes Conversations-Handbuch für Berlin und Potsdam zum täglichen Gebrauch der Einheimischen und Fremden aller Stände*, Berlin.

Zenz, Emil (1979): *Geschichte der Stadt Trier im 19. Jahrhundert, Band I*, Trier: Spee.

Index